# THE UNFORGETTABLE BUZZ

## The History of Electric Football and Tudor Games

Earl Shores | Roddy Garcia

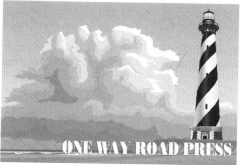

onewayroadpress.com

Printed in the United States of America

First Edition, 2013

ISBN: 978-0-9892363-1-7

Library of Congress Control Number: 2013906056

# THE UNFORGETTABLE BUZZ

## The History of Electric Football and Tudor Games

### Earl Shores | Roddy Garcia

theunforgettablebuzz.com

One Way Road Press
P.O. Box 371
Media, PA 19063-2414

Cover and Interior Design by **Michael Kronenberg**

For Norman Sas and his family, and for all the Christmas memories he created with electric football. For Lee Payne and his artistic visions of football in miniature. For Robin and Terri, who have put up with so much through the years. And to the "Famous One," without whom this project would have never happened. The Walk will long be remembered. Finally, this book is dedicated to anyone who found happiness while sitting over an electric football game.

Author Earl Shores Christmas morning 1968...the best present ever.

"Shores and Garcia have really done their homework
in opening a sacred portal to the past."

— Rick Burton
David B. Falk Professor of Sport Management
Syracuse University

# ORDER YOUR FAVORITE AFL & NFL TEAMS
## WITH THIS HANDY DELUXE PLAYER ORDER FORM

| HOW MANY DO YOU WANT? | | | | | | |
|---|---|---|---|---|---|---|
| DELUXE FIGURES $1.50 PER TEAM | | DELUXE PLAYER NUMBERS $.20 PER SET | | | | |
| DARK JERSEY | WHITE JERSEY | FOR DARK JERSEY | FOR WHITE JERSEY | NATIONAL FOOTBALL LEAGUE | | TOTAL COST |
| | | | | FALCONS | | |
| | | | | COLTS | | |
| | | | | BEARS | | |
| | | | | BROWNS | | |
| | | | | COWBOYS | | |
| | | | | LIONS | | |
| | | | | PACKERS | | |
| | | | | RAMS | | |
| | | | | VIKINGS | | |
| | | | | SAINTS | | |
| | | | | GIANTS | | |
| | | | | EAGLES | | |
| | | | | STEELERS | | |
| | | | | CARDINALS | | |
| | | | | 49ers | | |
| | | | | REDSKINS | | |
| | | | | AMERICAN FOOTBALL LEAGUE | | |
| | WHITE JERSEYS NOT AVAILABLE FOR AFL | | WHITE JERSEYS NOT AVAILABLE FOR AFL | PATRIOTS | | |
| | | | | BILLS | | |
| | | | | BRONCOS | | |
| | | | | OILERS | | |
| | | | | CHIEFS | | |
| | | | | DOLPHINS | | |
| | | | | JETS | | |
| | | | | RAIDERS | | |
| | | | | CHARGERS | | |

| How Many? | SOLID COLOR DELUXE FIGURES FOR PAINTING YOUR OWN TEAMS | |
|---|---|---|
| | Bags of 11 yellow figures ($1.00 per bag) | |
| | Bags of 11 white figures ($1.00 per bag) | |
| | DELUXE NUMBERS (2 through 89) in 9 colors — $.20 each | |
| | Black deluxe numbers | |
| | White deluxe numbers | |
| | Blue deluxe numbers | |
| | Navy Blue deluxe numbers | |
| | Green deluxe numbers | |
| | Purple deluxe numbers | |
| | Red deluxe numbers | |
| | Brown deluxe numbers | |
| | Gold deluxe numbers | |
| | 5 color paint pallets ($.20 ea.) | |
| | Paint brushes ($.15 ea.) | |
| | Bags of 22 green deluxe bases and 2 green deluxe quarterback bases ($2.00 per bag) | |
| | Green deluxe bases ($.20 ea.) | |
| | Green deluxe quarterback bases ($.20 ea.) | |
| | TOTAL | |

WRITE TOTAL OF PLAYER AND PARTS ORDER FORMS IN "GRAND TOTAL" SPACE ON OTHER SIDE OF THIS PAGE.

# CONTENTS

Tudor President Norman Sas (far left) discusses electric football with NFL Commissioner Pete Rozelle (2nd from left) in 1971. At the time, Tudor's electric football games were the No. 1-ranked moneymaking item for NFL Properties. (Personal collection of Norman Sas)

# TOYS FOR THE NFL

**N**orman Sas hadn't made many mistakes during his seventeen years as president of Tudor Metal Products, but this was shaping up as a big one. And as a meticulous decision maker, Norman now wondered what he had missed on that fateful day in 1960 when he declined to give away a 5% cut of his company's record-setting profits. The honest answer was nothing. Significant changes had come to the unique intersection of American business and culture that Tudor inhabited. Anyone claiming to have foreseen the events of the last five years was either a liar or a lunatic.

It was now the fall of 1965, and Tudor's specialized station in the world was that of toy maker, complete with a six-story factory and warehouse just off Flatbush Avenue near the entrance to the Brooklyn Bridge. The company had been founded by Norman's father Elmer Sas in 1928, but after two decades in business a dispute between Elmer and his partner pushed Tudor to the verge of a postwar liquidation. Only a last-minute deal brokered by the company accountant had saved Tudor from joining the Everest-like scrap pile of defunct toy manufacturers. Under the terms of the agreement Tudor stayed in business, but Elmer and his partner had to sell their halves of the company and "retire." Buying the partner's share of Tudor was sales manager Joe Tonole. Elmer's half of the company was sold to Norman, who was just a year removed from his college graduation. In addition to half of the company, Norman got something else – Elmer's job. He was just twenty-three years old and now the president of Tudor Metal Products.

Considering Norman's limited work experience – he'd spent the previous year working for General Electric – it was an enormous gamble to put him in charge of a struggling company of any kind. Yet by the time the annual American Toy Fair got underway the following year in March of 1949, Norman had invented the game that would make Tudor a household name. That game was electric football. Tudor had the electric football category all

Norman Sas from *Playthings*, December 1961.

to itself in the early 1950's, building the brand and profits as the game became a Christmas-morning staple. When a competitor finally stepped onto the vibrating gridiron in 1954, Tudor's electric football game was available in all forty-eight states. As the 1950's came to a close the Gotham Pressed Steel Corporation was struggling to pick up yardage against Tudor's popular and well-established Tru-Action No. 500 model. But Gotham's electric football games had become a regular part of both the Sears and Montgomery Ward Christmas catalogs, which at the time imparted almost biblical influence on Christmas shopping and toy marketing. Thanks to Sears, who was the country's largest toy retailer, Gotham still maintained championship ambitions for electric football.

Norman's mistake, at least as he viewed it now, had come in early 1960 when he received a phone call from a company that up until that moment, he had never heard of. On the line, long-distance from Beverly Hills, California, was Larry Kent, who introduced himself as the vice president of National Football League Enterprises, the newly created marketing arm of the National Football League. Kent's actual employer was Roy Rogers, with NFL Enterprises being a subsidiary of the extremely profitable Roy Rogers Enterprises. As Kent explained it, he had full command of the new entity and was prepared to offer Norman one of the first official licenses the NFL would ever hand out. In fact, Tudor had been targeted several weeks earlier during the foundational meeting of NFL Enterprises, a New York City event whose attendees included Kent, Chicago Bears owner and NFL legend George "Papa Bear" Halas, acting league commissioner Austin Gunsell, and... Roy Rogers. Also taking a prominent seat at the conference table on January 13, 1960, was the man who helped Kent pitch the NFL marketing concept, and who knew as much about the purpose of NFL Enterprises as anyone in the entire league. That man was Los Angeles Rams' general manager Pete Rozelle. Not long after the meeting adjourned, Rozelle was unexpectedly promoted to the position of NFL Commissioner.

Larry Kent from *Playthings*, December 1961.

NFL Enterprises represented the league's first ever attempt to market football merchandise on a national scale. Up until this point, teams sold pennants and other souvenirs on their own, with game-day stadium sales accounting for the bulk of their mostly meager proceeds. Kent's vision was much more ambitious. During his seven years with the "King of the Cowboys," Kent had created the Roy Rogers Corral, an exclusive in-store display area that sold only Roy Rogers merchandise. These Corrals were now a year-round feature in hundreds of department stores across the U.S., including major chains like Sears, Montgomery Ward, J.C. Penney, the May Company, and Macy's. Kent hoped to apply his Corral model to the NFL and impressed upon Norman that the fledgling merchandising program was a ground floor opportunity. All Norman had to do was put an NFL shield somewhere on his boxes and games, then give NFL Enterprises 5% of his gross sales.

That the NFL was getting more popular really wasn't in question. Just thirteen months earlier in December of 1958 the Colts and Giants had played the NFL's "greatest game," a championship contest won by the Colts in sudden-death overtime. Not only did the game capture the imagination of the sixty-four thousand fans in Yankee Stadium, it entertained a national television audience of more than 45 million people. Yet Norman still wasn't sure that the NFL's rising profile would automatically translate into additional electric football sales. Tudor had sold more than $1 million worth of electric football games in 1959 – if the company had been a licensee that year it would have handed over more than $50,000 to NFL Enterprises. After quickly doing the math in his head, Norman decided that an NFL license wasn't worth $50,000. Tudor was already selling out most of its electric football inventory. It honestly didn't need the NFL to help move games. Norman thanked Kent for the call, but politely passed on the NFL's offer.

Kent was stunned. Tudor and the NFL seemed like a perfect match – how could Norman not want to be a part of pro football? But Kent wasn't deterred. He had a backup plan, and soon found a company who thought that an NFL license for electric football was a great opportunity, 5% and all. That company was cross-town toy making rival Gotham Pressed Steel.

Recently ascending to the top of Gotham's organizational chart was toy veteran Eddie Gluck, who didn't need to think twice about signing on with the NFL. There were a number of motivations for Gluck's eagerness to be

Gotham President Eddie Gluck shows off his brand new NFL game in 1961. *Playthings*, June 1961.

associated with professional football. First, he had been the one who steered the Bronx-based company into electric football, and he had long grown tired of his company's second-string status behind Tudor. An NFL license offered Gotham a very visible way to make its electric football games different from Tudor's. Additionally, Gluck had been a professional basketball player in the 1920's and 1930's and carried a preference for the "pro" side of things. Sports licensing wasn't even a new concept for Gotham, as the company had sold baseball games endorsed by Jackie Robinson and Carl Hubbell during the late 1940's and early 1950's. Finally, there was the issue of being a former Tudor employee. Even though Gluck left the company three years before Norman was named president, he seemed to resent Norman's success with electric football. There had even been a bout of trash talk at the 1954 Toy Fair where Gluck threatened to bury Norman and Tudor. Perhaps with the NFL Gluck had finally found a shovel.

Production logistics prevented Gotham from producing an NFL game in 1960, but the Gotham-NFL licensing partnership wasn't a secret. Since Gotham's sales had never come close to equaling Tudor's, Norman wasn't overly worried about saying "no" to Larry Kent. Had he been aware of Gluck's plans for the NFL, he might have felt differently.

What Gotham unveiled in 1961 was the largest and most elaborate electric football game ever made. It was almost a foot longer than all previous games, and sitting along the sideline was a three-foot long metal grandstand that looked exactly like Yankee Stadium, complete with paper NFL pennants "flying" high above the stadium's distinctive façade. On the field were more innovations. Since Norman invented electric football in 1949 the players had been flat, two dimensional, and plastic, with the "team" component indicated by the color of the figures. (Tudor's current teams were red and yellow, while Gotham's were red and blue). Gotham had produced new plastic players that, although still flat, were tan in color. This generic color scheme served as a blank canvas for team creation, which came in the form of self-sticking paper jerseys and helmets. Seven sets of "removable" uniforms were included in every new Gotham game – each set came printed in an official NFL team color.

Whether Norman liked it or not he now had to go head-to-head with Gotham and the NFL. That meant Tudor would have to have its own oversized football game on toy store shelves for 1962, and considering Gotham's NFL muscle, Norman knew that he would have to come up with

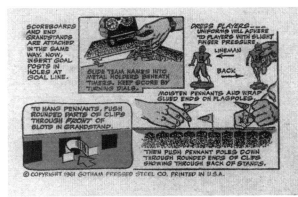

A page from Gotham's 1961 NFL Playbook. It was included in each NFL Gotham game. (Collection of Earl Shores.)

something that was more than simply "big." The new game would have to have a feature that made it clearly different from Gotham's NFL game. Norman's answer came from a talented young industrial designer whose name wasn't even officially on Tudor's payroll. Thanks to Calvin "Lee" Payne, all of Tudor's 1962 electric football games would have an electric football "first" – realistic looking three-dimensional players. And these new plastic players didn't need paper jerseys. They could be painted to look like a kid's favorite team.

Norman's response to Gotham in 1962 was timely in more ways than one, as Commissioner Rozelle had finally landed a league-wide national television contract. Starting in September, CBS began televising NFL games on each and every Sunday. The deal was groundbreaking because all the NFL teams were now "equal," receiving an equal cut of the CBS fee, equal benefit from the CBS promotional department, and equal access to the latest television production technology. Previously teams had negotiated their own individual television contracts, with the financial rewards being determined mostly by the luck of geography. Pressure for a league-wide single-network contract had come not only from Rozelle, but also from the rival AFL, who already had a similar television deal in place with ABC.

As the NFL made its debut on CBS, the league had another very special debut in the Sears Christmas Book. There at the top of page 344 was Gotham's NFL football game – in glorious full color. It was the first time Sears had elevated an electric football game to the status of a color catalog page, which at the time was very costly to print. It was a development that meant the nation's largest retailer giant viewed electric football as a toy whose star was on the rise.

Tudor's efforts to remain the dominant electric football brand in 1962 went beyond large games and 3-D players. Norman had convinced Montgomery Ward to carry Tudor's new game, as well as the smaller Tru-Action No. 500 model. Although this ended Gotham's Christmas catalog monopoly, Gluck still came away with better field position on the mail-order front. Montgomery Ward was the smaller of the two national chains, and the retailer did not use valuable color ink to show off Tudor's games. They also did not promote electric football in their Christmas advertising nearly as much as Sears did. Still, the Montgomery Ward relationship was very beneficial for Tudor. The opening of this substantial new market left Gotham's electric football gains for the year almost negligible.

An easy way to measure the impact of Tudor's new 3-D players was to look at a 1963 Gotham sales catalog. Gotham's newest feature was…3-D players. These players, while promoted as newly designed, carried a suspicious whiff of Tudor about them. But they certainly added another dimension of realism to Gotham's already lifelike NFL concept. Beyond the world of electric football, the NFL licensing program was continuing to grow. In fact it had grown so quickly that the NFL itself took over the management of the program in March of 1963. Larry Kent was now president of a new company called National Football League Properties. Finding himself on the NFL cut list in this new marketing arrangement was Roy Rogers. It was a betrayal that the King of the Cowboys would never forgive.

During the fall Norman could observe the new era of NFL marketing on CBS, or anytime he ventured over to Manhattan to check out the toy department at Saks Fifth Avenue. NFL Enterprises had made Saks the "official distributors" of New York Giants clothing, so displayed on special racks in The Boys' Shop were officially licensed Giants hats, warm-up jackets, pajamas, sweaters, and uniforms. Norman could also look at page 100 of the Sears Christmas catalog where Eddie Gluck had landed three NFL electric football models, all in a blitz of full color. At least the Sears page didn't blindside Tudor this year, as Montgomery Ward had elevated Tudor's electric football games to color status. Yet Norman was well aware that the NFL logos and shields gave Gotham's games a more authoritative presence. Also giving Gotham an authoritative sales presence was the dedicated advertising support that Sears provided during the 1963 Christmas shopping season.

Tudor's 1962 answer to Gotham's NFL – an oversized electric football game with 3-D players (Collection of Norman Sas.)

But Gotham still wasn't eating all that much into Tudor's electric football earnings. For the moment, anyway, the electric football market had actually expanded thanks to the high-end "deluxe" models that both companies were now selling. As 1964 opened it was clear to Norman that selling games was becoming increasingly about marketing and perception. More and more NFL items were being licensed, with American boys being the main target of this NFL promotional power sweep. Previously mundane items like parkas, raincoats, bathrobes, towels, blankets, and even lunch boxes, were now available with NFL team logos and the distinctive NFL shield. There were also other NFL items like seat cushions, juice glasses, transistor radios, plaques, decals, bobble-heads, uniforms – and, of course, Gotham's electric football games. The average ten-year-old boy probably didn't know or care that NFL television ratings were up, or that the league had just tripled its television money intake by signing a two-year $28 million deal with CBS. But young football fans did see and feel that there was "more" NFL all around them. Not only was it was on television every Sunday, it was on their heads and their backs as they walked to school in the morning; on the lunch table holding their chocolate milk and bologna sandwiches; and in the backyard – again on heads and backs – during after school pick-up football games.

Tudor was now fully engaged in a marketing battle with Gotham, coming up with a second-generation of 3-D electric players that were far and away the most realistic ever created. Payne's continued refinement

A new Tudor 3-D player in 1962 (Photo by Earl Shores)

had given Tudor unbreakable players that looked great and played great. The only thing they lacked was involvement with the NFL. That was still Gotham's domain, and Eddie Gluck had again placed three NFL electric football games on a lively color page in the 1964 Sears Christmas Book. Montgomery Ward did all it could for Tudor, giving electric football top billing on a full-color, all-sports Christmas catalog page. This left Sears and Ward battling to a stalemate on the holiday advertising electric football scrimmage line, but Gotham's market share began to edge upward.

The opening days of 1965 were filled with pro football headlines even though both the NFL and AFL seasons were long over. That's because the AFL New York Jets spent a pro sports record $400,000 to sign a University of Alabama quarterback named Joe Namath. The Jets were already on the rise, having tripled their attendance after moving to the newly opened Shea Stadium for the 1964 season. This was on top of a fully guaranteed five-year $36 million television deal the AFL had signed with NBC. (Much of the money used to sign Namath came from an NBC "advance" to the Jets.) The new league still wasn't viewed as an equal of the NFL, but the Namath signing gave an indication of just how hard they were going to fight – and how much they were willing to spend – to try and achieve parity with the older league.

Norman could only watch and scratch his head as the buzz from the Namath signing finally dissipated from the sports pages. The AFL was involved in licensing too, although not to the extent of the NFL. There were AFL shirts and slacks, and Norman had even owned the AFL electric football rights since 1961. But the AFL had nothing like what Hormel was going to sell in 1965 – Official NFL Training Table meats including bacon, hot dogs, and lunchmeat. And in the snack aisle of the grocery store you could find bite-size solid milk chocolate NFL footballs and NFL Touchdown Cookies. Saks had even more official New York Giants items for sale this year. Most of these items were in The Boys' Shop, but adults were finally being given the chance to be part of the NFL. Team logos were now appearing on Arrow shirts and Mighty-Mac stadium jackets.

But there was one NFL item in particular in 1965 that crystallized Norman's growing doubts about his decision to turn down the NFL. It appeared on page 442 of the Sears Christmas catalog, and was called the NFL Big Bowl Electric Football game. The game's maker was Gotham. With the Big Bowl, Gluck had taken the stadium concept to another level. Now sitting on top of Gotham's standard oversized NFL field was a thoroughly modern 3-D, double-decked, bowl-shaped stadium. It was stunning – even Norman conceded that the game looked "fantastic."

And that was the key point in 1965 – how the game looked. It didn't matter that the bowl design would make the game almost impossible to play with, or almost impossible for anyone younger than age twelve to reassemble once Christmas was over. It also didn't matter that Tudor had more realistic players and better playing games, not to mention grandstands that could be set-up and taken down in a matter of minutes. What mattered was this: Gotham had an NFL game with a thoroughly realistic and modern-looking stadium on full color display in the Christmas catalog of the largest toy retailer in the entire country.

For Norman, there was no doubt about it anymore. Saying no to Larry Kent and the NFL had been a mistake. The mistake wasn't really about sales figures, as 1965 would mark the sixteenth straight year that Tudor had the top-selling electric football model. Yes, the NFL would help Tudor sell more games, but Norman had simply grown tired of playing defense against the electric football whims of Eddie Gluck. It felt like Tudor had spent the last four years running from sideline to sideline on a muddy field trying to tackle Gotham and the NFL ball that the company held so tightly. Norman was sure that if he had signed on with Kent in 1960 he wouldn't

Gotham's large NFL game in 1963 with new 3-D players. (Photo Earl Shores.)

The game that made Norman pursue the NFL – the 1965 Gotham NFL Big Bowl.

now be wasting time and effort figuring out how to top the Big Bowl. Instead, Gluck would be the one calling an audible whenever Tudor had a new feature on their NFL games. Five years out, $50,000 seemed like a small price to pay to have Gluck and Gotham permanently anchored to the bench of electric football.

A simple solution was to make Gotham fumble the NFL license. Gotham had never come close to selling as many games as Tudor did annually, so there was no question that NFL Properties would make more money if the electric football license belonged to Tudor. And while the Big Bowl was undeniably inspired – and big – Lee Payne was now Tudor's Director of Product Development. In combining Lee's creativity with the NFL, Norman was certain Tudor could set an electric football standard that Gotham would never equal. Worrying about Gotham would be a thing of the past. Gluck would be left sprawled on the turf watching Tudor race towards the end zone with the NFL cradled under its arm. At least that's how it worked out in Norman's frequent daydreams. Reality, however, was going to be just a bit different.

Taking the NFL away from Gotham wasn't going to be easy. The fact that Tudor was the stronger company, and other than the Big Bowl structure, had a more realistic electric football platform, really didn't matter. What did matter was how Larry Kent felt about Norman and Gotham. Was Kent still feeling slighted over Norman's original decision? Was there a special relationship between the NFL and Gotham that transcended the basic elements of business? Had being in the right place at the right time in 1960 earned Gluck a permanent NFL license?

There was only one way to find out – call Larry Kent and ask. One problem Norman didn't have was admitting to a mistake, and he would acknowledge right up front that he had been wrong in 1960. Then he would pitch Kent on why Tudor could do more for the NFL than Gotham. Regardless of the outcome, Norman knew it would be a challenging conversation.

As Norman picked up the phone and dialed Kent's number he had no idea that he was about to change the world of toys and sports licensing.

Forever.

# 2 TUDOR'S POSTWAR STRUGGLES

**A**fter more than a decade of building Tudor Metal Products into a major toy maker, Elmer Sas and Eugene Levay now fought bitterly over the direction of the company. Levay, who was sixty-three years old, didn't want to put more money into research and development. He was comfortable with Tudor's current direction and didn't feel the company should take on any more financial risk than it already had. Elmer, who was the "younger" partner at age sixty-one, still held the same outlook that he did when Levay joined Tudor in 1936. He felt the company was worth investing in and expanding further – to make money, money had to be spent. As a result, by mid-1947 the two former friends were barely talking to each other.

The postwar years had been difficult ones for Tudor, and for the country in general. "Reconverting" from a war-based to a civilian economy had been difficult, and at this point far from successful. Millions of returning servicemen and women were being reabsorbed into the workforce (part of the genius of the GI Bill was delaying their reentry through a college education). Companies, including Tudor, had to wean themselves off the guaranteed profits of Uncle Sam's military contracts. And if these challenges weren't cause enough for uncertainty, inflation had been moving steadily upward since the government's strict war pricing controls expired in July of 1946. Within nine months inflation was nearing 20%, killing the demand for many nonessential consumer items. Prices had simply gotten much too high.

Accelerating the slump in demand was having multiple manufacturers selling the same item. During the war Tudor had invented and manufactured a cardboard toy Walkie-Talkie that became a best seller. In the postwar period Tudor now found itself competing with several Walkie-Talkie imitators who had priced their products well below Tudor's. And even without the specter of inflation, Tudor was carrying the expense of

Tudor's Brooklyn factory at 176 Johnson Street. (Personal collection of Norman Sas.)

a new Brooklyn factory (opened in December of 1945), new equipment, and rising employee costs thanks to the longstanding, and unusual for the time, company policy of providing health and retirement benefits. Mounting expenses and declining sales were not a good combination. Tudor's books had begun filling with red ink.

"Levay and my dad were going to liquidate," said Norman Sas. "It was that bad." With such an atmosphere of discord at the top of the company, Tudor moved carefully through the remaining months of 1947. Finally, as the year came to a close, Tudor's accountant, Charles Weisberg, came up with a solution that was agreeable to both Elmer and Levay. Sales manager Joe Tonole would buy out Levay, and Levay would leave the toy business. Tonole would also take over Levay's position as vice president of Tudor. Elmer would sell his half of Tudor to his twenty-three year old son Norman, who would also inherit his father's position as president of the company.

"My dad wasn't ready to leave the toy business," reflected Norman Sas, "but it was just too unpleasant to stay." So in the summer of 1948, Tudor got a new president and a new direction. The changes were announced in the July issue of the toy industry publication *Playthings* where an article talked about the "retirement" of Levay and Elmer Sas from Tudor. Photos of both Tonole and Norman accompanied the article, with Norman pictured wearing his U.S. Navy uniform. Whether intended or not, the uniform helped disguise just how young Norman really was.

Handing over a struggling company to a twenty-three year old – essentially a kid – would appear to be a foolish act of nepotism. Norman had spent some summers hanging around the factory, but since graduating from college, he had been working for General Electric. What could an ordinary twenty-three

The 1944 Toy Manufacturers of the U.S.A. dinner at the Hotel McAlpin in New York City. Tudor President Elmer Sas is on the left, his partner Gene Levay is on the right. (Collection of Norman Sas.)

year old possibly know about running a toy company? The key word here is "ordinary," and it's something that Elmer knew his son was not.

Norman had graduated from the Massachusetts Institute of Technology in the spring of 1947 with not just one degree, but two – one in business and one in mechanical engineering. He had also written a senior thesis titled *Characteristics and Problems of the Toy Manufacturer*. In researching his work, Norman visited nineteen different toy factories and interviewed twenty-eight different toy executives. Of course, one of the executives who contributed his knowledge readily was Elmer Sas. Throughout the pages of Norman's thesis, the toy industry was explored in surprising depth, including the difficult plight of the seasonal employees who made up the bulk of the toy workforce. Established straight away

The photo that appeared in *Playthings* (1948) announcing Norman's arrival at Tudor.

in the introduction was the fickle nature of toy acceptance or rejection and the general cloud of uncertainty that even the largest toy makers toiled under in a world that had yet to discover the focus group. Norman came to Tudor understanding a very basic yet very important aspect of the toy industry. In fact, it was stated on page two of his thesis: "The ultimate aim of all manufacturers is to promote an item that will be popular and long lasting."

Maybe this was a concept Norman could have learned from a book, but somehow it seemed this lesson was imparted from a far more authoritative source. An earnestness in Norman's written words left the distinct impression that he had taken this and a number of other pieces of toy wisdom completely to heart.

Tudor's 1950 Toy Fair Showroom, with Vice President Joe Tonole showing off the company's line of electric games. (Personal collection of Norman Sas.)

# 3 A TOY FAIR PRIMER

**N**o true toy story would be complete without a description and visit to the New York City Toy Fair. This book takes many trips to the Fair, and not only do the visits check in on the happenings in electric football, they offer a window to what's going on in the toy world in any given year. The basics of the Toy Fair are this: Each year, the Toy Industry Association, Inc., holds the American International Toy Fair in New York City. The first Toy Fair was held in 1902, and for both U.S. and international toy makers, the event has evolved into the most important week of the year. Great planning, effort, expense, and even secrecy still go into the presentations each company makes during the event. When Norman Sas took over Tudor in 1948 the Toy Fair was being held in March. The date of the event has migrated through the years to its current slot in early February.

All of the Toy Fairs referenced in this book took place in New York City's "toy district," an area just west of Madison Park, between 23rd and 25th Streets. The buildings located there were known as the International Toy Centers North and South, and home to hundreds of showroom suites where toy makers displayed their wares. In good economic times, large toy makers might have more than one suite; in some years Hasbro and Mattel had their own buildings. (Currently, the Toy Fair is based at the Javitz Convention Center on Manhattan's Westside.)

This showroom arrangement allowed toy makers to show off their new products and entice buyers to place orders for the coming year. In 1948 you would have found the owner of your local toy store at the Fair, but in today's discount driven, chain-store retail world, that type of toy buyer is almost extinct. What still holds true, just as it did in the earliest days of the event, is that a company's financial fate can be determined by buyer reaction during Toy Fair. Tudor's showroom at 200 Fifth Avenue

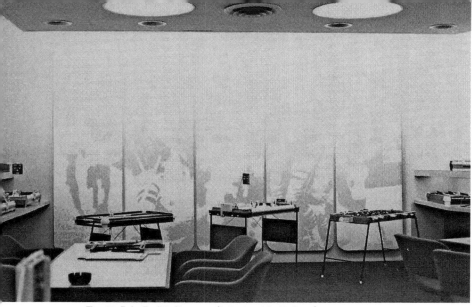

The 1974 Tudor Toy Fair Showroom. (Collection of Roddy Garcia)

was a vital part of the company's success, and events that occurred in the showroom will be recounted throughout the book.

Until 2010, the Toy Industry Association (known as the Toy Manufacturers of America before 2001) published a monthly trade journal called *Playthings*, which for over a century was *the* voice of the toy industry. *Playthings*' most anticipated issue was the one published during the month of the Toy Fair. It often contained ten times as many pages as a typical *Playthings*, with those extra pages filled by ads from the manufacturers attending the Fair. In strong economic times, companies would run multiple ad pages, or even have their own company insert.

The Toy Fair issue of *Playthings* served as a "Rosetta Stone" for deciphering what was happening in toys at any particular point in time. It was also the starting point for much of the research in this book. Electric football's story would be woefully incomplete without the history and context of the toy business provided by *Playthings*.

A number of other publications have covered the toy industry through the years, some with more success than others. *Toys & Novelties* was a monthly magazine that

The 1962 Gotham Toy Fair showroom. Seated on the right is Eddie Gluck. *Playthings*, page 97, April 1962.

began publishing in 1911 and continued covering the toy trade into the 1960's. It ranks second only to *Playthings* for longevity. *Toy & Hobby World* covered the toy industry for almost thirty years, beginning in 1963. One of the distinctive features of this publication was that it came in the format of a tabloid newspaper. A very ambitious journal called *Toys* also had a brief stint

The 1963 Tudor Toy Fair Showroom. *Playthings*, April 1963.

covering the industry from 1970-77. What made *Toys* ambitious was its full-color formatting – every page of the magazine was printed in color. Not even *Playthings* had evolved to full color by 1977. At the time, it was very expensive to print color pages. *Toys'* limited run makes it clear that the publishers couldn't extract enough ad revenue from toy makers to support a full-color magazine. The inexpensive tabloid printing format used by *Toy & Hobby World* allowed the magazine to charge a great deal less for ad space and also contributed to the publication's longevity.

Because of its direct ties to the Toy Industry Association, *Playthings* was the definitive toy-industry publication. But *Toys & Novelties*, *Toy & Hobby World*, and *Toys*, all made contributions to the toy world – and this book.

RUN
A

PLAYERS ACTUALLY
BLOCK AND TACKLE

# 4 NORMAN SAS
## OPENS HIS PLAYBOOK

orman arrived at Tudor knowing the company needed a new item, something to lift the Brooklyn firm out of its financial doldrums and also distinguish it from the dozens of other companies making metal toys. And he knew that a "fad" item, while nice for raising the company profile, might not be the best way to secure Tudor's financial future. Sometimes these toys, despite their super sales for a single Christmas season, didn't end up covering the cost of their development. What Norman wanted for Tudor was "popular and long lasting," and he reasoned that tying into the postwar culture might help accomplish these two objectives. It would also help if Tudor didn't have to spend major amounts of money developing the new toy. Perhaps the company had something lying around that, with some modifications, could be transformed into a totally "new" item.

One of the prewar items that never made it back into the Tudor line was a vibrating electric horse race game. Elmer and Gene Levay created the game, which evolved from Tudor's 1937 Electric Auto Race. The electric horse race had the unfortunate luck of debuting in 1941, and thanks to wartime metal shortages, that turned out to be the only year it was ever produced. Its concept was simple. Six miniature horses lined up on an oval track that was lithographed onto a 26" x 14" metal game board. When the game was turned on, an electro-magnetic relay device – a repurposed doorbell ringer – converted alternating current (AC) into game-board vibrations. Once the metal game surface began vibrating, the horses "ran" around the track thanks to a pair of copper reeds mounted on the bottom of each figure.

"AC changes 120 times per second, with the board cycling up and down sixty times," said Norman, explaining the electric vibrating game principle. "As the board goes down, the reed goes down with it, which brings whatever is on the reed a little forward. And as the board vibrates up, the reed straightens up causing forward motion."

Not long after the pleasantries and formalities of taking over Tudor died down, Norman pulled a long-forgotten horse race game out of a dusty factory back room. He'd always been fascinated by the vibrating concept, and in watching the horses run, Norman could see that while a couple were genuine Triple Crown contenders, the others banged along the rail, completing a rough and tumble lap where things looked more like roller derby than a horse race. It only took a few moments of pondering before the young Tudor president thought of another sport that might really lend itself to the vibrating game board – football.

Football didn't come to Norman through fond memories of autumn afternoons spent cheering in the crisp Boston air. Since its founding in 1865, MIT had never fielded a football team. But football, while not holding the iconic stature of baseball, was clearly growing in popularity. In New York City during the late 40's, football was hard to miss. During the fall, newspapers devoted pages of their Friday, Saturday, and Sunday editions to football, almost exclusively the collegiate type. On Sunday, college football coverage expanded to take up the first five pages of the *New York Times* sports section with details and results reported from games all around the country. (Previews of Sunday's professional football games were usually squeezed into a single column article on page 6.) The crowds major college football powers were drawing could boggle any sports fan's mind, as schools like Ohio State, Michigan, Penn, and Southern California were all averaging over 70,000 fans per home game. Providing an exclamation

The grandfather of vibrating games: Tudor's 1940 Auto Race Game. Norman's electric football was a direct descendant of this game.

Mid-October 1948: While Norman Sas worked on the details of electric football, just a subway ride away in Manhattan over 35,000 fans filled Baker Field to see visiting Penn pull out a last-minute 20-14 victory over Columbia. (© Bettmann/CORBIS)

point on college football's popularity were the spirited rivalries of Army-Navy and Notre Dame-Southern Cal. Both games were capable of selling out 100,000 seat stadiums.

Live football in the city consisted of Columbia University, which played a top-notch schedule and drew over thirty thousand fans per game to Baker Field in northern Manhattan. And several times a season Yankee Stadium became the home of Army, one of the top college football teams in the country. The 1946 "game of the century" between No. 1-ranked Army and No. 2-ranked Notre Dame drew more than 74,000 fans (the game ended 0-0), while a 1947 contest between No. 2-ranked Army and unbeaten Illinois drew 65,000 (another 0-0 tie). On the professional side there were now three teams in New York, with a professional football attendance record for the city being set just weeks after the Army-Illinois game. Attracting 70,060 spectators to Yankee Stadium were the New York Yankees and Cleveland Browns, who battled gallantly in a 28-28 standoff.

Norman Sas in 1949. (Collection of Norman Sas.)

The original New York City attendance record had stood since 1925 when the New York Giants hosted Red Grange and the Chicago Bears in a National Football League contest. Setting this new record were two teams from the two-year-old All-America Football Conference.

Yet there was something else going on in the New York City area that made its football scene unlike any other in the country. Almost all the college and professional football games played in the city were broadcast on television. In fact New York television manufacturer DuMont was enticing buyers with a fall advertising campaign using football. (It was no coincidence that DuMont owned WADB, the New York City television station that owned the broadcast rights to both the baseball and football Yankees.) With prices running $400 and up, there still weren't a lot of sets in U.S households. But it was the New York City area that had the greatest concentration of television sets and television stations. Local owners of the exotic and expensive new medium could watch a lot of football, especially the pro version, since the city was home to the NFL Giants and AAFC Yankees and Dodgers. Many times during the fall of 1947, television programming on Saturday and Sunday consisted of a single event – a football game.

So when Norman thought, "Gee, I could make a good football game out of that race game," he was taking into consideration more than just the toy world. He realized that 1948 might be an ideal time to create a football game, especially if that game looked and played unlike anything sports-loving boys had ever seen before. Football's popularity was likely to continue to grow, and maybe, just maybe, this television gadget could help football's popularity during the next couple of years. At least this is what Norman hoped. And this hope compelled Norman to move forward with designing prototype football game boards and football players. After several months of testing and going back to the drawing board, Norman finally approved the production of the first toy football game where the players would "run" around the field without any human help – the Tudor Tru-Action Electric Football Game Model No. 500. If everything worked as planned, the game would be on toy store shelves in 1949.

While offensive schemes of the late 40's football leaned heavily on the "three yards and a cloud of dust" philosophy, Tudor gambled and threw a bomb with its new game. "We spent a lot of money on the tools and dies, plastic molds, and other stuff for the game," said Norman. "Everything rode on electric football...if that game didn't work out, who knows what would have happened to Tudor."

RUN PLAYS FROM ANY FORMATION

PLAYERS ACTUALLY BLOCK AND TACKLE

Norman's new No. 500: "Everything rode on electric football...if that game didn't work out, who knows what would have happened to Tudor." (Personal collection of Norman Sas.)

Making such a decision in the toy industry today would involve boards of directors, CPAs, stock analysts, market studies, and of course, focus groups. And what was Norman's basis for his company to risk almost everything on a completely new and unproven game?

"It was a gut feeling," said Norman with a laugh.

Norman's gut must have felt pretty good as 1948 wound down. On Thanksgiving Day, 78,000 fans in Philadelphia watched Cornell defeat Penn for the Ivy League title. With a cable now linking television stations in the Washington-New York corridor, a lot of football fans got their first taste of a new Turkey Day tradition by watching the game in the comfort of their own living rooms. Two days later 102,000 fans packed Philadelphia's Municipal Stadium for the annual Army-Navy game, and both those in attendance and those watching on television knew they had witnessed something very special. The Midshipmen, who came into the game winless and a 20-point underdog, managed a 21-21 tie with the mighty Army team. But the biggest football game of the year was still to come. On December 5, undefeated and top-ranked Notre Dame played Southern California before a crowd of 100,571 in Los Angeles. For the fans, it was another exciting game. Unfortunately for the Fighting Irish, the 14-14 result handed Michigan the No. 1 ranking for 1948. With no television cable connecting the two coasts, football fans outside the City of Angels had to huddle around their radios to catch the game.

Almost afterthoughts to the collegiate football season were the NFL and AAFC championship games played on Sunday, December 19. In Philadelphia, the NFL title was decided in a snowstorm so intense that players from both the Eagles and Chicago Cardinals had to team up to drag a snow-covered tarpaulin off the field. When play finally commenced, the Eagles outlasted the visitors 7-0. Kicking off at almost the same time in Cleveland, were the Browns and Buffalo Bills. The Browns had no trouble winning their third straight AAFC title 49-7. Combined ticket sales for both games totaled 59,290, with the NFL accounting for the larger share (36,309). The senior league also got more media coverage with a national radio broadcast and an ABC network television feed to cities in the Northeast.

As 1949 began, Norman and Joe Tonole focused their energies on getting the new game into production and on the upcoming Toy Fair. They hoped to make a big impact with electric football, enticing buyers to place orders for the brand new item. One thing they had going for them was Tudor's reputation for meticulous work and dependable delivery schedules. This made it easier for Tonole to pitch electric football as a risk worth taking. Norman could also point out how attendance for college football games was at an all-time high (and skip over the declining professional attendance). Artwork for the new game was still being worked on, so Tudor's full-page ad in the Toy Fair issue of *Playthings* didn't have any illustrations. Listed were the usual Tudor toy items – pianos, xylophones, banjos, and banks – while text at the bottom of the page quietly introduced a new line of "Electrical Action" games. According to the ad, buyers would find three new electrical games in Tudor's showroom – Horse Race, Auto Race, and Football.

Tonole was essential to the selling of electric football at the Fair. He had been in the toy business almost nonstop since 1923, landing at Tudor in 1945 when he took over the sales manager position from the departing Eddie Gluck. Now fifty years old, Tonole had spent more than half of his life in toys, establishing valuable relationships throughout every layer of the industry. (Also well established in the toy world was Tonole's gregarious and straight-shooting personality.) Exposure in the Toy Fair issue of *Playthings* was vital for Tudor's new game, and it was Tonole who got the magazine to run a short piece describing electric football to the toy trade. Since Tudor's artwork wasn't available, *Playthings* published a headshot of Tonole instead. In many ways this worked to Tudor's benefit as Tonole was a very recognizable figure. Toy buyers who might have passed over an image of Tudor's new and unfamiliar game would stop and read about what was new at Joe Tonole's company. Toy people knew that Joe was a good guy who didn't do junk.

A 1949 Tru-Action No. 500 game pictured with its box. (Photo by Earl Shores.)

While the *Playthings'* article focused mainly on electric football, Tonole did mention the Horse Race game. But ultimately, only football made the cut for the 1949 Toy Fair. And it was in showroom 551 at 200 Fifth Avenue, where Norman unveiled Tudor Tru-Action Electric Football Game Model No. 500. It was like no other toy football game ever made before. It had an authentically "chalked" green metal 28" x 16" field, with yard lines every ten yards, and diagonal line patterns decorating the end zones. For a finishing touch of football realism, there were 3"-high metal goal posts rising from each goal line. The field, which sat 2" off the ground, was surrounded by an elevated bright red border that not only provided a pleasing contrast to the green "grass," it kept some very important things on the field – that would be 22 miniature football players who could run, untethered or unaided, wherever they wanted to.

The players were the key to Norman's innovative concept. Having two full teams of players (11 red and 11 yellow) that could, with the flick of a switch, run anywhere on the game board, brought a realism to sports toys that had never been seen before. Instead of flipping a card, spinning a spinner, or rolling dice to determine the outcome of a play, a kid could now line up his players in real football formations – both offensive and defensive formations were diagrammed in the rule book – and watch the action unfold before his eyes. It was like being at a game. And it was like being a coach. Give your fastest player the ball and watch him go.

A close up of Tudor's 1949 players. (Photo by Earl Shores.)

To the modern eye, the players look crude. They were made out of flat plastic (two dimensional), all posed in a crouched or "three-point-stance" position and attached to shiny metal bases which had two copper reeds mounted on the bottom. As in the horse racing game, the reeds allowed the players to run around the field. Gently bending or twisting the reed adjusted the direction and speed of each player – at least that was the theory. Yet even if the players ran in circles, well…it was 1949, and here was a football game where the players ran *all by themselves* in circles. The Tudor No. 500 model offered as much football realism to postwar boys as Playstation, Xbox, and Wii football games do for today's computer generation.

The most specialized player was the Kicker-Quarterback. Made out of metal instead of plastic, he was also posed in a crouch position. But mounted on his right side was a spring-loaded "arm," which allowed him to pass, punt, and kick a tiny felt football. Unfortunately there was no fine adjustment on the arm mechanism, so passing and kicking was strictly an all-or-none affair. If you wanted a 70-yard bomb, or a 70-yard field goal, there was no problem. (Unfortunately, Tudor's rule book prohibited any field goal that was longer than forty yards.) But a 5-yard out pattern? Better stick to a classic "T" formation" and put the ball in your fullback's arms.

Besides the game, Norman paid great attention to the packaging. The box for the game was an eye-catching yellow color, with two players – leather helmets, no facemasks – getting ready for a collision. Inside, the

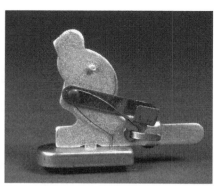

Tudor's 1949 kicker-passer figure. (Photo by Earl Shores.)

players were encased in a large jewel box that contained a mounting slot for each individual player, the goal post, and the down marker. Also in the box were rub-on letters and numbers for identifying the players and six felt footballs. It made a great display piece when the game was turned off.

Electric Football produced quite a buzz at the Toy Fair. Norman and Tonole were thrilled with the response the game received, and orders were ahead of what they had predicted, or even hoped.

Electric football had made its mark – and Norman was glad he had already registered the name "Electric Football" with the U.S. Patent and Trademark Office. From now on only Tudor could use the term. Any future imitators would have to call their game by another name.

To promote the new game, Norman and Tonole took the No. 500 to the National Sporting Goods Association Trade Show in Chicago a few months later. Once again, the game was well received, and more accounts were won as the miniature players buzzed their way into buyers' hearts. With so much of the company's capital funneled into producing the game, there were no plans for any extensive promotions beyond the Toy Fair and the spring visit to Chicago. But the stores who planned to carry Tru-Action Electric Football saw it as an exciting item that warranted display.

In September, Tonole went back to *Playthings* for promotion, this time with a photo of the game and a report on how well electric football was selling. According to Tonole, many stores that displayed the new game had already sent in reorders. This was evidence of "encouraging consumer acceptance" of Tudor's new game. One of those early retailers was the Abraham & Strauss department store in Brooklyn, who ran a sizeable ad in the *New York Times* on September 11. *"Men actually move in new electric football game! First at A & S!"* read the description, which hovered over a photo of the new game. It was quite an introduction for electric football, and it came very early in the shopping season. It would give shoppers a chance to save up the $5.95 needed to buy the game, or put the game on a lay-away account (today's dollar equivalent price is $55).

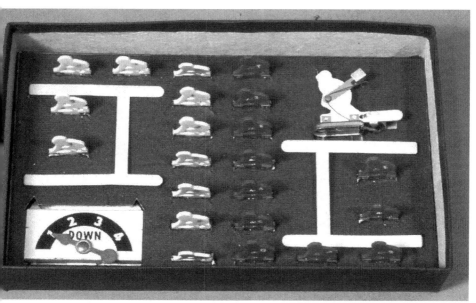

All of Tudor's new games came with a storage box for the players and the accessories.

The game was going to get a boost from football itself as the DuMont network planned to televise five Notre Dame football games in the fall, including one to be played in Yankee Stadium against South Carolina. NBC was also jumping on the college football bandwagon by announcing it would televise 24 games starting on October. Sponsoring this ten-week package was the American Tobacco Company. And despite nine of the ten NFL teams deciding to ban home game telecasts (this ban also extended to pro football telecasts of any kind into a city where a home game was being played), the league signed on to its first-ever television package with ABC. Fifteen NFL games would be televised, including a number of Saturday night contests. A very significant piece of this package was that twelve cities that didn't have NFL teams would finally get to see the professional game. Unfortunately, only four NFL games would be shown in the New York area. That's because the Boston Yanks had recently become the New York Bulldogs and were now sharing the Polo Grounds with the Giants. As a result, New York City had a "home" game every weekend.

College football's popularity seemed to have no limits as 67,000 fans filled Yankee Stadium on November 12 to see No. 1-ranked Notre Dame crush South Carolina 42-6. Notre Dame had now gone thirty consecutive games without a loss, and the crowd size was stunning considering that both teams were over 700 miles from their respective campuses. And just down the road in Philadelphia, 78,000 people watched undefeated Army edge Penn 14-13. Between the DuMont and NBC telecasts, both games reached a large television audience (for 1949 at least). Pro football, however, still seemed to be having attendance issues despite the home television ban. The very next day the NFL Bulldogs and AAFC Yankees could only lure a combined total of 18,000 New York sports fans to their games – even though neither game was on television.

Early December saw Notre Dame wrap up its third national title in four years. A few weeks later the professional season finished when the Philadelphia Eagles overcame the Los Angeles Rams and a California monsoon to earn a second consecutive NFL Championship. Surprisingly, there was not even local television coverage of the game. Only through radio could a fan follow the NFL's most important contest (most did through KCEA's national radio broadcast with Harry Wimser and Red Grange).

It was about this time that Norman and Tonole found themselves in a state of shock – the complete production run of Tru-Action Electric Football had sold out! Between the Toy Fair and the Chicago sporting goods show, they had managed to get the No. 500 distributed throughout the eastern half of the country. And the games available didn't hang around long on toy store shelves. There were going to be Tudor electric football games under Christmas trees in 1949 – lots of them.

"We didn't advertise much in those days, and there was no television either, so it was just word of mouth," said Norman. "Things built up, and built up, and then the game got so popular we couldn't meet the demand." A very pleased and now worldly 24-year-old Norman Sas had gotten the "popular" part right for electric football. The bigger challenge was making his game "long lasting."

# *Tudor* `TRU-ACTION` ELECTRIC GAMES

*The sensation of 1949!*

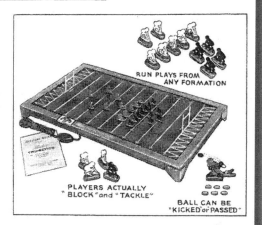

**RUN PLAYS FROM ANY FORMATION**

No. 500

`TRU-ACTION`
## ELECTRIC FOOTBALL

*We could not supply the demand!*

The ball is actually kicked and passed — the players run until tackled — plays can be run from any formation — line plays — end runs — forward passes — field goals — real TRU-ACTION Football right on the living room table!

**PLAYERS ACTUALLY " BLOCK" and " TACKLE"**

**BALL CAN BE "KICKED" or PASSED"**

**PLAYERS RUN THE BASES! BALL IS FIELDED AND THROWN!**

No. 550

`TRU-ACTION`
## ELECTRIC BASEBALL

*New!*

*The most amazing baseball game ever created!*

The players actually run the bases — a fielder and a batter — permanently magnetized ball — the batter makes a hit — he starts for first — the fielder picks up the ball and tries to throw him out — double plays — stolen bases — nearly every play in baseball . . . really TRU-ACTION Baseball!

*New!*

No. 525

`TRU-ACTION`
## ELECTRIC HORSE RACE

*The most realistic Horse Race Game ever made!*

Really TRU-ACTION — cannot be fixed! Every player has a chance at the start of every race. A fascinating adult sport! You will be astonished when you see the track-like things that happen when you're playing TRU-ACTION Horse Race! Ideal for the game room.

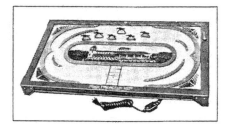

*All games 25 x 15¼ inches*
*Packing ½ dozen . . . wght. 27 lbs.*

**Also the famous TUDOR XYLOPHONES PIANOS and BANJOS**

ROOM **551**

# TUDOR METAL PRODUCTS CORPORATION

SHOWROOM 200 Fifth Ave., N.Y. City          FACTORY 176 Johnson St., Brooklyn 1, N.Y.

A Tudor sales flyer from 1950. These were handed out in the Tudor Toy Fair showroom. (Personal collection of Norman Sas.)

# 5 NO SOPHOMORE SLUMP FOR TUDOR IN 1950

I n addition to overseeing the New York City Toy Fair, the Toy Manufacturers of America (the forerunner of the Toy Industry Association) held an annual banquet during the first week of December. At its 33rd annual gathering, on December 5, 1949, Norman Sas and Joe Tonole took their seats at a large round table in the main ballroom of the Hotel New Yorker. Seated to the left of Tonole was the final member of the Tudor delegation – Eugene Levay. He was there as a courtesy. It was part of the agreement that allowed Norman and Tonole to take over Tudor.

Another part of the agreement required that Levay leave something behind at 176 Johnson Street in Brooklyn – patent no. 2,167,985. Down at the United States Patent Office in Washington, D.C., the file name of this patent was "Vibrating Propelling Device." It had been applied for in April 1937, the same month and year that Tudor debuted its now forgotten Auto Race Game to the toy world. Beginning in 1949 patent no. 2,167,985 appeared in small yellow text on the frame of every No. 500 game that Tudor sold.

While it's obvious that Levay relinquished control of his patent to Tudor – there is no way he would have ever let the company use it without compensation or legal action – by 1950, the paperwork for assigning the Vibrating Propelling Device over to Tudor had yet to be filed. According to the U.S. Patent Office, Levay was still listed as the owner. And surprisingly, it seems this vital paperwork was never *ever* filed. Sixty years later, Levay's name is the only one on the patent. Tudor, it turns out, never officially owned the patent.

In reality, though, it was Tudor's patent. And what Norman was able to achieve with the No. 500 was something that inventors and toy makers had only dreamed about doing since the first toy football game was patented in 1897. From that date on, the Patent Office became littered with attempts to create a realistic method for making football players "run" and "tackle" on a miniature game board. A finger-snap propulsion technique was patented for a 1905 game, and in 1926 an inventor named Robert Rubino obtained a patent for a game with miniature 3-D football players in two different poses – kneeling linemen and upright running figures. Rubino even proposed that his players could be "decorated to imitate uniforms or colors of schools, colleges, or clubs, and carry a number on their back." While forward thinking with his players, Rubino's method of locomotion was quite conventional. The teams would run around the field by taking alternate turns, like a game of chess or checkers.

In a 1933 patent, push rods were used to move two-dimensional players adorned with uniforms and numbers around a tabletop football field, and by 1937 player locomotion had evolved to dragging players using hand-held magnets on the underside of an elevated field. Electrical vibrations were considered for football as early as 1939 when James Hackman of Delaware obtained a patent for a vibrating football/car race game. His "vibrating device" was pretty simple – a battery-operated doorbell with the bell removed. It was "different" from Levay's patent in that Hackman used DC current instead of AC. Hackman's figures stood upright thanks to a tripod-like support base that included the player's feet plus a chest-mounted piano wire "guide." This left each player looking as if it had a golf club protruding from its chest.

For all of these inventors' efforts, there is no record that any of these games were ever produced. Like thousands of other patents whose apparatuses were functional, but not in a really meaningful or marketable way, these never had an impact on the real world. Norman, on the other hand, had not only been able to invent, he had managed to get his invention into production and on toy store shelves. He wasn't just a dreamer – or a slightly imbalanced person with too much time on his hands. Inventing a toy, in many ways, was the easy part. Producing a toy, one that was attractive, durable, and really worked as advertised, was something of a higher order altogether.

So Norman and Levay made an odd and uncomfortable pairing at the TMA banquet, but they did manage to make it a civil evening. As the courses of dinner were served, Levay must have had second thoughts about attending. He had to realize that while Norman was carving out a new legacy in the toy industry, his own legacy was fading fast.

By mid-January, Tudor was finally able to ship out a new batch of electric football games. Stores around the country that ran short during Christmas were eager to get this new shipment, going so far as to announce the game's arrival in local newspaper ads. Having electric football sell "out of season" – that is, a football game being popular during the indoor sports

Find the youngest man at the center table and you've found Norman Sas. On the far right edge of the photo is Joe Tonole. Seated to his left is former Tudor partner Gene Levay. (Personal collection of Norman Sas.)

months of January and February – confirmed the enormous and genuine appeal of Norman's new game.

Tonole again sought the influence of *Playthings*, reporting electric football's success on page 289 of the February issue. During the fall, "It was evident that we had not merely a good item, but actually an all-out best seller," said Tonole. Stores that had put in minimal initial orders found themselves sold out of Tudor's new game before the calendar reached Thanksgiving. All of these retailers were forced to reorder to have any electric football in stock for the actual Christmas shopping season. Tonole went on to claim that he was receiving orders almost daily from leading stores around the country who were continuing to sell – and sell out – electric football during the winter months. And the shrewd toy veteran saved his best quote for last: "It certainly looks like our Electric Football Game will occupy a prominent place on best seller lists for a long time to come." At least Norman and Tonole hoped that would be the case.

Tudor did not just stand back in 1949 and admire the spiraling popularity of electric football. Two more electric games were on display alongside electric football in Tudor's Toy Fair showroom – an all-new Electric Baseball Game and the long-lost Electric Horse Race Game. The Horse Race was a revival of Tudor's pre war model, with six horses running their way around an oval track that had been overlaid on the 25" x 15" electric football frame. Updated artwork and horses were the main differences between the new game and its older relative.

# Tudor TRU-ACTION ELECTRIC GAMES

The sensation of 1949!

No. 500

**TRU-ACTION ELECTRIC FOOTBALL**

We could not supply the demand!

The ball is actually kicked and passed — the players run until tackled — plays can be run from any formation — line plays — end runs — forward passes — field goals — real TRU-ACTION Football right on the living room table!

RUN PLAYS FROM ANY FORMATION

PLAYERS ACTUALLY "BLOCK" and "TACKLE"

BALL CAN BE "KICKED or PASSED"

A 1950 Tudor sales flyer announces the success of the No. 500 model. (Personal collection of Norman Sas.)

Adapting baseball to the vibrating method seemed a bit of a stretch given that the "electric" part of the game only applied to the players running the bases. A spring-type mechanism served as the "bat" (no balls were actually pitched), while another similar spring mechanism at the opposite end of the game acted as the "fielder." The fielder was supposed to throw out a base runner before he reached base. It was an awkward concept that wasn't helped by the rectangular Polo Grounds-like shape of the "field." But it was 1950, and players running the bases were as intriguing as players "running to daylight."

A full-page Tudor ad in *Playthings* pictured all three games with electric football getting the headline: "The sensation of 1949!" The game's description went even further to say, "We could not supply the demand!" Whether that would be the case in the coming year was open to question, but Tudor's showroom, again under command of the engaging Joe Tonole, was a busy place. The Fair ended with Norman having a sense that 1950 might be an even better year than 1949.

With its baseball game already in production, Tudor had the game on store shelves in time for the start of the Major League Baseball season in mid-April. The game sold steadily over the summer, but despite recreating the national pastime, it did not come close to matching electric football's sales figures.

Norman's hope of this being a better year was bolstered by football's rising profile. CBS, NBC, ABC, and DuMont were all televising college football games in the fall. As a result, a football fan who owned a television set in a major Eastern city could choose between four different collegiate games on most Saturday afternoons. These games usually included the best teams in the country – DuMont was broadcasting six Notre Dame contests, while ABC was showing all seven Penn home games. A significant chunk of both the Army and Navy schedules would also make it on to television.

The NFL wasn't as prolific on the television as the college game, but it did have a 15-game arrangement with ABC, using a "game of the week" type format, and it had finally dealt with the money and attention-draining specter of the AAFC by absorbing the rival leagues' three strongest franchises. The AAFC champion Cleveland Browns (who were actually the only champions the league ever had), the Baltimore Colts, and the San Francisco 49ers were all now members of the NFL. Seeking to gain even more attention for this newly merged alignment, the NFL scheduled the four-time AAFC champion Browns against the NFL champion Eagles for the opening game of the 1950 season. Over 70,000 people attended the game, which was played on Saturday night, September 16, in Philadelphia's Municipal Stadium. While the league was surely happy with the attention the game received, it probably wasn't thrilled with the outcome. The Browns walloped the Eagles 35-10. It turned out that, yes, the Browns were a very good football team – in any league.

Luckily, the local Eagles' fans didn't see the game thanks to NFL's home game telecast ban (Browns fans in Ohio did get to watch the rout). Unfortunately, this ban, which the owners were determined to uphold, was having some disastrous results. When the New York Yankees played at Detroit on Thanksgiving Day, it was only the third NFL game to reach New York City television viewers. It had taken eleven weeks for pro football to equal the number of college games that were usually televised during a single Saturday afternoon. This didn't seem like the best way to showcase the NFL to the area with highest concentration of television sets in the nation. But the league didn't want the Yanks and Giants playing in the city on the same day and take the chance of either team stealing paying fans from the other. So the teams alternated "home" dates, once again leaving New York with a home game – and television blackout – on almost every weekend.

As the Lions dismantled the Yanks 49-14 on the chewed-up Briggs' Stadium turf, people around the country were gearing up for the Christmas shopping season by sifting through their advertising infested newspapers. Tudor electric football was even more widely available this year, being sold not only at toy and department stores, but also at sporting good, auto, hardware, furniture, hobby, and drug stores. It was also a featured item in newspaper advertisements, often as the lead toy complete with a photo and description of how the game worked. The price of the game was usually $5.95, although some retailers didn't hesitate to price the No. 500 at $6.95.

The 1950 Toy Manufacturers of the U.S.A. dinner at The Hotel Park Sheraton in New York City. Pictured from bottom to top: Tudor President Norman Sas, former Tudor co-owner Gene Levay, and current Tudor Vice President, Joe Tonole. (Personal collection of Norman Sas.)

Sears, with its mail-order catalogs and growing chain of stores was the country's biggest toy seller. But it had yet to join the electric football huddle. The western influence was strong at Sears, with a number of official Roy Rogers' items. A Daisy Red Ryder 1000 BB repeater rifle – with a 2x scope – was $6.95. Other items electric football was competing with in 1950 were Lionel train sets (that were advertised on NBC television during *The Joe DiMaggio Show*), pedal cars, Radio Flyer wagons, and the Marx Service Station.

In an unusual but astute move Tudor ran a full-page advertisement in the December issue of *Playthings* aimed at harried retailers. "Working overtime; all orders will be filled!" said the headline, which referred specifically to Tudor's line of electric games. The ad went on to say that Tudor had taken care of its regular customers and could even fill some last-minute orders. For those retailers who had run out of electric football games, there certainly was a message in between the lines. If you become a "regular" customer of Tudor's, you'll never find yourself in this position again.

New York football fans found their luck picking up as the season wound down and the shopping season wound up. On Sunday, December 17, the Eastern Conference playoff game between the Browns and the Giants was televised to the New York area. Unfortunately, the Giants lost the game by an 8-3 score. A week later on December 24, New York and many other Eastern cities got to watch the Browns and Rams play the NFL Championship from Cleveland on ABC. (Television maker Admiral sponsored the game.) On a day so brutally cold that many players wore sneakers for traction on the frozen Cleveland field, the Browns kicked a last second field goal for a 30-28 victory. It was also a day where the cold made a mockery of the NFL's television blackout policy. Only 29,000 hardy souls went through the turnstiles at Municipal Stadium. This left the cavernous structure only 50,000 fans short of a sellout.

With the pro football season ending on Christmas Eve, it was a fortuitous time for Santa to have football items in his sleigh. For tens of thousands of boys, that item would be an electric football game. Certainly a number of those boys would spend the morning replaying the Browns-Rams game, having seen the action live on television just the day before. But there was also a large segment of the population who either didn't own a television or lived beyond the current range of live network broadcasts. (This out-of-range area included much of the South, and the expanse west of the Mississippi river, where Los Angeles had emerged as the hub of West Coast television.) And it was still a time when most football fans preferred the college game. A steady Saturday television diet of Notre Dame, Penn, Columbia, Princeton, Harvard, Army, and Navy games guaranteed that a large number of electric football games were playing out the upcoming New Year's Day Sugar Bowl contest between Kentucky and No. 1-ranked Oklahoma.

Regardless of which brand of football was projected onto the No. 500, it was another very successful year for Tudor. And it was a banner year for television makers as well. Six million sets were sold during 1950, bringing the estimated national total to more than ten million. What wasn't estimated was how many of these early sets were sitting in the repair shop.

# It's not too late YET

## Tudor

**TRU-ACTION**

**ELECTRIC GAMES**

No. 500
**TRU-ACTION**
ELECTRIC
FOOTBALL

WE are happy that we were able to give our customers such good service in 1950. We will do everything possible to continue this record, and will be looking for you at the Toy Fair . . . in

ROOM **551**

No. 525
**TRU-ACTION**
ELECTRIC
HORSE RACE

Also the famous **TUDOR**
**XYLOPHONES**
**PIANOS** and **BANJOS**

No. 550
**TRU-ACTION**
ELECTRIC
BASEBALL

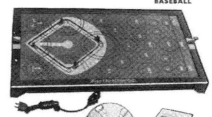

## Tudor
# METAL PRODUCTS CORPORATION

Showroom: 200 Fifth Ave., N. Y. C.     Factory: 176 Johnson St., Brooklyn 1, N. Y.

Tudor's full-page ad from the March 1951 *Playthings*. (Collection of Earl Shores.)

# 6 ELECTRIC FOOTBALL ELEVATES TUDOR IN THE TOY WORLD

**F**or Norman, 1951 should have been off to a flying start. Tudor had once again sold through its inventory of electric football games, and orders for winter and spring shipments were already coming in. The game's popularity was continuing to grow. Toy Fair was just weeks away, and it seemed certain the company would again have a record number of electric football orders by the time the nation's toy buyers left New York. Yet by mid-January the satisfaction of 1950 and anticipation of the coming year was completely pushed aside. Norman's mother Martha passed away on January 15.

Toy Fair had already been well planned, so when showroom 551 opened its doors, it was business as usual other than the occasional offering of condolences from buyers and toy makers. Joe Tonole did his usual showroom magic, keeping the atmosphere upbeat and collegial while chatting up potential clients. So the fact that Norman was less then fully focused on selling electric football games was hardly noticed. It was a period when Norman was grateful for Tonole's presence. His experience had kept things at Tudor running smoothly over the last couple of months – Norman's faith in his partner at this point was unwavering.

The full-page ad Tudor ran in the March issue of *Playthings* pictured all the Tru-Action games with a headline saying, "It's not too late YET." Implied was the idea that buyers should place their game orders early to ensure they had ample stock come the fall – at least for electric football. And whether influenced by the ad or the success of electric football, buyers did drop into showroom 551 and place orders in impressive numbers. It was another successful Toy Fair for Tudor.

And again Tudor would receive a boost from football's rising profile in the sports world. DuMont bought the television rights to the next five NFL Championship games (at $95,000 per game) and was also set to televise 63 NFL games during the 1951 NFL season. Most of these games would only go out to a localized region of the DuMont Network, and, of course, the NFL home-game ban was still in effect. But by early September an AT&T cable was finally going to make coast-to-coast broadcasting a reality. DuMont planned to take advantage of the new technology when the season started. A number of West Coast residents did too, creating a run on television sets as the World Series neared.

While the new cross-country cable and NFL schedule were putting more football on television, the NCAA had decided to drastically restrict the number of college games being televised in 1951. Fearing declining attendance, the NCAA instituted its own home-game ban and also took complete control of all telecasts. As a result, there would be a single college football television contract, with NBC and sponsor Westinghouse paying $1.2 million for 10 weeks of college football. In total, 40 different games would be broadcast over 52 NBC stations – but there was a catch. Only 7 games could be shown to any given area during the season. This meant that the New York City viewing area, which sometimes got to see 5 college games on a single fall Saturday afternoon in 1950, would only see 7 games during the entire 1951 college football season. Another NCAA imposed limitation was that no team could appear more than twice on NBC during the season. This left Notre Dame and Penn, teams with a long history of televising games, threatening to disobey the NCAA. But neither team did – and Penn didn't even make it onto NBC's schedule. The bottom line was, college football fans were going to have to plan their Saturday carefully if they wanted to see a game on television.

With football season underway, electric football games again became popular lay-away items at stores around the country. And, once again, this included many types of stores – department stores, toy stores, hardware stores, auto part stores, and hobby shops. In fact the Ohio-based Strauss department store chain ran a full-page newspaper ad in late September featuring ladies dresses, coats, sweaters and suits. The only non-women's garment item on the page was Tudor's electric football game.

By mid-October most Sears stores had opened their Toy Town departments, and this year Sears was advertising an electric football game. But it wasn't the No. 500 – it was called Foto-Electric Football and sold for the same $6.95 price as Tudor's model. The difference between the two games was obvious. Foto-Electric Football was basically a box with a light bulb inside. Two players picked their plays from transparent overlay cards, placed the cards on the "field," then turned the light bulb on to reveal the outcome of the play. So there was no mistaking the Tudor game for this Cadaco-Ellis game, at least on the toy store shelf. Newspaper advertisements, however, were another story. And Foto-Electric was not the only game in 1951 with "electric football" in its title. Jim Prentice Electric Football used a battery-

A Tudor No. 500 box from 1952. (Photo by Earl Shores.)

powered circuit board that was concealed beneath the game. When the players selected their offensive and defensive choices – by pressing a metal tab – an electric circuit was completed. The completed circuit then lit up a tiny light bulb to reveal the outcome of the play. Again, no boy or parent would ever confuse Jim Prentice Football with a Tudor No. 500...in person at least. But thanks to the popularity of Tudor's game many retailers had begun conveniently advertising "electric football" generically without any designation as to what particular type of electric game they were selling. One giveaway was that the Prentice game usually sold for around $3, while the Tudor No. 500 cost double that amount. Despite the confusion the Prentice and Cadaco-Ellis games were causing, Norman did not take legal action against either company. Tudor had been the owners of the "electric football" trademark since March of 1949.

Not that the world of football was devoid of legal action in October of 1951. Just days before Sears opened its Toy Town departments, the Justice Department filed an antitrust lawsuit against the NFL over the league's television blackout policy. A number of factors prompted the suit, but a major impetus was the unfortunate situation that had arisen in New York City, home of the four major television networks, and the nations' highest concentration of television sets, as well as, unfortunately, the NFL Giants and Yanks. Thanks to the Giants and Yanks alternating home dates, New York City football fans were going to see only a single NFL game on television during the entire twelve-week season. It was not a great way for the NFL to win over new fans. But after the Rams attendance declined by over 100,000 fans in 1950 (during an official NFL "experiment" that allowed home game telecasts to the Los Angeles metropolitan area) the owners were more determined than ever to keep their blackout policy in place.

On Thanksgiving Day, New York City fans got to see their first and only NFL game on television when the Lions hosted the Packers in Detroit. The game was a television and, arguably, a cultural landmark as it was the first ever coast-to-coast Thanksgiving Day football telecast. For better or for worse, dinner plans for this Thursday holiday have never been the same. And by this point in the football season, there were unhappy fans stretching well beyond the New York area. The new collegiate television plan had angered a lot of people, including powerful ones in Congress. As a result, the Justice Department had issued an opinion declaring that the NCAA restrictions on college football broadcasting were illegal – but the Department was not prepared to take action until there was a verdict or settlement in the NFL suit. Another reason the Justice Department was reluctant to file another suit was that this season's NCAA broadcast restrictions were set to end on November 24. Perhaps the NCAA would be more open to television next season thanks to the opinion alone.

With the NCAA's broadcast restrictions lifted, football fans got an eyeful the following Saturday when NBC televised the collegiate double-header of Army-Navy and Notre Dame-Southern California. None of the four teams were ranked, and Navy made quick work of Army in their 42-7 win. But viewers got to enjoy the Irish and the Trojans sliding around in the fog and mud of a Southern California rainstorm (Notre Dame prevailed 19-12).

The three nationally televised football contests were a good way for Tudor to catapult into the heart of the Christmas shopping season. Final payments were being made on lay-away No. 500's, and those shoppers fortunate enough to lay-away had guaranteed they would get their hands on a very popular Christmas item. In 1951 electric football was more than holding its own against Lionel and American Flyer train sets, wind-up Dick Tracy squad cars, Marx Army play sets (with 145 pieces), and the Red Ryder line. The going price for electric football this year was $6.95, which placed it somewhere between a Marx Metal Service station and an entry-level tricycle.

Fewer and fewer No. 500's were to be found as Christmas neared, and any remaining games got last minute help from the NFL, who played their championship game on Sunday, December 23. The game was historical from the standpoint that it was the first ever coast-to-coast telecast of an NFL Championship game (it was also just the second NFL game televised to New York City in 1951). With the game being played in Los Angeles, it was a true illustration of the power of a national television cable link-up. Of course local Ram fans didn't get to see their team's 24-17 victory, thanks to the NFL blackout policy. No video record of the game exists. DuMont's telecast now resides on the Museum of Television and Radio's "Lost Programs" list.

For any child receiving an electric football game on Christmas morning, their imagination would surely be influenced by the "recency effect" of the

NFL Championship game. The college football regular season had been long over, and fewer games had been televised, so the NFL's stature had likely gotten a boost during the year. But when you consider that there were only 12 NFL teams, and only 10 NFL cities (both New York and Chicago were home to two teams), there were large swaths of the country where the college game was king. The kind of buzzing a No. 500 was doing was still based in large part on geography.

College football finished its season on New Year's Day with the first-ever national telecast of the Rose Bowl, as well as a Sugar Bowl match-up between top-ranked Tennessee and third-ranked Maryland. Thanks to cable limitations allowing television broadcasts into New Orleans, but not out, the country couldn't see Maryland pull off a 28-13 upset of the Volunteers. Because the season's final rankings were etched in stone weeks before the game, Tennessee would still end up with the No. 1 ranking despite the loss.

For the third year in a row, Tudor's No. 500 proved to be so popular that retailers took out newspaper ads when they received new shipments of the game in January and February of 1952. To have a toy football game in demand in February – at a $6.95 price – was quite an accomplishment. Electric football was proving to have more staying power than even Norman had dreamed. Not only was the game "long lasting," at the moment it seemed to be in a phase of "ever lasting." It was able to sell year round – this was well beyond the expectations Norman had when he was working on game prototypes back in 1948.

At Toy Fair in March, a record 5,500 buyers jammed the hallways of 200 Fifth Avenue and the McAlpin Hotel during the first two days of the event. A *New York Times* article even joked that the toy sellers were getting writer's cramp from the number of orders they had to write up. Norman and Joe Tonole did their part writing orders, having a game that was in demand not only throughout the country but also throughout the year. By the time the Fair was over, 11,000 buyers had attended. Many manufacturers reported record sales for the ten-day event. Tudor was one of those manufacturers.

While electric football's place in the toy world seemed pretty well defined in 1952, both pro and college football were struggling mightily to define what role television should play in growing their sports' popularity. The NFL had a federal antitrust suit sitting on its doorstep, thanks to the league's home blackout policy. In hoping to incur the good graces of the government, the owners voted to move the financially struggling New York Yanks to Dallas. This would free up the New York airwaves for at least 6 Giants games in the coming season. And these games would be televised by DuMont, who signed a season-long deal not only with the Giants, but

The color sales flyer that Tudor handed out at the 1953 Toy Fair. (Personal collection of Norman Sas.)

also the Eagles and Steelers. Away games would be shown to each city, with non-NFL Northeastern cities like New Haven, Providence, Boston, and Syracuse getting to watch all 12 Giants games. DuMont started its 1952 NFL schedule in August with the first coast-to-coast telecast of the College All-Star game. Since 1934, a team of college all-stars had faced off against the reigning NFL champions in Chicago during the preseason, with the college players winning 6 times in 18 tries. Viewers of the 53 DuMont stations around the country were treated to another very competitive contest, as the Rams needed 10 fourth-quarter points for a 10-7 win.

To counter criticism of its stingy football television policy, the NCAA had paid $50,000 for a study of television's effect on college football. It was no surprise that the "study" offered, at least according to the NCAA, conclusive proof that television was hurting game-day attendance. And as a result of the study, only a single college football game would be televised each fall Saturday, with no major teams appearing more than once. NBC got the college football contract for 1952 – General Motors was the sponsor – for 12 NCAA games over 63 stations. Again, Notre Dame was not happy with the limitations imposed by the NCAA. CBS found a way to work around the NCAA rules by getting a contract with the U.S. Military to broadcast 12 armed forces games. These games did not include any of the military academies under NCAA jurisdiction; they were limited to "base teams" (for example game, Fort Belvoir vs. the Quantico Marines) but there would two networks showing Saturday afternoon football.

In early October, Sears signaled the start of the Christmas shopping season by opening their Toy Town departments. Mail-order and retail competitor Montgomery Ward was not to be outdone, busily readying the Toyland sections of its own stores. Curiously, neither of these retail powerhouses had approached Tudor about selling electric football, despite its growing popularity. (J.C. Penney had shown no interest either.) And Norman felt no compulsion at this point to push his game on any of these national retailers. He was doing just fine, continually emptying his warehouse by selling games through just about every type of retailer other than Sears, Ward, or J.C. Penney. There would certainly be prestige and profit in being carried by one of the nation's mail-order giants, but selling to Sears or Ward would add pressure to the production line. It might also hasten the "long lasting" part of the electric football equation. If the game became too easy to find, then it might lose some of its appeal. In the fall of 1952 demand was still increasing, and Tudor was making a nice profit. Norman didn't see any reason to change his approach to marketing the game.

Someone who was changing his approach to his "game" was NFL Commissioner Bert Bell. With the antitrust suit hanging over the league, and players' salaries escalating, Bell proclaimed during a Football Writers Association luncheon in October that professional football "is no longer a sport – it's a big business." And some of its businessmen were losing money. Bell estimated that only four of the twelve teams would show a profit for the 1952 season, despite record attendance. Considering the NFL's contentious relationship with television, Bell did say something very surprising. He called the revenues from television and radio broadcast "life savers."

As the business of Christmas picked up in November, Tudor's electric football games were moving off the shelf in record numbers. Some of those games were off the shelf, but not yet out of the store, as the popularity and $6.95 price of electric football again made it a trendy lay-away item. Any football related items were also going to get some help from television during Thanksgiving week. On the Saturday before the holiday, a national television audience watched undefeated USC battle undefeated UCLA before an overflowing Coliseum crowd of 96,000. USC earned a New Year's Day trip to the Rose Bowl with a 14-12 victory.

On Thanksgiving Day, the popularity of television was illustrated far beyond the NFL double-header that the DuMont broadcast over 48 stations during the afternoon and early evening hours. The Grand Marshall of Macy's nationally televised Thanksgiving Day parade was CBS television personality Jackie Gleason. Just two days later, Navy topped Army 7-0 in front of 102,000 fans and a national NBC television audience. Those couch-bound football fans who stayed tuned after the game was finished got to see bonus coverage of Notre Dame-USC from South Bend. Although the Irish were having a less than stellar year, at least by Notre Dame standards, they squashed USC's national title hopes by handing the Trojans their first loss of the season. The next day, the Sunday sports section of the *New York Times* devoted its first six pages to college football results. Found on page seven, next to the Brooklyn Dodgers' spring exhibition schedule, was a preview of that day's NFL games.

With the calendar turning over to December, the Christmas shopping season was in full swing. Toys were getting bigger and more expensive, with metal pedal cars, pedal tractors, and Lionel train sets all rubbing up against or exceeding the $20 mark. And besides train sets, Lionel had a number of elaborate and expensive accessories for its trains, like an operating milk car and a cattle car where the cattle actually loaded themselves on and off the train. The cattle's method of movement, though few toy buyers realized it, had been borrowed from an unlikely source. Before boarding their special car, Lionel's bovine passengers waited patiently in a fenced-in pen for their date with destiny. Once the train arrived, the bottom of the pen and the bottom of the cattle car started to vibrate, and the cattle could do nothing but follow the irresistible urge to trundle onto the train. So if a boy got bored on Christmas and put his Lionel cow on a Tudor No. 500 he could see quite a sight – a cow "run to daylight." Levay's 1937 vibrating patent was even cited in Lionel's patent application for "Toy Railroad Trackside Accessories."

A Tudor Playthings' ad from 1953. *Playthings*, page 701, March 1953

Electric football was widely available again this year, with Tudor making shipments to stores even in December. (The arrivals of Tudor shipments were still being announced in local newspaper advertisements.) Many of these December sales were coming on top of the record orders Tudor had taken at the Toy Fair, so it was shaping up as the company's most profitable year ever. Football's still growing popularity was helping, and this year Christmas ended up being sandwiched between a nationally televised NFL playoff game on December 21 (the Lions beat the Rams 31-21 for the

Western Conference title), and the NFL Championship game on December 28. Both games were televised by DuMont, who managed to get the title game broadcast over 63 stations. With Christmas falling on a Thursday, there was still plenty of buzzing going on by the time the Lions and Browns lined up in Cleveland on Sunday afternoon. The Lions held off the Browns 17-7 to claim the NFL 1952 title.

1953 opened with the first-ever New Year's Day television football orgy, as the Sugar Bowl, Orange Bowl, Cotton Bowl, and Rose Bowl, were all broadcast nationally. For football fans around the country this was the exclamation point to a bountiful season, even with the NFL's home blackouts and the NCAA's strict one-game-a-weekend policy. Many areas without a home NFL team had seen a televised professional game on every weekend of the 1952 season. Even New York City viewers got to watch ten NFL games this year. So ending the season with a television football quadruple-header was a landmark event. Without remote control, any kind of recording technology or onscreen "crawls" updating watchers with every detail of every game being played, viewers pretty much picked their favorite game and stuck with it. The only disappointment of the day might have come from the No. 1 team not being in action. Undefeated Michigan State was only a provisional member of the Big Ten, and not yet eligible for the Rose Bowl.

In March, Toy Fair continued to reflect the growing postwar economy and birth rate, expanding to 1250 exhibitors in 1953. Fair attendance was on the increase too, with opening day registration running 1500 buyers ahead of last year's total. Having a record number of buyers didn't guarantee record orders, but business was brisk for most of the established toy makers. Lionel was reporting that its entire planned production run had been booked after just two days of the Fair. Obviously, Lionel's production plan would change in the coming days. Tudor was having a good Fair too, with the No. 500 again in demand even with the new football season being months away. It was a nice situation for any toy company to be in. Norman and Joe Tonole headed home from the Toy Fair confident of another record year for Tudor.

Sweating through the early months of 1953 were Commissioner Bell and a number of NFL team executives, as they all found themselves testifying in front of Federal Judge Alan Grim over the leagues' limitations on television and radio broadcasts. Judge Grim was incredulous after Detroit's general manager Nicholas Kerbawy claimed that the champion Lions had lost money during 15 of the last 17 seasons. Grim was curious as to how a business survived such a predicament – not many others could. As the Justice Department lawyers turned up the heat, the NFL searched for profitable ways to get more football on television while maintaining the sanctity of the home blackout. With the help of DuMont, Westinghouse, and Rams' owner Dan Reeves, the NFL came up with its first true national television contract in May.

Under the terms of the deal, Westinghouse paid the league $1.3 million for the rights to 20 games. DuMont would televise the games over 87 stations, getting the NFL into 45 areas of the country that had previously not been able to watch pro football. One of the contingencies for Westinghouse to complete the deal was a guarantee that NFL cities would see a televised game on each and every week of the season – even if the local team was home. Without 12 weeks of airtime in each NFL city, there was no deal. The solution came by having the league play Saturday night games during 8 weeks of the season and having the Rams play afternoon home games on the first two Saturdays of December. (None of the Midwest or Eastern owners wanted any part of night games in December. Los Angeles had a temperate climate and a three-hour time difference – a 2:00 p.m. West Coast start translated to a 5:00 p.m. television slot in the East. An extra $40,000 payment from DuMont helped the Rams "see" the benefits of playing on Saturday.)

The new television arrangement worked as follows: if the Giants were playing at home on Sunday afternoon, DuMont would show an NFL game to New York City on Saturday night. And if the Eagles were home on Saturday night, then DuMont would televise a game to the Philadelphia area on Sunday afternoon. It was also possible to see games on both Saturday and Sunday if your local team was playing away from home. To end up with 19 viable telecasts, DuMont was planning on covering 48 different NFL games – or two-thirds of all the league's games. Commissioner Bell hoped the Feds would look upon this innovative package as proof that the NFL was truly open to television and that the home game blackout was necessary to protect the interest of the teams.

In college football, NBC and the NCAA (with General Motors as the sponsor) had come up with a 12-week package, similar to the previous year. Only a single game per Saturday would be shown, but sometimes that game would actually be a "panorama," or portions of four different games. Again the NCAA held to a single appearance by any team, even the major teams like Michigan State, Notre Dame, and USC.

By the time Sears stores opened its Toy Town departments in early October, the college and pro football seasons were several weeks old. DuMont had already started its NFL telecasts, and electric football was sure to benefit from the new exposure the NFL would receive with each passing week. Tudor's game was again a featured lay-away item, joining Lionel trains, doll carriages, pedal cars, and Radio Flyer wagons as a must-have toy that parents would pay for on the installment plan. Neither Sears nor Ward had looked in electric football's direction yet, and Norman was still content to not have to deal with the added pressures of delivering product to the country's largest retailer. He still had no trouble selling out the No. 500.

Someone who had no problem delivering items to Sears was Roy Rogers. The popular "King of the Cowboys" had made a name for himself through dozens of western movies in the 1930's and 1940's, and since late 1951 his television show had been a fixture of NBC's Sunday night schedule. Underneath Mr. Rogers' easygoing cowboy persona was a smart man who was very good at something that kept his popularity consistently high – marketing. For years, the Roy Rogers Rodeo toured arenas throughout the country, selling a variety of official Roy items at every stop. And by 1953 Roy's merchandise had become a staple of Sears, with over 50 Roy Rogers' items – ranging from a $4 Marx Double R Bar Rodeo play set, to a $20 Roy Rogers Chuck Wagon (a very fancy Radio Flyer with a canvas cover) – gracing the pages of the catalog. Responsible for the licensing and promotion of these items was the marketing arm of Roy's financial empire, Roy Rogers Enterprises [RRE]. Under the direction of marketing manager Larry Kent, the RRE-Sears relationship had been quite profitable. Sears had sold $7.5 million worth of Roy Rogers merchandise in 1951 – an amount that equaled 35% of RRE's total sales for the year. Already planned by Larry Kent for the coming Christmas shopping season was a full-page Roy Rogers' ad in *Life* magazine.

Unfortunately, just days into November, the month turned tragic for Tudor. Joe Tonole passed away on November 4. It was a shock to the company and devastating for Norman. Tonole was a trusted friend by this point, having never doubted Norman's ability to run the company, and the knowledge and connections Tonole offered Tudor had played a large part in electric football's success. The fact that the No. 500 was seemingly everywhere during the Christmas shopping season was of little consolation. For Norman, 1953 would always be remembered as the year his business partner "died too soon."

Just as the month reached the halfway point, Judge Grim handed down a verdict in the NFL antitrust case. He allowed the league to maintain the right to blackout home game telecasts, but NFL teams could no longer have sole control of their home television airwaves when the team was playing away. The ruling would open the door to something football fans currently take for granted – the Sunday double-header. Both the government and the NFL claimed victory. In Commissioner Bell's view, the league had "won the most important part of its case." The gate receipts of the home team had been protected.

On Thanksgiving morning, newspapers bulging with Christmas advertising were delivered around the country. Prominently featured in

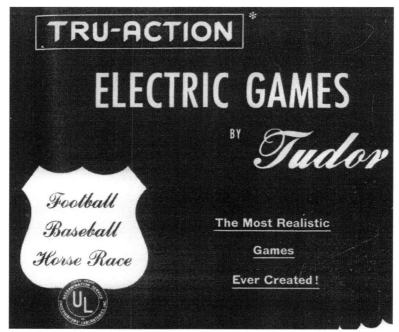

Tudor's Toy Fair ad in 1953. *Playthings*, March 1953.

these ads was the Tudor No. 500, which again was available at nearly every type of retailer in existence (except for large mail-order retailers like Sears, Ward, and J.C. Penney). And by 11:00 a.m. that morning – 8:00 a.m. on the West Coast – professional football was flickering across television screens throughout the country as the Packers visited the Lions in Detroit. NBC was adding a second game to the day, televising the Brigham Young-Utah game a few hours later. Fortunately, all the day's football would be done by the time the turkey came out of the oven.

December rolled forward at a quick pace. Electric football was an established part of toy advertising, even to the point where retailers mentioned how they ran short of the game in 1952. The game was now frequently mentioned in the Dear Santa letters published in local papers throughout the United States. But even as the game became a regular in the Christmas toy line-up, there was not a lot of joy in the hallways of Tudor. There was still an empty office and a silent spot in the Tudor hierarchy that was once filled by the ebullient Joe Tonole.

Christmas landed on a Friday in 1953, giving a long weekend to those not on a school vacation schedule. It also gave the feeling of an extended holiday, which was not really over until DuMont signed off from its broadcast of the NFL Championship game on Sunday afternoon. A record 130 stations across the country carried the Browns-Lions game from Detroit (only 63 stations broadcast the 1952 contest; 114 stations had shown the recent World Series). Viewers were treated to a thrilling game as the Lions scored a touchdown with just over two minutes left in the game for a 17-16 victory. Since it was the only football game on television that weekend, the electric football buzzing of Christmas morning had to be at least slightly influenced by the professional game. The following weekend five collegiate bowl games would be televised, including four on January 1. Any electric football games still in the living room "play" rotation by that point surely had teams full of players on athletic scholarships.

# New!

## GOTHAM

The Gotham Pressed Steel Corporation joins Tudor on the electric football scrimmage line in 1954.
(Gotham sales catalog; collection of Earl Shores.)

# 7 A COMPETITOR TAKES THE FIELD

or both the NFL and Tudor, 1953 turned out to be the most profitable year ever. Electric football was an item that stores wanted to have on their shelves, even in January. And at the moment, Tudor was very adept at getting their game to almost any store in the country that wanted it. Thanks to the expanded television contract with DuMont, the NFL had also been very adept at getting pro football into households across the country, at least ones with television sets. Television money had allowed 9 of the 12 NFL teams to be profitable in 1953, with the Giants and Steelers reporting that DuMont dollars were the sole reason both teams made money. College football had done well too with the networks paying a combined sum of $900,000 dollars to televise the four major bowl games on New Years Day.

As the preparations for Toy Fair got underway, the loss of Joe Tonole was still very much on Norman's mind. Electric football by now could sell itself, so it wasn't necessarily Tonole's sales prowess that Tudor would miss most. But Tonole's presence and input certainly would be missed. And there was something else that Tudor needed to have at the Toy Fair this year that Tonole could have offered – perspective. Among the record 1,400 exhibitors in 1954 was a company called the Gotham Pressed Steel Corporation. Incorporated in 1930, the Bronx-based company was hardly a new face at the Fair. But they had a new item for 1954 – an electric football game.

Gotham wasn't a newcomer to the sports-action category either. In the mid-1930's Gotham created the first toy hockey game with rotating metal players, and the company was already running multi-page color *Playthings* spreads before Elmer Sas and Gene Levay pointed Tudor down the road to being a toy maker. By 1940 Gotham's toy line included a popular bowling game, multiple bagatelle games, child-size pool tables, toy sweepers, and elaborate metal Chinese Checker sets. In *Playthings'* advertisements published throughout 1941 Gotham claimed to have "America's Foremost Line of Action Games." After the war, the company branched out into basketball and baseball games with the baseball line featuring models endorsed by big league stars Carl Hubbell and Jackie Robinson. Football had never really interested Gotham – that is, until the company saw how much success Tudor was having. After sitting on the sideline through the early 50's, Gotham decided to strap on its helmet and step onto the vibrating gridiron.

"Gotham was the first company to copy us," said Sas. "They showed up at the 1954 Fair with a game of their own." Although imitation may be the sincerest form of flattery, and Norman had acknowledged in his MIT thesis that "competition in the toy industry takes the form of copying," he was less than amused by Gotham's "competition" for reasons that went beyond plain business. Gotham's new game, as Norman recalls, came with trash talk that would be more at home in the machismo of the new millennium than in the mid-1950's. "Gotham's vice president threatened to bury me and Tudor."

The name of Gotham's vice president was...Eddie Gluck.

Yes, it was the same Eddie Gluck that Elmer Sas and Gene Levay had hired to be Tudor's sales manager in 1938. And it was the same Eddie Gluck who in mid-1945 jumped at the chance to become Gotham's vice president and treasurer – an event of such import that Gotham President Charles Anderson announced it in the December 1945 issue of *Playthings*. Replacing Gluck, of course, was Joe Tonole who went on to become half owner of Tudor and Norman's partner. Somehow this missed opportunity seemed to haunt Gluck, even though he hadn't been on the Tudor payroll for close to a decade. He was jealous of Tudor's current success and not shy about showing his disdain for Norman.

"Eddie was an older man who really knew the toy business and all the toy buyers – to him I was still a kid," said Sas. "The more successful we got with the No. 500, the more bitter he got."

In addition to his extensive toy background, the 52-year-old Gluck had a very impressive sports background. He had played professional basketball during the 1920's and 1930's, as a 5' 7" guard. Although this was short even for the period, "Sonny" Gluck's solid 190-pound frame and scoring skills landed him on the rosters of some of the best teams in the country, including the Original (New York) Celtics and Philadelphia Warriors of the American Basketball League. But with substitutions being a rare part of 1920's basketball, and the talent level on both teams being so high (many Celtic and Warrior players are enshrined in the Basketball Hall of Fame), Gluck never saw significant playing time in either city. By 1928 he had moved on to become the starting guard for the Brooklyn

An unusual photo from the 1946 Toy Manufacturers Association dinner. Left to right: Eddie Gluck, his wife Pearl, Gene Levay, Joe Tonole, and Elmer Sas. (Personal Collection of Norman Sas.)

Dodgers, an independent pro team who defeated the Negro-champion Harlem Renaissance along with many others while barnstorming through the Northeast during the winter of 1929. This initial era of "big time" professional basketball disappeared with the Depression, leaving Gluck to finish his career in the mid-1930's toiling away in the New York State Basketball League.

What's crucial to understand about basketball of this era was that it was far from a glamorous profession. It was a rough and tumble period for the sport, when on-court fights were common, and a now familiar nickname was developed for those who played the game. Professional basketball players became known as "cagers" because often a chicken wire or rope cage was erected around the court. This kept rowdy fans, bottles, and other unwanted items off the court. Lit cigarettes, however, often still made it through the screens. So besides points and rebounds, players could compare burn marks and bloody tic-tac-toe cage marks at the end of the game.

It was in this sporting crucible that Gluck molded his competitive instinct. Threatening the opponent, in this case Norman Sas, was likely just part of how Gluck learned to play the "game." Still, there's no question that challenging Tudor in electric football was more than just business – Gluck wanted to show Norman just how difficult the toy business could be.

What Gotham had on display in showroom 221 of the Fifth Avenue building was the G-880 All-Star Electric Football game. Measuring 28" x 15", it was three inches longer than the Tudor No. 500, with a 2"-high simulated wood-grain metal frame. And instead of a metal playing surface, the Gotham field was made of laminated fiberboard ("Masonite Pressedwood" was the official name). Field composition was just one of a number of features where Gotham differed from Tudor.

Gotham's players, like Tudor's, were made of flat plastic and mounted on metal bases. But the similarities ended there. Each Gotham player was posed upright and running, with a "straight arm" extended out. Clearly visible on each player were a helmet, face, hands, uniform outline, and shoes – details that were a stark contrast to Tudor's smooth, essentially naked players. Gotham's men were almost twice as tall as Tudor's men; when the G-880 was set up, it looked as if it had a red team and a blue team of miniature Heisman trophies.

Having a field not made of metal allowed Gotham to go "magnetic" with their footballs. So instead of felt footballs, each Gotham game came with ingeniously shaped miniature wooden footballs that contained a magnet on one end. A player "ran" with the ball by having the magnetic end of the ball attached to his metal base. On Tudor's metal game boards, this magnetic running technique would have resulted in the player being stuck to the field. The magnetic ball concept also led to a different kind of passing and kicking game. Instead of an actual quarterback/kicker figure, Gotham had a wedge-shaped "spring shooter" device. Although the shooter couldn't run and looked awkward, those weighty wooden balls allowed Gotham's passing and kicking game to be more accurate than Tudor's. Finishing touches for the game were two wire goal posts and a metal first down marker.

Surprisingly, there wasn't much of a rollout for the G-880. There were no special announcements in *Playthings*, or even a mention of electric football in the business-card-sized Gotham ad run in the Toy Fair issue (Gluck did mention his new electric basketball game). But Eddie wasn't going to quietly let his G-880 play second string to the No. 500. As a toy industry veteran, he knew how to promote his game and gain a foothold in electric football. Up until this point, Tudor and Gotham hadn't really competed directly against each other for dominance in the toy marketplace. That would soon change.

Another thing about to change was the NFL's television policy. To comply with Judge Grim's verdict, the league would now allow telecasts of other "neutral" games into a city even when the local team was playing away. Under the old policy, the home team had exclusive rights to their territory. When the Eagles visited the Giants in New York, the Eagles-Giants game was the only NFL contest that could be televised to the Philadelphia area that day. Under the new rules, Philadelphia fans might now also be able to watch a late afternoon NFL contest from the West Coast after the Eagles game was finished.

As a result, DuMont eagerly renewed its NFL television contract with the promise of showing a record number of games. The network would continue Saturday NFL games (nine at night, and two late afternoon West Coast games), guaranteeing each NFL city at least a game a week

– and likely more. In all, 60 of the league's 72 regular season games were going to be televised. And DuMont was starting things off early, with 4 national preseason telecasts. It was an ambitious schedule, yet one the network was more than happy to undertake.

In a bit of a coup, ABC took college football away from NBC for the coming fall (offering $4 million to the NCAA didn't hurt). ABC was set to televise 12 games in all – again the NCAA was limiting college football to just a single game per Saturday. Unfortunately, the network was having a hard time coming

Featured in the display case at The Toy Center in Brookline, MA – a pair of Tudor No. 500 models. *Playthings*, page 89, August 1954.

up with a sponsor. GM, who helped NBC defer the costs of college football in 1953, was not interested. At least not at the price ABC was asking.

It was May when Gluck finally broadcast Gotham's new additions to the toy world in a four-page color *Playthings* layout. Leading the way on the first page was Gotham's new All-Star Electric Basketball game, which was no surprise considering Gluck's past. The game was the same size as Gotham's football game, with 10 plastic and metal players who vibrated around the "court." At each end was a large metal backstop that included a basket, scoreboard, and lithographed crowd scene. Players "dribbled" by carrying the magnetic ball on their metal bases (player construction was identical to Gotham's football players), and shot the ball with a spring shooter device. The game was advertised as "A Sure Shot For Big Sales."

On the next page was a new 40" x 22" floor model pool table, complete with collapsible metal legs. Three other pool tables were advertised on this page, including a smaller table model that had been Educator Approved by the Toy Guidance Council. It wasn't until page 3 that the new football game showed up with the headline "This Is It! The much talked about All-Star Electric Football Game with Magnetic Football." Like all the artwork in the layout, the game was hand drawn and illustrated in color. It was a very attractive and accurate depiction of the G-880, all the way down to the blue and red players and wood-grain frame. A number of football puns finished the ad: "Don't be caught 'off side' by not carrying this number.

The Penalty will be Lost Sales." Retail price for the game was suggested at $6.98, the same as the basketball game. And when you looked closely at the basketball shooter and football quarterback, you couldn't help wonder if Gluck came up with the basketball game first, then decided he might just get a football game out of the same concept and parts.

Finishing out the Gotham layout was a new electric Bingo game, whose method of operation was a complete mystery. But it was an impressive and colorful spread that left the impression that Gotham was serious with its new items and new electric direction. All the games had a large "wow" factor. And the following month Gluck's picture appeared in *Playthings* along with a three-paragraph article describing the new games. Gluck added that Gotham had completely modernized its factory. With these "increased production facilities" the company would be able "to take care of reorders promptly."

Gotham's 1954 Heisman player. (Photo by Earl Shores.)

Throughout the summer, Norman had wondered what kind of impact Gotham's electric football clone would have on Tudor's sales. Tudor had a five-year head start with electric football, and the retailers who dealt with the company over that period were unlikely to switch allegiances – unless they had been already carrying other Gotham products. Gluck would surely offer those retailers the G-880 at a discount, allowing more profit to be made from a Gotham electric football game than a Tudor game. And Gluck would surely be dangling the promise of discount wholesale pricing to any store that took on multiple Gotham items. Like Levay, Gluck had decades-old relationships with toy buyers. There was no doubt that he would use those connections to place his game.

In July, Tudor picked up an added selling point to the No. 500, as the Toy Guidance Council endorsed the No. 500 as an "Educator Approved Prestige Toy." Tudor could now put a large TCG symbol on the boxes of the No. 500 (it looked much like a Good Housekeeping logo) announcing the game's enhanced status to toy shoppers everywhere.

The rising profile of football could be seen in the fact that three of the four major networks now saw the sport as important enough to have as a regularly scheduled part of their fall lineup. NBC, who earlier in the year lost their NCAA contract, was determined to have football on the air during the fall of 1954. So in an innovative move, the network looked north

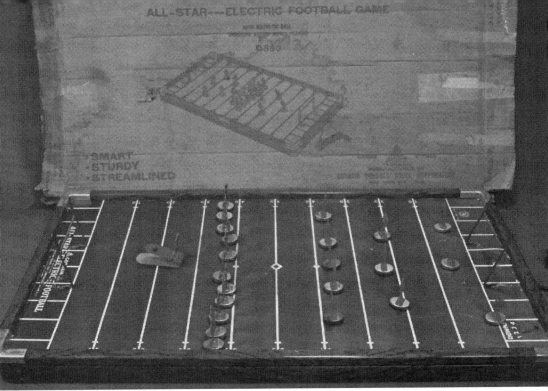

**Gotham's 1954 G-880 All Star Electric Football Game. (Photo by Earl Shores.)**

– to Canadian professional football. NBC signed on to show 13 Saturday afternoon Canadian games, including the Grey Cup Championship game in November. Press releases explaining the different rules of the Canadian game were sent out by the network. NBC also had the good fortune of handing the play-by-play microphone over to future football and baseball Hall of Fame sportscaster Lindsey Nelson.

Not only was there going to be more football on television, there was going to be more electric football on toy store shelves. Norman was still uneasy as the football season started in mid-September. No one really knew what the impact of either was going to be. On the second weekend of the NFL season Washington D.C. football fans got their first taste of the loosened television rules. DuMont televised three NFL games into the area – one on Saturday night followed by a Sunday double-header that finished with the Rams-49ers game from Los Angeles (93,000 fans packed the Coliseum for the 24-24 tie). By the following weekend, Sears had kicked off the Christmas shopping season by opening the Toy Town section of its more than 400 stores, and the Sears *Christmas Book* was arriving in mailboxes around the country. Fortunately, there were no surprises for Tudor from the nation's largest retailer. Cadaco's Foto-Electric football was the only electric football game being sold by Sears.

**Gotham's 1954 kicker/passer device. (Photo by Earl Shores.)**

But when a slightly smaller national retailer put out its catalog a few weeks later, Norman's uneasiness was confirmed. Eddie Gluck had gotten his Gotham electric football into the Montgomery Ward Christmas catalog. Although Ward was only doing a third of the business that Sears did, it was still selling close to a billion dollars of merchandise a year. That's a significant sales figure, even by current standards. And it was an electric football landmark because it was the first time that a major national retailer decided to sell the game. Using his carefully cultivated toy contacts, Gluck had broken new ground in electric football marketing. While it didn't exactly send Norman scrambling for a national retailer of his own, he knew he needed to keep an eye on Gotham. Gluck was making a serious effort to sell his game.

Unfortunately, Ward's efforts didn't quite equal Gluck's. The G-880 was pictured from overhead. It was a very unflattering perspective that rendered all of the game's features into a flat one-dimensional image. In fact, it was really hard for shoppers to figure out what type of game they were looking at. But Ward was selling electric football, even calling the game "electric football" in spite of Tudor's trademark. And they were featuring the G-880 as a lay-away item for $6.95.

The fall continued with lots of NFL on television and lots of newspaper ads featuring electric football games. Tudor's No. 500 was the dominant model heading into the Thanksgiving holiday, even being advertised as a Prestige Toy by a number of retailers. After the morning papers were scattered on the floor and NBC finished with their Macy's Thanksgiving Day Parade broadcast, the Packers and Lions kicked off for their noontime game on the DuMont Network. Set to kickoff the very next morning was the all-important Christmas shopping season.

Electric football was a visible part of toy advertising throughout the holiday weekend and into December. Ward eventually included electric football in its Christmas campaign, but the game was not seriously promoted. In fact it usually wasn't even pictured, just mentioned in line item fashion (Electric Football Game ------$5.85). That it was a vibrating-type game made by Gotham Pressed Steel wasn't made clear. Over the next few weeks, many retailers selling the Gotham G-880 were conveniently vague about the brand of electric football game they were selling. Gotham games were usually promoted generically as "electric football," whereas Tudor retailers seemed much more determined to include the name of the No. 500's maker when the game was advertised. It was, after all, a Prestige Toy. The Toy Guidance Council had yet to issue any edict for the G-880.

Thanks to its greater availability, the No. 500 outsold Gotham's model as December moved along toward its penultimate day. And with Christmas falling on a Saturday, it was another perfect year to manufacture a connection between the holiday and football. On Sunday afternoon – while the leftovers were heating and two different kinds of electric football game were still buzzing – the Lions would play the Browns for the NFL Championship. The other connection between the NFL and Christmas was television. Almost seven million sets were sold during 1954. Many of those new sets would be Christmas presents, and one of the first major events they would show was the NFL Championship. (In the New York City area, this would be the 19th televised NFL game of the season.)

The G-880, though not educator approved, wouldn't have been a disappointing gift on Christmas morning. Electric football was pretty basic – the crux of the concept was still 22 figures vibrating around a field. Gotham's men looked different, but they still looked like football players. And the fields, although made of different material, were pretty much identical. While Tudor did have an edge in construction and durability, the Gotham model was certainly sturdy enough to remain intact over the holiday.

With the Browns thrashing the Lions 56-10 on Sunday, and five televised bowl game the following Saturday (DuMont was adding the East–West Shrine Game to the New Year's Day bowl lineup), it was a good week to receive an electric football game. And it had been a great year to sell them.

The electric football page from Tudor's 1955 sales catalog. (Personal collection of Norman Sas.)

# 8 THE TUDOR-GOTHAM RIVALRY HEATS UP

**F**ootball fans who figured they had one more game to watch before the pigskin was put away for the winter were in for a rude mid-January surprise. DuMont cancelled its telecast of the NFL Pro Bowl just days before the game. The network's official explanation was a mix up in scheduling a time slot on AT&T's cross-country television cable (the game was being played in Los Angeles). This explanation sounded fishy, not only to football fans but also to an embarrassed NFL hierarchy. But it was a worried hierarchy too. DuMont's on-air presence was now down to just a handful of programs.

In covering the Toy Fair in March, the *New York Times* reported on the record number of toy makers (1,400) and toy buyers (14,000) who were in attendance. The *Times* also reported on how many manufacturers were replacing wood and metal items with ones made completely out of plastic. A company who was doing just that was Tudor, as they were introducing new all plastic players for the No. 500. The credit for these new players belonged to plant manager Joe Modica, who had spent quite of bit of time and effort creating the new small, yet sophisticated, electric football players.

Tudor's new high impact Styrene figures were three-dimensional (technically, at least) and came in two different poses. For blocking, there was Tudor's traditional crouching lineman, but now there was a running back, who came complete with one arm bent to cradle the football while his other arm projected straight out to fend off tacklers. In this running back figure, Modica had created the first electric football player who could actually carry the football. Also part of each new Tudor pose were realistic and detailed features, all the way down to jersey wrinkles, chinstraps, and shoes with spikes. Another well thought out part of the player was the new base. On the old players the base was metal, and the player needed to be attached to the base with clips. This point of attachment proved to be

New Tudor electric football players for 1955. (Photo by Earl Shores.)

the weak spot of the players and the place where most breakage occurred. On the new Tudor players, the base was molded directly to the player's feet. This design change along with the use of styrene made for an almost unbreakable figure. It was very refined work on Modica's part.

Protruding from the base was a set of flexible nylon "legs," which couldn't be broken and also didn't pose an injury hazard (Tudor's old metal legs often scratched the field, not to mention skin). It was also claimed that the new legs had a smoother running action since the softness of the nylon provided a shock-absorbing quality, transmitting the vibrations from the game board to the players less harshly than metal.

Each game would come with 11 red players and 11 yellow players, with the pose ratio of each team being 7 crouching lineman to 4 running players. Tudor was also including a set of positional stickers, which could be mounted on the leading edge of each player's base. At the least the stickers offered the chance to mark the best running players on each team. Remaining unchanged for 1955 was the quarterback figure.

Norman announced the new upgrades in a full page *Playthings* ad, listing five "NEW" improvements on the No. 500. Beyond the new players, the game now had styrene corners that would eliminate scratching on tables and floors; a tri-color box featuring oversized renditions of Tudor's new players, as well as a large seal of approval from the Toy Guidance Council and *Parents Magazine*; and the game was now Canadian Standards Approved – it could be sold in Canada.

Tudor's new players and features were no accident. They were a way to try and keep Tudor ahead of Gotham in the world of electric football. If Eddie Gluck wanted to compete with Norman, then a competition it would truly be. With only a year of electric football under its belt, Gotham was not yet in a position to start tinkering with its players. And surprisingly, Gotham again did very little to promote its game at the Toy Fair. There was no mention of the game in any of the ads Gotham ran in *Playthings* or any special feature in the publication introducing new items. The G-880 All-Star Football game was in the showroom – and it seemed the only way to know about it was to visit Gluck in Suite 214 during the Fair.

Even with Gotham's low profile, it was hard for Norman to come out the Fair with same type of optimism he felt when Tudor had electric football all to itself. The new players looked great on the game and on the box; they were clearly more realistic looking than the Gotham players. But as Norman knew well from his studies and now from his hands-on time in the toy world, the best product wasn't always the winning one. So many factors played into the popularity of a toy, not the least of which was placement. Eddie had already put the G-880 into Ward. Norman worried that Gluck might have more surprises in the future.

One factor that played into Tudor's favor was having the No. 500 again be named a Prestige Toy by the Toy Guidance Council. In fact the updated No. 500 was displayed at a New York City TGC

A, B—TUDOR ELECTRIC Tru-Action GAMES afford all the exciting action of real sports on their 25" x 15½" lithographed metal playing fields. Motion results from electrical vibration. Each game U.L. listed, operates 110 volts, AC. Instructions included.
A—Football Game. Steel "gridiron" with styrene corners, 22 three-dimensional styrene "players" with nylon "legs", felt "football". $6.98*.

Tudor's No. 500 model in the influential Toy Yearbook. This official publication of the Toy Guidance Council provided toy recommendations to parents. *Toy Yearbook* 1955-56 edition. (Collection of Earl Shores.)

press preview in mid summer, with a large photo of the game making it into the *Washington Post*. Unfortunately, by this time there was bad news for the NFL on the television front. The Pro Bowl debacle foreshadowed deep financial problems at DuMont. The network never renewed its contract with the NFL and sold off its rights to the 1955 NFL Championship game to NBC. By late summer, DuMont was in such dire trouble that it cut its schedule down to one program a week – boxing from St. Nicholas Arena in Manhattan. DuMont planned to honor its commitment to broadcast Giants games once the NFL season started, but with the entire network now consisting of only two stations (in New York and D.C.), the Giants probably wished they had another outlet for their games. Like the Giants, the rest of the NFL teams were going to have to fall back on local stations for television exposure. In the past, DuMont had left these agreements in place, working around the local stations while constructing a national television package. But the money paid by local advertisers was nothing like what Westinghouse had brought to the league in 1953 and 1954.

Without a national package from DuMont, the NFL had a bunch of scheduled Saturday night games that were television orphans. No local network affiliate was going to bump the *Perry Como Show* or *Your Hit Parade* (NBC), *The Lawrence Welk Show* (ABC), or *The Honeymooners* and *Gunsmoke* (CBS), for an NFL game.

While the NFL suffered through more television-induced growing pains, the NCAA decided to pull back many of its television restrictions in 1955. As a result, there was going to be more college football on television than at anytime since 1950. Both CBS and NBC got a piece of the pie, with the networks even being allowed to televise games on the same day, even at the same time. CBS had exclusive rights to the Big Ten and the Pacific Coast Conference, while NBC got Notre Dame, who was going to appear three times during the fall of 1955.

On the eve of the NFL season, Commissioner Bell admitted that national Saturday night telecasts were essentially finished. None of the three remaining networks had any interest in the games, and the NFL couldn't afford to buy time on the cross-country cable to show the games themselves. (Without DuMont, the NFL would pay triple the rate that CBS, NBC, and ABC did for cable time.) The Saturday games according to Bell were being priced out of existence. Losing prime time television exposure was a setback for the NFL.

The Toy Guidance Council logo. This appeared on the boxes of recommended toys. Toy Yearbook 1955-56 edition. (Collection of Earl Shores.)

Change wasn't just confined to pro football, as there was a significant change in electric football that became fully apparent when the Sears Christmas catalogs started arriving in households around the country. There on page 202 was a Gotham electric football game. And it wasn't just the basic G-880, it was a brand new game that Gotham was making exclusively for Sears – the new "deluxe" G-940 Electro-Magnetic Football game. It was hard to tell from the photo, but the field was the same size as the G-880 (28" x 15"). What was also hard to see was that the frame was twice the height of the old game, so the field sat a majestic four inches off the ground. Easy for any shopper to see was an electric football first – a grandstand. Actually there were two grandstands, one mounted behind each end zone. Both stood six inches tall with a colorful lithographed

Tudor's new box in 1955 with an "Educator Approved" Prestige Toy logo. (Photo by Earl Shores.)

crowd scene looking out over the field. And at the dead-center top edge of each grandstand was another electric football first – a two-dial scoreboard. Not only did a boy get a football game, he got a stadium too. Gotham's players may have not been as detailed as Tudor's in 1955, but the No. 500 was yet to have a stadium or a scoreboard.

Sears had priced the G-940 at $7.49, which was a pretty good deal considering the added grandstands and scoreboards. Unfortunately the game wasn't a featured item, it was casually pictured with a Gotham basketball game and several other bagatelle-like sports games. But for the first time ever, electric football had made it into the Sears catalog. Through his years of cultivating important contacts in the toy business, Eddie Gluck had been able to land his football game in the catalog of the biggest toy seller in the country.

Gotham's achievement didn't go unnoticed by Norman, although he was more impressed by Gluck's endeavor to land Sears than the G-940 itself. Whatever game Gotham put in Sears would sell more just because it was in Sears. The grandstand feature wasn't really going to make that much of a difference this year because the G-940 was only being sold through Sears. Tudor wasn't going to have to compete with the game beyond the catalog page. Most of Tudor's comparison-shopping competition was going to come from the Gotham G-880, and it didn't have a grandstand. And with the new Tudor players and new box, Norman felt his No. 500 was the more appealing game. It would be the winner in any town that had stores selling Tudor and Gotham electric football games. Plus the No. 500 was still reaching parts of the country that Eddie Gluck could only dream about getting his games

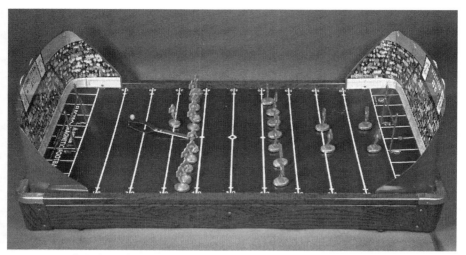

Gotham's new G-940 Electro-Magnetic Football game, complete with the first grandstands ever used on an electric football game. The G-940 was a Sears' exclusive in 1955. (Photo by Roddy Garcia.)

to (although both Sears and Ward were helping Gluck with his distribution issues). So Norman would keep an eye on the G-940, but there was no panic at Tudor. Gotham still had a lot of catching up to do.

Ward was still involved in Gluck's quest to bury Tudor, having the G-880 pictured on page 234 of its 1955 *Christmas Book*. Unfortunately, Ward again did Gluck no favors by placing an overhead photo of the game in the upper right hand corner of the page. Like the year before, it was really hard to tell exactly what the game was supposed to be. It just seemed to float on the page, thanks to Ward's text description being miles away from the photo. Even the large heading saying "Electric Football, Carrom, and Shooting Games" was a half a page down. Any shopper curious for the price of the G-880 ($5.69) had to search really hard to find it.

But any slight Gluck may have taken by the Ward catalog presentation was made up for as the fall unfolded. Starting in October, Ward began making the Gotham electric football a featured part of nearly all its Toyland newspaper advertising. From Troy, New York, to Waco, Texas, to Reno, Nevada, to Bismarck, North Dakota, toy shoppers across the country were seeing the G-880 in Ward's Christmas ads. And Ward had upgraded and modernized shelf displays throughout the country, making electric football an easy game to find in all 567 of its stores. Although this still didn't quite rival the depth of Tudor's distribution, it was quite a step forward for Gotham, especially with the G-880 only in its second year of being sold.

Much to Norman's relief, Sears did not make Gotham's G-940 part of its newspaper advertising. There was an electric football game that got occasional print time – Cadaco's Foto-Electric Football – but Gluck had to be content with page 202 for now. One of the more interesting toy items Sears was featuring was a Roy Rogers Sports Kit, complete with a "double R" football, basketball, baseball, and carrying case. While it was a bit unusual for Roy to venture over into the sports world, it showed how attuned Roy and Larry Kent were to the rising role of sports in America. They were also feeling the heat from Disney, who unleashed Davy Crockett on the world with a three-part television biography in late 1954. Soon afterward, a Crockett craze – helped by Disney's clever marketing including a big-screen movie that rolled all three Davy Crockett episodes together – raced through schoolrooms and backyards across the country. Disney marketed hundreds of Davy Crockett items, and Sears was doing its part to "help the cause." In Crockett-mad 1955, a Roy Rogers Sport Kit was one way not to be completely overshadowed by coonskin caps and Alamo play sets.

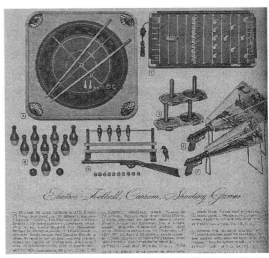

Gotham's G-880 electric football game in the 1955 Montgomery Ward *Christmas Book.* ©Montgomery Ward 1955.

Thanks to the lack of a DuMont-like television contract, NFL fans had to be content watching whomever the home team was playing in 1955. So even though it was an essentially meaningless contest, a lot of football fans around the country were grateful to ABC for telecasting the Lions and Packers nationally on Thanksgiving Day. It gave Eastern Conference cities a chance to watch two teams they didn't see very often and sustained the fledgling tradition of people anchoring themselves in front of the television on the fourth Thursday of November for the Macy's Parade and an NFL game. Also turning into a tradition was the use of electric football games in newspaper toy advertisements throughout the holiday weekend. Sears purchased hundreds of pages of advertising during this period, although the only football game to benefit was the one made by Cadaco. Retailers throughout the country were grateful for the date of Thanksgiving this year – November 24. It gave the Christmas season an extra week of shopping days.

Gotham was more visible outside of Sears and Ward this year as once again retailers spent little effort in naming the manufacturer in their ads.

The Tudor No. 500 in the 1955 Spiegel Christmas Catalog (page 226).

9.95

BOY'S 4-PC. FOOTBALL UNIFORM
• Plastic helmet . . . shoulder pads
• Padded pants with kidney guards

A boys' football uniform kit from Spiegel. 1955 Spiegel Christmas Catalog, page 50.

Electric football was electric football – Tudor, Gotham, what was the difference, as long as it sold? But for Norman Sas and Eddie Gluck in 1955, who sold what and where did make a difference. With two different kinds of games available, appearance was important – and that was exactly why Tudor developed its new bright tri-color box. It shouted "action" to any child who saw it while assuring parents it was a worthwhile "Prestige Toy." Gotham's plain brown boxes just didn't elicit the same kind of "I gotta' have it!" impulse that Tudor's boxes did.

As the shopping season heated up in December, the NFL season quietly wound down with only the Eastern Conference having any drama left on the final weekend of the season. The Cleveland Browns ended the drama by scoring 21 fourth-quarter points in a 35-24 victory over the Cardinals. This gave the Browns the Eastern title and also a championship date with the Rams in Los Angeles on December 26.

Christmas fell on a Sunday exactly two weeks after the NFL finished its regular season schedule. And with the college regular season also long over, no football had been seen on television since December 11. But that didn't mean it wasn't an exciting day to receive a football gift. Scheduled for the very next day (Monday!) was the NFL championship game, and a record seven college

Cover of the 1955-56 Toy Yearbook, which was published by the Toy Guidance Council. (Collection of Earl Shores.)

bowl games would be televised on the following weekend. Christmas week in 1955 had turned into the consummation of the entire football season.

In electric football this year, there would be few disappointments. Games were readily available – including for the first time through Sears – and there were even three different models to choose from. Tudor's updated players added a new dimension of realism to electric football, as did the grandstands on the new Gotham game. Electric football, in just its sixth year of existence, was a "must-have" Christmas toy.

Unfortunately for NBC, the Browns intercepted seven passes in demolishing the Rams 38-14. It was only the second nationally televised NFL game of the season, and without DuMont, fewer NFL games were seen throughout the country (New York City viewers only saw eight games, including the championship). But on the plus side 7.6 million televisions were sold in 1955, and it was estimated that 74% of all the homes in the country had a television set. So even with fewer games, more people may have been watching. There was no question that more people were watching the NFL in person, as the league set an attendance record in 1955. And just a month earlier one of the most prominent sportswriters in the country, Arthur Daley of the *New York Times*, declared in a lengthy Sunday Magazine article that, "the best football in the land is fashioned each week by the NFL."

The profiles of both electric football and the NFL continued to rise in 1955.

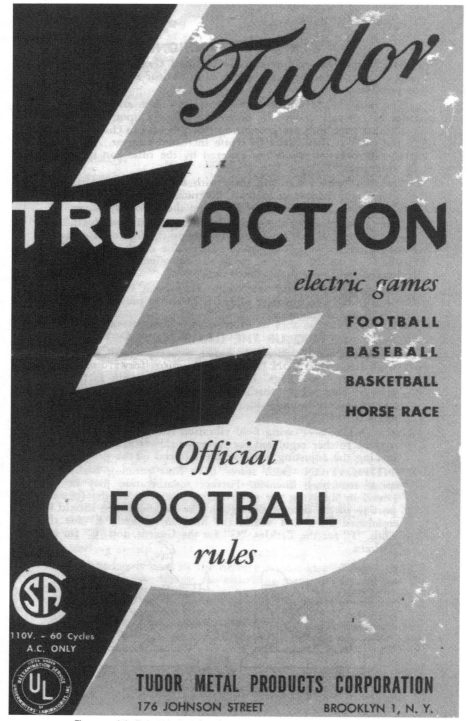

The cover of the Tudor Rule Book (1956).

# GROWING POPULARITY FOR
# TUDOR AND
# THE NFL

O f the four New Year's Day bowl contest (which were actually played on January 2nd this year because the NCAA didn't permit Sunday games) the most interesting game was the Orange Bowl where No. 1 ranked Oklahoma faced off against No. 3 Maryland. Both teams came to Miami with 10-0 records, so it was a true national championship game even though the final Associated Press poll rankings had been issued at the end of November. Whoever won would be the nation's top team – at least in the eyes of college football fans. After trailing 6-0 at the half, Oklahoma rebounded for a 20-6 victory. It was clear that the undefeated Sooners were the best college football team in the country.

By the end of the month, Toy Fair preparations were well under way for both Tudor and Gotham. Neither company was planning any electric football changes. The increasing visibility of Gotham models had not taken a significant chunk out of Tudor's sales. Norman, who had recently won a two-year term on the Toy Manufacturers of America board of directors, still thought he had the best product. There was no need to chase down a Sears or a Ward or spend money adding extraneous features to electric football. The way Norman saw it, Gotham was chasing Tudor, and they would be for some time to come.

Although Gluck was always looking for a new angle, there wasn't much more he could do with electric football in 1956. He was in the game, his line was being sold by two of the biggest toy retailers in the country, and he had an electric football model that was unlike any ever made. This was all accomplished after just two years in electric football. It seemed that Gotham's foray onto the vibrating gridiron would be a lasting one.

Throughout the toy industry, there was an air of optimism when Toy Fair opened in early March. A record 1,655 manufacturers turned up this year, and some toy makers quickly began reporting that sales were 15% ahead

Tudor's 1956 Playthings' ad page. *Playthings*, March 1956.

of last year. Helping drive the increase in orders were volume buyers like Sears and Ward, who were now allowed to place orders before the Fair officially opened. By the time ordinary toy buyers made their way through the doors at 500 Fifth Avenue, Lionel had announced that most of its current inventory was sold out. (They would, of course, produce more trains.)

Another change in the industry was that more self-service stores were selling toys. These retailers, who usually advertised themselves as "discounters," didn't have a lot of salespeople roaming the aisles or standing behind counters to push the items on hand. This made overhead costs cheaper but also required shoppers to wander around the store and make their own choices about what to buy. Thanks to this self-service trend, packaging was becoming a vital part of the toy industry. Toy boxes had to be attractive because more and more shoppers were making buying decisions based solely on an item's picture. A toy might have a single chance to get a buyer's attention. This was an area where Tudor was well ahead of Gotham. The fact that Gluck's G-940 had a colorful grandstand was completely lost on most Sears shoppers. Neither the catalog nor the box provided an appealing image of what the game actually looked like.

Norman Sas at the 1956 Toy Manufacturers of the U.S.A. dinner. Norman was now on the TMA Board of Directors. *Playthings*, page 122, January 1956.

As the Fair moved through its run, many manufacturers, including Tudor and Gotham, received a record number of orders. And by the time the event closed on March 15, the TMA claimed that overall sales were up 10-15% from 1955. For most toy makers 1956 was shaping up to be a remarkable year.

Gotham's G-940 Electro Magnetic Football Game. It was the first electric football game to have a grandstand. (Photo by Roddy Garcia.)

Things were also looking up for the NFL, at least in terms of television. CBS stepped forward to do regional and national Sunday telecasts for the 1956 season. It wasn't a league-wide contract as CBS was only able to reach agreements with seven of the twelve NFL teams. But that still left the network with 63 different games, and those games would reach 187 cities throughout the country. Any football fan who lived within range of a CBS television signal would have access to more than 16 regular season NFL games in 1956 (fans in many NFL cities would see at least a dozen). An additional contest was possible provided your area had an NBC affiliate and your home team didn't end up hosting the NFL Championship game. Commissioner Bell was proud of the NFL's increasing television presence. He made a point to bring it up whenever he was interviewed.

This ad appeared in "The Market Place" section Playthings. It ran there every month. Playthings, page 814, March 1956.

Over the summer the No. 500 was once again named as a Prestige Toy. Being "educator approved" was turning out to be a useful marketing device that kept Tudor distinct from any Gotham electric football game. It didn't hurt that the Parent's Magazine seal of approval looked very official on the No. 500 box. So as the summer days drained away and the serious toy-selling season became more visible on the horizon, Norman was not particularly worried about Gotham. Tudor had the better game, the more attractive

A box from the Gotham G-940 Electro Magnetic Football Game. Although not as colorful as a Tudor No. 500 box, it was the first electric football game to have a grandstand. It was also being sold in the 1956 Sears *Christmas Book.*

box, and six years of experience getting the No. 500 to the far reaches of the U.S. (and they'd even put the game in Canada in 1955).

By the time the NFL season opened on the last day of September, electric football games were already being put in lay-away storage rooms. And before the second weekend of NFL contests were played, Sears opened many of its Toy Town departments. In Toy Town, as well as in Sears' recently mailed Christmas catalogs, the Gotham G-940 could be found. This year's price was up to $7.98, making it the most expensive electric football game ever sold. (Gluck was also selling his basketball game and a new Push-Button Baseball game in Sears.) Not to be outdone, Montgomery Ward stores around the country were readying their Toyland departments for shoppers. Available in both Ward stores and Christmas catalogs was the Gotham G-880, which was initially priced at $6.95. It was also being used as a featured item in the company's newspaper advertising, along with Monopoly and Lionel trains.

Ward continued to feature electric football in its November newspaper ads, even dropping the price to $5.66 during "Early Shopper Specials." This discount was very attractive considering that many Tudor retailers were easily selling the No. 500 for $6.95, the game's suggested retail price. Sears had the G-940 in its Thanksgiving Day newspaper ads, hoping to piggyback sales onto the nearly five hours of football being televised that afternoon. The retail giant went on to use the G-940 in ads throughout the Thanksgiving weekend.

One result of Sears and Ward so actively promoting electric football during the Christmas season was that the competition between Tudor and Gotham became keener. Ward did its share to heat things up by pricing the G-880 at $5.66 through most of December. But in general, Tudor games moved steadily even when priced higher than Gotham models. Toys overall were having another record year with sales up 12% from 1955.

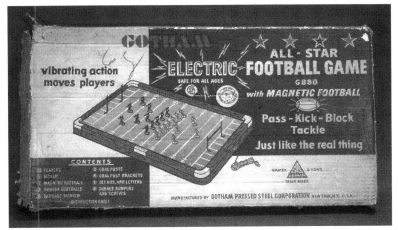

By 1956 Gotham had started to make colorful boxes to compete with Tudor. A G-880 All-Star Electric Football Game box. (Photo by Earl Shores.)

Surprisingly, the same couldn't be said for televisions. Over 39 million sets were now in use, including 300,000 color sets, and sales were dropping. In fact, there were so many unsold television sets in warehouses and in showrooms that more than 7,000 electronics workers had been laid off by General Electric, Motorola, Philco, and Admiral. The economy was as strong as it had been during the entire decade, so it wasn't that people couldn't afford a television. It came down to this: everyone who wanted a television had one. In late 1956 there was a glut of televisions. The companies had overproduced.

While there were some overproduction issues in the toy world – Davy Crockett items were practically glued to shelves in 1956 – it was not a problem for electric football or items like the elaborate Electronic Radar Rocket Cannon (a miniature missile-launching console, complete with rocket), or the sci-fi inspired walking and talking Robby the Robot. One of the unique boy's items being sold this year could be found

Gotham's G-940 in the 1956 Sears *Christmas Book* (page 284). At $7.98 it was the most expensive electric football game being sold. ©Sears, Roebuck & Co. 1956.

exclusively on the West Coast in the sporting goods department of May Company stores – an official Los Angeles Rams uniform set. Complete with a helmet featuring the Rams' famous horns, the kit also included a Rams' jersey, pants, and a vividly illustrated cardboard carrying case. The uniform was one of the first NFL items ever marketed. Unfortunately for young Rams' fans, their team finished at the bottom of the Western Conference in 1956.

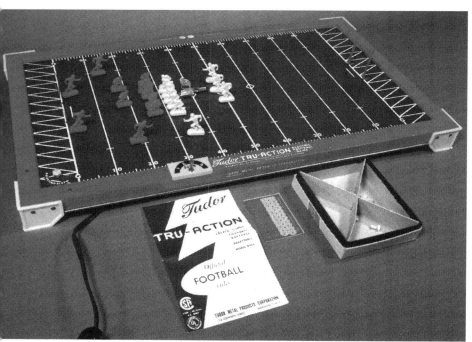

Tudor's No. 500 in its 1957 configuration. (Photo by Earl Shores.)

In the days leading up to Christmas, which fell on a Tuesday thanks to 1956 being a leap year, there were two nationally televised football games (the Aluminum Bowl on Saturday, and the Redskins-Colts game on Sunday). The main course of televised football would come the following weekend, with three college bowl games on Saturday and the NFL championship game on Sunday. Whether the four televised New Year's Day bowl games were dessert or simply a second main course was open to debate, but all those football games on television during the holiday season meant one thing: it was a very good year for Santa to leave football stuff.

More Gotham games appeared under trees this year thanks to Sears and Ward, but fortunately, Tudor and Gotham had yet to create a situation like the one that idled the nation's television makers. Demand for electric football games was still strong. And interest in football was continuing to grow, despite the NFL championship game falling 10,000 fans short of a sellout. (Single-digit wind chills in Yankee Stadium didn't help – many Giants swapped cleats for sneakers during their 47-7 rout of the Bears.) An emphatic bottom-line statement about football's popularity came from NBC, ABC, and CBS, who combined to broadcast ten nationally televised football games over a ten-day period.

In spite of the number of bowl games played on New Year's Day of 1957, there wasn't a lot of drama left in the college football season. Oklahoma had already been declared the country's top-ranked team and they weren't

Norman Sas demonstrates Tudor's new basketball game at the 1957 Toy Fair. *Playthings*, page 108, April 1957.

playing on January 1. The Big Seven Conference, which annually sent their champion to the Orange Bowl, didn't allow a team to make consecutive trips to Miami. So, much to the dismay of television viewers, CBS, and the Orange Bowl organizers, the Big Seven sent runner-up and unranked Colorado to the game. For the first time in ten years the Orange Bowl did not sell out (Colorado beat Clemson 27-21).

New Year's Day again proved to be the end of televised football, as the NFL Pro Bowl got caught up in a cross-country cable availability crunch for the second year in a row. Commissioner Bell laid the blame at the feet of ABC, but there was likely more going on with Pro Bowl than the commissioner cared to reveal. The league hadn't even bothered to arrange radio coverage for the contest.

There weren't any significant changes in the works for Toy Fair, either in terms of the number of toy makers, toy buyers, or electric football games being offered. Tudor's No. 500 and Gotham's G-880 again remained unchanged for 1957. What did change was that Norman was now the assistant treasurer of the Toy Manufacturers Association. This ascent through the TMA hierarchy seemed to reflect Tudor's growing stature in the toy-making community.

CBS decided to continue its coverage of the NFL, paying $1.2 million for the rights to seven NFL teams. This gave CBS 63 total games, and it was claimed by the network that 175 cities from Maine to Seattle would see the NFL in 1957. Besides three preseason games, CBS would televise during the regular season on thirteen Sunday afternoons, two Saturday afternoons, one Saturday night, and Thanksgiving Day. Viewers in cities with NFL teams would still have to dance around the home game blackout issue, while cities without NFL teams were guaranteed at least one NFL game on each weekend of the season. It was another season where pro games would outnumber college games on television, as the NCAA limited NBC to showing just nine games during the coming fall.

Electric Football $7.64

Players realistically race down field. Plastic players, kickers, passers. 2 magnetic balls, goal posts. Masonite Presswood field. 28x15x8 inches. UL approved. 110-120 volt, 60-cycle AC. Rules.
79 N 0236—2pg. wt. 7 lbs. ........ $7.64

10% down on orders of $20 or more, on Sears Easy

The 1957 Sears *Christmas Book* (page 270). Gotham's G-940 was still the only electric football game being sold b y Sears. ©Sears, Roebuck & Co. 1957.

The Tudor No. 500 was still a Prestige Toy in 1957 with retailers able to display the game alongside other Toy Guidance Council approved items like the Marx Metal Service Station and the Thunder Electric Burp Gun. And even electric football games without the distinction of a Toy Guidance Council endorsement were being presented as featured items, as many Sears stores christened the opening of Toy Town with newspaper ads featuring the Gotham G-940. At $7.39 it was still the only electric football game over the $7 mark. Almost simultaneously in October, Ward opened its Wonderland of Toys, selling the Gotham G-880 model for $6.95 (this was also the Ward Christmas catalog price). But within weeks of Sears and Ward inaugurating the Christmas shopping season, they found themselves competing with a Tudor No. 500 model that many retailers were pricing for less than $5.

Ward made the Gotham G-880 a mainstay of its newspaper advertising throughout the fall, keeping the $6.95 price even as the Payless Drug Store chain lowered the price of Tudor No. 500 to $4.43 in mid-November. While retailers could still be found selling Tudor's game for its $6.95 suggested retail price, there seemed to be a distinct trend for the game to be priced for less than $5. By Thanksgiving, Ward caught on to this trend and lowered their Gotham electric football model to $5.97.

Finally in early December, Ward broke the $5 electric football barrier and discounted the G-880 to $4.88. The retailer also continued to highlight electric football in its print advertising for the final weeks of the shopping season. Having direct competition between Tudor and Gotham was one reason for electric football's price drop, but other economic pressures had a hand in creating the lowest prices ever seen in the history of the vibrating gridiron. Christmas sales were struggling all around the country, as a downturn in the economy had to led to layoffs and workweek cutbacks for many major industries. Television sales were running behind 1956, car sales were down 31%, and New York City was about to embark on an eight-day subway strike that would sharply curtail retail sales throughout the region.

So retailers everywhere were jittery this season, not wanting to get stuck with excess inventory. And with more and more discount houses joining the toy business (the discounters profit model called for rock-bottom prices, slim profit margins, while moving a large volume of a particular item) there was beginning to be a whiff of "eau de oversupply" in electric football. This left most toy sellers searching for a price point that moved their items, even if the price resulted in minimal or no profit. As a result, the No. 500 was turning up more and more with a sub-$4.50 price, even hitting $4.28 during an electric football price war among the retailers in downtown Chester, Pennsylvania.

Procrastinating shoppers benefited from the deep discounts in electric football. And all those retailers trying to move discounted football merchandise got a push from the NFL, which ended up holding a Western Conference playoff game on the Sunday before the holiday. With the game being played in San Francisco, most of the country was treated to a late afternoon national CBS telecast of a contest that saw the 49ers run out to a 27-7 third quarter lead before losing 31-27 to the Lions. It was the NFL at its best – West Coast sunshine, a sold out Kezar Stadium overflowing with more than 60,000 fans, and the biggest comeback in NFL playoff history. The next day, *New York Times'* television critic Jack Gould praised CBS's camerawork and finished up his summary of the broadcast quite succinctly: "Professional football is now just about the best sport to watch on TV."

Of course, lots of boys around the country watched the game. They now fervently hoped that Santa read their Christmas lists carefully...and that Santa's verdict would render them in the "good" column. Any boy with a last-minute electric football wish was in luck, as plenty of electric football games were available in 1957. In fact, thanks to the discount houses, electric football might have been starting to seem a bit ordinary this year. But with the help of the NFL – the Lions and Browns would play for the championship just days after Christmas – electric football was still a prized toy. Surely many were still buzzing when the Lions dismantled the Browns 59-14 before a national television audience on December 29. It could be argued that far from being ordinary, electric football had simply developed into a Christmas morning staple.

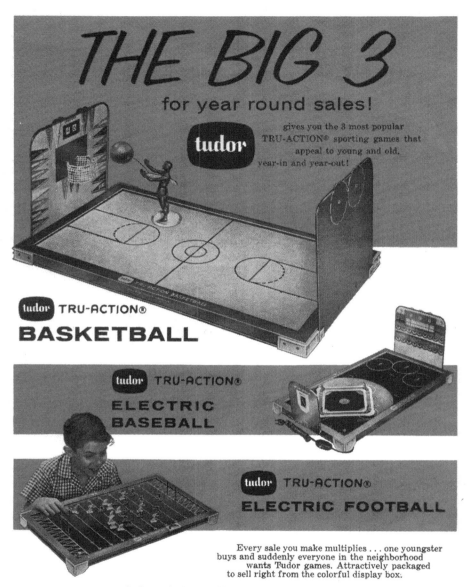

# THE BIG 3

## for year round sales!

**tudor** gives you the 3 most popular TRU-ACTION® sporting games that appeal to young and old, year-in and year-out!

**tudor** TRU-ACTION®
## BASKETBALL

**tudor** TRU-ACTION®
### ELECTRIC BASEBALL

**tudor** TRU-ACTION®
## ELECTRIC FOOTBALL

Every sale you make multiplies . . . one youngster buys and suddenly everyone in the neighborhood wants Tudor games. Attractively packaged to sell right from the colorful display box.

*Write today for complete literature. Glossy photos, mats, electros available for your promotional activities.*

## TUDOR METAL PRODUCTS CORPORATION
**SHOWROOM:** 200 Fifth Ave. (Room 551), New York 10, N. Y. **FACTORY:** 176 Johnson St., Brooklyn 1, N. Y.

MARCH. 1958—PLAYTHINGS                                                                    95

A full page Tudor ad in the Toy Fair edition of *Playthings.* March 1958.

# 10 LANDMARKS FOR THE NFL: A GAME AND A MARKETING AGREEMENT

our more games hit the television airwaves on New Years' Day. The most anticipated contest was the Rose Bowl, where Ohio State lived up to its No. 1 ranking by beating Oregon 10-7. Played in California, the Rose Bowl was the last game of the day and also the last collegiate game football fans would see on television until September. When the final gun sounded in Pasadena, the NCAA hierarchy was able to bask in a neat and tidy finish to the 1957 season.

During the early days of January, sales figures made it clear that Christmas wasn't as bad as retailers and manufacturers had feared. Toy volume, it turned out, had increased for the seventh straight year, even if overall profits were slimmer. So despite the economy technically being in a recession, there was optimism as toy makers geared up for the Toy Fair in March. There hadn't truly been any successful fad items in the toy world since the Davy Crockett craze, but a definitive theme was shaping up for 1958 – space. Thanks to the Soviet Union's launch of Sputnik I and II in late 1957, and the subsequent U.S. Explorer launch in January, there was a new term in the world vocabulary: "space race." And with the Americans and Russians racing to see who could conquer space first, toy makers jumped on board, political ramifications be damned. Russia's late launches, at least from a toy design and production standpoint, meant that manufactures had to hustle their prototypes together quickly to show them at the Fair. It also meant production schedules would be balanced on a knife's edge. Any delays or difficulties would be very costly, perhaps more in reputation than in dollars.

Not joining the space race this year were Tudor and Gotham. Tudor brought to the Fair "The Big 3 for year round sales!" promotion, featuring electric football, electric baseball, and a new non-electric basketball game. This basketball game came with a unique 3-D shooter figure that had been recently designed and patented by Joe Modica. Modeling a crew cut and high-top sneakers, the new player illustrated Modica's eye for detail. But only basketball received an update; the No. 500 and Tudor's baseball game remained unchanged from the previous years. Tudor promoted "The Big 3" in the showroom, and also with a full-page ad in the Toy Fair issue of *Playthings*. According to the ad, "Every sale you make multiplies...one youngster buys and suddenly everyone in the neighborhood wants Tudor games."

Gotham arrived at 200 Fifth Avenue with no major design changes to any of its sports games. The metal "legs" of the electric football and basketball players had been replaced with "vinyl plastic activators," which were simply plastic versions of the original legs. Gluck discovered what Tudor had several years earlier – that plastic legs put less wear and tear on the game board and on the flesh of preadolescent fingers. With a major safety issue taken care of, Gotham, without a hint of irony, included instructions in both its basketball and football games to boil the activators if the players did not run properly.

By the time the Fair wrapped up, it was estimated that a record 16,000 buyers had come to New York. And even though some buying had been a bit cautious, toy makers were confident another sales record would fall by the end of the year.

Another organization feeling confident was CBS, who eagerly signed on to televise the NFL again in 1958. The new contract was almost identical to the previous year's, including two games on the first Saturday night in October, the Packers and Lions on Thanksgiving Day, and West Coast games on each of the final two Saturdays of the season. CBS would also televise any playoff games that needed to be played, but they didn't have the championship game. That was still the property of NBC.

The NFL gave both networks a chance to make more money in 1958 by approving what is now known as a "television timeout." NFL officials were instructed to pause a game for 90 seconds during the opening 10 minutes of the first or third period if a) there was no score, or; b) no timeouts had been called by either team. Ninety seconds gave a network just enough time to run three 30-second commercials. Anyone who has watched a recent NFL game knows this original 90-second idea has been extended in a way that hasn't necessarily made a positive impact on professional football.

Within days of the NFL season kickoff on September 28, Sears and Ward began opening their in-store Christmas toy departments. Catalogs for both companies had already been arriving around the country, with Gotham maintaining its electric football monopoly in the mail-order giants. Sears had the deluxe G-940 model for a $7.79 price, while Ward was showing off the $5.75 Gotham G-880 in full color! This was a momentous achievement for electric football, as color toy pages were still rare in both the Ward and Sears catalogs. Color pages were very expensive to print, so both companies carefully considered what items were placed on a color catalog page. The fact that Ward thought electric football was worthy of color said a lot for the game's ranking in the 1958 toy hierarchy.

Despite the prominent placement Sears and Ward gave electric football in both their catalogs and toy departments, neither company used the game in print advertising during the fall. Perhaps they didn't need to – the economy was bouncing back and toy sales were strong. By the November 27 Thanksgiving Day national telecast of the Lions and Packers (the home Lions came away with a 24-14 victory), retailers around the country were feeling pretty good about the Christmas selling season. Electric football games were moving off of shelves with the same regularity they had in previous years. And also as in previous years, prices moved downward as the calendar counted toward to Christmas.

By early December, the No. 500 could be found for as low as $3.99 in communities where multiple retailers were battling for the electric football dollar. This was good for the shopper, but it was raising concerns about whether the electric football market was getting oversaturated. Sports games of all types were also battling with space and Cold War toys like the Marx Cape Canaveral Missile Base play set, the American Flyer "Satellite" Train, Ideal's Atomic Cannon, and the Gilbert Star Finder set. Still going strong in spite of the race to space was the old West, thanks to numerous Western-themed television shows. The latest character added to the Western television and licensing canon was a masked swordsman named Zorro. Sears and Ward were both promoting dozens of Zorro items, ranging from a Hacienda playhouse tent to an eighty-piece Zorro play set. Responsible for the Zorro phenomenon was one of the biggest names in marketing – Walt Disney. Calculating how the sword-swinging "Z-man" could leave his mark on parents' pocketbooks started long before the first script of the television show was ever completed.

Electric Football Game

Players race up and down, tackle and block. Ball can be kicked, passed or run. Masonite Presdwood surface with a steel frame. Hidden vibrating motor, UL approved for 110 to 120-volt, 60-cycle AC. 22 players, 2 magnetic footballs, goal posts, markers, instructions. 28x15x8 inches high.
79 N 0236—Shpg. wt. 7 lbs. . . . $7.79

Gotham's G-940 in the 1958 Sears *Christmas Book*, page 346. ©Sears, Roebuck and Co. 1958.

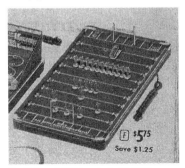

The Gotham G-880 in color in the 1958 Montgomery Ward *Christmas Book*, page 22. ©Montgomery Ward, Inc. 1958.

On December 14, the final Sunday of the NFL season, there was drama to focus the attention of football fans. The New York Giants needed a win in their final game to create a two-way tie for the Eastern Conference title. Their opponents for the afternoon were the Cleveland Browns...who also happened to be the team the Giants would tie with a victory. Playing such an important game at home should have been a big advantage for the Giants, but the Browns had never lost in Yankee Stadium. This undefeated streak not only stretched over nine NFL seasons, it also included the Browns' 1946-49 run as champions of the All-America Football Conference. But thanks to a dramatic 49-yard Pat Summerall field goal, the Giants defied history and came away with a 13-10 win. They also earned a playoff date with the Browns the following Sunday in Yankee Stadium.

Originally, there were no NFL games scheduled for December 21. Now there was an important NFL playoff being nationally televised just days before Christmas. This was positively good news for electric football makers, although many toy retailers were already in clearance mode. In many areas of the country there were electric football bargains to be had, with the No. 500 selling for less than $4. But in areas with less electric football competition, the game was still a "most wanted toy," and carried a premium $6.95 price (equivalent to just over $54.00 in 2012). By day's end, the Giants had handed the Browns a second consecutive Yankee Stadium loss, 10-0. That set up a NFL Championship game meeting with the Western Conference Baltimore Colts.

The NFL game that would go on to obtain larger-than-life status in American sports history was simply an upcoming championship game when the presents were opened on Christmas Day. This was true for ordinary football fans of the time and even dedicated NFL fans in Baltimore and New York. Contributing to the subdued anticipation of the game in New York was the fact that the media capital of the world was in the midst of a newspaper strike. Giants fans weren't getting their daily dose of championship hype from any of the ten striking papers in the area. Out-of-town newspapers were selling out within minutes of their appearance on New York newsstand shelves.

For electric football, it was turning out to be another strong Christmas. In the days leading up to the holiday, the game was one of the most mentioned items in newspaper Santa letters. And throughout the country electric football games were a standard part of holiday toy ads. Going hand in hand with this increased visibility was the fact that there were plenty of games to be found in 1958. Gotham's share was creeping slightly upward thanks to the help of Sears and Ward, but Tudor still held a major advantage in sales. Both companies were happy to have Christmas arrive on a Thursday. This fortuitous timing assured that lots of games would still be set up and running when the Giants and Colts lined up for battle on Sunday afternoon.

Much has been written and said about the NFL's "Greatest Game." ESPN even colorized and digitally enhanced old footage of the game for a television special commemorating the 50th anniversary of the Colts 23-17 sudden-death victory. So there's really little new to add to the lore of the 1958 NFL Championship. Was it truly the NFL's greatest game? Maybe. (Can a game that didn't even sell out really be the "greatest?") What it was, beyond a doubt, was the most important NFL game ever played. The timing of Johnny Unitas's winning touchdown drive couldn't have been more perfect: it was late on a Sunday afternoon when the NBC telecast of the game was unopposed by any other nationally televised sporting event; late in the month of December after the regular segment of the college football season was long over; late in the decade, when more than 84% of the U.S. population owned a television set (the were over 50 million sets –

**TUDOR METAL PRODUCTS CORPORATION**
176 JOHNSON STREET, BROOKLYN 1, N. Y.

No C.O.D. orders accepted — No Stamps please.

* Please Note: When ordering complete games or xylophones, $.50 must be added to the price to cover the cost of mailing and handling. THANK YOU.

* TUDOR PRODUCTS — 1958

| | |
|---|---|
| #450 — TRU-ACTION JUNIOR BASEBALL | $ 4.00 |
| #475 — TRU-ACTION BASKETBALL | 6.00 |
| #500 — TRU-ACTION ELECTRIC FOOTBALL | 7.00 |
| #525 — TRU-ACTION ELECTRIC HORSE RACE | 7.00 |
| #550 — TRU-ACTION ELECTRIC BASEBALL | 7.00 |
| #575 — TRU-ACTION ELECTRIC BASKETBALL | 7.00 |
| #300 — READY MONEY BANK | 3.00 |
| #100 — 8 NOTE COLOR XYLOPHONE | 1.50 |
| #125 — 8 NOTE COLOR XYLOPHONE | 3.00 |
| #150 — 12 NOTE COLOR XYLOPHONE | 4.00 |
| #175 — 25 NOTE CHROMATIC XYLOPHONE | 10.00 |

8

The 1958 Tudor product line with mail order instructions. From the 1958 Tudor Rule Book.

more homes now owned televisions than bathtubs); and finally, on the day the New York newspapers ended their strike.

It was clear when Colts fullback Alan Ameche appeared as a guest on the popular *Ed Sullivan Show* later that evening that it hadn't been just another NFL Championship game. (Sullivan settled for Ameche after Unitas turned down a $300 appearance fee.) It also turned out to have been more than just another Christmas for toy makers and toy sellers. Early in the New Year, both Sears and Ward would report all-time record sales for the month of December. Also adding to the good news was the U.S. Commerce Department, who reported that retail sales for all of 1958 set a new record ($200.3 billion). Tudor and Gotham were both beneficiaries of the new record.

None of the four collegiate bowl games on the opening day of 1959 could match the Colts-Giants epic, although No. 1 ranked LSU did confirm its place as the top college team with a 7-0 win over Clemson in the Sugar Bowl. So this year it was the NFL that carried a football "buzz" into the New Year, inspiring many electric football games to buzz well beyond the boundaries of Christmas vacation. Summing up the NFL's stature dramatically was *New York Times'* Pulitzer-Prize-winning sportswriter Arthur Daley, who opened his January 6 column with "Watching pro football on Sunday afternoons was getting to be as habit forming as taking hashish or smoking opium." Millions of football fans throughout the country were beginning to feel the same way. Between DuMont and CBS (with assists from NBC in 1949 and ABC in 1950), NFL games had been broadcast on a regular basis for a decade now. The ritual of sitting down in front of the television on a fall Sunday afternoon to watch the pros play was well established, and the overtime Colts-Giants game cemented the NFL as a major-league sport.

In March of 1959 Commissioner Bell received a proposal to create a comprehensive league-wide merchandising program for the NFL. Bell was eager to figure out how the NFL could reach its growing legion of fans – beyond the stadium and beyond the television screen. So he formed a committee to look into the feasibility of such a program. Two of the three members Bell picked were NFL heavyweights. George "Papa Bear" Halas was a pro football legend. In addition to being the owner and coach of the

Electric football in the 1959 Tudor sales catalog. (Collection of Norman Sas.)

# FREE DEALER AIDS AVAILABLE!

Be sure to write today for these traffic-building, profit-making free dealer aids, including newspaper mats, glossy photos, reproduction proofs, electros! Just write: Tudor Metal Products, Room 551, 200 Fifth Avenue, New York 10, N.Y., and we'll rush your request.

NO. 500
**tudor** TRU-ACTION®
ELECTRIC
FOOTBALL GAME

Tudor's advertising acumen was the reason the No. 500 was the best-selling electric football game. 1959 Tudor sales catalog. (Collection of Norman Sas.)

Chicago Bears, he played a major role in founding the NFL back in the mid-1920's. He also had marketed and sold Bears' items for decades, including through his George Halas Co. store in Chicago. The other committee heavyweight was Carroll Rosenbloom, who owned the Baltimore Colts... the now World Champion Baltimore Colts, thanks to the "Greatest Game" ever played. Compared to these men, the final committee member's identity might have left the average football fan scratching their head. At least in 1959. He was the 32-year-old General Manager of the Los Angeles Rams, Pete Rozelle.

But the junior member of the committee was not there just to warm a seat. Rozelle had been the Rams' publicity director from 1952-55 but then left to work on the 1956 Sydney Summer Olympics for the international public relations firm P.K. Macker. When he returned to the Rams as general manager in 1957, he initiated the licensing of official Rams' items, including bobbing head dolls, t-shirts, and pennants. (Rozelle could also take credit for the kid-sized Rams-uniform kit sold by the May company during the 1956 Christmas season.) Not only were these items sold at the Coliseum on game day, they were also sold out of the Rams' Store, an official team-sponsored business located near the team offices. Commissioner Bell was impressed by Rozelle's innovative efforts. The Rams were well ahead of all the other NFL teams in terms of merchandising and marketing.

And there was one more thing...Rozelle had been the one who presented the merchandising proposal to Bell.

Rozelle played the role of messenger, as someone else had written the proposal. That "someone else" was an acquaintance of Rozelle who had helped the young general manager set up the Rams' elaborate merchandising program. This acquaintance was also something of a marketing expert, and in fact worked for a national marketing powerhouse that had grossed $30 million in sales in 1958. Not only did the company have sales agreements with Sears, Ward, J.C. Penney, and most major U.S. department stores, its accounts were so large that these retailers dedicated special sections of their stores exclusively to the company's items. The cover letter accompanying the proposal that Commissioner Bell received was signed by Rozelle's acquaintance. His name?

Larry Kent.

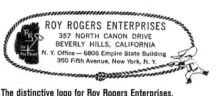

The distinctive logo for Roy Rogers Enterprises.

Yes, the same Larry Kent who was the marketing mastermind for Roy Rogers Enterprises. The connection between the two men made sense. RRE was headquartered in Beverly Hills, not far from Rozelle's office. And Rozelle truly admired what Kent had accomplished with Roy Rogers. In working together on merchandising the Rams the two men had come to share a vision on the licensing and marketing potential of the NFL.

Kent's letter pointed out that this would be the first time RRE ever took on an outside client, but the company was "convinced that this proposal merits an all out effort on our part." Much of this willingness to take on an outsider could be traced to the dominant force of the decade – television. *The Roy Rogers Show* was canceled in June of 1957 after six years as a Sunday night television fixture. It had been bumped off the air by a wagonload of newer Westerns that offered a grittier portrayal of America's past. Among these shows was top-rated *Gunsmoke*. (Eight of Nielsen's top ten television shows for the 1958-59 season were Westerns.) And, thanks to television, the licensing and marketing landscape was changing dramatically. Walt Disney, the undisputed pioneer and king of licensing, now had a popular hour-long television show on ABC *and* a Disney-themed amusement park in southern California. So it was an ideal time for Roy to blaze some new licensing trails.

Other than what the Rams were doing, the NFL had no licensing or marketing strategy to speak of. Kent would be starting totally from scratch. But he liked a challenge. Plus if the proposal went through as written, the NFL would be Kent's baby almost entirely. He could take it in whatever direction he saw fit. And he was sure he could work the same magic for the NFL that he had worked for Roy Rogers Enterprises. Rozelle was going to be happy if just a little of Roy Rogers' magic rubbed off on the NFL. He liked the proposal and was convinced that Kent was the right man to promote the league. When the owners gathered again in April, the Roy Rogers Enterprises proposal would be on the agenda.

In the meantime, the Toy Fair had come and gone with great optimism for sales but without Tudor or Gotham showing off anything new in electric football. But thanks to the success of 1958, Tudor was running monthly full-page ads in *Playthings* with each ad placed prominently in the front of the magazine. Dominating these ads was a large letter "T" and the slogan: "Build on the Big 'T' Build The Big Volume." Sitting on top of the T, which stood for "Tru-Action," were an electric football game, an electric baseball game, a xylophone, and two new Tudor Tru-Action race games. Both the Electric Sports Car Race and the Electric Horse Race game were Joe Modica creations featuring a vacuum-formed plastic overlay that functioned as the game board surface. (Modica and Tudor earned a patent for this plastic-on-metal technique.)

The NFL owners were intrigued by a partnership with Roy Rogers Enterprises. After the April meeting in Philadelphia, the two sides went into serious negotiations. If they moved quickly, some type of merchandising might be available for the fall of 1959. But hammering the contract's details turned out to be slow process. Some of the owners were having problems with the idea of sharing the merchandising profits equally. It didn't seem fair that a team whose licensed items might only account for 1/50 of the total sales would still get a 1/12 share of the profits. And a popular team whose licensing might account for a significant percentage of league sales would only get 1/12 of the profit pool. Often Rozelle and Bell were pitching the sharing idea much harder than the licensing program.

Successful negotiations were carried out during the summer between the NFL and both CBS and ABC. For $1.5 million, CBS got the rights to televise 66 games. ABC landed 5 exhibition games, plus Saturday night contests on the first two weeks of the season. NBC once again only had a single NFL telecast during the season, but it was a big one – the NFL Championship game for which it paid $200,000.

Larry Kent (seated) and Lou Banks oversee a summer meeting of Roy Rogers' licensees in New York City. *Playthings*, page 136, August 1959.

Another event taking place during the summer was the board of directors meeting for Roy Rogers Frontiers, Inc. (RRF was parent company of the entire RR empire.) Roy Rogers was there, as was Larry Kent, who had recently been promoted to vice president and general manager of RRE. Not long after the meeting ended Kent told *Playthings* that RRE was planning a large-scale expansion of its licensing program. A major new project was in the works, although Kent wasn't at liberty to disclose the parties involved. An official announcement regarding the expansion would happen in the very near future.

A few weeks later, Kent and RRE's vice president of sales and promotion, Lou Banks, hosted a manufacturers' dinner at an exclusive New York restaurant. Neither Kent nor Banks offered any news on the new project. Instead, they laid out the company's marketing plan for the fall. Kent and Banks – who was headquartered in the Empire State Building – detailed the promotions and display techniques RRE would use to entice retailers to sell Roy Rogers merchandise. The marketing might of the organization was on display as Mr. Banks listed all the cities and department stores he would be visiting in the coming weeks. It was a *Who's Who* of the most successful retailers in country.

Heading into the selling season Tudor still had the No. 500 as a Prestige Toy and had continued showing its toy muscle with heavy monthly advertising in *Playthings*. By contrast Gotham was almost invisible, both at the Toy Fair and in *Playthings*. It appeared that Eddie Gluck was leaning heavily on Sears and Ward to do the bulk of Gotham's marketing in 1959. Sears had the G-940 for $7.89, titling it as a "Thrill-a-Minute Football Game." For the first time ever, the game received prominent placement on the upper half of a catalog page. It also benefited from the largest space and photo Sears had ever devoted to electric football. The field, the players, the grandstands, and the goal posts were all clearly visible. Sears even tried to help shoppers visualize the game this year. Accompanying the photo of the G-940 was a hand-drawn illustration of a boy and a girl playing the game. (A Munro table hockey game got the same instructional treatment.) A notable addition to the Sears sports game page was the new Tudor Electric Sports Car Race. It was the first Tudor item to make it into a Sears Christmas catalog.

Despite the upgraded presentation the G-940 received in the *Christmas Book*, Sears offered no print-advertising support as the fall unfolded. For those kids lucky enough to visit a Sears Toy Town, there were large display boards showing off the monstrous 180-piece Marx Blue and Gray Civil War battlefield play set. The set, which came complete with an antebellum Union headquarters building, also had a reasonable $5.98 price tag. Sears' newspaper ads were plentiful and mostly devoted to bicycles, dolls, and trains. The mainstay item of all the Sears' ads was the Allstate Service Station. It came in three different configurations. A battery-powered car elevator was the star attraction on the deluxe model.

Surprisingly, Ward didn't use electric football in any of its advertising either. Instead, the retailer's big item was a Wells Fargo train set, one of the officially licensed toys spawned by NBC's popular television show *Tales of Wells Fargo*. Other toys Ward advertised heavily through the fall were Remco's Coney Island Penny Arcade claw machine and the Yankee Doodle Rocket Test Center. Like many other retailers of all sizes, Ward also planned to tie in with a national television ad campaign by Marx. While not revealing how much they were spending, Marx was modestly calling it "the most powerful TV advertising barrage the toy industry has ever known." The company had bought airtime on the all three major networks, including time on all the key "kiddy" shows – *Captain Kangaroo*, *Rin Tin Tin*, *Rocky and Bullwinkle*, *Howdy Doody*, and *Heckle & Jeckle*. It was an unprecedented plan. No toy company had ever devised an ad campaign that would reach so many viewers on both a national and local level. (Marx estimates put the figure around 45 million viewers per week.) Central to the new campaign was an animated character called "Magic Marxie." Playing the role of television ringmaster, Marxie was set to introduce seven new Marx toys beginning in October.

| OTHER FINE TUDOR PRODUCTS 1959 | |
| --- | --- |
| #500 — Tru-Action Electric Football Game | $ 7.00 |
| #525 — Tru-Action Electric Horse Race Game | 7.00 |
| #530 — Tru-Action Electric Sports Car Race Game | 7.00 |
| #550 — Tru-Action Electric Baseball Game | 7.00 |
| #575 — Tru-Action Electric Basketball Game | 7.00 |
| #300 — Ready Money Bank (assorted colors) | 3.00 |
| #100 — 8 Note Color Xylophone | 1.50 |
| #125 — 8 Note Color Xylophone | 3.00 |
| #150 — 12 Note Color Xylophone | 4.00 |
| #160 — 17 Note Black and White Xylophone | 7.00 |
| #175 — 25 Note Black and White Xylophone | 10.00 |

The 1959 Tudor product line from the 1959 Tudor Rule Book (a rule book was included in every Tudor game).

Also heavily into television this year was Lionel, who planned to run ads during NBC's broadcast of the Macy's Thanksgiving Day parade. In addition, Lionel would run ads during *The Lone Ranger Show* (already in reruns) and have promotional tie-ins with General Mills and Colgate. Further print exposure for the company would come in the form of full color double-page spreads in *Look* and *Life* magazines.

Nothing that dramatic or costly was happening in electric football. But by early fall the Toy Manufacturers Association was reporting that toy orders were running 18% ahead of 1958, with some factories already on twenty-four hour production schedules. Television advertising was surely playing a part in the increased demand. And even without massive ad campaigns, both Tudor and Gotham were benefiting from the increased foot traffic toy departments were receiving.

After six months of negotiations, Roy Rogers Enterprises and the NFL agreed to the terms of their new relationship. This wasn't exactly the "very near future" that Larry Kent had predicted to *Playthings* back in the summer, but finally the league gave verbal approval on October 1. The contract created National Football League Enterprises (NFLE) that would operate as a new division of Roy Rogers Enterprises. Kent would be the vice president and general manager of NFLE and hold the exclusive rights to grant licenses for the use of the names, emblems, and colors of the twelve-team NFL. The contract also gave NFLE the sole discretion in choosing licensees. In other words, Kent was in charge of deciding who could manufacturer any NFL-licensed item. Royalties would be collected from the licensees by NFLE, and the league would receive 50% of the annual gross...that would be split evenly among the twelve teams. Terms of the contract would go into effect on January 1, 1960, and continue until March 31, 1962. Beyond that date, the contract would be renewed on a year-to-year basis. The NFL became the first major sport to have a fully structured and professionally managed licensing agreement.

## TRU-ACTION®     No. 500
## ELECTRIC FOOTBALL GAME

This is the famous electric football game that's so real, so exciting, so fast-moving you'll really think you're right in there playing the game yourself. You get 2 teams with 22 players that move up and down the field. They actually carry the ball . . . pass . . . kick . . . knock each other down in rough and tumble tackles. You can play coach, too, and plan your own real football plays and strategy. Game comes complete with Passing-Kicking figure, Yard Marker, Goal Posts — everything you need to play real Football.     **$7.00**

**The No. 500 model as advertised in the 1959 Tudor Rule Book.**

Sadly, the man who started the NFL on the road to sports-licensing history never got the chance to make the contract official. On Sunday, October 11, Commissioner Bell suffered a heart attack and died while attending an Eagles game in Philadelphia. NFL Treasurer Austin Gunsell was named acting commissioner just a few days later. It was his signature that authorized the NFL-Roy Rogers relationship.

In spite of not being featured by Sears or Ward, electric football was very visible in other print advertising throughout the fall. Retailers of all kinds viewed the game as an anchor item for the Christmas season that consistently generated easy sales. Dozens of newspapers across the country carried electric football ads on Thanksgiving Day with Tudor's No. 500

appearing more often than the Gotham G-880 by a 6-1 margin. At this point in the selling season the No. 500 was priced in the $5 to $6 range (the Pay-Less chain was down to $4.77). The G-880 was costing shoppers a bit more, usually between $6 and $7.

After putting the papers down on Thanksgiving Day, many shoppers would see Lionel ads during the Macy's Parade on NBC. (Magic Marxie had already been busy on the air during the morning cartoon shows.) And all it took was a quick look at the television listings to see the growing influence of television as THE selling medium for America's kids. Hosting ABC's telecast of the Hudson Thanksgiving Day Santa Parade from Detroit was children's entertainer Shari Lewis and her puppet Lamb Chop. Overseeing the *Thanksgiving Parade Jubilee* on CBS – a program showing parts of the Macy's, Hudson, and Gimbel's parade in Philadelphia – was Captain Kangaroo.

At noon the CBS airwaves gave way to the Packers and Lions game in Detroit, which Green Bay won 24-17 to keep their slim playoff hopes alive. When the pros finished, the dedicated football fan could switch over to NBC for the Duke-North Carolina game, although only the truly hard-core football junkie would have stayed around for the final gun of the 50-0 North Carolina rout. Prying the males away from the television in time for turkey was not a problem in 1959.

As December began the Toy Manufacturers Association reported that toy shipments were up 10% from 1958. It was also predicting that retail toy sales would hit an all-time record this year. This news was not a great surprise, but it certainly was a relief. The optimism felt by the industry coming out of the Toy Fair back in March was well founded. Marx continued its advertising blitz though the opening weeks of December; during the same period Lionel unveiled its full-color magazine spreads. Endorsing Lionel's train line in both *Look* and *Life* was Chuck Connors, the star of ABC's popular *The Rifleman* television show. Pictured in full Western gear, Connors was offering a manly aura to Lionel. Connors also helped Lionel compete with Ward's Wells Fargo train, which was cheaper than most Lionel sets…and was made by Marx.

Also enjoying increased demand were Tudor and Gotham. Tudor games were easier to find throughout the country, with many retailers dropping the No. 500 under the $5 mark as the serious time of Christmas shopping arrived ($4.77 and $4.88 seemed to be popular price points). Tudor's games were much more prominent in retailer advertising, and less expensive, although the accessibility of Gotham's models through Sears and Ward made those games an easy choice for shoppers around the country. For both companies, it was a good year to sell electric football. After a decade on the toy "field," electric football was still a highly desired gift.

The NFL headed into its final weekend with a nationally televised Saturday afternoon contest on December 12 that could decide the Western Conference title. Playing on the road in Los Angeles, the Colts scored 21 unanswered fourth quarter points to defeat the Rams 45-26. It was the fifth victory in a row for the Colts, who would again face the Giants again for the NFL Championship on December 27. Only this time the game would be played in Baltimore.

Gotham's G-940 game in the Sears 1959 *Christmas Book,* page 405. ©Sears, Roebuck and Co. 1959.

Within days of the season's end, Austin Gunsell received a letter from Larry Kent thanking the acting commissioner for all his efforts in finalizing the NFL-Roy Rogers partnership. According to Kent, Roy Rogers himself had personally executed the contracts. The paper Kent used for the letter was not the standard issue RRE stationery. In fact, the letterhead at the top of the page read: "National Football League Enterprises – the exclusive licensing organization of professional football." Also part of the preprinted text was Kent's new title as NFLE's vice president and general manager.

Without an NFL playoff game, the weekend before Christmas was devoid of any type of football game. Not that sales of electric football games would be hurt. By that point Ward, J.C. Penney, and many other retailers were in clearance mode. Tudor's No. 500 could be found in many places for just over $4. Ward shifted to 50% in the final days before Christmas, putting any in-stock Gotham G-880's at the $3.50 mark. But it would take a lot of luck to land one at this price. Parents with a definitive electric football request for Santa would have been foolish to wait until the last minute.

Christmas once again offered good cover for football items. The Friday holiday opened a weekend that included three national football telecasts, with the final game being the NFL Championship on Sunday. Two college all-star games filled out the Saturday schedule, with NBC broadcasting the Blue-Gray game from Alabama at 1:45 p.m., and CBS debuting the Copper Bowl from Phoenix as the late game. But these games were just warm-ups for the main event, the rematch of the 1958 NFL Championship game. For much of Sunday afternoon it looked like the Giants would get

An official Roy Rogers' store display that included Roy, Trigger, and a variety of officially licensed items. *Playthings*, page 91, April 1958.

their revenge. With just fifteen minutes left to play, they held a 9-7 lead over the struggling Colts. Unfortunately for the Giants, Baltimore showed its championship pedigree, scoring 24 fourth-quarter points for a 31-16 victory. Johnny Unitas again led the comeback with help from defensive back Johnny Sample. Sample picked off two Giant passes in the final quarter, returning one of them for a touchdown.

**tudor** Tru·action® *Electric*
# football game

Deservedly America's best selling electric football game, duplicating the thrills and excitement of the stadium.

Ever-popular with stay-at-home coaches, it permits endless offensive and defensive formations and strategies.

Game is solidly constructed with steel frame and colorful playing field, "Mr. Kickoff", yardage marker and full instructions included in sales-stimulating box.

• EXCLUSIVE "Mr. Kickoff" kicks ball and throws passes.
• 22 electrically-operated plastic players in life-like action postures run on Nylon legs.
• Both teams line up, players carry ball, block, tackle, pass and fumble as in real football.

**No. 500**
BOX SIZE: 27" x 16½" x 2⅛"
½-DOZ. CTN. WT. 26 LBS.
**ONLY $7.00 RETAIL**
110 VOLTS A.C. ONLY

## TUDOR METAL PRODUCTS CORPORATION • 200 FIFTH AVE., NEW YORK 10, N. Y.

The Tru-Action No. 500 as pictured in the 1960 Tudor sales catalog. (Personal collection of Norman Sas.)

**EARL SHORES | RODDY GARCIA**

# 11 A NEW DECADE BEGINS

I t was truly an outstanding bowl lineup on New Year's Day, with undefeated and No. 1-ranked Syracuse squaring off against No. 4 Texas in the Cotton Bowl; No. 2 LSU and No. 3 Mississippi meeting in the Sugar Bowl; and No. 6 Wisconsin playing No. 8 Washington in the Rose Bowl. By the end of the day, Syracuse had affirmed its place as national champions with a 23-14 win in Dallas. In the other games, higher ranked teams fell with a mighty thud. Mississippi routed LSU 21-0, while Washington was totally overrun by Wisconsin, 44-8. The Cotton Bowl was the only game with any drama. It easily won the New Year's battle for television viewers.

During the early days of the month, the January issue of *Playthings* began arriving in offices throughout the toy industry. Page 137 contained an obituary for a long-time toy veteran – Eugene (Gene) Levay. He had died on December 15 in Miami Beach at the age of 74, having retired from the world of toys just a few years earlier. Many of Levay's accomplishments were recounted in the article, yet his tenure at Tudor, arguably the most successful part of his toy career, was never mentioned. In fact, the obituary seemed carefully written around those Tudor years. Such was the depth of the acrimony still lingering from the 1948 breakup. Not even in death could Tudor be mentioned.

While the toy world was still discovering Levay's passing, history was being made in New York City. On Wednesday, January 13, National Football League Enterprises held its inaugural meeting. In attendance were Acting Commissioner Gunsell, George Halas, Eagles Vice President Joseph Donoghue, and, of course, Pete Rozelle and Larry Kent. Oh yes, there was one other person whose presence was fitting considering how this meeting can be pinpointed as the big bang moment for the sports-marketing phenomenon that currently overwhelms American culture. That person was Roy Rogers himself who admitted to reporters covering the

Larry Kent called Norman Sas in early 1960 to offer and NFL license to Tudor. *Playthings*, page 100, July 1959.

meeting that he had never played football. But Roy was certainly an "all-pro" at marketing. He was confident the NFL could be a profitable property, especially under Kent's guidance.

The meeting was more than just a formality. Kent knew the newly formed NFLE would need to reach out and recruit manufacturers into the licensing program. So Rozelle, Kent, Halas, Gunsell, and Donoghue quickly got into the nitty-gritty details of what type of items should be targeted. It was a productive discussion, and through Kent's leadership the league seemed to have a promising direction for the new decade – at least in terms of marketing. However, when the NFL owners gathered for their annual meeting in Miami the following week, marketing would not be at the top of the agenda. The league powers needed to elect a new commissioner, which was no minor proposition considering how the personality and perspective of this individual would play a major role in determining the future of the league. And while sitting poolside beneath the palms the owners no doubt saw imaginary storm clouds gathering on the horizon. It wasn't a hurricane, but this storm did have a name, and it frightened the NFL owners more than any winds or waves created by Mother Nature.

It was called the American Football League.

Ten years after disposing of the All-America Football Conference, the NFL once again found itself in competition for players, coaches, fans, and dollars with a rival professional football league. The NFL had nothing but its own success to blame for bringing the new league to life. It was the excitement created by the 1958 Colts-Giants championship game that convinced AFL founder Lamar Hunt to organize a new league. With World War II Medal of Honor winner and former South Dakota governor Joe Foss already in place as commissioner and an inaugural season slated for September, the AFL was creating professional football havoc just days into the new year. In fact, Rozelle and his Rams were suing the AFL Houston Oilers over their "illegal" signing of Heisman Trophy winning running back Billy Cannon.

Electing a new commissioner who could deal decisively with the AFL was the main mission for NFL owners in Miami. The commissioner would also need a thorough understanding of the growing stature of professional football in American culture. Agreeing on the perfect man for the job turned out to be not an easy task. After 22 ballots and a weeks' worth of political infighting, no candidate had earned the required vote majority to get the job. Finally, on the 23rd ballot, a commissioner was elected. Although his name wasn't on the first 22 ballots, the NFL's new commissioner was...Pete Rozelle.

Larry Kent must have wondered whether a new commissioner would be as enthusiastic about the national merchandising program as Commissioner Bell had been. With Rozelle's election, Kent would worry no more. Not only did he have an advocate in the commissioner's office, he had the man who knew more about the agreement and its purpose than anyone else in the NFL. And just minutes into his new job, Rozelle set the tone for the league's new attitude by announcing that NFL headquarters would soon move from Philadelphia to New York. Rozelle knew that the best way to sell the league

Norman Sas listened carefully to Kent's offer, but did not reveal Tudor's previous electric football earnings. *Playthings*, page 69, December 1961.

was to put the commissioner's office just blocks from America's cultural power center – the executives of network television and the ad agencies of Madison Avenue.

As Rozelle settled into his new position, Kent began contacting the makers of the items discussed during the NFL Enterprises' January meeting. One of the people receiving a call from Kent was Norman Sas. Kent laid out to Norman what NFL Enterprises was about, and what the league was trying to accomplish with their new marketing program. With the success and status Tudor carried in electric football, Kent thought the company was perfect to become an NFL partner, and Kent was giving Norman a chance to be one of the league's first licensees.

Norman listened carefully to Kent's NFL pitch. The stature of the league was growing and the chance to make Tudor's electric football game an exclusively licensed NFL product – very much a "ground floor" licensee, at that – was tempting. Surely it was an ideal match. Yet Norman didn't jump at Kent's offer. The NFL's asking price for the license was 5% of Tudor's gross electric football revenue.

"Kent probably didn't have any idea how much business we were doing," said Sas. "And I wasn't going to tell him – he was just looking for companies to license." So what Kent didn't realize was that in 1959, Tudor took in over $1 million in electric football alone. Norman did the math in his head and reacted like the savvy businessman he was: "I thought, 'Geez, who needs to give the NFL $50,000? They are not going to help us sell more games.' And at the time, it was true. The NFL still wasn't that big of a deal." Norman turned the NFL's offer down.

Kent hung up the phone disappointed. The country's most prominent maker of electric football games had passed on the NFL. Kent had been certain that he would soon be telling Commissioner Rozelle about one of the first ever officially NFL licensed products – electric football. Not surprisingly, Kent had a plan B, and he planned to unveil his audible at the upcoming Toy Fair in March.

THE COMPLETE LINE OF SPORTS GAMES AND XYLOPHONES

Cover of the 1960 Tudor sales catalog showing off the entire Tudor line. (Personal collection of Norman Sas.)

Kent was a Toy Fair regular, turning up on most years to inspect the special displays that all Roy Roger Enterprises' licensees were required to have in their showrooms. There was also a fair amount of schmoozing and licensee egos to massage, so even though RRE didn't have its own showroom, both Kent and vice president of sales Lou Banks spent long days at 200 Fifth Avenue during the Fair. This year Kent planned to make a special stop in showroom 214 – the showroom of Gotham Pressed Steel.

Heading Gotham's showroom was Eddie Gluck. With his background in professional sports, not to mention Gotham's second-class status in electric football, Gluck was very interested in becoming an NFL licensee. But at the moment, Gotham was dealing with a recent move to a new factory (actually it was an old factory, being the same Welsh Avenue site in the Bronx that Gotham had occupied between 1930 to 1940) and the declining health of company president Charles Anderson. So despite Gluck's interest, the timing really wasn't right for a Gotham-NFL partnership. The company needed to get settled in its new location and feel comfortable in getting ready for this year's production schedule. Gotham didn't even have any new items for the Fair, due to the effort required in moving an entire factory from 133rd Street to 144th Street.

Tudor had two new games to introduce, and both items combined to constitute an entire new line for the company – table hockey. Canadian hockey makers Munro (sold by Sears) and Eagle (sold by Ward) were doing very well with their games in the U.S. Gotham had even jumped into the table hockey fray in 1959, buying gears, players, pucks, and nets from Munro to complete its games. It was clearly a case of Tudor engaging in some good old toy industry "borrowing" in table hockey, but at the same time it was something the company had to do to remain competitive. Now Tudor could provide a retailer with a complete lineup of sports games – football, baseball, basketball, and hockey. No longer would an extra call have to be made to Munro, Eagle, or Gotham to fill the shelves with table hockey games. Gotham's ability to entice retailers into becoming all-Gotham shops was diminished by Tudor's entry into table hockey.

Tudor was going all out to promote the new hockey line to the toy trade, purchasing a two-page spread not far from the front cover of the Toy Fair issue of *Playthings*. Like Fifth Avenue storefronts, ad pages in this part of a Toy Fair issue (Tudor had gotten pages 10 and 11) were exclusive

**tudor** Tru·action® *Electric*
**football game**

Deservedly America's best selling electric football game, duplicating the thrills and excitement of the stadium.

The Tru-Action No. 500 as pictured in the 1960 Tudor sales catalog. (Personal collection of Norman Sas.)

pieces of real estate. It was an emphatic way for Tudor to let the buyers know it was serious about table hockey.

Toy Fair ran for ten days in 1960, twice as long as previous editions of the Fair. And by the end, it seemed most manufacturers preferred a hectic five-day event to a more leisurely yet longer selling period. A five-day Fair was over before the sellers even knew it. The final days of this years' Fair seemed to drag on forever.

In early April, Charles Anderson passed away. Fortunately, he left his affairs well in order, having already created a trust to oversee his estate, which included the Gotham Pressed Steel Corporation. The trustees of the estate, Anderson's wife and his four children, could have liquidated Gotham. They had power to take this route if they wanted. Instead, Eddie Gluck was given the presidency of the company. His vice president would be Anderson's son Curtis. Gotham would stay in business and be run just as it had been for the last 30 years.

Well, actually things were going to be a little different. Eddie Gluck was determined to put his mark on the company and convinced that with a little more ambition Gotham could challenge Tudor for sports game supremacy.

Not long after assuming the president's chair, Gluck contacted Larry Kent. Landing the NFL license was just the start of Gluck's plans to make Gotham a sports game heavyweight. With the NFL's help, Gluck was sure he could lead Gotham to be the dominant brand in electric football. Kent, for his part, was just glad to have another licensee to tell Commissioner Rozelle about.

While Norman was unaware that the electric football competition was about to move to another level, the AFL boldly moved forward in its battle with the NFL. In June, the new league announced a season-long national television contract with ABC. The new deal guaranteed 14 weeks of televised AFL games and would pay the league just over $2 million annually for five years. Foss convinced the owners that the only way the league could survive was through splitting the $2 million equally among the eight teams. For the AFL, this was major step toward legitimacy. For the NFL, it was an embarrassment. The league had recently failed to close a $3 million television deal with CBS because the owners couldn't agree on revenue sharing (revenue sharing for the NFL Enterprises was one thing – television money was a more serious matter). This left NFL teams again negotiating separately for television deals. By mid summer the NFL television tally was ten teams on CBS, two teams on NBC, and one team on an independent network. When the league offices officially moved to New York in July, Rozelle expressed his desire for an AFL-type television contract.

The American Football League started their season two weeks earlier than the NFL, and planned a longer 14 game schedule (NFL teams would only play 12 games). 1960 Fleer AFL Decal.

In September, the AFL got the jump on the NFL by starting their season on the weekend of the 10th, two full weeks earlier than the established league. This gave television viewers two Sundays to sample the goods of the new AFL without any competition. Perhaps in two weeks American football fans would establish a little affection for the underdog league? The AFL was also giving football fans a longer regular season, playing a 14-game schedule (the NFL was playing their usual 12-game schedule). It was no coincidence that the final day of the season would be the same for both leagues. Both ABC and the AFL were determined to make the NFL take notice. Just the fact that most television viewers would have a choice of two professional football games every Sunday was a topic of concern for anyone occupying a newly painted NFL office on Park Avenue.

By the time the NFL season started on September 25, hopeful eyes from coast to coast were scouting the pages of the Sears Christmas catalog. The retailer had even opened up some of its key Toy Town departments

Gotham's G-940 game in the 1960 Sears *Christmas Book* (page 451). It was the largest electric football presentation yet in Sears. ©Sears, Roebuck & Co 1960.

already, giving the Christmas shopping season almost a summertime start. Gotham again was Sears' featured electric football maker, but unfortunately Gotham's licensing deal with the NFL was completed too late for the company to create a special game for the country's largest toy seller. Kent already knew there would be an ordinary Gotham G-940 in the Sears catalog.

Giving both Kent and Gluck a hint of things to come was the first officially NFL licensed item ever to grace a Sears' catalog page. It was a boy's "Pro-style" NFL uniform, complete with authentic team helmet, road jersey, shoulder pads, and white pants. All thirteen NFL teams were available, although Sears was selling them on a regional basis. (For example, catalogs sent to the Northeast offered only the Eagles, Steelers, Giants, Colts, and Redskins as choices). The uniforms were branded under the Sears J.C. Higgins label, which meant Sears' itself was the manufacturer. Considering Kent's long history with Sears, it was no surprise that he was able to land an account with the retailing giant. While the uniforms looked great, they came with a $10.47 price tag. By comparison, a pair of J.C. Higgins boy's hockey skates costs just $6.98.

Montgomery Ward Christmas catalogs were also showing up in mailboxes although Ward didn't seem to be in the same rush to open its toy departments as Sears had been. Ward's sole electric football game was the G-880, again giving Gotham control of the major Christmas catalogs. Most Ward Toyland departments were open by mid-October when the selling of electric football games was already well under way at retailers like Sears, Western Auto, and Gibson's.

November began with the expansion Dallas Cowboys still looking for their first NFL victory, and NFL Enterprises getting a big push from a nationally published *Parade* magazine article. (*Parade* was, and still is, a free magazine that appears in Sunday newspapers throughout the U.S.) Above an article titled "There's gold in the sidelines," was a picture of Roy Rogers surrounded by NFL merchandise. In the text of the piece, Roy said the NFL came to him because the owners didn't want to be bothered selling the stuff. "I've got the merchandising setup, the organization," said Rogers, who summed up his role succinctly. "Merchandising is merchandising."

He also summed up the operations of NFL Enterprises for the fall of 1960, saying that there were 45 manufacturers making 300 different products. Over 3,000 stores were selling NFL merchandise, with bobble-head dolls being the best sellers at the moment. NFL team sweatshirts and caps were doing well too.

At this point, Eddie Gluck had to feel a bit left out of the NFL, even

Roy Rogers never played football, but he was a licensing and marketing "all-pro." Over 300 different NFL licensed products were already being sold by Christmas 1960 *Playthings*, page 128, April 1961.

though Gotham games were starting to get an advertising push from Sears and Ward. The G-940 was priced at $6.98 in Sears' newspaper ads. Ward had the G-880 going for $4.99. Both of these prices were still more than what the average Tudor No. 500 was costing. Tudor's game had been under the $5 mark with most retailers since September and was even being featured as low as $3.99 at some of the discounter/wholesaler outlets.

On Thanksgiving Day there was lots of football on the television and in newspaper ads. Sears and Ward used electric football in their holiday toy advertising with Sears even dropping the G-940 to $5.66. But outside of the catalog giants, Tudor No. 500's were seemingly everywhere, getting equal billing and listing with toys from industry heavyweights like Mattel, Remco, Ideal, and Marx. (Marx toys were usually billed as "the fabulous Magic Marxie toys you've seen on TV.")

For the first time since the days of the All-America Football Conference, there were two football games from competing professional leagues on television on Thanksgiving Day. The AFL decided to get a jump on the NFL and tradition by starting their game at 11 a.m. This meant the New York Titans and Dallas Texans were going to kickoff on ABC at the same time NBC was just starting its telecast of the Macy's parade (led by the cast of *Bonanza* on horseback). Play in Detroit between the Lions and Packers was scheduled to start at noon, just before the AFL would go to halftime. With most households still owning only a single television, there were tough viewing decisions to be made that morning.

The AFL game was a wild and sloppy affair, with 70 passes being thrown to score 76 total points. But if the defenses were invisible, so were the spectators. Only 14,000 New Yorkers showed up for the game, making the cavernous Polo Grounds look vacant on television. Those who did choose the home Titans over New York parade tradition were rewarded with a 41-35 victory. They also got to see Titans' quarterback Al Dorow throw for an AFL record 301 yards. Passing yardage for the game totaled 536 yards...an unheard of total for pro football in 1960. In fact, the Lions and Packers combined for only 245 passing yards during the Lions' 23-10 win. Detroit's sold out Briggs Stadium certainly made the NFL game look "superior" on the television screen.

Electric football was a prominent part of December print advertising, not only for Sears and Ward, but also for hundreds of other stores throughout the country. Prices continued to remain low, thanks to the pressure exerted by the discount houses. Many retailers were describing the game as a bestseller. An Albuquerque retailer reported to a local newspaper that his electric football sales were "terrific."

Both the NFL and AFL finished their seasons on December 18, leaving just a week until Christmas. This was a good lead-in for any Christmas

**National Football League**
## JUNIOR FOOTBALL UNIFORM OUTFIT ★ $.
### $10⁹⁵
No.
- Helmet, shoulder pads
- Jersey and pants
- BEARS OR COLTS Colors
- Quality built for safety

**$1 National Football**
## LEAGUE OFFICIAL
## FOOTBALL $4⁹⁹

Success for NFL Enterprises: Sears and other retailers began selling officially licensed junior NFL uniforms in 1960, just in time for Christmas. *Chicago Tribune*, Display Ad 189, November 24, 1960.

football items. Even better was the follow-up coming over the next nine days. At noon on Monday, December 26, the NFL championship game between the Eagles and the Packers was going to be played in Philadelphia (the early start time was needed because the Eagles' Franklin Field didn't have lights). So with barely any time to shake off the toy hangover from the previous day, football inspiration was going to come streaming into living rooms across the nation. Certainly there were lots of electric football games buzzing on Monday as the Eagles upset the Packers 17-10. A significant portion of those games were carrying the Tudor label. And there was much more live football to come. The following Saturday, three bowl games were televised. Then on Sunday, New Year's Day, the AFL would play its championship game with ABC doing a national telecast. Finally on Monday, four more bowl games would fill the nation's television screens. In all, eight games would be televised nationally over the three-day period. Never before had so much football been shown in 72-hours.

December 17, 1961: The Giants clinched the Eastern Division title in Yankee Stadium after a bruising 7-7 tie with Browns. Thanks to Eddie Gluck and Gotham many boys around the country would soon find a miniature Yankee Stadium under their Christmas tree. Photo by Art Abfier ©Bettmann/CORBIS

# 12 GOTHAM BRINGS THE NFL TO ELECTRIC FOOTBALL

O n New Year's Day of 1961 the Houston Oilers became the first champions of the AFL with a 24-16 win over the visiting Los Angeles Chargers. More than 30,000 fans showed up for the game, and with the AFL having the television airways all to themselves, thousands of football fans who weren't followers of the new league tuned in for a Sunday afternoon football fix. Fans were in for more compelling television on January 2, when the Orange Bowl, Sugar Bowl, Cotton Bowl, and Rose Bowl games occupied the nation's television screens for seven hours. Washington upset top-ranked Minnesota in the Rose Bowl 17-7, essentially invalidating the final polls of the Associated Press and United Press International. Both organizations had declared Minnesota No. 1 back in early December because the AP and the UPI based their rankings solely on play in the regular season. Bowl game results didn't count. It was just exhibition football.

But by 1961, most college football fans thought it was silly to declare a No. 1 team before *all* the college games were played. The Football Writers Association of America agreed, and this season they weren't going to choose a top team until all the bowl games were finished. After considering Minnesota's dismal Rose Bowl performance, the FWAA declared undefeated Mississippi as college football's national champions.

With the weekend finally over, *New York Times* television critic Jack Gould summed up the overload of football that had been beamed into living rooms across the country. "Twenty hours devoted to passing, running, tackling, kicking, taking time out, and half-time marching," said Gould, "is only telethonic madness, not sport."

The day before the Pro Bowl, AFL Commissioner Joe Foss sent Pete Rozelle a telegram inviting the NFL to participate in an NFL-AFL world championship game at the end of the 1961 season. Rozelle declined, citing an antitrust lawsuit the AFL had filed against the NFL. Said Rozelle, "You don't consider playing games with people who are suing you for $10 million."

Rozelle was envious of the AFL, at least of its television contract, and was working hard to get the NFL owners to play nice and agree to a similar revenue sharing arrangement with a single network. However, the league was being warned by the Justice Department that such a contract might violate antitrust laws. This view left both league lawyers and owners confused because the AFL, the NBA, the NHL, and college football all had some type of single-network contract. Why an NFL television deal might trigger antitrust laws when other existing agreements did not remained a mystery, but Rozelle continued pushing his owners towards just such a deal.

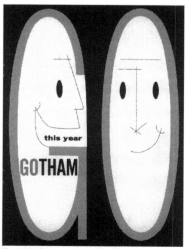

The 1961 Gotham sales catalog. (Collection of Earl Shores.)

Toy Fair in 1961 was really a tale of opposites. Most of the 1,500 manufacturers who showed up for the March event came in with an optimistic attitude, as toy sales had set a record in 1960. Multiple themes had been established in toys for the coming year, including space (NASA had manned launches scheduled), the Civil War (it was the 100th anniversary of the conflict), and television shows. Marx covered all these themes in their showroom with multi-piece play sets named Cape Canaveral, Battle of the Blue and the Gray, the Untouchables, and the Flintstones. Many retailers, however, had a less cheerful take on the toy industry – at least the direction it was currently headed in.

A price war had broken out during the Christmas shopping season, with the discount

Gotham's new NFL G-1500 as featured in the 1961 Gotham sales catalog. (Collection of Earl Shores.)

and wholesale retailers driving prices into the territory of little or no profit (aggressive retailers sold the Tudor No. 500 for as little as $3.44 in 1960). In fact many stores, including major department stores, joined the war and turned some of the most popular TV-advertised toys into "loss leader" items. This meant a toy would be sold at or below its wholesale costs, giving the retailer red ink for each sale. While this seems like a really bad business model, the bottom-line thinking for the loss leader concept was that it was better to have a shopper in your store than to have them go to a competitor down the street. It was hoped the shopper would make a loss leader purchase and then buy additional toys that actually contained a profit margin. It was a desperate strategy, which incensed many long-time toy retailers who had no choice but to join the cost-cutting frenzy. They viewed it as shortsighted and ultimately destructive to the entire toy business.

So despite record toy sales for 1960, retailer profits were another matter entirely. Hardest hit were the independent toy and hobby shops that had no other merchandise such as clothes, shoes, electronics, etc. to lean on for profits. For many of these retailers, the Christmas of 1960 was completely lost. There was genuine concern within the industry that it couldn't afford to lose retailers who sold toys all year round. Discount houses selling toys for convenience and profit during the holiday season had little interest in selling pools, swing sets, and wiffle-ball bats when Christmas was over.

Into this atmosphere of unhappy retailers pushing for lower wholesale prices, Eddie Gluck introduced the most expensive electric football game ever made – the Gotham Official National League Electric Football G-1500.

The game was the culmination of nearly a year's worth of planning, and Gluck had little trouble taking credit for the new model (he would eventually title himself a "pioneer" in a future issue of *Playthings*). There was good reason for Gluck to be proud of the G-1500, as it was a pioneering game on a number of levels. For starters, it was the first electric football game to be licensed by the NFL. It also had a huge 36" x 21" field that made the G-1500 the largest electric football game ever to hit toy store shelves. But these two firsts were just the start of what was the most elaborate electric football game ever created.

The field sat upon a 4"-high bright white metal frame that contained not only the NFL's instantly recognizable red, white, and blue shield, it also

Gotham's highly detailed G-1500 grandstand. It looked very much like Yankee Stadium, especially with a set of NFL team pennants flying above the stadium's distinctive façade. (Photo by Earl Shores.)

included the logos of all 14 NFL teams (the Minnesota Vikings were set to become NFL team number 14 in 1961). At the back of each end zone sat a 3"-high metal grandstand complete with a highly detailed and colorful lithographed crowd scene. Gotham's "crowd of thousands" featured suit-and-tie-and-fedora wearing men seated next to stylishly dressed women who modeled a variety of chic Eisenhower-era chapeaus. The hand-drawn details went as far as to having some fans wearing eyeglasses. Topping the grandstand was a metal 4"-high "Official National Football League" scoreboard. Besides having two prominent NFL shields, the board also had a place for the nameplate of an NFL team (cardboard name plates of all 14 teams were included). Finishing details included a down counter, a yards-to-go counter, and two scoring dials.

Yet as striking as the end-zone grandstands were, they were really only the "second-string" parts of the G-1500. The most extraordinary piece of the game ran from end zone to end zone and stood almost a foot tall. It was Gotham's new colossal metal grandstand, beautifully lithographed with the same stylish crowds that occupied the end zone seats. But thanks to a number of exquisite additional details, it was clear that this crowd was sitting in Yankee Stadium. From the support posts to the famous rooftop façade, there was no mistaking the look of the G-1500. There were even paper pennants of all the NFL teams to fly on the roof of the stadium. Anyone who watched the 1958 NFL championship game, or saw newspaper or magazine pictures of the game, would instantly recognize the scene Gotham had recreated.

Also new for the G-1500 were detailed plastic goal posts, and a metal first-down marker featuring a referee. The only things that weren't new were the players, which were the same red and blue Heisman models Gotham had been making since 1954. But they were sheathed in new stick-on paper uniforms that, theoretically at least, were supposed to give the teams an official NFL look. Gluck was promising newly designed players by the time the G-1500 hit the toy stores.

It was a very ambitious toy, and its debut was being announced in an equally ambitious four-page color layout in both *Playthings* and *Toys & Novelties* that stated things simply: "This year GO

The colorful frame of the G-1500 made contained the logos of all 14 NFL teams. The backside of the grandstand was detailed with images of fans entering the stadium. (Photo by Earl Shores.)

Gotham." Also introduced in the ad was an oversized Gotham hockey game, complete with metal grandstands and overhead scoreboard. A game that wasn't pictured in the new ad, the electric football G-880 model, had gotten a makeover for 1961. The Gotham Professional Electric Football game now had a white frame just like its big brother. Big brother's influence also came in the form of Gotham's new goal posts, and a sideline grandstand that would appear on special G-880 models. Gluck hadn't bothered to design an entirely new grandstand for the G-880. He simply borrowed an end zone grandstand piece from the G-1500 and mounted it on the sideline of the smaller game.

Dropping in to visit the new Gotham line was Larry Kent. As usual he was pulling double duty at the Toy Fair these days overseeing the licensees of both Roy Rogers and the NFL. But he didn't mind. He was very excited by the NFL side of things and took time to linger over the G-1500. It was a majestic-looking game, truly NFL worthy. And it was one of the best looking items that NFL Enterprises had in 1961. Kent viewed the G-1500 as a bull's-eye for one of his biggest targets – American boys. What better way to promote the NFL than to put it on the living room floor at Christmas time?

Tudor had nothing to compete with the G-1500, at least in terms of games. But Norman had planned a very ambitious advertising campaign, one that would put Tudor ads in *Sports Illustrated*, *Boys' Life*, and the *New York Times Sunday Magazine* during the height of the Christmas shopping season. The campaign was announced with a dramatic two-page spread in *Playthings* and *Toys & Novelties* – "Nationally Advertised" ran in bold font across both pages with Tudor claiming their new ads would reach 14 million readers. For any retailer, these new ads would be "Your Ticket To More Big-Ticket Sales." While the proof of this claim wouldn't be decided for many months, orders for most toy makers were running ahead of 1960. And although Tudor's advertising plan wasn't nearly as extravagant as the one planned by Ideal Toys, who announced during the Fair that they would be spending an industry record $3 million on television and magazine advertising in 1961, Norman knew it was important to raise the visibility of his company. Especially in light of Gotham being able to charge out of the Toy Fair with the official electric football game of the NFL.

The growing popularity of the NFL was demonstrated in early April by the television contract NBC signed with the league to broadcast the 1961 and 1962 NFL Championship games. NBC agreed to pay the league $615,000 per game. This was a record sum – the most ever paid by a network for a single sporting event. It was triple the amount NBC paid for the Eagles-Packers title game just months earlier, and if the network fees for the Sugar Bowl, Cotton Bowl, and Orange Bowl were combined, and then

# TUDOR

**TUDOR ALL STAR FOOTBALL**
ADMIT ONE · BOX SEAT
★★★★★★★★★★★★★
SEASON TICKET

## YOUR TICKET TO "BIG-TICKET" SALES

**NOW**

*Nationally Advertised*

TO 14 MILLION READERS

**tudor**

TUDOR Tru · Action® Electric Sport Games
featured in dramatic FULL PAGE ADS in

☆ SPORTS ILLUSTRATED
☆ BOYS' LIFE
☆ NEW YORK TIMES MAGAZINE

TUDOR METAL PRODUCTS CORP., Rm. 551, 200 Fifth Ave., N.Y. 10

Photo courtesy "Titans of New York" American Football League

| Electric Football $7 | Electric Baseball $7 | De Luxe Hockey $16 | Electric Basketball $7 | Electric Sports Car Race $7 |

A month after Gotham unveiled the NFL, Tudor had enlisted the AFL for licensing help. In the photo, New York Titans QB Al Dorow carries the ball against the Denver Broncos. Dorow would be part Tudor's advertising in 1961. *Playthings*, April 1961.

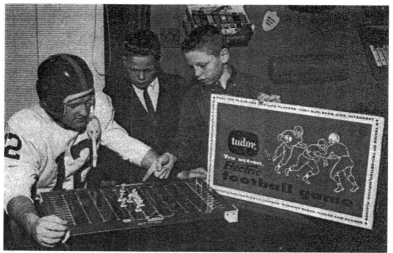

Al Dorow, quarterback of the AFL New York Titans, discusses football strategy over a No. 500 model in the Tudor showroom. Dorow was now part of the "Tudor sports game advisory staff." *Playthings*, page 103, April 1961.

*doubled*, the total still didn't equal what the NFL was going take in from a single championship game. Perhaps the most significant part of the money equation was that NBC agreed to pay that amount because they were sure they could make a profit. That is, they could sell a lot more than $615,000 worth of advertising during the game.

Evidence that the NFL's growing popularity was finally a concern for Tudor came in the form of an addendum to the nationally advertised program. Appearing in the April issue of *Playthings* was a full-page Tudor ad featuring an action photo of Al Dorow – the starting quarterback of the AFL's New York Titans (the photo was labeled "courtesy of the American Football League). The same issue also included an article about Tudor's ad campaign which introduced Dorow as a member of Tudor's sports game advisory staff. For his introduction, Dorow was shown in the Tudor showroom wearing his helmet and jersey while demonstrating football strategy on a No. 500 model to two "young admirers." Dorow was the perfect AFL player for this type of demonstration. Not only was he the Titan's quarterback, he was the AFL's chief scout…and chief public relations man.

By the end of April, Eddie Gluck had to be feeling good about his decision to become an NFL licensee. First, there was Tudor's reaction to the NFL G-1500 and their apparently hurried decision to link the No. 500 with the fledgling AFL (an organized Tudor would have unveiled the AFL relationship during Toy Fair). Next, Rozelle had already announced that NFL Enterprises had more than $2 million in total sales in 1960 – it was a pretty nice figure to start with. Finally, at the spring NFL owners' meeting, the owners approved a massive all-encompassing television contract with CBS. It was a two-year regular season deal with CBS paying the league $4.65 million per year. Thanks to Rozelle, this amount would be split equally among the 14 teams. The commissioner had lobbied hard to convince the owners that the league needed an AFL-type deal, including the revenue sharing concept. After watching the AFL on ABC all season long, the owners needed less convincing than the year before. So come the fall, boys and girls throughout the country would see the NFL games every Sunday – and Gotham's new NFL games in every Sears Christmas catalog.

In the June issue of *Playthings* Gotham ran a bold full-color two-page ad featuring a hatching toy chick asking, "What's New? Everything!" More exclamation points were peppered throughout the text, further claiming Gotham had "redesigned, re-tooled, and renewed" at their new factory. When the page was turned, there was a full-color G-1500 under the headline "Only at Gotham" – the capital "O" in "only" having been turned into a football. Also prominent on the page was the NFL shield, making the game's lineage crystal clear. But that wasn't the end of the Gotham hype in this edition of *Playthings*. On page 88 there was an article about Gotham and the new game, complete with a picture of Gluck playing with a G-1500. Within this piece Gluck was portrayed as a "pioneer" and "master-mind," not only for signing on with the NFL, but also for the major expansion at Gotham that "covers every phase of the operation from product design and plant facilities to showroom display and sales promotion." It was all characterized as "Mr. Gluck's dynamic new expansion program for Gotham." Gluck also went on to describe how television had educated the average viewer about sports strategy and that toy consumers now had higher expectations for realistic game play and game appearance. Gotham's new line was specifically designed to meet this untapped demand.

But just when it seemed that both Gotham and the NFL had assembled the perfect marketing plan for the 1961 season, Federal Judge Allan K. Grim voided the CBS television deal due to antitrust violations. Coming on July 20, the ruling sent a shock wave through all of sports, as it seemed to question the legality of any current single-sport television contract, including those held by the AFL, NCAA, and National Basketball Association. (Within days of the ruling, the AFL was claiming that their contract was "different.") Without the league package, and with the NFL season set to start in less than eight weeks, teams went scrambling to resurrect their individual television deals. During an appeal of the ruling, Rozelle declared that the NFL needed the package to compete with AFL and that it would be "an economic disaster for the league" if the CBS agreement was nullified.

Despite this dire prediction, the ruling was upheld. Grim's decision cost the league over $2.2 million dollars in television revenue.

In spite of the letdown, Gotham continued to ramp up the promotion of its sports games with another two-page color ad in the August issue of *Playthings*. "SIZZLING!" was the headline this time, with the accompanying text: "It's not just weather – it's GOTHAM! We're turning on the heat to bring you the hottest line ever!" (Once again the copywriter, who perhaps was Eddie Gluck himself, was heavy on the exclamation points.) On the flip side was the Gotham Professional Basketball game, which essentially was an all-metal version of Bas-Ket. It didn't quite have the impact of an NFL-endorsed game, but it was presented in a serious and expensive *Playthings* layout. Glossy color pages were still quite costly in 1961. But *Playthings* wasn't the only place where Gotham was promoting its games. By mid-month Gluck had landed the NFL G-1500 into an Associated Press "New Products" article that was published in newspapers throughout the country. From smaller papers in communities like Grand Rapids, Michigan, to the *Washington Post*, readers were told that, "Gridiron fans will find new dimensions of realism at their own firesides." In addition to describing Gotham's new stick-on NFL uniforms and realistic steel grandstand, the article claimed the company had developed the most realistic spring action kicking and passing game ever achieved in a board game. Football season still wouldn't kickoff for another month, yet Gotham was clearly in midseason promotional form.

Gotham and Tudor both had ads in the September *Playthings*. Tudor focused on hockey, using a large black and white photo of an NHL game to remind clients and potential buyers of their upcoming nationally advertised campaign. Gotham again went full color over two pages with an eye-catching "action" image of an apple being shot off a boy's head. Joining the dramatic photo was the headline "Pro-Action!" – along with a paragraph of exclamation-laden text. The game being promoted on the flip side of the page was Gotham Push-Button Baseball, which Gluck obviously hoped to tie in with the upcoming World Series. But with baseball season just about at an end, it was fair to wonder how many baseball game sales were really left in 1961.

Also in *Playthings* was a special pullout section from Ideal Toys showing in detail how the company spent its television advertising budget. The company was sponsoring three network shows: *Mighty Mouse* on CBS; *Bullwinkle* on NBC (which appeared in evening prime time); and the popular western *Maverick* on ABC. It was also sponsoring an incredible 149 local shows throughout the country. Included in the pullout was a state-by-state breakdown of the geographical areas where Ideal ads would be shown. It was a thorough illustration of television's power in the toy world.

Gotham's hard charging public relations campaign took a hit when the Sears *Christmas Book* came out in mid-September. In both *Playthings* and *Toys & Novelties*, the G-1500 had appeared in full color glory – it was clearly a grand game. Sears, on the other hand, ended up squeezing the G-1500 into the top corner of page 371. And not only did they squeeze the game, they posed Gotham's flagship model at a sharp angle to fit on the page. As a final insult, the G-1500 was photographed in black and white.

The striking colors and creative details of the G-1500 completely disappeared into a muddle of sepia shades as Sears even let a photo of the old G-940 overlap part of the new game. Gotham's new players weren't in production when the photo was taken, so even though the catalog description promised stick-on uniforms, the old Heisman players sat on the new field naked as ever. It wasn't exactly a perfect presentation of Gotham's premier game. Still, the impact of the company's hard work was not totally lost, as there was a total of six Gotham sports games on page 371. But would Santa think this giant new electric football game was worth the extraordinary price of $12.99? Or would children gravitate to the smaller, yet more reasonable $7.99 G-940? Elsewhere in the catalog $13 could buy an all-metal pedal car. The 95-piece Marx Disneyland Play Set, advertised in full color on the back cover, was a relative bargain at $9.77.

Gotham President Edward Gluck tries his hand at firm's new game.

**Gotham President Eddie Gluck shows off his brand new NFL G-1500 game in 1961.** *Playthings,* page 88, June 1961.

Montgomery Ward wasn't carrying the G-1500, but the electric football game they were selling, a Gotham Professional Football G-880 model, was in full color on page 388 of the Christmas catalog. The new "professional" game had an all-white frame like its big brother but had miniature pennants with NFL city names lithographed on the sides of the frame instead of official team logos. Ward's G-880 was also one of the special models that would come with a grandstand.

On the final day of September, President Kennedy signed into law a bill that exempted single-network sports television contracts from antitrust regulations. The law wouldn't go into effect until January 1, 1962, leaving the NFL with its piecemeal television schedule for the current season. It was a bitter pill for Rozelle to watch ABC orchestrate AFL telecasts while

Game instructions from the 1961 Gotham NFL Playbook. A copy was included in each NFL G-1500.

the NFL scrounged around trying to get visibility for their marquee teams and games.

By mid-October, with both the NFL and AFL seasons a month old, Sears began running newspaper ads throughout the country that prominently featured the G-1500. Sears made it clear in the ads that the game was an official NFL electric football game and had even come up with a special $10.99 price. The G-1500 became a fixture of Sears' toy advertising as the fall moved on, sharing pages with Lionel train sets, Mattel's Tommy Burst Machine Gun, and even the Disneyland Play Set.

Thanksgiving Day arrived with the NFL and AFL once again set to battle for holiday television viewers. The AFL would get on the air first, with the New York Titans and Buffalo Bills kicking off at 11:00 a.m. Eastern Time. (Like 1960, New Yorkers had a choice between attending the Macy's Parade or an AFL contest – most chose the former as only 12,023 showed up at the Polo Grounds). As per NFL Thanksgiving tradition, the Packers were visiting the Lions with the game starting at noon. It was a crucial game, given that the Packers and Lions were sitting in first and second place respectively in the Western Conference. By mid-afternoon the Titans and Packers were celebrating victories.

Of course, it was traditional for Thanksgiving Day newspapers to be bulging with holiday advertisements. In many areas of the country, Sears had given the G-1500 headliner status, placing the game at the top of its ad pages while vividly illustrating the unique details of an NFL electric football game. Some ads even featured a second image of the G-1500, with a young boy and girl playing the game. Sears presented a range of prices

The first officially licensed NFL electric football game: Gotham's 1961 G-1500. (Photo by John Doub.)

for the game (from $9.88 to $11.88), the amount being saved off retail was always emphasized. It seemed the NFL had put Gotham in the big leagues, at least at Sears.

During the holiday weekend the United Press International published a "game" article, which contained a fawning paragraph about the G-1500. This piece appeared mostly in smaller community newspapers, the type of publications that would be looking for free copy during a long holiday weekend. It was advertising Gotham didn't have to pay for. While the article looked like an official review of 1961 toys, it was little more than a feel-good public relations piece for all the games mentioned. Yet it was typical Eddie Gluck. Any plug for Gotham was a good plug – especially if it was free.

The NFL G-1500 was turning up on toy shelves beyond Sears, but retailers in general seemed cautious about taking on an enormous game with a $13 price tag. One thing that the big push from Sears did for the G-1500 was to raise expectations (kid-wise that is) and give the game the appearance of being a reasonable Christmas item. Over at Ward, however, it was not the same story. Ward had been using Gotham's smaller G-880 in its Christmas advertising, but electric football wasn't a headlining toy item like it was in Sears. When a Gotham game did appear in a Ward ad, it was given no special status. As in past years, it was just an electric football game.

As usual, Tudor was selling just about everywhere else outside of Sears and Ward. And the No. 500 was selling because thanks to Gotham taking on the NFL, Tudor had the most affordable electric football game on the market with the average price of a game ranging between $4 and $5.

Gotham's G-880 didn't have paper uniforms or pennants, and most didn't have grandstands. The game did come in a fancy colorful box that said "Professional Football," but the box didn't even display an NFL shield. So during side-by-side comparison on a store shelf, the main difference between the Tudor and Gotham at the all-important electric football entry level was…price. It was a battle Tudor had been winning since 1954. This year was no different.

Tudor's highly publicized national advertising campaign finally made its appearance in the November 27 issue of *Sports Illustrated*. The ad ran on page 86 where Al Dorow was in uniform, "demonstrating gridiron strategy to young admirers" with a Tudor No. 500. Dorow's photo took up the top half of the page, with the complete line of Tru-Action Electric Sport Action games filling in the space below the photo. "Family Fun with Tudor" was the overall theme of the ad, and it appeared at a very convenient time. Just days earlier the UPI had headlined a nationally syndicated article about the AFL's Thanksgiving Day game with "Dorow Stars As Titans Whip Bills." (Dorow threw a 67-yard touchdown pass and ran for another touchdown in the Titans 21-14 win.) By the end of the week the same ad appeared in the December issue of *Boys' Life*, and the December 3 issue of the *New York Times Sunday Magazine*.

Surprisingly, Tudor wasn't the only toy company who bought space in *Sports Illustrated* in 1961. Just pages away from Tudor and Al Dorow was a two-page Strombecker spread promoting its line of 1/32-scale slot cars. The following week Aurora bought a quarter-page layout for its very popular HO Model Motoring slot cars. There were certainly positives for Tudor in the new ad campaign. Sales were strong, so strong in fact that in the December issue of *Playthings* Norman announced the appointment of special factory sales representatives for six geographical regions of the country. The only states now not covered personally by a Tudor sales rep were Alaska and Hawaii. Employing a sales force to cover 48 states was a serious commitment for any business, let alone a toy manufacturer. So in a very different way from Gotham, Tudor had entered the big time.

But Gotham would not go away or concede an inch this year. Less than ten pages beyond Norman's announcement in *Playthings*, Eddie Gluck was claiming that his NFL G-1500 had brought electric football to a new level of realism. Gluck also announced that Gotham was running Christmas-season television commercials for the G-1500…in Philadelphia. One set of Gotham commercials was running during the Sunday pro football pre-game show on WCAU-TV (channel 10), the CBS affiliate who televised the Philadelphia Eagles. Another set of G-1500 commercials was running on Philadelphia's NBC affiliate, WRCV-TV channel 3. These aired on Saturdays during a college football pre-game show called *NCAA Football Kickoff*.

The G-880 in the 1961 Montgomery Ward *Christmas Catalog* (page 388). This game has no official NFL designation. The pennants on the frame of the game contain city names, not team names. It's also being shown with a grandstand. ©Montgomery Ward, Inc. 1961.

Like the G-1500 itself, Gotham's television ads were an electric football landmark. And it was a very ambitious step to take. It was obvious that being part of the NFL provided Gluck with the self-assurance to take the game to a place it had never been before. At the same time, he wanted to show Kent that Gotham was an innovative and completely modern toy company. It's true that sticking a toe into the Philadelphia television market was minor league stuff compared with Ideal's $3 million television budget, but it was a case of thinking big to be big. Gluck was determined to make Gotham an all-star in the toy world.

In considering Gluck's ambition, it's fair to wonder why a Bronx-based toy company would run its first ever television ads only in Philadelphia. The wonder only increases upon discovering that the New York Giants were occupying first place in the Eastern Conference at the time. But there is an explanation for why Philadelphia was more attractive for Gluck's television experiment than the home market of New York City – money.

Gluck might have been thinking big, but he still had a bottom line at Gotham. It was simply cheaper to put a television commercial on the air in Philadelphia than it was in New York. Gluck claimed that Philadelphia was attractive because the Eagles were the NFL's defending champs, and the city had a strong tradition and interest in professional football. This was all true. Yet it's easy to argue that New York had an equally strong pro-football tradition. Anyway, in 1961 Eddie Gluck saw the Philadelphia television market as a gamble worth taking, even if his new G-1500 looked a lot like Yankee Stadium.

All the thrills, all the plays, all the strategy of major league sports!
Operate on house current! UL approved for safety!

Tudor's 1961 ad featuring QB Al Dorow of the AFL's New York Titans. *Boys' Life*, page 93, December 1961.
©*Boys' Life* 1961.

Gotham got a strong endorsement from an unlikely source – the December 11 issue of *Sports Illustrated*. The unlikely part was that Gluck hadn't paid to run an ad in the magazine; the positive press came from a "Shopwalk" column titled "Imaginative Sporting Games That the Whole Family Can Enjoy Are Good Presents for Christmas." Essentially, it was a shopping guide for the year's best sports games, but it also served as a powerful illustration of just how prominent sports games and toys had become by 1961.

In the article, Gotham was given top game honors in baseball and hockey. Accolades for Slide Action Hockey and Push Button Baseball came from the magazine in the form of both text and photos. Eddie Gluck must have been ecstatic to see his games pictured and described on a *Sports Illustrated* page...for free!

The article did contain a result that could only be described as an upset – neither Tudor nor Gotham won the endorsement in the football category. That honor went to Mag-Powr Football, a game that was played using magnetic wands to make players run and tackle (the field was elevated, allowing the wands to control the players from under the game board). Positioned prominently at the end of the article's first paragraph was a black-and-white photo of a Mag-Powr Football game. By coincidence, it was the same photo the company had used for a full-page Mag-Powr advertisement in the November 20 issue of *Sports Illustrated*.

Only in the final paragraph did Tudor get a mention, and this was a paragraph that Norman probably wished the magazine had left out. It described the Tudor Electric Horse Race Game as "the most realistic of the various vibrating games." Unfortunately, this was a backhanded compliment. The previous sentence had completely trashed the entire genre of vibrating games. It must have been galling for Norman to see the nation's leading sports magazine proclaim that "electric vibrating games on the whole do not offer much of a challenge and make an awful racket." Especially since this blistering critique appeared just weeks after Tudor forked over thousands of dollars for an ad in *Sports Illustrated*.

And not only did the article insult the entire genre Tudor had created and nurtured, it insulted the company further by making its main competitor, Gotham, sound like the standard bearers in the action game market. What *Sports Illustrated* neglected to mention was that Gotham made vibrating games and had recently created the largest vibrating game the toy world had ever seen!

Despite the nationally published slights, Tudor was doing well in the month of December. Its games were advertised and available through more retailers than Gotham with the price of the No. 500 rarely going above the $5 mark. Gotham had Sears using the G-1500 in newspapers ads until mid-month, while Ward totally abandoned electric football in the weeks before Christmas. And the G-880 was rarely seen below the $5 mark; $4.98 was a standard "sale" price. By contrast, if a shopper was willing to do a little legwork, No. 500's could be found for a little as $3.99. But this was as low as the pricing seemed to go for 1961.

There was still cutthroat pricing in toy departments throughout the country. TV toys were once again being served up as loss leaders, especially at discount retailers who needed to attract shoppers in volume to turn a profit. Electric football, despite Eddie Gluck's best efforts to turn it into a TV toy, didn't need a gimmick for strong sales. The game was a Christmas morning staple and able to stand on its own in the toy world.

Both the NFL and AFL finished their seasons on December 17 with a cosmic football coincidence leaving the Eastern Conference in both leagues up for grabs on the final week. Although the Giants could only manage a 7-7 tie with the Browns, this result was good enough to earn them a championship date with the Packers on December 31. The AFL got its

# Action Toys for Children of Every Age!

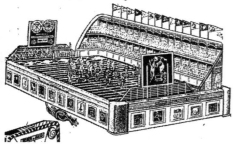

## National League Electric Football

You can almost hear the roar of the crowds in this action packed game! Fast moving activators with improved v i b r a t o r, spring action passer and kicker." Magnetic football, stick-on official uniforms in color. Full colored Official emblems around stadium and full colored official pennants.

Regular $12.98

**9**⁹⁹

A Thanksgiving Day newspaper ad for Gotham's NFL G-1500 game. Sears ran this in the *Chicago Tribune*, the largest newspaper in the Midwest. *Chicago Daily Tribune*, page N12, November 23, 1961.

Eastern champ late in the day after the Oilers destroyed the Raiders in Oakland by a 47-16 score. On the following Sunday, December 24, the Oilers and Chargers would meet in San Diego for the AFL title game.

This week carried meaning well beyond football as Christmas shoppers rushed to finish their lists before the arrival of the holiday. Fortunately the AFL game was in San Diego with a scheduled kickoff of 1:30 p.m. Pacific Standard Time (4:30 Eastern). This gave shoppers and sports fans in the East an entire afternoon to finish any last-minute loose ends before settling in front of the television set. When the gun finally sounded in San Diego, Houston had defeated the Chargers 10-3. Christmas Eve was officially underway.

On Christmas morning, it was clear that a new era in electric football had begun. Any boy who found a nearly three foot long piece of Yankee Stadium under the tree knew he was on Santa's good list. Gotham's G-1500 was a stunning toy, holding its own with almost any toy the reindeer could haul. Through the majesty of the field, frame, and grandstand, it was almost possible to overlook the shortcomings of the new players and the paper uniform concept. Without question, Gotham had opened up new possibilities in electric football.

Tudor didn't have a game to compete with the G-1500, but most families didn't have $12.99 for Gotham's new game. So at least for 1961, the status quo was unchanged. Tudor remained the major player in electric football. Still, for both companies it was a good year to be in electric football and a good year for any sports-minded boy to receive an electric football game. A big reason for this was television. The AFL Championship game was just the first of *fourteen* football games that the networks were going to televise over the next two weeks.

Ten of those games were going to be shown on the following weekend. Saturday would have five bowl games, Sunday was the NFL championship game, and then New Year's Day on Monday would bring four more contests to the tube. A televised football overload? Certainly. But it would keep electric football games buzzing throughout the holiday period, further reinforcing the Christmas vacation-football relationship. G-1500's all over America would surely be set up to play and replay the NFL Championship game. Whether kids would take the time to outfit the Gotham players in blue paper jerseys and helmets (Giants) and green paper jerseys and helmets (Packers) was another question. Getting a Gotham team in and out of uniform was a tedious and time-consuming process. "Undressing" the players offered the biggest challenge. Serious ripping and tearing problems had cropped up before Christmas Day even finished, and it was obvious that there were only so many applications a Gotham uniform could withstand. The more they were used, the more fragile they became. And finally, since Gotham had generously provided uniforms for seven different teams, there was the problem of keeping track of 77 unstuck jerseys and helmets.

Having the Giants in the NFL championship game almost made Gotham seem clairvoyant for designing the G-1500 with a Yankee Stadium grandstand. But the serendipity of the situation was ruined by the fact that the Packers got to host the NFL Championship game thanks to a better record. This left the Giants not only dealing with Vince Lombardi's Packers but also a near zero wind chill. (It was so cold that scalpers were reduced to selling $10 tickets at a 5-for-$15 rate). The Giants had no answers for the Packers or the cold, rolling over meekly in a 37-0 rout on the final day of the year.

Any championship game played on a G-1500 would have easily been more competitive.

Lee Payne's brass master prototype fullback figure, which was created in 1961. It was never put into production. (Collection of Roddy Garcia.)

# 13 TUDOR GETS A KEY PLAYER

 orman Sas had not been overly concerned that Gluck would snap up the NFL licensing after Tudor passed on it. "It may have crossed my mind, but it didn't make any difference," said Sas. "We had a good game and the NFL didn't mean that much." But it wasn't long after seeing the G-1500 that Norman realized that passing on the NFL was a mistake. The Sears picture, said Sas, was worth more than a thousand words. "When Gotham came out with that big game...the way it looked in the catalog, man, it looked fantastic."

And there was the NFL's television contract. Tudor caught a break when the deal was voided in 1961, but it was just a matter of time before the NFL became an even larger part of the Sunday afternoon television landscape. With increasing doses of the NFL reaching across the country, the profile of the league, and of the licensees of NFL Enterprises, would certainly rise. The stakes in electric football were rising. Eddie Gluck seemed to be almost unleashed after Charles Anderson's death, creating new and larger games while pouring money into an aggressive advertising campaign that even included television commercials. Gotham was on the offensive and applying pressure.

Tudor now had one choice – to step up and answer the competition.

"If you're a car manufacturer and hybrids are getting popular, you better get into hybrids, otherwise you're out of it," said Sas, who had little choice with his biggest decision since betting Tudor's entire existence on electric football back in 1948. "Our response was to make our own big game."

From a manufacturing standpoint, it wasn't that difficult for Tudor to make a bigger model and a metal grandstand (Tudor had already created a nearly 40"-long hockey game in 1960). But that would only get them even with Gotham in the "flash" department. Tudor might still be behind because of the NFL factor. Norman wanted more. He wanted something to make Tudor's game unique. But how could Tudor go one step, at least, beyond Gotham? Norman started contemplating ways to improve his game and got his answers from someone who wasn't even a Tudor employee.

Lee Payne was hired as an industrial designer by Walter Dorwin Teague Associates on August 1, 1960. Payne's path to a position at one of New York's renowned industrial design firms included a degree in fine arts from the University of Georgia in 1955, a degree in industrial design from the University of Cincinnati in 1958, and two years of experience with design firms in Ohio and Georgia.

Lee Payne, 1951, starting offensive tackle and defensive end for the undefeated and Aiken County (S.C.) champion North Augusta H.S. Yellow Jackets. (Collection of Roddy Garcia)

When Teague Associates hired Payne, Tudor happened to be one of the company's clients. "Teague already had the Tudor account," said Payne. "Before I arrived they had redesigned the xylophones and done a hockey game." After a few months on the job, Payne was working on the Tudor account. Up to that point, according to Payne, Teague hadn't done much with electric football. "Their designers weren't into sports... they didn't relate," said Payne, referring to a firm that had designed items ranging from the Kodak Baby Brownie Camera to the interior of Boeing 707 jets. "I played enough football to be dangerous. I took to it like a duck to water."

Actually Payne was more than "dangerous" with football. He knew his stuff and, in fact, had played the game at a level that most people never reach. During his high school days, he played for the North Augusta Yellow Jackets in Aiken County, South Carolina. Located just across the Savannah River from Augusta, Georgia, Aiken County in the early 1950's was a high school football hotbed. Schools there had already established a "Friday night under the lights" tradition, with games between local rivals drawing 4,000 fans. Payne was a starting offensive and defensive lineman for North Augusta, lettering in both 1950 and 1951. Making Payne's achievement truly impressive was the fact that North Augusta High was the undefeated champion of Aiken County in both of these seasons. Payne continued his football career into college, playing a season of freshman football at the University of Georgia before finally hanging up the cleats to concentrate on his books.

Just weeks after the G-1500 appeared at the 1961 Toy Fair, Norman recruited the football savvy Payne to work on a Tudor "big game." By the time the NFL signed its full-season television contract in April, Payne was in charge of the Tudor account – and the designing of Tudor's answer to the Gotham's NFL game.

Payne, like Norman, appreciated details. His vision for improving electric football was simple. "Lee really came up with 'let's make this realistic'," said Sas. "That's what we had tried to do in the past. I let him go."

Payne saw a number of areas where more realism could be added to electric football. Even the G-1500, with all its detail, left the young designer less than impressed. "I knew Gluck was our hated competitor, but I didn't see my work as a response to Gotham," said Payne. "We were just trying to make the game better." To Payne's artistic eye, the part of electric football most in need of a major makeover was obvious – the players.

Back in 1955 Tudor laid claim to having 3-D players, but this was a stretch. After six years of production these players were barely wider than a pocket comb. And Gotham, even with the grandeur of the G-1500 and the NFL, was still using the same nickel-width players that they'd entered electric football with back in 1954. Payne felt the time had come to give the players a trait they sorely lacked...a realistic third dimension.

With this extra dimension, Payne envisioned his players with protruding pads, facemasks, and

Lee Payne's 1961 defensive back brass master figure. Lee used himself as the model for this figure. (Collection of Roddy Garcia)

arms that could hold a football. Getting the new dimension out of the mind's eye and into production – profitable production at that – was going to be a monstrous challenge. If it were a simple process, Tudor or Gotham would have done it already. When Payne talked with Norman about making 3-D players, Norman remained skeptical. Payne needed to do something to convince the Tudor owner that the concept was feasible.

He presented his idea to friend Euclides "Lou" Theoharides who was a graphic designer and an accomplished New York sculptor. After talking over his plan, Payne commissioned Theoharides to sculpt six 3-D wax players. The players were individually posed to represent an offensive lineman, a

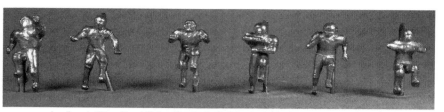

Lee Payne's "Magnificent Six" – offensive back, defensive back, defensive lineman (tackle), fullback, end, and offensive lineman. (Collection of Roddy Garcia)

defensive lineman (tackle), a defensive back, an end, a running back, and a fullback. When Theoharides's work finally met Payne's approval, the wax figures were used to cast a set of six "brass master" players.

In this process, the wax players were mounted in clay, and molten brass was poured into the molds. The hot brass melted the wax player, and, after cooling off, left behind a "brass master." Payne and Theoharides filed and sanded each master figure to their liking, then made a rubber mold of each player (hot rubber was poured over the brass then peeled off, creating a hollow rubber mold). In the last step, Payne poured hot wax into the six rubber molds multiple times, creating two complete teams of wax players. The finishing touch for each team was a careful paint job by Payne. The players looked so good, there was only one thing left to do – show them to Norman. Quickly.

Lee Payne's 1961 brass master defensive lineman figure. This would eventually become Tudor's "tackle." (Collection of Roddy Garcia)

"The players were very, very, fragile," said Payne. "It was strictly a one-shot deal."

Although there had been talk of the players, Norman was unaware how far Payne had moved forward with the process. "I was creating them more or less on my own, and just decided it was time to show Norman," said Payne, who still chuckled when recalling Norman's reaction to the wax teams. "He almost fell out of his chair."

Payne's players provided the realism Norman wanted – and then some. Gotham may have had the NFL, but they didn't have anything like the miniature scrimmage line that sat before Norman. On the spot, Payne got the approval to move forward with getting the players into production. It was too late to get the players into any of Tudor's current models, but come 1962, the company would provide electric football with a level of realism never seen before.

Payne's creative genius wasn't limited to the players. Norman let him loose on Tudor's entire electric football line. They both wanted a grand game to debut the players on, so during the rest of 1961, Payne spent much of his time working on the new Tudor large game, which would eventually be known as the No. 600 model.

When the word came down in July that the NFL's television deal had been declared illegal, both Norman and Lee breathed a sigh of relief. Gluck had the NFL game, but now he wouldn't get an extra push from television. With Payne continuing to make progress on the new game, Norman felt confident that Tudor could level the scrimmage line at the 1962 Toy Fair.

Payne used Tudor's DeLuxe Hockey game as a template, designing a new frame for the football game that was 38 " x 21" (by comparison the No. 500 dimensions were 25" x 18"). And at 3" tall, the frame allowed the field to sit down in the game and be completely surrounded by a stadium "wall." To add to the wall's realism, Payne would lithograph yard markers every 10 yards.

The field was also included in Payne's quest for realism. Up to this point, Tudor and Gotham electric football game fields had always been a monochrome green. This was not good enough for the new game. Although Payne entertained thoughts of having worn muddy spots, he finally settled on

Lee Payne's 1961 brass master end figure. (Collection of Roddy Garcia)

a light green/dark green speckle pattern, which looked very much like a real grass field. The yard lines and hash marks (this would be the first Tudor field with hash marks and yard lines every 5 yards) were created with breaks and feathered edges to simulate the exact look of chalk when it's applied to grass. Lines on all previous games – including the G-1500 – had a perfectly "machine" solid appearance.

Perhaps the most distinctive thing about the new Tudor field was not its colors but its composition. For the first time in twelve years of making electric football, the company was abandoning its trademark metal field. The playing surface of the No. 600 was going to be masonite...just like Gotham's. Was this a concession to Tudor's rival? Not really.

"At that point, we really didn't know how to attach a metal board to a metal frame [the No. 500's were a one piece design]," said Sas. "We were afraid the games might bend or break in shipping." Tudor already had a hockey game with a metal frame and a fiberboard rink that could be shipped around the country without much problem. So the decision was made to stay with the hockey template – it would save money because the company was already producing the same components. This left Norman and Lee searching for an acceptable technique for making the new field vibrate evenly.

Lee Payne's 1961 brass master offensive back figure. (Collection of Roddy Garcia)

After much trial and error and effort, Payne came up with the "Isopad." The Isopad – essentially a metal clip with a foam rubber lining – would attach the field to the frame. Not having a hard mount for the frame allowed the vibrations of the field to work their way around the game more evenly and also deadened the noise made by the vibrator. Or at least that was the theory. A plain fact was that each game would need fourteen Isopads to hold the new field in place.

While the game took shape, Payne continued working on the players. After getting Norman's word to move forward, a second set of master players was designed. These players were the same size as the original brass masters, but made out of white metal. To keep the game profitable, only four of the six player poses made the final cut for production; the lineman, the end, the defensive back, and offensive back. The unique ball-carrying fullback and Payne's beloved tackle figure were relegated to Tudor's toyshop workbench for the 1962 season. But Payne did design a new metal 3-D quarterback with a spring-loaded leg that could actually kick the ball.

This figure would be the first real kicker in electric football history. Initial production plans called for Tudor to cast all their players straight from molds made by the new metal masters.

The crucial part of Payne's 3-D concept was painting the players. Payne thought the Gotham idea of individualizing players had merit, but the paper-jersey concept was a cheap and not very realistic way to go about it. Customizing electric football players with paint seemed like a much better method. Tudor planned to include a paint palette, thinner, and a paintbrush, as well as two sets of stick-on numbers in the new game to allow kids to personalize their teams. Surprisingly, the minor detail of paint had a profound effect on the final design of the players.

Not all types of plastic hold paint well. Harder plastics (like styrene used for car models) provide a great platform for paint. But styrene's rigid nature, while providing strength, introduces something not necessarily desirable in a child's toy – a distinct crunch-ability. A soft plastic like polyethylene (green army men for example) can be twisted and flexed and still stay together, but paint flakes off it like drying mud off football cleats. Payne had to come up with a functional player that could be painted and have an element of durability.

Lee Payne's 1961 brass master lineman figure. This would become Tudor's "guard." (Collection of Roddy Garcia)

His solution was to make the final Tudor player out of two parts: a high impact styrene body that could be painted, and a green polyethylene base with eight "legs." The players and bases would be included in the game on separate plastic sprues (the plan for the No. 600 was 34 total players – 17 white and 17 yellow). Assembling the players would be done by the owner of the game...or Santa.

Norman and Lee spent the summer of 1961 anxiously waiting for Eddie Gluck's new players to appear. These players were going to be a crucial piece of the G-1500. If they looked good and added to the realism of Gotham's massive stadium, they would surely help sell the game. The players would also give Tudor an idea of whether Payne had created something truly special with his own players. It wasn't until September that

Gotham's "Martian" players. Fully dressed in helmet and jersey. (Photo by Earl Shores)

the G-1500 finally started hitting toys store shelves, and when Norman and Lee finally got their first look at Gotham's new players, they were stunned – and practically giddy. They knew that all the frantic work of the previous months was worth every single bead of sweat. Gotham may have had the NFL and innovative stick-on uniforms, but wearing those uniforms were the ugliest electric football players ever made.

Boys expecting the Heisman players were surely in shock when Gotham's bizarrely bubble-headed backs and lineman tumbled out of the G-1500's box. At least with two poses, Gotham had finally caught up with Tudor, but...the new players looked like something that stepped off a Roswell Alien Invasion play set.

Like the old Heisman players, the new players were still flat and two-dimensional. But they were made out of an odd tan color. Presumably it was flesh tone. The only problem with this color concept was that Gotham didn't provide paper pants. If you wanted to take miniature realism to its logical conclusion – and Eddie Gluck had pushed the realism factor hard in all his interviews with *Playthings* – then Gotham's new players were naked from the waist down.

In fairness, the eye would likely adapt to the coloring issue. But when combined with the new player poses, the Gotham players created an overall image that was too disturbing to ignore. For starters, the running backs looked like Radio City Rockettes who were about to launch into their trademark can-can kick. Continuing with the dancer theme, the linemen, with their bizarrely stretched fingers and deeply bent arms and knees, also looked like a chorus line of dancers about to strut their way through a show-stopping number. But things got even stranger. To accommodate the helmet stickers, Gotham enlarged the players' heads – significantly. Lining the players up on the field made the G-1500 looked like it had been captured by 22 men from Mars.

These Gotham figures, now referred to as the "Martian Players," were galaxies away from the realistic vision of electric football that Norman and Payne forged in secret during 1961. As the year closed, the two men felt confident that they had created a better looking and better playing game than the G-1500, despite Gotham's NFL ties and Gluck's advertising blitz. Norman knew that 1962 was guaranteed to be a year of change – and of challenge.

# tudor® SPORTS CLASSIC — *Electric* FOOTBALL

EACH TEAM INCLUDES—

LINEMEN    ENDS    OFFENSIVE BACKS    DEFENSIVE BACKS    KICKER-PASSSER      COLORING SET

## NEW! "Sculpt • action" players create the most realistic football game ever!

• *Exclusive* 3-dimensional "Sculpt • action" players—34 of them—simulate the action of real football games! Coloring set and press-on numerals permit the ultimate in realism.

• Actual offensive and defensive formations are now possible—players run, block, tackle, pass and kick as never before!

• A Kicker-Passer for each team actually kicks with foot and passes with arm—another Tudor first!

• Yardage and down markers—even a 10-yd. marker to take on to the field to measure "the close ones"—all simulate the real thing! The Bowl crowd is an actual photo.

• Players run on new, more durable Vibra-Action "legs".

• Gridiron has exclusive "Isopad" mounting for consistently smoother, quieter performance.

• Handsomely illustrated display box, commands attention —sells the game!

**No. 600**
BOX SIZE: 21½" x 39" x 3¼"
¼ DOZ. CTN. WT. 30 LBS.
110 VOLTS A. C. ONLY
$16.00 RETAIL

Tudor's 1962 answer to Gotham's NFL – an oversized electric football game with 3-D players. (Collection of Norman Sas.)

# 14 GORILLAS ON THE FIELD

**B**owl game results went pretty much as expected on New Year's Day of 1962. Most of the day's football drama was over by mid-afternoon when top-ranked Alabama beat Arkansas 10-3 in the Sugar Bowl. Even without an exciting end to the Bowl season, the following morning presented a major challenge to football fans. They were coming off a three-day bender of televised football. Ten games had been televised during the last 72-hours – it was a new record. Sitting bleary-eyed over cups of instant coffee, football fans would have to wait five days until the NFL runner-up bowl on Saturday for their next football fix.

On January 10 the NFL finally signed a legal season-long television contract with CBS. It was essentially the same agreement the league tried to sign the year before, a two-year deal guaranteeing the NFL $4.65 million annually. The money was to be split evenly between the league's 14 teams. There's no question that $322,000 per team sounded good, especially to the Eagles and Green Bay, who both earned less than $130,000 from television in 1961. But the Colts and Steelers were less than thrilled. As the only NFL teams on NBC in 1961, the Steelers and Colts were broadcast nationwide over 135 stations stretching from Portland, Maine, to Yakima, Washington. The Colts' television earnings for the season totaled $445,000, while the Steelers took in $355,000. Both

Lee Payne's unique Kicker-Passer figure. This white metal master was used for catalog photos and Toy Fair demonstrations in 1962. (Collection of Roddy Garcia.)

would have to take a pay cut in 1962...for the good of league. Finally the NFL would be on even television footing with the "evil empire" of the AFL. Competition between the two leagues was heating up.

Also coming to a boil was the rivalry between Tudor and Gotham. With the NFL television contract finally signed, Eddie Gluck could ride high into the 1962 Toy Fair. Besides appearing in the Sears catalog, Gotham's G-1500 was going to make a full-page appearance in the 1962 NFL Enterprises catalog. Included with each G-1500 game this year was an NFL season schedule featuring a cover page that placed the Gotham logo and the NFL logo side by side. It was a striking graphic that made a direct link between the game and the league.

Gotham gave its players a slight redesign for 1962, molding them from red as well as tan polyethylene plastic. Having a red team and a tan team in each Gotham game would make the paper uniform concept much less important, as it would now be possible to open a G-1500 and start playing the game without bothering to "dress" your teams.

Keeping a new toy secret is vital to success in the toy industry. If your competitor finds out what you have under wraps, they may beat you to the market with an item and may even make it better. One year with an exclusive item is better than no exclusive at all. The secrecy Tudor maintained about its electric football innovations would have made James Bond proud. Gluck had no idea what Payne had been up to over the last year.

The only hint came in the February *Playthings* where a full-page Tudor ad announced, "There's a new dimension in electric sports games." Farther down on the page, Norman – for the first time ever – took direct aim at Eddie Gluck and Gotham: "No matter how sophisticated a buyer you think you are, your eyes will pop...when you see realism never achieved before." This teasing ad served its purpose. It left the toy trade guessing about what Tudor was up to. Especially uneasy was Gluck.

When the Gotham reconnaissance team entered Tudor's showroom in early March, the new Sports Classic No. 600 model hit them like a blitzing 250-pound linebacker. Sitting on perhaps the most realistic looking "grass" electric football field ever made, were two teams of fully three-dimensional players. These "Sculpt-action" players, as Tudor called them, stood 1 ½"-high and were perfectly proportioned in every way. Helmet, hands, arms, legs, and facemasks; they looked like football players who had been put in a miniaturization machine. Each team had players in four different Payne poses: the lineman, end, offensive back and defensive back. And then there was Payne's ingenuous kicker-passer figure. Proportioned in the same scale as the other players, this player had a special arm to throw passes as well as a spring-loaded leg to kick punts and field goals (both actions used

Tudor's white felt footballs). Topping off all the players was a meticulous Lee Payne paint job, giving the home team white helmets, red jerseys, and white pants, while the visitors took the field in blue helmets, white jerseys, and yellow pants. Press-on player numbers completed the personalization of the teams. The players were stunning and realistic.

Of course, Payne's refined vision of realism went beyond the players. Not satisfied with a hand-drawn crowd scene, Payne attended a Princeton-Yale football game in November of 1961 and took a photo of the Palmer Stadium crowd on the other sideline. This photo was printed on sheet metal, and now served as the grandstand for the new Tudor game. The goal posts and first-down marker also received 3-D treatment, being molded of white styrene plastic. With all these pieces assembled on a featured table in the Tudor showroom, there was no question that Norman and Lee had done exactly what they set out to do: create the most realistic looking electric football game ever made.

Tudor's realism theme was carried off the field too. Box lids for the new game were going to feature a color photo instead of a hand-created illustration. Gracing nearly the entire front of the

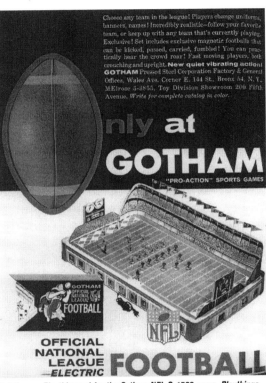

A full-page *Playthings* ad for the Gotham NFL G-1500 game. *Playthings,* February 1962.

No. 600 box were two crew-cut topped boys playing a No. 600 game. The background looked like the paneled wood wall of a typical rec room, and the boys' smiles spoke eloquently – "Tudor electric football is fun!"

Payne had recruited the boys. They were the Drummond brothers, sons of Archie Drummond, the production manager at Teague Associates. And the Drummonds were going to be an integral part of Tudor's No. 600 marketing. Not only were they on every box, they were on page two of every Tudor sales catalog. It all fell in with the theme of realism. Here were two real boys,

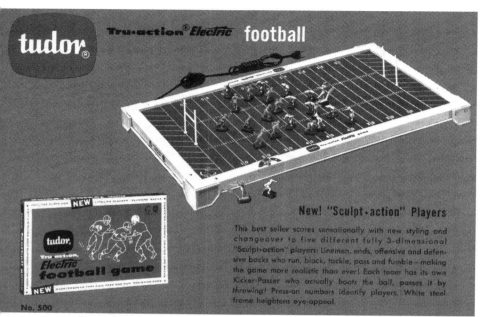

tudor®

Tru·action® *Electric* football

**New! "Sculpt·action" Players**

This best seller scores sensationally with new styling and changeover to five different fully 3-dimensional "Sculpt·action" players: Linemen, ends, offensive and defensive backs who run, block, tackle, pass and fumble — making the game more realistic than ever! Each team has its own Kicker-Passer who actually boots the ball, passes it by throwing! Press-on numbers identify players. White steel frame heightens eye-appeal.

No. 500

The redesigned Tudor No. 500 in the 1962 Tudor sales catalog. (Personal collection of Norman Sas.)

looking over this new realistic football game, in a realistic setting. Any kids who saw the box could easily put themselves in the picture.

Obviously Tudor's emphasis at the Fair was the new game, but the No. 500 model was not forgotten. Tudor was still making its top-selling game, and it would be updated this year with Payne's new 3-D players. Payne also redesigned the No. 500, giving it a bright white frame and a new dark green field with feathered hash marks and yard lines every five yards. Other additions were Tudor's new goal posts and down marker. One thing the No. 500 didn't get was a grandstand.

Tudor's showroom was abuzz during the Fair. The new games had been promoted by a four-page color spread in *Playthings* that ran the headline: "There's a new dimension in electric sports games, and Tudor's got it!" Included in the layout were Drummond boxes as well as a close-up of a new player – one that had been expertly painted by Payne. Buyers huddled around prototype No. 600 models that displayed this same player and his hand-painted teammates. Most unusual were the gasps of disbelief being uttered by world-weary "seen-it-all" toy buyers, who often sounded as if they were watching a live 100-yard kickoff return instead of a toy.

Gotham may have had the NFL, but Rozelle had yet to award expansion teams to Venus or Mars. Several AFL teams had weird-looking uniforms –

A photo of the 1962 Gotham Toy Fair showroom. Seated on the right is Eddie Gluck. *Playthings*, page 97, April 1962.

the Denver Broncos' vertically striped socks come to mind – but no teams looked as strange as the Gotham men. Tudor's new players were comparable in detail to the best miniature toy figures being made. But there were several caveats that went with the players Tudor displayed in room 551.

First, these were white metal prototype players, not production players. (Taking prototypes to the Toy Fair is still a standard practice.) A New York area plastics manufacturer would soon start making the real players. It was safe to assume there would be slight differences between the players in the showroom and the players Tudor ended up shipping to retailers in the fall.

Qualification number two was that although the showroom players were beautiful, their level of detail depended on someone having the steady hand and artistic eye of Lee Payne. The average 10-year-old was probably not going to coax the same captivating appearance out of Tudor's paint palette, brush, and thinner. Leaving an item's finishing touches to the owner was a common practice in the hobby world, so Tudor wasn't doing anything out of the ordinary. And poorly painted Tudor 3-D players were arguably more attractive than the most perfect press-on uniform Gotham players. Payne had clearly set the bar for how realistic electric football could be – it was just that maybe he set it at world record height.

So the battle was on. Gotham came into the Toy Fair advertising heavily. A full-page color ad for the G-1500 had already run in the February issue of *Playthings*, and Gluck had placed another double-sided color ad in the Toy Fair issue. In a clever layout that had a toy owl perched on a pair of eyeglasses, the ad asked, "Look sharp and see...what's been going on at Gotham?" The text below the question provided the "right" answer – Gotham had been expanding its production and redesigning its games and packaging. On the other side of the page was Gotham's oversized Slide-Action Electric Hockey game. (The "electric" part was battery-operated goal lights.) Gotham also landed a three-paragraph, two-photo blurb on page 488 that introduced Gotham's new Pro-Action Electric Speedway game and redesigned bowling game. The Speedway model was truly electric, having a G-940 frame with a vacuum-form plastic racetrack mounted over a vibrating piece of masonite. This overlay technique was obviously borrowed from Tudor and Joe Modica.

The Toy Fair ended with Gluck knowing he had seen the future of electric football on someone else's game. Sas and Tudor had countered Gotham's NFL coup with realism and taken electric football to places Gotham designers had yet to dream of. And Sas was even highlighting the differences between the two companies in Tudor's *Playthings*' ads! The G-1500 still had the Yankee Stadium grandstand and the NFL logo-lined frame, but in every other area Tudor had moved ahead, even in packaging. Perhaps the biggest realism gap fell on the quarterback, where Gotham still had a spring-shooter device that was basically a piece of metal. Tudor had a quarterback who not only looked like one of the other players, he could pass, kick, or run if needed.

Tudor's new realism had already cost Gluck a major retailer – Montgomery Ward. Come the Christmas shopping season, Ward would be selling Tudor's new line of electric football games. This ended Gotham's exclusive seven-year control of the mail-order Christmas market. It was also the first time Tudor had placed its electric football games in a major Christmas catalog. Gluck and Gotham needed to do some careful evaluation over the coming months.

Also doing some hard thinking by the end of the Fair was the toy industry itself. Specifically, the industry had to come up with a way for retailers to offer competitive prices and make a profit. Loss leader pricing had again been a major issue during the Christmas of 1961, and its negative consequences were only heightened by the fact that for the first time ever the discount houses were handling a greater volume of toys than department stores. As a result, department stores were threatening to reduce or eliminate toys altogether because toy profit now ranged from tiny to nonexistent. Competing with the discounters required selling many toys at a loss. A number of major department stores were saying it simply wasn't worth the hassle to be in toys anymore.

Hardest hit, as usual, were the independent mom-and-pop toy stores. Surviving the vicious high-volume/no-profit trap was almost impossible for

Tudor's new 3-D player lineup for 1962. Lee Payne's reaction when he saw the new players was: "They looked like damn gorillas!" (Photo by Earl Shores.)

these stores, and the reason was very simple. Discounters frequently had retail prices that were less than what smaller toy-only stores were paying for the same item *wholesale!* Because the discounters sold in volume, they were allowed to order toys – in volume – directly from toy makers. And because of the size of the orders, the discounters received a discounted wholesale price. Numerous small toy stores reported to *Playthings* that it was cheaper during the Christmas season to restock their shelves with toys bought from a discount store rather than buying more inventory directly from the toy maker or a jobber (the middlemen of the toy business). Some retailers, in fact, admitted to using just such a strategy during the crunch time of Christmas.

The toy industry hierarchy was certain that it couldn't afford to lose any year-round toy retailers. But it wasn't sure what it owed the independent retailers and department store chains. Those retailers had little doubt as to what they needed from the toy makers – the same wholesale prices that the toy makers were offering the discount houses.

For the NFL, the month of March marked a landmark; it was on the 31st that the original two-year NFL Enterprises contract was set to expire. The owners had already voted to renew it, even though the amount of revenue the teams saw from licensing wasn't very significant. Rozelle was still a big NFLE supporter, viewing the organization as an image booster more than a bottom-line booster. Surprisingly, a major player was now missing from the NFLE equation: Larry Kent. He had resigned from Roy Rogers in late 1961 to become the director of marketing at Scientific Industries, a toy model maker that was planning a big entry into educational toys in 1962. Kent's departure was surprising. He loved working with the NFL and was proud of how far NFLE had come in a short time. A lot of people were left scratching their heads. This included Eddie Gluck.

Kent might have been gone, but Gluck still had the NFL, and he continued to promote electric football heavily in *Playthings*. In the April issue, Gotham ran another two-sided color ad for the G-880 electric football game. A little farther inside the magazine there was photo of the Gotham Toy Fair showroom with Gluck and his sales staff gathered around a Slide Action Electric Hockey game. But before reaching this photo, Gluck was in for a rude surprise. Tudor had purchased a color four-page spread that included two full pages devoted to electric football. "Tudor scores again" ran the caption over the redesigned No. 500 model, which included a detailed photo of the new Sculpt-action players. All four poses were clearly visible, as was the quarterback, who was posed with a ball in his throwing arm. "Each one is a little masterpiece – a miniature work of art," said the text in the ad.

On the following page the new No. 600 Sports Classic Football game received the royal ad treatment. Again the Drummond boys were shown in mid-game, but, as an added bonus, there were individual close-up photos of each player pose with the players painted in splendid detail. The running back, end, and quarterback figures were the "visitors" – yellow pants, blue helmet, blue socks, black shoes, and flesh-tone hands and face. Actually, these players looked a lot like they were wearing the away uniform of the AFL New York Titans. There was even a yellow stripe going down the center of the helmets; the markings were identical to the helmets real Titans wore. The "home" team, represented by Payne's lineman and defensive back, wore red jerseys, white pants, red socks, and a white helmet with a red stripe.

When a toy buyer looked at the players in the Tudor ad, then compared them to the players Gotham had lined up in their G-880 ad – the differences posed a dramatic contrast. And really there was no comparison. Tudor's new players were spectacularly more realistic than Gotham's players. Heisman or Martian, it just didn't matter. Tudor was far ahead in the "realism" battle now.

Gluck, however, was ready to concede absolutely nothing and proceeded to run another color two-page ad in the June issue of *Playthings*. In addition to the ad, which featured Gotham's Push Button Baseball game, Gluck landed a four-paragraph feature on page 138. A photo of the baseball game sat above the text, but more significant was the headline above the photo that read "Gotham's Pro Action Sports Game Line Scheduled for Network TV."

Eddie Gluck had gone big-time with his advertising. Just like Ideal, Marx, and Mattel, Gotham was going to promote its games on national television. The Gotham plan was going to be a little different than the ones used by the toy industry's "A team" in that it was much more focused. Gluck had picked a single show to advertise on, a popular ABC game show called *Seven Keys*, which aired on weekdays from 2:30-3:00 p.m. Beginning on September 1, Gotham's line of sports games would receive "dramatic national TV exposure." The games would be demonstrated on the show throughout the fall and right up until Christmas. (This was still a time when a commercial would consist of the show's host walking over to a sponsor's display to pitch the items live to the cameras.) It seemed that Gotham's Official National Football League G-1500 game would be pretty well known by Christmas time. There was no doubt that the Yankee Stadium grandstand was going to look good on television.

During the summer, Gotham unveiled a new electric Tank Battle game. An ad in the July issue of *Playthings* gave the game a color debut into the toy world, with the other side of the page devoted to three Gotham games, including the G-940 Electro-Magnetic Football game. In the August *Playthings*, Gotham began promoting the new G-980 Electric Race Car Speedway with a full-page ad. While the Speedway game was news, Gluck had even bigger news printed on page 179. There a large headline declared "TV Star Art Linkletter to Present Commercials on Gotham's Hockey."

Gotham was going to advertise on a *second* national television program. And this second program arguably had a higher profile than *Seven Keys*.

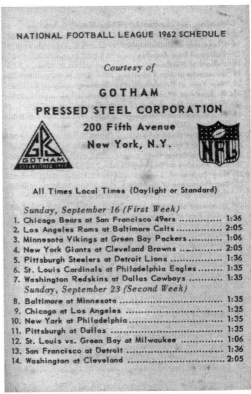

The official Gotham NFL Schedule included in all 1962 G-1500's.

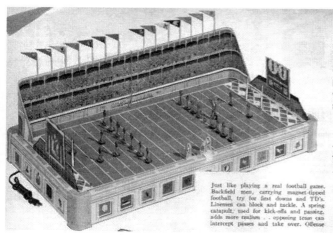

It's just like real football with plenty of body contact and broken field running. When the big 36x21-inch electrically-controlled field starts to vibrate, all of the 22 men are set in motion.

## $12⁴⁴

### National League Electric Football

Just like playing a real football game. Backfield men, carrying magnet-tipped football, try for first downs and TD's. Linemen can block and tackle. A spring catapult, used for kick-offs and passing, adds more realism . . . opposing team can intercept passes and take over. Offense controls the push-button vibrator. The hardboard field is set in steel frame. Includes emblems, pennants, stick-on uniforms, goal posts, markers, metal scoreboard and rules. Operates on 110-120-volt, 60-cycle AC. UL listed.
79 N 404L—Shipping weight 13 lbs. . . .$12.44

Gotham's NFL G-1500 on full color display in the 1962 Sears *Christmas Book* (page 344). It was the first time that Sears put electric football on a color page. ©Sears, Roebuck & Co. 1962.

It was a daytime variety show called *House Party*, which ran on CBS in the very same time slot as *Seven Keys*. The show's host was Art Linkletter, one of the most popular personalities in all of television. Linkletter himself would give a live demonstration of Electric Slide Action Hockey during Gotham's designated commercial slots. The commercials would start running the week after Labor Day and continue to be part of the Linkletter show until Thanksgiving.

Advertising nationally on ABC and CBS was a major step for Eddie Gluck and Gotham. There was no question that millions of consumers would now be exposed to the Gotham brand. And Gluck was in good company. Mattel was spending a toy-industry record $5 million on television commercials this fall in order to "pre-sell the children and parents in your community."

As if Tudor didn't have enough concerns with Gotham running nationwide television commercials on two major networks, the company was also having an issue with the most important part of the 1962 line, the Sculpt-action players. The molders of the new players had missed the original delivery date and were evasive about when the players would be shipped. As more weeks passed, Sas and Payne became increasingly troubled. Other than the players, the No. 600 games were complete and ready to be shipped. What could possibly be going on with the company molding the players? Would they be delivered at all, or would Tudor, after all the 3-D hype, be forced into the disastrous situation of substituting old players on the new games?

Finally, the new players arrived in Brooklyn – Sas and Payne were livid.

"The molders got their hands on the players and took artistic license," said Payne. "They really screwed them up." The production players had some resemblance to Payne's detailed metal masters, but they were clearly not a precise copy of what Tudor sent out months earlier. On each of the four different poses, the player's torso was badly out of scale with the rest of his body. In particular, the shoulders and arms of the figures were too thick, especially considering that football players of the 60's wore much less padding than modern players. (They also didn't have year-round weight-lifting programs, the science of supplements, and another unseemly "s-word" that can stay on the sidelines for the sake of electric football innocence.) Completely lost was the upper-body detail Payne painstakingly imparted upon the metal masters. Necks had been lost too, and out of the players' puffed-up sleeves, protruded tiny hands. Payne and Theoharides's first generation of brass masters had been scaled more accurately.

The scale issue affected more than the players' looks, as the increased mass of the upper body made the figures top heavy. In testing, the players fell over much too easily as the game board vibrations increased. Creating games with somewhat limited playability was not the Norman Sas way of doing business. Tudor had put so much effort into the new game, and now they found themselves several yards short of the goal line of perfection. Sas was faced with a difficult decision.

"They looked like damn gorillas," said Payne. "And since we didn't get them until the eleventh hour, Norman had no choice but to put them in the game." So each No. 600 was packed with 17 white and 17 yellow plastic gorilla players. The game also came with a single figure that escaped "gorilla-ization" – the quarterback. For whatever unknown reason, the quarterback figures came back looking much like Payne's original master. With their unique design unaltered, realistic passing and kicking finally arrived in electric football. The quarterbacks proved what could be done with an electric football figure. And Tudor's gorilla teams were several branches up the electric football evolutionary tree from Gotham's big-helmeted 2-D space-invaders. Still, Sas and Payne were deeply disappointed. It was hard to accept putting out players they didn't really believe in.

The fall unfolded with the NFL and AFL again battling every Sunday afternoon on network television and Tudor and Gotham battling on the Christmas catalog pages, *Playthings'* pages, and retailers' shelves. Sears had the Gotham G-1500 on full-color display in the *Christmas Book*, with the game taking up the top third of page 344. Flat players and all, it was an eye-catching presentation. The price had even dropped $0.55 from the year before to $12.44. Just below the photo was the redesigned G-940 Electro-Magnetic Football game that, despite some upgrading, did not have the impact of its bigger and flashier NFL brother. Both of these games were part of the most extravagant sports game presentation ever seen in a Christmas catalog. Laid out over two full-color pages were 15 different sports games, including four football games, three race games, two basketball games, three hockey games, and three baseball games. Landing the most games was Gotham, who had six models being sold by Sears (NFL G-1500, G-940 Football, G-980 Car Race, G-900 Basketball, G-850 Baseball, and a less expensive version of Slide Action Hockey). Tudor had a single game – its new Track Meet game. There was little doubt that Sears was going to help Gotham sell games this year.

But there was good news for Tudor over in the Montgomery Ward catalog. The No. 500 and new Sports Classic No. 600 model were both prominently on view at the top of page 366. Ward hadn't been quite as ambitious as Sears, offering up only a single page of sports games. And in another more significant way, Ward had been less ambitious than Sears – the Ward sports page was printed entirely in black and white. All of the details Sas and Payne worked so hard to perfect on the No. 600 vanished in the printing process. Ward had taken a stunning toy and made it look ordinary, just as Sears had done with the G-1500 the year before. Even worse, they made it look almost the same as the toy it sat next to – the No. 500. In another unfortunate case of artistic license, Ward scaled both games so they looked equal in size. The reduction of the No. 600 was so drastic that it was hard to notice the painted players, let alone the new field and grandstand. (Both games were shown with Tudor's new metal grandstand; it's possible that Ward actually sold a No. 500 in this configuration, but it has never been confirmed by the either of the authors.)

Undoubtedly many Christmas shoppers, even savvy ones, had a hard time understanding why one game cost $12.44, and the other one just $5.44. Okay, one had "Deluxe" in its title, yet the deluxe aspects of the game really weren't obvious. It wasn't much of a stretch to interpret the expression of the young boy Ward had posed over the No. 600 as reflecting puzzlement instead of excitement.

Tudor did have the run of Ward's sports page with three of the seven games. But in yet another case of unfortunate placement, the new Tudor Sports Classic Baseball game was placed right next to a Gotham Baseball game. In black and white, the two games looked very similar. So it was again puzzling to shoppers why the Tudor game cost almost twice as much as the Gotham game. While it was great to have taken over the Ward electric football slot in 1962, there was surely disappointment in the Tudor camp when the Ward catalog hit the mail routes.

The *Playthings* advertising battle continued in September with Gotham running another two-page color ad showing off eight games, but surprisingly there was no NFL G-1500. Tudor kept things simple, saying

Tudor's new Sports Classic No. 600 model in the 1962 Montgomery Ward *Christmas Catalog* (page 366). ©Montgomery Ward, Inc. 1962.

that its new games, styling, realism, and packaging had resulted in the "biggest demand ever for Tudor Electric Sport Games." Which was true. It was a good year to be a toy maker. Some of the most iconic toys ever made were available in 1962. The toy departments of both Sears and Ward were full of items like King Zor, Chatty Cathy, Magnatel, Mr. Machine, Kenner Girder and Panel sets, Aurora Model Motoring sets, and Marx Blue and Gray Civil War play sets. There were also Cold War influenced toys, the most notable being Remco's line of oversized plastic "battle" toys: the 3-foot long Barracuda Atomic Submarine; the Sky Diver Jet with parachute ejector pilot; the massive battery operated Bulldog Tank; and the 2-foot long Whirlybird Rescue Helicopter. All of these toys were getting a push from heavy television advertising (and they soon would receive a subversive push from the Cuban Missile Crisis).

One place where Tudor and Gotham weren't competing was on television. With *Seven Keys* and Art Linkletter, Gotham had cornered the sports game market on television. By early November, Sears began running newspaper ads featuring Gotham's Electric Slide Action Hockey – the game that Art Linkletter was pushing on *House Party*. As the Linkletter promotion entered its concluding weeks, Sears finally started promoting the G-1500. Electric football seemed more of an afterthought for Sears this year, as Gotham's hockey game was clearly the headline item. It's likely that the Linkletter promotion influenced Sears' choice of a feature game.

In the No. 500 Tudor still had the most affordable football game in 1962. Considering the costs Tudor had to absorb in developing and

**No. 600—TUDOR CLASSIC ELECTRIC FOOTBALL**
Every football fan is sure to get a great kick out of playing this game which features 3-dimensional "Sculpt-action" players—34 of them! You can now set-up actual offensive and defensive formations with players who run, block, tackle, pass and kick as never before. A "Kicker-Passer" for each team actually kicks with his foot and passes with his arm! Included is a coloring set plus numbers, yardage, ball and down markers — even a 10-yd. field chain for "close ones"! $16.00

Tudor's No. 600 game as pictured in the 1962 Tudor Rule Book (a rule book was included in every Tudor game). Lee Payne recruited the Drummond brothers to be part of Tudor's 1962 advertising. They were the son's of Dorwin Teague's production manager, Archie Drummond.

manufacturing new players, this might have been a bit of a surprise. But Norman was determined not to abandon Tudor's carefully cultivated reputation for affordability. Profit could be made by the sheer number of No. 500's the company sold every year.

By Thanksgiving Day, the price of a No. 500 was hovering around the $4 mark. In contrast, Gotham's G-880 football game was rarely found for less than $5. Over the holiday weekend Gotham got a promotional push from J.C. Penney, who featured the G-880 in its newspaper advertising throughout the country for $5.98. Things were a little different in the battle of the "large" electric football games, as Gotham's NFL G-1500 was priced consistently lower than Tudor's new No. 600 model. Sears set the benchmark price for the G-1500 at $12.88. Any other retailer who carried the game would have to match or beat this price to stay competitive. Overall, retailers seemed unsure how to handle the Sports Classic No. 600. Price tags bearing Tudor's suggested retail price of $16 were not uncommon, making the No. 600 the most expensive electric football game ever sold. (Perhaps the colorful box picture and extra players led retailers to put a special premium on the game.) This distinction didn't really fit in with Tudor's affordability mantra. Norman didn't think a whole lot of retailers would stick with the full retail price because the $7 suggested retail price for the No. 500 was ignored by almost every store in the country. Retailers facing direct competition from the G-1500 seemed to be the only ones who felt pressure to adjust the No. 600's price, usually to just under the $14 mark. This left Tudor's new game still costing a dollar more than a Sears G-1500.

As the shopping season hit high gear in December, Sears was using the NFL G-1500 consistently in print ads. And once again *Sports Illustrated* felt the need to enter the fray of Christmas sports games. In this year's article, titled "Beneath the Christmas Tree," there was an electric football endorsement – for Cadaco's Foto-Electric Football Game. Also reviewed were Golferino, Carrom Nok-Hoky, and Tudor's redesigned Electric Horse Race Game. Surprisingly, Tudor got a thumbs up this year with the writer saying it was "a good one for the intermediate horseplayer." Not receiving any mention for any type of game this year was Gotham. What a difference a year, and a different writer, could make.

A topic *Sports Illustrated* didn't cover was the ongoing toy price wars, which this year included electric football. Many discounters had dropped the No. 500 below $4 with extreme examples of price-cutting coming from stores like Thrifty Acres Toy Town in Holland, Michigan, which was advertising the No. 500 for $3.44. Big retailers got in on the act too, with Sears lowering the price of the G-1500 to $9.88 by mid-December. The G-1500 then appeared in a Sears "Last Minute Life Savers" promotion for $8.99. Tudor's No. 600 wasn't immune to discounting; by December 20 Thrifty Acres was clearing the game out for $8.11. Not far away in Benton Harbor, Ward had started its toy clearance sale with most of the remaining inventory being offered for 50%-75% off. And with just two days left to Christmas the Gibson Discount Center chain dropped out the bottom on the No. 600, offering the game for just $7.66. There were certainly plenty of bargains for lucky procrastinators.

Those not out doing last-minute shopping on December 23 could watch the AFL Championship game on ABC. It was an all-Texas affair between the Houston Oilers and the Dallas Texans, with the Texans dramatically taking the title 20-17 after 17 minutes and 54 seconds of overtime. Even before the sudden-death finish, the game had been an exciting one for

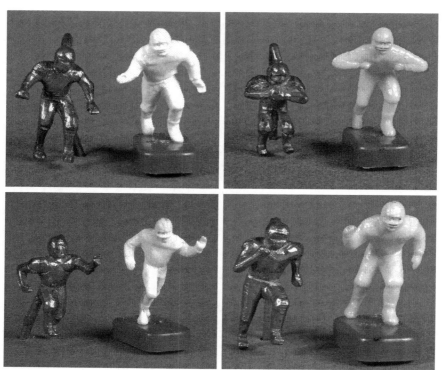

Lee Payne's brass masters with their plastic production descendants. Clockwise from upper left: defensive back, lineman, end, and offensive back. (Collection of Roddy Garcia.)

television viewers. It also marked the third nationally televised football game of the weekend, and for most of the people around the country it was the sixteenth televised football game of December.

With both Gotham and Tudor creating oversized electric football games and oversized expectations (at least from a parent's point of view), it's easy to say that 1962 was a "big" Christmas for electric football. Receiving a handsome No. 600 or G-1500 would have made for a memorable Christmas morning. On the flip side, it's hard to imagine that many kids would have put the smaller No. 500 or G-880 on their Christmas lists over Tudor's or Gotham's big models. There were certainly some disappointments on Christmas morning.

For Tudor, the new 3-D Sculpt-action players were a giant step forward, although there would have been some understandable frustration for No. 600 owners at not being able to reproduce the beautiful Lee Payne players that the Drummond boys were enjoying on the box of the game. One thing that was likely to keep many electric football games vibrating through the Christmas holiday period were the eight nationally televised football games scheduled for the upcoming weekend. Included among the eight was the NFL title game on Sunday, December 30.

While the NFL was glad to have the AFL season out of the way, the league still found itself in a familiar battle – it was being sued over the impending blackout of the championship game. The uproar hit close to NFL headquarters in 1962 as the Giants were hosting the Packers in Yankee Stadium. A New York City U.S. district court judge did what all other judges had previously done when presented with a challenge to the NFL's television policy. He upheld the league's legal right to blackout all home games. So the most densely populated area in the country would not watch the NFL championship game.

On a bitter windy day that was even colder than Green Bay's weather the year before, the Packers beat the Giants 16-7. A plus for Gotham was that families with a G-1500 could have recreated the game in their living room with impressive miniature accuracy. The stadium would have been perfect. All that was missing was the 13-degree temperature and the 40 miles-per-hour wind gusts. (Gotham's paper uniforms, unfortunately, were another matter entirely.) Giants' fans certainly would have welcomed the opportunity to play the game to a more favorable conclusion.

Despite the less than perfect players, Norman was happy with his new games. The players, no-necks and all, had been well received. Retailers also appreciated that the wholesale price of the No. 500 remained almost the same even after a complete redesign. Another decision Norman made turned out to be one that every NFL and AFL coach would envy. He decided not to bring AFL quarterback Al Dorow back for a second season as Tudor's electric football spokesperson. Norman, in football terms, had put Dorow on waivers. By early October, the Buffalo Bills – who obtained Dorow in a preseason trade – had done the same thing.

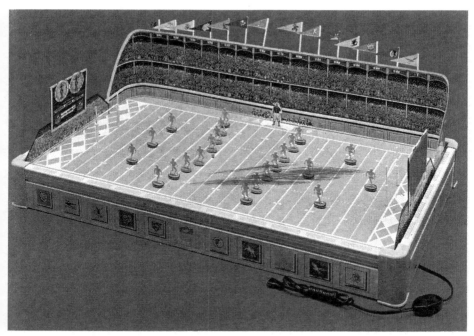

# Be a NFL coach...on your couch at home.

#G-1500—Official National Football League Electric Football Game

At last, those who often groan aloud, "Oh, why did he call for a pass at a time like this?" can now coach their favorite NFL team to victory every time. You call the plays, then watch your team go into action at the mere touch of your finger. There are thrills galore as the teams run . . . kick . . . block . . . tackle—and it is so realistic that you can practically hear the crowd roar! It is good sport and healthy competition for NFL fans from nine years of age on. Everything needed is included in this intriguing set. There are twenty-two fast-moving plastic players, both crouching and standing, with activators attached. A sheet of pressure-sensitive, colorful football jerseys and helmets is included for dressing the players to represent your favorite team. In addition, there are plastic goal posts; fourteen flagpole sticks and NFL team pennants; a snap-action kicker or passer; three magnetic footballs that can be kicked, passed, carried, or fumbled; and, to make sure that the enclosed "Rules for Playing" are obeyed, there is a referee attached to a metal yardage marker. The ruled-to-scale, highly varnished Masonite playing field is enclosed in a multi-color steel stadium frame with rounded plastic corners for smoothness and safety. The colorfully designed grandstand and scoreboards are steel. The vibrating coil, cord set, and switch, attached underneath the game, are UL and C.S.A. approved, and are for use with 115 volt AC current.

Suggested retail ......................$15.95

## GOTHAM PRESSED STEEL CORP.
### New York, New York

23

Gotham's NFL G-1500 as featured in the 1962 NFL Enterprises catalog (page 23). ©NFL Enterprises 1962.

# HOW **BIG** SHOULD A FOOTBALL PLAYER BE?

There was little question that the Rose Bowl was the game of the day on January 1. In reality, it was the game of the season as top-ranked USC was set to play No. 2-ranked Wisconsin. The winner would be the unquestioned national champion (nobody wanted to think about the ramifications of a tie). Heading into the 4th quarter, the outcome of the game seemed already decided with USC leading 42-14. But Wisconsin came back and scored 23 unanswered points, leaving USC clinging to a slim 42-37 lead with just minutes left in the game. Television viewers were on the edge of their couches – could the Badgers pull off one of the greatest comebacks in college football history? No, they could not. USC was able to hang onto their five-point margin and also their No. 1 ranking.

When the final gun sounded at the Rose Bowl, it marked the end of more than just a football game. It also marked the end of a record setting period for nationally televised football games. Between December 1 and January 1, twenty-four football games had been televised to most parts of the country. Just a few years earlier this would have constituted an entire season's worth of telecast.

Records outside of sports were also set in December 1962. Sears reported record sales for the same period, and it wasn't just a December record, it was a record for any month in the company's history. Total December sales topped $610 million. This was good news for Eddie Gluck, as Gotham would have benefited from the sheer number of people who did their Christmas shopping at Sears. But the Sears retail paradigm was changing. Although Sears was still mailing out millions of catalogs each year, about 75% of all sales now came from its retail outlets. Sears already had 748 stores in the U.S., with 27 more scheduled to open in 1963. And on top of the full-service stores, there were 950 catalog outlets servicing smaller communities. (At catalog outlets shoppers could place orders directly to

Sears, then go back and pick up their item when it was delivered to the outlet.)

For Gotham to take full advantage of its Sears relationship, the company needed to have games in stores all over the country. It was a task that Gluck was still finding a challenge despite the two-year investment in Gotham's "all-things-new" campaign.

When the NFL owners met in January, they had an unexpected issue to deal with. It wasn't something the AFL had done; it was something that their own players were accused of doing – betting on NFL games, including the ones they had played in. Since the bets had been placed with illegal bookies, the Senate Racketeering Committee was leading the investigation. Even though gambling wasn't officially on the meeting agenda, it was discussed in secret.

NFL bobbing heads, one of NFL Enterprises' top-selling items. 1962 Montgomery Ward Christmas Book, page 182. ©Montgomery Ward, Inc. 1962.

The official meeting agenda did have an item that was a bit surprising. That was the formation of a new NFL-owned business endeavor called NFL Properties. NFL Properties would replace NFL Enterprises, whose contract with the league was set to expire on March 31. It wasn't that Rozelle or the owners were unhappy with Roy Rogers Enterprises management of NFLE. RRE had done quite well in marketing the league. But thanks to the ever-growing popularity of the NFL – besides the millions watching on television, over 4 million people attended league games in 1962 – Rozelle was having second thoughts about letting RRE continue to take a 50% cut off the top of NFLE earnings. Now that Rozelle and the owners were getting a hint that NFL licensing might be lucrative, they wanted an agency that the league would own and control entirely. In many ways this new organization was based on a simple equation – if the NFL could simply equal the licensing sales of 1962, it would double its money.

And just who proposed this new entity to Rozelle and ultimately presented NFL Properties to the owners? Larry Kent.

Yes, Larry Kent had left NFLE in late 1961, but he wasn't finished with the NFL. He enjoyed his work with the league much more than his work for Roy Rogers Enterprises. Kent also realized that the popularity of the "Old West" was starting to decline. *Bonanza* and *Gunsmoke* were still

## SPORTS CLASSIC
### Electric
# football

**An immediate success — and a sure-fire repeater this year!**

● From first kick to final tick 34 exclusive "Sculpt-action" players simulate the play of major pro and college teams.

● Actual offensive and defensive formations are now possible — players run, block, tackle, pass and kick as never before!

● Each team's Kicker-Passer is a marvel of ingenuity: he runs, his foot kicks the ball, his arm throws passes! Only Tudor captures this real-life quarterback action!

● And only Tudor offers these added sales features: "Isopad" mounting, Bowl photo grandstand with scoreboard, coloring set, press-on numbers, yardage, down and ball markers — even a 10-yard "chain" to measure the close ones.

● Interest is stimulated, and buying impulses are aroused with this full-color display box illustrating exclusive playing features that make this Tudor game so popular!

**NO. 600**
Box size: 21½" x 39" x 3¼"
¼ Doz. ctn. wt. 29 lbs.
110 Volts, A. C. only
$16.00 retail

The 1963 Tudor sales catalog with the Drummond brothers playing the Sports Classic No. 600 model. (Collection of Earl Shores.)

top-ten rated programs, yet times were changing. Heroes with ten-gallon hats were being replaced by heroes wearing helmets – like John Glenn in space or Johnny Unitas on the football field. During the 1959-60 television season, 30 westerns were airing regularly on NBC, ABC, and CBS. By the 1962-63 season, the number was down to 13. How tough things had gotten was illustrated by Roy Rogers' own return to television in the fall of 1962. Roy's new show was cancelled and off the air before Thanksgiving Day.

So although Kent was officially not part of the NFL in 1962, he still had Rozelle's ear. And it didn't take much to convince Rozelle that it made much more sense for the league at this point to have complete control of its marketing program. But just who could manage the new program? Why, Larry Kent of course.

Obviously, Kent knew exactly how the program worked. He had recruited most of the current NFL Enterprises licensees and still had contacts throughout the toy and marketing world. A cynical observer might wonder if Kent and Rozelle had come up with the idea for NFL Properties before Kent left Roy Rogers Enterprises in 1961. In fact, it may have been the reason that Kent left Roy Rogers. There were certainly clauses in Kent's contract that would have prevented him from walking into Roy's office in early 1963 and saying, "You know, I'm kind of tired of this cowboy thing. So I'm leaving – and by the way, I'm taking the NFL with me." The legal repercussions of such a scenario would have been swift and brutal.

Kent had not worked for Roy Rogers for more than a year now. This was likely enough time for any legalities regarding the NFL to lapse. So Kent was free to create NFL Properties and pitch it to the NFL owners. Thanks to Rozelle's enthusiastic support of Kent, approval of the new organization was a formality. The organization's first president would be...Larry Kent. Vice-president would be former advertising executive Carl Schroeder. NFL owners George Halas, Carroll Rosenbloom (Colts), Art Moddell (Browns), and Bill Boyer (Vikings) would comprise NFL Properties' board of directors. Licensees would still pay a 5% licensing fee in 1963, the difference now being that the league would keep the entire fee.

Kent envisioned a bright future for NFL Properties, which he would run out of an office in Sherman Oaks, California, along with Schroeder and graphic artist Dave Boss. In focusing solely on the NFL, Kent could take the league to loftier promotional summits. One of his ambitions raised some eyebrows – and some snickers. As he had been able to do with Roy Rogers, Kent proposed getting an entire page of NFL items in a future Sears Christmas catalog (for reference, in 1962 there had been exactly one NFL item in Sears...the Gotham G-1500 electric football game). Most owners didn't feel very strongly about seat cushions and bobble-head figures, at least at the moment. But at the top of the NFL organizational chart sat someone who was quite passionate about marketing. In going back to his days with the Rams, Rozelle was really the NFL's original "market-teer."

Rozelle, Kent, and the NFL were happy with the new marketing arrangement. One person who was not amused was Roy Rogers. He had lost a valuable client whose marketability had increased by leaps and bounds since the first NFL Enterprises contract was signed in 1959. And the NFL hadn't been just lost. In Rogers' eyes the league had been stolen – stolen by a former member of his inner circle. For more than a decade, Kent had been trusted to run large chunks of Roy Rogers' marketing empire. Roy couldn't believe that Kent would do such a thing. Rogers remained hurt and bitter over the loss of the NFL for the rest of his life.

Gotham's new 3-D players in 1963: offensive back, tackle, lineman, and defensive back. (Photo by Earl Shores.)

Not being an NFL licensee, Norman Sas had no reason to be concerned about the backroom machinations of Larry Kent and Roy Rogers. He and Tudor were focused on the coming year, determined to keep Gotham from taking a larger piece of the electric football market. Once again Tudor started its advertising in February, announcing in *Playthings* that the company had a new showroom, having moved from room 551 to suite 526. "So what's new?" asked the ad – the answer was the showroom. Tudor also teased that it had new electric games and selling features.

Gotham passed on advertising in February, but what was more surprising was that the company had no advertising in the most important *Playthings* of the year, the March Toy Fair issue. In contrast, Tudor piggy-backed on its February ad, loading up with a color four-page layout that introduced four new games – Electric Track and Field, Electric Horse Race, Electric Mickey Mouse Treasure Hunt, and electric Baseball. Both Treasure Hunt and the Baseball game were unusual for Tudor in that they were square in design. The new track and horse race games had Tudor's traditional rectangular shape, but no longer had a plastic overlay playing surface.

On the final page of Tudor's elaborate spread the company showed off its best-known games – the No. 500, Sports Classic Football and Baseball (again with help from the Drummond brothers), DeLuxe Hockey, Sports Car Race, and electric Basketball. A small article on page 443 provided extra print and photo exposure for the Baseball and Treasure Hunt games. Tudor was out of the gate fast in 1963, at least in *Playthings*.

In any normal year Gotham's lack of advertising would have been surprising. But what left toy buyers shocked by the total lack of promotion was that Gotham had come to the 1963 Toy Fair with new electric football players. They were 3-D.

Gluck had only prototypes to show at the Fair, and by some strange "coincidence," Gotham's new players came in four poses. Just like Tudor. And Gotham had named those poses "offensive back," "tackle," "lineman," and "defensive back" – just like Tudor. Gotham's players even had some distinctly gorilla-like characteristics, including a lack of upper-body detail. They also didn't seem to have any necks. Tudor's Sculpt-action players clearly served as models for Gotham. It wasn't hard to imagine Gluck's designers taking a hot butter knife to Tudor's players, changing the

Gotham also designed a new metal quarterback/kicker figure in 1963 to go with their new 3-D players. (Photo by Earl Shores.)

pose slightly, then making a direct mold from these altered figures. Except there were some noticeable differences. The offensive back looked like a 3-D version of Gotham's trademark Heisman player, complete with one leg high-stepping in midair. This particular pose was an important figure to Gluck. And, overall, the new players were a giant improvement over the previous Martian models.

Another significant difference was the material Gotham used to mold the players. Both the figures and bases were molded entirely from flexible and forgiving polyethylene plastic. This would make Gotham's men more durable than Tudor's, as Tudor was having an issue with the hard plastic players breaking off from their soft plastic bases. But in turn, Gotham was going to have a different problem.

Gotham had retired the paper jersey concept, and this year was including a paint palette in its G-1500 models. It's possible that the laws of chemistry were different up in the Bronx (as over in Brooklyn, paint would not adhere very well to polyethylene). But it's more likely that Gluck was well aware of the painting issue and just needed 3-D players on his game in 1963 at any cost.

Taking his place with the new 3-D players was a new Gotham quarterback figure. He was made of metal, but not 3-D, being lithographed onto a flat piece of sheet metal. And while he was able to throw Gotham's magnetic-tipped footballs with his "arm," and kick with his "foot," he was still a stationary figure, unable to scramble out of the pocket like Tudor's triple-threat quarterback. So while more realistic than Gotham's old spring-shooter quarterback gadget, the new quarterback was still lacking in the realism department. Also still having a "realism" issue was Gotham's ball-carrying technique. Even with new 3-D figures Gluck stuck with the original magnetic-ball-on-the-base method of possession. It was hard to believe that none of the new Gotham players had been posed to carry a football. Tudor had three different players who could carry the ball under their arms just like real football players.

In addition to the new players, Gotham came to the Fair with two new electric football games, although one of the games was actually a case of addition by subtraction. A new G-1400 model was really a G-1500 game without the distinctive Yankee Stadium grandstand piece. It came with the large field, the two end zone grandstand/scoreboards...and a cheaper price tag. The new NFL G-890 was actually a remodeled G-880. On the frame were NFL shields, while mounted along the sideline were two end zone grandstands from the G-1500. But the only way to find out about Gotham's new items was to visit the showroom.

Gotham's new players didn't really surprise Norman. Actually, he would've been surprised if they hadn't come up with 3-D figures. "We all copied each other," said Sas. "All the toy manufacturers did in those days." But there was no borrowing going on in the 1963 Tudor showroom. In fact, there wasn't even a single change or modification to be found in Tudor's entire electric football line. To discover why the No. 500 and No. 600 models remained unchanged from the previous year all a toy buyer had to do was look at the 1963 Tudor catalog.

With bold print the No. 600 description declared the game "An immediate success – and a sure-fire repeater this year!" That was just the beginning of a paragraph in which a Tudor catalog mentioned pro football for the first time ever. Other highlighted selling points were the "real-life" quarterback, and the buying impulses "aroused" by Tudor's full-color photo boxes (the Drummond effect). Over in the description of the No. 500 model, more bold text trumpeted Tudor's success from the previous year: "The firmly established leader grows increasingly popular! The public has fallen in love with our Sculpt-action 3-dimensional players."

Obviously, this was a sales catalog, meant to drum up sales. But it wasn't Norman's style to go in for a whole lot of hyperbole. Reaction to the gorilla players, warts and all, had been very positive, especially on the most important level of electric football – the entry level. When comparing the Tudor No. 500 to the Gotham G-890, it was obvious that Tudor had more realism. With the Gotham game, you got NFL city names on the frame, maybe a grandstand, but you also got Martian players (at least in 1962). The field, although a few inches longer than Tudor's, was only detailed

Gotham's vibrant G-1500 box, highlighting the Gotham-NFL connection. (Photo Earl Shores.)

with yard lines every 10 yards, and the quarterback not only couldn't run, it didn't even look like a football player.

The Tudor No. 500 offered true 3-D players who could actually carry the football like real players did; a realistic quarterback figure, who could throw, run, and kick; and an authentic looking field with yard lines every 5 yards. Tudor's games were also being sold around the $4 mark. This made the entry level of realism offered by Tudor quite remarkable and affordable.

Publicly, Norman was pleased. Business was good, even with Gotham trying to make inroads in electric football. Yet privately, Norman and Lee knew there was more work to be done. The gorilla figures were still much more realistic looking than Gotham's new 3-D players, but they needed improvement to truly be up to Tudor's standards. Once again, Lee would turn to the sculpting expertise of Lou Theoharides for help in upgrading Tudor's players.

Within the toy industry, much of the hand wringing over loss leader pricing and the plight of the independent toy store seemed to be dissipating. The march of the discount chains and roadside strip shopping centers was not going to be halted. Or at least the toy makers themselves realized they couldn't stop what was a cultural change in the way Americans did their shopping. A thoughtful manufacturer could try and give smaller retailers the same wholesale price breaks that bigger clients received. Unfortunately, that very basic solution was complicated by the fact that many small retailers supplied their stores through jobbers (the middlemen of the toy world). A toy maker who was solely interested in profit could just stand back and watch retailers slit each other's throats trying to win customers. It's debatable whether an annual pricing free-for-all was a great long-term business model, but by 1963 TV toys and loss leader pricing were accepted practices of toy selling. And there were a lot of toys to be sold in 1963. Many of them would turn out to be long lasting symbols of a toy golden age.

On April 1, National Football League Properties officially took over the licensing and merchandising commitments of the NFL. Just a few weeks later, Larry Kent's faith in the potential of the NFL was reinforced when NBC paid $926,000 for the television rights to the 1963 NFL Championship game. This was the largest sum ever paid for a single-day sporting event. (The previous record was the $615,000 that NBC paid for the 1962 NFL Championship.) What NBC agreed to pay was almost 20% of the sum CBS was paying to televise the entire 14-week NFL season. And this $926,000 sum was more than 25% of what it cost NBC to televise the World Series. In doing a little simple math, it was clear that the rights to the NFL Championship game cost more than the rights to an individual World Series game – for the first time ever. NBC viewed the NFL and Major League Baseball as equals in their ability to draw viewers and sell advertising. The National Pastime was starting to require a helmet and a pair of shoulder pads.

Another individual who surely felt proud of his gamble on the NFL was Eddie Gluck. When Gotham became one of the first NFL licensees back in 1960, the NFL's profile was still in the midst of a methodical climb up the public sporting ladder. Yet in just three short tumultuous years, the NFL found itself sharing the top sports rung with Major League Baseball. Kent, with all his optimism, would have never promised such an audacious outcome during the initial Gotham-NFL conversation. Gluck, with all his years in toys and sports, wouldn't have believed Kent anyway. But it had happened. In spite of the AFL, or maybe with thanks to the AFL, football was arguably the most popular spectator sport in the nation. By taking up Kent's offer back in 1960, Gluck now had the officially licensed electric football game of the country's most popular professional league. And this game was now prominently featured in the Christmas catalog of the country's largest retailer – Sears. Add in Gotham's new 3-D players, and 1963 seemed to be shaping up as an "all-star" year for the company.

Yet Gluck seemed uncertain about exactly what to do with his seat on the NFL bandwagon this year. There had been no advertising of any kind in the March issue of *Playthings*, and there was nothing in the April issue, despite Tudor running another eye-catching multi-page spread showing off the complete Tudor line. "Most popular because most realistic!" read a headline beside a photo of the Drummond boys earnestly enjoying the Sports Classic No. 600 football game. *Playthings'* coverage of the Toy Fair even had a photo of Tudor's new showroom, and a small photo and article on page 119 describing Tudor's new Horse Race game.

Sixteen pages later, Gotham finally had its 1963 *Playthings* debut – with a hockey game. The new Electric Floor Model Hockey Game (G-1650) was in a small feature, similar to the one showing off Tudor's Horse Race. From the photo it was obvious that Gotham's new game was a massive full-feature model, having not only collapsible legs, but also 3-D hockey players "whose uniforms may be painted with a special paint set packed with each game." Clearly, Lee Payne's painting concept was having wide influence in 1963. While there were some interesting features on the G-1650, the game still didn't rise to the level of "stunning." That was left to the suggested retail price of $19.95.

Gotham clients were likely confused at this point, as the company seemed to have little direction for the coming year. Being the first company to sell a $20 sports action game wasn't necessarily a positive promotional strategy. And where was the NFL? Wasn't that a connection that still deserved to be front and center in Gotham's advertising?

| CHECK LIST | |
|---|---|
| **GOTHAM** | **OTHERS** |
| 1. Priced to sell at $7.00. | 1. Priced to sell at $7.00. |
| 2. Exclusively licensed to use NFL name. | 2. Not licensed. |
| 3. Wide, lithographed frame for sturdiness and realism. | 3. Narrower frame, not lithographed. |
| 4. Hardboard base for quiet vibrating action. | 4. Metal base, noisier action. |
| 5. Large 3-D football players in four different playing positions. | 5. Smaller figures. |
| 6. Large no-tip base for players. | 6. Smaller base. |
| 7. Players activated by built-in polystyrene "legs". | 7. Similar. |
| 8. 3" metal unbreakable kicker-passer. | 8. Small plastic device. |
| 9. Goal posts with realistic simulated padding. | 9. Straight plastic sticks. |
| 10. Copyrighted magnetic football makes it possible to pick up a loose ball while moving. | 10. Felt football |
| 11. Full rounded plastic corners, sturdily constructed and accident-proof. | 11. Straight plastic edge. |

Gotham's very direct and audacious "checklist" from the summer of 1963. It made a side-by-side comparison of Gotham and Tudor electric football features. *Playthings*, June 1963.

Over in Brooklyn, Tudor was already looking to 1964. Lee had kicked the quest for functional and realistic 3-D electric football players into high gear. In order to get as much detail in the men as possible, Lee had Theoharides's skillful hands sculpt new wax models that were almost 2.5 times the size of the final player. And with Norman's approval Lee added a fifth player pose to Tudor's lineup. This new figure would be Lee himself – the tackle.

A new process was developed for creating the figures, one that Lee devised in order to head off any future artistic-license issues. In this new technique, a set of large, highly detailed brass masters would be molded from Theoharides's wax players. The molding company would then use an industrial pantograph to trace the large brass master figures, while simultaneously carving wax players 2.3 times smaller than the master. The pantographic technique would transfer much of the detail of the large master to the smaller players. From these smaller wax figures, the company would make production molds for Tudor's electric football players.

Throughout the summer, Norman and Lee made a number of decisions that would make these new players significantly different from any previous

Tudor electric football men. Besides being highly detailed, the new players would be molded, base and all, out of one single piece of soft polyethylene. This would take care of the breakage issue Tudor was experiencing with the current gorilla players. It also eliminated the "living room floor assembly issue," which factored into the breakage. The new players would be field ready as soon as they were removed from their molding sprues. At the moment, Gotham's new 3-D men were going to require a set-up period to get the body, metal plate (for carrying the magnetic football), and running base assembled as a unit.

To solve the wobble factor of the top-heavy gorilla figures, Payne designed a wider player base with rounded front and square back. The bottom of each base contained only four single legs, compared with eight (four pairs) on the green gorilla base. Some speed would be lost by this leg reduction, but the molding process would be simpler and less costly. It was a fair compromise. The compromise that Norman and Lee lingered over the longest was player painting. The all-polyethylene players were pretty much allergic to paint – at least the enamel-based kind that required paint thinner. But it turned out there were safety issues with having paint thinner in a children's game. And sometimes the thinner bottles leaked during shipping, ruining the game. So Norman and Lee decided to go with nontoxic water-based paints for the new players. Watercolor would adhere to polyethylene. It wasn't going to look as good as enamel paint, but nobody would get hurt – unless the players were given a bath.

While Tudor quietly went about designing its new players, Gotham finally fired up its 1963 advertising campaign – and aimed it directly at Tudor. It surfaced in the June issue of *Playthings*, with a color photo of three shoppers standing in a returns line. The text accompanying the photo was not the upbeat happy talk usually seen in toy ads:

> *Are we insisting on customer dissatisfaction? Every year, the lines at the Return window get longer. Cheaply-made toys break down fast, don't give the play value they were made and paid for. The consumer, too often disappointed, is getting mad. Massive TV selling becomes less effective. Even the kids are getting cynical. Slowly, the emphasis is shifting from gimmickry and price to quality. Are you ready for the Big Change?*

Gluck had laid out a very insightful snapshot of the toy industry in 1963. Toys had become bigger and more elaborate in the early 60's, with plastic being used more and more for all the moving parts. Some toys proved to be great fun...for a short period of time. Other toys were just bad designs that never worked as advertised. It was hard to tell how much of the "return" issue was from Gotham's own experience, or perhaps even pointing a finger at Tudor. But Gluck's lament about television selling becoming less effective was an obvious admission that Gotham's own television advertising campaign in 1962 had not been a success. In reading between the lines of the ad, it seemed clear that Gotham was announcing that it would not be doing any more television advertising.

The line in the ad about "shifting from gimmickry and price to quality" was true, but Gluck was on thin ice here. What was the giant Yankee Stadium grandstand on the NFL G-1500 other than a large gimmick? And those 3-D players on the new Gotham hockey game – were they a gimmick or simply a natural evolution of table hockey? As for the emphasis on quality, Norman Sas would argue that quality was what Tudor was founded on. Quality and price always trumped gimmickry. Norman had written as much in his 1947 MIT senior thesis.

On the next page Gluck went after Tudor. Occupying the top half of the page was a color photo of the new Gotham G-890 Official Electric Football game. It was new because it was the first time one of Gotham's small electric football games was licensed by the NFL. The previous edition of the game had been called Professional Football and did not include any NFL team names or markings. This new G-890 had the NFL shield on the frame in multiple places.

Also placed in the photo was a close-up image of Gotham's new players and metal quarterback figure. But what really made the ad unusual was something below the photos – a 12-point checklist comparing Gotham electric football games to "Others." Everybody in the toy business knew there was only one "other." That would be Tudor.

The first point of comparison was price, where Gotham claimed that both the G-890 and the Tudor No. 500 were priced to sell at $7. While this was technically true, neither game sold for this price. And if the past was any indicator, the No. 500 usually had a lower price tag. Gotham's next point of comparison was NFL licensing, which Tudor couldn't match. Frame width was Gotham's third comparison, but it was filler more than anything. At number four, Gotham claimed its fiberboard field was quieter than Tudor's metal field. The point was true, but again, a minor one. Both games "buzzed" pretty well. Beyond point four is where things got more serious. At number five, Gluck was claiming that he had larger 3-D players than Tudor, and number six piled onto a major gorilla issue. Gotham was claiming that is now had a "large no-tip base for players."

Of the final six comparisons, two were remarkable for their blunt criticism of Tudor. Gotham's number eight claim was a "3-inch unbreakable kicker-passer" compared to Tudor's "small plastic device." The "unbreakable" dig was making light of the problem Tudor was having with throwing arms and kicking legs. But Gotham conveniently ignored the fact that the "small

CORRECT SIZE—
CORRECT WEIGHT

# HOW BIG

## SHOULD A FOOTBALL PLAYER BE

**?**

If he plays pro football the bigger the better! But if he's an Electric Game player he must be engineered to exactly the correct size and weight for lively playing action. And the teams must be sized in logical proportion to the gridiron area—otherwise there is not enough room for player movement and strategy.

Tudor responds to Gotham's June checklist by asking, "How Big Should A Football Player Be?" in the September 1963 issue of *Playthings*.

plastic device" was an actual 3-D player who, when healthy, could run, pass, and kick. Perhaps the sharpest of Gotham's critiques came at point nine where "goal posts with realistic simulated padding" contrasted with Tudor's "straight plastic sticks."

Tudor wasn't alone in taking fire from Gotham. Gluck had a hockey checklist on the very next page of the ad, this time offering up five points of critique for Eagle Toys of Montreal and Munro Games of Ontario. What Canada's table hockey giants made of Gluck's comparisons isn't known, but the checklist gimmick didn't go unnoticed in Brooklyn. Norman answered back in the September *Playthings* with a full-page Tudor ad asking in headlined-sized font: "HOW BIG SHOULD A FOOTBALL PLAYER BE?" Above the text was a color photo of a life-size hand holding a life-size Tudor quarterback between the thumb and index finger. Adjacent to the quarterback were four words: "Correct size – correct weight."

The rest of the ad took Gotham to task for its June electric football checklist. After prefacing that in pro football the bigger the player the better, the Tudor ad explained the company's view on sizing players. "But if he's an Electric Game player he must be engineered to exactly the correct size and weight for lively playing action. And the teams must be sized in logical proportion to the gridiron area – otherwise there is not enough room for player movement and strategy."

A less diplomatic way to say this would have been "when the players get out of scale with the field, the game looks really dumb." This concept was reinforced when the ad went on to implicitly compare and contrast Tudor's quarterback with the new metal Gotham quarterback: "He not only LOOKS like a gridiron star but ACTUALLY kicks, passes, and runs throughout the game!" said Tudor's text. Tudor also noted that its games included TWO quarterbacks, not just one. It was a little surprising to see Tudor fire back at Gotham so pointedly, but Norman and Lee had worked very hard on developing 3-D players and bringing them to production. And once again, all Gluck had done was "borrow" another electric football concept. Then he had the audacity to turn around and criticize the original creators. It was a tactic that didn't sit very well with anyone at Tudor.

Kicking off earlier than ever was the AFL, whose regular season started on the weekend after Labor Day. The Sunday, September 8 start date even beat out the college boys, who wouldn't start playing until the following Saturday. And the very next day, Sunday the 15th, the NFL would finally get underway. For both Tudor and Gotham this timing was all very convenient as the Sears and Montgomery Ward Christmas catalogs were just beginning to appear in mailboxes throughout the country.

This year, Ward had Tudor's No. 600 model at the top of page 318 in full color. It was the first time Tudor had gotten color treatment. It was fitting, as this year's catalog photo featured Lee Payne's painted metal

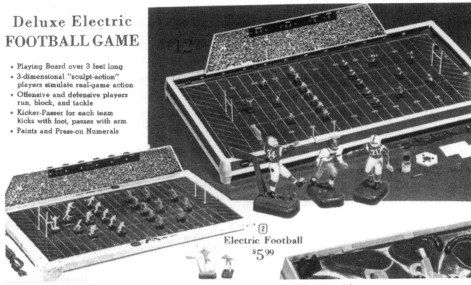

## Deluxe Electric
## FOOTBALL GAME

- Playing Board over 3 feet long
- 3-dimensional "sculpt-action" players simulate real-game action
- Offensive and defensive players run, block, and tackle
- Kicker-Passer for each team kicks with foot, passes with arm
- Paints and Press-on Numerals

② Electric Football
$5⁹⁹

The Montgomery Ward's color electric football page, with the Tudor No. 600 and No. 500 models. Montgomery Ward 1963 *Christmas Book*, page 318. © Montgomery Ward, Inc. 1963.

prototype players. The game looked incredibly realistic with the players accurately scaled to the size of the field. Also the No. 600 was given more space in the catalog than the previous year – it was clear as to why the "Deluxe" game was the more expensive model. Featured in the foreground of the No. 600 were enlargements of two painted metal players, and an actual production quarterback that Lee had painted for Ward. Up close and in color, the players were stunning.

Just below the No. 600 was Tudor's No. 500. The Ward version of the No. 500 would come with a metal grandstand, just like its big brother. On the field were production gorilla players – one team of yellow and one team of white players. There were no close-up shots of these players. They looked great from the vantage point Ward was offering. Norman and Lee were very pleased with Ward. It was the most glorious presentation Tudor electric football had ever received from a national retailer.

Eddie Gluck was also feeling good; Sears had made the NFL G-1500 the full-color focal point of page 100 of its catalog. And framing the G-1500 from the left margin were color photos of both the NFL G-1400 and NFL G-890 models. Sears had also enlarged and prominently displayed two of Gotham's new 3-D players in the foreground of the G-1500. Both figures were meticulously painted – and seemingly hand drawn. It was difficult to figure out which two NFL teams the players were painted to represent. But even with a paint job these players did not look as realistic as Tudor's men. In terms of scale and painting, Tudor had the edge. Of course, Tudor's painted metal prototypes didn't look exactly like their production gorilla players either. Both companies were doing a little "extra" salesmanship in the 1963 Christmas catalogs.

For NFL Properties, Larry Kent's goal of getting a full page of NFL items in Sears remained just a goal. Only three NFL items made it into the *Christmas Book*, and they were the G-1500, G-1400, and G-890. Sly old Roy Rogers still had the marketing upper hand. Scattered throughout the catalog were more than a dozen Roy Rogers' items, including a guitar, robe, boots, slippers, cap pistols, and Western play outfits for both boys (Roy) and girls (Dale). But even Roy couldn't match the exposure Sears was giving to slot cars in 1963. Sears devoted nine pages to this very hot-selling segment of the toy world, with sets ranging from $10 to $45 in price.

*Watch these 3-dimensional football players go into action . . and run off exciting plays on a big de luxe gridiron*

### National League Electric Football $11 88

Two full teams in realistic on-the-move positions . . ready for you to paint with special paints and brush included

A vibrating coil in the field puts "a-c-t-i-o-n" in this game. All team players block, tackle, run for yardage and TD's . . even receive passes from the spectacular kicker-passer, using a magnet-tipped football. Set up your offensive and defensive formations . . set back and watch. Hardboard playing field, 36x21 in., set in steel frame.

Big grandstand section in center with worked scoreboards at each end. Includes pennants, goal posts, 3-man yardage marker, instructions in NFL plays. Coil and cord attached underneath board. Operates on 110-120-volt, 60-cycle only. UL approved.
79 N 1051—Shipping weight 15 pounds . . . $11.88

The Gotham NFL G-1500 in the 1963 Sears *Christmas Book*, page 100. ©Sears, Roebuck & Co. 1963.

Larry Kent might not have had the success he hoped for with Sears, but he was having success with a new program that enticed retailers to take on a full line of NFL team items. Most prominent of the NFL Properties' sellers was Saks Fifth Avenue, who had become the official New York City area distributor of Giants clothing (most items were in the boys' department). A smaller but significant retailer, Schlafer's in suburban Green Bay, had become an official NFL seller of Packers items. Packers' stadium cushions, footballs, helmets, bobble-heads, jackets, and Hartland figures were available at Schlafer's. They even offered home delivery.

The fall moved forward with football fans seeing the same amount of football on television as the previous year – that would be a lot. CBS had college football on Saturday and the NFL on Sunday, while ABC continued its weekly AFL telecasts. Fans not living within a 75-mile radius of an NFL or AFL team were guaranteed three televised pro football games each weekend.

Most Sears Toy Town and Ward Toyland departments had opened by mid-October. Surprisingly, neither retailer was pushing electric football very hard, despite the lavish catalog layouts. Tudor No. 500's were abundant as usual with discount retailers setting the price of the game at just under $4. Gotham NFL G-890's were available, too, although not as widely as Tudor's game. And this is where the flaw in "Item No. 1" of Eddie Gluck's checklist became all too apparent – none of his G-890's were priced under $5.

Then a seemingly normal year turned tragic. On the afternoon of Friday, November 22, President John F. Kennedy was assassinated in Dallas. With ABC, NBC, and CBS all providing unbroken nonstop coverage of the unfolding events, the country turned to television for the news. And when Jack Ruby shot Lee Harvey Oswald live on television three days later, the medium of television took an elevated position in American culture. Neither radio nor print could transmit the immediacy of an event the way television could. By the time President Kennedy was laid to rest in Arlington National Cemetery on the afternoon of the 26th, life for most Americans had revolved around the television set for almost five full days. Television had become the medium for the news and collective focal point for America.

$988

NFL Electric Football
played on 36x21-inch gridiron

Sears promoted the Gotham NFL G-1400 in Thanksgiving Day newspaper ads. The game didn't have the metal Yankee Stadium grandstand piece – but it did have a sub-$10 price tag. Sears 1963 *Christmas Book*, page 100. ©Sears, Roebuck & Co. 1963.

One thing America didn't see on television during that weekend was football. Most college games were cancelled, as were all the games in the AFL. Commissioner Rozelle, however, decided the NFL should play its full schedule. Broadcast partner CBS wanted no part of the games, spending Sunday afternoon covering the grief of thousands of Americans as they filed by the President's coffin in the Capital Rotunda. There was loud and immediate criticism of Rozelle's decision, but most stadiums had normal attendance.

It was a subdued nation that tried to conjure joyful thoughts during Thanksgiving Day weekend. Normal activities – parades, football games, turkey eating, and Christmas shopping – went on as planned even though there was hardly anything normal about Thanksgiving this year. And retailers still had selling to do as it was still the most lucrative of selling seasons.

A 1963 Gotham NFL G-1500 as it might have looked on Christmas morning in 1963. (Photo by Earl Shores & Roddy Garcia.)

Sears finally started promoting electric football, running color newspaper advertisements throughout the country featuring the Gotham NFL G-1400 game. Since this new model came without the trademark Yankee Stadium grandstand, it wasn't quite as grand as the G-1500. But the price was clearly right. For $9.99 a shopper could pick up a large, NFL-endorsed electric football game with 3-D players. Ads for the game ran throughout the weekend, usually including a Gotham hockey game with an identical $9.99 price. But unlike last year, Gluck was not spending any money on television advertising.

Outside of the Sears shopping bubble, Tudor electric football games continued to outnumber and outsell Gotham models. Gotham still had pricing issues at the entry level. Tudor's No. 500 was widely available for $4 or less, while most G-890's were at the $5.50 mark. Was an NFL endorsement worth an extra $1.50? For most adult shoppers the answer was "no," the two games were equal. One just cost much less than the other.

Sears continued advertising the G-1400 in December providing a big boost for Gluck. Ward, unfortunately, was not doing the same favor for Tudor. But Norman didn't really care. He was selling almost all the games he could make. And he was also pleased with Lee's progress with the new players, which would be ready for 1964. Beyond electric football, loss leader pricing was taking less of a toll in the toy world this year. Many TV toys had held their value, with Sears even selling some of the in-demand Remco toys for more than the catalog price. Remco was a leader in the bigger-is-better category, with its ever-expanding line now including the plastic 3-foot long Mighty Matilda aircraft carrier, and the 2.5-foot long Big Caesar Roman Galleon battle ship. (Battery power brought to life 16 rowing oars, yet it was advertised as "Not a Water Toy.") Marx had its 2-foot long Big Shot missile launcher, Ideal had its 2-foot long Dick Tracy Copmobile, and there were slot car sets that seemed to be getting bigger by the month. It was estimated that $80 million worth of slot cars would be sold in 1963.

Toy clearance sales appeared on the weekend before Christmas, but the discounts weren't as deep as in other years. Those Americans who weren't out bargain hunting or frantically finishing off their shopping lists were likely to be found at home on their couches doing one thing – watching football. Cementing the relationship between the Christmas season and football were three college bowl games on Saturday and the final day of the AFL season on Sunday (the season being extended a week because of the Kennedy assassination). A dedicated football fan or even a casual one could have spent more than ten hours watching football on December 21 and 22.

Christmas Day finally arrived on Wednesday, and Santa's delivery of Tudor and Gotham electric football games helped many boys

**NFL Electric Football played on 28x15-inch gridiron**

Put all your football know-how into action with these teams of 3-dimensional players. Flip the switch and they're in motion . . passing, kicking, blocking. Paint them in your favorite team colors with the paint and brush set included. Metal scoreboards, goal posts, kicker-passer, magnetic ball, yardage marker and instruction sheet with NFL plays. Hardboard field is set in steel frame. UL approved for 110–120-volt, 60-cycle AC.
79 N 141C—Shipping weight 6 pounds. $5.32

The Gotham NFL G-890 in the 1963 Sears *Christmas Book*, page 100. ©Sears, Roebuck & Co. 1963.

buzz away the pall hanging over the final week of 1963. How big was the disappointment if a G-1400 showed up instead a G-1500? Not as much as if a small game – either the G-890 or Tudor No. 500 – showed up instead of a large game. The stakes in electric football were being raised through game size, grandstands, 3-D players, and even paint. Gotham had tried to get back in the game this year with their new 3-D players. How successful the company had been was still an open question. At least Gotham's Martian players had returned to their own planet.

Most electric football games were still in use the following Saturday when the Bills and Patriots met in Buffalo for the AFL Eastern Conference title (San Diego had already won the West). This game would be televised nationwide,

What Tudor had to compete against on the toy store shelf – a colorful 1963 Gotham electric football game box (G-890), highlighting the Gotham-NFL connection. (Photo Earl Shores.)

as would two other collegiate games – the Gator Bowl and the East-West Shrine game. The AFL and Gator Bowl were going head-to-head in the early afternoon time slot, while the Shrine All-Stars wouldn't step on the field in San Francisco until late afternoon. The Patriots headed into the fourth quarter with a 16-8 lead, and it really seemed like anybody's game. The Bills only needed a touchdown and two-point conversion to tie the score. But the Patriots had other ideas, pulling away for a convincing 26-8 win.

On Sunday, most Gotham NFL games got a workout when the Bears and Giants met in Chicago for the NFL title. It was a tense and brutally cold afternoon (just 8 degrees at halftime) during which the Bears defense intercepted five passes. Two interceptions led to touchdowns, and that's all the Bears needed for a 14-10 victory. It was a very frustrating day for the Giants. This marked their third straight NFL Championship game loss, and fifth NFL Championship game loss in six years.

Surprisingly, the title game came up 200 tickets short of a sellout despite the television blackout in Chicago. But for the rest of country the game was "must see" television. How popular was the NFL at this point? The very next day, *Sports Illustrated* named Pete Rozelle its "Sportsman of the Year." It was the first time the magazine had given the honor to a non-athlete. Rozelle's face was on the cover of the magazine, along with the helmets of all 14 NFL teams. For the NFL, it was a fantastic way to end 1963. In the meantime, the AFL had to spend the week looking at Rozelle's face on the cover of *Sports Illustrated* while waiting for its championship game to be played on January 5.

Baltimore Colts defensive back Bobby Boyd runs onto the field during pre-game introductions at the Los Angeles Coliseum. Taking the photo from his sideline vantage point was Tudor's new Director of Product Development, Lee Payne. Lee was determined to bring "sideline" realism to electric football. (Photo by Lee Payne; Collection of Roddy Garcia.)

# 16 NEW PLAYERS AND A NEW NO. 500 FOR TUDOR

**T**elevision viewers had to be choosy on the opening day of 1964 as the Sugar Bowl, Orange Bowl, and Cotton Bowl all kicked off at 1:45 p.m. Eastern Time (the Rose Bowl started at 4:45 EST). Most viewers chose the Cotton Bowl where undefeated and No.1-ranked Texas was going up against No. 2-ranked Navy. Enhancing the glamour of the game even more was that Navy had Heisman Trophy winner Roger Staubach at quarterback. Unfortunately, Texas held a 28-0 lead by the start of the fourth quarter, giving television viewers a good reason to get up and change the channel to a different bowl game. Staubach scored a fourth quarter Navy touchdown, but it was too late. The 28-6 rout gave Texas its first ever football national championship.

With New Year's Day on a Wednesday, football fans only had to wait two more days for another television fix, the Senior Bowl from Mobile, Alabama. Then on Sunday, the AFL would crown a champion, but it would do so only after the NFL Playoff Bowl finished up in Miami. Watching the NFL's second-place teams battle was an event that only hard-core NFL fans could love. The players themselves weren't too keen on the game, despite its being played in balmy Miami. There was also the irony of the league's runner-up teams getting to play in the Florida sunshine, while the championship teams lined up on a bitter December day in Chicago.

Finally at 4:30 p.m. EST, the AFL got to play its championship game on ABC. San Diego was hosting the Patriots, and the game was everything that fans had come to expect from the AFL. The Chargers scored 21 first-quarter points, and held a 31-10 lead at halftime. Those hoping for a Patriots comeback were disappointed, as the Chargers stretched out for a convincing 51-10 win. A television viewer couldn't help but be impressed by the Chargers' offensive prowess.

Just a few days later, the retail world began reporting some very impressive figures. Toy makers had expressed confidence that 1963

L. John Swedlin

Norman A. Sas

The official announcement of the Toy Manufacturers' 1964 Officers and Directors. Courtesy of The Strong®, Rochester, New York

would be a good year, and now there were actual sales figures to support this optimism. Although the exact earnings for toys had yet to be calculated, nine major retail chains – including Montgomery Ward, Woolworth, J.C. Penney and Sears – were reporting record sales for December. Sears was especially impressive, not only surpassing its old December sales record by more than $100 million, but also pulling in a record $5 billion in total sales for 1963. These figures had to be encouraging to Gluck. For Norman, December was a landmark month in another way. He had been elected vice president of the Toy Manufacturers Association.

A record of a different kind was set between December 21 and January 5. Fifteen football games were televised nationally during this period making it the largest cluster of televised games ever seen. It averaged out to almost a game a day. The major networks, it seemed, were eager to have football on their airwaves. This was something Commissioner Rozelle kept in mind as he negotiated a new television contract for the NFL during the opening weeks of the New Year.

On January 24, Rozelle waved his magic marketing wand and produced a television contract that stunned the sports world and even surprised sorcerer Pete himself. Instead of following the league tradition of negotiating a deal with a single network, Commissioner Rozelle invited competitive bidding on the new contract. Essentially, Rozelle bet that the whims of ambitious and covetous television executives would provide the league with an economic bonanza. As usual, his instincts were dead on the mark. He knew the NFL had a strong hand. A.C. Nielsen was reporting that the average 1963 Sunday afternoon NFL telecast drew over 15 million viewers, while stadium attendance was up another 4%. Both of these numbers were league records. In fact, both of these figures had been rising steadily since 1960 – the year Rozelle became commissioner. The NFL was becoming America's game, or at the very least, America's television game. Just being the network that televised the NFL was starting to carry its own cachet. So ABC, NBC, and CBS did exactly what they still do today. They threw money at pro football.

Coming in last was NBC with a $21.5 million bid (all bids were for two seasons of coverage, 1964 and 1965). Runner-up was ABC with a $26.1 million offer. The winner, and continuing NFL broadcast partner, was CBS who brought a whopping $28.2 million to the table. It was more than triple what they paid for the NFL in 1962. With this new deal, each team in the league was set to receive over a million dollars per season in television money. It would be hard to feel sorry for any NFL team with red ink on their books at the end of 1964.

There was speculation from within the television industry that it would be impossible for CBS to turn a profit. One thing the network already planned to do was increase the amount of commercial time per game from 16 to 18 minutes. Other rumors had CBS upping the cost of a commercial during a game from $45,000 to $70,000. Rozelle was keenly aware of the network's financial constraints. He had a plan to make sure that CBS did see a profit from its generous commitment to the NFL.

When Rozelle and the owners convened for the annual NFL winter meeting on January 28, an easy solution was devised for CBS to get more advertising money. The network would simply televise more games. Thus, the NFL double-header was born. After the professional baseball season concluded in October, CBS would start showing back-to-back NFL games on Sunday afternoons. (Unfortunately, there would still be no games when your team was home.) Not only would the double-header allow CBS to sell more advertising, it would allow the NFL to be on the air for five straight hours. And it also created a minor by-product that nobody from the NFL camp minded – absolute and unavoidable head-to-head television competition with the AFL. In the AFL's previous four seasons, the league had tried not to televise games directly up against an NFL broadcast. For example, a city seeing a 2:00 p.m. NFL game on CBS would likely get a 3:30 or 4:30 p.m. AFL game from ABC.

Finally, television football watchers would have to make a choice. Would their loyalties lie with the NFL or the AFL? The NFL was sure it knew the answer. According to the A.C. Nielsen ratings, AFL games were drawing fewer than half the viewers of NFL games (about 6.2 million per game). Perhaps this head-to-head challenge of the 1964 season would be the beginning of the end of the junior league.

But the NFL's television gauntlet had barely hit the table when the AFL not only answered the challenge, they left the senior league simmering in its own rich juices. NBC, who was still smarting from its last place finish in the NFL bidding process, had taken its spurned money and swiftly made a deal with the rival league. And so it was, that less than 24 hours after the NFL's very public double-header declaration, the meeting rooms of Miami's Kenilworth Hotel were set abuzz when NBC and the AFL announced a five-year television deal...worth $36 million. The deal wouldn't start until 1965 (ABC still had the league for the 1964 season), but the contract, as written, was "non-cancelable." The money was completely guaranteed. If the AFL was going to fold, it probably wouldn't happen until 1969. In the meantime, each of the eight AFL teams would receive $900,000 a year from NBC. And if the league could expand by two teams, NBC would kick in an extra million dollars a year during the last two seasons of the contract.

Guaranteed money and expansion for the AFL – these were not issues the NFL owners were thrilled to be dealing with at their meeting. But it was a sign of the lucrative and changing times. In just a single week, network television had promised over $64 million for the rights to broadcast professional football. Major League Baseball teams could only dream of such riches (though they were watching closely). There was no official declaration, yet it was clear from the networks' staggering financial commitment: professional football was the nation's most profitable sport.

And the football television bandwagon kept on rolling. On February 10, the day after the Beatles television debut on the *Ed Sullivan Show*, ABC and the Ford Motor Company announced an agreement to nationally televise five Friday night NFL games. This was possible because the CBS-NFL deal only covered 93 of the 98 total NFL games to be played in the 1964 season. The television rights to the five games not covered by CBS were controlled by the teams involved in these games. While Rozelle was probably pleased that these "uncovered" games were considered hot television properties, he was surely less than pleased that the current network of the AFL now had a piece, however small, of the NFL pie.

The very next day, Major League Baseball attempted to get in on the sports television gravy train by pitching a Monday night "Game of the Week" package to any network that would listen. Their pitch was low and away, drawing little interest while being cynically viewed as a way to salvage the national pastime's pride amongst the pigskin profits. An unnamed network source succinctly summed up baseball's problems: "The leagues have got to put more excitement in their regular season and not just in the World Series."

By early March, the NFL announced it would not allow national telecasts of Friday night games. Both the NCAA and the National Federation of High School Athletic Associations had lobbied Congress, fearing that competition from the professionals would damage attendance and interest in scholastic football. Rozelle was reluctant to have the league look like the neighborhood bully and closed the issue down before the Senate Antitrust Committee got geared up for an investigation. Any Friday night games – according to Rozelle only one was scheduled at this juncture – would be televised only to the city of the visiting team.

**THE BEST SELLING OF ALL FOOTBALL GAMES
FOR THE LAST 15 YEARS...BUT THAT
DIDN'T STOP TUDOR FROM IMPROVING IT...**

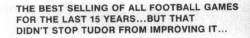

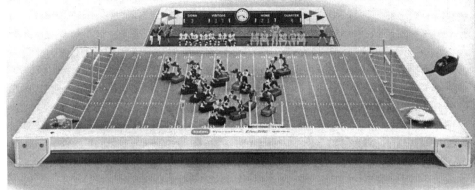

| Automatic timer | Action poses duplicate live game realism | Triple threat quarterback |

**Tru·action.**

## *Electric*
# Football

**Check these new features about this consistent leader...**

NEW  All the features and action of the game described right on the cover of the box in a beautiful full-color illustration ... perfect for P.O.P. display in self-service operations.

NEW  Exclusive timer that automatically starts and stops with each play.

NEW  Colorful grandstand with adjustable score board.

NEW  Larger figures in five realistic 3-dimensional action poses...ends, tackles, guards, offensive backs, defensive backs...plus an additional kicking, passing, running quarterback for each team.

NEW  Virtually unbreakable figures with increased stability.

NEW  Brush and water soluble paints to color the players.

NEW  Magnetic ten yard marker with movable chain marker to measure the close ones out on the field.

NEW  Magnetic down and ball marker.

NEW  Four goal line flags.

NEW  Speed control improved with printed dial and plastic knob.

NEW  Brighter, livelier, gridiron color.

NEW  Movable goal posts for college or pro positions.

**Plan your own offensive and defensive strategy!**

**No. 500**
Box size: 27" x 16½" x 2⅛"
⅓ doz. ctn. wt. 25 lbs.
110 Volts, A.C. only
$7.00 retail

**The Tudor sales catalog listing all the new electric football features for 1964. (Collection of Norman Sas.)**

Lee Payne's redesigned Tudor's 3-D players for 1964. (Photo by Earl Shores.)

Finally, after two of the most eventful off-season months in professional sports history, the Toy Fair opened on March 9. Although retail sales had been strong for the Christmas season, it turned out that 1963 had been a mixed bag for toy makers. Some did very well, and some didn't, even with increased toy volume. Loss leader pricing had not completely disappeared, and although there was less gnashing of teeth over the issue, it still squeezed retailer profits. Again, there were durability issues with even popular toys, and there was a new criticism for toy makers to deal with. Outside the buildings of 200 Fifth Avenue, Parents Against the Encouragement of Violence manned picket lines protesting the increasing production of military toys. In a strange twist of fate, the 1964 Fair would mark the debut of the most successful and recognizable military toy ever made – Hasbro's GI Joe.

The Toy Manufacturer's Association was painting the usual rosy picture, pointing out that the toy industry was still expanding and wholesale toys sales would likely be a record $1.2 billion in 1964. On advertising alone, toy makers were spending over $120 million, with Mattel's $9 million advertising budget accounting for a significant chunk of that total. To kickoff its "MattelZapoppin" promotion, the company had an eight-page color layout in the March *Playthings*, including a page trumpeting the details of its ad campaign. To call it an onslaught was an understatement. The company was claiming that 90% of the toy commercials shown on Saturday morning network television in the fall would be for Mattel products. Mattel would also be putting messages on the famous scrolling electronic screen in Times Square from October to December.

Other toy makers who experienced success in 1963 were easy to pick out in the current *Playthings*. Marx had a large spread extolling its past and upcoming TV promotions ("A Simple Statement about Marx TV in 1964"). Topper Toys, who previously only sold its line in food stores, had a multipage color insert explaining why the company was expanding into traditional toy retailers for 1964. The answer was pretty simple – to better sell its hit 1963 item, the Johnny Seven One Man Army Gun.

Another company with a multipage color layout was Tudor. The lead page was devoted to electric football, specifically the newly made over No. 500 model. "The best selling of all football games for the last 15 years...but that didn't stop Tudor from improving it" read the headline at the top of the page. Pictured just below the text was a photo of the new game, along with a list of twelve new electric football features. Key among these were "larger figures in five realistic 3-dimensional action poses" who were also "virtually unbreakable with increased stability." Tudor's second page was devoted to two new items, Jr. Magnetic Baseball and Magnetic Basketball. Pool tables filled out the third page, while the final page showed off the rest of the items in the 1964 Tudor line. It was an impressive promotional display – even without the promise of television advertising.

Far above the protesters on the street and far removed from the lofty predictions of the TMA, Norman and Lee were proudly showing off the prototypes of their new players.

These players were larger, more detailed, sturdier, and better balanced than any previously made electric football players. And Lee was gloating like a proud papa over the new tackle figure. Tudor was now literally one up on Gotham. Watercolor paints added to the kid-friendly changes made by Norman and Lee. At least now the mess a kid made while painting his players would be easy to clean up.

Tudor's quarterback had been the most fragile player in the gorilla lineup, with an unfortunate tendency to snap at the ankle or break at the elbow of the throwing arm. The small spring in the kicking leg also experienced its share of problems, sometimes getting "sprung" or dislodging entirely. Eddie Gluck had alluded to these issues in *Playthings* back in June. But Lee had now taken care of these player weaknesses. Tudor's new quarterback was made out of the same soft polyethylene as the other players and had only two pieces, the body and the kicking leg. The leg was activated by pressure. Pull back on the quarterback's arm, and the leg sprung forward. The figure embodied Lee's ultimate goals as a designer – simplicity and functionality.

All of Tudor's new electric football features were from the imagination of Lee Payne. From the new full-color No. 500 display box, to the new

Lee Payne helped design The AMF Monorail Station for the 1964 New York World's Fair. Postcard by Dexter Press, West Nyack, NY.

automatic game timer, to the plastic end zone flags and first-down marker, Lee had created it all. He also made the grass on the No. 500 a brighter green color and transferred this shade over to the fiberboard field of the No. 600. A vibrant new cardboard grandstand was also included with the No. 500. Using this same cost-saving technology, Tudor replaced the metal grandstand on the No. 600 with an identical looking cardboard version.

There was another first for Tudor in 1964. For the first time ever, Tudor put electric football on the front of its sales catalog. Taking up the entire page was a close-up of electric football players in action. It was surprising that the company had never before featured its marquee toy in a cover shot. But this year was different. There was no question it was the most important game in the Tudor lineup.

Unlike the color *Playthings* ad, Tudor's entire sales catalog was printed in black and white. Perhaps this was done to camouflage the true identity of the players on the cover and in the catalog. As much as Norman and Lee wanted Tudor's new players in the catalog, they weren't available when the photos were taken in November of 1963. That meant that all of the players on display in the 1964 catalog were of the gorilla variety. Lee gave them a very neat and basic watercolor paint job, using the paints that would actually come in the new games. This turned out to be a surprisingly effective way to mask the players' true identity. Only with careful study was it clear that Tudor had gorilla players on their new No. 500 model. It was the first time gorilla players had ever appeared in a Tudor catalog, an ironic distinction considering they were no longer in production. With new players and all the new changes to electric football, Tudor was again attending to the details. And these details went all the way down to the entry level. The No. 500 was, after all, "the best selling game of all football games for the last 15 years."

Eddie Gluck may have regretted calling out Tudor's weaknesses in Playthings during the previous summer. Other than hanging onto their "straight plastic sticks" for goal posts, Tudor had voided many of the items on Gluck's electric football checklist. And Tudor's new 3-D players looked better than Gotham's players. Even with the NFL license and the NFL's perpetually growing popularity, Gotham was a quiet presence at the 1964 Fair. Subdued might be a better description.

Gluck had only a short three-paragraph article in Playthings about pool tables. And the photo accompanying the article was...of Eddie Gluck. Even stranger, it was the same photo of Eddie that Playthings first used back in 1941. The young man from that photo was now 61 years old. Even young Eddie probably wondered why current Eddie was pontificating on the virtues of pool. Where were the full-page Gotham ads? Where in the world was the NFL?

Perhaps Gotham played it cool in 1964 because there were really few changes to the Gotham line. Or maybe Gluck felt that when your licensing partner was shifting the entire landscape of professional sports all you needed to do was hang on and enjoy the ride. He still had the NFL shield on his games, and he still had Sears, the country's largest retailer, selling his games. But to not promote Gotham's NFL lineup with any type of ads? It was likely that Larry Kent had some questions for Gluck when he visited the Gotham showroom.

The NFL television bandwagon kept on rolling in April when CBS bought the rights to the 1964 and 1965 NFL Championship games for

Page 124 in the Sears 1964 *Christmas Book.* Almost the entire page was taken up by electric football games... Gotham electric football games. ©Sears, Roebuck & Co. 1964.

## Classic Electric Football Game

$12⁴⁴

- Gridiron Board 3 ft. long
- New Larger Figures in 5 Realistic Action Poses
- Offensive and Defensive Players can Run, Block, Tackle
- Triple-threat Quarterback for each Team can Run, Kick and Pass
- Paints, Press-on Numerals

Electric Football Game
$5⁶⁶

Pro Football Game
$8⁸⁷

Electric football in the Montgomery Ward 1964 *Christmas Book* (page 276). Both the Tudor No. 600 and No. 500 were featured. Tudor's gorilla players were on the games because Lee Payne's new players weren't ready in time for Ward's photo submission deadline. ©Montgomery Ward, Inc. 1964.

$1.8 million per game. This was almost double the previous year's contract and set a new record for the amount paid for a single-day sporting event. It also gave CBS the NFL lock, stock, and barrel, which was exactly what Rozelle wanted. No other networks were even invited to bid on the games, an event which left ABC and NBC – who broadcast the previous nine championship games – completely miffed. According to Rozelle, the reason the other networks weren't included in the process was simple. Both NBC and ABC currently had contracts with the AFL. It was "in the best interest of the NFL to keep the championship game free of any conflict of interest." On a day when most people were caught up in the euphoria of the opening of the 1964 New York World's Fair, Rozelle delivered a body block on two of the most powerful media entities in the country. Baseball was again left in the NFL's wake. The NFL Championship game now cost twice as much as a single World Series game.

Gotham finally got around to buying some print advertising in the June issue of *Playthings*. (Ad rates were not as expensive during the summer months.) It was a four-page color insert, and, not surprisingly, the first three pages were devoted to Gotham's pool tables. Only on the final page were there any sports games, with Gluck promoting a giant new 42"-long Super Deluxe Electric Hockey game with 3-D players, a large grandstand, scoring lights, and protective "glass" behind each goal. But electric football wasn't anywhere to be found in the ad. It also didn't get mention on page 94, where Eddie Gluck again had his picture accompanying a two-paragraph Gotham blurb. This time, at least, it was "contemporary" Eddie, who proudly looked on as a smiling girl and boy tried out one of Gotham's new pool tables.

By early summer Teague Associates' "Festival of Gas" had established itself as one of the most striking pavilions at the World's Fair, and the firm was enjoying the attention its futuristic five-story-open-air structure was receiving. Much smaller in scale was another recently completed Teague Associates' item, which, despite its diminutive stature, would prove to have a much longer shelf life than the Festival of Gas. Thanks to Teague and Chiffon, margarine would soon be available in the first easy-to-use resealable tub.

The designer of the Chiffon Margarine tub was Lee Payne, who also had a hand in designing the AMF Monorail stations at the World's Fair. It was an innovation that would change the lives and buying habits of millions of American consumers, yet dairy section conquest was not something Lee would linger over. It wasn't a big secret that he enjoyed his work with Tudor much more than his other Teague assignments. Norman had essentially given him free rein with his creativity. As a result, Tudor's electric football games were now almost entirely Lee Payne creations. And Lee simply loved sports. His efforts with Tudor's football, baseball, basketball, and hockey games were labors of the heart. Margarine tubs and World's Fairs were one thing, but electric football players and realistic miniature recreations of sports were quite another. Working with Norman, Lee got the chance to come up with his own ideas, his own designs, and his own creations. It was an ideal marriage of skill and desire.

The single NFL item in the Montgomery Ward 1964 *Christmas Book* – boys' pajamas (page 128). ©Montgomery Ward, Inc. 1964.

Early on, Norman recognized the enormous talent that Lee brought to Tudor. This was clear in the major responsibilities handed over to the young Teague designer. Great things had happened, and Norman now wanted to bring Lee onto the Tudor team full time. But how could Norman lure Lee away from the glitz of a nationally renowned Manhattan design firm to the cozy confines of a Brooklyn toy company? He created a new position. In July of 1964, just as Tudor's new players were arriving from the injection molder, Lee Payne became Tudor's first Director of Product Development.

In this position, Lee became the primary creative force at Tudor, responsible for both product and packaging development. Electric football, or course, would still be his main focus. It was the company's signature product, as well as its chief moneymaker. With fall Sunday afternoons setting up to ingrain professional football deeper into American life, Norman was hopeful that having Lee's creativity full-time would translate into more electric football profits.

When the Christmas catalogs starting appearing in September, it was apparent that the retail world had taken notice of football's increasing popularity. Just three years earlier electric football games were treated pretty much as just another toy – pictured in black and white, with the game size scaled the same as the toys on surrounding pages. Now in 1964, Sears and Ward gave electric football games "featured toy" status. Both companies presented the games on full color (expensive to print) pages that included large, detailed photographs.

Perhaps the most unique official NFL item available in 1964, the Aladdin NFL Quarterback lunch box. The Browns and Giants were pictured on the other side.

The big games were clearly BIG. Electric football had become an important part of the Christmas sales season. Another illustration of this came from a relative newcomer to the Christmas catalog fray, J.C Penney. The company, who had just published its first-ever Christmas toy catalog in October of 1963, made sure it had electric football covered this year. And which company did the Penney's catalog have a slot for in 1964? Surprisingly, it was Gotham.

Sears devoted the most space to electric football, letting the NFL G-1500, NFL G-1400, and NFL G-890 take up about two-thirds of page 124. This edition of the G-1500 came with 44 players that you could paint, theoretically at least, to look like the four hand-drawn players in the foreground of the game photo. Again, Gotham outfitted these enlarged figures in uniforms that were not identifiable as any particular NFL team. The players set up on the game, interestingly enough, were left unpainted. At least it was an honest view of what the G-1500 would look like on Christmas morning.

Since Ward required that all toy photos be submitted by January, it was Tudor's gorilla players who made their second and final appearance in the retailer's Christmas catalog. The No. 500 game was the new prototype model from the Toy Fair, while the No. 600 was the soon-to-be obsolete speckle field model, outfitted with the new end zone flags and game timer. A description next to the No. 600 said "New Larger Figures in 5 Realistic Action Poses," although the gorillas gracing the field were only in four poses. Payne's modest yet neat paint job, done with watercolor paints, made the players look quite different from the year before. It was difficult to tell that these players weren't the new Tudor figures.

In the cost battle, Ward had knocked the price of the Tudor No. 600 down to $12.44 (this was a $0.55 decrease from the 1963 price). Sears had the G-1500 below the $12 mark for the first time ever, pricing the game at $11.66. Even with these decreases, both games still carried lofty price tags for the toy world. GI Joe cost less than $3. Mattel's new short-order-grilling Creepy Crawler Thingmaker cost less than $7.

NFL items in the Christmas catalogs were still scarce. Sears had two different types of NFL items this year – Gotham electric football games and bobble-head figures. Ward had new NFL boys' pajamas, which seemed to be targeted perfectly. With all the professional football games on television in the fall, it was a safe bet that there would be an outbreak of boys dozing off with NFL dreams. It was also something Larry Kent was counting on. He again had lined up Saks Fifth Avenue as the official New York area seller of Giants merchandise, with the 1964 line expanding beyond jackets to include sweaters, bathrobes, and pajamas. Like the previous year, these items were available only in boys' sizes.

One unique item Kent had licensed for the year was already showing up in elementary schools around the country – an Aladdin brand NFL quarterback steel lunchbox. How much a lunchbox would add to NFL Properties' profits, reported to be a meager

An eye-catching Gotham G-890 box from 1964. (Photo Earl Shores.)

$36,647 for the 1963 fiscal year, was open to question. But like the jackets, robes, and pajamas, it was a simple yet effective item for making the NFL an everyday part of life...an impressionable young boy's life. The entire concept of NFL Properties was to promote the league, not necessarily make money – at least that was the company line. Kent was certainly building the promotion part, and he was sure there were significant profits to be made. All he needed was time.

Before September ended, many Sears retail stores had opened Toy Town departments. Ward wasn't far behind, getting its Toylands' open during the early days of October. Sears immediately started featuring the Gotham NFL G-890 game in some of its earliest print advertisements for the sale price of $3.99. Ward joined the sale-pricing bandwagon, advertising the Tudor

A 1964 Tudor No. 500 as it would have looked on Christmas morning 1964. (Photo Earl Shores.)

No. 500 for the same price a few weeks later. Although both retailers' advertised these prices as "sales," a $3.99 price tag was fairly standard for the No. 500 in October of 1964. Safeway grocery stores were selling it for that price; the Gibson Discount Center chain had it for $3.88, and some discounters were even advertising the game for $2.99.

One of the sure football winners as the fall moved on was the AFL New York Jets (formerly known as the Titans). After moving from the dilapidated Polo Grounds to a new stadium not too far from the World's Fair, New York's once struggling AFL franchise was averaging more than 43,000 fans through the first six games of the season. (This represented an incredible 260% increase over 1963 attendance figures.) The large sparkling bowl-shaped structure the Jets shared with the National League Mets was called Shea Stadium, and it was just the tip of a multipurpose stadium iceberg that would soon impact the American sports scene.

While AFL television ratings were down from previous years, game day attendance – thanks in large measure to the Jets – was up 40%. And on November 8, an AFL record crowd of 60,300 saw the champion Bills beat the Jets at Shea Stadium. Making the figure even more impressive was that at the very same time, 63,031 fans were sitting across town in Yankee Stadium watching the Giants beat the Cowboys. It would seem the AFL was the winner in this match-up, proving that it could hold its own when the leagues went head-to-head. But both leagues came out looking good. What the networks and potential advertisers saw was this: on a single afternoon in New York City, almost 125,000 people paid over a half a million dollars to watch professional football. What other sport could match those figures?

In the toy world, both Tudor and Gotham looked like winners as the calendar ticked toward Thanksgiving. Sears had the NFL G-1400 in heavy use in newspaper advertising, while Ward made a $3.99 Tudor No. 500 a staple of its Christmas print ad campaign. Sears often prominently presented the G-1400 – there was always a large photo of the game in the Toy Town ads. Ward was more sporadic in selling the No. 500 with an illustration, but the $3.99 price was never hard to miss. Outside of Sears' push, however, Gotham didn't really have any heavy promotion going on. And when compared to the television blitz Eddie Gluck had run in 1962, Gotham had pulled back dramatically in spending money on advertising.

During the Thanksgiving holiday weekend Gluck was relying on a brief press release he wrote and sent to hundreds of small newspapers around the country. The "Sports Games Sure to Score" article that appeared in publications like the *Kokomo Morning Times* (IN), the *Oshkosh Daily Northwestern* (WI), *The Morgantown Post* (WV), *The Benton Harbor News Palladium* (MI), and *The Gettysburg Times* (PA) talked about NFL electric football with a magnetized ball and a realistic kicker-passer. But there were no photos or even a mention of the Gotham brand. It really didn't seem like a very dependable way to sell games.

On Thanksgiving Day, television viewers didn't have to choose between the NFL or the AFL. They could actually watch both thanks to the Packers and Lions doing their traditional noontime kickoff, while the Chargers and Chiefs game started at 3:30 p.m. On Sunday afternoon the two leagues would go at it again, but one of the biggest NFL-AFL battles of the entire year was going to take place on Saturday when both leagues held their college player drafts. Actually the draft was just going to lay out the battle lines, with the actual "war" taking place over the coming weeks. But what made the 1964 draft perhaps the most monumental in pro football history was that NBC had handed over a $250,000 check to each of five different AFL teams. This money was an advance on NBC's upcoming television contract with the league. It was done for a very a simple reason – so AFL teams could outbid the NFL for players in the draft. NBC was determined to ensure the quality of its investment, even though the network had yet to televise a single AFL game.

NBC throwing its weight into the mix made sense, but it was particularly galling to NFL owners. After five years of bidding wars, they were angry and wary of spending their own newfound television bounty on unproven players. Especially when rookie salaries and signing bonuses were adding up to significantly more than NFL stars were making (of course, now the stars had to be paid more to keep them happy). The owners saw themselves in a "damned if you do, damned if you don't" predicament. They could lose their profits by signing new players, or they could lose on the field by not signing new talent. Losing on the field would soon translate into losing at the ticket office. At least they would still have the television money.

There were a couple of nightmare scenarios for owners in 1964. One was to waste a draft pick on a player who ended up signing with the other league. The other was to spend money on new players and get lousy results on the field. There was a long history in the NFL draft of collegiate stars who never became even average professional players. With the player-signing atmosphere now so heated, mistakes and misjudgments were bound to happen. An owner prayed hard that it wouldn't happen to him.

Owners' worries aside, there were some promising players in the 1964 draft. The Bears, with three first-round picks, chose Illinois linebacker Dick Butkus and Kansas halfback Gayle Sayers. Taken second overall in the AFL draft and eighth in the NFL draft was a quarterback from Alabama. His name was Joe Namath.

Sears continued to push the G-1400 in ads throughout December with the game being offered at either $9.99 or $10.99 (it was usually paired with Gotham's Pro League Hockey). And Tudor's No. 500 model continued showing up in Ward print advertising, usually at the $4 mark. This was a price Ward had to meet to be competitive, as the No. 500 was being sold for less than $4 at many toy discounters. The G-1400 hovered around the $10 price until the Monday before Christmas when Sears began clearance sales. At this point, the Gotham game dropped to $7.88. (A Sears ad in Washington state was clearing out the smaller Gotham G-890 NFL games for $1.88!) Tudor No. 500 models could be found near the $3 mark.

The only problem Tudor had this year was that it sold so many No. 500 games it ran out of the new picture boxes. Many games at the end of the year were shipped covered in the old green box lids with the words "NEW" stamped prominently in the box border. Fortunately Tudor had plenty of new players to put in their games. This mattered a lot more than box lids.

Tudor appeared to be the clear winner in the 1964 electric football Christmas battle. Their new 3-D players were more detailed, attractive, and sturdier than Gotham's players. And they even came in the No. 500, the most affordable electric football game on the market. For all of Sears' efforts, the $10 electric football game was a tough sell. (Tudor didn't have earth-shattering sales numbers with the No. 600 model either, but Norman knew he needed this game to compete with Gotham's large electric football models.) Regardless of what brand of electric football was under the tree, this particular Christmas was more of a football Christmas than any other. For the first time ever football was being televised on Christmas Day. Being shown by ABC at 3:00 p.m. Eastern Time was the North-South College

Tudor's No. 600 Sports Classic model as it would have looked on Christmas morning 1964. (Photo Earl Shores.)

All-Star game from Miami.

This was also the first day of three consecutive days of televised football. With Christmas falling on a Friday in 1964, the AFL scheduled its championship game for the very next day (the Sun Bowl would also be televised on Saturday). And the day after that, the NFL would play its championship game. It was quite fitting that the days following Christmas would be the ultimate championship football weekend, as 1964 was really the ultimate year for televised football. Many cities around the country were able to watch more than 30 professional games during the regular season. Add that to the 11 college bowl games and 4 professional contests that would be televised nationwide between December 19 and January 3, and it was clear that 1964 had been an "all-time" year for football on television. The weekend unfolded with televisions blazing and electric football games buzzing. By Sunday evening the Buffalo Bills were the AFL champions, while the underdog Browns routed the Colts 27-0 for the NFL title in front of almost 80,000 delirious Cleveland fans. And in just a few days, the year would come to a close with another nationally televised three-day blitz of football.

When Shea Stadium opened not far from the Gotham factory in 1964, it inspired Eddie Gluck to update his NFL G-1500. Gluck's update, in turn, inspired Norman Sas to go after the NFL. (AP Photo)

**EARL SHORES | RODDY GARCIA**

# 17 TUDOR MAKES A PLAY FOR THE NFL

The New Year's Day bowl schedule had a new twist this year – the Orange Bowl would be played at night. This would allow NBC, who also was covering the Sugar Bowl and the Rose Bowl, to televise over ten consecutive hours of football on Friday, January 1. Besides showing prime time football on New Year's Day, NBC was also breaking technical ground by doing the first color broadcast of a night outdoor event. New lights had been installed in the Orange Bowl to make the telecast possible.

The game itself was already the marquee match-up of the day, featuring undefeated and top-ranked Alabama going against No. 5-ranked Texas. Adding further intrigue was Alabama's star quarterback Joe Namath, who was reportedly ready to sign with the AFL. Namath played well enough to be named the game's MVP, but he couldn't finish off a goal-line quarterback sneak that would have given Alabama the lead late in the game. Texas got the ball back and was able to hold on for a 21-17 win. Alabama's heartbreaking loss surrendered the national title to Arkansas.

The very next day, Namath soothed his Orange Bowl loss by signing a contract with the New York Jets. While it was always noteworthy when a star college player signed with the AFL, this particular signing had a number of factors that made it, well, just a bit more remarkable. First off, the best quarterback in the draft was heading to the AFL. But it wasn't just any AFL team – it was the AFL franchise that played in the sports media capital of the world. This was no accident. Namath had expressed his desire to play in New York, and the AFL was happy to oblige him. After all, NBC headquarters and Madison Avenue were just a long post pattern from Shea Stadium. The NFL knew this too, and rumors had the St. Louis Cardinals trading their draft rights for Joe to the New York Giants. Unfortunately the senior league was just a bit tardy in trying to make such an arrangement.

But obviously the most remarkable part of the Namath signing was the money. For signing his name on the dotted line, Namath was paid over $400,000. He hadn't even thrown a pass as a professional, and he was already the highest paid athlete in team sports. And now he was probably one of best-known professional athletes in all of sports because the signing made headlines throughout the country. NBC had rolled the dice to invest in the AFL, and the Jets took the network's money to invest in Namath. Only time would tell whether both bets would pay off, but the message in the money was clear – the AFL was here to stay. Come fall, people would surely tune into NBC to see just how good a $400,000 quarterback was. The NFL would have to learn to live with its rival.

One immediate thing Namath's signing accomplished was to overshadow the weekend's football games, which included the Gator Bowl and Shrine Game on Saturday, and the NFL Runner-Up Bowl on Sunday. One team in the NFL game had already been a runner-up – the St. Louis Cardinals.

A few weeks later, there was the usual anti-AFL grumbling at the NFL owners meeting. But other than Namath, the NFL had good success in signing draft picks. Top pick Tucker Fredrickson had signed with the Giants, while the Bears landed both Sayers and Butkus. Talent for the league was not really an issue. Marketing the league, however, was an ever-evolving concern, and the 1965 meeting was the scene of a little known tryout that ended up putting a face on the NFL. Besides having a marketing arm (NFLP) to sell the league's image, Rozelle had another plan for promoting the NFL – a league-owned film company.

Most teams were already creating their own season highlight films, so why not create an entity that would do it, do it well, with the league maintaining control over content and quality? A number of production companies made their pitch at the 1965 meeting to become the official filmmaker of the NFL. The winner was a small firm that didn't even show any images, still or moving, to the owners. Blair Motion Pictures was owned by Ed Sabol, a former overcoat salesman from Philadelphia. Blair was not as well known as some other competitors, yet Sabol's salesmanship had enabled the company to film the previous three NFL Championship games.

## SPORTS CLASSIC
# *Electric* Football *for '65*

**Tudor Sports Classic games are for those who demand the very best in realistic play action and styling...this one has all the exciting new features of the 500 Electric Football Game plus...**

- A gridiron 3' long which provides the scale necessary for realistic play patterns
- Deluxe quality game rail construction
- Exclusive Isopad game board mounting which eliminates dead spots usually found in game boards of this size...continuous action is assured.
- Colorful grandstand is a photo reproduction of an actual football crowd.
- Four color palette of water soluble paints for coloring uniforms on players.
- Handsome "self-service" display box with full color illustration of the game in use plus detail illustrations explaining play action.

**No. 600**
Box size: 21½" x 39" x 3¼"
¼ doz. ctn. wt. 32 lbs.
110 Volts, A.C. only
$16.00 retail

Getting a half-page photo in the 1965 Tudor sales catalog was the No. 600 model. (Collection of Norman Sas.)

In fact, it was Sabol who suggested to Rozelle that the league should have its own film company. With the owners' approval and seed money from each of the teams (about $168,000 total), NFL Films was born.

Thanks to strong toy sales in 1964, the Toy Fair opened in early March on a decidedly positive note. Discount houses and loss leader pricing were still problems, but the toy world seemed to have simply gotten used to them. Sears and Ward again set sales records for 1964, with Sears' total sales figure going over the $6 billion mark for the first time ever. These retailers unquestionably helped the toy industry with its profits.

But the profits made by several 1964 toys were drawing unwanted attention. GI Joe turned out to be the most popular boy's action figure ever made, while Remco sold 1.6 million Johnny Seven One Man Army Guns. The nearly life-size gun, which featured seven ways to "kill" an enemy, was again the target of picket lines from groups protesting against the selling of war toys. This year's large assortment of James Bond inspired toys, including camera pistols and bullet firing attaché cases, surely had the protestors reserving their rooms for next year's Fair.

Tudor arrived at the Fair with the same electric football lineup the company had in 1964. The No. 600 and No. 500 were unchanged, although Norman and Lee could finally show off the actual production version of

## magnetic quarterback

### THE GAME OF FOOTBALL STRATEGY

- Players choice of 14 offensive plays and 8 defensive formations give quarterback all the action, suspense, and realistic scoring of the top pro games.
- Diagrams of offensive plays printed right on metal gameboard match up with defensive formations printed on transparent "defense card" overlays.
- Tudor magnetic arrow determines final outcome of every play.
- Grandstand-scoreboard keeps track of score and time.
- Magnetic 10 yard marker measures for first downs.
- Diagram of actual football formation serves as ball marker.
- Full color display box.

**No. 400**
Box size 20½ x 20½ x 1¾
½ Doz. Ctn. Wt. 19 lbs.
$5.00 retail

**Lee Payne's newly designed Magnetic Quarterback game was Tudor's headline item in the 1965 Toy Fair issue of *Playthings*. 1965 Tudor Catalog. (Collection of Norman Sas.)**

the new one-piece players. Also unchanged from the previous year was the electric football section of Tudor's sales catalog. Considering the fact that the new players were available, it was a little unusual not to have taken new catalog photos. But this lack of change showed the confidence Tudor had in its games, including the new Magnetic Quarterback Strategy Game. Lee designed this non-electric spinner-based board game, aiming it at the "mature" football fan who wanted strategy beyond vibrating figures. The main appeal of the game was realistic play outcome. Lee also added a classic touch of 3-D reality with a colorful foldout cardboard stadium. Tudor was giving the Magnetic Quarterback a serious promotional push, publicizing the game in a full-page *Playthings* advertisement.

Gotham's Toy Fair electric football lineup also stayed the same in 1965, with the NFL G-1500 as the focal point, and the NFL G-890 as the entry-level model. The G-1500 had lost its end zone grandstand pieces, replaced by a modernistic cardboard scoreboard that mounted up along the team flag line. Leaving off the end zone pieces didn't significantly change the game's appearance, but it did significantly change something else very important – the game's price. Gotham's largest electric football could now retail for less than $10. And by some strange coincidence, Gotham also showed up at the Fair with a new football strategy game. It was called the NFL Big Play Electric Football Game (G-1000). This game had a Gotham G-890 frame as a base, but the field didn't vibrate. A battery powered Selectro-matic Quarterback device was the reason that "electric" was part of the game's official name. The Big Play also had a feature that set it apart from any toy football game that had ever been displayed at the Toy Fair.

What was modestly described in the 1965 NFL Properties catalog as a "modern bowl-shaped stadium," was in reality a giant double-decked cardboard grandstand that surrounded the Big Play on three sides. With dozens of pieces, it was the most elaborate stadium ever designed for a toy football game, and it also had another very distinguishing characteristic – it looked a lot like Shea Stadium. (Since the AFL Jets played in Shea, the proper NFL reference was the Redskins' four-year-old District of Columbia Stadium.) Gluck's designers had obviously studied stadium photos and made good use of them. They also followed Lee Payne's lead and finally made a photo-based crowd scene grandstand instead of one with hand-drawn spectators. The Big Play stadium was amazingly realistic – the "wow" factor was enormous. And with all its parts, it might take more time to put the game together than it would to actually play it.

Surprisingly, Gluck had nothing in the March issue of *Playthings* other than a small box ad in the back of the magazine. A lot of effort had obviously gone into creating the Big Play. It was unlike Gluck not to broadcast the arrival of the new game to the toy world – especially considering the NFL aspect of the game.

Gluck finally did present the NFL Big Play to the toy world in the April issue of *Playthings*. But it wasn't done with a full-page ad, or even a *Playthings'* piece with a photo of the game. Instead, it was an anonymous paragraph in the bottom right corner of page 102 with the headline "Gotham's game will tie in with NFL TV program." While details about the television program were vague, Gluck was not shy about the virtues of the game. "Gotham believes their new NFL Big Play is the most significant advance in football realism in a decade," said Gluck (the football realism "advance" of 1955 being Gotham's entry into the electric football market). Again, it was not the usual promotional splash from Gluck for a new NFL product. But he was getting help from NFL Properties, which had the Big Play and G-890 Official NFL Electric Football game taking up a full page in its color catalog. The Big Play's description touted the game's "modern bowl-shaped stadium."

A number of cities were now building modern bowl-shaped stadiums, including the city of Atlanta. The recently completed Atlanta structure was an enclosed bowl just like the stadium in Washington, D.C. And like D.C.'s Stadium and Shea Stadium, it was a multipurpose structure. That is, it would be able to accommodate baseball and football. The unusual thing was, when Atlanta started building its stadium, it had no professional teams of any kind to put in it. Yet the city was creating a blueprint that many cities would follow in the future – build it, and they will come. "They" being expansion or disenchanted professional sports teams. The National League Milwaukee Braves had already made arrangements to become the Atlanta Braves starting in 1966.

Atlanta's vision seemed to have been rewarded for a second time in early June when the NFL announced that it would expand from 14 to 16 teams by 1967. Rozelle didn't mention Atlanta specifically, yet it was a foregone conclusion that, with its nearly completed state-of-the-art sporting structure, the city was at the top of the commissioner's expansion list. For years the NFL's "Southern" team had been the Redskins, so the South was regarded as a particularly ripe area for professional football, especially given the region's passion for the college game. For Rozelle, it was just a matter of time before professional football came to Atlanta. As usual, the commissioner was right. Three days later, the AFL announced that it was expanding from 8 to 10 teams and that the league's newest franchise would be in…Atlanta.

The deal, however, was far from complete. What the AFL had done was award a franchise to the Cox Broadcasting Corporation for a stunning $7.5 million. But Cox didn't have the rental rights to the new stadium, which Atlanta's Stadium Authority was conveniently withholding until July 1. And the reason for the delay? Money. Under the AFL's television pact, expansion teams didn't get any money until 1968, and even then it was only a partial share of $250,000. An NFL franchise would not only be more prestigious, it would be more profitable. The Stadium Authority was betting that the NFL would not let the AFL have Atlanta without a fight – and they were right. At a special meeting in New York on June 21, the NFL owners unanimously awarded Atlanta a league franchise for the 1966 season. With a revenue stream that included a full share of NFL television money, stadium rental rights were a mere formality for the new ownership group.

As usual, the AFL didn't back down. Instead, they called an audible and looked further south, ultimately giving the AFL's ninth franchise to a Miami ownership group that was headed by television icon Danny Thomas. Since this team wouldn't take the field until 1966, proud Miami fans would have to get their football fix from CBS or NBC, who were combining to televise a record 14 preseason games this year (Score: CBS/NFL 10 – NBC/AFL 4). The profitability and interest generated by these essentially meaningless games showed off the ever-growing popularity of professional football.

Also enjoying a rising profile was NFL Properties. A national United Press International article in August highlighted the growing line of NFL items: socks, hats, mittens, gloves, sweatshirts, t-shirts, sweaters, pajamas, uniforms, tankards, fitness sets, stadium boots, pennants, helmet plaques, posters, badges, buttons, and bobble-heads. NFL Properties even gathered a number of NFL-licensed companies together at an upscale New York

### G-1000 NFL "BIG PLAY" ELECTRIC GAME

**Size:** 32¼" long x 22½" wide x 17" high

Experts call "The Big Play" the most exciting new football game to be invented in years. Excitement builds for fans when red light flashes as plays are properly defended. Countless combinations of plays to be found in a typical NFL game. Offensive team runs draw plays, end runs, short and long passes, off-tackle slants and host of other key moves. Defense counters with linebacker rushes and zone moves.

Selectro-matic Quarterback set in modern "bowl-shaped" stadium triggers the exciting pro action. Now for the first time NFL fans can call their own plays and enjoy the fast moving action of realistic play on the field.

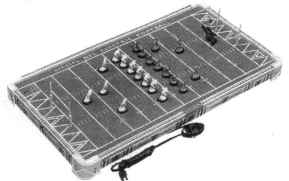

### G-890 OFFICIAL NFL ELECTRIC FOOTBALL

**Size:** 28¼" x 15¼" x 2¼" high

**Construction:** Playing surface—Hardboard. Frame: steel, with full-formed rounded plastic corners. Vibrating Coil with Cord Set and Switch attached underneath game, for use with 115 Volt AC current only. UL and CSA approved.

**Finish:** Playing surface—mounted with multi-colored, glossy label. Frame—multi-colored. Corners—plastic.

**Accessories:** 22 3-dimensional "life-like" styrene players, mounted on polyethylene base. One metal snap-action Kicker/Passer with metal figure attached. 1 molded magnetic football; 2 plastic goal posts. 1 metal yardage marker. Rules for playing with sheet of key NFL plays.

**Packing:** Each in 200 lb. test corrugated box, printed in 3 colors. 6 only to shipping carton. (MAILABLE.)

**Weight:** 32 lbs. to shipping carton.

**For ages:** 7 to 15 years.

### GOTHAM PRESSED STEEL CORPORATION   Top Division Showroom: 200 Fifth Avenue

Factory & General Offices: Wales Ave., Corner E. 144th Street, Bronx 54, New York • MOtthaven 5-4800

19

---

**A full page Gotham ad in 1965 offered hints at the "big" changes to come in electric football. (Collection of Earl Shores.)**

restaurant for a clothing show. NFL coats, parkas, and rain gear were unveiled to the sound of a 56-piece marching band. (They were seated; they didn't march.)

The UPI article also pointed out that this was another area where the AFL was not backing down. Joe Namath was already endorsing a line of slacks, and the AFL did have an official clothing line of its own. But there was no AFL Properties – even off the field, the AFL still couldn't match the NFL.

This marketing deficit wasn't from a lack of effort. From 1960-62, all

AFL licensing and merchandising was handled by the most powerful talent agency in the world, the Music Corporation of America. But it wasn't just a licensing agreement, as MCA acted as the league's agent in negotiating the first AFL television contract with ABC in 1960. MCA, whose client list included Marlon Brando, Kirk Douglas, Tony Curtis, and Sophia Loren, was derisively known as "the octopus" in Hollywood, creating many enemies for the power it wielded in the entertainment industry. It turned out that MCA was in fact too powerful, as evidenced by an antitrust lawsuit filed against the company in 1962. MCA got out from under the lawsuit by dissolving its talent agency in July of 1962. (It held onto its even more profitable television production company.) Many of the agents working for MCA jumped to other talent agencies, taking their famous clients with them. Some agents opened up their own talent agencies. One of those opening their own agency was Frank Mincolla.

Handling the licensing for the AFL was former Music Corporation of America agent Frank Mincolla. *Playthings*, page 68, December 1962.

Mincolla had spent ten years at MCA as the vice president of MCA Enterprises, the character-licensing division of the company. One of his claims to fame was creating the marketing plan that helped Alvin and the Chipmunks become a household phenomenon in 1959, but he also spent time working with the AFL. When MCA ceased to exist in mid-1962, Mr. Mincolla was able to persuade the AFL to become one his clients. The new office of Frank T. Mincolla Associates would be located in the Time-Life Building in Rockefeller Plaza.

Mincolla was no doubt eagerly watching as the AFL started its season on Saturday, September 10, hoping the charismatic Joe Namath would give the league greater merchandising opportunities. But it wasn't until the Jets' second game, with over 53,000 people in Shea Stadium watching, that the $400,000 man threw his first professional pass. Namath performed like a typical raw rookie, and the Jets lost to the Chiefs 14-10. Knowledgeable football fans weren't surprised by Namath's lack of success. Being a professional quarterback was perhaps the most difficult job in all of sports. It would take some time to learn all the nuances of the game and the savvy to succeed. Being a professional was about more than just throwing passes.

To see what being a savvy professional was all about, Joe might have taken a peek at the recently published Sears Christmas catalog. On page 442, Eddie Gluck had sprung a flea-flicker of a surprise on Norman and Lee. Taking up almost a third of the page was the new Gotham G-1503S game. The "S" meant the model was a Sears exclusive, although it also could have stood for "secret," since exclusive toys were never shown at the Toy Fair. Until the Christmas catalog hit the mail routes, only Gluck, Kent, and the Sears' toy buyers knew the G-1503S existed.

Gotham's new game was called NFL Big Bowl Electric Football. The Big Bowl consisted of the G-1500 game board and the elaborate grandstand from the non-vibrating Big Play game. It was the most stunning electric football game ever made. Surrounded on three sides with the gigantic double-decked grandstand, complete with overhanging roof, the Big Bowl looked a lot like the new stadiums in New York and Washington. And just like the Big Play, the Big Bowl was going to be a near perfect match with the soon to be opened stadiums in Atlanta and St. Louis. Gotham's stadium concept was almost as complex as it was ingenuous, requiring nearly 40 interlocking pieces of cardboard. With the colorful NFL team logos on the frame border and the words "Big Bowl" sandwiched between two NFL shields high up on the center roof section, the game was one of the most remarkable toys in the entire toy section. Electric football...the NFL...a modern stadium...the Big Bowl had it all.

Gotham's rather ordinary 3-D players almost seemed to be an afterthought, swallowed up by the majestic bowl. Heck, a kid could put plastic green army men on the field and it would still look good. Also coming in as an afterthought on page 442 was Gotham's G-1500. Sized in the catalog at two-thirds the scale of the Big Bowl, Yankee Stadium now seemed a bit dated. An NFL G-890 finished out the page, as did the new Gotham Big Play game. The Sears version of Big Play, however, came with no grandstand at all. Sears wanted absolutely no confusion between the Big Play and the Big Bowl, especially since Big Play was cheaper. Only one game in Sears was going to be allowed to have a stadium. The G-1503S seemed the right choice.

Norman and Lee knew they had been scooped. Even though Ward gave the No. 600 a very nice full-color half page, it didn't generate the same visual awe of the Big Bowl. Lee's new players looked good, being colorful and painted realistically, but the No. 600 was $11.99 – the same price as the Big Bowl. Tudor always had an advantage over Gotham due to the quality of its game boards. Yet in the catalog beauty pageant of 1965, Tudor was clearly the runner-up.

"Gotham came up with the stadium idea to sell to Sears," said Sas. "The Big Bowl looked terrific in the catalog." And just like the NFL-AFL battle, the Tudor-Gotham battle was becoming more and more about marketing. With the elaborate layouts electric football was getting in Sears and Ward, image was very important, perhaps more important than how the game actually worked. The Big Bowl was a great idea, but it did have a bit of a flaw – you really couldn't play the game with the bowl wrapped around it. This was especially true if two kids were trying to play with it. But it looked great on the page and would sell games; just as a handsome charismatic rookie quarterback would sell seats and slacks and make the Jets the professional team that everyone wanted to see.

Officially NFL-licensed items were becoming more common in 1965. Spreading out to NFL rugs was Montgomery Ward. 1965 *Christmas Book*, page 158. ©Montgomery Ward, Inc. 1965.

All outward appearances pointed to Gluck and his company being on a roll in 1965. He had the NFL, and his designers were extending the realism of electric football by keeping up with the trends of multipurpose stadium architecture. The Big Bowl was an action toy landmark. No other sports game – basketball, hockey, or baseball – had ever taken stadium or arena design to such a realistic and complex level. And, of course, Gotham had Sears too. Page 442 was one of the most attractive pages in the entire Christmas catalog. Things were looking up for Gotham...or were they?

Not long after seeing Gotham's new monster game, Norman Sas began working on a secret of his own. "The NFL's popularity was growing, it had become obvious the licensing was important and would help us sell games," said Sas. "So I picked up the phone and called Larry Kent."

Kent's reception was cool to say the least. He felt a genuine sense of loyalty towards Gluck, who was one of NFL's original licensees. Back in 1960, Eddie had believed in the NFL, and Norman hadn't. Kent still resented this lack of faith, seeing Norman's previous rejection as a personal slight rather than a careful business decision. It would have been easy for Kent to tell Norman that he missed his chance to carry the ball for the NFL five years ago, but Kent didn't slam the door (or the phone) on Tudor. He was too smart to burn his bridges. Kent told Norman he would have NFL

Properties Vice President John Carney "look into things." Carney would get back to Tudor in a few weeks.

Besides being NFL Properties' No. 2 man, John Carney had another unique qualification – he was Kent's son-in-law. Recently graduated from college, Carney was a relatively young man compared to Gluck and Sas. But he was not in over his head at NFL Properties. He was not the boss's relative that everybody made fun of. Carney was a quick study and had a sharp business sense. He also had Kent's ear, which certainly equaled power. Upon looking into Gotham's relationship with the NFL, he discovered something startling. Although Gotham's games were distributed throughout the country by Sears and Alden's catalog orders, the company didn't have that many active retail accounts outside of the Northeast part of the country. The farther you got away from New York City, the less likely you were to find a Gotham game of any kind on a store shelf.

Tudor, on the other hand, had relationships with a number of major national chains including True Value Hardware, Western Auto, Skaggs, the Otasco Stores (which included the Economy Auto Stores chain), and the ever-growing Gibson Discount Center chain. With 145 stores in 11 states throughout the South and Southwest, Gibson's was a large and powerful retailer who held its own trade show every summer in Dallas. Over 300 toy makers, including Tudor, attended Gibson's most recent event. And in 1962 Norman had appointed six special factory sales representatives, each one assigned to a specific geographical region of the country. The only states that didn't have an assigned sales rep were Alaska and Hawaii. It was one of the reasons that, year in and year out, Tudor always sold the most electric football games. Tudor games were the most readily available throughout the U.S. When Carney reported Gotham's shortcomings to Kent, he was instructed to call Norman and see what else Tudor could offer the NFL.

Norman's pitch to Carney was pretty simple – Tudor made the better game. The players looked more realistic, the field vibrated better (at least the smaller metal No. 500 did), the games were better constructed, and Lee's artwork was better. Tudor had the better product. Norman didn't really get an argument from Carney on these points, but Gotham's games were decent enough, and NFL Properties had a good relationship with Gluck. What else could Tudor offer? How about the fact that Tudor was always the leader in electric football game sales? Giving Tudor the license would automatically mean more money for NFL Properties. Carney knew this was absolutely true, but he reminded Sas that the NFLP wasn't totally about profit, it was about enhancing the image of the league. Could Tudor do something, other than slap an NFL shield on its games, to promote the league? Could they come up with something different, something beyond what Gotham had already done with the NFL license?

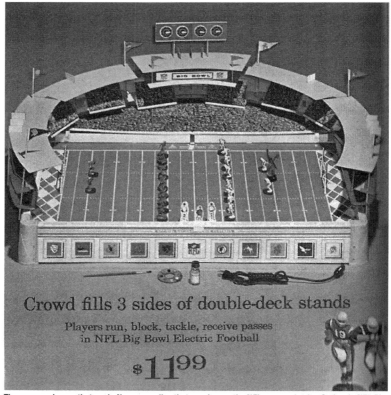

**Crowd fills 3 sides of double-deck stands**

Players run, block, tackle, receive passes
in NFL Big Bowl Electric Football

$11⁹⁹

The game and page that made Norman realize that passing on the NFL was a mistake. Gotham's NFL Big Bowl, along with the G-1500, G-890, and NFL Big Play – all on one page. Sears 1965 *Christmas Book*, page 442. ©Sears, Roebuck & Co. 1965.

Norman was sure he and Lee could come up with the kind of innovation Carney was looking for, but he needed time. Could he get back to Carney? Norman was starting to wonder if his chance at the NFL was slipping away, but little did he know that Carney himself was having questions about Gotham. So Carney's reply was a pleasant surprise. "See what you can come up with, and get back to me." The door to the NFL was still open. It was only a crack, yet Norman could see the light. This opportunity was one Norman was determined not to miss.

Lee was surprised to find out that Tudor had a shot at the NFL... surprised and intrigued. He could think of no better test for his skills than to design for the NFL. The challenge Norman offered – to improve on both Gotham's NFL games and Tudor's games – got Payne's competitive juices flowing. Not that he thought there was much competition. Gotham's designs never impressed Lee. From the 3-D players that were obviously

It was clear where Eddie Gluck got the idea for the Big Bowl. Just across the East River in Flushing Meadows, where Shea Stadium opened in 1964. (AP Photo)

copies of his own, to the thin sheet metal of the frames, Lee felt Gotham cut too many corners in the tooling process. And corners actually were a problem for Gotham. Made out of a soft plastic, Gotham's corners attached to the metal parts of the frame with two rivets. These rivets had a habit of working their way out of the plastic, leaving the metal sides of the frames vulnerable to warping as well as damage during shipping. Tudor's games had hard high-impact plastic for corners, and heavier metal in their frames. Frame warp was seldom an issue on a Lee Payne-designed game.

Lee told Norman that he could refine the players further, adding even more detail. This would serve to distance Tudor's players from Gotham's. And while Tudor already had a better-looking field than Gotham's, it would be a pleasure to make it even more realistic, more NFL-like. Lee would check out some photos of recent NFL games and see what he could come up with.

Again Lee called on his friend Lou Theoharides to help with new figures, and discussions soon started on what could be done to give more detail to Tudor's players. As for field details, Lee noticed that some teams had moved beyond placing generic stripe or diamonds patterns in their end zones. For the last several seasons the Giants had placed a large "NY" behind each goal post, and more and more teams were starting to personalize their end zones. It was a trend that Lee knew he could use for Tudor's NFL effort.

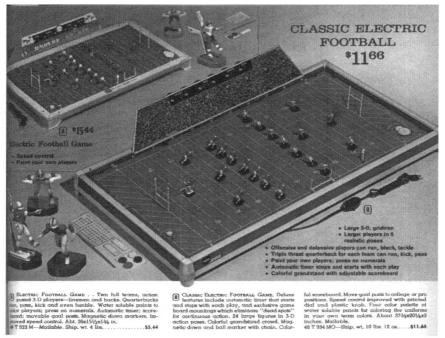

The fall moved on with Joe Namath and the Jets drawing big crowds to Shea Stadium, parents deciding whether an NFL Big Bowl was worth $11.99, and Norman and Lee trying to gain John Carney's approval. Lee's work with Theoharides was coming along nicely, the results being superbly detailed metal players that were unquestionably the best work Tudor had done. Based on the current players, each figure was more refined at every turn – thigh pads, shoulder pads, facemasks, faces, socks, and spikes. As for the games, Payne wanted to go beyond Gotham's basic field markings. He wanted to make the fields distinctive, make a kid know he had an NFL game. So with the Giants' field marking in mind, Payne came up with a prototype game featuring a large "NFL" in the end zone behind the goal post. This prototype was based on the No. 600, and it was photographed with the new prototype metal players on the game. The photos were sent to Carney for his evaluation.

Carney thought Tudor was going in the right direction, but he still wasn't convinced there was a significant difference from Gotham. Tudor hadn't even tried to match the Big Bowl's grandstand. But that was about to change. The toy buyers at Montgomery Ward wanted something from

Tudor to rival the Big Bowl, so Lee's efforts were now extending to nights and weekends in his apartment. Norman assured Carney that a bowl-like grandstand could be done if that's what the NFL wanted.

NFL Properties was continuing to make headway at Sears; there were now over a half a dozen NFL items in the Christmas catalog. Adding to the ever-present Gotham NFL games were three NFL kids' books, an NFL Board Game, and an interesting fellow by the name of Johnny Hero. Johnny was a GI Joe-inspired sports action figure, who instead of having camouflage fatigues and machine guns for accessories had the uniforms of all the teams in the NFL as a possible wardrobe. Kent probably wasn't thrilled that the uniforms of all the AFL teams were available as well – and that Johnny had bright blue eyes much like Namath's. At least the NFL uniforms were listed first. Sears also had Johnny sporting an NFL Colts uniform in the catalog photo. And 1965 was another year where Saks Fifth Avenue carved out a special area in its boys' departments to sell official New York Giants clothing.

The long-promised Gotham Big Play promotion was finally unveiled in late October. Thanks to Larry Kent, NFL players in nine different cities were set to make personal in-store appearances endorsing the Big Play game. The players would not only greet fans and demonstrate the realism of the new game, they would also take on some lucky fan in an actual Big Play competition. The Woodward & Lothrop department store ran a full page ad for the game in the *Washington Post*, enticing local boys to come out: "Hey Fellows, Beat Redskins star Dick Shiner at his own game with the new Gotham Big Play Football Game."

With more help from Kent, the Big Play was distributed beyond Gotham's usual range of retailers. In fact some regional department store heavyweights were backing the new promotion – Dayton's in Minneapolis, Wannamaker's in Philadelphia, Higbee's in Cleveland, Hechts in Baltimore, and the May Company in Los Angeles, to name a few. In many ways it was a groundbreaking promotional campaign. Gluck publicized the promotion in the November issue of *Playthings*, hoping to entice new retailers to sell the game through the popularity of the NFL. But despite all of Kent's help, there was no mention of the television tie-in that Gluck had promised back in the spring.

Neither the Big Play nor the Big Bowl was getting any advertising help from Sears in October. Instead, the NFL G-1500 was being featured in Sears' toy ads for $9.99. The retailer continued to ignore the Big Play and Big Bowl in November, maintaining its focus on the G-1500 while occasionally trotting out the smaller G-890. Meanwhile, Tudor was getting the usual support from Ward, who had the No. 500 advertised for $4.44. This was an attractive price, yet a number of retailers were already advertising Tudor's best-selling game for less than $4.

Sears had begun featuring the G-1500 and a Gotham pool table prominently in its toy advertising, but the Big Bowl and Big Play were still nowhere to be found. Finally, over the Thanksgiving Day holiday period, the Big Play started showing up in newspapers around the country. But Sears, surprisingly, had nothing to do with these appearances. Eddie Gluck had sent out Gotham press release packages to dozens of publications, and, luckily, some happened to need filler material over the holiday. Gluck's package included a photo of a Big Play being played by two boys (with dad looking on), as well as seven paragraphs of text hyping the Big Play and Gotham's oversized table hockey game.

**Punt, Pass and Kick Library**

$1.66 Each or
$1.48 in Sets
Ea. of 3

For Boys Ages 9 to 12. Here are four titles kicking off the new Punt, Pass, and Kick Library.

01 **Heroes of the NFL.** Tells of famous stars who overcame such limitations as size, illness, fear and physical handicaps.
02 **How to Punt, Pass and Kick.** Informative and exciting, with expert advice on all the football basics.
03 **Great Quarterbacks of the NFL.** Stories about your favorite heroes.
04 **The Big Play.** Tells about exciting moments in the history of the NFL. Please state title numbers of books desired. Ship. wt. 1 lb.
253T734..3, $4.44; Ea. $1.66

Pete Roselle

**Latest Editions**

THE STORY OF FOOTBALL—For Ages 9 and Up. A colorful history of America's exciting gridiron sport. Famous stars and coaches of college and pro football. Loaded with illustrations. 53 T 739–Wt. 4 oz.$3.23

THE STORY OF BASEBALL—For Ages 12 and Up. A lively history of America's favorite game—the outstanding highlights, the outstanding teams, the colorful personalities, Hall of Fame, World Series winners, etc. Packed with photographs. Revised edition. 53 T 738–Wt. 2 lbs. 5 oz.$3.23

Sears and Ward were both selling the NFL's official line of boys' books. Ward was using Pete Rozelle's face - and misspelled name - as a stamp a proof of authenticity. Montgomery Ward 1965 *Christmas Book*, page 304. ©Montgomery Ward, Inc. 1965.

The results of Gluck's mailing campaign were spotty. Sometimes Gotham's entire package made it into print, other times it was just the Big Play photo with a caption, and sometimes it was only the text. But it was hard for Gluck to complain. He had to be grateful that newspapers in places like Cedar Rapids, Iowa; Hays, Kansas; Racine, Wisconsin, and Centralia, Washington were looking for toy-oriented material during the holiday weekend. It was free advertising for Gotham. Sears continued to do its part for Gotham, running full-page ads in hundreds of newspapers during the holiday period. Again, the only games being featured were the NFL G-1500 and the Gotham pool table. Ward had a much smaller advertising presence than Sears, but Tudor No. 500 games were the most common game seen in holiday newspapers, priced anywhere from $6 to less than $4 (the Gibson Discount Center chain was selling the game for $3.88).

On Thanksgiving Day, the NFL and AFL were competing for television viewers, although once again not directly. Kicking off at noon were the Colts and Lions, while later on the West Coast, Buffalo was visiting the Chargers for a replay of the 1964 AFL Championship game. In a strange twist, both games ended up as ties. The Colts and Lions finished deadlocked at 24-24, while a late Bills field goal gave the AFL game a 20-20 finish.

Saturday's sports' focal point should have been the nationally televised Army-Navy game, but the NFL and AFL seemed determined to divert attention from the collegians in 1965. Both leagues were holding their college player drafts on Saturday. The AFL originally planned to hold its draft on the 20th, but bowed to pressure from the NCAA for a later date. Adding extra drama to draft day were accusations of tampering and foul play from both sides. Persistent rumors asserted that the AFL had already held a secret draft in late October, while "unnamed sources" claimed the NFL had a list of 13 players who were to be signed at "all costs." Regardless of the innuendo, both leagues knew their top picks were going to exceed Mr. Namath's price. The first pick of the NFL went to the expansion Atlanta Falcons, who took Texas All-American linebacker Tommy Nobis. With the first pick in the AFL draft, the expansion Miami Dolphins took Illinois running back Jim Grabowksi. Army and Navy continued with the on-field theme of the weekend, finishing up in a 7-7 tie.

During the opening days of December, electric football became very prominent in print advertising. Sears was prolific in showing off the G-1500 (still $9.99), although sometimes the smaller G-890 was mistakenly pictured in the ads. Ward picked up its pace, presenting the No. 500 in numerous ads for $4.96, even though the going price for a No. 500 was around the $4 mark (Giant Tiger Discounters in Ohio and some Rexall Drug Stores had the game at $2.99). Heading into the final weekend of both the NFL and AFL seasons, Sears was still giving the G-1500 a strong $9.99 push. And by this stage of the month Ward had the large Tudor No. 600 on sale for $11.44.

Fans around the country were all set for a heavy dose of televised football on the weekend of December 18 and 19. Four games would be on the air on Saturday, two bowl games, along with an NFL and an AFL game. Sunday would also feature an NFL and an AFL game. It turned out to be a dramatic final day of the season, at least in the NFL. During the fading seconds of a late afternoon West Coast game, which many football fans across the country were watching on CBS, the 49ers tied the Western Division-leading Packers. The game was still tied at the final gun, with the result dropping the Packers into a tie with the Colts. A playoff game was now needed to see who would play the Browns for the NFL Championship.

Over in the AFL, the Bills and Chargers would again face off for the league championship. Not making the playoffs were the Jets, who ended up with the exact same 5-8-1 record it had in 1964. Did this mean that the team's $400,000 rookie quarterback was a failure? Not at all. Despite this seemingly mediocre record, Namath had done exactly what the league had hoped – he created a buzz. AFL attendance was up 25% (Jets attendance had finished at almost 55,000 fans per game), while AFL Nielsen ratings were nearly double that of the previous year. About 4 million people were watching the AFL on Sunday afternoons, compared with 7 million watching the NFL.

Namath even got a nod of approval from the city's hard-boiled sportswriters when the *New York Times* published a Thanksgiving Day

Joe Namath not only helped fill Shea Stadium seats in 1965, he was named AFL Rookie of the Year. ©Bettman/Corbis

article with the headline "Namath Has Proved that Price Was Right." The article took a clear-eyed view of Namath's on-field progress, declaring that despite the team record, it had been a very successful season for the rookie quarterback. And being named the Associated Press AFL Rookie of the Year a few weeks later provided an exclamation point to Namath's first season as a pro.

In the week leading up to Christmas, Sears continued its widespread promotion of the G-1500. The game was part of clearance sales for $8.88 and also a "Last Minute Gifts" item for $7.88. Gotham's large game was not the only electric football model being discounted, as Tudor's No. 600 dropped to the $10 mark. But none of these discounts could match what happened to the Big Play. Sales, despite the NFL player in-store promotions, had been

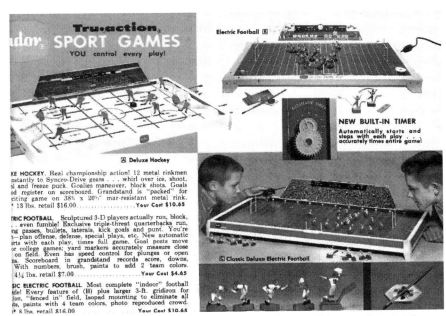

**Tru·action,**

**SPORT GAMES**
YOU control every play!

Electric Football **B**

**NEW BUILT-IN TIMER**
Automatically starts and
stops with each play . . .
accurately times entire game!

**A Deluxe Hockey**

**XE HOCKEY.** Real championship action! 12 metal rinkmen
nstantly to Syncro-Drive gears . . . whirl over ice, shoot,
l and freeze puck. Goalies maneuver, block shots. Goals
d register on scoreboard. Grandstand is "packed" for
citing game on 38½ x 20½" mar-resistant metal rink.
· 13 lbs. retail $16.00 . . . . . . . . . . . . . . . . . . **Your Cost $10.65**

**TRIC FOOTBALL.** Sculptured 3-D players actually run, block,
. . even fumble! Exclusive triple-threat quarterbacks run,
ng passes, bullets, laterals, kick goals and punt. You're
h—plan offense, defense, special plays, etc. New automatic
irts with each play, times full game. Goal posts move
or college games; yard markers accurately measure close
on field. Even has speed control for plunges or open
ss. Scoreboard in grandstand records score, downs,
With numbers, brush, paints to add 2 team colors.
4¼ lbs. retail $7.00 . . . . . . . . . . . . . . . . . . **Your Cost $4.65**

**SIC ELECTRIC FOOTBALL.** Most complete "indoor" football
de! Every feature of (B) plus larger 3-ft. gridiron for
ion, "fenced in" field, Isopad mounting to eliminate all
ts, paints with 4 team colors, photo reproduced crowd.
·· 8 lbs. retail $16.00 . . . . . . . . . . . . . . . **Your Cost $10.65**

**C Classic Deluxe Electric Football**

Tudor had an entire page in the 1965 First Distributors Christmas Catalog. First was a Chicago area discount retailer.
©First Co. 1965.

slow. The Big Play list price was $9.95, but as Christmas neared, retailers
had now reduced the price to as little as $3.97. There had been no support
from Sears (plus the Sears version did not include the bowl grandstand), and
Gluck's main ad support for the game consisted of sending out press releases.
Perhaps Gotham expected more support from the NFL. The lack of support
and advertising for the brand new game remains a mystery.

It's hard to imagine Santa ever losing his cool, yet his patience was surely
tested by the life-like construction requirements of Gotham's Big Bowl
and Big Play games. It's likely that Santa found himself running behind
on Christmas night. The earlier he got started at your house, the more
likely you were to have a completed game. Squeals of disbelief filled the
air of those households lucky enough to receive a Big Bowl on Christmas
morning – at least one that was already assembled. Boys who had to punch
out and painstakingly assemble the many pieces of the Bowl on Christmas
morning may have uttered less optimistic adjectives. Was the Big Bowl
worth the extraordinary effort? For most boys it was. The sheer scale of
the game made Christmas memories for a lifetime.

And once again, Christmas Day was the perfect time to receive an
electric football game. Two college all-star games would be on television
later in the day (around dinner time) and two professional playoff games
were on television the very next day, including the AFL Championship.

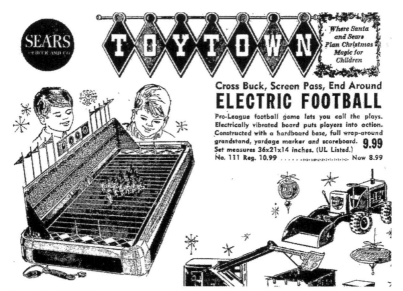

Sears put the G-1500 into heavy newspaper ad rotation in December of 1965. The art for the ad, unfortunately, didn't provide an accurate rendition of the game (common for the time). *The Oneonta Star (NY)*, page 8, December 18, 1965.

Any boy receiving a Big Play game – at least a boy who didn't have the game on his list – would have been puzzled for sure. While on the box the game said "electric," the only electric part of it was the battery-operated Selectro-matic Quarterback. What someone ended up with was a very cool looking stadium structure surrounding a game board where nothing really happened. Some levers could be pulled, and the ball marker could be moved up and down the field, but otherwise nothing happened. The game didn't generate excitement for very long – especially the basically naked Sears Big Play version.

While Sunday turned into a tremendous day for pro football fans, for the AFL it had turned into something much less than the league had hoped. The AFL had chosen December 26 for its championship because no NFL games were scheduled for that day. It was supposed to be an AFL day all the way. But when the Colts and Packers ended up with identical 10-3-1 records, an NFL playoff game was needed to decide the Western Conference title. So the AFL now had to share the day and the television with the NFL, who would play first at 2:00 p.m. EST. Adding to the drama of the NFL game was the fact that Colts running back Tom Matte was forced into quarterback duty because of injuries to Johnny Unitas and back-up quarterback Gary Cuozzo. Thanks to Matte's valiant performance, the Colt's led 10-7 with just over two minutes to go. That's when the game entered the realm of NFL infamy. Packer's kicker Don Chandler kicked a 22-yard field goal, which appeared to be wide right by several feet. But the lone official under the goal post called it good, and the Packers went on to win the game in overtime 13-10. (Although the NFL never admitted a mistake was made on Chandler's field goal, the league increased the height of the uprights by 10 feet for 1966.)

Compared to the NFL's drama in Green Bay, the Bills 23-0 victory over the Chargers made the AFL Championship a bit of a snooze fest, unless you were a Bills fan. New York City area Arbitron television ratings confirmed this devastating fact. During the half hour when the two games overlapped – thanks to overtime – the Packers-Colts game garnered a 26.5 rating. The Bills and Chargers turned in a meager 1.7 rating (an Arbitron rating equaled the percentage of sampled homes tuned into to a given program). Regardless of anyone's rooting interests, college, NFL or AFL, the weekend of games would certainly have left electric football games buzzing into the holiday week.

Another big football television weekend was on the horizon, but before that got under way, the NFL announced some significant television news of its own. The league signed a new two-year television contract with CBS. It would pay the league $18.8 million in 1966 and 1967, which averaged out to $1.2 million for each of the 15 NFL teams. With the package totaling $37.6 million, it was the largest sports contract in television history, just eclipsing AFL's deal with ABC. Surprisingly, Rozelle didn't get everything he wanted, as CBS passed on a commissioner-proposed series of nationally televised Monday night football games. But Rozelle did get his foot in the door. CBS agreed to do three national nighttime broadcasts during the 1966 season.

As the year came to an end on Friday, December 31, a glorious three-day football weekend was just kicking off. At 2:00 p.m. ABC would televise the Gator Bowl from Jacksonville, which would end just in time for football fans to switch over to NBC for the 4:30 p.m. East-West Shrine game kickoff. And whether someone chose an early or late New Year's Eve bedtime, there were ten hours of televised football to absorb the very next day.

Tudor's answer to the Big Bowl. The game was made for and sold exclusively by Montgomery Ward in 1966. (Photo by Earl Shores.)

# 18 1966 A YEAR OF CHANGES

J anuary 1 of 1966 was an extraordinary day for football fans, as the tension built with each game that was played and televised. In the Cotton Bowl, second-ranked Arkansas lost to LSU 14-7. Then top-ranked and two-touchdown favorite Michigan State was upset by UCLA in the Rose Bowl 14-12. This put all eyes on NBC and the prime time Orange Bowl game, where No. 3 Nebraska would play No. 4 Alabama. Since Michigan State and Arkansas had both posted New Year's Day losses, it was likely that the Orange Bowl winner would end up as the new national champion. Alabama led 24-7 at the half and never really looked back in their 39-28 win. In just a few days the final Associated Press poll would declare Alabama the nation's best team.

Saturday's events provided a great lead-in for Sunday's NFL Championship game. Green Bay even had real football weather – three inches of morning snow, which gave way to a numbing afternoon rain. By the end of the game, the players were so covered with mud it was hard to tell one team from the other. It was the kind of day that should have been etched into football mythology. But it was not to be. Although the Packers held only a slim 13-12 lead at the start of the second half, the Browns never scored again. And the 23-12 final score actually made the Browns look good. As the Packers celebrated their third NFL title in four years, the Brown's legendary running back Jim Brown walked off an NFL field for the final time.

By the time the NFL's all-stars lined up for the Pro Bowl on the following Sunday, the 1965 draft war between the two leagues had mostly been settled. And the clear winner was the NFL. Of the 111 players drafted by both leagues, the signing score was NFL 79-AFL 28, with four players undecided. The score was made even more impressive by the fact that the NFL signed 14 of its 16 first-round picks, including the No. 1 overall pick in both leagues, Texas linebacker Tommy Nobis. (He signed with the NFL despite a plea from orbiting Gemini 7 Astronaut Frank Borman to sign with the AFL Houston Oilers.) It was the expansion Atlanta Falcons who landed Nobis, but he wasn't cheap. Following the rookie windfall standard set by Namath the season before, Nobis's three-year deal was reported to be in the $700,000 range. Beyond Nobis, the Packers paid each of its top two draft picks more than $600,000. Once again, the players were the big winners in the draft. The combined sum of the twenty most lucrative rookie contracts from both leagues totaled more than $7 million.

So it was a less than happy group of AFL owners who gathered in Houston for the league's annual meeting on January 15. Although league attendance reached an all-time high in 1965, the AFL owners were smarting from the drubbing by the NFL in the draft, the NFL hijacking the television ratings on the day of the AFL Championship game, and the embarrassment of losing the Atlanta franchise. The object of their ire was AFL Commissioner Foss. Beyond the grudges festering between Foss and several key owners, there was league-wide perception that the commissioner was distant and a weak leader. The four-day meeting ended with the owners putting on their best "All Is Well in the AFL" faces. But an unpleasant undercurrent was engulfing AFL executives. Commissioner Foss had to go – the sooner, the better.

It was no coincidence that on the same day the AFL meeting started, the city of New Orleans initiated a public relations blitz about a new retractable roof stadium called the "Superdome." In reality the stadium was still a plastic model sitting on a conference-room table, but with the NFL and AFL both promising to expand, it was just the kind of exquisite bait needed for landing a professional football team. A lot of the "conditions" required for the stadium to be constructed – like the donation of 100 acres of city real estate – depended upon New Orleans landing an NFL team. Still, it couldn't hurt the city to catch the attention of the AFL, seeing that the AFL was having an official league meeting just a few hundred miles to the west.

It was in this post-Christmas period that Norman took his final pitch to John Carney and Larry Kent. What Norman unveiled, to Kent and Carney's complete amazement, was a miniature NFL. Standing before the NFL Properties' execs was a set of Tudor electric football figures painted in fine detail to look like the teams of the NFL. Lee had carefully painted players wearing both the home and away uniforms of each team; he even had the players wearing numbers corresponding to well-known stars of the NFL. The plan was simple, yet stunning. Tudor would make NFL electric football games that included a pair of hand-painted NFL teams. And beyond the teams in the game, all the teams of the NFL would be available from Tudor by mail. If a boy's favorite team didn't come in the game, he could get the figures from Tudor. Something else he could get from Tudor

Tudor won over NFL Properties with painted 3-D players. Lee Payne had been working on the concept since 1962. His refinement of the process paid off with an NFL license for Tudor. 1962 Tudor sales catalog. (Collection of Norman Sas.)

would be a miniature number sheet in matching team colors. With some basic scissor work and a bit of rubbing, an NFL team, including favorite star players, could be created.

This was exactly the type of special idea Carney was looking for. In fact, Carney was bowled over by the concept. The visual impact of the painted players was enormous, yet there was something more to the miniature team concept. It personalized the NFL. A boy could root for his favorite team on Sunday afternoon and play with that team all week long. Eddie Gluck may have had a relationship with Larry Kent and Sears, but he didn't have a miniature NFL. The closest Gotham had come was the paper jersey Martian players of 1961-62. After that failure, Gotham's designers focused more on electric football stadium development than on player development. Gluck had no match for hand-painted NFL teams, not that he was even going to get a chance to counter Tudor. Kent and Carney already knew Tudor had better games and better distribution. And Norman was offering them an NFL product like no other. In their marketing crystal ball, Kent and Carney foresaw boys in far reaches of the U.S. being indoctrinated to the NFL right in their own living rooms. Norman was given the electric football contract on the spot. Commissioner Rozelle would soon hear of the NFL's newest licensee.

Norman and Lee were elated. They had done what they set out to do – win the NFL. Yet even though they had the contract, the reality of it was far from simple. What they had won was the NFL electric football license

Gotham's NFL Big Bowl. Sold only by Sears, it came with 44 players. (Photo by Roddy Garcia.)

for 1967. Gotham would still have the NFL for 1966. Tudor wouldn't be able to unveil its NFL line until the Toy Fair of 1967. Which was a good thing, because there were a lot of details that still needed to be figured out.

"We wanted the NFL so bad," said Sas, "that we never gave any thought to the cost of creating the players." Now that Tudor had the license, they had to figure out how to get the painted players into production. Norman was pretty sure he could get them produced; yet the profitability of producing the figures was a question mark. "I had a friend who was importing painted items from Hong Kong," said Sas. "He gave me the name of someone who he thought could do our players."

At the NFL owners meeting in mid-February, the television gravy train continued to fill the leagues' trough as CBS paid $2 million for each of the 1966 and 1967 NFL Championship games. This $2 million payout set a new television record for a single-day sports event, and combining this $4 million with the two-year regular season deal CBS signed just after Christmas meant the network was paying $41.6 million for two years of NFL television rights. Thanks to CBS, the NFL was now the most expensive sports property on television. And it wasn't too much of a stretch to say that CBS's millions confirmed that the NFL was the most popular sport on television.

The league was pretty popular in person, too, as another NFL season attendance record was set. Over 4.6 million people paid to see an NFL game. Fifty-seven of 98 games sold out, stadium capacity averaged 83%, and the average game attendance was 47,286. Most importantly, all 14 teams made money in 1965. With the help of these stats, as well as a presentation by Harris Poll head honcho Lou Harris, Commissioner Rozelle convinced the owners to lift the total television blackout that occurred on the day an NFL team played at home. In a poll taken by Mr. Harris, fans said they would still come out to the stadium even if another NFL game was on the tube the same day. So CBS was given the go-ahead to broadcast an NFL game into "home game" cities. Many owners felt attendance was sure to decline, but they went along with Rozelle anyway. The commissioner did have a pretty good track record with the television issue.

Just a few weeks later the Toy Fair opened in New York. Toy sales had set another record in 1965, and many large retailers including Sears, Ward, and Woolworth also set sales records. So there was an optimistic feeling in the hallways at 200 Fifth Avenue, probably more optimistic than in a number of years. Mattel showed up with 25 new toys in its line, while Eldon had a complete new line of sports action games, including Willie Mays Baseball, Bob Cousy Basketball, and Don Carter Bowling. A six-page color layout in *Playthings* was helping to introduce the new Eldon games to the toy world.

Many toy makers came to the show heavily mortgaged in the officially licensed items of a new television show that had its premiere just days before the AFL owners met in January. Those who rolled the dice on the comic book-inspired *Batman* series were now bouncing off their Fifth Avenue showroom walls. The show was an instant hit and turning into something more – a cultural phenomena. Bat-mania was spreading around the country. But the campy on-screen tension between Batman and the Penguin was nothing compared to the real-life tension that existed between Norman Sas and Eddie Gluck. There may have been brave faces in the Gotham showroom, but there was no way around the fact the distinctive NFL shield would not be part of the company line in the future.

Gotham seemed to be simply limping away from the NFL. There were no full-page ads in *Playthings*, only a small photo and two paragraphs announcing that the Big Play would be one of the prizes in a "U.S. Historic Jingle Contest" being run by the Sealright Company. Sealright made containers for dairy products – they also published a comic book explaining the "story of milk." So it was in those comic books and in the dairy aisle where the contest and the Big Play would be promoted. Somehow the Sealright campaign didn't carry the weight of an NFL player making a department store appearance with a Big Play under his arm.

Besides the Big Play, the Yankee Stadium G-1500 and the smaller G-890 game filled out Gotham's NFL line. Gluck, unfortunately, couldn't use his Sears-exclusive NFL Big Bowl to pump up buyers for this final Toy Fair with the NFL license.

**tudor**

No. 500
Box Size: 27" x 16½" x 2⅛"
½ Doz. Ctn. Wt. 25 Lbs.
110 Volts, A.C. Only
$8.00 Retail

# *Tru·action.* *Electric* Football

Tudor's No. 500 game as pictured in the 1966 Tudor sales catalog. It was the first time that Lee's singe-piece 3-D players made it into the catalog. 1966 Tudor sales catalog. (Collection of Norman Sas.)

Over in the Tudor showroom, a quiet glow exuded from Norman and Lee. That's because they both envisioned a very different looking showroom come next year. But for now, they had to keep the NFL news to themselves. If all went as planned, there would be plenty of profit and publicity in the not-so-distant future.

What Tudor brought to the Fair, at least in electric football, was very basic. There was the "best-selling" No. 500, and larger Sports Classic No. 600 model. Both games were presented in color in the Tudor catalog, which made it the first catalog with color photos of Lee's now not so new one-piece players. What wasn't shown in the catalog or on display at the Fair was Tudor's answer to the Big Bowl. After Gluck's two-tiered "monster-piece" appeared in the Sears catalog, Ward asked Tudor if it could make a Ward-exclusive game that had the same kind of awe-inspiring catalog presence. Lee had managed to design an accordion-like cardboard grandstand structure that, when stretched, went almost two-thirds of the way around the large No. 600 game board. It didn't have a second deck, but it would come with 120 interchangeable scoreboard team names covering both college and professional teams. AFL and NFL teams were cleverly represented by only their city names.

Despite the lack of changes in the electric football line, it was a very important Toy Fair for Tudor. Over a half dozen new items were on display, including two new hockey games, both of which were the product of a new manufacturing arrangement with Canadian table hockey giant Munro Games Ltd. (Munro hockey games were a Sears catalog staple.) There was also a trio of colorful easy-to-play Snap-Action games, which were aimed at the pre-electric age group. To promote these new games Tudor had run a single-page "So What's New?" ad in *Playthings*, and curious toy buyers found many ways to have fun during a tour of the showroom. Of course, the Toy Fair bottom line is business – serious business. And in 1966 a man walked into the Tudor suite hoping to land a major role in the company's forthcoming NFL line.

"I met Norman at the Toy Fair," said Albert Sung, who was the president of the Hong Kong-based MCX International Ltd. Through his company, Sung could set up the entire manufacturing process for Tudor's new NFL players – from molding and painting to shipping to Brooklyn. Sung listened as Sas explained the basics of what he would need. In Sung's mind, painted NFL players could be done. It would be a challenge. Coming up with a meticulous production schedule, and then following it carefully, would be key to getting all the figures delivered on time (in 1966 there was no FedEx to bail anyone out). Sas was pretty sure he had found the right man for the job. He felt comfortable talking with Sung, and it turned out the feeling was mutual. Sung was certain he wanted to be involved with Tudor. Before the meeting ended, Sung was

The business card of the man who played a major role in bringing Tudor's miniature NFL to life. (Courtesy of Albert Sung; collection of Earl Shores.)

given sample players to take to Hong Kong and have painted. If Norman and Lee liked these samples, then Tudor and MCX had a deal.

While the NFL was coming to life, in miniature at least, the family feud brewing in the AFL finally boiled over. In early April, Commissioner Joe Foss resigned at the owners' request. The new AFL Commissioner was Oakland General Manager and Coach Al Davis, who didn't hesitate in setting a tone for his tenure. "My goal is to make the AFL the best league in pro football," said Davis on April 8, the day he was named commissioner. At a New York press conference a few weeks later Davis said that, despite the rumblings of some other AFL owners, he was not interested in a merger with the NFL. Rather he was ready to take on the senior league in every aspect of the game. In summing his position up succinctly Davis said, "We'll do anything we think necessary."

Not long after Davis's declaration, Norman received the painted sample players from Sung in the mail. He and Lee were pleased with Sung's product – the players definitely captured the realism Tudor wanted. Sung was given the O.K. to move forward with laying the groundwork in Hong Kong for making the players. He also started working on a production schedule which would let Norman and Lee know when the final brass masters and paint schemes needed to be completed.

The month of May saw the NFL owners attend to some unspoken business regarding goal posts (see the Colts-Packers playoff game). Starting in the 1966 season, all goal posts would have uprights extending 20 feet above the crossbar. This doubled the present minimum, with the extra footage of upright soon to be known as the "Baltimore Extension." The new rules additionally mandated that all posts be offset from the goal line and painted bright gold – better to see the uprights against a foggy sky. And instead of a lone official, a pair of officials – one under each upright – would make the call on all future field goals.

In an odd coincidence, the Giants made a significant change to their kicking game the day after the refurbished goal posts were approved. Pete Gogolak became the highest paid kicker in the NFL, signing with the Giants for three years at $32,000 per season. The deal, even at such a price, made sense. During the 1965 season, Gogolak made 28 of his 46 field goal attempts. The Giants' kicking game, meanwhile, had only made 4 field goals in 28 tries. Gogolak's accuracy would be a huge addition to the Giants' offense. There was just one minor issue with the first soccer-style kicker in professional football. His previous employer was the AFL Buffalo Bills.

Legally, Gogolak had every right to sign with the Giants. He had played out his contract and option with the Bills, so technically he was a free agent. And he certainly wasn't the first player to jump leagues. But despite the animosity between the NFL and AFL, there had been an unspoken agreement that the leagues would not go after each other's star players (star draft picks were a different matter altogether). Both sides feared a signing war that could potentially bankrupt professional football. Though only a kicker, Gogolak had been the AFL's second leading scorer in 1964 and 1965. He was certainly one of the AFL's most valuable players. Still, was the signing of a kicker enough to start the war that every owner feared?

Yes.

Three days after the Gogolak signing, the AFL Chargers made offers to three Giants. Over the coming weeks Commissioner Al Davis would lead the charge on the NFL, claiming to have signed Los Angeles Rams' star quarterback Roman Gabriel for his own Raiders. The Oilers then went after 49ers quarterback John Brodie, offering a reported $750,000. AFL teams bearing six-figure contracts also approached Lions' star Alex Karras and Bears all-pro end Mike Ditka. The interleague war was underway.

Even though these pirated star signings seemed certain to sink professional football into a sea of dollar bills, Lee was at work finishing up Tudor's new players. He was going back to a two-piece design, much like the gorilla players. Because of the extensive paint jobs the players would receive, Tudor needed the body of the players to be made of the hard paint-holding polystyrene plastic. Making a working one-piece polystyrene player was impractical, if not impossible. From a durability standpoint, Tudor might as well make the players out of glass. The vibrating base legs, as well as the player's legs, would be too fragile. So Payne came back to the eight-legged gorilla bases.

He had always liked the vibrating properties of these bases and also liked the green polyethylene against his green fields. It was more realistic. But he was going to make a significant change to the mounting design. Instead of having pegs on the bottom of the players to mount permanently into the green polyethylene base (like the gorilla design), the player would be molded on his own thin rectangular polystyrene base. And this base would have a hole in the center to allow the entire player to slide over a new tooth-like protrusion on the vibrating base. It may sound complicated, but what Payne had created was simple. He had created removable players' bases.

In the conceiving Tudor's NFL players Lee Payne returned to the gorilla design for inspiration. Tudor's new players would consist of polystyrene player and separate green polyethylene base – that would be removable. (Photo by Earl Shores.)

The removable base idea was ingenious for a number of reasons. By not having to mold an entire base to each player, the NFL teams would be cheaper to make. This was good because the labor of painting was already going to add significantly to Tudor's production costs. And the removable bases would also make it cheaper for young NFL fans. A kid could have half a dozen teams but only need two sets of bases. If he felt like playing with a different team, all he had to do was take the bases off one team and put them on another one. But perhaps the biggest change the removable base system made to electric football involved the playing of the game itself. In the past, players who were the best runners often weren't the players who were designed to carry the ball. Many a boy lamented having a team with a guard or tackle figure who could not only run 100 yards in a dead straight line, he ran it in 9.0 seconds flat (electric football scale, that is). Invariably, this same team came with ends and running backs that spun in perfect five-yard diameter circles. If only you could turn your guard into a running back. With Tudor's new base system a kid would be able to do just that. It would be possible to take the best running bases and put them on the team's "money" players. Again, the solution was classic Lee Payne – simple yet elegant with a major impact.

In late May, Eddie Gluck had a different kind of problem to solve at Gotham. His solution was to take a $300,000 second mortgage on his Bronx factory. It wasn't totally out of the ordinary for toy companies to leverage their buildings for the cash needed to make a production run. But Gotham hadn't done any serious advertising in *Playthings* since 1963, and the promotion for Gluck's Big Play, had been lackluster to say the least. If the Big Play really was the most important game Gotham had invented in a decade (and Gluck himself said as much in *Playthings*), was sending out hopeful press releases to small town newspapers really the best the company could do? Or was something more going on at Gotham? The lack of advertising and promotion, when added to the $300,000 second mortgage, seemed to confirm that the company was facing serious financial issues.

With both leagues going after each other's star players, the coming season was shaping up to be a turbulent one. Then on June 6, word leaked out to the press that a truly startling thing was happening. The NFL and AFL were secretly negotiating a merger. While most people speculated that the Gogolak signing spurred these discussions, the merger talks had started back on April 4 with Rozelle's blessing.

These NFL-AFL talks began rather humbly, in a car in an airport parking lot. The car belonged to Cowboys General Manager Tex Schram, who met up with Kansas City Chiefs owner Lamar Hunt during a layover in Dallas. In a scene straight out of a cheap Cold War spy novel, Schram and Hunt sat among a sea of deserted cars making plans to change the world – the football world, that is. The meeting was just the start, as the secret merger talks continued even through the signing wars of May. It turned out that most NFL owners knew of and approved the clandestine encounters between Hunt and Schram. On the other side, however, only a select group of AFL owners were aware the meetings were taking place. It might be reasonable to assume that Commissioner Davis's "fight the NFL" bluster was a smokescreen to allow the negotiations to move forward. But Davis was speaking from his heart. The secret meetings were a secret to the AFL Commissioner.

On June 8 the merger was officially announced. NFL owners voted unanimously to accept it, while the AFL came in with a 7-2 vote. The Jets, and not surprisingly, Al Davis' Raiders were the nay votes. Besides the humiliation of the AFL owners going behind his back, Davis had another reason to object to the merger – Pete Rozelle was going to be commissioner of this new league.

The merger was set to take place incrementally over the next three years, culminating with NFL and AFL merging into one entity with a common schedule in 1970 (this date was chosen largely due to the television commitments of both leagues). But pro football fans wouldn't have to wait until 1970 to get the game they wanted. Starting this season, the winners of the NFL and AFL would play each other for the championship of all of

NFL President Tex Schramm, NFL Commissioner Pete Rozelle, and AFL founder and President Lamar Hunt officially announce the merger of the NFL and AFL during a news conference in New York City on June 8, 1966. ©Bettman/CORBIS

pro football. And soon after this game, the leagues would hold something that, to the owners at least, was perhaps more important than a combined pro football championship – a combined draft of college players. Those outlandish rookie-signing wars would be a thing of the past.

So would the bitter interleague battles over the placement of expansion teams. Under the merger agreement, the NFL would expand first in 1967. The AFL would then get its chance to expand in 1968, with the expansion fee going entirely to the NFL. Also going to the NFL was a $2 million merger fee from each current AFL team. For the privilege of being part of the NFL, the AFL paid $18 million. There would be antitrust issues to discuss with the Justice Department, but with Rozelle at the helm, any major legal problems were sure to be solved. The only losers this day were the players. Their ability to have absolutely crazy money thrown at them had just vanished in the merger maelstrom.

Norman and Lee, like everybody else, were stunned by the merger news. Stunned but elated. It was going to be the biggest sports story of the year, and Tudor was part of it. Finally it was Norman's turn to look like a toy-licensing

A capacity crowd fills the big double-deck stands . .

Players run, pass and receive the ball as defensive team blocks and tackles . .

**NFL Big Bowl Electric Football Game**

EXCLUSIVELY AT SEARS $11.99

Strategically set up your formations, then watch 3-D players click on 36x21-in. field. Vibrating coil beneath keeps your men in action. Kicker-passer throws and boots magnetic ball. 3-man yardage marker and scoreboards keep track of game. Includes pennants, goal posts, 4 magnetic footballs, instructions and NFL plays. Paints and brush for painting players. Steel frame, plastic corners. Cord, coil operate on 110-120-v., 60-cycle AC. UL listed. Partly assembled.
79 N 296L—Shipping weight 12 pounds . . . . . . . . . . . . . . . . . . . . . . . $11.99

Includes 44 players plus paints so you can make 4 different teams

Gotham's NFL Big Bowl was still the most prominent and colorful electric football in the Sears 1966 *Christmas Book* (page 562). ©Sears, Roebuck & Co. 1966.

visionary. By pushing forward with John Carney, Norman aligned Tudor with a sport that was well on its way to being a cultural force in America. Norman had signed on for one league and now had all of professional football.

Actually, Norman had both leagues before the merger. Tudor had owned the electric football rights to the AFL since the Al Dorow/New York Titans promotion back in 1961. And Norman had held onto the rights for a very simple reason: to prevent Eddie Gluck from creating a potential NFL-AFL monopoly. The AFL fee was pretty nominal – Norman viewed it as an insurance policy. But now that the two leagues would eventually become one, Carney and Kent could really have no objections to Tudor creating a miniature AFL.

The summer of 1966 moved forward with Lee continuing to refine the realism of Tudor's NFL. Part of this realism came down to which teams to feature in the new games. Norman and Lee decided that using well-known division rivalries would create the widest appeal in selling the games. The new NFL flagship model (based on the No. 600) would feature the Eastern Division Giants and Browns. These two teams were bitter rivals, and over the previous 15 seasons, they had combined to win the Eastern Division 14 times. It was a brilliant pairing despite the Giants' recent struggles, and it also didn't hurt for a Brooklyn-based company to put its "home" team on a game. Tudor's No. 2 NFL game, a smaller No. 500-sized model, would come with the Colts and Packers. Besides combining to win the Western Division title seven times in the last eight years, these two teams were part of that memorable playoff game back in December that led to the Baltimore extension rule change. Yet the pairing of these two teams might have boiled down to even simpler terms for Norman and Lee – how can we go wrong with a game featuring Bart Starr and Johnny Unitas?

Tudor's final NFL game wasn't quite final yet, but the company interested in selling the game was quite a surprise. Sears had a new toy buyer handling sports games, and Norman had approached him with the idea of putting a Tudor

Ward put Tudor on almost equal footing with the Big Bowl this year, giving the Ward-exclusive No. 600 "accordion" game nearly half of a catalog page. Montgomery Ward 1966 *Christmas Catalog*, page 317. ©Montgomery Ward, Inc. 1966.

NFL electric football game in the 1967 Sears lineup. This game would be a Sears exclusive and a completely new Tudor electric football model. To further entice the Chicago-headquartered retail giant, Norman and Lee would put the Chicago Bears on the new game, although it's likely that some members of the Sears corporate hierarchy wouldn't have completely cast their football loyalties with the "monsters of the Midway." From 1938 to 1960, the Cardinals (now in St. Louis) played in Chicago. Even with the cross-town rivalry five years gone, fan conversion was far from complete. Much to Norman's surprise, Sears said yes. It was another big blow for Eddie Gluck. He had already lost the NFL, and now he would have to share Sears with Tudor's NFL.

A large part of Tudor's realism refinement would come from the NFL Properties' Creative Services office. The purpose of Creative Services was to advise and approve the designs and artwork of any NFL-licensed product. A licensee couldn't just slap an NFL shield on a something and stick it on a shelf. All products had to be reviewed by Creative Services to make sure they had the right color scheme (each NFL team had a league approved uniform color chart), and the appropriate packaging. Within this office was graphic artist and Art Director Michael Gaines, who was working closely with Lee to finalize the uniform designs for Tudor's mini NFL. With the players being so small, reproducing the helmet logos and sleeve striping patterns of many teams was a serious challenge. Not that the designs couldn't be reproduced faithfully. They could if one person, Lee for example, took his time and painted small groups of players over the course of several days. But on the large-scale assembly line Albert Sung was going to oversee in Hong Kong, exact uniforms weren't going to be practical. Some compromises were going to have to be made to make sure the production of the teams was practical and profitable.

Lee and Creative Services were going to have to decide whether Tudor should reproduce things like the Giants' "NY" helmet, the Rams' famous helmet horns, or the Packers' and Browns' triple-stripe sleeve and sock patterns. If these uniform features proved to be beyond the realm of assembly-line practicality, then Lee and Mike Gaines were going to have to come up with acceptable substitute stripes and logos.

While Lee dealt with the creative part of NFL Properties, Norman approached Kent and Carney with the idea of making AFL teams. Tudor already owned the rights, and the merger was being finalized. Didn't it make sense to have all the teams available? It did make sense, even if the NFL Properties hierarchy was less than thrilled. The two leagues would soon be one league, with the operative word being "soon." NFL Properties did not yet control the marketing of the AFL, and Kent had viewed Tudor's team's concept as an exclusive NFL item. If a New York kid bought the Jets instead of the Giants, or a Bay area boy bought the Raiders instead of the 49ers, it was money out of the NFL's pocket. (Actually the money was negligible, it was more the loss to the rival league.)

Norman wasn't really asking permission – he didn't have to. He already had an agreement with Frank Mincolla for the AFL's electric football rights and could do what he wanted. Kent knew this. It was more of a professional courtesy to let NFL Properties know it was going to happen. And it wasn't unprecedented for a company to own both NFL and AFL rights. Rosco-Steele had made both NFL and AFL uniforms for its Johnny Hero figure, Technigraph was still making its eye-catching helmet plaques for NFL and AFL teams, and Sports Specialties had been doing bobbing heads for both leagues since the birth of the AFL. In the long run, having AFL teams was, in fact, promoting the NFL. Kent and Carney swallowed hard, and agreed it was probably a good idea. Lee would soon be in touch with Frank Mincolla to set up the uniform details for nine more teams.

All these summer decisions – which teams would go in the new games, the NFL uniform details, and the addition of the AFL – affected Albert Sung. When player production started in the fall, there would have to be enough Browns, Giants, Packers and Colts to put into all the NFL games Tudor planned to make. And the uniform design instructions he received needed to be practical enough to allow all those Browns, Giants, Packers, and Colts (and all the others teams) to be painted and shipped from Hong Kong to Brooklyn according to the soon-to-be finalized production schedule. Throwing the AFL into to the mix meant that Sung would have a total of 24 different teams to produce – and 24 sets of uniform details to keep track of.

By the time a disenchanted and disgusted Al Davis resigned as AFL commissioner on July 25, Lee was finalizing the new 7" brass masters. Two sets of masters were made, and with five player poses, there were a total of ten brass figures. One complete set was going to Hong Kong with Albert Sung. All of Tudor's NFL players would be the offspring of these figures. The five remaining figures were divided up among the central

Albert Sung took one set of 7" brass masters to Hong Kong. A second set of brass masters was divided up among Lee Payne, Norman Sas, Larry Kent, John Carney, and Pete Rozelle. This is the original 1966 NFL brass master tackle figure that Lee Payne kept for himself. (Collection of Roddy Garcia.)

"players" in the Tudor-NFL relationship. Lee kept the tackle for himself, and Norman got one. The final three went to Larry Kent, John Carney... and Pete Rozelle.

Albert Sung flew back to New York in August to pick up the production set of brass masters and the official instructions and paint chips for each NFL team. For further guidance, Sung also got to look at some teams that Lee had painted using the NFL specifications. Norman and Albert then went over the details of the upcoming production schedule, which would get under way in just a few weeks when Albert returned to Hong Kong. The first step in the schedule was scaling down Lee's brass masters to create production-size masters. Then injection molds would be made from the production masters, and large-scale production of the players would begin. As soon as the players were being produced, Sung would send both painted and unpainted sample players back to Brooklyn. Once Norman approved the players, Sung would move forward with full-scale production of the painted teams. Since the details of the AFL were still being finalized, Sung would receive instructions for these teams during the fall.

August was also the start of the professional football television schedule. With both leagues modifying their blackout rule (allowing the broadcast of a game into a city where a home game was being played), there was going to be a whole lot of professional football on television. In fact, combining the NFL and AFL television schedules together produced a staggering sum – 159 professional football games would be broadcast during the 1966 season. Not only was professional football going to be on the airwaves often – CBS was planning a record 12 double-header Sundays as well three prime time evening broadcasts – it was also getting off to an early start. CBS began televising the NFL preseason on Friday, August 12, the first of four consecutive Friday nights on which the network planned to show preseason football. Friday was typically a big attendance night for Major League Baseball, so the NFL was doing a bit of muscle flexing with its ever-growing popularity. The same could be said of the not-so-accidental ten-week overlap that professional football now had with professional baseball.

Lee Payne and Normans Sas were never totally happy with the Isopad/fiberboard field design. The fields didn't vibrate as well as expected, and sometimes undulated up and down between the Isopads. All of Tudor's electric football fields would be metal in 1967. (Photo by Earl Shores.)

Also reflecting the league's growth was NFL Properties. In early September an Associated Press article about the organization appeared in hundreds of newspapers around the country. Just a few days later the *New York Times* was inspired to tackle pro football licensing in its regular advertising column, talking to both Larry Kent at NFL Properties and AFL licensing agent Frank Mincolla. Kent told the AP and the *Times* pretty much the same thing – that the NFL Properties now had 66 licensees selling team blankets, team sweatshirts, helmet banks, helmet radios, electric football games, and even official NFL children's football outfits. The expected licensing fees for 1966 would exceed $600,000. This was a new record, and a long way from the first year (1963) fee total of $150,000. Kent made sure the NFL Properties mantra made it into the article. "Our job is not really to make money for the league," said Kent; "The promotion is worth more than the money we earn." But surely the owners liked the extra money. And Kent's dreams of significant profits were coming true.

It was no accident that the *Times* was talking to Kent. In just a few days, the NFL season would start – and so would NFL Properties' biggest ever promotion. The September 16 edition of *Life* magazine was going to have a spread of 13 consecutive full-color pages advertising the "Selected Official Training Table Foods" of the NFL. (It was also going to have a nearly naked Sophia Loren on the cover.) Kent had rounded up seven of the biggest names in food manufacturing – General Foods, Nabisco Cereals, Pillsbury, Heinz, Kraft, Hormel, and Del Monte – and convinced them to pay NFLP $15,000 for each product advertised in the *Life* layout. The fee also entitled the companies to put a special "NFL Selected Official Training Table Food" logo on the packaging of each item. The Training Table Food program actually started in 1962, with 34 bakeries in NFL cities making Official NFL Training Table Bread. Now in 1966, grocery shoppers around the country would find Tang, Birds Eye vegetables, Nabisco cereals, Pillsbury pancakes, Kraft cheeses, Hormel chili, Heinz ketchup, Heinz soups, as well as Del Monte raisins and prunes – all displaying the official NFL "SOTTF" symbol on their packaging. In all, it was estimated that 1.2 billion food packages would carry the new logo. Like much at NFL Properties, the Training Table program had come a long way.

September marked the kickoff of NFL Properties' biggest ever promotion – the NFL Selected Official Training Table Foods program. *Life*, September 16, 1966.

On the AFL licensing side, Frank Mincolla had to be thrilled to see the AFL merchandising program on equal footing with the NFL – at least on the pages of the *New York Times*. Mincolla was coy in not giving out any dollar figures to the paper, but he did claim that the AFL had 40 licensees for 1966.

Both the NFL and AFL started their seasons on the second weekend of September. As usual, the AFL got underway first with a nationally televised Friday night contest between Namath's Jets and the league's newest franchise, the Miami Dolphins. The expansion Dolphins played surprisingly well in the 19-14 loss. Namath, who was recovering from a knee injury, didn't see action until the second half and struggled to make an impact on the game.

Kicking off on Saturday night was the NFL, enticing the nation's television viewers with a rematch of the Western Conference championship between the Packers and Colts. Besides the competition on the field, the NFL was in a serious competition on the television as Bart Starr and Johnny Unitas went head-to-head with the Miss America Pageant on NBC. The 24-3 beating the Colts took on the field was just about equal to the beating the NFL took in the Nielsen ratings (in the New York City area Miss America won 39.1 to 8.1).

Over the next week *Life* would deliver Ms. Loren's Venus-like visage and the NFL Training Table promotion to millions of U.S. mailboxes. Fighting for space in many of those same mailboxes was a Sears or Ward Christmas catalog. Between *Life* and Sears, Larry Kent had to be feeling pretty good. Gotham's NFL Big Bowl was still the headline electric football game for the country's largest retailer, taking up almost half of page 562. Filling out Sears full-color sports action game page were Gotham's NFL G-1500 and the smaller G-890. A new Gotham game, Pro League Baseball, gave the company four of the six games on the page. But not returning to Sears this year was the NFL Big Play. Eddie Gluck was hurt by this exclusion. It added to his mounting disappointment over losing the NFL.

Kent could even feel good this year looking at the Ward catalog because he knew he was seeing the future of electric football for the NFL. And it looked fantastic. Taking up the top third of the Ward electric football page was the now not-so-secret Tudor "accordion" No. 600 model. Advertised with a subtle tweak at the Big Bowl – "when the game's over the grandstand folds easily for storage" – the new stadium looked impressive ringing the No. 600 game board. It still didn't make quite the impression that the Big Bowl did, but if Kent wanted NFL games with a stadium, he knew he could have them. The Tudor No. 500 model assumed its usual second-string spot, getting slotted just below its big brother.

Having an all-NFL Sears page was still just a dream for Kent, although more NFL items were creeping into both catalogs. A line of NFL Punt, Pass, and Kick books, including titles such as *Heroes of the NFL* and *The Big Play*, were in the children's book section in both Sears and Ward. Just a few pages away in the Ward catalog was one of NFL Films' earliest ventures: NFL team highlight reels for a battery-operated 8mm projector (it was sold on the same page as Kenner's Easy Show Projector). Outside of Sears, another long-held Kent idea had now come to fruition. One of Kent's innovations with his previous employer was the Roy Rogers "Corral," an area of a department store that was devoted singularly to Roy Rogers' items. Most cities throughout the NFL now had a department store with an official NFL Team Shop. In Cleveland, the Higbee's Team Shop carried nothing but Browns' merchandise, while Saks in New York carried Giants items. Throughout the season, NFL players would make appearances in the shops to help promote NFL merchandise.

As U.S. mailmen tested their shoulder muscles with bags full of the thickest Christmas catalogs ever delivered, Albert Sung worked in Hong Kong scaling down Lee's brass masters to production size. The masters were seven inches tall, and the production players were scheduled to be an inch and a half tall. Reducing the players, as before, required a pantographic machine, which "traced" the original masters and cut smaller scaled models using a separate arm. "The masters were cut down three times," said Sung. "Each time we had to measure the model and make corrections before going on to the next scale." It was a painstaking process that required numerous trials, but Sung finally got the production-size figures he liked. The injection molds for producing the thousands of future players could be made.

While Sung worked overseas, Lee continued to put in long hours in Brooklyn. As a result, another major change was in order for Tudor's electric football line – all of the company's large games would come with a metal field.

"We were never happy with how the fiberboard field vibrated," said Lee. "Finally we got some steel thin enough and strong enough for the large frame." Lee also maximized the strength of the metal by rolling the edge of the field over and riveting it to the frame. Norman and Lee were confident the new design would stand up to the rigors of shipping and be the "truest" vibrating large electric football game ever made. Also receiving final touches was Tudor's new Sears NFL game. It was based on the No. 600 template, with a field and frame sized between the No. 500 and No. 600 models. The new "midsize" model would use Lee's new metal field and frame design.

**Triple-action 8mm Film Projector**

Both Sears and Ward were selling battery-operated 8mm projectors that included official NFL highlight films. Sears 1966 *Christmas Book*, page 541. ©Sears, Roebuck & Co. 1966.

Another concept that Norman and Lee weren't completely happy with was the accordion grandstand that was now being used on the Ward No. 600 game. It was expensive to produce, and the folded cardboard was turning out to be much more fragile than expected. And truth be told, the game was difficult to set up. Not as challenging as a Big Bowl but more challenging than any previous Tudor model. Norman and Lee wanted realism, but both agreed that on future models, simpler would be better – at least in terms of grandstands. For the last two years, Tudor's Racing game had come with a Lee Payne-designed flat clip-on cardboard grandstand. It was less expensive to make, easy to set up, and the wear and tear it accumulated through repeated uses was minimal. Lee was sure he could transfer the clip-on concept to electric football. It would be one more item to add to his ever-expanding to-do list.

The final piece of the NFL-AFL merger fell into place on October 21, when Congress passed a bill exempting the leagues from antitrust action.

This landmark was quickly followed by another groundbreaking NFL event on Halloween night. Before a national television audience, the Cardinals beat the Bears 24-17 in St. Louis's newly opened and packed to the arched rooftop Busch Stadium. An NFL game on Halloween wasn't a particularly unique event, but this year October 31 fell on a Monday...Monday night football had been born. The very next day, with the buzz of the game still making the rounds at the office water cooler, the NFL awarded a team to New Orleans. This unnamed team was scheduled to start play in 1967, even though an owners group didn't currently exist. Whoever won ownership of the new team was going to have to move quickly in the coming months.

**NFL Electric Football ..
36x21-in. gridiron**

2 full teams of 3-D players plus a separate kicker-passer meet on vibrating gridiron. 2 magnetic footballs, 3-man yardage marker, goal posts, plays and instructions. Steel-framed hardboard. UL listed, 110-120-v., 60-c. AC.
Shipping weight 12 pounds.
79 N 301L. . . . . . . . . . . $9.99

Sears made the Gotham NFL G-1500 a regular part of their December newspaper advertisements. Sears 1966 *Christmas Book*, page 562. ©Sears, Roebuck & Co. 1966.

A group moving quickly now were the NFL and AFL owners, who met jointly in early November to decide the date and site of the new championship game (the game was already being called the "Super Bowl"). The date and site of the new joint player draft also needed to be decided. It was quite a change from past Novembers, the traditional draft month for both leagues, when acrimonious accusations and ferocious finger-pointing between the NFL and AFL seemed to reach a zenith. While the exchanges in this meeting were more cordial, the only decision made was that the joint draft would take place on January 31.

By this time Sung had gotten the injection molds up and running and the first production players had reached Brooklyn. Along with the players, Sung had sent word that he would need the final team uniform designs by the end of December. Although Sung had the NFL paint chips, the reason the team designs weren't final was simple.

"Once the players were finished, the figures were so small that some of the uniform standards had to give," said Sung referring specifically to sleeve striping and helmet logos. "For production, we had to simplify the logos to a dot, or an olive, or something." Norman and Lee were very pleased with the players but agreed that changes had to be made. And it was important that Sung and Lee were on the same page when Lee started painting the NFL players he would photograph for the Toy Fair sales catalogs. Even with the unveiling of the new teams still a long way away, Norman and Lee knew they didn't want the teams in the catalog looking different from the teams the kids would actually receive in the games. The kids would know the difference.

So over the next couple of weeks, with input from Mike Gaines at NFL Creative Services, the final uniform designs were completed. For some teams, there were no changes. The Colts horseshoe and the Bears "C" could easily be replicated, and with a little more effort the Rams "horns" and the Eagles "wings." But for complex logos like white and green "G" on the Green Bay helmet, a simple green oval would have to do (in production terms it was an "olive;" also getting an olive, albeit a red one, was San Francisco). Another logo getting simplified was the Giants famous "NY," which would be represented by two perpendicular lines. The standard came down to what could realistically be done with one or two brushstrokes of the same color paint. Sung didn't want the production line to get bogged down on one part of the player.

Tudor had also been getting uniform input from Frank T. Mincolla Associates. Lee's hand-painted prototype AFL players received quick approval from an awestruck Mincolla, and a set of AFL paint chips and uniform instructions were now on their way to Hong Kong. Norman hadn't come up with an exact figure yet, but he knew the run of AFL teams would be smaller than the NFL. Mincolla had few complaints about a smaller production run. He was just happy that the AFL was included.

In the selling of electric football, Ward had started in October by putting the No. 500 in heavy ad rotation. Sears waited until almost November to start using electric football in its ads, offering the NFL G-1500 for $9.99. During a special November sale, Ward dropped the No. 500 to $3.49, giving the retailer a chance to compete with the numerous discounters who were selling the game for under $4. Throughout the month, Sears continued to give the G-1500 scores of ad appearances, often pairing the game on the page with Gotham's Pro League Baseball game. By Thanksgiving Day it was hard to find a toy ad that didn't have an electric football game in it. Sears often had the G-1500 as the headline item, with a picture that was larger and more detailed than all the other toys on the page. Ward wasn't quite as generous with the space it gave electric football (Tudor's No. 500) but made up for it with volume. In terms of sheer numbers, Ward had run more ads promoting electric football than Sears.

Gluck still had the NFL, and for 1966 he also had a redesigned baseball game and a brand new Pass-N-Shoot basketball game. The latter game was enormous. Using the G-1500 frame and spinning metal players, it was like a combination of table hockey and Bas-Ket. Since basketball was Gluck's favorite sport, it's no surprise that the game was highly detailed, including a large grandstand and transparent plastic backboards. A lot of effort went into the details of the game (and probably much of Gotham's second mortgage). With these two new games, and a final Christmas selling season with the NFL license, it was an ideal time for a well-funded ad campaign supporting the Gotham line. In taking a hard look at Gotham in 1966, it could be said that serious promotion was something the company desperately needed.

Instead, Gluck sent out another deluge of hopeful press releases to newspapers around the country. Again, the takers were mostly small publications looking for filler over the Thanksgiving holiday. While it was mentioned that the NFL "sponsored" an electric football game, the name of the company who sold the game wasn't. In one published version, the new Pass-N-Shoot game was even described as the brainchild of former pro basketball star Eddie Gluck. But just who Gluck worked for or what company he owned was never divulged. Also not to be found was any mention of the Big Play game. At this crucial juncture in Gotham's history, was press-release promotion really the best the company could do?

Luckily for Gluck, Sears made the G-1500 a hard-to-miss item over the holiday, although sometimes the ads gave the shopper a "Your Choice" for $10.99: football, hockey, or pinball. Ward showed off the No. 500 at every chance, even giving the game "first item" status by placing it in the top left corners of their advertisements.

As the year and the football season headed into their final weeks, it was clear that 1966 had been a momentous year for pro football. The sport had nonstop publicity, and television was confirming its ever-growing popularity. Nielsen ratings for the NFL were up 14% from the year before with over 8.5 million television sets being tuned into the league each Sunday. Ratings for AFL games were the same as 1965 (about 4.1 million viewers each Sunday), but the Jets gained on the Giants. Both teams commanded more than a 30% share of the New York area television audience whenever they played. The most impressive ratings, and most exciting to NFL officials, were from the prime time games. Nielsen reported that the Halloween night Cardinals-Bears game drew an almost 40% share of the national television audience, while Arbitron – whose ratings come from phone sample surveys – reported that 42% of all television sets turned on Thanksgiving night were tuned into the Cowboys-Browns game. And still to come was the biggest game of the season.

The date and place of the NFL-AFL Championship game was finally decided in early December. Los Angeles was the winning city, with the game scheduled for Sunday, January 15 in the Coliseum. It's hard to imagine a city having only six weeks to prepare for a Super Bowl. Today most Super Bowl cities get at least five years of prep time. It would also be unheard of today for two different television networks to end up with the broadcast rights to football's ultimate game. But that's what happened in 1967. Both CBS (the NFL network) and NBC (the AFL network) bought the rights to the game for $1 million apiece. CBS was not very happy. As a matter of fact, they felt they were being played for suckers. The network had already paid $2 million for the NFL Championship game – a game that was now the second most important game of the season. And then they had to put up an extra million to get the Super Bowl. CBS demanded a rebate. They didn't get it.

On the weekend of December 17 and 18, both leagues finished their seasons. It was a busy television weekend too, with four pro games plus the Bluebonnet Bowl being broadcast nationwide. Saturday's schedule had a 1:00 p.m. AFL game, a 4:00 p.m. NFL game, with the Bluebonnet Bowl on for good measure at 2:15 p.m. The Western Division of both leagues had been decided with the Packers and Kansas City Chiefs both heading to their respective league championship games. Television's early Saturday AFL game could decide the Eastern Division – if the Patriots beat the Jets, they were champs. And by coincidence, the televised NFL game could decide that league's Eastern Division. If the Browns beat the Cardinals, then Dallas was champion. By the end of the day, only the NFL had been decided. Cleveland routed the Cardinals 38-10. In the AFL, the Jets upset the Patriots 38-28. Boston would have to hope Denver could beat the Bills on Sunday.

A Montgomery Ward toy ad featuring slots cars and Tudor electric football. *San Antonio Express*, page 9-E, December 1, 1966.

The Bills-Broncos game from Buffalo was the nationally televised AFL game on Sunday. NBC was clairvoyant in this decision, as the game had been on the network's television schedule since September. So the members of the Patriots got to watch their playoff hopes disappear live on TV, right before their eyes. Denver never made a game of it, losing 38-21.

Sears and Ward continued to push electric football in their advertising throughout December. Many other retailers were doing the same thing with the No. 500 hovering around the $4 price point, while Sears kept the G-1500 around the $10 mark. Toys overall were doing well in 1966. Sales were heading for another record despite higher prices outside of electric football. Other popular items this year were scaled-down pool tables (made by Tudor, Munro, and Gotham), and monster-size slot car sets by Strombecker and Eldon. Some these layouts had over 30 feet of track and would completely fill a 4' x 8' train platform. Ranging in price from $30-$50, these sets were quite an investment too. And it was really no surprise that many of them were put on "super sale" as Christmas got near. Also discounted during the final shopping week before Christmas was the

The Montgomery Ward Tudor "accordion" No. 600 game as it would have looked on Christmas morning. (Photo by Earl Shores.)

G-1500. Some Sears stores were selling the game for less than $7. By this point Ward was discounting its version of the Big Bowl, giving the Tudor accordion No. 600 model a $9.88 price.

Again, as in 1965, one of the most shocking developments was that the Big Bowl never appeared in a Sears Christmas ad. Perhaps it didn't need to be advertised because it was selling just fine. But if that were the case, if the Big Bowl had been a significant seller, it's unlikely that Gotham would have lost the NFL.

Christmas came on a Sunday in 1966, and, as a result, not a single professional football game was played during the entire holiday weekend. The AFL Championship game, which had originally been scheduled for Monday the 26th, was moved to create an AFL-NFL Championship double-header on Sunday, January 1. It was moved in the spirit of cooperation...and profit. Despite this timing, it was again an ideal year to find an electric football game under the tree. The Blue-Gray All-Star game and the Sun Bowl were played and televised on Saturday, so it wasn't a weekend barren of football. And unquestionably the profile of pro football had risen to new heights in American culture – or at least to the height of the breakfast or dinner table. A Sears Big Bowl or a Ward accordion No. 600 could easily produce a lifetime of Christmas morning wonder. (One of the authors can speak from experience, having found a Big Bowl dominating his family's tiny living room in 1966.)

No football was scheduled until the following Saturday, making five days where electric football games would have to vibrate along without the spark of televised football to enhance interest in the toy. But what a football bonanza the weekend was going to be. Three games were being televised on Saturday, December 31 – the Cotton Bowl, the Gator Bowl, and the East-West Shrine game. The collegiate lineup would provide ample warm-up for a professional football Sunday afternoon unlike any ever seen.

1966 had become the most important year in professional football history. From television ratings, to training table pancakes, to advertisers body-blocking each other for Super Bowl commercial time, professional football was the "it" sport. It was the sport with the buzz, the one that major U.S. corporations were trying to align themselves with. And it was no accident. Both Rozelle and Kent had been working for this type of acceptance and recognition since 1960. With Rozelle in charge of the newly merged NFL, the sky seemed to be the limit for professional football.

But the ride was over for Eddie Gluck. He had climbed on the NFL bandwagon back when it was made mostly of cardboard and rubber bands, and now it was a sleek silver jet airliner...with someone else sitting in his seat. That someone was Norman Sas. The NFL never brought Gluck the golden football he was looking for. While the NFL G-1500 was a groundbreaking item, and still a decent-selling game, neither the Big Bowl nor the Big Play turned into the type of items Gluck needed to oust Tudor from the top spot in the sports action market. And in the entry level, the G-890 never competed very well with Tudor's No. 500 in terms of price. First time electric football buyers were usually looking for bargains not NFL logos. If Gluck couldn't catch Tudor with the NFL, what chance did he have without it?

So as the league and NFL Properties taxied to the runway of 1967 and future riches, all Gluck could do was stand at the gate and watch.

CATALOG 67

tudor.

Lee Payne created the distinctive cover for Tudor's 1967 sales catalog using metal master football players. There was no need for any text – the photo said it all. (Personal collection of Norman Sas.)

EARL SHORES | RODDY GARCIA

# 19 THE NFL COMES TO LIFE IN MINIATURE

**T**he New Year's Day Championship double-header kicked off in Buffalo, where the Bills hosted the Chiefs. It was briefly an interesting game, with the score tied 7-7 early on. But then the Chiefs scored 24 unanswered points for a convincing 31-7 win. In the late game, the Packers were cruising until the final five minutes. After cutting a 14-point deficit to 7, the Cowboys had the ball first-and-goal from the two-yard line with less than two minutes left in the game. Three plays later the Cowboys were still two yards from the goal line. On fourth down Dallas quarterback Don Meredith found himself immediately under heavy pressure (NFL lore includes an incorrect play call, a botched substitution, and a missed block) and threw a fateful pass that was intercepted with 28 seconds on the clock. The Chiefs would play the Packers in the first Super Bowl.

On the following day, not long after football fans were done reading newspaper accounts of the NFL and AFL Championship games, the Sugar, Rose, and Orange Bowl games served up nine consecutive hours of televised gridiron action. Conveniently, NBC was televising all the games, meaning a viewer wouldn't even have to get out of his or her chair to change a channel. Missing this year was any drama, as the Associated Press had already declared Notre Dame the nation's top team. The No. 1 position was assured because Notre Dame did not accept bowl bids, so they weren't in action on the most important bowl day of the season. And neither was second-ranked Michigan State who, thanks to Big Ten conference rules, was not allowed to make consecutive appearances in the Rose Bowl.

While it's impossible to add to the fairy-tale status of Super Bowl I, there were some events in the two-week run-up to the game that have long been forgotten by the NFL's mythmaking machinery. First, another NFL game was played during that period. In the Runner-Up Bowl on January 8 the Colts beat the Eagles 20-17. Second, a fascinating and critically

# NFL joins TUDOR's Champions-- Watch 'em go!

Ride the tide of football popularity with Tudor's Tru-Action, Sports Classic and NFL Electric Football Games.

The original artwork for Tudor's ad in *Playthings* (March 1967 issue). It was conceived and created by Lee Payne. (Collection of Roddy Garcia.)

No. 510
Box Size: 16½" x 27" x 2½"
½ Doz. Ctn.  Wt. 27 Lbs.
110 Volts, A.C. Only

*Electric* Football

Introducing tudor NFL

Tudor's new NFL No. 510 with the Colts and Packers. From the 1967 Tudor sales catalog. (Personal collection of Norman Sas.)

acclaimed television documentary called *Pro Football's Shotgun Wedding: Sonny, Money, and Merger* ran in prime time. For 60 minutes the program carefully examined the NFL-AFL merger, ultimately crediting Jets owner Sonny Werblin for setting the wheels in motion by signing Joe Namath. The producer and host of the show was a sportscaster named Howard Cosell. Third, famed trumpeter and part-New Orleans team owner Al Hirt announced that the newest NFL team would be named the Saints. (Norman and Lee could breathe a sigh of relief as they now had a logo and color scheme to forward to Albert Sung.)

Finally, much is always made about the thousands of empty seats in the Coliseum on the day of the game. What isn't mentioned is that Commissioner Rozelle admitted the day before the game that he wasn't surprised there were unsold seats. In fact, he himself felt many of the seats, especially the ones at the far end of the stadium, were overpriced. Chief's owner Lamar Hunt even joked that these seats might be beyond the television blackout area. And of course there was the bottom line – the Packers beat the Chiefs 35-10.

There were lots of ways lots of people could feel good about the success of the first World Championship game. (In these early days, Rozelle didn't like the Super Bowl moniker.) The NFL confirmed itself as the best league. There was no debate now that the matter had been settled on the field of play. Obviously, the AFL wasn't happy with the result, but the league owners would feel better when the joint player draft took place in March. The draft would mark the place where the AFL could start to level the field with the NFL. And the divided broadcast wasn't such a horrible thing

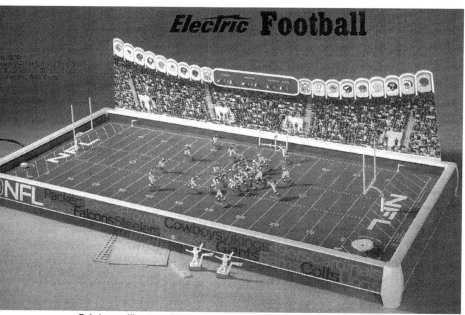

*Electric* **Football**

Tudor's magnificent new NFL No. 620 with the Giants and Browns. From the 1967 Tudor sales catalog. (Personal collection of Norman Sas.)

after all. Both CBS and NBC sold out their entire 18-minute allotment of commercials weeks before the game, with CBS charging $85,000 a minute, and NBC charging $70,000 (this was double NBC's regular season rate). When the Nielsen ratings for the game finally came out, there was good news for the leagues, the networks, and the advertisers. It was reported that over 50 million people watched the game.

Never in his wildest toy dreams could Norman have invented a scenario like the one that had unfolded over the last seven months. Being tied into the NFL was one thing, but to be tied into the biggest sports story of the year, followed then by the hype surrounding the biggest professional football game ever played – it was overwhelming. Norman didn't know for sure what being part of the NFL-AFL story would ultimately mean to Tudor. But it had to be a lot better than not being part of the story. And there was a lot of work still to be done to make sure Tudor made the most of this extraordinary opportunity.

In less than six weeks, Tudor would unveil its new NFL line at the 1967 Toy Fair, and Lee was doggedly working to get all the NFL prototype games – six of each – into a state of presentation perfection. With the help of Mike Gaines, Lee was working on a tentative design for the new Saints uniform. If the Saints were going to be part of Tudor's lineup in the fall, the

**NEW NFL TEAMS IN OFFICIAL UNIFORMS!**
All 16 NFL Teams will be available.
Consumer may order favorite teams in both light and dark jerseys.

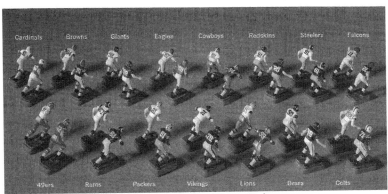

From the 1967 Tudor sales catalog. (Personal collection of Norman Sas.)

team's paint chips and uniform diagrams needed to soon be on their way to Hong Kong. Also needed was Norman's decision on how many AFL teams to produce. The molding of the plastic players was finished – that is, Tudor had all the plastic players they were going to have for the season. It was too late to go back and order a larger production run. So Norman had to figure out how to use the inventory wisely. The NFL was already promised in both home and away uniforms. Should Tudor do the same with the AFL?

No, there was no way Norman could take a chance on coming up short with the NFL. Not only was it the best and most popular league, it would make Tudor the most money. The AFL teams would only be painted in their dark, or "home" uniforms, and in significantly smaller numbers than NFL teams.

Instructions for the AFL and the Saints would be wired to Albert Sung who now had a factory in Hong Kong with over two hundred workers painting players. During the next several months, these workers would paint hundreds of thousands of tiny NFL and AFL players, all by hand. Each sock stripe, each Ram horn, each Colt horseshoe, was the stroke of a human hand. It was a labor-intensive venture being done on a very challenging scale. Shipments of teams for Tudor's NFL games (Browns, Giants, Colts, and Packers) were set to start in March. Once shipped, it would take a month for a player to make it from Hong Kong to an individual team bag in Brooklyn. Tudor's NFL success was balanced upon Sung's ability to align the painting and shipping schedules.

Both the NFL and AFL owners had meetings in February. Pete Rozelle was present at each event, where the main discussions involved the

There was a sigh of relief in Brooklyn when Albert Sung's painted NFL teams started arriving in Brooklyn. A 1967 Los Angeles Ram. (Photo by Earl Shores.)

upcoming player draft and the selection of the next Super Bowl site. The NFL owners once again took up a goal post issue, officially adopting the new single-standard slingshot style goal post for league play. With no posts on or near the goal line, it was a design that would minimally interfere with play, and more importantly, minimize the chance of player injury. And they would all have to be painted NFL gold and have 20-foot high "Baltimore Extension" uprights.

When Toy Fair officially opened on March 6, the hot topic among toy insiders was the 5-10% wholesale price increases most major manufacturers were demanding. This was a highly contentious issue for the industry as profit margins continued to remain low for many toy retailers. For better or for worse, loss leader pricing had become an accepted way of doing business. Toy makers seemed to have grown tired of trying to referee the loss leader issue, and now in 1967, were essentially telling retailers to figure out their own way to turn a profit.

Surprisingly, the Batman craze of 1966 was already over with sales of "caped crusader" merchandise heading downward since before Christmas. One trend that was predicted for continued success was slot cars. Strombecker, Revell, and Eldon were still riding a wave of demand that started early in the decade, and even with some of the clearance and inventory concerns of the previous Christmas, toy analysts and company executives remained optimistic. Even more elaborate sets were being marketed this year, some in the bigger "professional" 1/24 modeling scale (1/32 scale – meaning cars were 1/32 the size of life-size cars – was the standard home slot car scale). While larger slot cars were singled out as winning items, the popularity of model trains, especially large scale models, had sunk to an all-time low. Lionel was in such bad financial shape that it had made no new trains – its entire 1967 line consisted of leftover trains from the year before.

Tudor's official NFL kickoff appeared in the March issue of *Playthings*. Taking up all of page 109 was a Lee Payne-created ad featuring a photo of two real NFL players in action centered underneath large bold black letters: "NFL Joins TUDOR's Champions – Watch'em go!" Following the ad was a four-paragraph feature on page 324 that was headlined "Tudor Set for 1967 Kickoff With Electric Football Games." A small picture of the new No. 620 game offered the first glimpse of an actual Tudor NFL game, but there was no way the magazine could make the same impact as seeing the games in the showroom.

With only a handful of cosmetic frame and field modifications, the new NFL No. 510 wasn't dramatically different from the standard No. 500 model. Yet Lee's changes made it a completely different game. By adding blue to the outer rim of the frame and a green border on the far frame edge, the No. 510 became a more "serious" looking game. Having

Albert Sung had lots of teams to paint in 1967, but he didn't have to paint them for Tudor's redesigned Sports Classic football game. Renumbered the No. 610, the game was a new "mid-size" for Tudor. It came with Lee's new two-piece players – in unpainted form. 1967 Tudor sales catalog. (Personal collection of Norman Sas.)

"NFL" printed in white against the blue frame background, also added more authority, as did a new clip-on cardboard color-photo grandstand. Printed on the grandstand were pennants of each team and a scoreboard that allowed NFL team names to be easily interchanged. But what really separated the No. 510 from the No. 500 was the bold "NFL" in each end zone – and the beautifully painted Colts and Packers.

For the new NFL No. 620, no comparisons were necessary. The game was pure awe at first sight. Drawing attention first was the field, which looked huge and very realistic. The next thing the eyes were drawn to were the end zones where large white block letters spelled out "N-F-L." And mounted almost in the center of each "F" was a perfectly scaled, official "NFL gold," single posted slingshot-type goal post. There was even a perfectly scaled goal post pad around each base. Although the NFL had officially adopted this type of goal post just weeks earlier, Payne had been working on the miniature versions for months.

More realism came in the No. 620's clip-on grandstand, which was much larger than the No. 510, and again, perfectly scaled for the size of the new game. Payne wanted a modern look for the big game (the No. 510 still used the Princeton crowd), so he went to Atlanta's new stadium during the fall of 1966 and took crowd photos during a Falcons game. The results were impressive; visible on this new grandstand were not only football fans, but also ushers, security guards, and vendors. Across the "façade" of this new Tudor stadium Payne placed the helmets of each NFL team, and a scoreboard with the interchangeable name feature.

Eventually the eyes dropped to the center of the playing field where beautifully painted Giants and Browns waited for a young quarterback to call a play. No other electric football game had ever been so "real."

Yet there was more. When the teams on both the No. 620 and No. 510 were examined closely, two things became apparent. First, the players were numbered after actual football players. Quarterbacking the Packers, of course, was no. 15, Bart Starr. Second, the teams were integrated. That is, each NFL team had three African-American players. So lined up in the backfield behind Starr was not only no. 31 Jim Taylor, but also no. 22 Elijah Pitts. And flanked out wide on offense for the Browns was star receiver no. 42, Paul Warfield. Compared with the goal posts, the grandstands, and painted NFL uniforms, this might seem like a small detail. Surely to a generation raised on cable and the Internet, it seems like an obvious thing to do. But at the time, it was a major step for Tudor to take. And it made Tudor's NFL much more real. How could you have an NFL, even a miniature one, without Gale Sayers, Jim Parker, or Herb Adderly? You couldn't, and Norman Sas knew that you couldn't. It was his decision to produce African-American players. This seemingly small detail would earn Tudor a loyal following of boys who finally found a toy they could truly identify with – electric football.

Equally as impressive as the No. 620 and the No. 510 was Tudor's display of NFL teams. With their brilliant details and colors, they were sure to be a major selling point for the entire Tudor NFL line. Yet individual teams were not going to be available for retail sales. The only way to get an NFL team that didn't come in the game was to order it from Tudor. Norman decided to do this so Tudor could have complete control of the inventory and know the exact sales numbers for each team. It also allowed Tudor to keep the teams affordable, preventing any type of price gouging on the most popular teams. The mail-order price of a 1967 NFL or AFL team was set at $1.50 plus shipping.

Also on display in the showroom were the No. 500 model and the new midsize No. 610 Sports Classic Football game. In an earlier year, the No. 610 would have been the electric football highlight of 1967. But in the year of the NFL, the game was almost an afterthought. It did come with Lee's new two-piece players in unpainted form, and you could order any of the new NFL teams to go on it. Still, even though it was quite a nice looking game, it was basically just a slightly shrunken version of last year's Sports Classic model. And along with the completely unchanged No. 500, the new No. 610 sat there completely overshadowed by its NFL brothers.

As Norman threw open the showroom doors in March of 1967, he wasn't sure what to feel. After waiting over a year to "officially" be an official NFL licensee there was a strong sense of relief, which now mixed

## ELECTRIC FOOTBALL

Set up your formations .. players block, tackle, pass and receive. You control direction players move by turning each slightly to the left or right. Vibrating coil under field keeps magnetic football in play, makes action different every time.

### $12⁶⁶

A capacity crowd fills the stands! Set up your formations strategically, then watch 3-D players clash on big 21x36 inch field. Kicker-passer throws and boots magnetic ball, defensive team blocks and tackles. Vibrating coil beneath field keeps men in action.

Paint players in the colors of your favorite teams. Game includes 3-man yardage marker and scoreboard, colorful pennants, goal posts, 3 magnetic footballs, instructions. UL listed, 110–120-v., 60-c, AC. Plastic players. Metal unit. Partly assembled.
79 N 65218L—Shipping weight 12 pounds.... $12.66

Includes 44 players (4 teams) plus paints. Now you can have your own bowl games!

ctric Pro Football .. rlerback your team **$6⁹⁹**

witch on 29x15-in. gridiron and 2 f 3-D players plus kicker-passer go ion. 2 scoring devices, magnetic ball, r marker. Steel and hardboard. UL 110–120-v., 60-c, AC.
04C—Shipping wt. 6 lbs.... $6.99

Foto-electric Football with lighted gridiron **$7⁵⁹**

"Hall of Fame" game includes offensive and defensive plays, dials for kicks and runs, scoreboard. Lighted gridiron shows plays in action. Laminated cardboard. UL listed, 110–120-volt, 60-cycle, AC.
79 N 114C—Shipping wt. 3 lbs.... $7.59

### NFL ELECTRIC FOOTBALL
32x18-inch vibrating gridiron. Game includes all key plays of NFL teams, two 3-D teams.

### $9⁹⁹

Gotham's generic Big Bowl was now side-by-side with a Tudor NFL No. 613 game on the Sears' electric football page in 1967. Sears 1967 Sears *Christmas Book*, page 461. ©Sears, Roebuck & Co. 1967.

with the exhaustion of showroom set up and the efforts of keeping his NFL line a secret. Yet there was an excitement he could barely contain. This was Tudor's most important Toy Fair ever – and Norman saw it as his company's finest moment. The best and most creative toy efforts Tudor had ever produced were riding on the coattails of the most notable year in professional football history and the most publicized professional football game ever played. Tudor couldn't have hand picked a better year to become an NFL licensee.

Buyer reaction was everything Norman and Lee hoped it would be. The Tudor showroom buzzed and bustled in ways that neither man had experienced before in the toy business. Lee's beautifully photographed sales catalogs, with a full-color macro close up of the Packers and Colts on the cover, disappeared faster than Super Bowl tickets, and orders for the NFL games exceeded Norman's expectations. Even toy buyers who for years had only ordered No. 500 models were tempted to gamble on the allure and extra expense of filling their shelves with NFL games. The games were beautiful; there was little doubt they would sell. Tudor's NFL coronation became official when three visitors from beyond the toy world entered the showroom – Larry Kent, John Carney...and Pete Rozelle. They congratulated Norman and Lee on their innovation and persistence, and left 200 Fifth Avenue feeling pretty good about giving the NFL to Tudor (and also about the fact that the only sign of the AFL was in the sales catalog description of the No. 610).

A Dennis the Menace theme ran throughout the Sears *Christmas Book.* Just below the Tudor NFL No. 613 Dennis and Joey were playing electric football (with a Big Bowl...) Sears 1967 Sears *Christmas Book,* page 461. ©Sears, Roebuck & Co. 1967.

In another showroom at 200 Fifth Avenue, the atmosphere was a bit gloomier. For the first time in six years, there were no NFL logos to be found anywhere in the Gotham showroom. Surrounding Eddie Gluck were G-1500 and G-880 models that seemed almost naked. Games that just the year before would have sported the distinctive Gotham NFL frame – bright white, with the red-white-and-blue NFL shield at the midpoint and colorful team logos spreading in each direction – now had a very sedate pattern of black and brown stripes. Eye catching they were not. It might be said that the frame matched Gluck's mood. The loss of the NFL was devastating for Gotham. Also devastating was the fact that Gotham's exclusive electric football run with Sears was about to end. While the Big Bowl was still going to be the featured item on the electric football page, Gluck was going to have to share the page with Tudor. Tudor and the NFL that is.

If Gluck planned on staying in the electric football business, he needed to come up with something to compete with Tudor. Revenue from electric football was what made the company profitable. Obviously company sales were going to take a hit in 1967, so finding extra money in the Gotham budget for product development was going to be difficult. In 1966 Gluck had to take a second mortgage to meet his production schedule. But something had to be done. Without a significantly new electric football concept, there might not even be a showroom in the very near future.

Ward's version of the NFL No. 620 in 1967. It appeared to come with a scaled down version the accordion grandstand. Montgomery Ward 1967 *Christmas Catalog*, page 275. ©Montgomery Ward, Inc. 1967.

Just as the Toy Fair was wrapping up, another monumental pro football event was taking place blocks away. At 10:00 a.m. on March 14, the first joint NFL-AFL draft was held in the Hotel Gotham. The expansion Saints had been awarded the first pick, but they traded it to the Colts, who drafted future star Bubba Smith.

March continued to be busy for both the NFL and Tudor. During the month's final days, Larry Kent and National Football League Properties hosted a show of NFL licensees at the Warwick Hotel in New York. Besides Tudor, 36 other manufacturers were invited to display their official NFL items. So just weeks after becoming an NFL licensee, Tudor found itself sharing the stage with some of the largest companies in the country – Jansen Sportswear, Reynolds Metal, Ideal Toys, Random House, and MacGregor Sporting Goods. If Norman had any doubts about how much the NFL could mean to his company, all he had to do was look around.

Adding to the heavyweight atmosphere of the event were sales representatives from all the department stores who handled NFL Properties merchandise. These reps were a cross section of some the biggest stores in the biggest retail markets in the country, including Macy's, Gimbel's (Philadelphia), Higbee's (Cleveland), and The May Company (Los Angeles). For Norman, exposure of this magnitude was something he only dreamed about for Tudor. Before the show ended, things got even better. NFL Properties announced that it was launching a program to get NFL-licensed merchandise in major stores located within 100 miles of NFL cities. This was in addition to the NFL Team Shops in retailers like Macy's,

Tudor's NFL No. 620 was a hot item when it hit toy store shelves in the fall of 1967. (Photo by Earl Shores.)

Gimbel's, Higbee's, and H.C. Prange. Tudor's already strong distribution got even better; Gotham's distribution issues were only going to intensify.

The satisfaction produced by the events of March was well deserved, but Norman and Lee could hardly start feeling smug about a few weeks of success. They hadn't put a single NFL game on a shelf or received the first shipment of NFL teams from Hong Kong. The teams were on their way; it wouldn't be long before the supply line was established. Still, there were questions of quality control once the teams did arrive. Would the level of painting be acceptable? Would the "NFL" part of the teams be recognizable, or would it be a flashback to the gorilla player fiasco? Sung had done great work so far. He had given no one any reason to worry. Still, it was human nature to have concerns. Especially about the key piece of Tudor's giant NFL puzzle.

When the first shipment of teams arrived in Brooklyn, Norman and Lee were thrilled. The teams were easily identifiable, and some of the painting details were really extraordinary considering the number of players being processed by Sung's assembly line. Tudor's production of the actual NFL games was also moving along smoothly in Brooklyn. Orders for the games

Sears used the Tudor No. 613 in newspaper ads throughout the Christmas shopping season. A studio photo taken by Lee Payne in 1967. Look closely at the helmet in bottom left hand corner of the photo. It has no logo. That "place holder" would eventually become the Saints. (Collection of Roddy Garcia.)

were continuing to come in throughout the spring, and Norman's concerns were starting to shift just a bit. It was possible, just maybe, that the demand for the new games was going to outstrip production. There were certainly far worse problems to have. The result of this problem would be a record sales year for Tudor. Just before Memorial Day, pro football owners created more work for Lee and Albert Sung, by approving a tenth AFL team for the city of Cincinnati. The owners also decided to play the next Super Bowl in Miami on January 14, 1968. At least the city got seven months to prepare for the game.

Seven months is about how long it took for Albert Sung to finish up the initial run of painted NFL players. Although there had been intermittent problems getting enough paint, Sung kept things going until he filled Tudor's entire order. Still left were thousands of unpainted players. They would be included in the new No. 610 model, and were also part of Tudor's mail-order plans. As the summer moved forward," then continue on as it is. As the summer moved forward, Norman watched the NFL game orders amass beyond his sunniest expectations – and this was before Sears and Ward unveiled their exclusive NFL games in the coming Christmas catalogs. By the time the NFL and AFL training camps opened in late July, Tudor was on its way to a profitable year.

Following the template of previous years the pro football preseason once again expanded. This year it would be six weeks long with the AFL playing its first preseason game on July 29 and the NFL following on August 2.

Between the two leagues there would be 80 preseason games in all, 51 in the NFL and 29 in the AFL. But length of the preseason was not the biggest news of 1967. The most notable aspect of the preseason was the 16 interleague games – that is, 16 games where NFL teams played AFL teams.

Most football experts say that exhibition games mean very little. Such conventional wisdom is true for most seasons; in 1967, however, there was no question that AFL teams would be out to prove themselves. On the other side of the field, no NFL team wanted to be accused of letting the "superior" league down. And this was a bonanza for both NBC and CBS. They got to televise ostensibly meaningless preseason games…that now had meaning. The interleague rivalry paid dividends quickly, for on August 5, the Denver Broncos beat the Detroit Lions 13-7. It was the first time an AFL team ever defeated an NFL team.

Also warming up in the preseason was Larry Kent and NFLP, who again recruited the Training Table Food sponsors to back a 36-page insert in the September 8 issue of *Life*. Measuring 5" x 7," the removable booklet was titled "A Family Guide to Football." The goal of the booklet was to help those who might not grasp the appeal of America's new pastime (women), to understand football. An even better outcome than understanding the game was if mom got inspired to put some of that Official Training Table Food on the family table.

It wasn't long after the NFL season started on September 17 that the Christmas catalogs started to appear. The sports games in Sears received a beautiful full-color two-page spread, with table hockey (Munro Games) and basketball games taking up the left side while football dominated the right. This year, even Dennis the Menace got into the electric football act, as a cartoon in the bottom corner of the football page depicted Dennis and Joey in the middle of a game. The main feature was Gotham's Big Bowl – without the NFL (Dennis and Joey appeared to be playing with an NFL version). Even to the unbiased observer, the game had lost something. It didn't have the impact on the eye that the game did in 1965 and 1966. And once you were done reading the description of the Big Bowl, your eye dropped right down to Tudor's new NFL No. 613 model.

In some ways, Lee had borrowed just a bit from Gotham. The frame of the No. 613 was bright white like the NFL Big Bowl models. But instead of team logos, he used team helmets to decorate the frame. The effect was spectacular, as the exact replica single-bar facemask helmets seemed to jump off the frame and announce how realistic the game was. Lee had also come up with a new grandstand design. Using the metal mounting brackets from last year's Ward accordion game, Lee created a grandstand, which bent slightly back and upward when mounted on the No. 613 frame. And a slightly enlarged version of Lee's Atlanta stadium photos gave this

An original Lee Payne studio photo that didn't make into any of Tudor's advertising. Despite being the most expensive game in Tudor's line, the NFL No. 620 would sell out in 1967. A game as Santa might have left it. (Collection of Roddy Garcia.)

grandstand Tudor's signature modern touch. The game also had the Bears and Cardinals on the field. Not only was this pairing an intense Midwestern rivalry, it was a re-creation of last season's very successful foray into Monday night football. The only minus to the No. 613 was Tudor's old style H-shaped goal posts. Yet it would be hard to imagine any boy being disappointed by Santa delivering a No. 613. The game has long been considered one of the most striking NFL models Tudor ever made.

Besides being an official NFL game, the No. 613 had one extra thing going for it – its price. The Big Bowl was selling for $13.29. Aligned on the page just inches below the Gotham behemoth was the No. 613, and the price for the NFL was a mere $10.49. It was a harsh juxtaposition for Eddie Gluck. But this wasn't the only bad news for Gotham. To produce this year's run of games the Gotham factory had once again been put up as collateral on a $300,000 loan.

It was no surprise that Tudor's NFL got a more impressive presentation in the Ward catalog. The retailer was not about to be left out of the NFL derby and had requested that Tudor make Ward an exclusive NFL model. Although Tudor didn't make an entirely new game, what Ward got was still pretty extraordinary. It was an NFL No. 620 with a more manageable version of the accordion grandstand. This No. 620 took up the entire top third of page 275 and even came with a larger-than-life photo of a player from each team. By having a painted player from the Browns and Giants in the foreground, Ward did a better job than Sears of illustrating exactly what Tudor's NFL was about.

Serious NFL fans would notice that the Browns player on the Ward page wore no. 36 – for the real Cleveland Browns, this was running back Nick Pietrosante. The number of the Giants player on the page was no. 29 – the real Giant with this number was running back Chuck Mercein. Add in the Ward-highlighted "Center-post goal post in NFL gold" sitting in the middle of the "N-F-L" in the end zone, the hand-painted NFL players, the 3-foot long grandstand, and the accurately numbered players, and Tudor's NFL concept was clear. Realism. Electric football had never before seen such attention to detail.

September ended with both leagues well underway and another Larry Kent *Life* magazine promotion. Kent was aiming at men this time, with a 32-page booklet in the September 29 issue titled "This Is Football." All the "Golden Helmet Award Products" advertised in the booklet were men's toiletry icons – Gillette razors, Right Guard, Listerine, Desenex, and Lectric Shave. In addition to the ads, there were detailed play diagrams and text that described the philosophies of offense and defense. *Life* again regionalized the booklets. Readers received a guide featuring the nearest NFL team.

Larry Kent and John Carney had to be pleased with the overall progress of NFL Properties. It was obvious that the influence of the NFL was growing well beyond the field of play. In September alone, some of the biggest companies in the U.S. had put up over $1.5 million to be part of NFL promotions. NFL Properties was still waiting to get a full page in Sears. (Surprisingly, Roy Rogers still had his.) But Kent and Sas were both happy to see that Sears was already using Tudor's NFL No. 613 game in newspaper advertisements.

The popularity of Tudor's NFL line continued to grow through the fall. But by the time of the NFL's next Monday night game on October 30 (Green Bay 31 – St. Louis 23), it was clear that Tudor had a problem. There was no way the company was going to keep up with the demand for the games. Stores that sold out of No. 620's and No. 510's were now looking at backorders on Tudor's NFL games. For the moment, Tudor was able to keep up with the NFL team orders that were arriving in Brooklyn by mail. All of those orders were thanks to Tudor's new "rule book" which came in every Tudor electric football game. Besides the rules, there was a 4-page full-color spread of the NFL No. 620, the NFL No. 510, and all the NFL and AFL teams. On the back page of the book was an order form for teams, number sheets, and game accessories. Including photos of the games and teams in the rule book was a touch of genius on the part of Norman and Lee. It quickly turned into a book of dreams, generating almost as much wonder as a Sears or Ward Christmas catalog.

Word of Tudor's success with the NFL had reached Hong Kong where Albert Sung was already gearing up for next year. A new set of production-size masters had been made from Lee's large brass master players, and molds for the run of 1968 players were just about finished. Sung had also been informed that because of this success, he would have a larger number of players to paint for the coming year. New molds needed to be made because under standard Far East production agreements of the time, Tudor did not own the player injection molds – the company in Hong Kong making the players owned them. These companies did not have the space or the ambition to store hundreds of different injection molds from American toy makers, so instead of making a set of master molds in 1967, and then using this master year after year, the company melted down and recycled the old player molds as soon as a production run was finished. This is why Tudor's NFL 1967 players are larger and more detailed than any other Tudor players. It would also lead to other player variations over time.

In the early weeks of November Sears had the NFL No. 613 as a featured item in most of its newspaper ads. The game was always clearly pictured, usually at the top of the page accompanied by the caption "Go Team Go! Play NFL Electric Football Game." All the features of the game were described, including the five different player poses of the Cardinals and Bears. Depending on the geographic location, the No. 613 was priced anywhere from $8.99 to $11.99 (the Sears catalog price was $10.99). Ward was running the No. 500 in its print ads during this period although the retailer wasn't giving electric football the same push as Sears. Top toy spots at Ward were reserved for giant slot car sets and space action figure newcomer Major Matt Mason.

Sears continued having the No. 613 in heavy ad rotation right up to Thanksgiving Day when the company shifted gears over to slot cars and the "Greatest Road Race Sale." Making no changes to its advertising was Ward, who used the No. 500 throughout the holiday weekend (Ward's pricing on the No. 500 ranged from $4.88 to a hefty $6.99). On Thanksgiving Day, a new record was set for televised football games – five. Thanks to the AFL adding a second game, there were two NFL games, two AFL games, and a significant college game – Nebraska vs. Oklahoma – vying for viewers. With the first game kicking off at noon EST, and the final game starting at 6:00 p.m. there would almost be nine continuous hours of televised football. In contrast to football's overexposure on television, Gotham was completely invisible during the holiday weekend. Sears was still carrying

Tudor's NFL teams being painted in Hong Kong. Each painter had a stack of "pallets," with each pallet holding more than 200 players. (Personal collection of Albert Sung.)

the Big Bowl but was too busy promoting Tudor's NFL No. 613 to bother with a Gotham model. And Tudor just seemed to be everywhere this year. Retailers, it appeared, weren't wasting paid ad space on Gotham games. A final blow to visibility was that Gluck hadn't even bothered sending out any press releases this fall. Outside of the Sears catalog, it was almost as if Gotham didn't exist.

By the start of the final Christmas season push in early December, electric football was still occupying a prominent place in the advertising of both Sears and Ward. Norman was pleased with the visibility from Sears and pleased that Tudor's NFL games were doing well. He was a little surprised to learn that even the Giants-Browns No. 620 game, the most expensive electric football game on the market, would likely sell out.

Not far away in Queens, another New York organization was doing pretty well. The Jets were 7-2-1 and seemed a lock to make the AFL playoffs for the first time ever. But three consecutive December losses sent the Jets into the final week of the season trailing the Houston Oilers in the Eastern Division standings. This final AFL weekend was setting up as a tense one, and not just because of the undecided Eastern playoff race. Thanks to expansion, the NFL now had four divisions of teams. And by an unfortunate coincidence – or premeditated hubris, depending on which league you asked – the NFL's new "semifinal" playoff games were scheduled

Tudor's NFL No. 613: Neither the Cardinal nor Bears made the NFL Playoffs in 1967, but they would still be in action on Christmas Day. (Photo by Roddy Garcia.)

for December 23 and 24. Which happened to be the weekend the AFL regular season was scheduled to end.

Despite the coming merger, there was no love lost between the two leagues on the television front. The AFL and NBC had begun doing their own double-header broadcast on Sundays in 1967, significantly increasing the already overwhelming amount of pro football on the airwaves. (Areas of the country without a "home" team had seen more than 50 professional regular season games.) On Saturday, December 23, the Rams visited the Packers for a 2:00 p.m. Western Conference title game. In front of a CBS national television audience, the Packers dismantled the Rams 28-7.

Later that evening in Miami, the AFL had a game scheduled that could decide the Eastern Division. If the Oilers could beat the Dolphins, they would be the champs of the East and face the Raiders in the AFL Championship game. A loss by the Oilers would give the Jets an opportunity to force a playoff game. Such an important game on a Saturday night in late December seemed ready-made for a national telecast, and a significant Nielsen rating. But it was not to be. Only fans in Houston saw the Oilers 41-10 victory. For the rest of country, NBC showed *Get Smart* and *Saturday Night at the Movies*.

The Oilers' win made Sunday's Jets-Chargers game meaningless. It was an unfortunate break for the AFL, as this was the league's "prime" television game – the one the league was counting on to keep things competitive against the NFL playoffs. Being played in San Diego, the kickoff was set for 4:30 p.m. EST, or two hours later than the start of the Cowboys-Browns game in Dallas. Since the AFL playoff teams were already determined, it seemed that football fans would have little reason to change the channel. But something unforeseen happened. The Browns forgot to show up in Dallas. After three quarters of play, the Cowboys had a 45-7 lead (the final score was 52-14), and die-hard football fans were looking for something else to watch. The Jets-Chargers game filled the bill nicely, having all the excitement and drama the NFL game lacked. After a wild first half in which the two teams traded touchdowns, the Jets led 28-24. And the New Yorkers never trailed again. Namath was spectacular, throwing for four touchdowns and 343 yards in the 42-31 victory. He also set a new AFL season passing record of 4,007 yards. It was the first time an AFL or NFL pro quarterback had broken the 4,000-yard barrier.

After a full weekend of pro football games, it was now Christmas Day...Christmas in a year that started with the hoopla of the first ever Super Bowl and was now headed for a finish on New Year's Eve day with a double-header of the NFL and AFL Championship games. And it was into this remarkable football year Tudor had introduced its NFL line. Tudor's timing, as it had been all through the odyssey of obtaining and creating a miniature NFL, bordered on the miraculous. Had there ever been a better Christmas to receive an electric football game than 1967? A Tudor NFL electric football game, that is?

In living rooms all over the U.S., tens of thousands of tiny Browns and Giants, Colts and Packers, Bears and Cardinals were vibrating into each other, and into the hearts of young boys. There were probably more than just a few disappointed children, as Tudor, who sold more games than ever before, could not keep up with the demand for the NFL models as the Christmas season accelerated to its finish. A generic Tudor No. 500, of which the company had plenty, was small consolation for those dreaming of single-posted "NFL gold" goal post glory. At least the disappointed ones could order their favorite team from Tudor when the Christmas season finished (and hope their team was still in stock).

Unless you had asked for a Tudor NFL game, receiving a Gotham game for Christmas really wasn't a major disappointment. But once you knew of the existence of Tudor's miniature NFL, perhaps from a neighbor lucky enough to get a No. 620, the Big Bowl didn't seem quite so big anymore. (It wouldn't take long for boys to figure out that Tudor NFL teams looked pretty cool and worked just fine on any Gotham model.) For Eddie Gluck, however, Christmas was a major disappointment. Sales of electric football games were down from the year before, and this trend wasn't going to be easily reversed. And for two consecutive years Gotham had to borrow funds to meet production, using its Bronx factory as collateral. This was far from a perfect way to compete with Tudor and the NFL.

The Packers' Ray Nitschke would still be in action in real life, and on your living room floor. 1967 was the year of the Ice Bowl. (Photo by Earl Shores.)

Much to Norman's delight and Gluck's chagrin, a great year became a legendary one. The early game on December 31 had the Cowboys and Packers playing in Green Bay for the NFL Championship. On a day when the high temperature reached minus 13 degrees, both teams skated around the "tundra" of Lambeau Field – and into football history. Thanks to a last-second Bart Starr touchdown plunge, the Packers came away with a 21-17 victory. And thanks to television, which prevented the game from being postponed to a later date, the "Ice Bowl" became one of the most famous games in NFL history. The Raiders' 40-7 win in the AFL Championship game has faded to a pro football footnote.

Tudor's 1968 NFL Championship "Ice Bowl" prototype game. Designed by Lee
Payne, the game was never put into production. (Collection of Roddy Garcia)

# 20 TUDOR AND PRO FOOTBALL NEGOTIATE A YEAR OF NATIONAL TURMOIL

**A**s New Year's Day 1968 dawned, there was no time for a football hangover. Dedicated football fans would have already taken in six nationally televised games during the weekend. In addition to the NFL and AFL Championships, four collegiate games had been played on Saturday (the Gator Bowl, the Sun Bowl, and the Blue-Gray and East-West all-star games). Monday, January 1 was all set to cap off the weekend with four bowl games and nine more hours of televised football. Most viewing interest fell on the Rose Bowl and Orange Bowl games. The Rose Bowl had top-ranked USC going up against No. 4 Indiana, while the Orange Bowl had No. 2 Tennessee playing No. 3 Oklahoma. If Indiana upset USC that would leave the national title honors open to possibly three teams. USC took all the drama out of the day by beating Indiana 14-3.

With the college football season officially over, football fans could concentrate on the professional game. The Super Bowl wouldn't be played until the 14th, leaving plenty of time for fans to thaw out from the gridiron epic poem composed by the Packers and Cowboys. In the meantime, those needing a professional football fix would have to settle for the Playoff Bowl –

now being labeled the "Superfluous Bowl" by some – that was scheduled for January 7. Before a sparse Orange Bowl crowd, the Rams dismantled the Browns 30-6 to claim the dubious crown of third-best NFL team.

Taking place amid the other hoopla in Miami during Super Bowl week was the annual gathering of the National Football League Players Association. Since its creation in 1956, the NFLPA had won some battles with the league over medical benefits and pensions, but in general, it was viewed as a weak organization. Many of the men who buckled their chinstraps and played the game each week didn't see the NFLPA as representing their best interests. As a result, the NFL hierarchy didn't lose much sleep worrying about the NFLPA.

But the merger agreement had killed more than just the bidding for rookie players; it killed salary increases throughout the league. The players now watched as television money poured into the NFL and their share of the pie got smaller. Making the rounds through NFL locker rooms in 1967 was the idea of forming a new players' union, with Cleveland players going so far as to ask the Teamsters for help. Despite their dissatisfaction with the NFLPA, most players were wary of being represented by an outside organization. And the Teamsters came with their own baggage, namely racketeering and organized crime. So during meetings on January 10 and 13, the NFLPA set out to make itself a stronger organization. Under the guidance of a new president, Detroit Lions lineman Tom Gordy, the players voted to reject the Teamsters and make the NFLPA the sole bargaining agent of the NFL players. Legally it wouldn't be a union, but it would act in the same capacity. (The term "de facto union" was used in the press at the time.) At the conclusion of the second meeting, Gordy issued six demands that the owners needed to take up immediately. Demand number one was increasing the minimum player salary from $5,000 to $15,000.

While not exactly unnoticed, Gordy's demands were overshadowed by the media buildup for the Super Bowl. And within 48 hours, the NFLPA was completely buried by the Packers' 33-14 victory.

After back-to-back Super Bowl victories, it was clear that the NFL was the superior league. But the AFL got a chance to close the talent gap on January 30, when the second combined draft commenced at the Belmont Plaza Hotel in New York City. Not far away in Brooklyn, Tudor was dealing with the post-Christmas rush of team orders, which included a heavy run on Raiders in dark and Packers in white. (This was the first Super Bowl where Tudor had both teams available in the uniforms they wore during the game.) Norman was also trying to come up with realistic production numbers for games and teams for the coming year. One thing was obvious – Tudor needed to make more games. They also needed to get ready for the fast approaching Toy Fair. Lee was busy prepping games and

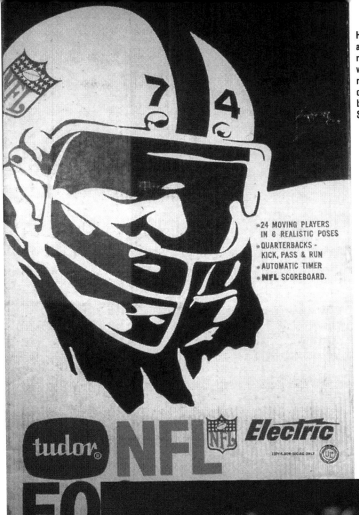

Helping to inspire a post-Christmas rush on NFL teams was Lee Payne's remarkable artwork on the Sears No. 613 box. (Photo by Earl Shores.)

• 24 MOVING PLAYERS IN 6 REALISTIC POSES
• QUARTERBACKS - KICK, PASS & RUN
• AUTOMATIC TIMER
• **NFL** SCOREBOARD.

tudor® NFL Electric

Lee created the No. 613 box art from this slide. The player is Cleveland Browns' defensive end Paul Wiggin, who is about to put a hit on the Cardinals' Charlie Johnson during an NFL game in 1966. Lee cropped the slide to use Wiggins' helmet and facial expression. Lee also changed the number – Wiggins wore no. 84. (Collection of Roddy Garcia.)

tinkering with new electric football ideas. As always, he felt he could lend more realism to the game. Albert Sung had just shifted the 1968 painting schedule into high gear and was also very busy. It wouldn't be long before the second season of Tudor teams would start shipping from Hong Kong.

It seems almost unthinkable today that any coach with consecutive Super Bowl victories would consider retiring. Yet it wasn't a major surprise when Vince Lombardi stepped down as the Packers' coach in early February. Rumors had circulated for some time – many were expecting the announcement to come in the locker room after the Super Bowl. By taking over the job as the Packers' general manager he wasn't completely out of

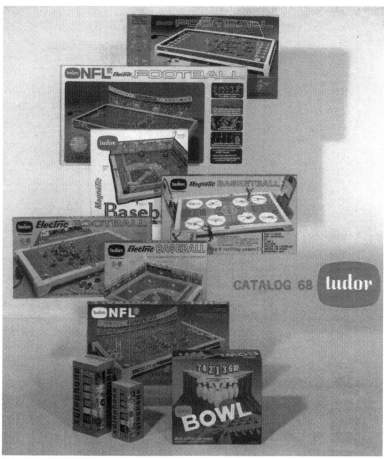

Tudor's 1968 sales catalog. "Selling the NFL games was easy," said Norman Sas. "We had the game everybody wanted." (Collection of Norman Sas.)

football, but he was removed from an obviously aging team that, despite being league champion, wasn't viewed as the NFL's best team in 1967.

A few weeks later, the owners of both leagues met in New York to start to work on the details of the merger. During the meeting, league attendance figures were announced with both the NFL and AFL setting new records. It was a seventh consecutive record year for the NFL. While a new team in New Orleans was an obvious reason for increased attendance, the per-game average was up by more than two thousand people. And there were other numbers further illustrating pro football's ever-rising popularity. A 1967 Harris Poll showed football to be the favorite sport of people under 35 years old, beating baseball 34% to 25%. Football was also the favorite sport of people earning more than $10,000 a year (football 37%; baseball 29%). This meant football's fan base was an advertiser's dream – the young and affluent.

There was, however, a small gray cloud on the horizon. That was the NFLPA. Since the owners had agreed to recognize the organization once the Teamsters were rejected, they now needed to make good on this promise. So an owner-appointed committee met with the NFLPA on February 21. One of the committee members listening to the players' demands was an ex-coach named Vince Lombardi. No progress was made in this get-to-know-you session, but any owner counterproposals could be directed to the newly opened New York City office of the NFLPA.

When the Toy Fair opened on March 11, there was unusual optimism even for the perpetually optimistic Toy Manufacturers Association. Major toy companies were putting record sums into their advertising budgets, leading to predictions that wholesale toy purchases could rise by as much as 10% in 1968. Much of this advertising was scheduled to come during Saturday morning and weekday afternoon children's shows. Besides unveiling Talking Barbie, Mattel was in the second year of its Hot Wheel blitz. Their advertising budget for the year was going to be $15 million. Also spending freely this year was Milton Bradley, who set aside a company record $4 million for advertising. But one company not planning on spending millions on advertising was Tudor. They didn't need to. By being tied to the most popular sport and league in the country, things had taken care of themselves.

"Selling the NFL games was easy," said Norman. "We had the game everybody wanted." In fact, Tudor NFL games were so "wanted" that the company became NFL Properties top-earning licensee for 1967. No other product made as much money for NFL Properties as electric football. Norman was surprised by this success, but he also knew that sometimes a company just happened to be in the right place at the right time. And the tricky part to being a successful toy company was making a wanted item be

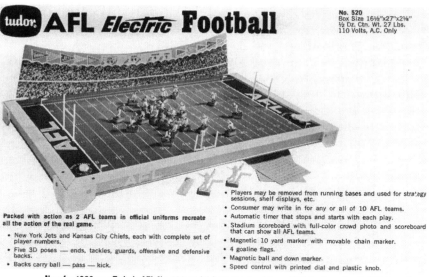

# tudor AFL *Electric* Football

No. 520
Box Size 16½"x27"x2⅛"
½ Dz. Ctn. Wt. 27 Lbs.
110 Volts, A.C. Only

**Packed with action as 2 AFL teams in official uniforms recreate all the action of the real game.**

- New York Jets and Kansas City Chiefs, each with complete set of player numbers.
- Five 3D poses — ends, tackles, guards, offensive and defensive backs.
- Backs carry ball — pass — kick.

- Players may be removed from running bases and used for strategy sessions, shelf displays, etc.
- Consumer may write in for any or all of 10 AFL teams.
- Automatic timer that stops and starts with each play.
- Stadium scoreboard with full-color crowd photo and scoreboard that can show all AFL teams.
- Magnetic 10 yard marker with movable chain marker.
- 4 goaline flags.
- Magnetic ball and down marker.
- Speed control with printed dial and plastic knob.

New for 1968 was Tudor's AFL No. 520 model featuring the Jets and Chiefs. From the 1968 Tudor sales catalog. (Collection of Norman Sas.)

wanted for more than a single year. With that thought in mind, Norman and Lee came to the 1968 Fair with an expansion of the Tudor pro football line. Being content with success was not going to be the company's downfall.

Tudor's new item was the No. 520 model, the first-ever AFL electric football game. Based on the NFL No. 510 game, it featured the Kansas City Chiefs and the New York Jets. Norman and Lee had again been thoughtful in their choice of teams, making sure both the Eastern and Western divisions of the AFL were represented. The Chiefs had played in a Super Bowl and were always one of the best teams in the league. The Jets, on the other hand, while not yet the best team in the East, had arguably the best-known player in all of pro football as their quarterback. By putting the Jets in the game, Tudor made Joe Namath part of its line. They couldn't put Joe's name on the box, but as long as there was a no. 12 on the number sheet in the game, Namath's Tudor presence was assured. For a Brooklyn company, it was smart to have the Giants and the Jets as an integral part of your toy line.

The Chiefs were the home team in the No. 520, wearing their bright red jerseys, while the Jets were resplendent in another Tudor first for the AFL – white away uniforms. It was the first time Tudor made any AFL team available in an away uniform (one more team for Albert Sung to paint). But the Jets would be the only away AFL team available in 1968.

Overall the differences between the NFL No. 510 and the AFL game were slight but significant. The grandstands were identical in size and shape, but differed in color scheme and league allegiance. On the field there were only two differences, those being the orange yard-line numbers and the large orange "A-F-L" in each end zone. And where the frame edges were blue on the No. 510, they were orange on the No. 520. Once again, it was a classic and clean Lee Payne design. The No. 520 was a worthy addition to the Tudor lineup.

And that lineup was up to five electric football games with the generic No. 500 and No. 610 complementing the AFL and the NFL No. 510 and No. 620. Tudor still had the games people wanted and that included Sears and Ward. Both had again requested exclusive models for Christmas; Norman was delighted with how Sears had promoted the NFL No. 613 model during the previous fall. There was little doubt that Tudor's sales were going to pick up in cities like Houston, Buffalo, Miami, and Kansas City. Oakland was a question mark owing to the fierce rivalry the Raiders had with both the Chiefs and the Jets.

Another positive thing about having the game everybody wanted was that it helped sell the rest of Tudor's line. Besides football games, stores would be more willing to put other Tudor games on their shelves. Norman

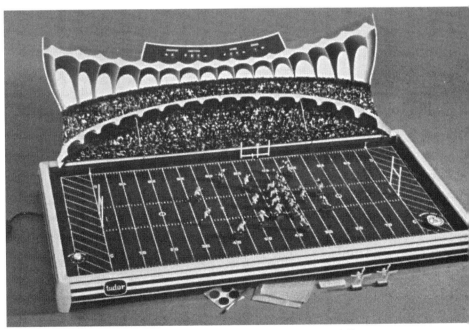

An unpublished original Lee Payne photo of an NFL prototype game that was never produced. The grandstand would appear on the Montgomery Ward version of the NFL No. 620 game. (Collection of Roddy Garcia.)

could leverage the games so a store would be guaranteed a certain number of NFL games only if they took on a designated number of the other Tudor products. This would help Tudor's other new 1968 game – a National Basketball Players Association model complete with the lithographed likenesses of ten NBA all-stars – get off to a strong start.

Buyer reaction was again overwhelming. The showroom was even more crowded than the year before, a circumstance that left Norman in disbelief and was surely heartening to the NFL Properties contingent when it dropped by to offer words of encouragement and thanks. It was clear now that Tudor was selling more than just electric football games.

After six years of sampling the buzz of NFL prestige and profits, Eddie Gluck was desperate for a way to reinvigorate his electric football line. No games had been changed or updated for 1968, and the Yankee Stadium game and basic G-883 (simply a renumbered G-890 game) were the only electric football models appearing in the Gotham showroom. Sears would again get a generic Big Bowl for Christmas, but the gap between Tudor and Gotham was getting wider. The differences between the two companies could be seen in the current issue of *Playthings*, where Tudor ran a color two-page photo spread while Gotham ran a tiny text-only ad in the back pages. When the Fair finally packed up, Norman was confident it would be another record year for Tudor.

But within weeks, the entire tone of 1968 was changed. On the evening of April 4, Martin Luther King was assassinated in Memphis. Reaction to the death of the man who was the face of the American civil rights movement was swift and fierce. Rioting broke out in cities throughout the U.S., overwhelming local police forces. To help restore order, the National Guard was sent into half a dozen cities, including Chicago, Detroit, and Boston. In the nation's capital, regular Army troops guarded the White House and helped the National Guard enforce a curfew. Racial tensions were high – a senseless act of violence had cast a pall over an entire nation. Cities smoldered for days as people around the country dealt with the emotional aftermath and struggled to regain a sense of normalcy.

It was a time when news from the off-season of the pro football world seemed trivial. Did anyone really care that the Houston Oilers were going to be the first pro football team to play indoors and that they were in the process of testing shoes on the nylon "grass" of the Astrodome? Or that Rozelle had extracted a second Monday night game from CBS for the coming season (an Ice Bowl rematch) and continued to push for an entire season of Monday night football games? Or that a lack of progress in recent meetings with the owners had a frustrated Players Association murmuring the dreaded labor "S" word – strike? There were more important things on most people's minds.

Throughout 1968 Lee Payne developed prototype electric football games at Tudor. The ultimate "lost" game is the NFL Championship "Ice Bowl" model, as seen in an unpublished original Lee Payne photo. (Collection of Roddy Garcia.)

Of course, within the grand scheme of ordinary lives, things did move on. For Tudor, Sung was keeping the team delivery schedule on target while game board production was under way again in Brooklyn. Lee, as usual, was experimenting with concepts to make electric football more realistic. The result of his late-night brainstorming would soon see the light of day.

A voice vote by the NFL and AFL owners in mid-May sent the Super Bowl back to Miami. Also discussed at this gathering were the Players Association demands, but the owners weren't in the mood to make any pronouncements on the topic. When the owners and players met again on May 23, the players officially broke off the negotiations with John Gordy claiming that the owners "refused to budge on any economic issue." No date was set for the resumption of the labor discussions. For Norman, there was concern but no alarm yet about the disagreement between the two sides. There was still plenty of time for things to get ironed out before training camps opened in July.

But it wasn't long before sports were again relegated to the bin of triviality. In the early morning hours of June 5, Massachusetts Senator

More of Lee Payne's creative work in 1968: a prototype Sports Classic electric football game that was never produced. (Collection of Roddy Garcia.)

Bobby Kennedy was shot in the head after winning the California presidential primary election. Gravely injured, Kennedy died the next day, becoming the second prominent national figure to be murdered in eight weeks. The California victory didn't guarantee Kennedy the Democratic presidential nomination, but at the least, he and his supporters were going to be a major force at the upcoming August convention in Chicago. Once again, the entire nation found itself in mourning. When Bobby was laid to rest next his brother, President John F. Kennedy, in Arlington National Cemetery, the nation was forced to confront emotions of grief and loss that reached beyond the deaths of three individuals.

As June came to a close, the NFL players and owners decided to resume their negotiations. Training camps were set to open in a few weeks, but neither side exuded any optimism for an agreement. Talks continued through July 2, when the Players Association rejected an owners' offer and then told all veteran players not to report to their training camps. The 68-game pro football preseason schedule, which included 23 interleague games, seemed in serious jeopardy. With the players instructed not to report, the owners responded a few days later by claiming that training camps would not be open to NFLPA players. Only rookies and free agents would be welcome. So were the players on strike – the first strike in modern professional sports history – or were they "locked out?" It all depended on your perspective. Talks continued through the 9th, when the owners rejected the players' most recent proposal (pension payments were the sticking point). Negotiations were stopped. The previously infallible NFL was a mess, with bitter parties on both sides. In the Packers camp, Vince Lombardi found himself "ejecting" 11 veteran players, including Bart Starr and Ray Nitschke.

When the NFL owners threatened to play an entire season with rookies and free agents, it seemed that maybe in 1968 there would finally be no argument over which was the better league. The AFL owners and players had quietly negotiated a new labor agreement that would cover the league up to the merger, and the AFL players had voted not to honor the NFL strike. So would the second Sunday in January see a thoroughly skilled and professional AFL side dismantle a semiprofessional team that was NFL in name only? It was hard to imagine the NFL owners letting such a scenario play out.

But for the moment, they were not giving in to the Players Association's demands. For Norman, it was an unsettling period. His NFL was in place. Sung had delivered almost all of the players from Hong Kong, game production in Brooklyn was in full swing, and complete games were boxed, stacked, and waiting for shipment to retailers around the country. Negotiations were even underway with Sears for another new game, spurred on by prototypes designed by Lee. With his typical quest for realism, Lee had come up with an NFL Championship game featuring the Packers and Cowboys. This "Ice Bowl" prototype, like the actual field in Green Bay, had a red, white, and blue NFL shield at midfield. It also had all white end zones...the frozen tundra had come to Tudor.

So while it was exciting to be the NFL's top licensee, what would it mean to be part of a league that might end up being a shadow of its former self? What if the owners finally decided the rookie and replacement players weren't good enough to carry the league for an entire season? Who wanted to be the top licensee of a league that didn't exist? Maybe Tudor would end up as just another toy industry one-year-wonder.

Norman received assurances from John Carney that the labor issue would be resolved. Reputations and revenue were riding on the season. The repercussions of a scab season would be enormous, from angry advertisers and television execs to apoplectic season ticket holders. Finally, a settlement was reached on July 14, with owners agreeing to increase pension contributions and medical benefits. The season would move forward without delay despite some training camps opening a few days behind schedule. As scheduled, the preseason would start on August 1 when the Houston Oilers would welcome the Washington Redskins to the brave new world of indoor football. Millions of football fans exhaled in mid-July. So did Norman Sas.

It was a good start for the AFL, as the Oilers beat the Redskins 9-3 in the Astrodome. The trend continued through the month, with the AFL holding their own in exhibition games, and sports fans looking forward to the upcoming pro football season. Unfortunately, before the season got started, the nation suffered another blow to its fragile sense of well-being.

Robert Kennedy's death left a giant void in the Democratic Party, so it was a fractured gathering that showed up in Chicago to nominate a presidential candidate in late August. Up for grabs at the national convention were Kennedy's delegates and the direction of the party. Adding to the official party views expressed on the convention podium were thousands of antiwar protesters who had gathered in several Chicago parks to express their own views on a war they blamed on current Democratic President Lyndon Johnson. With discord the dominant theme both inside and outside the convention, there was violence between protesters and police on each of the first two nights.

With 4 teams you can have your own championship playoffs

**Big Bowl Electric Football**
$13⁷⁷

**NFL Electric Football**
$10⁶⁶

The 1968 Sears' electric football page. Gotham still had the headline slot, but Tudor had the NFL. Sears 1968 *Christmas Book*, page 468. ©Sears, Roebuck & Co. 1968.

On the third night, the violence took place near the Chicago Hilton, which housed television crews from the major networks covering the convention. As Chicago police waded into the protestors with nightsticks, shields, and tear gas, they were taunted with the chant, "The whole world is watching." At the least, the whole country was watching as another violent and unsettling episode unfolded in an already turbulent year for America. The trail of those left bloodied and beaten by Chicago police included not only protesters, but also the candidacy of Democratic presidential nominee Hubert Humphrey.

So even for the most casual of sports fans, the start of the pro football season a week later was a welcome diversion. And it would be another busy year for football on the tube. Both the NFL and AFL were sticking to their double-header formats, meaning that most cities would see over 50 pro football games on television.

In starting their season a week sooner than the NFL, the AFL got to be front and center on the television screen for an entire weekend. And they made the most of it, opening with a prime time national television broadcast on Friday, September 6, in a game debuting the AFL's newest team, the Cincinnati Bengals. The Bengals surprised many viewers by going into halftime tied 10-10 with the Chargers, but in the second half the Chargers turned it into the game most people expected, winning 29-13. After the Patriots beat the Bills 16-7 on Sunday afternoon, the Astrodome welcomed the eyes of a national television audience for a Monday night battle between the Oilers and the Chiefs. The Chiefs prevailed 26-21 in a game that not only beat the NFL Monday night debut by a week, it pre-empted the first half hour of NBC's *Tonight Show*. (This did not sit well with Johnny Carson, who was so angry that he refused to do a show that night.) For the AFL, the weekend was a running start into the regular season. Adding to a sense of optimism was the fact that the league had won 13 of the 23 preseason games played against the NFL. That was ten more games than the AFL won during the 1967 preseason.

Shortly after the NFL started its season on September 14, the toy season officially got underway with Sears and Ward Christmas catalogs arriving on doorsteps across the country. Reflecting cultural change was the fact that war toys had an extremely low profile at the recent Toy Fair. Most major manufacturers were quietly moving away from the genre altogether. Perhaps the best example of the antiwar influence was illustrated on the 1968 Sears' GI Joe page. America's most famous fighting man now had no guns. He was an astronaut or a frogman – his enemies were meteors or sharks. If Joe wanted some ammo, he could find a very limited supply in the Montgomery Ward catalog.

Fortunately, Norman didn't have such worries about his top toy. What worries he had concerned Gotham and the new Sears catalog. For the fourth year in a row, the Big Bowl was the main electric football feature. Positioned on the upper left-hand side of page 468, the game took up over half of the full-color page. It was the same generic Big Bowl as the year before, yet displayed prominently in the foreground were four oversized and well-painted Gotham players. Painted players were not a new Gotham feature, but the uninformed shopper might not completely grasp this unless he read all the fine print or looked closely at the game picture. Lined up on the Big Bowl field was a generic red team and a generic white team – tucked along the edge of the game was a paintbrush and paint pallet.

Once again Tudor's NFL No. 613 was located directly below the Big Bowl. The photo was a bit sharper this year, so the NFL helmets lining the frame did catch the viewer's eye. But with only a third as much space as the Big Bowl, it was hard to see how beautifully detailed the NFL Bears and Cardinals really were. It was a point of frustration for Norman. He knew Tudor's players looked better than the Gotham impostors printed on the page. Yet Sears wasn't going to great lengths to make the differences between the two games absolutely clear. Eddie Gluck had been selling electric football games to Sears since 1955, and Sears' toy buyers felt it was in their best interest to have several different suppliers of similar items. It kept everybody "honest." The competition also did something else. It kept prices low. In fact both the No. 613 and Big Bowl were cheaper than the year before.

Not following the lower price trend was Gotham's G-883 Pro Electric Football game, which sat completely overshadowed in a tiny layout next to the Big Bowl. Priced at $7.49, it made Tudor's larger and more detailed NFL No. 613 seem like a bargain for $9.99. Although he didn't get the top spot, Norman had made up ground on Gotham this year. In addition to the No. 613, Tudor also had its electric baseball game on the page. This made Tudor and Gotham "equal" for 1968 – both companies had two games on page 468.

Over in the Ward catalog, Tudor had electric football all to itself. Taking up the top two thirds of page 311 were three Tudor games, including a new Ward version of the Sears No. 613 model. Since Ward and Sears wanted exclusive items, this game was numbered No. 619 and was advertised as coming with the Rams and 49ers. (Anyone with a magnifying glass could see the Cardinals and Bears on the field.) The frame did not have the unique NFL helmet design of the Sears No. 613, but there really wasn't much difference between the two games. Lee had made just enough changes to give Ward an exclusive, without working himself too hard. Both Ward's and Sears' models were priced at $9.99.

The No. 620 was clearly Ward's featured game, and it, too, had a new grandstand design. Life-size Tudor players were again part of the Ward layout, except this time the realism got a little confused. In the middle of the page a Cleveland Brown figure wore no. 42, which corresponded to real life Brown, Paul Warfield. The only problem was, the figure was one of Tudor's white players, and Warfield was African-American. Somewhat hidden near the bound edge of the page was a New York Giant figure, wearing no. 11. When the catalog went to the printer earlier in the year, no. 11 was Giants backup quarterback Earl Morrall. Unfortunately, by August he was a Baltimore Colt. But inaccurate player numbering did little to distract from the grandeur of the No. 620. The game still looked fantastic.

And so did the new Ward Tru-Action No. 501 model. The No. 501 differed from the No. 500 in that it debuted a brand new and very modern looking Lee Payne-designed grandstand. Unlike the hand-drawn and somewhat cartoonish looking regular No. 500 grandstand, this one included a real crowd scene photo and even came in a double-deck configuration. It definitely enhanced the realism of Tudor's entry-level game.

Despite the quirks of the Ward page, Norman and Lee felt good about their relationship with the NFL and the coming Christmas season. Negotiations for a new Sears game were going well. Norman was confident

### Wards NFL electric football
with 3-ft. grandstand
... complete scoreboard **12**<sup>88</sup>

3-D players give their all on the vibrating gridiron. Triple-threat quarterbacks run, pass, kick. Offensive-defensive players run, block and tackle. 24 players, including passer-kicker, wear the official team colors of the Cleveland Browns and the New York Giants. Includes automatic timer and speed control. Magnetic down and ball marker with chain. Center-post goal posts in official "NFL Gold." All figures hand-painted for complete accuracy. Big grandstand, jammed with loyal fans, folds easily for storage. Game about 37¾x20¼x3 in. high. UL listed.
48 T 14510 A—Ship. wt. 11 lbs. 13 oz.... .........12.88

**42**

NFL electric football **9**<sup>99</sup>

Tru-Action electric football **5**<sup>99</sup>

Full of excitement! Game includes two full teams, 24 3-D players in all. Quarterbacks run, pass, kick, even fumble. Automatic timer, speed control. Magnetic down markers. Complete scoreboard. Paint your own teams with paint set included. About 26x15½ in. UL listed.
48 T 14505 M—Ship. wt. 4 lbs. 13 oz......5.99

Thrilling electric football between the San Francisco 49ers and the Los Angeles Rams. The 24 players, including 2 passer-kickers, can do everything the real teams do except get injured. Automatic timer, speed control. Full scoreboard. About 31½x17½ in. UL listed.
48 T 14509 A—Ship. wt. 9 lbs. 14 oz......9.99

It was all Tudor in Montgomery Ward, including a No. 620, the new NFL No. 619, and a No. 500 with an exclusive grandstand (numbered No. 501-S). Montgomery Ward 1968 *Christmas Catalog*, page 311. ©Montgomery Ward, Inc. 1968.

that a Tudor game would take the place of the Big Bowl on the Sears electric football page in the very near future. Gotham sales were falling, and the company's innovation was nonexistent. Tudor, meanwhile, continued to be NFL Properties No.1 licensee. Games were flying out the doors in Brooklyn as soon as they were boxed. If Sears wanted to make some real money on electric football, the company would have to change its loyalties.

Another person who was pleased with Tudor's success was Larry Kent. He was a little surprised to find electric football as his top seller, but it was a great item. Tudor's miniature NFL concept was a perfect way to market the league to the country's most impressionable segment of football fans – preadolescent boys. Kent was also having success with the Team Shop concept, which had expanded to even more retailers and cities this year. And there were a record 90 NFL licensees for 1968, including more Training Table offerings than ever before. About the only place Kent wasn't making ground was in Sears. There were still only two NFL items in the

Christmas catalog – Tudor's No. 613 and a line of NFL books for boys. (Ward was up to three items now – Tudor's No. 620 and No. 619 models, plus the NFL books.) But Kent had finally caught up with his old employer. Roy Rogers was down to two Sears items in 1968, a pair of children's boots and a guitar.

Team orders picked up for Tudor as the season rolled along, and demand for the new AFL was strong as well. Despite upping the production numbers from the year before, it was clear that the stock of some teams would not make it to Christmas. It was hoped no games would run short of teams. The likely suspects were the Chiefs and Jets, and the 49ers and Rams.

As the World Series got underway in early October, Sears, Ward, and J.C. Penney were already featuring electric football in their advertising. Sears again focused its promotional efforts on the NFL, using Tudor's No. 613 model in newspaper ads to announce the opening of their Toy Town departments. Like the catalog, Ward's advertising had some quirks, as occasionally an ad promoted NFL electric football – in price and description – while the game pictured was a No. 501 model. Where Ward was able to matchup text and photos, the No. 501 had a very attractive $5.19 price tag. The wild card and surprise in electric football was J.C.

The NFL had scheduled a nationally televised Ice Bowl rematch on Monday, October 28th. In Lee Payne's photography sessions he covered this matchup, lining up Cowboys and Packers on a No. 620. Unpublished original Lee Payne photo. (Collection of Roddy Garcia.)

Penney, who decided to push Gotham's large G-1500 game for $12.88. That put the game at the same price point as Tudor's NFL No. 620 and Gotham's own Big Bowl.

Pete Rozelle and the NFL spent much of October promoting the Monday night Ice Bowl rematch of the Packers and Cowboys. Scheduled for the 28th, the Monday night aspect of the game was more important than the rematch component. Rozelle was determined to land the NFL a weekly Monday night slot, and the ratings following the game would hopefully give him the leverage to push the concept on the television networks. Unfortunately, the Packers were not the same team they had been in January. Due to age and injury, they came into the game with a 2-3-1 record. (Lombardi knew what the future held.) The Cowboys, meanwhile, were an undefeated 6-0. Dallas fans, hoping to gain revenge for the previous two NFL Championship game losses, had months earlier made the game a scalper's paradise. But what the Cowboys' faithful saw was Bart Starr throwing four touchdown passes in a 28-17 Packers victory. Halfway into their 9th NFL season, the Cowboys had yet to defeat the Packers.

From the depths of the Cowboys' sorrows came the numbers Rozelle wanted. According to the national Arbitron ratings, the game drew a 44% share of the television audience. This made the game the sixth-highest rated show of the new fall television season. It seemed clear that a lot of people would watch football on a Monday night. And a lot of those people must have been women who could potentially attract a more diverse set of advertisers to pro football. Network executives still had questions about whether people would watch pro football on fourteen consecutive Monday nights, but Rozelle had all the evidence he needed. There was even talk of the NFL starting its own network once the leagues merged in 1970. So if neither CBS nor NBC wanted to televise Monday night games, Rozelle might just pick up his football league and go home.

Perhaps more than the Monday night ratings, an AFL game played on Sunday, November 17, demonstrated the raw emotional power of televised pro football. For almost 59 minutes the Jets and Raiders played the kind of offensive-overdrive game the AFL was famous for, with the Jets kicking a field goal for a 32-29 lead with 65 seconds left. It was now almost 4:00 p.m. in Oakland, where the game was being played, and almost 7:00 p.m. back on the East Coast, where the bulk of a national television audience was perched on the edge of its proverbial couch. After the Jets kickoff, most television viewers got to see only two more Oakland plays before NBC left the game and switched to a heavily promoted special program – the television adaptation of the children's book *Heidi*. While the story of Heidi unfolded, the Raiders scored two touchdowns in nine seconds for a 43-32 victory. Fortunate West Coast viewers sat stunned at the final gun (Oakland viewers were blacked out). East Coast viewers, on the other hand, went...nuts.

So many calls came into the NBC switchboard in New York City that it broke down. People who couldn't get through to NBC started calling the police department whose emergency phone number became overloaded – and stayed that way for several hours. Those who couldn't get through to NBC or the police directed their calls to the New York Telephone Company and the *New York Times*. Operators at both places got an earful from frustrated football viewers. The incident made the front page of the *Times* the next day, and within a few days NBC promised not to cut away from future football broadcasts. Somewhere in his Park Avenue office, Pete Rozelle was smiling.

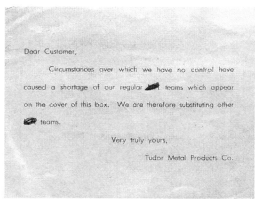

Dear Customer,

Circumstances over which we have no control have caused a shortage of our regular ▓ teams which appear on the cover of this box. We are therefore substituting other ▓ teams.

Very truly yours,

Tudor Metal Products Co.

**By late 1968 teams were being substituted in Tudor's NFL and AFL games. This note was from an AFL game. The "NFL" had been scribbled out. (Collection of Earl Shores.)**

Also doing a lot smiling at this point in the season was Norman. Sears once again had the NFL No. 613 a featured item in its print advertising, and NFL electric football games could be seen in newspaper advertising throughout the country. Retailers who regretted passing on Tudor's miniature NFL in 1967 were not making the same mistake this year – even the Gibson Discount Center chain had the Tudor NFL No. 620 in many of its stores. For a retailer that focused mostly on toys under $7, having the $11.88 No. 620 on the shelves was a testament to the popularity of Tudor's NFL electric football games.

While the popularity of Tudor's games made Norman smile, the popularity came with an occasional grimace. Besides record game shipments, Tudor had been overwhelmed with team orders. In fact, boys had begun walking right into the factory office in Brooklyn, money in hand, hoping to buy their favorite NFL or AFL team. As hard as it was for Norman and Lee to believe, teams were starting to run short. That meant disappointed kids when a Tudor box arrived at the doorstep minus that one coveted team. The team shortage began spilling over into the games too. Thanks to the Jets and Chiefs both having strong seasons, demand for the AFL game exceeded Norman's initial production numbers. Tudor could make more AFL games and boxes in Brooklyn as the fall moved on, but the team numbers were fixed. Albert Sung was already getting ready for the 1969 run of teams. As a result, by Thanksgiving Day, Tudor's AFL

More from Lee Payne's 1968 photography sessions: the Colts and Packers on a No. 620. Unpublished original Lee Payne photo. (Collection of Roddy Garcia.)

games were being shipped with a note of apology – and Bills and Dolphins in dark jerseys.

By December, Tudor NFL Games were so popular that retailers were using newspaper ads to announce when new shipments arrived. Many stores were selling both the No. 510 and the No. 620, giving shoppers the full range of NFL options for Christmas. Sears continue its heavy newspaper use of the No. 613, sometimes offering the game for as low as $8.88. Ward also gave electric football a high profile during the closing weeks of the season, mostly focusing on the generic No. 501 game. It might seem a little surprising that Ward's two NFL games rarely made the company's toy ads. But why would a retailer waste advertising space on games that were selling themselves?

Gotham's electric football picture in early December was a bit different. Not only were the games not selling, they were almost non-existent in toy advertising. At this point in the selling season, Eddie Gluck really needed all the promotional help he could get, even if it came from a clearance sale.

When an article about the toy industry appeared in the *New York Times* on Sunday, December 15, an anonymous "toy insider" answered the question, "what makes a toy a bestseller?" Television was the answer. In 1968 over 300 toys had been promoted on television – an industry record. Manufacturers had even come up with a formula for the expected

The new AFL No. 520 model was so popular that Tudor ran out of Jets and Chiefs long before Christmas. (Photo by Roddy Garcia.)

benefit from television exposure: $10 in sales for every dollar invested in a television spot. An exception to this was Tudor's NFL lineup, although it could be said that Tudor's advertising ran on CBS every Sunday afternoon between 1:00 p.m. and 5:30 p.m.

Toy clearance sales at Sears and Ward began during the final days before Christmas with both retailers offering savings of up to 50%. Usually the deepest discounts came on items that hadn't sold very well in the first place, a situation that wouldn't describe electric football in 1968. Santa letters this year had gotten very specific, with boys asking for NFL electric football games instead of generic ones. (This was one area the *Times'* toy insider forgot to consider – the contents of Dear Santa letters.)

After such a turbulent year, it was a relief for many people to finally make it to the Christmas season. It felt good to slow down and experience some Christmas spirit in 1968. Unfortunately by mid-December, seasonal joy in the NFL was limited to four teams – the playoff bound Colts, Cowboys, Browns, and Vikings. Over in the AFL, the Jets and Joe Namath won the East, while the Chiefs and Raiders finished tied at 12-2 in the West. The tie meant that the weekend before Christmas would have three playoff games, two NFL plus the AFL West tiebreaker.

Thanks to their quarterback, Earl Morrall, the Colts were favored to win the NFL. A preseason injury to Baltimore-legend Johnny Unitas allowed Morrall to leave his usual spot on the bench and lead the Colts to a 13-1 record. Coming from a player who spent nine of his twelve NFL seasons as a backup quarterback, this performance was a huge surprise. It also won Morrall the NFL Player of the Year award. And after the Browns beat the Cowboys 31-20 on Saturday, Morrall continued his winning ways by guiding the Colts to a 21-14 win over the Vikings in Sunday's early playoff game. Later that afternoon in Oakland, the favored Chiefs collapsed against the Raiders and took a 41-6 pounding. Meeting for the AFL title would be the Jets and Raiders. In the NFL, the Colts would get a chance to avenge their only loss of the season, which had come at the hand of the Browns.

Every year television offers a sleigh full of holiday specials, which mostly miss the mark in capturing the spirit of the season (the exception being *A Charlie Brown Christmas*). But anybody watching television on Christmas Eve 1968 experienced an unexpected and genuinely uplifting moment. Earlier in the day, the three astronauts of Apollo 8 became the first humans to orbit the moon. At 9:30 p.m. Eastern Standard Time, they began a 30-minute television broadcast from their capsule, viewing the earth as no humans ever had before. The astronauts concluded the broadcast by taking turns reading from the Book of Genesis, starting with, "In the Beginning, God created the heaven and the earth." By the time Commander Frank Borman signed off with "good night, good luck, a Merry Christmas and God bless you all – all of you on the *GOOD* earth," it was clear that one of most poignant moments in human history had just occurred. In fact so momentous were these few minutes of dialogue that *Time* magazine named the Apollo 8 astronauts its "Men of the Year" a mere week later.

Christmas morning was brighter all around thanks to the Apollo 8 astronauts. And it was even brighter if you found a Tudor NFL or AFL game under the tree. Any boy receiving a No. 620, No. 510, or No. 520 – at least a No. 520 with Jets in the game – now had a Tudor team that would be playing in one of the actual championship games on Sunday. With Christmas coming on Wednesday, smack in the middle of the pro football playoff week, it was an opportune time to get an NFL electric football game. Neither a Bears-Cardinals No. 613 from Sears nor a Rams-49ers No. 619 from Ward would have diminished the thrill of a Christmas morning. Finding a generic No. 500 or a Gotham game, however, surely would have conjured a whiff of disappointment to mingle with the scent of pine and roasting turkey. The Big Bowl might come with four complete teams, but none of them were playing for an NFL or AFL Championship on Sunday. They looked more like one of the teams from the North-South Shrine All-Star Game that would be televised later that afternoon.

Lagging sales had retailers completely on edge during the Christmas shopping season, with blame being spread on everything from the Hong Kong flu to the upcoming presidential changeover. But the last days before the holiday turned out to be record setting with some retailers reporting a 40% increase in sales from the equivalent period in 1967. And Sears, Ward, and J.C. Penney would all report sales records for December, as well as the entire year of 1968. December sales at J.C. Penney were up almost 20% from the year before. This figure may have given Gotham a boost, but with Ward being Tudor-exclusive and Sears heavily promoting the NFL No. 613, the major beneficiary from these sales figures was Tudor.

Most electric football games were likely still in the play rotation by Friday evening when the Tangerine Bowl launched a six-day period of televised football unlike any other before. Scheduled for the tube on Saturday were four more collegiate games, including the Gator Bowl, the Sun Bowl, and the Blue-Gray and East-West Shrine All-Star games. It was a full plate of televised football, providing almost seven full hours of games. But for most football fans, these were just appetizers for championship Sunday.

Surprisingly, the NFL and AFL had not cooperated very well with their starting times. The Jets and Raiders would kickoff at 1:00 p.m. in Shea Stadium, while the Colts and Browns got underway at 2:35 p.m. in

A scrimmage line of Cowboys and Cardinals, expertly painted and numbered by Lee Payne. On the Cowboys side are linebackers Dave Edwards (no. 52) Lee Roy Jordan (no. 55), and Chuck Howley (no. 54). Carrying the ball (top of the photo) is Cardinals running back Bobby Joe Conrad (no. 40). Photo by Lee Payne. (Collection of Roddy Garcia.)

Christmas morning 1968. The game had been moved from the living room floor to the kitchen table in order to accommodate the "crowd." (Photo by Doris Shores.)

Cleveland. It was a day when Broadway Joe Namath fulfilled his $400,000 promise, passing the Jets to a 27-23 win in front of 62,000 delirious New Yorkers. And by the time the Jets started showering each other with champagne, the NFL game was essentially over. A zero wind chill and a fired-up Colts team immobilized the Browns, who were humiliated in a 34-0 drubbing. In two weeks, the Colts and Jets would meet in Miami for Super Bowl III. By Monday morning, Las Vegas sports analyst Jimmy "The Greek" Snyder had declared the 15-1 Colts to be 17-point favorites.

But the year wasn't over yet, and neither was the televised football schedule. On Monday night, football fans could watch LSU and Florida State in the inaugural Peach Bowl game from Atlanta. New Year's Eve football entertainment would then come from the first Bluebonnet Bowl to be played in the Houston Astrodome. Then came the four traditional bowl games of New Year's Day.

January 12, 1969: Super Bowl III proved to be a landmark event for both professional and electric football. (AP Photo/NFL Photos)

# 21 A NEW STAR FOR PRO AND ELECTRIC FOOTBALL

The must-see game on New Years Day was the Rose Bowl, where No. 1 Ohio State was playing No. 2 Southern Cal. By early evening, Ohio State's 27-16 victory left no doubt that the Buckeyes were the nation's top team. Hard-core fans could still view football late into the night thanks to the Orange Bowl. Those who stayed up for the game were rewarded with a thrilling finish, as Penn State scored a last-minute touchdown and a two-point conversion for a 15-14 win over Kansas. When the Orange Bowl telecast finally signed off, it marked the end of something unprecedented in football's relationship with television. It was the end of six consecutive days of nationally televised football games.

In the Super Bowl buildup Rozelle had already announced the team uniform scheme – the Colts would wear their home blue jerseys while the Jets would wear their white away jerseys. And the brash Namath was already speaking his mind to reporters, providing bulletin board ammo for the Colts by claiming that Daryle Lamonica of the Raiders was a better quarterback than Earl Morrall. On the Sunday before the Super Bowl the Cowboys and Vikings provided the entertainment, with the Cowboys claiming the No. 3 spot in the NFL during a rain-soaked 17-13 victory. Not holding up well during the game was the freshly sodded Orange Bowl field, which came apart in chunks under the feet of the players. Field conditions for the biggest game of the season were now a question mark. But questions about the field were soon forgotten. While speaking at a Miami Touchdown Club dinner on Thursday night, a frustrated Namath lashed out at several heckling NFL fans and guaranteed a Jets victory. By Friday morning, Namath's "guarantee" was the story of the week.

At 3:30 p.m. on January 12, NBC began its Super Bowl III broadcast. The Colts were seething from Namath's insults. They were sure their suffocating defense was going to make Namath eat his words, and some of the plentiful Orange Bowl mud as well. But the game unfolded in a way that few people expected. When the final gun sounded, the Jets had a 16-7 win. And not only had Broadway Joe delivered on his guarantee, he was the game's MVP. The AFL was finally the equal of the NFL. Actually, on this day they were better. It was a bitter loss for the Colts and the NFL, a loss made all the more bitter when an invited special guest failed to show for a postgame chat with Commissioner Rozelle. It's usually not a good idea to a let your future boss stew in a hotel suite for twelve hours, but that's exactly what Namath did.

**AFL-NFL teams in official uniforms!**
Consumer may write in for any or all of 10 AFL and 16 NFL teams at additional cost.

AFL teams available in dark jerseys only.*
NFL teams available in both light and dark jerseys.
*JETS available in both light & dark jerseys.

Inside the Tudor sales catalog Norman and Lee hinted at things to come from Tudor. (Collection of Norman Sas.)

Over 75,000 spectators filled the Orange Bowl, and over 50 million viewers watched the game on television. One person who viewed the upset from a very good seat in the Orange Bowl was Norman Sas. He was there as a guest of NFL Properties, discovering that being the NFL's top-earning licensee had some very special perks. The event was mostly for pleasure, but some work was being done while the game went on. Camera in hand, Norman took photos of the elaborate markings painted on the field by the Super Bowl groundskeepers. Lee would study the photos carefully once the film was developed in Brooklyn. Norman had also sent word to Albert Sung to start painting thousands of Jets in white and Colts in blue.

The 1969 Tudor sales catalog made sure the company's connections with professional football would not be missed. 1969 Tudor sales catalog. (Collection of Norman Sas.)

While Norman was enjoying the Florida sun and a Super Bowl for the ages, Eddie Gluck was attempting to put Gotham back in the sports action game. In both *Playthings* and *Toy & Hobby World*, Gotham ran a full-page ad for a new Denny McLain baseball game. McLain was a Detroit Tigers pitcher who won 31 games on his way to the American League Cy Young and MVP awards. His Tigers also won the World Series. The ad claimed that "Gotham Brings Santa Back" for spring and summer sales. These ads were significant for several reasons. First, there was Gluck's initiative to go out and land an endorsement deal with McLain. It was a gamble, but the star's stature would help Gotham sell games. And second, it was the first time Gotham had run a full-page ad in *Playthings* in over four years. The question was, did Gluck really have a plan, or was it a last gasp attempt to stay competitive with Tudor?

Baseball's Denny McLain shakes hands with Gotham sales manager Jack Barry.

Gotham attempted to jump start 1969 by running a full-page ad in *Playthings* for their new Denny McLain baseball game. *Toy & Hobby World*, page 63, January 6, 1969.

January finished with the Buffalo Bills picking first in the NFL-AFL draft. Without hesitation they chose the best and best-known college player in the country – one O.J. Simpson. Added to the recent Jets Super Bowl victory, it was one more AFL step towards parity with the NFL.

Just a few days after the draft, a once-retired coach decided to make his way back to the sidelines. The Packers were not happy to free Vince Lombardi from his general manager obligations in Green Bay, but ultimately they had no choice. So the coach who was once the face of the Packers franchise became the coach and executive vice president of the Washington Redskins. If it was a challenge Lombardi was looking for, the lowly Redskins fit the bill perfectly. The team's last winning season came in 1955.

Already Norman knew two sure things about this coming year – he was going to sell more No. 520 AFL games and more Washington Redskins than the year before. A fair number of Washington teams were already stockpiled in Brooklyn, so upping their production numbers wasn't necessary. But his No. 520 projections were going to be moved upward. The most famous player in all of pro football, Joe Namath, was part of the game. It was going to be a game that people wanted. Norman was also hopeful that Sears' new exclusive model would be successful. Only Sears' toy buyers had seen it so far and they were ecstatic.

February, as always, was crunch month for Toy Fair preparations. Lee was busy in the Tudor showroom, but this year he was there in a slightly different capacity. He was no longer Tudor's director of product development. He was now the head of his own graphic design firm, Lee Payne Associates. The change had taken place during the previous fall with the new firm being located outside the city in Hastings-on-Hudson, New York. But Lee still wasn't very far away from Brooklyn. And his main client was Tudor. He had spent nearly a decade refining electric football, and it was clearly a prized part of his creative identity. Besides, who could walk out on NFL Properties' top-selling item? Lee was going to remain intimately involved with Tudor.

In some ways setting up in 1969 would be simpler than in other years because all of Tudor's electric football items for the Fair were in production. There wouldn't be any finicky prototype games to nurse through the daily grind of toy-buyer exhibitions. But next year would be different. The merger of the NFL and AFL would be the biggest sports story of 1970. Norman and Lee were already discussing ways to feature the merger in next year's Tudor line.

Tudor's Toy Fair showroom in 1969, with buyers placing their orders for Tudor's popular NFL electric football games. *Toy & Hobby World*, page 2, March 17, 1969.

Eddie Gluck, at this point, was involved in a different kind of discussion. Despite the Denny McLain splash in *Playthings*, Gotham was still having financial issues. On February 25, Gluck signed the factory over to the widow of former Gotham owner Charles A. Anderson for the grand sum of $1 (technically it was sold to the Charles A. Anderson trust). The estate would assume Gotham's debts, which now included $119,000 left on the original 1959 mortgage and $55,000 left on the second mortgage that was taken out in 1967. While it might appear to be a noble gesture by the Anderson family to assure that the company their patriarch founded would stay in business, a more realistic view was this: the family assumed the debt to make sure Gluck didn't mortgage Gotham into oblivion.

For both toys and professional football, March was a critical month. The Toy Fair would be the center of the toy universe during the opening days of the month, while just a short time later the NFL and AFL owners were scheduled to get down to the nuts and bolts of merging the two leagues. Television was a driving force in both worlds. Pro football needed to sort out its details so a new television deal could be signed. The sooner the owners could secure their major stream of income, the happier they all would be. In toys, the overriding theme was the amount of money major toy companies were going to spend on television advertising. Ideal, Remco, Kenner, and Hasbro were all pouring record sums – almost $25 million combined – into getting their products presented to both kids and parents through the magic of television.

It was no accident that space-themed toys had prominent placement when the Toy Fair opened on March 2. NASA's successful Apollo program, helped by the Christmas Eve broadcast of Apollo 8, was inducing a severe case of space fever among all Americans. Benefiting from some fortuitous timing was the Fair itself, as Apollo 9 was scheduled to lift off on the afternoon of March 3. Toy manufacturers were also looking into the future. If all went well, two Apollo manned moon landings would happen by December. To help kids relive any moonwalk memories, Mattel's Major Matt Mason and Eldon's Billy Blastoff would be ready for duty on Christmas morning.

Not needing any help from the heavens was Tudor. For the second year in a row, electric football was NFL Properties' top-earning product. Again, the company sold all the NFL games it had and could have sold even more. Tudor was playing up its link to professional sports and the NFL with a two-page *Playthings* spread. The ad theme picked for 1969 was "go to the pro," the pro of course being Tudor thanks to its licensing relationships with the NFL, AFL, Major League Baseball (new for 1969), and the Players Associations of both the NBA and NHL. Included in the ad was a list of all the professional games Tudor was making. At the top of the list were the company's NFL and AFL models.

What the ad did not include was any promise or mention of television advertising. Norman still didn't see any reason to join the crowd. He was already selling out his entire stock; why waste money on television spots? And really, Tudor had an expansive national television spot every Sunday afternoon from September to January. No other toy company could claim such visibility.

There was only one electric football change in 1969. Tudor was abandoning the generic No. 610 Sports Classic game. In two years of availability it had never been a big seller, mainly due to its cost (it was priced higher than the NFL No. 510 and AFL No. 520). The only time its sales picked up was when the NFL games were scarce. Only then were retailers willing to take on the No. 610. And it still was not an easy sell. But the game wasn't a complete failure, as this medium-size game board template had become a successful part of both the Sears and Ward NFL

**SUPER DOME ELECTRIC FOOTBALL**

No. 1512

Gotham's elaborate 1969 Super Dome Electric Football game, which followed the stadium trend for indoor football. The Oilers were now playing in the Astrodome, and the City of New Orleans was in the planning stages for an indoor stadium that would share the same name as Gotham's new game. 1969 Gotham sales flyer. (Collection of Roddy Garcia.)

lineup. The loss of the No. 610 left Tudor with only four electric football games – the NFL No. 620 and No. 510, the AFL No. 520, and the ever-present Tru-Action No. 500. The Tudor game drawing the most attention during the Fair, much to John Carney's chagrin, was the AFL Jets-Chiefs game. What toy retailer wouldn't want the Super Bowl champs and Joe Namath on its shelves? In addition to the champion Jets, the rest of Tudor's line was pretty strong. The NFL Champion Colts were on the No. 510.

The AFL was playing a bigger role in the 1969 Tudor sales catalog as well. Not only did the AFL shield make the cover of the catalog, for the first time ever, all nine AFL teams were pictured inside sharing a color page with the teams of the NFL. Serving as a tease for coming attractions, Tudor included a close-up photo of a Jets player in a white uniform posed next to a Colts player in a dark uniform. Once again, it was a strong Fair for Tudor. Norman and Lee had created a core of highly recognizable NFL products.

Not far away in the Gotham showroom, however, Eddie Gluck was set for one of his most ambitious Toy Fair presentations in some time. Despite the company's financial issues, he had not been idle during the last year. There was the new Denny McLain Baseball, which even had a miniature

Denny McLain as the pitcher. And Gotham's designers had been hard at work trying to keep their electric football line viable against Tudor.

For 1969 Gotham had come up with a midsized electric football game, and an endorsement deal with the National Football League Players Association. Gluck couldn't get the NFL, so he did the next best thing – just as Tudor had done with basketball and hockey. (Although if the previous season's NFL strike had lasted months instead of days, an association with NFLPA might not have been particularly attractive.) The new G-895 NFLPA game measured 30" x 17" and came with a large wrap-around grandstand that was streamlined and much easier to assemble than the Big Bowl. Gotham designers created a clever football-shaped logo that emphasized the "NFL" part of the NFLPA. The "Players Association" part of the logo was printed in much smaller text. Another new feature was 48 "self-stick name tabs" featuring the names of star NFL players. This would be the Gotham way of personalizing the players.

And in "bigger" news, Gotham had discontinued the Big Bowl. In its place was a new flagship electric football game, the G-1512 Super Dome. Standing 21" high, the Super Dome game was inspired by Houston's Astrodome, the stadium that introduced the world to indoor football during the previous season. New Orleans also had a domed stadium on the drawing board, so football stadiums with a roof and a rug seemed like an obvious new direction. It wasn't the first time that Gluck had gotten an early jump on a stadium architecture trend.

The Super Dome, at least the dome itself, was an innovative and inspired concept even though the top of the dome wasn't actually enclosed. Sitting on a large G-1500 game board was a colorful metal and plastic grandstand that fully encased the game from three sides. More like a tent than a stadium, the dome rose inward and upward instead of sloping away from the game like the Big Bowl grandstand did. So for practicality, the Super Dome was in the form-over-function category. It was going to be even more challenging to play with than the retired Big Bowl.

On the frame was a new design incorporating the NFL Players Association logo. Other standard game equipment included the 48 NFLPA self-stick player name tabs. Unfortunately, both Players Association models still had Gotham's antiquated players, goal posts, and quarterback.

The players remained the same unpainted and poorly molded players that Gotham introduced back in 1963. And on each goal line sat the same H shaped goal posts that first appeared back in 1961. Gotham's metal quarterback, with his high-top shoes and un-quarterback like number looked like a football dinosaur. (Seriously, how many years had it been since an NFL quarterback wore no. 32?) It was simply a strange mix of parts. The stadiums on the G-895 and the Super Dome were modern and

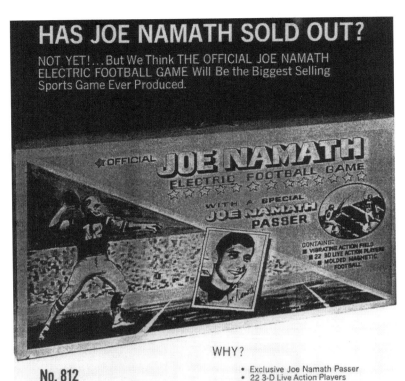

## HAS JOE NAMATH SOLD OUT?

NOT YET!...But We Think THE OFFICIAL JOE NAMATH
ELECTRIC FOOTBALL GAME Will Be the Biggest Selling
Sports Game Ever Produced.

★ OFFICIAL **JOE NAMATH**
ELECTRIC FOOTBALL GAME

WITH A SPECIAL
**JOE NAMATH**
PASSER

CONTAINS:
■ VIBRATING ACTION FIELD
■ 22 3-D LIVE ACTION PLAYERS
■ MOLDED MAGNETIC
  FOOTBALL

WHY?

**No. 812**

• Exclusive Joe Namath Passer
• 22 3-D Live Action Players

Gotham's 1969 sales catalog didn't appear until April, and when it did there was large surprise. The
Gotham G-812 Joe Namath Electric Football Game. 1969 Gotham sales catalog. (Collection of Roddy
Garcia.)

in full color, while the players and the field looked like leftovers from the
black-and-white television era. Perhaps Gluck did all he could in the face
of declining sales. It was just a question of whether he had come up with
enough special innovations to get back on the field with Tudor.

But Gluck hadn't survived over thirty years in the toy industry without being
resourceful. In the April issue of *Playthings* a full-page Gotham ad challenged
the toy world: "If these 3 Action Games don't make money for you, the other
9 will." The games in the ad were the Super Dome, the NFLPA G-895, and
the Denny McLain Baseball game. Also promised was "Gotham games will be
backed by the biggest advertising and promotional campaign ever." It wasn't
clear what this meant, whether it was the biggest campaign in toy history or in
Gotham history. Those in the toy trade would know right away it wasn't the
biggest campaign in toy history. And considering that Gluck had recently sold
his building off for a dollar, it was really hard to believe that Gotham could even
muster the biggest campaign in company history.

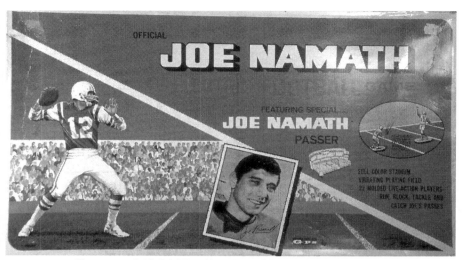

After a summer that included Namath's "retirement," Gotham's Namath model finally appeared on toy store shelves. (Photo by Earl Shores.)

Eddie Gluck then had one more trick play to unveil before April finished. Late in the month Gotham finally issued its 1969 sales catalog. In it was the toy equivalent of a "Hail Mary" pass. A new electric football game would be available in August. It would be numbered the G-812. Oddly, the catalog didn't have a photo of the game, just the mock-up of a box lid. And the player whose photo was on the game was unmistakable. Gotham's new game was...the Official Joe Namath Electric Football Game.

Somehow in the weeks since the Super Bowl, Gluck had landed a personal endorsement deal with the hottest name in all of sports – the Super Bowl MVP, the man with the guarantee, the one, the only, Broadway Joe. The text introducing the game asked, "Has Joe Namath Sold Out?" Of course he had, but the coy Gotham response was "Not yet...But we think the Official Joe Namath Game will be the biggest selling sports game ever produced." While the reality of that claim was open to debate, the game would be the first player-endorsed electric football game ever produced.

The selling point of the game was a special Joe Namath passer figure – which Gotham had yet to design. So toy buyers were being asked to take on faith that Gotham could produce a decent looking Joe and, therefore, a viable game. It was a bold move on Gluck's part. Super Bowl III was one of the biggest football stories ever – the hype of the Jets' victory still reverberated throughout the country. Perhaps Namath could do the same thing for underdog Gotham that he had done for the underdog Jets?

At Tudor, there was some unease about what Gluck was going to put on his Namath model, but there was greater concern about the pro football owners not being able to figure out the merger issue. A joint NFL-AFL meeting had taken place in mid-March, but the only decision made was to have the coming Super Bowl in New Orleans. For Tudor, there were games to plan for 1970, and the sooner Lee could start the design process the better. There was also the issue of knowing what teams to produce in "game" amounts. Getting the new line of merger games and teams right outweighed any issues Gotham could throw at Tudor. Norman also thought that Gotham might take another sales hit in the fall despite having Namath. Norman's confidence was founded by a simple fact – Gotham had lost its featured electric football slot in Sears. That slot was now Tudor's. And in this new Sears slot would be Tudor's own "Namath" model.

During meetings that began on April 30, the NFL and AFL owners finally made real progress toward the merger. It was agreed that the new league would be divided into 2 conferences of 13 teams, with each conference having 3 divisions. (Two divisions with 4 teams, and a single division with 5.) A playoff format was also devised, with 4 teams from each conference qualifying – the 3 division winners, plus the best second-place team. What wasn't decided during the five days of deliberation was exactly who would be in each conference, but the consensus scenario had 3 NFL teams combining to form a conference with the 10 AFL teams. The problem was, NFL teams weren't exactly lining up for a transfer to the AFL.

A week later, the owners went at it again, and on May 12 Rozelle announced that the Colts, Browns, and Steelers had agreed to move to the new American Conference. This new conference even had its division alignment set up, unlike the 13-team National Conference, whose owners still couldn't agree after 22 more hours of discussion. The American League teams were pleased with the deal as they had gained the defending NFL Eastern and Western Conference Champions along with a number of star NFL players. More importantly, an American Conference package would be attractive to any television network.

Even without the details of the NFC divisions, the alignment made things easier for Tudor. Decisions could finally be made about the games Tudor would produce for 1970 and what teams would be manufactured for these new games. A decision had already been made to produce all the teams of the merged NFL in both home and away jerseys. Albert Sung would have ten more teams to produce. His job would be further complicated because some teams were planning on changing their uniforms in the new NFL.

On May 26, another one of Pete Rozelle's visions was fulfilled – the NFL signed a three-year Monday night football deal with ABC. Starting in 1970, the network would televise 13 Monday night games per seasons. Both CBS and NBC had been offered the contract, but they turned it down saying it was too risky to put sports on regularly in prime time. The cost of

Super Bowl III MVP Joe Namath passed for 206 yards against the Colts in January. The Gotham designers studied photos like this one and took extra care in... (AP Photo/NFL Photos)

...creating one of the most distinctive electric football pieces ever made. The Gotham Joe Namath passer figure – white shoes, white wristbands, dirty pants and all. (Photo by Earl Shores.)

the contract was not announced at the time, but it turned out to be $8.6 million per year. Prime time exposure for the NFL would certainly help Tudor sell more games.

Eight days later, the owners met again to finalize the realignment of the National Conference. Although they cut the number of realignment plans from 20 to 9, they couldn't get any further. No plan was agreed upon by the time the meeting adjourned on June 6. Rozelle vowed that the owners would meet in July to finalize the lineup of the new conference.

But something else happened on June 6 that sent shudders through the sports world – and Eddie Gluck. Joe Namath retired from football. Earlier in the week Namath had been asked by Rozelle to sell his half-ownership in the New York restaurant Bachelors III. The reason, according to Rozelle, was that well-known gamblers were frequenting Namath's establishment. Since a possible suspension had been mentioned during the course of the conversation, Namath perceived the commissioner's "request" as a threat. (Perhaps if Namath had visited with Rozelle in the hours after the Super Bowl, Bachelors III wouldn't have turned into a hardball issue.) Upset over Rozelle's methods, Namath decided to quit football. It was estimated that between lost salary and endorsements, Namath's premature retirement would cost him about $5 million in future compensation.

The details of Namath's deal with Gotham aren't known. It's likely that the quarterback was going to get a cut of each game sold. But whatever the arrangement, Namath's decision to quit football was a devastating blow to Gluck. After watching Tudor steal the NFL and climb to the top rung of NFL licensees, Gluck was hopeful that the Namath model would put Gotham back on the path to profitability. How could the Super Bowl MVP miss? Every pass he threw would be an advertisement for the Gotham G-812 model. But what kind of market would there be for a player who never stepped on the field again? Even for a player as famous as Namath

# Strange But True...

In September of 1969, the New York Jets were holding their practices on the grounds of the Rikers Island prison, which sits in the East River near La Guardia Airport. The Jets were practicing at the prison because the New York Mets were making their improbable run to the World Series. Both teams shared Shea Stadium, and the Jets also held their in-season practices there. So the Jets were now doing their part to be good neighbors and keep the stadium field as pristine as possible.

The prisoners at Rikers Island were allowed to watch the practices, and were enjoying their up-close-and-personal view of Joe Namath and the Super Bowl champion Jets. And Joe wanted to give the prisoners a chance to do more than just spectate his pinpoint passing.

In a promotional event that was surely masterminded by Gotham President Eddie Gluck, Namath donated a number of his personally endorsed electric football games to the prison. Supposedly Namath was showing his appreciation for the Jets being able to use the prison field. But it didn't hurt that Namath's generosity was written up in a nationally syndicated column by Leonard Lyons.

Warden Buono reportedly didn't miss a beat, thanking Namath for his generosity:

"That's nice, Joe. The boys here haven't got any place to go at night."

There was no word on how quickly the prisoners put together an NFL team order to Brooklyn...

The 1969 Sears' electric football page. Sears left no doubt as to which game was the headline item. Sears 1969 *Christmas Book*, page 472. ©Sears & Roebuck, Co. 1969.

The realism Tudor tried to impart to its new Super Bowl game was clear to see. (AP Photo/NFL Photos)

the answer was, a diminishing one. And undoubtedly the retirement was tainted. Despite Rozelle saying that "we know of no illegal activity on the part of Joe Namath," the insinuations were clear. Joe Namath owned a joint where gamblers hung out. It seemed that any hope Gluck had for resurrecting the Gotham line had vanished. Gluck thought he had a sure thing. But his horse never made it to the starting gate.

What could Gluck do? The games were already in production, as were the Joe Namath quarterback figures. Money had been spent on advertising, orders were taken, and delivery promises were made. Did production of the Namath line grind to a halt, or did Gluck roll the dice that a 26-year-old quarterback, one who was arguably the most famous athlete in all of sports, wouldn't really hang up his famous white shoes? That an agreement of some type would be reached, and that come September, Namath would be thrilling capacity Shea Stadium crowds and national television audiences with the same determination he was now using to battle Rozelle? Without Namath, Gotham's future was bleak. Gluck had to make as many games as he could, and hope for Namath's return to football.

Fortunately for Tudor, the success of its line was based on the collective aura of the NFL and AFL rather than on an individual player. Still, the Namath retirement wasn't welcome news in Brooklyn either. The fame and accomplishments of the Jets quarterback would surely help sell all Jet-related Tudor items – and the grandest Jets item was yet to be unveiled. Sales would be stronger if Namath were on the field, but Norman also knew that new stars would emerge during the coming season and in the next Super Bowl. Tudor would have ties to any pro football star, no matter what team he was on. It was a very different situation from Gotham's. But like Gluck, Norman hoped that Namath's retirement would be short lived.

And it was. On July 18, Namath and Rozelle held a joint press conference announcing that an agreement had been reached. Namath would sell his interest in Bachelors III and return to football, reporting to the Jets training camp a week late. It was the second consecutive July where pro football fans let out a sigh of relief. Namath's return was good news to a lot of people, and certainly few people were happier than Eddie Gluck. His company still had life. Perhaps 1969 would turn out to be one of the best years in some time.

Within 48 hours, pro football's family squabble was pushed aside by a much more meaningful event. Just before 11:00 p.m. on July 20, American astronaut Neil Armstrong became the first human being to step onto the moon's surface. Witnessing the event was fellow astronaut Buzz Aldrin as well as a worldwide television audience numbering in the hundreds of millions.

It took a decade, but Larry Kent finally got his "all-NFL" page in Sears. Sears 1969 *Christmas Book*, page 213. ©Sears & Roebuck, Co. 1969.

It was a rusty Namath who led the Jets to narrow victory over the College All-Stars on August 1, opening an exhibition season that would feature 33 interleague games. Over a million fans paid to see the 23 interleague games played in 1968, so having 10 more NFL-AFL contests was good business. And in this season with an AFL team reigning as Super Bowl champion, there was speculation that NFL teams would be seeking revenge for their lost prestige. Also on the preseason schedule was the first ever meeting between the Giants and the Jets. (New York City newspapers had already titled the game the "Gotham Bowl.") Over 70,000 fans filled the Yale Bowl when the two teams kicked off on Sunday,

August 17, but that number paled in comparison to the 500,000 people who, at the moment, were gathered on a muddy hillside in Bethel, New York (aka Woodstock), listening to Joe Cocker. Namath completed 14 of 16 passes, including 3 for touchdowns, as the Jets dismantled the Giants 37-14.

With the Bachelors III crisis past, and Joe generating positive headlines, Gotham began delivering its new Joe Namath game. It was a midsized game based on the NFLPA G-895 model. On the left side of the carrying case box was a large color drawing of Namath in action; centered along the bottom edge of the box was a black-and-white photo of Broadway Joe. The colors of the box were vibrant, with the top half orange and an electric blue sky forming the background for Namath's green jersey and white helmet. Namath's name was printed twice on the orange part of the box in large white letters. A very accurate yet small hand-drawn stadium was pictured below the second "Namath." The only thing missing was a picture showing what the special Namath passer looked like.

Only upon opening the box could the first personalized quarterback figure in electric football history be found. It was a shame that there wasn't a picture on the box because Gotham had done a nice job. Instead of the generic metal Gotham quarterback in a red-and-white uniform, there was a lithographed Broadway Joe. And Gluck's designers had been thorough. Joe came complete with white shoes, his white away no. 12 uniform, white wristbands, and the same facemask he wore during the Super Bowl. There was even dirt on his pants! There was only one thing missing – the New York Jets logo. Since the endorsement was with Namath and not the league, the logo couldn't be reproduced.

The dark green field had Joe's handsome face on the 50-yard line, and the game's metal frame contained photos of Namath in action. Combined with the 12" tall cardboard grandstand, it was a distinctive looking game. It was a shame that the rest of the games pieces – the standard generic Gotham players and the H goal posts – weren't an equal match for the great looking passer. But Gluck had a game endorsed by the most famous athlete in pro sports, not to mention a lifeline for his company.

In the September 1 issue of *Toy & Hobby World*, Gluck claimed that demand for the Namath model was so overwhelming that Gotham had doubled its production of the game. Gluck also claimed the game would be promoted on local television, although there were no details about where and when the ads would run. And it was fair to wonder if the ads would ever appear. Since the Joe Namath model appeared in the Gotham catalog back in April, Gluck had done very little to promote it. Nothing had appeared in the all-important toy trade publications. No announcements, no teasers, no ads – nothing. And this was a game that Gotham did not have at the Toy Fair. Considering how important the model was going to be for the company (and only Gluck truly knew what a critical financial juncture Gotham was at), relentless promotion of the new Joe Namath game was the most basic thing to expect. Yet in the toy publications, the Namath game was almost a secret.

For both leagues, the coming season was a landmark one, and not just because of the pending merger. The AFL, which started play on September 14, was now in its tenth year of existence. The NFL, which began the regular season a week later, was celebrating its golden anniversary, the fiftieth year for organized professional football. With Namath back, the Jets were viewed as league favorites, even though they would have to survive an extra layer of playoffs in 1969. (Division winners now had to play the second-place team from the opposite division.) In the NFL, the Colts were tentative favorites, depending on the condition of Unitas's surgically repaired arm.

As both leagues got their seasons underway, Christmas catalogs from Sears and Ward began arriving in households around the country. And it was obvious that Gotham had a couple of problems. First, they had lost their featured electric football spot in Sears. After almost a decade of dominance with the Yankee Stadium model, and then the Big Bowl, Gotham was relegated to a small slot underneath a Tudor game. Next, despite counting on Namath's charm and golden arm to carry them through the season, there was no Namath game for Christmas shoppers to see. Or more precisely, there wasn't a Gotham-made Joe Namath model for shoppers to see. Hovering majestically above the Super Dome was Tudor's brand new No. 633 Sears Super Bowl game.

It was genius on Norman and Lee's part. They had conceived and produced an electric football game that recreated the most important game in pro football history. Tudor had taken January 12, 1969 – the day the AFL became equal with NFL, the day Broadway Joe backed up his prediction, the day that changed pro football forever – and frozen it in miniature. No game of any type had ever captured such an exact sporting moment. It was a landmark toy on every level.

This status came from the details Lee put in the game. The Colts and Jets were wearing their exact Super Bowl uniforms, Jets in white, Colts in blue. That meant that somewhere on the field a Jet was wearing no. 12. So Tudor had Joe Namath, and they had him in the most important game he ever played. It was a much more realistic presentation than Gotham's G-812, and Norman wasn't even paying Namath for his name. While getting the teams right was important, it wasn't breaking new ground for Tudor.

What elevated this game into the realm of a landmark was the field. It looked exactly like the Orange Bowl field. In fact, it took some hard

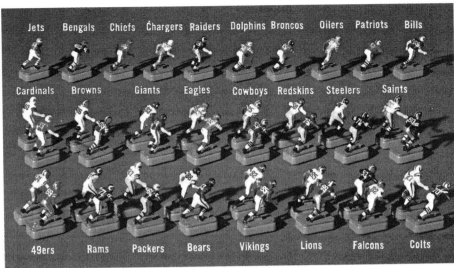

The NFL team page from the 1969 Tudor Rule Book. Tudor's AFL teams were still on available in dark jerseys.

observation to notice any differences at all. Both end zones were light blue – one had an NFL shield in the top corner, while the other had an AFL shield (these were the first league shields on any Tudor field). At midfield was a carefully painted Super Bowl trophy, framed by a light blue square that stretched from 45-yard line to 45-yard line. Even the white yard line numbers were outlined in an alternating pattern with red surrounding the odd numbers, while blue surrounded the even numbers. Only in the end zones did Tudor's field differ from the field millions of people saw on television. Instead of a team name in each end zone, Tudor's Super Bowl had "AFL" in one end zone and "NFL" in the other. With the font and layout identical to the actual Super Bowl field – block white letters with black outline – even a careful observer might think the fields were identical.

The new features didn't stop with the field. Bold white letters on the frame announced "SUPER BOWL," and a newly designed grandstand graced the game, featuring a photo crowd in a very modern triple-decked stadium. There were even faux floodlights lining the stadium's "roof." It was far and away the best-looking game Tudor had ever made and possibly the best looking electric football game ever. It completed a decade of evolution for Tudor and Lee. This was the pinnacle of realism in sports games, easily rivaling the kind of obsessive attention to detail found only in custom-built train layouts. It looked great on the catalog page. And even though at $14.99 it was the most expensive electric football game ever made, the price didn't seem outrageous. This was a very special item.

As many as 300 painters worked on Tudor's NFL teams. Playoff teams had priority and were painted in greater numbers than teams who finished at the bottom of the standings. Teams like the late 1960's Redskins, Eagles, Steelers, and Lions were only painted in quantities of a couple thousand bags a year. (Personal collection of Albert Sung.)

For Eddie Gluck, there was little consolation in having his flagship Super Dome pictured right below the Super Bowl. Sears had shrunk the Dome down to about a quarter of the size of the Super Bowl game – the photo was so small it was hard to see the field. The game's main selling point, the dome, was a liability on the catalog page. Another liability for Gluck was the price. At $13.99 the Gotham Dome cost just a dollar less than the Super Bowl. It was clear to even the casual catalog browser that the Jets and Colts were worth an extra dollar. For such a small price difference, there was no comparison.

Displayed in an equally small photo directly below the Dome was Tudor's Cardinals-Bears game (the game's model number had been changed to No. 618). This year's description didn't mention which teams came in the game, allowing Tudor to improvise according to its stock of teams. Norman was not fond of putting apology notes in his games, or having his product associated with disappointment.

Over in Ward, the electric football page was again an all-Tudor affair, with only a single change from 1968. The Rams-49ers No. 619 dropped in price by $0.50 to $9.99. This made the Ward game two dollars cheaper than the Sears No. 618, and since they were pretty much the same model, Ward shoppers were getting a bargain. Ward's No. 620 model with the Browns and Giants again looked sharp, dominating the entire top half of the page. The only electric football negative for dedicated Ward shoppers was in not knowing that Tudor had a new Super Bowl game. But that was okay with Norman. It was just how the toy business worked. The bottom line was this – Tudor was now the main electric football game supplier for the two biggest toy retailers in the entire country. The company had the games that everybody wanted.

The Sears Christmas catalog was home to another significant NFL accomplishment in 1969. Larry Kent had finally gotten his wish: taking up *all* of page 213 were children's NFL and AFL sweatshirts (in 1969, only boys were pictured). Each sweatshirt came with a matching team poster, so not only could a boy wear his favorite team, he could put them on his bedroom wall. It was a clever way to further nurture any fledgling team bond. The posters themselves came with a pure NFL pedigree. They were taken from original oil paintings done by NFL Creative Services Director Mike Boss.

Many Sears stores had already opened their Big Toy Box departments by the end of September. A staple item of newspaper ads announcing these openings was Tudor's NFL No. 618 game. Not to be overshadowed, Ward also featured Tudor's NFL models in ads announcing the opening of its Circus of Toys.

Electric football was seemingly everywhere in October. Both Sears and Ward were using Tudor NFL models heavily in their ads. This was a general trend, as more retailers than ever were running print ads with NFL models. Even the large Browns-Giants No. 620 game was making regular appearances – this was the game seen in most of Ward's newspaper ads. Retailers had discovered that shoppers wouldn't hesitate to pay $12 or more for Tudor's miniature NFL. (The Giants' unexpected 3-1 record in mid-October was helping boost New York area sales.) Sears' toy ads focused solely on the NFL No. 618 game. Surprisingly, the new Super Bowl was nowhere to be found in the retailer's advertising. The response to the game was so overwhelming that it didn't need any promotional help.

Even more NFL games were advertised in November. The NFL No. 620 had become as common as the No. 500, with retailers like the Gibson Discount Center chain selling NFL and AFL games. Tudor's AFL model was selling out within days of hitting a seller's shelf, thanks to the success of the real-life team included with the game. The Jets were still riding the popularity of their Super Bowl victory, and were now in the middle of a six-game winning streak. Also pulling their own weight in selling the game were the Chiefs, who hadn't lost a game since September.

In the midst of Tudor's dominance, Eddie Gluck was barely staying afloat in electric football. Gotham games were just starting to populate toy advertising, but like a third-string NFL quarterback their appearances were sparse. Gluck caught a break when the Gimbels department store chain began using the Joe Namath model in full-page newspapers ads. Its $9.99 price placed it right in between two other electric football games that Gimbels had on its shelves – the $7.49 Tudor AFL No. 520 and Tudor's $12.99 Giants-Browns No. 620. Gotham attempted to stay connected with the NFL by having the photos of dozens of NFL player photos printed on the boxes of the Players Association and the Super Dome games. But even though stars like Dick Butkus, Gayle Sayers, and John Brody were on a Gotham box, kids knew the players weren't inside. Butkus and Sayers, as well as many other Chicago Bears players, were in the NFL No. 618 game. John Brody and his 49ers teammates could be found in the NFL No. 619 model. And Namath was in the AFL No. 520 and Sears' Super Bowl game.

By Thanksgiving both Sears and Ward were setting records for electric football advertising. Never had the game appeared as frequently in print ads as it did in 1969. Sears still hadn't advertised the Super Bowl yet, but the retailer didn't need to. The game was nearly sold out. And outside of the country's giant retailing chains, lots of different toy sellers were featuring NFL games in their holiday advertising. NFL models seemed to be the new standard. Lots of No. 500's were available and still being advertised, but there was a marked change from even 1968.

Whether it was the Jets' Super Bowl victory, the soon to be completed merger, or the full page of NFL items in Sears, pro football was more

Christmas morning dreams in 1969 with Tudor's No. 633 Jets-Colts Super Bowl game. (Photo by Roddy Garcia.)

popular than ever. Being blitzed by the NFL over the holiday period was Gotham. Joe Namath couldn't compete on the electric football field. Gluck's claims of "increased demand" were starting to seem pretty hollow.

Thanks to a late date for Thanksgiving, this year's holiday weekend ended on the cusp of December. In New York, Lee was busy putting the finishing touches on Tudor's 1970 line of games, while in Hong Kong, Albert Sung was overseeing the molding of a record number of Tudor players. When painting began in January, it would be Sung's most challenging season ever – 26 NFL teams and 52 different uniforms. The color combinations were staggering. As December moved on, the NFL No. 618 appeared in Sears' toy ads throughout the country, with prices ranging from $8.99 to $10.99. The No. 618 was often the featured item, with the ads including a large illustration of two very excited boys playing the game. Also by this time Tudor was subbing teams into the game; the Bears and Cardinals were in short supply. Not in short supply, but also not in demand, were Gotham's NFLPA G-895 and the Super Dome games.

The AFL's season ended on December 14 with the Jets and Raiders as conference winners. In a fortuitous coincidence, Tudor turned out to be selling a 1969 AFL playoff game – the Jets were going to play the Chiefs thanks to the new layer of AFL playoffs. The other AFL playoff match-up would feature the Oilers and the Raiders, with both games scheduled for the following weekend.

For football fans, Saturday, December 20, and Sunday, December 21 were going to be great days to spend in front of the television. Kicking off at 1:30 on Saturday afternoon were the Jets and Chiefs, while just a half-hour later the Sun Bowl would get underway from El Paso. Tudor had gotten one thing wrong for this particular Jets-Chiefs contest – the team uniforms. Since the Jets had home-field advantage, they were wearing their green jerseys. The Chiefs were in white, and a long way from Kansas City. But the Chiefs, who had a better regular season record than the Jets, proved to be the better team overall with a 13-6 win.

In the NFL, Sunday marked the end of the season, and also the long time intradivision rivalry between the Browns and the Giants. Since the Browns came into the league in 1950, the two teams had met forty times. Many of the games came in the wind chill of December with the Eastern Division title on the line. For this last game, it did happen in December, but the Giants were out of the playoff picture, while the Browns had already wrapped up their division. They would be moving on to the NFL playoffs and to the AFC in 1970. Tudor's No. 620 game was now a piece of NFL history. With the Colts also on their way to the AFC, the same could be said for the Packers-Colts No. 510 game.

Fortunately for the AFL, the NFL division races were already settled. That left the nationally televised Oilers-Raiders playoff game going up against a

A Joe Namath game as it might have appeared on Christmas morning. Gotham did a great job with Joe and the stadium. The rest of the game couldn't match Tudor's level of detail. (Photo by Earl Shores.)

meaningless CBS Colts-Rams telecast late on Sunday afternoon. Most football fans would rather tune into a game of significance, but it was likely on this day that they wouldn't tune in for long. The Raiders were up 28-0 by the end of the first quarter, while on their way to a 56-7 victory. It was a result that reflected the true gulf between the 12-1-1 Raiders and the 6-6-2 Oilers.

On Monday morning, Sears and Ward began having toy clearance sales. But any shopper inspired by the pro football games of the weekend was out of luck. There wasn't much left to clear in electric football, especially the NFL games made by Tudor. No matter where the NFL games had been – Sears, Ward, Gimbels, Macy's, True Value, the Gibson Discount Center chain, or Western Auto – they disappeared quickly. And even if a retailer still had a few NFL games hanging around, they were being sold at or near the original retail price. With just three shopping days left until Christmas, some parents were now desperately hunting down a Tudor NFL game. That was obvious by looking at all the electric football requests in the Santa letters that appeared in local newspapers. Boys had even gotten so thorough as to name the specific Tudor NFL model they wanted. A game being named often this year was Sears' Super Bowl.

Christmas came on Thursday, and it was a super year for electric football – especially for those who received Tudor's No. 633 Jets-Colts game (again, one of the authors can vouch for this experience). Not only was the game a magnificent sight sitting by the Christmas tree, the box was pretty amazing too. Lee had created a large dramatic silhouette image of a Jets receiver catching a ball while being tackled by a Colts defender. It was an enhanced version of the No. 613 and No. 618 box, which immortalized former Browns defensive lineman Paul Wiggin with the same technique. The game, box and all, was a masterpiece. It's hard to ask for much more out of a toy.

With Tudor's sales figures again reaching a new record (both Sears and Ward would set December sales records, while J.C. Penney would have its first $500 million month), there were a lot of No. 510's, No. 520's, No. 618's, and No. 620's to be opened on Christmas morning. In a bit of fortunate timing, both the No. 520 and the No. 620 could replay actual games from the previous weekend. And besides the Chiefs, two other Tudor game teams had a chance to make it to the Super Bowl. The Rams would meet the Vikings in the NFL Western Conference playoff on Saturday afternoon. In Sunday's Eastern Conference playoff game, the Browns would travel to Dallas.

For Gotham, neither Joe Namath nor a domed stadium offered the type of realism that Tudor had so skillfully assembled. Any boy who wanted a Tudor Super Bowl and ended up with a Super Dome would be a bit grim on Christmas morning. Compare the Super Dome to the Super Bowl: for one thing, you could hardly see inside the Gotham game, let alone get your hands inside to play with it. But mostly it came down to what you were putting your hands on. With Tudor, you were picking up a real player – Emerson Boozer, George Sauer, Tom Matte, or Bubba Smith – and placing him in his real position. Getting a Namath game might have been a bit more acceptable, but the Super Bowl MVP was throwing to an out-of-focus blue player, or a red player, or a white player. It was almost like

Super Bowl MVP Joe Namath with his decidedly second-string Gotham teammates. (Photo by Earl Shores) (Photo by Earl Shores.)

Broadway Joe was playing in an exhibition game, especially with those antiquated players and H-shaped goal posts.

Namath did help Gotham stay on store shelves and increase sale numbers from the year before. But Namath wasn't lending his persona for free, and neither was baseball's Denny McLain. Just because Gluck sold more games than the year before didn't mean he made more money. Gotham was still in a financially precarious position, owing its solvency in large part to Sears' generous practice of sustaining as many toy suppliers as possible. This year, for example, although Sears was selling only one Gotham football game, they had taken on a second Gotham basketball game. Despite not offering up any ad support, Sears was still giving Gluck an opportunity to make money. At this point, Eddie needed every opportunity he could find.

Keeping electric football games buzzing on Christmas day was the North-South Shrine game, hitting the television airwaves at 4:30 p.m. Then the independent and sports-oriented Mizlou Television Network picked up the ball on Friday, televising the Tangerine Bowl live from Orlando. That led into a busy Saturday with the Gator Bowl on NBC at noon, the Vikings and Rams playoff game on CBS at 2 p.m., and the East-West Shrine game

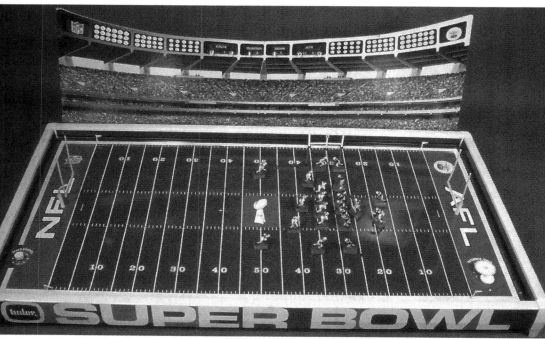

Tudor brings the Orange Bowl and the greatest moment in pro football history to your living room floor. Sears' Super Bowl III. (Photo by Roddy Garcia.)

on ABC at 4:30. In the main game of the day, the Vikings came from behind to beat the Rams 23-20. With the AFL taking the week off, the NFL had the Sunday airwaves all to themselves. Unfortunately, the NFL Eastern Conference playoff game wasn't as engaging as the previous day's contest. The Browns crushed the Cowboys 38-14.

Football took a breather on Monday, but the 1969 schedule wasn't finished yet. On Tuesday, Mizlou televised the Peach Bowl, while the Hughes Sports Network covered the Astro-Bluebonnet Bowl on New Year's Eve. That made eight nationally televised games since Christmas. And just hours away was the annual New Year's Day football overload.

A wholesale Tudor Price List that was turned into an order form. This retailer's plan was to sell the No 500 and the NFL No. 620. The No. 500 was Tudor's most popular model, while the No. 620 was the most profitable. (Personal collection of Michael Kronenberg)

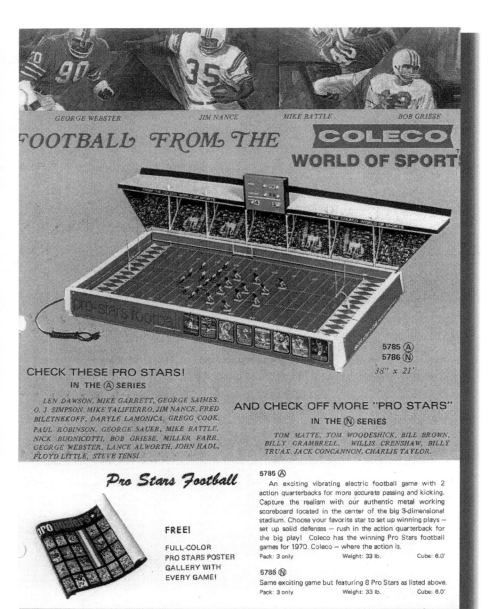

GEORGE WEBSTER     JIM NANCE     MIKE BATTLE     BOB GRIESE

# FOOTBALL FROM THE COLECO WORLD OF SPORTS

5785 Ⓐ
5786 Ⓝ
*38" x 21"*

## CHECK THESE PRO STARS!
### IN THE Ⓐ SERIES

*LEN DAWSON, MIKE GARRETT, GEORGE SAIMES, O. J. SIMPSON, MIKE TALIFIERRO, JIM NANCE, FRED BILETNEKOFF, DARYLE LAMONICA, GREGG COOK, PAUL ROBINSON, GEORGE SAUER, MIKE BATTLE, NICK BUONICOTTI, BOB GRIESE, MILLER FARR, GEORGE WEBSTER, LANCE ALWORTH, JOHN HADL, FLOYD LITTLE, STEVE TENSI.*

## AND CHECK OFF MORE "PRO STARS"
### IN THE Ⓝ SERIES

*TOM MATTE, TOM WOODESHICK, BILL BROWN, BILLY GRAMBRELL, WILLIS CRENSHAW, BILLY TRUAX, JACK CONCANNON, CHARLIE TAYLOR.*

## Pro Stars Football

### FREE!

FULL-COLOR
PRO STARS POSTER
GALLERY WITH
EVERY GAME!

### 5785 Ⓐ

An exciting vibrating electric football game with 2 action quarterbacks for more accurate passing and kicking. Capture the realism with our authentic metal working scoreboard located in the center of the big 3-dimensional stadium. Choose your favorite star to set up winning plays — set up solid defenses — rush in the action quarterback for the big play! Coleco has the winning Pro Stars football games for 1970. Coleco — where the action is.

Pack: 3 only     Weight: 33 lb.     Cube: 6.0'

### 5786 Ⓝ

Same exciting game but featuring 8 Pro Stars as listed above.

Pack: 3 only     Weight: 33 lb.     Cube: 6.0'

Coleco blitzes into electric football in 1970. From the 1970 Coleco sales catalog. (Collection of Earl Shores.)

# 22 AND COLECO MAKES THREE

E ven without an epic contest like last year's Rose Bowl, there was plenty of intrigue on New Year's Day 1970. Three undefeated teams were in action: No. 1 Texas (10-0) was playing Notre Dame in the Cotton Bowl; No. 5 USC (9-0-1) was playing Michigan in the Rose Bowl; and finally, No. 2 Penn State (10-0) was up against No. 6 Missouri in the Orange Bowl. The outcome of these three games left a number of possibilities for who might be the nation's top college team by the time the television lights dimmed in the Orange Bowl. A determined Texas team put an end to any speculation with a 21-17 victory over Notre Dame. It was possible that a Penn State blowout of Missouri could create some controversy as the Nittany Lions were riding a 29-game unbeaten streak. Penn State earned a 10-3 win, but it wasn't enough to steal the No. 1 spot away from Texas. But it still was a great day to spend in front of the television set.

After watching twelve games in eight days, football fans only had a short wait for their next dose of televised football. In fact it was less than a 48-hour wait until the American Bowl (college all-stars) kicked off at noon on Saturday. Finishing the day was the NFL Runner-Up Bowl at 3:00 p.m. on CBS. It was certainly a strange sporting twist that had the Cowboys and Rams – the previous week's losers – earning a trip to sunny and warm Miami, while the Browns and Vikings got ready to play a championship game in Minnesota's Arctic-like winter weather.

The NFL had the early slot on championship Sunday, and by noon the temperature had reached a balmy 9 degrees in Metropolitan Stadium. It was no surprise that only the Vikings could negotiate the frozen field and function in the subzero wind chill conditions. The Vikes took a 24-0 lead at the half and finished with a convincing 27-7 victory. In the day's late game, the AFL's two best teams had their third meeting of the season in Oakland.

Tudor's Super Bowl model was such a success that Sears had ordered a second one. Lee Payne's eye-catching artwork on the box of Tudor's Jets-Colts Super Bowl III. (Photo by Shores & Garcia.)

Despite playing at home, the Raiders couldn't pull off the difficult task of beating the Chiefs for a third time. After taking a 7-0 lead, Oakland was shut out, losing 17-7. The Chiefs would join the Vikings in New Orleans.

For the first time ever, there was only a single week between the championship games and the Super Bowl. This limited the amount of hype the game could generate, not that the stoic Vikings or veteran Chiefs were going to delve into any Namath-like prognostications. Many of the Chiefs had played in Super Bowl I and were eager to have another crack at the NFL. They were even more eager after Jimmy the Greek made the Vikings 13-point favorites. Jimmy and many others viewed the Vikings "purple people-eater" defense as just too much for the Chiefs. Regrettably – for Vikings fans – the god of gambling odds turned out to be as inaccurate as he had been the year before. On a cold and wet New Orleans day, the Vikings were completely dominated by a quicker and smarter Chiefs team. In many ways the 23-7 score was misleading. The game wasn't even that close.

So now that the AFL was a true equal – the first four Super Bowls were split evenly at 2-2 – it had to dissolve. Equality wasn't necessarily the result NFL owners were hoping for, but it was far from a bad thing when viewed in the big merger picture. According to the Nielsen ratings, over 60 million people watched the Super Bowl on television, making it the largest audience ever to watch a single sports event. Equality also extended to the Nielsen ratings for the NFL and AFL Championship games. More people than ever were watching pro football. This interest, along with the obvious on-field parity of the two leagues, would help Rozelle move forward those all-important network television deals.

One of NFL Properties' special guests for the game was again Norman Sas, who carefully took notes as the players slid around a field that NFL Films' Steve Sabol has described as "mud with green paint." Norman had already wired Albert Sung to start painting thousands of Chiefs (in home red) and Vikings (in white). By the time Rozelle decided to hold a realignment lottery on Friday, January 16, Lee was almost finished with the field artwork for Sears' next Super Bowl game.

After four meetings and sixty-four hours of realignment discussion, Rozelle had had enough. None of the five realignment plans for the new National Conference had received unanimous approval from the owners, and the league needed to complete the television contracts and get on with scheduling the coming season. So Rozelle took it upon himself on the morning of the 16th to solve the issue. He wrote the five plans on a blackboard in the NFL's New York office, numbered each plan, and put a corresponding number into a flower vase. Then he asked his secretary Thelma Elkjer to reach in and pull out a number. The plan she pulled out was number three. That meant the National Football Conference would look like this:

Standing second from the right in the photo is Coleco founder Maurice Greenberg. His sons Leonard (2nd from left) and Arnold (far right) were running the company in 1970. Courtesy of The Strong®, Rochester, New York

Eastern Division – Giants, Eagles, Redskins, Cowboys, Cardinals
Central Division – Vikings, Packers, Bears, Lions
Western Division – Rams, 49ers, Falcons, Saints

Although chosen by chance, this plan preserved many traditional rivalries within the NFL. It was also the only plan that left the Central Division intact. With the conference finally decided, Rozelle could push television negotiations into the final stage. And Tudor could finally ready its new National Conference games for the Toy Fair and for production.

On January 26 Rozelle announced that the NFL had signed a four-year $142 million television deal with CBS and NBC. Each season the NFL would receive $33 million from the networks, with CBS paying $18 million to broadcast the NFC, while NBC paid $15 million for the AFC. Each network also got two Super Bowls, paying $2.5 million per game. The bounty of television money for each NFL team was $1.6 million a year. Rozelle, in a convenient coincidence, was just a day past his ten-year anniversary as commissioner. During his decade as NFL chief, he had negotiated $285 million worth of pro football television contracts.

The very next morning, Rozelle was busy overseeing the NFL draft at the Belmont Plaza Hotel. Taken first overall by the Steelers was a blond quarterback from Louisiana Tech named Terry Bradshaw.

When the calendar turned to February, the AFL officially ceased to exist. Parts of the NFL and AFL had already combined, including the two Players Associations. Baltimore receiver John Mackey was the new president of this essentially brand-new organization, and with the merger complete, the players needed a contract for the coming season. (Negotiations between the owners and players were scheduled for April.) In other league news, plans for a domed stadium in New Orleans had been completed. The new 84,000-seat home of the Saints would be called…the Louisiana Superdome. This surely had to put a smile on Eddie Gluck's face. Now he just needed to make sure his Gotham Super Dome game got distribution in Louisiana.

As the Toy Fair opened on March 1, it was clear that television was going to continue to be a crucial part of selling toys in the new decade. In 1969 toy manufacturers spent almost $60 million on television advertising, splitting this almost equally between spot ads (shown during local station programming), and network ads (shown during nationally broadcast programming). Toy buyers were now eager to screen television ads themselves and were becoming selectively receptive to toys and games that came backed with some type of formal advertising campaign that included television. The retail climate was tilted toward large discount chains as the main outlet for toy sales. And in the ever-growing miles of toy aisles, it had become difficult – by design – to find an employee to answer questions or show off how a toy worked. So a toy without advertising behind it was now viewed as a tough sell. If a

A Coleco World of Sports Ad in early 1970. (Collection of Earl Shores)

customer wasn't already familiar with the toy before he or she entered a store, that item was thought to have little chance of moving off the shelf.

There were a number of interesting themes at the Fair. The most unusual was an interest by toy makers in the occult. Some of the biggest names in toys (Parker Brothers, Remco, and Milton Bradley) were presenting new games based on the Zodiac, astrology, or witchcraft. In the ever-evolving world of die-cast cars, Mattel was fending off Topper's Johnny Lightning challenge by supplementing its Hot Wheels line with battery-powered cars called Sizzlers. Venturing into the realm of sports games was Ideal, who had a trio of new plastic Sure Shot games. Basketball, hockey, and baseball were the sports Ideal chose to market first; there was no football. Despite

Coleco's small Pro Stars Electric Action Football game in 1970. From the 1970 Coleco sales catalog. (Collection of Earl Shores.)

Ideal being a toy heavyweight, these Sure Shot games were of little concern to Tudor.

And really there should have been little that concerned Tudor coming into the Fair. The company had enjoyed its most profitable year ever and was introducing a new lineup of NFL games. Gotham, even with Namath, had become almost a nonfactor. At Sears the Super Bowl sold out and was such a big hit that Lee was working on a second one. Something else Lee had in the works was a new exclusive game for Montgomery Ward, who, after seeing the Super Bowl, wanted a super luxury model of its own. Finally, for the third straight year Tudor was NFL Properties' No. 1 licensee. The company sold every single NFL game that it made in 1969.

Demand was sure to increase in the coming season, especially with the NFL being televised on all three major networks and in prime time on Monday nights. While the saying "always leave them wanting more" might work in show business, in the toy business, it leads to something else – competition. Norman knew this well. So he wasn't completely surprised when Coleco Industries showed up at the 1970 Fair with a line of electric football games.

Like Tudor, Coleco was a family-owned business that traced its origins back to the Depression years. Founded as a leather products manufacturer in 1932 by Maurice Greenberg, the Connecticut-based Coleco changed course a bit over the next thirty years and went on to become the world's largest manufacturer of above ground pools. By the mid-1960's, Maurice's sons Leonard and Arnold were at the helm of Coleco, and the brothers felt the company could be more profitable if it had items to sell during the lucrative Christmas shopping season. Currently, Coleco's business was based on spring and summer sales – above ground pools just didn't have much of a yuletide tradition.

A decade of record profits allowed Coleco to go on a buying spree, purchasing Playtime Products (makers of baby carriages and strollers) in 1966 and Klauber Games (makers of shuffleboard and table tennis equipment, basketball backboards, and hoops) in August of 1968. Then in October of 1968, Coleco purchased Eagle Toys of Montreal for $1,675,000. Eagle's most popular items were National Hockey League table hockey games. Being the NHL's official licensee meant that the metal players on Eagle's hockey games wore authentic NHL uniforms, complete with the team crests on their chests. So the Montreal Canadiens came with their famous "CH" logo, while the Toronto Maple Leafs sported their distinctive maple leaf. This licensing distinguished Eagle's games from those of long-time table hockey rival Munro who, without any official league affiliation, could only put city names on its games and players: the Canadiens were Montreal; the Maple Leafs were Toronto. (Also limited to carrying only a city name were all the hockey players that Munro produced for Tudor.)

Since debuting in American Christmas catalogs in the mid-1950's, both Eagle and Munro table hockey games had become under-the-tree staples. Eagle sold its games in both Ward and Sears up until 1964 when Sears aligned exclusively with Munro. By this time hockey games had become so popular that, just like electric football, they were getting full-color

**Coleco World of Sports**

- TV Spots in 18 Major Markets
- Ads in Stadium Programs
- Personal Appearances by Sports Stars
- National Advertising in Sports Illustrated
- And more. Ask Us for Details

You'll find the Coleco World of Sports in Room 1453 for Pro Star games, Room 450 for Official Team games.

*Come In. Get Some of the Action!*

COLECO Coleco Industries, Inc., 945 Asylum Avenue, Hartford, Conn. 06105. Telephone (203) 278-0280.

Coleco was promising an extensive promotional campaign for its new World of Sports. (Collection of Earl Shores)

## tudor Tru-Action *Electric* Football 500 New for 70

Tudor's newly redesigned No. 500 model. From the 1970 Tudor sales catalog. (Collection of Norman Sas.)

presentations in both catalogs, usually near or on the same page as electric football. In 1968, Eagle did a quarter of its total business (about $1.0 million) in the U.S. And this was all in table hockey sales. A large percentage of this amount could be credited to page 311 in the 1968 Ward Christmas catalog, the page which Eagle shared with Tudor's electric football games.

Eagle Toys became a division of Coleco, and in 1969 the newly created Coleco-Eagle organization began selling pools and table hockey games in both the U.S. and Canada. It was a nice fit. Company executives on both sides of the border were happy with what they gained in the sale. Eagle had previously relied on a loose network of individual distributors to sell its hockey games in the U.S., including the games sold through Ward and Sears. In this arrangement, there were often problems in getting Eagle's games to where they needed to be – the exclusive Munro-Sears table hockey relationship may have evolved through Eagle's distribution failings. Having the distribution and marketing muscle of a Coleco behind its hockey line was something Eagle executives had previously only dreamed about.

But Leonard Greenberg had more than table hockey on his mind when he bought Eagle Toys. He had seen page 311 in the Ward catalog. The headlining item on the page wasn't Eagle's NHL Stanley Cup hockey, it was

**EARL SHORES | RODDY GARCIA**

Tudor's NFL No. 620 model. And he had seen Gotham's Big Bowl get star treatment in Sears during the previous four years. Now Tudor and the NFL were taking off. Greenberg knew there was a growing market for electric football games. So he had a vision, a vision of Coleco making a giant splash in sports games. That vision was "The Coleco World of Sports."

Not only would this new "world" include Eagle's hockey games, it would also include a brand new line of electric football games, two new baseball games, and an NBA basketball game. The purchase of Eagle instantly gave Greenberg the manufacturing capacity to make the games, as well as designers to create them. Greenberg then had Eagle Toys purchase a Montreal injection mold company called Herlicon Metals & Plastics. This final puzzle piece gave Coleco control over every stage of production for the new World of Sports.

Once the games were being made, Greenberg was confident that Coleco's marketing influence with pools and table hockey would easily land his World of Sports on toy store shelves. If Tudor couldn't meet the demand for electric football, then Coleco would.

In early 1969 Greenberg gave Eagle's hockey designers the job of creating Coleco's new world. They did the whole job from scratch in Montreal, designing new game frames, game boards, and grandstands. Out on Eagle's shop floor, entire new sets of tools were created to make the new games. It was a given that Greenberg would have to come up a unique marketing angle for his electric football games. Tudor had the NFL, and Gotham had the NFL Players Association...what didn't anybody have?

Canada.

Other than quickly abandoned attempts by Eagle and Munro to sell electric football games in the early 60's, the Canadian market was untouched. Tudor and Gotham games had been available in Canada since the mid-1950's, but neither company spent much energy marketing electric football to our northern neighbors. With Coleco's new games being made in Montreal, and Eagle having a well-built Canadian distribution chain through table hockey, it was a simple decision to sell games in Canada. Coleco even signed a licensing deal with the Canadian Football League to make official CFL electric football games. The games would have the CFL logo on the frames and in the end zones and have a real CFL field with a 55-yard line.

Games for the American market were going to require more creativity, so Greenberg came up with the Coleco World of Stars. This world consisted of over 30 NFL players, half a dozen NHL players, 4 NBA players, and 4 Major League Baseball players, who had personally endorsed Coleco's games. It wasn't clear how an NFL player could lend his name to a company through the Players Association and then go out and sign a personal services contract of his own, but apparently Coleco's lawyers had found a way for

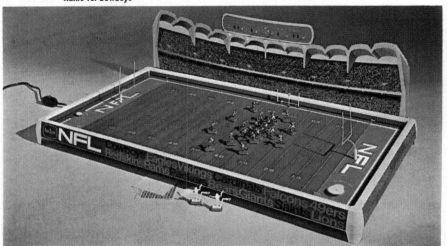

Tudor's new No. 620 NFC Conference game featuring the Cowboys and the Rams. From the 1970 Tudor sales catalog. (Collection of Norman Sas.)

it to happen. This allowed Coleco to show up for the 1970 Toy Fair with two different Worlds and two-dozen sports games. In fact, they had so many games that they used two showrooms to display them all (rooms 450 and 1453). There were a total of 6 electric football games for the American market, including 4 Pro-Stars models, and 2 collegiate games.

Eagle's hockey games had always been attractive well-made toys, and Coleco's new football line proudly displayed this lineage. Fields were fiberboard with realistic grass color and well detailed. The cardboard grandstands were large and elaborate multipiece 3-D designs, complete with a metal scoreboard on the stadium roof. Along the frame of the game were actual game photos of Coleco's stars in action. The stars you saw on the game depended on which Coleco model you had.

In this Pro Stars line, there were four games, two large (38" x 21") and two small (33" x 17"). The large 5785A and smaller 5765A came with American Conference stars, including Super Bowl-winning quarterback Len Dawson, pictured on the box and the frame. Coleco's National Conference stars – there were only eight stars total – were featured on the large 5786N, and a smaller 5766N model. The college models also came in two sizes, with the College Bowl being the large game and Collegiate Football the smaller version. Both of these games were star-less.

Coleco had done its homework and was equipping all of its games with single posted goal posts. A modern look to the game was very important. Yet they were not planning on painted players of any kind. In a novel scheme to create the illusion of different teams, Coleco had created all-polyethylene (soft plastic) players with interchangeable legs and torsos. By molding these parts in four different colors – red, blue, yellow and white – Coleco theoretically had twelve different team combinations. Although the players were molded with more detail than Gotham's, they only came in two different poses, that of a blocker and a runner. Also like Gotham, the ball was a magnet. Each player had a metal plate on his polyethylene base to allow the ball to be carried.

The lack of player innovation was made up somewhat by Coleco's new "action quarterback," which was unlike anything seen before in electric football. Standing almost as tall as the goal posts, he was a giant polystyrene figure with a spring-loaded passing arm and a spring-loaded kicking leg. Both of these monstrous appendages were powerful enough to throw and kick Coleco's heavy magnetic footballs the entire length of either the large or small field. But the arm had a surprising touch that, with a little practice, allowed for an accurate passing game. Unfortunately, due to his size he was immobile. There would be no scrambling while he was on the field.

Another unique aspect of the quarterback was that he came painted, in great detail, like one of the team combinations (for example, white jersey with red pants). This gave Coleco the honor of having the first-ever pre-painted quarterbacks in electric football history. While there was no questioning Coleco's innovation with this new figure, a lot of "borrowing" had occurred to get electric football ready for 1970. A close look at the Coleco sales catalog revealed thinly disguised Tudor players on all of Coleco's games. And the goal posts and first-down markers were obviously Tudor's. These photos were also on all the prototype boxes that Coleco brought to the Fair.

Overall, the Coleco line was much more attractive than Gotham's. But without the NFL, they were still short of Tudor in terms of realism and detail. The Eagle pedigree would give them a quality edge over Gotham, at least in retailers' eyes. A very important part of the toy equation that Coleco had right was distribution. The NHL hockey games were popular items, but more importantly, Coleco made more above ground pools than anybody else. If retailers wanted pools in the spring and summer, they would have to make room on their shelves for Coleco football, hockey, and basketball games in the fall and winter. In preparing to meet the anticipated nationwide demand for Coleco items, the company had built a massive three-acre distribution center in Mayfield, New York, and also a West Coast production and distribution facility near San Francisco.

Something else Coleco was promising for the World of Sports was a promotional campaign unlike anything ever seen before in the sports action game category. A four-page full-color *Playthings* layout not only announced

# Play the greats!

Tudor NFL figures come complete with a set of easy-to-apply numbers (2 through 89) so that you can watch your favorite NFL stars in action.

All NFL teams available in their official home and away uniforms by special order from consumers direct to Tudor.

A close up photo of Tudor's Conference games. The players are numbered as actual players – the quarterbacks are Roman Gabriel (no. 18) and Joe Namath (no. 12). The runners with the ball are Elijah Pitts (no. 22) and Matt Snell (no. 41). (Collection of Norman Sas.)

the coming of the World of Sports, it spelled out the promotions Coleco would unleash in the fall. There would be TV spots in 18 major markets, ads in stadium programs, personal appearances by their sports stars, and advertising in *Sports Illustrated*. It was an extraordinary debut on Coleco's part.

Norman, however, wasn't exactly in panic mode. The NFL Properties' executives were still visiting only Tudor's showroom, not only to see the new line of NFL games but to say thank you for $6 million of electric football sales and $300,000 of licensing fees. Tudor's theme for 1970 was "pride and performance," as laid out in a four-paragraph message on page one of the new sales catalog. Toy buyers were told that Tudor, like the NFL, was an organization of great pride. And with the company's reputation for quality games and great service, a retailer couldn't go wrong.

Because Tudor's new electric football line wasn't in production yet, preparations for this Toy Fair had been especially arduous. Tudor had to create and show off prototypes of six new models – and they needed six copies of each game. So Lee had worked much like a Tudor employee since the start of the New Year. Even the No. 500 game had been redesigned, taking on many features of Tudor's NFL models. It had a new field design, a new crowd photo grandstand, and now came with unpainted deluxe (two-piece) Tudor players. This signaled retirement for Tudor's polyethylene "standard" players. After seven years of valuable service, they had been asked to turn in their playbooks. (Only Tudor could afford to abandon the standard players – at either Gotham or Coleco, they would have been considered "state of the art.") The redesigned No. 500 even got prominent placement on page 2 of the 1970 Tudor sales catalog, being lauded as "the all-time, best selling favorite!"

For those retailers without an exclusive Tudor electric football creation, the flagship games were the new No. 610 and No. 620 models. Both were large games based on the original NFL Giants-Browns No. 620 model, with the No. 610 being Tudor's American Football Conference game and the new No. 620 keeping a "national" affiliation to be the National Football Conference game. The No. 610 AFC game came with the Jets in their home green and the Browns in white, which they wore both home and away. A new field design gave the "grass" a brighter look, and a thick white sideline (the NFL's mandatory six-foot sideline "safety zone") bordered the field. Centered in each new yellow end zone was a white "NFL" outlined in orange. Standing just in front of each "F" was Tudor's still unique "NFL Gold" single-posted goal post. The frame of the game was orange and listed all the names of the AFC teams. Rounding out the No. 610 was a new and larger clip-on crowd photo grandstand, which offered no specific conference allegiance.

This grandstand was a cost-saving measure on Tudor's part because it allowed the same grandstand to be used on the new No. 620. Featuring the Rams and Cowboys, this game turned out to be a rematch of the recent Playoff Bowl (the Rams won 31–0). The Cowboys were in their home white jerseys, while the Rams were in their away dark jerseys (yes, both teams had their home and away jerseys the opposite of most NFL teams). Other than using the blue color scheme of the NFC – blue end zones and a blue frame listing all the NFC teams – the No. 610 and No. 620 were almost identical.

Down in the No. 500 level of Tudor's NFL line, the model numbers had been switched in order to keep the conferences "aligned." The No. 510, which had been the NFL Colts-Packers game, was now the American Conference Chiefs-Colts game (Chiefs in red, Colts in white). And the No. 520, which had been the AFL Jets-Chiefs game, was now the National Conference Giants-Bears game (Giants in blue, Bears in white). Both games had brighter fields, a new and larger 3-D grandstand, and a new scaled-down version of Tudor's NFL Gold goal post. The NFC frame was blue, while the AFC was orange.

Another new feature for 1970 was that all 26 NFL teams were going to be available in home and away jerseys. But it was no coincidence that the away teams on the AFC games – the Browns and Colts – were former NFL teams. They had been in production before, and there were extra teams from past years sitting in Brooklyn. Norman wasn't going to take a chance on having shortages or appearance issues with new away AFC teams. And it was no coincidence that six of the eight teams had appeared on Tudor NFL games before. These teams had been produced and painted in large numbers already; Sung could pretty much keep doing what he had done in the past. Some of these teams, including the white Cowboys and dark Jets, were going to find themselves lined up on the exclusive models from Sears and Ward.

The updated Tudor line was impressive. The "pride and performance" theme was more than just a meaningless catch phrase. Tudor was proud of its relationship with the NFL, and it showed.

Outwardly, things seemed upbeat in the Gotham showroom in 1970. Gluck had an ad running in the current issue of *Playthings* claiming that the Namath game was "the hottest football game ever." The ad also introduced a new electric football game endorsed by Rams' star quarterback Roman Gabriel, and also the slogan "SCORE with Gotham's Family of Sports Stars." This family of stars had expanded to seven in 1970. Besides Namath and Gabriel, Gluck had NBA stars Willis Reed, Walt Frazier, Lew Alcindor, and John Havilcek endorsing Gotham basketball games, while NHL stars Phil and Tony Esposito were endorsing Gotham hockey games. In baseball, Mets' star pitcher Tom Seaver replaced former Gotham endorser Denny McLain. (The talented but unscrupulous McLain had recently been suspended from Major League Baseball due to bookmaking allegations.)

Having all these stars lend their names to Gotham did give the games an air of substance. But a closer examination of the company's 1970 line revealed that the only truly new thing about these games was the packaging. They were basically the same models from the previous year – models that hadn't sold particularly well in the first place – with different artwork. There was no innovation. Other than the Gabriel quarterback figure, the only new feature on the G-818 Gabriel game was the inclusion of 24 extra players. This idea was called "two-platoon" football. Rather than an improvement, putting 48 outdated Gotham's players in a game seemed like an act of desperation. Why would a company take one of its weakest electric football components...and double it? The two-platoon concept only seemed to emphasize that a box full of Gotham players couldn't equal a single Tudor NFL team.

Reality for the rest of the Gotham electric football line was just as unforgiving. The G-883 and G-886 were the same game, just with a different box. The G-895 NFLPA game hadn't performed very well, and the G-1512 Super Dome was an unplayable showpiece. Despite being featured in Sears in 1969, it hadn't sold well. It was expensive to make, expensive to sell, took a lot space on toy store shelves, and didn't have an ad campaign backing it. But the harshest part

of 1970 for Gluck was this – Sears didn't want the Dome back. In fact, Sears didn't want any Gotham electric football games for its upcoming Christmas catalog. For the first time since 1955 Gotham wouldn't have an electric football game in Sears. It was a major blow for Gluck, softened only slightly by J.C. Penney's willingness to take on the game for its 1970 Christmas catalog.

Piling on to Gotham's loss of Sears was Coleco. They wouldn't be able to muscle Tudor and the NFL off toy store shelves, but Gotham would be a different story. Coleco had come to the Fair promising a national ad campaign to promote its World of Sports. Gluck knew that the modest success of his Namath game and the introduction of the Gabriel game wouldn't be enough to dissuade toy buyers from trying out Coleco's electric football line (and hockey and basketball line). Serious advertising, like the national Big Play campaign in 1965, had been a stretch in Gotham's best years, and now the company's solvency was hanging by a thread. Gluck couldn't even squeeze extra capital out of his factory anymore, having turned the deed over to the Anderson family for a $1. After all the years in the toy business, creating games, constructing showrooms, and hustling for accounts, Gluck could

Gotham's electric football ad in the March 1970 Toy Fair issue of *Playthings*. Courtesy of The Strong®, Rochester, New York (Collection of Earl Shores.)

**No. 818**

OFFICIAL

## ROMAN GABRIEL

**GPs**

**GOTHAM**
PRESSED STEEL CORPORATION

# \ ELECTRIC /
# FOOTBALL GAME

**SUPER STAR OF LOS ANGELES**

- Two Platoon Electric Football Game
- Contains: 44 3-4 live action players
- 44 metal plates to catch forward passes
- Magnetic Football
- Exclusive Roman Gabriel passer
- Goal Posts
- Autographed picture

Gotham's new Roman Gabriel Electric Football game, as featured in the Gotham Toy Fair sales catalog. (Collection of Earl Shores.)

feel things slipping away. The business that he dedicated his life to just seemed to be getting harder, colder, and brutally competitive. And at 67-years-old, Gluck was no longer the driven man who once threatened to bury Norman Sas. But he still had one thing that was never in short supply at a 200 Fifth Avenue showroom. Hope. If one or both of his star quarterbacks could make it to the Super Bowl this season, maybe, just maybe, Gotham could get back in the positive column of the ledger book.

All of the companies selling electric football were now leaning heavily on pro football to help the sell games. Tudor was NFL's only official licensee, while Gotham had games endorsed by Joe Namath, Roman Gabriel, and the NFL Players Association. And this year Coleco had added its galaxy of pro stars to the electric football endorsement mix. This growing trend to hop on the "pro" bandwagon was not unnoticed, especially by Larry Kent and John Carney. So in the Toy Fair issue of *Playthings*, NFL Properties took out a half page ad that took direct aim at Gotham and Coleco. The most noticeable element was the large NFL shield, but the true power of the ad came in the text:

*Manufacturers are warned that the use of the name, symbol, or initials of the National Football League, or the names, colors or symbols of the 26 teams that comprise both conferences of the National Football League is subject to appropriate license from National Football League Properties, Inc., the holder of all rights to such names, symbols, and colors for commercial purposes. The address of such firm is 115720 Ventura Boulevard, Encino, California, 91316.*

In other words, there should be no Jets or NFL logos anywhere on a Namath game, no Rams horns on a Gabriel game, and no "accidental" NFL shields on Gotham Players Association models. Also, Coleco needed to make sure all its football Pro Stars were wearing photo-doctored logo-less helmets in any and all photos, wherever they appeared – in advertising, on boxes, or on the frames of the games. NFL Properties made it very clear. It would not tolerate any "inadvertent" and unofficial uses of the NFL.

The Toy Fair ended with Tudor and Coleco looking forward – and Gotham looking for answers.

Sears 1970 *Christmas Book*, page 488. Sears is selling three electric football games – all made by Tudor.
©Sears, Roebuck and Co. 1970.

# 23 MORE ELECTRIC FOOTBALL THAN EVER BEFORE

**T**he first postmerger meeting of NFL owners took place in Honolulu on March 17. By the end of the gathering, the owners had adopted the old Wilson NFL ball as the official ball; adopted the AFL rule that all players must have their last names on the back of their jerseys; elected George Halas president of the National Conference; elected Lamar Hunt president of the American Conference; and awarded the 1971 Super Bowl to Miami. Finally, they set up a Players' Relations Committee to negotiate with the newly merged NFL Players Association. A few days after the owners adjourned, Players Association President John Mackey held a press conference to talk about what the players wanted in a new contract. Increased pension benefits were a major priority, as was the reworking of the option clause in the standard player contract. Another thing the Association wanted was a larger share of product licensing revenue, particularly from bubble gum cards.

The spring moved forward with Tudor, Coleco, and Gotham all focusing on electric football. Tudor and Coleco both had completely new lines to deliver, with Tudor having the obvious edge in experience. Norman knew what it was like to unveil and supply a new line of games having done it before when Tudor debuted the NFL in 1967. He and Lee were old pros by now, as was Albert Sung in Hong Kong. For Tudor's games it was more of a "tweak" than a complete retooling as it was mostly the artwork that had changed. Otherwise game production in Brooklyn would be just like any other year. Sung had to deal with more teams, but this was his fourth year of team production – new teams were just part of the job. Norman knew Tudor could deliver. They always had.

Coleco, on the other hand, was in new territory. Eagle Toys had plenty of game-making experience, but the company plant in Montreal now had to produce vibrating football games as well as its prized NHL games. And before those giant quarterbacks arrived in Montreal, they took a journey around the globe that only a hard-core world traveler could love. After being made in Portugal the quarterbacks were shipped to Hong Kong for painting. They then continued across the Pacific to Canada, where they were sorted, boxed, and readied for another border crossing into the U.S. This supply chain had numerous places for kinks, and there was no back stock of quarterbacks to bail Coleco out. An ample supply had to make it to Montreal, or the launch of Coleco's electric football line would be reduced to a fizzle. At least the company didn't have the burden of getting the regular players painted.

Gotham's new Roman Gabriel quarterback figure. (Photo by Earl Shores.)

For Eddie Gluck, the new Roman Gabriel figure was a matter of routine production. The burden on Gotham at this point was keeping up a flow of capital so production could continue. (In April, the Anderson family took out a $100,000 second mortgage on the Gotham factory – presumably Gluck was a beneficiary of the loan.) Gluck was doing all he could to limit production costs, even going so far as to start making the frames of his baseball games out of cardboard instead of metal. What Gluck really needed in the summer of 1970 was a break of some kind. What he didn't need was one of his main endorsers – the NFL Players Association – filing an unfair labor practices charge with the National Labor Relations Board.

When the NFL owners broke off contract talks in early June, the players went before the NLRB and accused the owners of "not bargaining in good faith." So now that good faith was exasperated on all sides, the players sought a government order to reopen the talks. Negotiations resumed in early July with the talks taking place in secret to keep media scrutiny to a minimum. Then on July 9, the Players Association instructed veteran NFL players not to report to training camp until an agreement was reached. A few days later, the owners decided to prohibit Players Association members from attending training camps, and talks were broken off. It was the second labor strike in two years for the NFL. Over the next week, players and owners aired their grievances in the media, exchanging barbs and charges. The two sides couldn't agree on how much money the owners should be putting into the players' pension fund. A mere $7.6 million separated the players and owners.

Both sides agreed to federal mediation on July 23. The meetings took place in Philadelphia, and a baby step toward starting the season occurred when the Players Association agreed to let the Chiefs report to training camp in order to save the NFL-College All-Star Game on July 31. But just two days before the game, the owners asked the federal mediator for an "indefinite recess." The players were stunned and angry. Their anger grew the next day when the owners tried to break the strike by opening their training camps to any Players Association members who wanted to report. When only 21 of 1300 players crossed the picket lines, the players' unity was preserved – and the 1970 football season was in serious jeopardy. (Despite the strife and just a week or preparation, the Chiefs chalked up an easy 24-3 victory.)

Negotiations had been ongoing for four months now, and even the inclusion of a federal mediator hadn't made much of an impact. Two weeks of training camp had been lost, the first of 75 exhibition games were less than a week away, and the players felt the owners were trying to bust the Association. Who could wave a magic wand and get the season started? Why, Pete Rozelle of course.

Rozelle "summoned" the owners to a special meeting in his NFL New York office on August 2, and mediated 22 consecutive hours of negotiations between the players and owners. An agreement was reached the next day when both sides compromised their pension positions. For the first time ever, the players would get disability payments, as well as maternity, dental, and widow's benefits. Neither the players nor owners were completely happy, but there would be a season.

The agreement allowed the exhibition season to start on schedule…just five days later. Ten games were played during this first preseason weekend, leaving 65 more before the regular season started on September 18. Fifty of these exhibition games would match an NFC team against an AFC team. With the preseason finally under way, a lot of people were breathing easier. Besides the fans, this group included network executives, advertising executives, and electric football makers. Tudor, with its official relationship with the NFL, seemed to have the most to lose. But this was the second time around for Norman with an NFL strike. So as the players and owners bickered away the month of July, game production at Tudor continued without hesitation. Norman was betting on a season. The commissioner, the owners, and the players were too smart to let all those television dollars float away on a "principle."

For Eddie Gluck, there had to be a season. No pro football could lead to no Gotham in 1971. And even with the season moving forward, the Players Association's actions did Gotham's G-895 and Super Dome games no favors. Who called the strike? The NFLPA. Who endorsed these Gotham models? The NFLPA. It wasn't the kind of publicity that Gotham wanted.

# American Conference 610 New for 70
### Jets vs. Browns

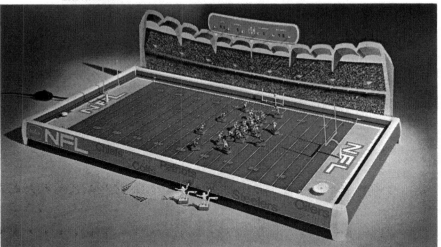

Tudor's new AFC No 610 model recreated the first ABC Monday Night Football game, even down to the correct uniforms worn by the Jets and Browns. 1970 Tudor sales catalog. (Collection of Norman Sas.)

Newcomer Coleco was surely sweating out the days of the strike, as it would have been a serious case of bad luck to debut its new games into a pro football vacuum. Coleco would still have the Canadian Football League season to help sell the Canadian games, but the real electric football market, the money market, was in the U.S. A year without the NFL would be a year without profit from electric football. Coleco's new games could flop solely through bad timing. (It wouldn't have been the first toy to suffer such a fate.) But all of these worries were things of the past. By the time the NFL season started and electric football games hit the toy store shelves, the strike would be long forgotten. Rooting hardest for this collective consumer amnesia was Eddie Gluck.

Before the season started, however, the entire professional football community found itself in mourning. On September 3, Vince Lombardi died of stomach cancer at age 57. In 1969 he had led the Redskins to their first winning record (7-5-2) in fourteen years, and the team was looking forward to greater success in 1970. But after his cancer was discovered in June, Lombardi lived just ten weeks. Howard Cosell narrated a nationally televised ABC special about Lombardi's life the very next evening. No commercials were shown during the 30-minute program.

The first regular season game of the merged NFL was played on Friday, September 18. In a night game that was not nationally televised, the host Los Angeles Rams defeated the Cardinals 34-12. On Saturday night in

New York, the Bears beat the Giants 24-16 in another NFL game that received only local television coverage. It wasn't until Sunday that the season truly got started when ten games were played, including a nationally televised rematch of the Super Bowl. At home in Minnesota the Vikings took revenge on the Chiefs 27-10. Then came the game that Rozelle had worked toward for the last seven years. On Monday night, 85,000 fans filled Cleveland's Municipal Stadium to watch the Jets play the Browns. Watching the game at the same time was a national prime time television audience. Joe Namath was intercepted three times during the official debut of *ABC Monday Night Football*, and the Jets lost 31-21. But it turned out that the Jets were the only losers that night. Nielsen ratings had the game capturing 35% of the Monday night viewing audience. This helped ABC finish the evening in second place overall, just behind CBS. It was a big improvement over the network's usual last place finish in the Monday night ratings race.

In a serendipitous sign of just how well things were going for Tudor, it turned out that the new No. 520 NFC model recreated the season opening game between the Giants and Bears, even down to the exact uniforms the teams wore for the game. Even more impressive was the No. 610 model, which now served as a re-creation of the first *ABC Monday Night Football* game ever played. Again, even the uniforms were correct, with the Browns in white and the Jets in green. It seemed appropriate that this event was represented by one of Tudor's large flagship games. And it was a complete coincidence. When Norman and Lee decided on the teams for these new games, the NFL season had yet to be announced. In fact the 1970 NFL schedule didn't come out until May, two months after the games were shown at the Toy Fair. But no matter how it happened, it served to strengthen the links between Tudor and the NFL.

The newly issued Sears and Ward Christmas catalogs were also playing a major role in firming the Tudor-NFL connection. Page 488 in Sears was stuffed with three full-color Tudor electric football games, including the "Sears Best" No. 633 Super Bowl model with the Chiefs and Vikings. This game immediately drew the attention of any reader – it was Lee's most extraordinary work yet. The field was almost an exact re-creation of the Super Bowl field in New Orleans, right down to the purple end zone that said "Vikings," and the yellow end zone that said "Chiefs." Besides having the team names in each end zone – this was the first Tudor game ever personalized with team names – each team's logo was in the top corner of its respective end zone. Further details included a midfield Super Bowl trophy framed by a Vikings helmet and a Chiefs helmet (each were centered on opposing 45-yard lines). The yard line numbers alternated being outlined in red and blue, and the Chiefs were in their home red jerseys while the Vikings were in their road white. Lee finished off the game with the same grandstand from the year before, and Tudor's distinctive NFL Gold goal posts. It was a thoroughly heart thumping re-creation...even for Vikings fans.

At $15.99, it was the most the expensive electric football game ever sold. Sears made it clear that this was an exclusive, leading into the description of the game with "Sold only at Sears." Pictured in the foreground of the game were a Viking and a Chief, each with a number corresponding to a running back that played in the Super Bowl. The Vikings player was no. 41, Dave Osborne. The Chiefs player was no. 21, Mike Garrett, who scored the game's first touchdown. Unfortunately, Sears seemed to think there was a piece of Super Bowl reality that was a bit too much for some youngsters to handle. In Sears no. 21 was a white player; the real life Mike Garrett was African-American. (Each Tudor team now featured four African-American players.)

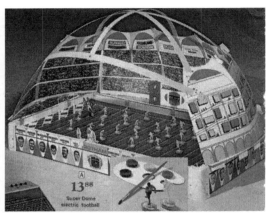

Eddie Gluck had lost Sears in 1970, but he was still getting help from J.C. Penney. 1970 J.C. Penney *Christmas Catalog*, page 342. ©J.C. Penney, Inc. 1970.

Other Tudor games on the page were a redesigned No. 618 game and a No. 515 AFC game. Both were Sears exclusives. Lee had updated the old Sears No. 618 game by adding the helmets of all 26 NFL teams to the frame, a new grandstand, and a set of NFL gold goal posts. The field, too, got a redesign, now having a large red, white, and blue NFL shield at midfield (borrowed from the 1968 prototype Ice Bowl game) and a colorful red, white, and blue diamond pattern in each end zone. Tudor's teams for this game were the Rams in dark and the Packers in white. It was a somewhat unlikely uniform combination in the real NFL, as the Rams currently wore white jerseys at home.

The Sears No. 515 model was basically an AFC No. 510 with the Jets in green and the Raiders in white. It cost $8.97, while the No. 618 was priced at $11.97. Completing the page was Tudor's MLB Electric Baseball and Ideal's Sure Shot baseball. There was nothing on the page from Gotham. The only obviously Gotham item in the entire Sears catalog was located on the opposite page in a small corner photo just under two large Munro hockey games. From that position, Gotham's Pro-League Basketball game competed with Ideal's Sure Shot Basketball and Cadaco's Bas-Ket for a shopper's attention. In addition to the undersized photo, the $14.39 Pro-

Wards NFL electric football

with 3 American and
National Conference teams **15⁷⁸**

3-D players give their all on the vibrating gridiron.
Triple-threat quarterbacks run, pass, kick. Offensive-defensive players run, block and tackle. 36
players, including passer-kicker, wear the official team colors of the Kansas City Chiefs, Cleveland Browns and Los Angeles Rams.
Includes automatic timer and speed control.
Magnetic down and ball marker with chain.
Center-post goal posts in official "NFL Gold." All
figures handpainted for complete accuracy. Big
3 ft. grandstand, jammed with loyal fans, folds
easily for storage. Game about 37¾x20¼x3 in.
high. UL listed. Wards Exclusive!
48 T 14519 A—Ship. wt. 11 lbs. 13 oz.........15.78

Pro-star
electric football **10⁷⁹**

Full of excitement! Game includes two full teams, 24 3-D players in all. Quarterbacks run, pass, kick, even fumble on vibrating field. Magnetic down markers
and footballs. Complete grandstand, scoreboard. Licensed by Professional
Football Players Assoc. 14x27 in. poster includes 42 action shots.
48 T 14523 M—Ship. wt. 9 lbs. 10 oz. Abt. 33x17 in. UL listed.............10.79

action shot poster

Bas-Ket **4⁶⁹**

Enjoy real basketball in miniature with Bas-Ket. Full of excitement for "cage" fans of
all ages. Fast, competitive
action every minute! Players control shots from anywhere in the court with
mechanical levers. Sturdy
construction, tested steel
mechanisms. Court, score-
board, game ball included.
Large playing court is about
20x12 in. Wt. 3 lbs. 10 oz.
48 T 14610............4.69

NFL electric football **12⁴⁹**

Thrilling electric football between the Dallas Cowboys and the New York Jets. The
24 players, including 2 passer-kickers, can do everything the real teams do
except get injured. Automatic timer, speed control. Full scoreboard. About
31½x17½ in. UL listed.
48 T 14521 M—Ship. wt. 7 lbs. 6 oz.....................................12.49

**Tudor and the NFL were well represented in Montgomery Ward. The 1970 electric football page included two exclusive Tudor games – and also a game by Coleco. Montgomery Ward 1970 *Christmas Catalog*, page 423. ©Montgomery Ward, Inc. 1970.**

League Basketball cost three times as much as the other two basketball games in the catalog. It was hardly a favorable presentation. Fortunately, Gluck could take solace in the J.C. Penney catalog, which gave his Super Dome game a full-color display, and a $13.88 price tag.

Over in the Ward catalog, which this year featured a mail-order puppy on the cover, Tudor had a game that was almost as impressive as the Super Bowl. It was the Ward NFL No. 627. This exclusive came with the field of the large AFC No. 610, but from there it was different from all other Tudor NFL games. On a yellow frame were the names of all 26 NFL teams, and with the game came not two, but three NFL teams – the NFC Rams in dark, and the AFC Browns and Chiefs, both in white jerseys. This made

An all-NFL page to make Larry Kent proud – Rawlings NFL team uniforms. Montgomery Ward 1970 *Christmas Catalog*, page 177. ©Montgomery Ward, Inc. 1970.

it the first interconference Tudor game. And the Ward presentation broke the catalog color barrier, as among the larger Tudor players pictured in the game's foreground was an African-American Cleveland Browns tackle. Finishing off the game was the grandstand that had been used on the Ward No. 620 models in 1968 and 1969. It was a grand looking game, and a $15.78 price made it $0.22 cheaper than Sears' Super Bowl.

Ward also had its Tudor NFL No. 619, which had the same frame and grandstand as the previous two years, but now came with the new field Lee had designed for the Sears No. 618 (red, white, and blue end zones, NFL shield at midfield). This too was an interconference model, having the NFC Cowboys in white and the AFC Jets in dark. With these new features the price of the game was up $2.50 from 1969, to $12.49.

As in previous years, Ward had a third electric football game for sale. But this year it wasn't a Tudor No. 500 model. It was a small Coleco Pro Stars Football game – and its grandstand was overlapping Tudor's extravagant No. 627. The photo was so small that it was impossible to tell whether the game was an American or National Coleco model. Yet with a sharp eye, other details could be discerned. Coleco finally had its own players and goal posts on display. One team had white torsos with red legs, while the opposing team had blue torsos and yellow legs. The goal posts were single posted and white in color. Overall it wasn't a bad look, but it wasn't one you were going to see until you opened the game. All Coleco boxes in the fall would come with photos of Tudor players, goal posts, and first-down markers. Ward's reason for taking on the Coleco game could be found on the opposite page where three Coleco NHL Hockey games and a Coleco NBA Basketball game took up 90% of the space. To continue selling the NHL, Ward agreed to sell other items from the expanded Coleco World of Sports.

NFL Properties, after absorbing the AFL teams (Frank Mincolla Associates received a "severance" payment), continued to make strides in both catalogs. Sears had a full page devoted to boys' NFL jackets and

*ACCEPTING SEARS "SYMBOL OF EXCELLENCE" AWARD is Norman A. Sas (center), president of Tudor Metal Products. Making presentation are John Waddle (l), Sears national merchandise manager; and Clyde Peterson, Sears toy buyer.*

**Tudor and Norman Sas earn their first-ever Sears Excellence Award.** *Toy & Hobby World,* **page 6, December 7, 1970. (Collection of Norman Sas.)**

**NFL**

**NFL teams in official uniforms—
available in both light and dark jerseys!**

Send for your favorite NFL deluxe teams! Use handy order form in back of book. Be sure to order player numbers with your new teams (specify team name and dark or white jersey). Order more DELUXE running bases too.

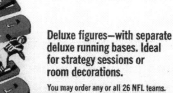

**Deluxe figures—with separate deluxe running bases. Ideal for strategy sessions or room decorations.**

You may order any or all 26 NFL teams.

Tudor's 1970 Rule Book. It was the first time the teams of the AFL – now AFC – were available in white jerseys. (Collection of Earl Shores.)

hats, as well as several partial pages featuring boys' NFL pajamas. But the best-looking NFL page belonged to Ward. Taking up almost all of page 177 was a display of child-size NFL "Pro" team uniforms. Made by Rawlings, all 26 teams were available, with each outfit having a replica team helmet, a team jersey, shoulder pads, pants, and iron-on numbers. What made the page so striking was a full-color display of all 26 Rawlings NFL helmets. They were beautiful – it was easy to imagine a Christmas morning transformation into your favorite NFL player.

And NFL Properties was now publishing *PRO!*, the official program sold in all the NFL stadiums on game day. Within issues of *PRO!* there was a "Time Out!" column that promoted NFL items. Also within each issue was a full-page madcap cartoon ad promoting the NFL Team Shop concept. Carefully placed within the zany world of the Team Shop ad were two electric football games. One was front and center just outside the entrance of the "shop," while the other was on the shop roof (don't try this at home boys and girls). NFL Team Shops were now a standard part of the retail world, spreading this year to the cities of former AFL teams. Larry Kent had devised the Team Shop concept in the mid-1960's, and he was surely reveling in its growing success. But now it was from outside the confines of the NFL. In June he left NFL Properties. Taking his place as president was merchandising chief Bob Carey. (Not only did NFL Properties have a new president, it had a new address, moving from Los Angeles to the NFL offices on Park Avenue.)

Thanks to the groundwork laid by Kent, Bob Carey was enjoying the still growing popularity of NFL Properties' top moneymaker – Tudor's NFL electric football games. By late September, many retailers were already using NFL games in their advertising. This included Sears, who was using the Tudor Super Bowl model as the lead item in newspaper ads announcing the opening of the "Big Toy Box" Christmas departments. Sears was even offering the game for a discounted $13.88 price. Ward wasn't far behind, using the new Tudor NFL No. 627 model to kickoff the opening of its "Circus of Toys," also with a discounted $12.88 price tag. (Both the Super Bowl and the NFL No. 627 would be advertised at these prices throughout the entire fall.)

The Super Bowl's appearance was significant – it was the first time the game had appeared in any Sears advertising. And in early October, Ward and Sears offered up another electric football first when both retailers produced ads showing off TWO electric football games (for Sears it was the Super Bowl and the NFL No. 618; for Ward it was the NFL No. 627 and the No. 500). Kmart was selling Gotham's Joe Namath game this year, while many Gibson Discount Center stores were promoting the NFLPA G-895. But Gotham wasn't alone in Kmart. The Namath games were sitting on the shelf right next to Tudor NFL models and Coleco Pro Stars electric football games.

Another NFL creation that was having great success in 1970 was *ABC Monday Night Football*. It moved through the fall with strong ratings and unanticipated cultural changes. *Variety* magazine reported that Monday night movie attendance was down significantly, a casualty of people watching football. And they weren't necessarily staying home to watch the game, as restaurants and bars were successfully attracting Monday night business by setting up more and larger televisions and tuning them to football. Perhaps the most significant "canary-in-a-coal-mine" change was taking place in the alleys...the ones with pins at the end. Monday was traditionally the most "male" bowling night of the entire week. But in the fall of 1970, Monday night men's leagues throughout the country were looking for ways to move to a different night. Once again, Rozelle was visionary in his convictions.

Visionary was not a word Norman Sas would be comfortable with, but his vision was rewarded in very dramatic fashion in November. At a New York luncheon held by Sears, and attended by Toy Manufacturers of America president Edwin Nelson Jr., Tudor received Sears' prestigious "Symbol of Excellence Award." Only 300 of Sears 20,000 suppliers earned the award in a given year, and for 1970, just 10 of those 300 winners were toy companies. Sears' national merchandise manager John Waddle and Sears' toy buyer Clyde Peterson presented Norman with the award, "In recognition of the outstanding performance of its [Tudor's] management and employees in manufacturing superior quality products for Sears during the past year." In reality, Tudor hadn't serviced Sears much differently than they had in past years. But they never had a Super Bowl game before. Sears was pleased with how the game looked and how it sold. It was a very special item. That played a big part in Tudor earning the Symbol of Excellence Award.

Tudor's success was continuing at Sears, with the Super Bowl being the lead item in the retailer's November toy ads. But Tudor was getting just as much support from Ward. It seemed like the NFL No. 627 appeared in nearly every toy ad that Ward published. Both retailers were using large illustrations of their respective electric football models. The impression throughout the country was that electric football was everywhere. Tudor had even regionalized some games already, selling a Vikings-Packers No. 620 model in the Midwest. Coleco's models were finally starting to have a presence, with Kmart featuring the small Pro Stars game for $5.97. Another significant toy seller also began promoting Coleco electric football – Toys R Us. While not yet the dominating force of today, Toys R Us was expanding aggressively and willing to sell any item that met its demanding wholesale pricing terms. Coleco's large electric football models were being actively promoted by the retailer, as were Tudor's NFL models and Gotham's Roman Gabriel game.

Newspapers were thick with toy ads over the Thanksgiving Day weekend. Brownwood Bulletin, page 7, November 26, 1970.

Coleco had made some bold promises at the Toy Fair about the advertising support they would lend to the World of Sports and its new electric football games. Somehow, Coleco's long-promised *Sports Illustrated* promotion never materialized during the fall, but there was an ad campaign in National Hockey League programs during November and December. Each program had a full black-and-white page devoted to the Coleco World of Sports, with the featured item being an NHL hockey game. Pictured right below the game was a Coleco electric football game, with a caption singing the praises of its "amazingly accurate" quarterback. At the bottom of the page was a list of local stores where Coleco's games were available. With the NHL having teams in fourteen major cities, it was a broad and ambitious effort on Leonard Greenberg's part.

But one of Greenberg's other promotional efforts that fall could only be viewed as ruthless and cynical. That would be a Pro Stars electric football television ad, which ran in a number of Eastern cities. When the ad was filmed, all Coleco had available was the prototype games that appeared in its 1970 sales catalog. So the players who were running around on the television screen were not Coleco's – instead, there were 22 crudely disguised Tudor players. The ad used a series of quick cuts, focusing on the features of Coleco's new quarterback (also shown in a never produced prototype design), but Tudor's players were easy to pick out. Norman and Lee were furious. Their players had been kidnapped and made to participate in the first television electric football ads aired since 1962.

Newspapers during the Thanksgiving Day weekend were full of electric football ads, the majority of them for Tudor NFL models. Sears and Ward did their share during the holiday, but even smaller retailers understood the value of the NFL. Tudor's games were truly dominant during this period. Coleco got a strong push from Kmart over the weekend, but the real surprise was Gotham's visibility. The Namath game appeared in ads from the Korvette's chain, while both J.C. Penney and the Gibson Discount Center chain gave the Super Dome a healthy dose of ad space. And Gluck had sent out a press release promoting his Namath and Gabriel games. It was just a few paragraphs long without any photos, and it was sometimes absorbed into a larger article about Christmas toys. But it did get Gotham free advertising in local newspapers throughout the country. With Coleco in the mix, Gluck needed all the help he could get.

More help came from a full-color J.C. Penney toy insert, which the retailer published in major newspapers on December 1. Prominently displayed on the "Action Toys" page was the Gotham Super Dome for $13.88. With the game positioned right next to GI Joe and Skittle Bowl,

Coleco's 5765A Pro Stars Electric Action Football game. The "A" model featured the images of AFC stars on the frame of the game. (Photo by Earl Shores.)

there was no question the Dome was being used as a "featured" toy. But just a few pages away in many of these papers were a couple of other featured items – the Sears Super Bowl and the Ward NFL No. 627.

Electric football had reached a pinnacle of popularity in December of 1970. There were more games on store shelves than ever before, more ads in print and on television, and in one of the most definitive "popularity" measurements of the Christmas season, more electric football requests in Dear Santa letters than ever before. Tudor was the most prominent company mentioned thanks to the NFL and its relationships with Sears, Ward, Toys R Us, Kmart, and hundreds of other major retailers. Gotham had a surprising presence thanks to J.C. Penney and the Gibson Discount Center chain, and also was getting help from Kmart with the Namath game and Toys R Us with Roman Gabriel model.

But Coleco in many ways was the straw that stirred electric football in 1970. Its entry into the market made retailers focus on electric football and the profitability that the game offered. Coleco also interjected an air of unpredictability for Norman and Eddie Gluck, as the company's distribution muscle automatically landed its electric football games in major chains like Kmart, Toys R Us, Kiddie City, the W.T. Grant chain, Ace Hardware, Alden's, Spiegel, and even Ward and J.C. Penney. Unfortunately, Coleco's muscle couldn't stop these same retailers from discounting Coleco's slower selling electric football line. These discounts only got deeper as the calendar neared Christmas Day.

Back on the real football field the eight-team playoff format was making the final day of the regular season very interesting, just as Rozelle and the owners had hoped. Things were particularly complicated in the NFC, where only the 12-2 Vikings had clinched a playoff berth. Six teams, almost half the NFC, were still in the running for the remaining three playoff slots, and determining the best second-place team (or the wild card team as we know it today) might come down to a coin flip. It was obvious the league would have to come up with more extensive tiebreaker rules in the near future.

In the AFC, the Colts and Raiders had clinched spots, with the latter team only having eight wins. The other two spots were just about decided. If the Bengals won their eighth game they would clinch the AFC Central in just their second year of existence. A win or a tie for the Dolphins would make them the best second-place team. It was even possible for both teams to lose and make the playoffs. With two former AFL expansion teams in line for their first playoff appearances, there were some major disappointments among the AFC team ranks. The Chiefs discovered what a heavy burden it was to be Super Bowl champs, and after struggling with key injuries, landed outside the playoffs. Another preseason favorite was the Browns, who had played in the 1969 NFL Championship game. They,

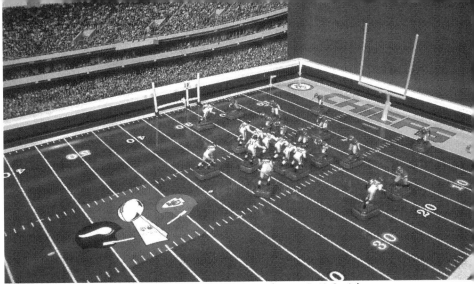

How Tudor's Super Bowl game might have looked on Christmas morning. (Photo by Roddy Garcia.)

too, had their share of injuries in 1970 and never recaptured their form of the previous season. The biggest disappointment, by far, was the Jets. Their playoff hopes were over long before play ever started on Sunday, December 20. Thanks to injuries to almost all of their star players, including Namath, they finished the season at 4-10. This kind of Jets performance was no help to Gotham and Eddie Gluck.

But Roman Gabriel did his part to carry the Gotham line on the season's final Sunday, throwing for two touchdowns in a 31-3 rout of the Giants in Yankee Stadium. It was a big game for New York – a Giants win would have put them in the playoffs for the first time since 1963. The Ram's impressive victory kept them in the playoff picture for at least a few more hours. And maybe, just maybe, it moved some Gabriel games off of toy store shelves.

By 4:00 p.m. it was clear there would be no coin toss in the NFC. The Cowboys destroyed Houston 52-10 to clinch the NFC East, and the Lions won their fifth straight game to clinch the "wild card" spot. In the AFC, both the Bengals and Dolphins capped off their surprising seasons with wins. All that was left was the NFC West title, which would be decided in the final and 182nd game of the NFL season, a nationally televised game between the 49ers and the Raiders. In the first regular season meeting between these bitter Bay Area rivals, the 49ers scored 35 unanswered points for a 38-7 victory and the NFC West crown. It was the first division title in the team's 25-year history.

As Monday dawned, there were only four shopping days left before Christmas. The usual discounts and toy clearance sales were occurring, but they just didn't include much electric football this year. Demand was strong for a number of models. Over the weekend J.C. Penney had offered the Gotham Super Dome for $11.88, just a $2 discount from the game's list price. The Gibson Discount Center chain joined in, advertising the Super Dome for $12.88, a price that was higher than what some Gibson outlets sold the game for in November. It was a pretty strong showing for Gotham's showcase game.

Tudor's NFL models were also in great demand, as evidenced by Sears advertising the Super Bowl for $14.88 on Tuesday, December 22. This price was a bargain considering how many Sears stores were completely sold out of all their NFL games. And then on Wednesday, just two days before Christmas, Ward advertised its NFL No. 627 for $12.88 - the same price for the game since September. It was clear that retailers knew shoppers were still looking for electric football games, even at this late date. All they had to do was read the newspaper Dear Santa letters, where boys again were asking for specific electric football items: Super Bowls, NFL No. 620's and No. 610's, favorite NFL teams, and even Super Dome and Joe Namath games. Santa truly had a tall task, thanks to the 20 different electric football games on the market this year. With that many choices available, not every electric football model was in high demand. Most of the discounted games this Christmas seemed to be ones made by Coleco.

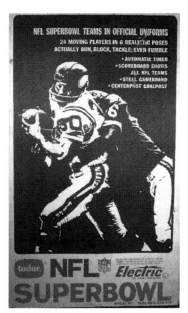

Lee Payne again did special box art for the 1970 Super Bowl game. (Photo by Earl Shores.)

When Christmas arrived on Friday, the game most boys wanted was an NFL game from Tudor. Sears' Super Bowl was the crown jewel of electric football, yet there would be little disappointment in receiving one of the other 8 NFL models in the Tudor line. The new games looked great – even the smaller No. 500 NFL line had enough updates (single-post goal post and bigger grandstand) to be very desirable games. A wider variety of teams were available, so the chances of getting a game with your favorite team were increasing. And game supply was up, so your chance of getting an NFL game was much better than in previous seasons. It was another strong year for Tudor. Their games would again produce a lot of fond Christmas morning memories.

What kind of memories Coleco and Gotham produced would depend upon a boy's expectations. Coleco's games were better looking and more modern than Gotham's. And they were better built, even if the main differences between Coleco's six models were "large" and "small." They had realistic looking single-posted goal posts (although in white), the fiberboard fields vibrated evenly, and the quarterback, however bizarre looking, was accurate in both the passing and kicking game. So other than lacking the NFL, Coleco had a very respectable electric football game. But anyone who saw a Gotham game next to a Coleco game on a store shelf would have been hard pressed to see much difference. If a Coleco game was sitting next to a Joe Namath or Roman Gabriel model, it might seem that a professional player endorsement meant Gotham had more to offer. The sheer audacity of the Super Dome stadium could lead shoppers to think "better," but the price might produce the conclusion, "not $4 better."

Although Christmas Day television would offer up the late afternoon North-South Shrine football game for entertainment and inspiration, the thing that would keep electric football games vibrating throughout the entire weekend would start the next day – the NFL playoffs. This made Christmas 1970 one of the best yet to receive an electric football game (the exception being those unfortunate boys who got an outdated Gotham G-880). Tudor still had four "game" teams left in the playoffs, the Cowboys, Vikings, Colts, and Raiders. It was a shame that neither the Rams nor Jets made the playoffs, for those teams were on three different Tudor NFL models, not to mention Gotham's Gabriel and Namath games. Perhaps even more kids would have been sitting in front of the television with their electric football games. (Of course, you weren't allowed to buzz it while the real game was on.)

Unfortunately, the Saturday playoff games offered up decidedly less drama than the final weekend of the regular season. In the early Saturday game, the Colts showed the Bengals what a real playoff team looked like, manhandling the second-year team 17-0. Later in the afternoon at Dallas, the Cowboys "pitched" a 5-0 shutout against the Lions in the lowest scoring playoff game in NFL history.

Sunday's games did a better job of showcasing the NFL and the excitement the league had to offer. An eight-degree Minnesota afternoon seemed to favor the favored Vikings, but the 49ers hadn't bothered to watch a weather report and stunned the home team 17-14. In Oakland the field was so muddy that the ball was changed after every play, and the treacherous conditions kept the Raiders and Dolphins tied 7-7 until late in the third quarter. Then the Raiders' defense turned the tide of the game by returning an interception for a touchdown. The Raiders added another touchdown early in the fourth quarter – an 82-yard pass thrown by Coleco Pro-Star Daryle Lamonica – and held on for 21-14 victory.

Football still wasn't finished for 1970. On Monday night, the Blue-Gray College All-Star game was televised nationally from Alabama (going up against the popular *Rowan & Martin's Laugh-In*), and the Peach Bowl filled out a prime time television slot at 8:00 p.m. on Wednesday. Finally, on New Year's Eve, the Bluebonnet Bowl ended the year, and a period where football was shown on national television during seven of the previous eight days.

A Lee Payne photo taken from the Cowboys' sideline during Super Bowl V in the Orange Bowl. Johnny Unitas awaits the snap. (Collection of Roddy Garcia.)

# 24 ANOTHER TOY MAKER BUCKLES ITS CHINSTRAP

The bowl games of New Year's Day 1971 offered up the most riveting day of college football ever seen on television. In the simplest of scenarios, top-ranked and heavily favored Texas would beat Notre Dame in the Cotton Bowl, and by dinner time all the drama would be gone from college football. But Notre Dame forgot to read the script, upsetting Texas 24-11 (the game also ended the Longhorns' 30-game winning streak). That result neatly moved television viewers to the next game of the day, the Rose Bowl in Pasadena, where undefeated and No. 2-ranked Ohio State could now claim collegiate football's top spot with a win over Stanford. Unfortunately, Stanford didn't cooperate, handing the Buckeyes a 27-17 loss. Once again, the outcome conveniently led television viewers to the final game of the day, the nighttime telecast of the Orange Bowl from Miami. Nebraska had started the day ranked No. 3, but by kickoff time against L.S.U. they were the only undefeated team left in the top ten. It seemed very likely that a Nebraska victory would give the team a very unlikely national championship. The Cornhuskers got a 17-12 win – and a few days later were crowned national champions.

Those not suffering a bowl-game hangover from Friday could watch the Gator Bowl and East-West Shrine games on Saturday afternoon. Truly meaningful football would begin again on Sunday when the NFL played its conference championship games. In the AFC, the Raiders traveled to Baltimore for their fourth consecutive appearance in a championship game that offered the winner a trip to the Super Bowl. Their chances seemed to fade when Lamonica limped off the field in the second quarter, but 43-year-old quarterback George Blanda had the Raiders all square in the third quarter at 10-10. Then "youth" took over, and 37-year-old Johnny Unitas led the Colts to a 27-17 win. Out in the San Francisco sunshine, the Cowboys gained over 220 yards on 51 rushing attempts, while their defense intercepted John Brodie twice. It was a tight game, but the Cowboys prevailed 17-10.

A two-week buildup to the Super Bowl allowed plenty of time for the sports writers to filet every detail of the game, all the way down to the Poly Turf carpet that would serve as the field. Who would have the advantage in the first "turf" Super Bowl, the Colts or the Cowboys? The Colts had yet to win on this particular surface, suffering both preseason and regular season losses to the Miami Dolphins. For the Cowboys, Poly Turf was going to be a completely new experience, but they were quite familiar with artificial grass. The field of their home stadium, the Cotton Bowl, was covered with Astroturf, and the Cowboys had played a total of 14 games in 1970 on surfaces that didn't require a lawn mower. Thanks to the Cowboy's decided edge in turf experience, Jimmy The Greek declared the game a toss-up.

After 59 minutes and 55 seconds of play – and also eleven turnovers and fourteen penalties – the Greek's powers of prediction were uncanny. The "blunder bowl," as the game would be nicknamed, was tied at 13-13. Fortunately, the deadlock was in jeopardy. The Colts were lining up for a game-winning goal which kicker Jim O'Brien mercifully made just as the clock ticked to zero. Finally, the Colts had their Super Bowl title. Both Johnny Unitas and Earl Morrall got a piece of redemption; Morrall had stepped in when Unitas was injured in the second quarter. Their reward for the 16-13 victory was the Super Bowl trophy, which acquired a new name in 1970. From this game forward, all Super Bowl-winning teams would receive the Vince Lombardi Trophy. Sitting in the stands again for an up close and personal view of the game was Norman Sas.

January finished with Albert Sung hustling to paint thousands of Colts and Cowboys in Hong Kong, and Nielsen ratings making Super Bowl V the highest rated sporting event of all time. In the final football event of the month, the Patriots made Stanford's Heisman Trophy-winning quarterback Jim Plunkett the top pick in the NFL draft. Yet to be discovered by television was the "drama" of a smoky hotel conference room filled with NFL executives making phone calls.

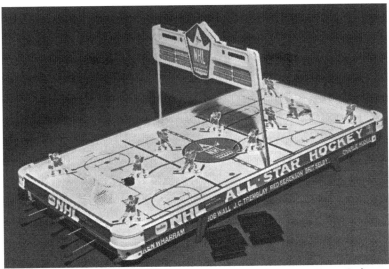

A Munro-made Tudor hockey game. From the 1970 Tudor sales catalog. (Collection of Norman Sas.)

Toy Fair had a late February opening this year, so preparations were already well under way at 200 Fifth Avenue. Lee, as usual, was working late hours setting up Tudor's still expanding electric football line. The merger year had been a good one for Tudor, but Coleco had made its mark. One of the new games in the Tudor showroom was a Lee-designed College Football game, complete with the checkerboard end zone pattern favored by perennial collegiate football powerhouses Alabama and Tennessee.

Norman had kept a close eye on Coleco in 1970, trying to anticipate what other electric football surprises the company might be contemplating. But while maintaining his vigilance with Coleco, Norman was blindsided by a different Canadian toy maker. Contributing to Norman's surprise was the fact that this company was a friend, not a foe. Since 1966 it had manufactured Tudor's hockey games, and in addition to making a high-quality product, the company's president had a great respect for Norman. Communication had always been very open, and there was never a problem the two men couldn't work out. Yet when Munro Games president Don Munro Jr. called Norman in late 1970, he knew he was about to put the Munro-Tudor relationship to a serious test.

"Norm, I want to buy a bunch of electric football parts from you," said Munro. "But I don't want to go through all this bullshit of one at a time through the mail."

"Uh-huh. Let me get this straight," said Sas. "You're going into competition with me?"

"Yeah, we are," said Munro.

"And with my own parts?"

"Yeah, at least for now."

Daryle Lamonica, Oakland Raiders' All Star Quarterback confirms his endorsement of the Super Pro Football Game with Nicholas D. Trbovich and Donald H. Munro.
1971 Munro sales catalog. (Collection of Earl Shores.)

"You've got the biggest balls I've ever seen," said Sas. "How many teams do you want?"

So just a few floors away at 200 Fifth Avenue, electric football rookie Munro was setting up its new line of games...with the help of 1,000 Tudor NFL teams.

Don Munro himself had no burning desire to jump into electric football. He was content to stay firmly committed to table hockey, the game and genre his father invented in 1932. Using an ironing board with nails as a starting point, Don Munro Sr. created a mechanical bagatelle-type hockey game from which all other modern table hockey games descended. Don Sr.'s game carried the company through the 1930's, 1940's, and into the 1950's, when both Munro Games and Eagle Toys started making hockey games with rods. Now under the guidance of Don Jr. and his brother Bill, Munro Games continued to do well in the late 1950's, even earning a spot in the 1957 Sears Christmas catalog. By 1963 Munro hockey games were prominent items in Sears, receiving large full-color presentations on the page adjoining electric football. This success occurred despite the fact that Munro Games didn't have a licensing agreement with the NHL. Unfortunately, as the company continued to grow in the 1960's, Bill Munro was tiring of the toy business.

"My brother didn't like the selling, didn't like the traveling – frankly, he just didn't like the business," said Don Munro. "So we decided he would get out and we would sell the business."

The suitors who courted Munro illustrated the company's stature in the toy industry. Mattel, Eldon, and General Mills all made offers for Munro Games, but in each case a deal was never completed. (General Mills moved on to buy Fischer-Price.) Eventually Don got a call from an A.C. Gilbert colleague who knew of an aerospace company in Buffalo that was looking to diversify. The company was Servotronics Inc., which produced servomotors for 747's, as well as rocket and missile guidance systems. Servotronics purchased Munro Games Ltd. in 1968 and immediately created an American version of the company, Munro Games Inc. Both Munro companies were subsidiaries of Servotronics, which held an 80% controlling interest above and below the American border. Don Munro was named president of the Canadian and American operations.

So Don was still president of the company his father founded in Burlington, Ontario in 1930, but he was no longer the boss. Final decisions about the direction of Munro Games now rested in the hands of Nick Trbovich, the chairman and president of Servotronics. Trbovich had already proven to be an ambitious hands-on type of boss. Not long after the ink dried on the purchase agreement, Trbovich initiated the construction of a new state-of-the-art Munro plant outside of Buffalo.

One of the items that was going to be manufactured in the new plant was Munro's flagship Bobby Hull table hockey game. Don had signed Chicago's "Golden Jet" to an endorsement deal in the mid-1960's, and the NHL's leading scorer continued to bolster the Munro line with stellar on-ice performances, including 58 goals during the 1968-69 season. With Servotronics' financial backing, Munro Games enlarged its reputation in 1969 by winning a Sears Symbol of Excellence Award (for the hockey games displayed on the page opposite Tudor's award winning Jets-Colts Super Bowl). In 1970 the company added NHL superstar Bobby Orr to its lineup and had even signed NFL star Daryle Lamonica to endorse a marble driven "computerized" football strategy game.

With both the company and the sports game marketplace expanding, electric football was under serious consideration at Munro Games in 1970 – at least by Trbovich. Don Munro still had memories of buying electric football vibrators, goal posts, and players from Eddie Gluck in 1960 and becoming the first Canadian company to make and sell electric football games in Canada. From 1960 to 1962 Munro sold about 5,000 electric football games to a less than enthusiastic Canadian market. This wasn't a profitable number, and Munro soon abandoned electric football. In the ensuing years, Don had been more than happy to leave electric football to his friend Norman Sas. Tudor knew what they were doing, and they did it well. As a fellow toy maker, Don could appreciate all that Tudor had done to be the electric football standard bearer. They had great looking games, the NFL licensing, plus good design and construction. And their games were available throughout the United States. It was really hard to improve on the Tudor model.

Trbovich, on the other hand, saw what Tudor was doing and thought he could do it better. If Tudor could make serious money in electric football, then Munro Games could make even more. When Coleco jumped in in 1970, Trbovich could be a spectator no longer. Munro Games had to get into electric football – the sooner, the better.

By the fall of 1970, Don was hopeful that Trbovich would sit on the electric football sidelines, at least for another year. Instead, Trbovich, whose ambitions were matched only by his impulses, had put on his helmet and buckled his chinstrap. The Servotronics president approached Don in early November.

Coleco's Vice President of Marketing, Brian Clarke. *Toys*, March 1972.

"We're going into electric football and we're taking it to the Toy Fair," said Trbovich. "We need 1,000 sets of men – can your people in Hong Kong turn them out in the next two weeks?"

"Nick, there's no way we can do that," replied Munro. "We can't even get the molds in two weeks." It was obvious at this point to Munro that despite repeated discussions over the last two years, Trbovich still didn't quite grasp how the toy industry worked.

"Why don't you call Norman Sas and see if you can buy them from him," said Trbovich.

"Norm has an instruction sheet where you can write in and buy the parts," said Munro.

The cost of an NFL team plus bases and a quarterback was $2.75 plus shipping in 1970. An unpainted team would cost $2.25. For Trbovich, this was too expensive.

"Yeah, it's going to cost a lot of money," lectured Munro, "if you want to get into the business, that's how it is."

Still, Trbovich remained undeterred. He knew what he wanted and knew who could get it for him. "You know Norm, why don't you phone him and ask if he'll supply the teams at cost?"

Don Munro was soon making his fateful call to Brooklyn.

While Norman's response to Don Munro was quite gracious, things were getting extremely tense in electric football. Putting up with Eddie Gluck all those years had been one thing, but having two more companies vying for a piece of the electric football market was a real cause for concern. So in a very stark ad published in the March issue of *Playthings*, Tudor issued a "Notice To The Trade." What the ad said, in a clear concise paragraph devoid of legalese, was that Tudor owned the trademark to

# Makes all other Electric Football Games Obsolete

## COMMAND CONTROL[T.M.] Football

Make the grandstand roar! You're the coach. Or you're the quarterback. But you're in complete control of a fabulous new game, attacking or defending the opposing team. Create a pro season series with your friends, building up to big bowl games.

You'll keep score on a metal working scoreboard nesting in a 3-dimensional grand-stand. Two action quarterbacks pass and kick. You direct the action backs of your choice by complete remote control. Get the game that lets you play real Pro Football!

### Check These Features!
- COMMAND-CONTROL[T.M.] Action
- Two Action Quarterbacks.
- Electric vibrating field with variable speed control.
- Working metal scoreboard.
- 3-D Stadium.
- Magnetic footballs.
- Yardage markers, corner flags, goal posts.
- U.L. & C.S.A. approved.

### Check This Play Action!
- Direct your offensive and defensive running backs.
- Run, block, tackle, reverse with complete COMMAND CONTROL[T.M.] Action
- Set up a surprise play and *completely control the players of your choice.*

| 5795 | 5775 |
|---|---|
| Pack: 3 only Weight: 33 lb. Cube: 6.0' | Pack: 3 only Weight: 24 lb. Cube: 2.7' |
| *Patent Pending | |

Coleco sales pitch for Command Control. From the 1971 Coleco sales catalog. The game in the ad is a prototype. When the actual Command Control games were released in the fall, the controllers were on the opposite sides of the game. (Collection of Earl Shores.)

Munro introduces its new line of electric football games in the 1971 Munro sales catalog. (Collection of Earl Shores.)

"electric football," and any other company who used this term should "be prepared to face the most drastic legal consequences." Whether it was in ads, in catalogs, on boxes, or in instructions, Tudor was the only company who could use the exact term "electric football." This ad was a warning. Any competitors, or even their distributors, who ignored the warning would be subject to "immediate litigation."

Tudor's announcement was a far cry from the gauzy and upbeat full-page ads that ballooned the Toy Fair issue of *Playthings* to an encyclopedic 300 pages. Yet Tudor had every reason to be defensive and prickly about a part of the toy landscape that it had carefully tilled since 1949 – especially with Coleco coming to the Fair with one of the most comprehensive promotional campaigns electric football had ever seen.

Coleco was sure it could build on its successes of 1970. "We were pleased with our results out of the gate," said Brian Clarke, who was then Coleco's vice president of marketing. The company even started its 1971 "buzz" the week before the Fair, hosting a "World of Sports" dinner for its most important toy buyers. Chief's quarterback Len Dawson was just one of a number of NFL, NHL, and NBA stars who mingled with the buyers at the dinner, pressing the flesh and praising the games that bore their likenesses. Of course, advertising was a major focus for the evening. "Coleco keeps your kids at home" was the theme of the new campaign. Besides television commercials during both local and nationally broadcast shows, Coleco was now a sponsor of two popular ABC sports programs, the *Wide World of*

*Sports* and *NCAA Football Highlights*. In print, there would be the usual ads in trade publications, but there would also be full-page "Coleco World of Sports" ads throughout the year in NFL and NHL programs. These ads would be most prominent during the pre-Christmas months when lists to Santa were being completed. Coleco was making an impressive commitment to electric football. The message of the night was clear – if you want to make money with sports games, Coleco is the company for you.

One of the things Coleco was not overly concerned with at the Toy Fair was the trademark issue. From the start, Coleco had been careful not to infringe on Tudor. In all official literature its games were clearly titled as "Electric Action Football." Granted, inserting the "action" in the middle of electric football wasn't a drastic departure from the official trademark, but it was legal, and that's how the toy business worked. There was always a lot of borrowing going on. The "action" this year, however, was going to be a little bit different. Coleco had come to the Fair with a new component for electric football. The company claimed it would make "other electric football games obsolete."

"Our hockey game designers in Montreal had been frustrated with the lack of player control in electric football," said Clarke. "They were motivated to come up with something more." On table hockey games, rods run underneath the surface of the game board and control the players. Each player has a rod and a slot on the game that he moves along. So the Coleco designers took their experience and came up with...a rod to go underneath the electric football game board. On one end of the rod was a handle, which came out of the side of the game. On the end of the rod under the game was a magnet, and this magnet was attracted to another magnet that was placed underneath one of the players on the field. The player could now be moved, without a slot, anywhere on the field. Coleco called their new invention Command Control.

Each game came with two Command Control rods (a single rod mounted on opposite sides of the frame) that allowed a single player on offense and a single player on defense to be controlled precisely. If the offensive line opened up a big hole, a kid could now guide his running back right through it. But he also now had to avoid his opponent's Command Control linebacker, who could fill the hole just as quickly and precisely as the running back. Thanks to Coleco's fiberboard field, the physics of this concept worked well. Sandwiching two opposing magnets over a metal field, like Tudor's, would create an enormous amount of friction. Any advantages of complete control would be rendered almost useless by the loss of speed and the amount of force needed to push the players over a game board that the magnets themselves were attracted to. Coleco was sure it had a winning concept. Command Control had already been made the star of all its electric football advertising. There would even be a new television commercial to show off the concept.

With Command Control, Coleco had expanded on the high-end of electric football for 1971. The two new Command Control models, a large 38" x 21" game and a small 33" x 17" game were going to be the company's most expensive electric football offerings. But Coleco had also learned enough from its first year in electric football to expand on the bottom end of its line. Tudor's bestseller was still the modest No. 500 model. The game could be found all over the country in a wide variety of retailers – super markets, drug stores, auto parts, and hardware stores were all places were a No. 500 could be bought. Cutting in on Tudor's domination of the entry-level game would give Coleco a stronger foothold in electric football. To do this, Coleco had two new smaller Pro Star models for 1971, a compact 27" x 17" model (it was 5" shorter than 1970's smallest Coleco game) and a 26" x 16" model. Both games sacrificed most of their end zone area to have a smaller frame size. In fact, the smallest Coleco model was so streamlined that the players could actually run completely off the end of the game.

Including a large Pro-Stars game without Command Control, Coleco had five games for American toy store shelves in 1971. (The two collegiate games from 1970 had been dropped due to lack of sales.) Coleco was confident that it was bringing a lean and calculated line of games to market for this second year of electric football. Command Control, with the help of television advertising, would certainly become a "must have" item. Coleco would continue to gain ground on Tudor – even with a fourth company jumping into electric football.

Munro's entry into electric football in 1971 wasn't supposed to be a secret. But in making a decision so late in the yearly toy cycle, Munro was now having a hard time getting the word out that it was in the business of selling electric football games. The ad deadline for the March issue of *Playthings* was long past by the time any prototype games were assembled, so in the most important issue of the most important publication in the toy trade, Munro had nothing. No photos, no announcement – not even an ad for the games of Bobby Hull or Bobby Orr. In an industry as competitive as toys, this was a far from optimal way to introduce a new line of games.

But Trbovich was undeterred. In fact, in the new sales catalog "consumer demand" was credited with "advancing" the introduction of electric football. So Don Munro found himself sitting in his Fifth Avenue showroom surrounded by prototype Munro games and thousands of Tudor NFL players.

"We showed up at the Toy Fair with Tudor men," said Munro. "We didn't even have time to repaint them for the Fair or the catalogs." A close look at the 1971 Munro sales catalog shows Tudor NFL Browns, Giants,

# MUNRO GAMES EAST COAST T.V. ADVERTISING
## FOR 1971 STARTING NOV. 1 FOR 7 WEEKS

SCORE MORE IN THE BIGGEST BURST OF TV ADVERTISING IN SPORTS GAME HISTORY.
DAZZLING NEW COLOR COMMERCIALS SCHEDULED TO SATURATE THE MARKET AT
PEAK VIEWING TIMES FOR 7 SENSATIONAL WEEKS. THRILLING LIVE ACTION FOOTAGE
WITH STAR ENDORSEMENTS TO BLAST THE MARKET WIDE OPEN.

**MARKET: NEW YORK CITY**

STATIONS: WNEW TV(5), WABC TV(7) & WPIX TV(11)

| TIME | PROGRAM | CHNL. | RTG. |
|------|---------|-------|------|
| 4:30 – 5 PM | Rifleman (2/Wk) | 5 | 5 |
| 4:30 – 6 PM | Early Movie (2/Wk) | 7 | 5 |
| 5 – 5:30 PM | Lost in Space (2/Wk) | 5 | 6 |
| 6 – 6:30 PM | Please Don't Eat Daisies (2/Wk) | 11 | 10 |
| 7 – 7:30 PM | I Dream of Jeanie (2/Wk) | 11 | 13 |
| 4:30 – 5 PM | Flintstones | 5 | 5 |

77 Announcements
Reaching 4,775,000 Homes Per Week, 33,425,000 Home Impressions

**MARKET: PHILADELPHIA, PENNSYLVANIA**

STATIONS: KYW TV(3), WKBS TV(48) & WTAF TV(29)

| TIME | PROGRAM | CHNL. | RTG. |
|------|---------|-------|------|
| 4:30 – 5 PM | Flintstones | 48 | 3 |
| 4:30 – 6 PM | David Frost | 3 | 11 |
| 5 – 5:30 PM | The Munsters | 48 | 3 |
| 6 – 6:30 PM | Star Trek | 48 | 6 |
| 7 – 7:30 PM | Dragnet | 29 | 2 |

35 Announcements
Reaching 530,000 Homes Per Week, 3,710,000 Home Impressions

**Munro's 1971 television advertising schedule. These schedules were given out in the Munro Toy Fair showroom. (Collection of Earl Shores.)**

Jets, and Chiefs, all sitting on white Coleco bases. The goal posts were also Tudor's, although no quarterbacks were pictured. That was one of the "minor" things that the designers at Munro Games were still working out. The type of quarterback the company picked would determine what kind of ball Munro football games would use, magnetic or felt.

Yet it was a credit to the Munro designers that for most buyers in the showroom, the players were far from the most noticeable feature of the new games. The models were large (38" x 21") with an attractive metal "Vibra-Turf" field, and a wind-up timer that ticked away actual minutes and seconds. But what really caught the buyer's eye was the first multi-tiered 3-D grandstand since the Big Bowl. Using a set of unique plastic support brackets, Munro designers were able to create a surprisingly sturdy stadium with both a sloped upper and lower deck. Adding to the concept was a color photo crowd, which mixed with the two tiers to create an intense dose of realism. And in doing their homework, these designers had already learned some important lessons about electric football stadium design. The structure only ran the length of one sideline. It didn't wrap around and interfere with play like some of the ambitious Gotham models had.

In creating its electric football games, Munro had done a lot of "borrowing." But one of these borrowed features must have come as a shock to Coleco. Sticking out of each end of Munro's flagship game, the 90541 Vibra Action Football game (no Tudor trademark violations here), was a white plastic handle. Attached to the handle was a rod that stretched under the game, and at the end of the rod was – a magnet! That magnet attached to a magnet on top of the field, and on top of this magnet sat an electric football player. Munro was calling it Play Action Control, but it was clearly Command Control. The only difference was Munro had the rods coming out of the ends of the game instead of the side.

Part of Munro's stealth entry into electric football had included some down and dirty undercover work. Command Control was going to be the pillar of Coleco's marketing in 1971. It was certainly not a feature they wanted a competitor to copy – at least not yet. Most toy innovations seemed to get at least a year of exclusivity, but Trbovich decided to play hardball. In his view, Play Action Control was Munro's innovation, just as Command Control was Coleco's. So the timing of these identical innovations was purely coincidental. Yet giving away Munro's role as the "borrower" was one small detail – the metal field. Unless Munro designers had found a way to suspend the laws of physics, there were two things Play Action Control was sure to do. Not work very well and scratch up the field.

So in many ways, it was a rocky start for Munro. But at least the games the buyers could see looked promising. Five different electric football models were on display in the showroom, although three of these models were simply variations of the Vibra Action 90541 game. A super-deluxe Munro model came with legs and Play Action Control, while a second tabletop game came without the controlling rods. Completing the line was a smaller electrical game and a smaller mechanically vibrating game that Munro claimed would "put the economy indoor/outdoor market in the palm of your [the buyers] hand." It must have been news to Norman Sas that there was a market for outdoor electric football games.

Despite the attractive games, it was painfully obvious that Munro was rushing into electric football. Buyers were going to have to take it on faith that the company could produce games, players, quarterbacks, goal posts, and other parts in time for the Christmas season. The largest leap of faith came in the form of the Tudor-like players the company was promising. Getting thousands of painted players into production in Hong Kong and then into boxes in Buffalo and Burlington by the fall was going to be quite a feat. But Trbovich was confident, and despite the apparent electric football obstacles, ready to sell Munro's line aggressively. And he was going to borrow again from Coleco to further his company's cause.

Munro Games was plunging heavily into television advertising. A schedule of commercials for the fall of 1971 was being handed out in the showroom with Munro claiming it would be "the biggest burst of TV advertising in sports game history." Starting on November 1, Munro would run weekday commercials in the television markets of New York

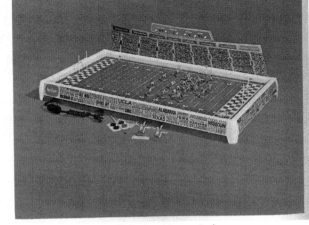

Not to be left out, Tudor introduces a new College model in 1971. (Collection of Norman Sas.)

City, Philadelphia, Baltimore, and Washington between 4:00 p.m. to 7:30 p.m. Kids' shows like the *Flintstones*, the *Munsters*, and *Lost in Space*, as well as adult shows like *David Frost*, *Dragnet*, and *Dark Shadows* were targeted. Over 200 Munro commercials were promised during a seven-week blitz, with 77 of those showing in the New York City market alone. Munro claimed the commercials would reach 4.7 million New York homes per week. And another 98 commercials were promised during the same period for the Buffalo, Syracuse, and Rochester, New York markets. It was an impressive and well-designed campaign. Perhaps it could make up for the inherent lack of deliberation and organization in Munro's electric football line.

In the Tudor showroom, all Norman could do was shake his head. He still had the NFL, and NFL Properties' president Bob Carey would soon be dropping by to congratulate Tudor for another year as the top-earning licensee. None of the other electric football makers could make such a claim. But things were starting to get crazy. The ad in *Playthings* demonstrated the serious concerns Norman had for his piece of the electric football market, which was bound to shrink no matter what Tudor did. The sheer volume of games produced by Tudor, Gotham, Coleco, and Munro would reduce profits for everyone. And all the television advertising...that was an expensive and uncertain path to start down. Norman didn't think the costs were worth it for Tudor. Essentially, they got free advertising with every televised NFL game.

Tudor still had Sears and the Super Bowl model. The company was also offering up more regionalized and customized NFL games in 1971.

This allowed retailers throughout the country to finally have a local NFL team sitting on their shelves. Games featuring the Packers-Bears and Raiders-49ers would surely help sway retailers from thoughts of defecting to Coleco or Munro. Most NFL teams had never been standard issue on Tudor's games before. These "home team" games were going to be bigger sellers than Coleco and Munro games with generic players.

Tudor had two new games for 1971, the previously mentioned College Football No. 600 game and an NFL No. 615 model. The new NFL game was midsize, having the same frame and field as the Sears No. 618 and Ward No. 619. But it didn't have the distinctive NFL helmet design on the frame; instead it had "NFL Football" in block white letters against a red and blue background. What made the No. 615 unique among Tudor's football games was that retailers would be allowed to pick their own team combination for the games. It was clever marketing on Tudor's part. It was a great looking game, yet it wasn't the largest and most expensive model in the Tudor line. So retailers could have the home team at an affordable price. Both of Coleco's Command Control models would cost more than an NFL No. 615.

The College Electric Football game, the Tudor sales catalog explained, was "designed to take advantage of the current TV boom in college football." This was true, but it was more specifically designed to compete with the now nonexistent Coleco Collegiate football games. It, too, was a midsize game like the No. 615, except it had the checkerboard end zone design and college names listed on the frame. It was a beautiful game; Lee had clearly put his heart into designing it. Since Tudor didn't have any kind of agreement with the NCAA, the teams were unpainted and no mascot names were used anywhere on the game.

For the rest of the NFL line, the only change was the addition of an NFL standings board to the No. 610 and No. 620 games. This clipped onto the end zone of the games and displayed all the NFL team names divided by conference and division. Besides keeping the standings, it also served as a storage area for all the scoreboard team names. No longer would they have to rattle around loosely in the bottom of the box.

The Tudor item getting the largest advertising push in 1971 was the nonelectric NFL Strategy game. Introduced in 1970, the Lee-created game was aimed at the expanding "intellectual" sports game market that included entries sold by 3M, *Sports Illustrated*, and Research Games. NFL Strategy was targeting the serious football fan – that is, a young male who had outgrown electric football. Instead of having random vibrations decide the outcome of a play, you could let your football knowledge be the deciding factor. The game included an official 36-page NFL Playbook and a "probability selector." A full-page ad for NFL Strategy was already running in the March issue of *Playthings*, and come the fall, Tudor planned a national advertising campaign with weekly advertisements in the NFL's *PRO!* magazine.

Over in a different area of the showroom sat Tudor's hockey games, which except for the artwork, were 100% made by Munro Games. Somehow Norman didn't feel as enthusiastic about his hockey line as he usually did.

For Eddie Gluck, the sports game waters were getting increasingly rough and shark infested. The sums of money that Coleco was pouring into marketing its World of Sports...Gluck could only dream of hosting a dinner in a four-star hotel ballroom so buyers could mingle with Joe Namath and Roman Gabriel. Company sales had suffered again in 1970, as stores that

A Gotham Toy Fair ad from 1971. (Collection of Earl Shores.)

previously carried only Gotham and Tudor decided to add Coleco to their shelves. As Gluck feared, Coleco's diverse line of products had muscled Gotham out of many accounts, some that dated all the way back to Gotham's 1954 entry into electric football. And Munro's debut, as wobbly as it was, wasn't going to make things any easier. While competitors were spending large sums on television time, Gluck was searching for ways to pinch pennies on each and every game. And in doing so, he decided to sacrifice the most recognizable piece on the best-selling game in his entire sports game line – the metal Joe Namath quarterback figure.

Not that there wasn't a quarterback in the game, but the detailed metal lithograph figure of Namath was gone, as was the metal Roman Gabriel figure. It was just too costly to make the metal quarterbacks anymore, especially compared with what the company could save by using an outside supplier. So Gotham's new quarterbacks were plastic, made in Portugal and painted in Hong Kong. They were also, in terms of electric football scale, the size of King Kong. Somehow Gluck had made a deal with the same company that made Coleco's quarterbacks. The Broadway Joe of Gotham's flagship game was now a towering human growth hormone mutant.

Not only was Namath a giant, he now had green pants and a green helmet to go along with his white no. 12 jersey. This wasn't a color scheme the Jets would wear until the 1980's (and it looked just as ugly then). The main selling point of Gotham's best-selling game was no more. Gluck must have gotten quite a deal

An original Lee Payne photo from 1971 of New York Giants' quarterback Fran Tarkenton. This photo appeared on Tudor boxes. (Collection of Roddy Garcia.)

on the plastic quarterbacks because he had been in the business long enough to know the change would not go unnoticed. Kids would open the box and be disappointed. Retailers would notice, too; they would be on the front line of returns and complaints from disgruntled parents. And retailers would notice when the games stayed on the shelves long past Christmas.

Yet even with the company in decline, Gluck continued to expand his "Family of Sports Super Stars." For 1971 he was adding a Dick Butkus electric football game, a Johnny Bench baseball game, as well as hockey games endorsed by Brad Park and Red Berenson. Increasing the number of games in the Gotham line while cutting costs (the Butkus model would not have a grandstand) might seem like conflicting business principles. However, to a toy insider, both actions reinforced the theme of desperation at Gotham.

"It was a pretty loose business," said Don Munro. "Names were used and photos were taken, but I don't think half of those guys ever got paid." So instead of paying up front for advertising, Gluck was gambling on increasing his sales with famous names. Gotham stars who earned a percentage of each game wouldn't be paid until after the sales figures were totaled. And it was possible they might not get paid at all.

Including the new Butkus model, Gotham was offering six electric football games for 1971. Filling out the rest of the line was the Namath game, the Gabriel game, large and small NFL Players Association games, and an entry-level G-883. All were coming with the new plastic quarterback, as well as single-posted goal posts. After ten years, the company had finally upgraded from its old H style goal posts – and this was the only upgrade in all of Gotham's electric football line. It was hard to see Gotham and its aging products staying competitive against the glossy modern games being offered by Tudor, Coleco, and Munro. There just wasn't enough sparkle in Gluck's Family of Stars.

In the days following the Fair, Don Munro focused his efforts on getting the new players into production. He had already been to Tokyo, where he left a number of Norman's players with an expatriate American sculptor. During Don's time in Japan, the sculptor made sketches from Tudor's men, incorporating changes to the poses as well as creating uniform designs for different teams. After Don returned to Canada, the sculptor made molds from the sketches and created prototype players. These players were sent to Munro Games in Ontario for a final evaluation.

Don told Trbovich that making five poses, like Tudor, was going to be a very expensive undertaking. With this advice in mind, Trbovich approved three electric football player poses. Since the sculptor had used Tudor players as his models, these new Munro players were going to look a lot like Tudor's. And not only were they going to look like Tudor players, they were going to be constructed the same way. The body would be molded from hard polystyrene and mounted on a separate green polyethylene base – just like Tudor's players. Only two different teams would be painted, but, like Tudor, these teams would be integrated. There were going to be two African-American players on each team. And there was only one place in the world where production could take place. Don knew that he had another long plane ride ahead of him.

"The teams were manufactured in Hong Kong," said Munro. "When you got into little parts with hand painting, that's where you had to go." And he ended up with the same kind of deal that Sung had arranged for Tudor. "The manufacturer charges for the molds, but they're not your property," said Munro. "We never had them in Canada or Buffalo." As long as Tudor or Munro continued to buy players from their respective manufacturers, they were guaranteed to be the only company getting those parts. So thanks to Don Munro's vast toy industry experience, Trbovich would have electric football players in time for the fall.

The year wasn't even three months old, yet it was a period of time unlike any other in electric football history. Coleco and Munro were determined to change how the game was played in the toy marketplace and shift the balance of power away from Tudor. The impact of their efforts would play out over the rest of the year.

An original Lee Payne photo that appeared in the 1971 Tudor sales catalog. A punt play between the Colts and Chiefs, with the punter being Johnny Unitas. (Collection of Roddy Garcia.)

# 25 TUDOR, GOTHAM, COLECO AND MUNRO ALL BATTLE FOR THE CHRISTMAS SHOPPER

**T**he NFL owners served up a surprise at their March meeting by awarding New Orleans the next Super Bowl. Miami and Dallas had been the front-runners, but New Orleans officials somehow convinced the Society of Air Conditioning and Refrigeration Engineers to start their convention a day later. This freed up 4,000 hotel rooms, which gave the city more than the number of hotel rooms required by the NFL. And in another "turf" battle, New Orleans promised to put artificial turf in aging Tulane Stadium. The field conditions for the 1970 Chiefs-Vikings Super Bowl had been described as "mud with green paint." The new field was going to cost somebody in New Orleans $250,000.

When the NFL owners met again in New York on May 26, they scrapped the coin flip as a method for deciding the final playoff team. In its place two more tie-breaking rules were added to the already complicated playoff formula. But it was a necessary change. After surviving the brutal battles of a 14-game NFL season, owners, coaches, and players wanted more than chance deciding their playoff fate. But that was the easy part of the meeting. The overriding issue still facing the owners was the labor agreement, which had been "agreed to" but never signed. That meant the player contract was far from official – actually, it wasn't even legal. And the Players Association had recently filed another complaint with the National Labor Relations Board, accusing the owners of illegally changing language in the contract.

Late in the day on the 26th, the NRLB issued a ruling that said the owners "had a duty" to sign the agreement as it was originally worded. The message of the ruling was clear, and before the owners adjourned on May 27, they extended an olive branch by setting up a charitable foundation to help needy former NFL players. There were many unique features of this new foundation, but perhaps the most interesting was its source of funding. Starting in 1973, profits from NFL Properties would help fund the foundation. (Despite millions in earnings, NFLP only claimed a profit of $260,000 – or $10,000 per team – in 1970.)

All the electric football manufacturers breathed a sigh of relief on June 17 when the players and owners finally signed the collective bargaining contract. After the signing, the players withdrew their complaint from the NRLB, and the season looked ready to move forward without any threat or thought of disruption. At Tudor, things were moving along at a less hectic pace than previous years thanks to a change in Sears' Super Bowl game. Waiting until

The full-page Coleco ad that appeared in the NFL's *PRO!* Magazine. *PRO!*, Volume 2, Number 1 (August 16,1971). ©NFL Properties 1971.

late January to start up the manufacturing process had put a lot of pressure on Tudor, especially with Sears asking for an earlier Super Bowl delivery date with each passing year. So this years' model would not have a replica Orange Bowl field. It would have Super Bowl trophy artwork at midfield, but otherwise would come with only conference designations. Neither the Colts nor Cowboys would have their names or logos on the game. This generic Super Bowl design allowed Lee to have the field artwork done well before the regular season ended. Games were already being manufactured in Brooklyn by the time the Toy Fair opened.

Coleco also had its electric football program in game shape as the start of the Canadian Football League season was just weeks away. In borrowing another page from Tudor's playbook, Coleco had created a Grey Cup CFL electric football game, complete with a miniature plastic Grey Cup Trophy. The company's new Command Control television commercials were set to run during CFL game broadcasts, and full-page Coleco ads would appear

The Sears' 1971 electric football page, complete with NFL logo. Sears 1971 *Christmas Book*, page 102. ©Sears, Roebuck and Co. 1971.

in CFL programs. This early start would give Coleco a chance to smooth out any kinks in its distribution or advertising program before the NFL season even began.

Munro Games, not surprisingly, was finding electric football to be a challenging endeavor. In spite of Don Munro's Far East efforts, the players hadn't made their way to North America yet. And in the manufacturing end, they were off to a late start. This left retailers with an official Munro-issued schedule for the times and dates of Munro television commercials, but with no schedule for when those advertised games would actually reach their stores. Tudor, Coleco, and even Gotham could provide games within days. Also, the product quality of Tudor, Coleco, and Gotham was already

**Thrill-packed Electric Football Game**

Executive Command Control® lets you direct $**29**^{95}$
player movement while plays are in progress!

Magnetic control rods move players to give play flexibility and bruising realism not possible in conventional electric football games. You're in complete command as the play unfolds .. direct offensive and defensive running backs to run, block, tackle, and reverse. You direct the players of your choice. Attractive wood-grained finished metal; game 38x21x32 inches. Pro-style goal posts, yardage markers, end zone flags, and realistic scoreboard help recreate colorful atmosphere of a championship game. UL listed for 110-120-volt, 60-cycle AC. Panel style legs. Canada.
6 C 25878N—Shipping weight 17 pounds. .................................. $29.95

98  [Sears]

Coleco's new Executive Command Control game. It was made exclusively for Sears. Sears 1971 *Christmas Book*, page 98. ©Sears, Roebuck and Co. 1971.

well known. If Munro's new line didn't measure up, a store could be facing a rash of returns on a profitable anchor toy item. There were a lot of questions to overcome before Munro could make an impact in the fall.

The 78-game NFL exhibition season opened in early August, and anyone skimming a *PRO!* program at those very first games would find a full-page Coleco electric football advertisement. Prominent in the foreground was a smiling boy playing a large Coleco Command Control game, while in the background a girl and another boy showed off Coleco's hockey, baseball, and basketball games. Coleco saved money by doing the ad in black and white but willingly incurred the extra expense of personalizing the ads for each NFL city. Listed in each ad were all the local stores selling the Coleco line. From this listing a boy could tell his parents exactly where to get a Command Control electric football game.

Another first-time *PRO!* advertiser was Tudor, although they weren't promoting electric football. NFL Strategy – "The brain game for serious football nuts" – was presented in a one-third-page column, using a smart black-and-white Lee Payne layout. It was clear from the ad that NFL Strategy wasn't a kid's game.

Also populating these preseason programs were advertisements for the NFL Training Table Foods and NFL Films. But not long after fans stopped scanning the pages of *PRO!* on August 8, an electric football maker who couldn't afford ad space in the NFL's glossy game day publication took a cruel promotional hit. Early in the second quarter of the Jets-Lions game Joe Namath threw an interception and severely injured his knee while trying to make a tackle as the play unfolded. Surgery was performed on the knee the very next day. Namath's doctor estimated that the quarterback might return to action in 12 weeks, but there was a significant chance the knee wouldn't heal until the season was over. It wasn't news that the Jets or Eddie Gluck needed. Namath's value to his team and to Gotham was incalculable. A long fall was shaping up for both organizations.

Getting underway before the NFL regular season was the new fall television schedule. A sign of how much American culture was changing in 1971 came from CBS, which cancelled a record 13 shows. And these were not just any shows; these were programs that had once been pillars of CBS, drawing powerhouse ratings that other networks envied. The most prominent casualty was Ed Sullivan, who lost his weekly Sunday night slot after 23 years on the air. Mr. Sullivan was now considered too "square" for the modern television audience. This quest for "hipper" television offerings also drove CBS to cancel the *Beverly Hillbillies*, *Green Acres*, *Hee Haw*, *Mayberry RFD*, and *Hogan's Heroes*. In addition, the network decided to move its hour-long biweekly news show to Sunday evening. It would now be a weekly show – except on those evenings when it was pre-empted by a late CBS football game. The name of the show was *60 Minutes*.

Also getting underway before the NFL season was the Christmas selling season. Montgomery Ward opened some of its Toyland departments just days after Labor Day, running newspaper advertisements with Tudor's NFL No. 627 model as a featured toy. Sears was not far behind, opening its Big Toy Box departments the following week. All ads announcing these openings had a Tudor Super Bowl or NFL No. 618 for a very inviting sale price.

*60 Minutes* made its Sunday debut on September 19, the day the 1971 NFL season opened. This timing was no coincidence, as late NFL telecasts would hand millions of viewers directly over to *60 Minutes*. Some viewers might get up and change the channel, but CBS was betting that a large majority of them would not.

Among the NFL teams favored to be lining up on New Orleans' new rug in January were the Cowboys, Vikings, Raiders, and the Colts. So it was no accident that the second season of *ABC's Monday Night Football* opened on the 20th in Detroit, with the Lions hosting the Vikings. ABC got the type of game it wanted for the new season – an exciting contest that kept viewers from wandering off to bed too early. After spotting the Lions 13 points, the Vikings came back to take a 16-13 lead. A Minnesota victory was finally assured when the Lions missed a field goal attempt with two seconds left in the game.

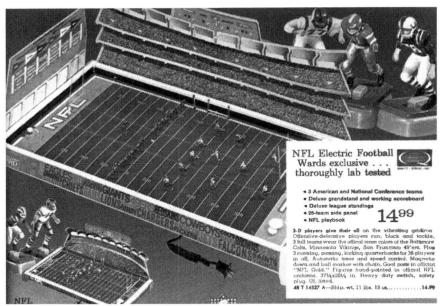

NFL Electric Football
Wards exclusive . . .
thoroughly lab tested

• 3 American and National Conference teams
• Deluxe grandstand and working scoreboard
• Deluxe league standings
• 26-team side panel
• NFL playbook

14⁹⁹

3-D players give their all on the vibrating gridiron.
Offensive-defensive players run, block and tackle.
3 ball teams wear the official team colors of the Baltimore
Colts, Minnesota Vikings, San Francisco 49'ers. Plus
3 running, passing, kicking quarterbacks for 36 players
in all. Automatic timer and speed control. Magnetic
down and ball marker with chain. Goal posts in official
"NFL Gold." Figures hand-painted in official NFL
uniforms. 37¾x20¼ in. Heavy duty switch, safety
plug. UL listed.
48 T 14527 A—Ship. wt. 11 lbs. 13 oz. . . . . . . . . . . . . 14.99

Tudor's NFL No. 627 model. The game was a Ward exclusive, and came with three NFL teams.
Montgomery Ward 1971 *Christmas Catalog*, page 431. ©Montgomery Ward, Inc. 1971.

By the end of September the Sears and Ward Christmas catalogs had been delivered. Tudor's redesigned Super Bowl got a "Sears Best" designation on top of page 102 which featured four other Tudor sports games. Lee's new Super Bowl field came with a red end zone with white "AFC" lettering, and a blue end zone with white "NFC" lettering. Both end zones also contained their respective conference logos. At midfield, the Lombardi Trophy was framed by a red helmet and blue helmet, both of which contained an NFL shield. Unchanged from previous Super Bowl models were the frame and the grandstand. The Colts and Cowboys came in their official Super Bowl uniforms, and Tudor even included team pennants and a booklet of Super Bowl history as special mementos. Overall, it was a nice electric football package that even had the same $15.99 price as the previous years' Chiefs-Vikings Super Bowl. But somehow this game didn't "pop" off the page the same way the Chiefs and Vikings did.

Sears had two other Tudor electric football exclusives under the Super Bowl: the midsize Lions-Rams No. 618 game and the smaller Jets-Raiders No. 515 model. Other than the Rams replacing the Packers, these were the same Sears models from 1970. Even the price of the No. 618 was the same at $11.99 (the No. 515 increased by $0.02 to $8.99). Finishing out the page was an NFL Strategy game, and a Tudor Major League Electric Baseball game. The only non-Tudor item was a Mattel Sure-Shot Baseball game, which was shown in a small photo near the bottom right-hand corner. For

Norman, this page was one of the highlights of his 23 years as Tudor's president. Nearly an entire Sears' page consisted of Tudor products. And right in the dead center of the page was a red, white, and blue NFL shield! Tudor wasn't a toy heavyweight like Mattel, Hasbro, or Ideal, yet it had the NFL and over 80% of a Sears Christmas catalog page. It was a "moon landing" achievement for a toy company of any size.

On the opposing page, displayed in color and just as large as Tudor's Super Bowl, was another "Sears Best" sports game – Munro's 36" x 21" Professional Hockey. It, too, was $15.99, and there was even a floor model with legs for $22.99. Lining up just below Professional Hockey were Munro's Pro-League Hockey and Pro-League Basketball games. This gave Munro Games two-thirds of the space on page 103. Both Don Munro and Nick Trbovich were pleased with Sears' presentation.

But not all the sports game makers were happy. Missing from the catalog for the first time in decades were any sports games by Gotham. Gluck hadn't managed to sell Sears a single item – not a basketball game, baseball game, football game, or even a pool table. There was nothing. For Don Munro, this development was long overdue.

"The problem with Gotham was, they never really had a good design," said Munro. "Their games – and not just football or hockey, but pool tables

*Coveted Sears "Symbol of Excellence" was garnered by Tudor Metal Products Corp. for the second successive year for quality and excellence of supply of its Electric Super Bowl and NFL Electric Football games. On hand for award presentation were (l-r) Clyde Peterson, Sears toy buyer; Pete Rozelle, National Football League commissioner; John Waddle, Sears national merchandise manager and Norman Sas, Tudor president.*

Tudor wins its second consecutive Sears Excellence Award in 1971. *Toy & Hobby World*, page 11, December 1971. (Collection of Norman Sas.)

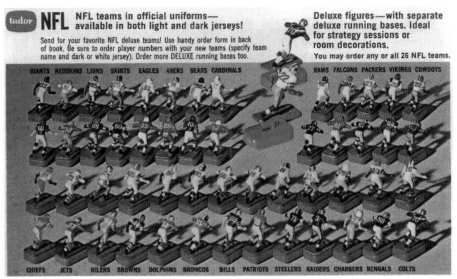

Tudor's NFL team page from the 1971 Tudor rulebook. (Collection of Earl Shores.)

and everything else – were very crudely designed." Don recalled an exchange with a Sears' toy buyer in the late 60's when he asked why Sears continued to buy Gotham pool tables when Munro's were obviously higher quality. The buyer told Munro that if Sears didn't buy from Gluck, Gotham might go out of business. Sears liked having competition among the toy suppliers and wanted to keep as many options as possible for buying toys. "Sears bought Gotham's stuff regardless of the quality," said Munro. "They wouldn't buy a lot, but they would try to keep Gluck in business."

By 1971, however, Sears saw little point in continuing to buy from Gotham. It was a devastating blow for Gotham to be dropped from Sears. And not only was the company dropped, it was replaced. A mere 96 pages later in the "Wish Book" toy shoppers could find a Coleco hockey game and a Coleco electric football game. Both of these Coleco games were stand-alone floor models complete with legs. An accompanying Sears' caption described the page as "Sports Table Games with legs...set up almost anywhere." They were also the largest and most luxurious models in the Coleco line, having been specifically designed as furniture for the family rec room. Nothing illustrated this fact better than the imitation wood grain that covered the metal frames. The usually bright and colorful graphics of Coleco's NHL and Command Control games were nowhere to be found.

Each game also came with a special timer-scoreboard apparatus attached to the side of the frame. Yet aside from the timer, the wood grain, and the legs, these games weren't any different from Coleco's basic models. There were no modifications or extra graphics on the playing surfaces – the "ice" and the "field" looked just like Coleco's other models. And the football game didn't even come with a grandstand. Ah, but Sears' description claimed it had "Executive Command Control." Was this a special advanced Command Control device available only on this game? No, it simply meant that Coleco viewed these games as "executive" models. (With their added wood grain sophistication they could look good in the office as well as the rec room?) This gave them license to add an extra adjective to their description. The word "executive" also seemed to give Coleco the idea that people would pay more money for these games. The hockey game was listed at $24.95 – two dollars more than Munro's stand-alone hockey game on page 103. And this new Coleco football game was priced at a whopping $29.95, making it the most expensive electric football game ever sold. It was almost double the price of Tudor's Super Bowl game, the acknowledged "Cadillac" of electric football. Would people really pay double for a non-NFL game with legs? Only time would tell. It was hard to imagine who at Coleco approved the idea of the $30 electric football game. (Perhaps it was the toy executives who stayed for "last call" at the Coleco World of Sports Dinner.)

Beyond electric football, NFL Properties now had over four pages of NFL merchandise in the Sears catalog. Pajamas, sweatshirts, jackets, clocks, watches, hats, and jewelry were all part of the expanding line of NFL items. Many of these items were receiving added promotion in the continuing weekly "Time Out" column of *PRO!* There seemed to be no stopping the gathering momentum of NFLP.

Tudor supplemented its Sears success in 1971 by occupying almost all of page 431 in the Ward Christmas catalog. Ward decided not to sell Coleco

Thanks to Munro's late entry into electric football, a Vibra-Action model like this one was a rare sighting on either side of the border in 1971. Pictured is a Canadian version. (Photo by Earl Shores.)

Munro's very Tudor-like players. They came in three poses: lineman, back, and end. The back is mounted on the special Play-Action Control base. (Photo by Earl Shores.)

electric football again and instead let Tudor offer a third model in the form of a small No. 515 game with the Cowboys and the Jets. This added to Tudor's large Ward No. 627 game, which this year featured the Vikings in white and the 49ers and Colts dark. Like Tudor's other large football games in 1971, this game came with the new NFL team standings board. While the No. 627's field and frame remained unchanged, the grandstand had been updated to an eye-catching triple-deck design. It was the tallest grandstand Tudor ever made, just bordering on the physical limits of what could be clipped onto the side of a game without falling over. Surprisingly, even with more grandstand the price of the game had dropped to $14.99.

The Ward No. 619 lost its marquee team matchup from the previous year (the Cowboys and Jets were instead on the new Ward No. 515), so the Chiefs and Bears were recruited to create a new Midwestern interconference rivalry. A new grandstand also graced the No. 619, while the field and frame stayed the same.

Even though Coleco didn't get a game on the Ward electric football page, the company had three hockey games and a basketball game on the preceding page. One of the hockey games was an "executive" model, complete with legs and a wood-grain finish. It was called NHL Table Hockey, and it differed from the Sears executive Coleco hockey model only in how the scoreboard mounted to the game. But like the Sears model, it was $24.95. Ward's "regular" Coleco hockey game – called NHL Stanley Cup Hockey – didn't really look all that different from Coleco's executive model, and it was cheaper by $9.

Throughout the fall, both Sears and Ward used electric football heavily in their print advertising. (Sears mostly featured the Super Bowl, while

Ward used the NFL No. 627.) But they were far from alone, and many other large retailers were giving shoppers a choice, selling models from at least three electric football makers. J.C. Penney, Toys R Us, and the Gibson Discount Centers were all lining their shelves with Tudor, Gotham, and Coleco games. Offering the most variety was Toys R Us, who was not only selling a full Tudor NFL line and the No. 500, but also large and small models from Coleco. Squeezed in between all these games was Gotham's Roman Gabriel model. It was the only game that Gluck managed to place with the nation's fastest growing toy chain. A major national retailer who surprisingly was not offering much choice was Kmart. For 1971 Kmart had cozied up with Coleco and was pushing Pro Action Electric Football with gusto during the early weeks of fall.

There was little surprise that the second season of *ABC Monday Night Football* was turning out to be even more successful than the first. An exclamation point to Rozelle's belief in weeknight football came when the Vikings beat the Colts 10-3 on October 25. Over 15 million homes tuned in to the game – it was the largest television audience ever to watch a regular season game. The only games having more viewers were Super Bowl and NFL Championship games.

Another illustration of the NFL's ever-expanding popularity came in early November, when Tudor won its second consecutive Sears Symbol of Excellence Award. Norman received the award during a luncheon at the 21 Club, with the presenter again being Sears' national merchandise manager

Munro's oversized quarterback figure. (Photo by Earl Shores.)

John Waddle. According to Waddle, the award was given for "the quality and excellence of the supply of its Electric Super Bowl game, and NFL Electric Football game." This year, NFL Properties president Bob Carey attended the luncheon, as did another NFL executive – Commissioner Pete Rozelle. Photos of Rozelle and Sas studying a Sears Colts-Cowboys Super Bowl game were published in the December issue of *Toy & Hobby World*. It was a proud moment for Norman. The biggest retailer in the toy business and the most powerful man in professional sports were both honoring the game he invented and nurtured for more than two decades. What could reinforce the relationship of Tudor and the NFL more than having the commissioner examine a game...and getting photographed doing it?

Gotham's oversized plastic Namath quarterback was a disappointing find on Christmas morning. (Photo by Roddy Garcia.)

Within a few days, John Waddle was at another Sears Symbol of Excellence Award ceremony, this time giving Munro Games its second consecutive award for supplying Sears with hockey games. For Don Munro, it was a reward for the many years his family had worked tirelessly as part of the toy business. Trbovich enjoyed these moments too, but besides getting a nice looking plaque to hang on the office wall, he saw an opportunity. To announce the Sears award to a broader audience, Trbovich held a special press conference in New York City. The "special" part of the conference, however, was not about the Sears award. It was to publicize Munro Games' "aggressive expansion" into sports action games in 1971, and its "heavy commitment to consumer and trade advertising." This was something people in the toy business already were aware of, but the Servotronics president was aiming for a different market. He was aiming at Wall Street and potential buyers of Servotronics stock.

"We are in the game business very seriously," said Trbovich, adding that Munro Games had committed hundreds of thousands of dollars to promote and advertise its games in 1971. He also dropped hints of further expansion of Munro Games, saying that serious negotiations were underway to acquire two more toy companies. Trbovich did not name names at this time, hoping that stock speculators would be willing to speculate. Munro's entry into making vibrating electric football games, according to Trbovich, was in response to consumer demand.

To illustrate further Munro's commitment to the game market, Trbovich bragged that Munro's super stars – Bobby Hull, Bobby Orr, and Daryle Lamonica – had all signed long-term endorsement contracts. Munro obtained the exclusive rights to Lamonica's name after winning a court settlement from Coleco. The Raiders' quarterback was featured as a Coleco Pro Star in 1970, but it turned out that he never gave the company permission to use his name. Coleco admitted as much in court and agreed it would no longer use Lamonica's name or image. Munro's monetary award was undisclosed.

While all that Trbovich said at his press conference was true, there was something he left out. Those electric football games were not showing up on many toy store shelves in the U.S. There might be ads, and there might be demand, but Munro wasn't exactly stepping up to fill the need. In trying to rush the game into production, there had been problems in the New York plant. So maybe it was a good thing that few retailers – the W.T. Grant's chain was one – had decided to take a chance on Munro's football games. Bobby Hull would sell, as illustrated by Toys R Us featuring the game prominently in its hockey line, but the prospects for a large, expensive, and generic Munro electric football game were still questionable. Tudor, Coleco, and Gotham could all fill the electric football entry-level price point for much less money and offer stores a greater profit. Since Munro didn't have the muscle of a Coleco to persuade retailers to take on the entire sports game line, few wanted to experiment on such an obviously rushed electric football offering.

The games that did turn up were impressive. Graphics on the metal fields were high quality, and Munro outdid Coleco by having its own "gold" goal posts. The grandstand was colorful, assembled easily, and looked very life-like despite not having a scoreboard. (The scoreboard was part of the frame.) Appearing for the first time were Munro's new players. Molded from polystyrene in three different poses, the players were very Tudor-like. In fact, it was hard to see where they differed from Tudor's men at all. Munro's blocking lineman, running back, and linebacker all looked like they stepped right out of the Tudor catalog. They were even the same size as Tudor men.

But Munro players differed from Tudor's in three distinct ways. The first was the color plastic the players were molded in: red and yellow. Tudor had started using yellow plastic players for specific teams (Packers, Redskins, and Steelers), but Munro's yellow was much brighter. The second distinction was the uniform designs, which were much more basic than Tudor's. Painted on the red players were blue pants, white socks, a white sleeve and helmet stripe, and black shoes. The paint scheme on the yellow players included black jerseys, a black helmet stripe, and black socks. Actually, it didn't even look like the players were wearing socks. Since there was no white paint above their shoes it looked a lot like this team was wearing boots. (Maybe they needed them for Canadian weather.) Munro then followed Tudor's method for realism by painting flesh-colored arms and faces – including two African-American players per team – and green "grass" on the player bases to blend in with the field.

The third and final way that Munro's players differed Tudor's was in how they mounted onto their green polyethylene running bases. On the bottom of each player were two molded plastic pegs, which snapped into matching holes punched in each base.

For its quarterback, Munro again borrowed from Coleco, producing oversized plastic figures with spring-loaded throwing arms and kicking legs. However, they weren't quite as large as Coleco's quarterbacks, even though both figures were produced in Portugal, most likely at the same manufacturing plant. The smaller size would save a bit in cost and look more realistic on the field. Adding to Munro's realism was a carefully detailed paint job that matched the colors of the teams in the game. But like Coleco's giants, the men would never scramble for yards or run downfield to make a tackle during a kickoff.

These large quarterbacks meant that Munro had committed to using a magnetic football, and again it appeared to be a part of the electric football concept that that needed more thought. Munro's new players had no way to carry the ball. Both Gotham and Coleco players had metal plates on their bases, allowing the ball to stick to a player and be carried. But there were no metal plates on the Munro players. And even if you did place the football on the player's feet there was another issue – the field was metal. The ball was going to have a slight attraction to the field and slow the runner the down. Gotham and Coleco avoided this problem by having fiberboard fields. Stuffing the magnetic ball under a player's arm was theoretically possible, but the weight of the ball would make the player top heavy. He was just as likely to tip over as run forward. Absent from Munro's Vibra Action game manual were any specific instructions about how the players carried the ball.

Of course the most obvious lapse in Munro's planning was the metal field. With the games on the market, it was finally clear – Play Action Control really didn't work.

Eddie Gluck's problems in 1971 were reversed from Munro's. He had football games that worked; he just didn't have hundreds of thousands of dollars in his advertising budget. But as Thanksgiving Day neared he again relied on the press release formula for free advertising. Hundreds of press releases extolling the virtues of Gotham sports action games were sent to small community papers looking for free Christmas shopping season copy. The results, as usual, were spotty. Sometimes the release ran intact complete with photos; sometimes it was edited so severely that electric football wasn't even mentioned. And often the copy ran in places where there wasn't a Gotham game available for miles around. It did consumers little good to know a Joe Namath game existed if they couldn't find one.

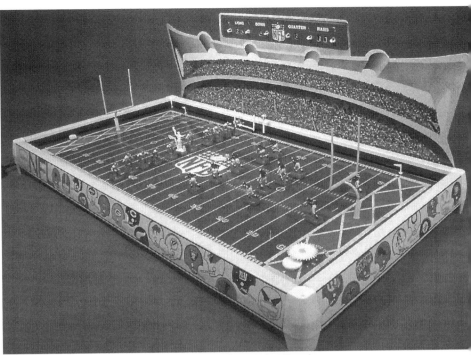

Sears' exclusive No. 618 model with the Lions and the Rams. (Photo by Earl Shores.)

Gluck had caught a break earlier in the week when Sunday papers around the country carried a color Toys R Us insert. Gotham's Roman Gabriel model was one of two electric football games pictured in the insert. That was the good news. The bad news was having Gotham's game sitting right next to a Tudor No. 500. Both games looked pretty much identical on the page, yet the No. 500 was $3 cheaper. At least Gotham's best-known endorser would soon be back in action. Word was out that Joe Namath would start the Jets' next game.

Gluck certainly needed all the help he could get because on Thanksgiving Day, Sears and Ward continued to make electric football a prominent part of their Christmas advertising (the Super Bowl and NFL No. 627 respectively). Toys R Us favored the No. 500 for its turkey day ads, while Kmart gave Coleco serious visibility. Aside from the assorted press releases, Gotham was nearly invisible during the four-day period. But there was a glimmer of hope. On Sunday, a returning Namath threw three touchdowns in a loss to the 49ers. While it was an encouraging performance, the Jets' season record was now a disappointing 4-7.

December shaped up as a busy month for both the NFL and electric football. Thanks to the college football season going on break until the bowl games of Christmas week, the NFL was able to televise games on Saturday, Sunday, and Monday during the first three weekends of the month. This helped stoke store-shelf showdowns in electric football, which

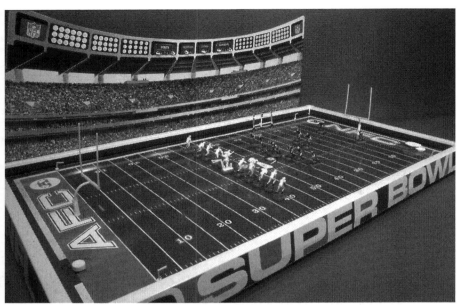
A Tudor Colts-Cowboys Super Bowl game as it might have looked on Christmas morning. (Photo by Roddy Garcia.)

were fiercer and taking place in more retailers than ever before. Coleco's Command Control television ads had run continuously through the fall, creating a demand for non-NFL games with the special feature.

"Command Control looked terrific on television," said Sas. "The ads were very effective." Besides helping Coleco increase its slice of the electric football market, it increased the pressure Coleco exerted on Tudor beyond the vibrating gridiron. In trying to entice more retailers to carry the Coleco brand the company had expanded its hockey line to have NHL "team specific" games (just as Tudor now had "regional" and "home team" games). If a boy lived in Chicago, he could buy a Black Hawks model, or a Flyers model in Philadelphia. Retailers were then "encouraged" to carry Coleco electric football games, lest they take the chance of running short of NHL games during the crucial Christmas season.

But Tudor still had the upper hand with Sears and Ward and remained the top-selling company in retailers like Toys R Us where multiple electric football brands were available. Taking the biggest hit from Coleco's increasing market share was Gotham. Despite the lift from Toys R Us, it was harder to find a Gotham product than in previous years, especially the Namath game. Gotham's widest distribution in 1971 likely came through the Gibson Discount Center chain. The downside of Gibson's was that the retailer didn't have any loyalty other than costs, so Gotham was usually sharing a shelf with Tudor's No. 500. But in many ways Gluck was still better off than Trbovich, who at this point in time could only dream about getting his electric football games to places like Brainerd, Minnesota; Commerce, Texas; or Greeley, Colorado. (The struggling W.T. Grant chain had gotten the new Munro games as far as Arizona.)

On the eve of the final weekend of the NFL season, *Sports Illustrated* published an article profiling the success of NFL Properties. No figures were disclosed, but NFLP was called one of the world's largest licensor of specialty items, now in the class with licensing behemoth Walt Disney. President Bob Carey told the magazine that over 200 official NFL-licensed items were now on the market. And what was the best selling item? Tudor's NFL electric football games. It's doubtful the article made an impact on Tudor's December sales figures, but it never hurt to have the head of NFL Properties tell the most popular sports magazine in the country that Tudor electric football games were No. 1. It was the kind of publicity that the lavish advertising budgets at Coleco and Munro couldn't buy.

Drama was not in abundance on the final NFL weekend. Only the Western Division of the NFC offered a hint of uncertainty, as a loss by the 49ers and a win by the Rams would put the new NFL tie-breaking procedures to the test. Otherwise the Cowboys, Redskins, and Vikings had locked up NFC playoff spots. Over in the AFC, the Chiefs, Browns, Colts, and surprising Dolphins were guaranteed post-season play. On Saturday, December 18, the Cowboys wrapped up the NFC East with a victory over St. Louis, making the Redskins the NFC's wild card team. The following day, the Dolphins took the AFC East crown with a 27-6 win over the now hapless Packers. Helping the Dolphins to the title were the Colts, who started the afternoon in control of their own destiny. All they needed to do to win the AFC East was beat the Patriots. This result would automatically relegate the Dolphins to the wild card slot. But the Colts couldn't stop rookie quarterback Jim Plunkett, who threw two touchdown passes in a 21-17 Patriots victory. Late in the day the eyes of the football world turned to San Francisco, where the 49ers needed a victory over the Lions to win the NFC West. A 10-yard fourth-quarter touchdown run by quarterback John Brodie gave the 49ers a 31-27 win and the division title. With the final team decided, the playoffs would start on the following Saturday – Christmas Day.

A sign of just how well electric football was doing in 1971 came during the final week of the Christmas shopping season. The games, at least ones made by Tudor and Coleco, were holding their value. That meant demand was still strong even in the frantic waning days of shopping. At Sears, the Super Bowl was $11.88, just a dollar below the "featured price" the game had been advertised for all during the fall. And by Wednesday, Sears' NFL No. 618 was still over the $10 mark. Over in Ward, the NFL No. 627 game was on "clearance" for $10.88 – just two dollars below its standard 1971 newspaper price. Discounts on Coleco models at Kmart were also slight, coming in at just a couple of dollars per game. Gotham, on the other hand, saw deep discounts on its large NFLPA game and player-endorsed models. Some Joe Namath games were being sold for less than $7.

Another sign of electric football's popularity could again be seen in the Dear Santa letters printed by local newspapers. Requests for electric football games – especially Tudor NFL models – had appeared throughout December. These requests appeared with even more frequency as more and more letters got printed during the final days before Christmas.

Tudor included a 22-page Super Bowl booklet in Sears Super Bowl game. On the cover were the Colts' Earl Morrall and Jim O'Brien. The photo was taken just after O'Brien kicked the game-winning field goal in Super Bowl V. ©NFL Properties 1971.

There were certainly no shortages of electric football games for Christmas morning in 1971. Including the catalog offerings of Sears and Ward, over 30 different games could be stuffed into Santa's sleigh. And there were still some stray Gotham Super Dome games floating around the aisles of discounters who specialized in liquidation. Tudor NFL games were again the most desirable, with Sears' Super Bowl being the crown jewel of Christmas morning. Finding one under the tree meant that you had definitely been "good."

Coleco's advertising, both in paper and on the television, had helped make the Command Control games popular items this Christmas. The company's promise to make all other electric football games "obsolete" was very appealing. What could be cooler than having an electric football player go exactly where you wanted him to go? Maybe Command Control would change electric football forever. At least that was the hope of every boy who put a Coleco Command Control game on his Christmas list.

Next to Command Control and regionalized NFL games, a Gotham electric football game didn't seem like a very appealing Christmas alternative in 1971 – especially if you had asked for a Coleco or Tudor game. For starters, Gotham's stars were shining less brightly than they once did. Namath was sidelined for most of the season, and without him the Jets staggered to a 6-8 record. There simply was no headline grabbing performance by either Joe or the Jets to stir up any thrill over a Namath model. Gabriel fared a little better during the season, leading the Rams to a winning record. But for the second straight year, the Rams didn't make the playoffs, once again finishing runner-up to the NFC West champion 49ers. And Gabriel himself was being overshadowed by the performances of 49ers quarterback John Brodie, who had won the NFL MVP award in 1970. It was almost sadly fitting that as Namath and Gabriel began to struggle on the field, their uniquely personalized electric football images were replaced with "lesser" and less attractive plastic figures.

Unfortunately, the Namath and Gabriel games were the best Gotham could offer in 1971. With the Bears, a middling team through most of the 1960's, the new Dick Butkus model would have little appeal outside of Chicago. It might have helped if Gotham had a plastic Dick Butkus figure that could go on the field and make bone-jarring tackles.

Gotham's NFL Players Association games had never generated much marketplace excitement. The reason for this was simple – the only time the NFLPA made headlines was when there was a dispute with the owners over money (not that the players' cause wasn't just). This kind of publicity wasn't going to sell electric football games. So it was another tough year for Gotham. It was also a tough year for any boy who found a Gotham game under his tree.

A Munro electric football game likely caused some Christmas morning puzzlement that was quickly followed by relief and delight. It wasn't a Tudor game, yet it wasn't Gotham either. With the metal field and the painted players it was Tudor-like, but it also had control rods like Coleco, as well as a cool-looking grandstand. So it really was a hybrid game that borrowed some of the best features in electric football. A disappointment it was not. Any disappointment associated with the Munro electric football line was confined to the Servotronics offices in Buffalo, thanks to the meager number of games that made it into the American market.

But no matter what kind of game you received, there had never been a Christmas day like this one. In fact, this had to be the best Christmas ever to get an electric football game. By midday (mid-morning on the West coast), the sounds of a live NFL playoff game would be competing with the buzz of vibrating game boards. In a stroke of total genius – or hubris – Pete Rozelle had decided to take on Santa Claus and baby Jesus. For the first time ever there would be NFL games on Christmas Day. Loyal Vikings fans were opening their presents in the frigid parking lot of Metropolitan Stadium, eagerly awaiting the 12:00 p.m. (local CDT) kickoff of the Vikings-Cowboys game. Fans in Kansas City got a bit of a reprieve; as their game wouldn't start until 3:00 p.m. For women around the country cooking dinner, Pete Rozelle was a modern day Mr. Scrooge ruining Christmas for everybody.

The Cowboys beat the Vikings 20-12, ruining the day for Vikings fans – a frozen dinner seemed fitting for them. But when the Chiefs and Dolphins

Lee Payne was now spending time, camera in hand, on NFL sidelines. His photos captured the detail that he was determined to put into electric football. John Brodie and the 49ers visit the Rams in the Coliseum. (Photo by Lee Payne, collection of Roddy Garica.)

An original Lee Payne photo that appeared in the 1971 Tudor sales catalog. Both the 49ers and Browns were involved in playoff games on December 26. The Browns lost to the Colts 20-3, while the 49ers bested the Redskins 24-20.

got under way, nobody knew it would finish as the longest game in NFL history. After 82 minutes and 40 seconds of play – or with 7:40 left in the second overtime period – Dolphins kicker Garo Yepremian made a 37-yard field goal to give Miami a 27-24 "sudden death" victory. A question for the ages is how many turkeys and possibly marriages turned to dust during the three and half hours the game was on NBC. Still, it's a safe bet that in numerous households throughout the country one sound continued on after the game was over...buuuzzzzzzzzz!

Two more NFL playoff games the next day left no time for a football hangover. Although by the time the sun set on Candlestick Park in San Francisco, most households had overdosed on America's pigskin pastime. In the early game, the Colts cruised to an easy 20-3 win over the Browns in Baltimore. John Brodie then thrilled the 49ers fans with another strong performance and gave the team a 24-20 win over the Redskins. It was hard to tell whether Santa or Pete Rozelle turned out to be the number one guy on this weekend, but tradition had taken a beating.

Something else that was taking a beating after two full days of "research by experts" was the Command Control concept. It turned out that it wasn't that realistic. Moving the players attached to the Command Control rod often gave the effect of having an Olympic sprinter lined up with the local high school track team. He could move so much faster that the action was anything but realistic. And the passing game became a great deal more complicated and time consuming because it often involved moving the Command Control rod to the pass receiver. The whole midplay magnet-rod changeover tango got old quickly. Finally, depending on how closely the rules were followed, the Command Control player could just be rammed through the entire offense or defense, knocking all the other players over. "You just put your guy on the magnet, shoved him forward, and you had a touchdown every time," said Sas. "It looked great on television, but it was a dumb idea."

Another problem was one of geometry. Having the controlling rods mounted on opposite sides meant there were positions where the two rods would interfere with each other, even though the offensive and defensive Command Control players on the field weren't touching. So a runner might not be tackled, yet he couldn't move forward because the defensive player's control rod was in the way. If a Command Control contest wasn't played in the spirit of true sportsmanship, then it wasn't much of a game. And when the "realism" and the sportsmanship wore off, boys soon discovered that the rods could be pulled out of the frame and turned into wonderful swords. This wasn't the kind of play value parents bargained for when a friend came over for a rainy afternoon indoors.

Depending on the child's determination to play electric football, the Munro Play Action control rods turned into swords even quicker than Command Control rods. This was due to the physical issue of trying to push two opposing magnets over a metal field. It simply didn't work. From the kickoff, there was simply no hope for the Play Action concept. For fencing, on the other hand, the rods were perfect.

The 49ers' victory on late Sunday afternoon did not mark the end of televised football for the week. It was really only just the beginning because college football would be televised in prime time on Monday, Tuesday, and Thursday nights. On Friday, New Year's Eve, three more games would be broadcast, having been opportunely scheduled to provide over eight consecutive hours of televised football. And that number would be topped the next day, thanks to a scheduling change by the Sugar Bowl.

Munro's groundbreaking 1972 Monday Nite Football game. 1972 Munro sales catalog. (Collection of Earl Shores.)

# 26 THE STAKES RISE AS ELECTRIC FOOTBALL "LIGHTS UP"

The Sugar Bowl had moved its kickoff up to 12:00 p.m., so by the time the Orange Bowl signed off the air late on Saturday night, over eleven consecutive hours of football would be televised into American households. And the Orange Bowl was the game that everyone wanted to see; it featured No. 1-ranked Nebraska playing No. 2-ranked Alabama. Both teams were undefeated, making it a winner-take-all game for the national championship. Nebraska came in as a 6-point favorite, and they did just a little better than that in a 38-6 mauling of the Crimson Tide.

There was little time to shake off the football overload of Saturday as Sunday brought the NFC and AFC Championship games. The NFC went first, with the home Dallas Cowboys shutting down the 49ers 14-3. In the late game, the Dolphins blanked the Colts 21-0 in an Orange Bowl stadium that had barely recovered from Saturday night's contest. Electric football sets buzzed through the weekend as nine football games had been televised nationally during a 72-hour period. But they did so in the "traditional" electric football way. By this point most Command Control or Play Action rods had been thoroughly abandoned – or confiscated by frustrated parents. Norman's original vibrating concept had hardly been rendered obsolete.

The promise of artificial turf played a big part in New Orleans' landing the upcoming Super Bowl, but doubts were being raised about whether football was meant to be played on a field of green plastic fibers. During the 1971 season the Players Association claimed that the new kinds of turf were producing an alarming number of injuries, the most common of which were burns caused by players skidding across a man-made surface. As a result, the players asked the league to halt future installations of artificial turf, at least until the league did a study comparing injury rates on turf against injury rates on grass. Concerns about artificial turf even made it to Congress, where hearings had been held to determine whether turf should be covered by product-safety regulations. Turf makers vehemently denied the injury claims, and the owners waved off any calls for a study. But the issue would not go away. Dolphins coach Don Shula had openly criticized the Orange Bowl's field in the days leading up to the AFC championship game.

Since both the Cowboys and Dolphins played their home games on plastic grass, there was no turf edge for this Super Bowl. But the Cowboys were granted a 5-point edge thanks to their previous Super Bowl experience. If only the odds makers had been that accurate. In a subdued and one-sided contest, the Cowboys ran the ball 48 times on their way to a 24-3 dismantling of the Dolphins. The 39-degree temperature made for the coldest Super Bowl conditions ever. Fortunately the cold didn't affect the field, which resembled a green Brillo pad with lines during the CBS telecast. It was a game that only a Dallas fan could love.

Yet the Super Bowl was now established as a true national event. Nielsen ratings were up from the previous year – over 65 million viewers, or 74% of all the people watching television on Sunday afternoon were tuned in to the game. This result was just one of many reflecting pro football's seemingly limitless popularity. *ABC Monday Night Football* Nielsen ratings increased by over a point during the 1971 season, and a Gallup poll had 36% of American adults naming football as their favorite sport to watch. Only 21% of poll respondents chose baseball. A Gallup poll taken a decade earlier had nearly the reverse result, with 34% of the respondents favoring baseball, while only 21% favored football.

Similar results came from an NFL-funded Harris poll. Baseball commissioner Bowie Kuhn was so infuriated – according to Harris, football's edge over baseball was 29% to 21% – that he held a New York City press conference to refute and question the poll's methodology. Kuhn told Pete Rozelle to "quit kidding the nation about football being the nation's No. 1 sport" and insinuated that the NFL had manipulated the Harris results. The timing of this rebuttal, January 31, was less than fortuitous. All Kuhn may have done was to remind the sporting world of an important NFL event that was taking place in New York the very next day – the NFL draft.

Toy Fair preparations were under way by draft day with most showrooms up and ready for visitors well before the official February 27 opening date. Coleco held its World of Sports dinner at the Essex House Hotel on the 21st, celebrating a successful year with invited toy buyers and NHL-legend Gordie Howe. But all was not well in the toy world. Some major companies were shaking off less than stellar results for 1971, thanks to the collapse of the die-cast car market. The "crash" actually started in 1970 when retailers found themselves with huge inventories of unsold

# THE COLECO WAY
# A total Merchandising Program for '72

**All From a Single Source**

- Taking proven basic items and improving them in our own unique way for better design, more play value, faster sale.
- Packaging these staple items in highly attractive, innovative packages for fast over-the-counter action.
- Promoting these same basic items with heavy TV — on leading family shows like Dick Cavett, Johnny Carson and on top sports shows like ABC's Wide World of Sports!

- All of these same basic values available from a single source!
- The Coleco Way — a way to build sales and profits for you with proven staple merchandise.

**All From a Single Source**

COLECO INDUSTRIES, INC., 945 ASYLUM AVENUE, HARTFORD, CONNECTICUT 06105 • IN CANADA - COLECO (CANADA) LIMITED, 4000 ST. AMBROISE ST., MONTREAL 207, P.Q.
©1972 — Coleco (Canada) Limited, Montreal, Canada.

Coleco's impressive 1972 Total Merchandising store display as featured in the Coleco sales catalog. (Collection of Earl Shores.)

Coleco's new line of smaller Command Control games. Not only did these games have a smaller playing surface, nearly half of the frame was made out of plastic. 1972 Coleco sales catalog. (Collection of Earl Shores.)

Hot Wheels to carry into 1971. With old cars still on the shelves, retailers had little desire to take on the new Hot Wheels line, so Mattel's die-cast sales declined dramatically throughout 1971. Red ink was spilled into the company ledger books for the first time since 1965.

Topper's Johnny Lightning car line also suffered from the die-cast downturn, so much so that the company was trying to work out deals with its creditors. But both Topper and Mattel came to the 1972 Fair feeling confident they would turn things around. Topper was holding off the banks with the promise of a new Sesame Street line, while Mattel planned to introduce a boys' doll named Big Jim. Mattel went out of its way to emphasize that Big Jim was a doll, not an "action figure." Somewhere in a damp dark attic, a forgotten Johnny Hero "doll" was shaking his head.

The troubles of excess inventory had yet to reach full bloom in electric football, although it was hard to imagine how 30 different electric football models all turned a profit in a single Christmas season. Yet this obvious crowding in electric football mattered little to Coleco and Munro. Both came to the Fair with aggressive plans for 1972.

Coleco's efforts seem to go mostly into marketing as they brought "The Coleco Way" campaign to the Fair. It was unveiled with a four-page color spread in *Playthings*, and at the World of Sports dinner. *(Playthings* was calling the dinner "one of the industry's major pre-Toy Fair week events.")* Part of the Coleco Way was a "Total Merchandising Program," which promoted the concept of getting all your sports games from a single source.

Instead of retailers getting their football games from Tudor, their hockey games from Munro, and baseball games from Gotham, they could get all their sports games from Coleco. A floor-to-ceiling store display full of Coleco sports games illustrated the concept. What boy could resist such a heavenly image?

The Coleco Way included promises of heavy television advertising. A national campaign was set to target *The Dick Cavett Show*, *The Tonight Show*, and *ABC's Wide World of Sports* – all during the Christmas shopping season. It was a serious show of product support on Coleco's part. These were all highly rated shows, broadcast to almost every corner of the U.S. and much of Canada. And Coleco was not about to overlook Canada. Aside from its obvious and vital relationship with the NHL, Coleco continued its relationship with the Canadian Football League. Once again, there would be a Grey Cup model and advertising in every CFL program sold during the 1972 season. Just the sheer scale of the Coleco Way was sure to impress potential buyers, maybe even more than the products did.

That's because there were no attention-grabbing electric football innovations for 1972. Command Control, with all its faults, would again be the main selling point of the Coleco line. And upon close examination, it was clear that Coleco was scaling down electric football. Instead of having two large games, Coleco consolidated down to a single Command Control configuration that came with or without legs. (Sears would again have an executive model, but this was not shown at the Fair.) While the large game remained mostly unchanged from the very first Coleco electric football prototypes, Coleco created a midsized and redesigned Command Control game for 1972. Unfortunately, this new design was based on the compact line of entry-level football games the company introduced in 1971.

Although the frame of the game was 32" long – just like the regular Pro Stars models – the field was shorter thanks to a new plastic framework that ate up 2 inches of each end zone. This left the end zones only as deep as the goal posts. Once your opponent reached the 10-yard line it became impossible to set up your team in a realistic defensive formation. When the offensive team reached the 5-yard line, you had to line up all eleven of your defenders on the line of scrimmage; and, if the scrimmage line got down to the 2-yard line, you couldn't set your team up at all. It was hard to understand why the Coleco designers ignored this issue. If Command Control was the height of electric football realism, why would Coleco sacrifice goal-line play on its most "realistic" game?

And it wasn't just the ends of this model that ended up being economized. The grandstand was trimmed down to a single piece of thin cardboard with a built-in cardboard scoreboard. The only metal parts on the game were the frame sides holding the Command Control rods. If things were

Munro debuted Monday Nite Football – the first electric football game with lights – at the 1972 Toy Fair. 1971 Munro sales catalog. (Collection of Earl Shores.)

going well in electric football why would Coleco scale down its entry-level Command Control model? Price. By adding more plastic and making a smaller grandstand, the game became cheaper for Coleco to manufacturer. Coleco could then sell this model at last year's wholesale price and increase their profit. Retailers could also hold the same price as the previous year (about $10.99), theoretically advancing Coleco's market share, especially if the price of Tudor and Munro games increased from 1971.

Another thing Coleco did to cut costs was to stop painting its quarterbacks. This left the towering giants looking pitifully naked, their unpainted faces now ghostly and blank. But what were looks versus the pennies Coleco was saving in every game?

While cutting in the middle, Coleco kept the bottom end of electric football the same as the previous year, offering two low-cost games to compete directly with Tudor's No. 500 model. They were even going after the pre-electric football crowd with a small nonelectric game called Power Play Football (aimed at the "Junior Pro," ages 4 to 10). Using "magnetic action" (hand-held magnets that slid along the underside of the 26" x 14" molded plastic field) junior coaches guided their teams to victory. It was a bit presumptuous on the part of the Coleco designers to think that 4-year-olds would know the X's and O's for a full eleven-man football team. The company could have done the kids a favor and saved some money by including six-player teams.

In contrast to Coleco, whose ambitions in 1972 seemed focused more on marketing than on game features, Munro's designers had been given a green light and a lot of greenbacks to produce an electric football "seventh wonder." Trbovich wanted a masterpiece, something so revolutionary that Munro would be the trendsetter of electric football, not just one of the followers. And cost would be no object. It's safe to say Trbovich got what he wanted in 1972. In 23 years of electric football there had never been anything like Munro's brand new Monday Nite Football game.

Measuring in at 40" x 25", it was the largest football game ever made. The field was so big that it even had a wind sprint track running along side of it. But what really made Munro's new game unlike any other was mounted on top of the double-deck grandstand – two battery operated floodlights. It was the first authentic "night" football game.

Munro had worked hard for many months to keep its new game a secret. "The secrecy before the toy shows…it was crazy," said Don Munro. "We even put up paper on the factory windows." Don joked that the security was so tight that getting into a Munro Games plant was like "getting into NASA." Considering how Munro Games had "borrowed" Coleco's Command Control the year before, the company had good reason for paranoia over its new game. Payback could have come in the form of Coleco "borrowing" the floodlight concept.

A lighted electric football game was an exciting idea on its own, but by calling the game Monday Nite Football, Munro Games could link the company with the NFL without actually having the NFL. Trbovich was determined to announce the game with a flourish, taking out a two-page color layout in the Toy Fair issue of *Playthings*.

A television screen on the page was "broadcasting" the image of an excited family playing the new Monday Nite game. The scene of the contest was the family's wood paneled rec room where father and son were playing the game (mom and sis were there too, but relegated to the cheerleader role). Text on the facing page described the game as "designed to tie in with the exciting games that flash across TV screens all over the country." Toy buyers were further encouraged "to sign up now for one of the biggest profit makers in sports game history." It was all heady stuff. And within the ad, Munro Games had started to call itself "The Innovators." This claim dripped with hubris, especially in light of a sentence highlighting Munro's *triple threat quarterback* who could "run, pass and kick with stunning accuracy." To make its utterly stationary quarterback figure run, Munro Games had to be more than innovators – the designers needed to be miracle

# Announcing Munro Monday Nite Football.

New Official Munro Monday Nite Football is designed to tie in with the exciting games that flash across TV screens all over the country. Official Munro Monday Nite Football, the most innovative game of '72. Sign up now for one of the biggest profit makers in sports games history.

Lights! Action! Lights! That's right. Powerful lights at the top of the game illuminate every play. Munro offers the fantastic realism of Monday Nite Football. There's even a sprint and warm-up track for the players. They can race or run wind sprints just before the game to get limbered up. Play action control adds even more play realism.

The Munro electric vibrator features variable vibration control for split-second timing. Triple-threat quarterbacks run, pass and kick with stunning realism. Panel-mounted scoreboard has dial controls for scoring, downs, and quarters. And interchangeable team placards are included for all pro-league games.

Official Munro Monday Nite Football! It rivals the real thing on television. Your sales and profits never had it so good. Available in all sizes of table and floor models.

See the Innovators in Room 803 in the Toy Center, North, 1107 Broadway.

Electric Vibra Action Football by Munro.

New exciting graphics make this game a real winner. Exciting three-dimensional players plus authentic 3-D full-color grandstand scene create extra realism. Play action control adds to player participation. Also a field-mounted Timer with time-in time-out control and a panel-mounted score-board for extra sales appeal. Mechanical vibra action games available.

Super-Pro Basketball by Munro.

The award-winning Game-of-the-Year in '71 is even better in '72. Skillful Munro engineering plus many new features make this the most realistic basketball game on the market today. Shoot from anywhere on the court— 10 movable plastic players. New, 4-color action graphics. Sales action is fast and furious. Make the most of it. Safety Value, Quality Approved by "Chicago Today."

Munro announces Monday Nite Football and also promotes itself as "The Innovators" at the 1972 Toy Fair. *Toys*, March 1972. (Collection of Earl Shores.)

workers. But the ad did its job. It was colorful and catchy, clearly presenting Monday Nite Football as the next "big thing" in electric football.

Once in the Munro showroom, there were promises of an extensive fall television campaign, as well as over 100 pages of trade publication advertising. This seemed more than ample support for the seven different Munro electric football games on display in 1972. In the Super Pro line there were three games, a 33" x 19" model with Play Action rods and a large (38" x 21") and small (33" x 19") model, both without the Play Action feature. There was only one size for the City Star line – a 38" x 21" game with Play Action rods – but the City Star model could be customized to feature a player from a specific city. At the Fair it was unclear if Munro had any NFL stars to feature on this game. (The City Star concept seemed more aimed at Canadian Football League cities.)

And finally there was the flagship Monday Nite line which consisted of three models. The "economy" Monday Nite game did not have Play Action rods and measured only 38" x 21", but it did have lights. Filling out the Monday Nite line were two super size 40" x 21" games with the Play Action feature. Only a single feature distinguished one game from the other. One was a stand-alone model with legs; the other was a tabletop game.

Any game 38" x 21" or larger came equipped with Munro's wind-up game timer, and most of the games on display in the showroom had metal fields. But these were only prototypes. Munro was promising fiberboard fields on all its games come the fall. This would make the Play Action feature more useful, although the entire Command/Play Action concept was being questioned by some of the most important people in electric football – the kids who played the game.

Electric football was just a part of Munro Games' grand Toy Fair presentation. Also on display were 12 hockey games, 4 basketball games, 3 pool tables, a soccer game, and a line of street hockey equipment. Despite the size of the Munro line, nobody in the company was anticipating any production issues this year. Besides the original Munro factory in Burlington, Ontario there was now a 100,000 square-foot warehouse for inventory storage. And the factory in Arcade, New York, had a 240,000 square-foot warehouse attached to it. High-speed assembly lines in both New York and Canada were capable of turning out 500 games per

More of Munro's "The Innovators" promotion at the 1972 Toy Fair.

hour. Trbovich was sure that every retailer who wanted a Munro game would get one.

For Norman, it was another year to look at the competition and shake his head. Munro's floodlight idea certainly was innovative, and even kind of fun, but making a profit with it was another story. Munro's wholesale prices on the Monday Nite line started at almost $12 – that meant at retail the game could end up costing $20 or more. Even though the executive Coleco football game at Sears had breached the $20 mark, and nearly hit $30, this was rarified territory. Norman was sure, for now at least, that $20 was more than the average consumer was willing to pay for electric football. If a game needed to be priced in that range, you just weren't going to sell a lot of games.

Norman also knew that despite Command Control's flaws, it had brought additional sales Coleco's way, and Tudor needed to come up with some type of competitive answer. Creating a control rod for a single player was never under consideration at Tudor. They had invented electric football and felt they understood the game better than any other company. Giving "control" to just a single player seemed unfair. Why couldn't you control the direction of all the players? This was one of the major things Lee worked on during 1971. Figuring out how to give directional control to all 22 players vibrating on an electric football field.

So at the Toy Fair in 1972, Tudor introduced Total Team Control bases. The new TTC bases were just like Tudor's regular green bases, except they didn't have a pair of front legs. Instead, a separate set of front legs could be snapped into the base and then turned to direct the player left, right, or straight ahead. These special bases and legs would be included in each Tudor TTC game. A small steering tool would also be standard equipment to help a coach make directional adjustments to his players. As usual, Lee only had prototype TTC bases for the Fair, and they worked well enough to demonstrate the concept. Production of the actual bases was under way in Hong Kong.

Only three Tudor games were going to have the Total Team Control feature, and those were a midsize NFL model and two large NFL conference models. They were numbered the No. 635, the No. 640, and the No. 650. The non-TTC equivalent of these games were the No. 615, the American Conference No. 610, and the National Conference No. 620. Other than the new TTC games, the rest of the Tudor line was unchanged from 1971. To support the line, Tudor was promising weekly advertising in the *PRO!* But Norman was not following Coleco and Munro into the costly world of television.

Tudor did not reveal the TTC concept in *Playthings*. Instead, on page 217 the company introduced a newly redesigned line of NHL Players Association hockey games. The extensive artwork, both on the players and on the game came from Lee Payne. He also designed a new automatic scoring system, as well as interchangeable player "sticks." A significant yet little noticed change was in the manufacturer of this new hockey line. Munro's aggressive charge into electric football left Norman little choice but to end the Munro Games-Tudor hockey partnership. Once again, the games would be made in Brooklyn.

As his company struggled, Eddie Gluck could take some solace in the fact that Gotham was not alone. But unlike Mattel and Topper, he didn't have a complete new line of toys to offer optimism for the coming year. And Gotham had lost the Toys R Us account. The nationwide chain decided to carry Munro's Monday Nite game instead of any Gotham models (they were still trying to get rid of last year's unsold Gotham games). There was no hope of getting back into Sears either, given that Munro had created a special Nite game for the 1972 Christmas catalog. Desperation was setting in. Game sales declined throughout 1971, and the number of retailers carrying any type of Gotham product was going to shrink even further in 1972. The company's viability was on the line. It was hard to see how Gotham could survive another year of battling with Tudor, Coleco, and Munro.

# NFL *Electric Football*® 635 New for 72

No. 635
Box Size: 18" X 32¼" X 3"
1/3 Doz. Ctn. Wt. 33 Lbs.
UL Listed 110 Volts, A.C. Only

Tudor introduces its new Total Team Control bases. 1972 Tudor sales catalog. (Collection of Norman Sas.)

And what did Gluck do in the face of such long odds? He again expanded the Gotham electric football line. Two new endorsers were added to the Family of Sports Super Stars: Cowboys All-Pro defensive tackle Bob Lilly and 1971 NFL Rookie of the Year Jim Plunkett. The G-1400 Lilly game even came with Gotham's large 38" x 21" field. Like the Dick Butkus model, the Lilly game came with 44 Gotham players as standard equipment. Besides this two-platoon feature, Lilly had his image printed on the 50-yard line. The Plunkett model had the quarterback's picture at mid-field, but it was a small 28" x 15" game with only two teams. And like most other Gotham electric football games in 1972, it didn't have a grandstand.

The reason that only the Namath model and the large G-1506 NFLPA game had grandstands was simple – cost. Gluck was cutting costs on his games any way he could, even if he wasn't cutting the number of games Gotham was offering. Of the nine electric football games Gotham was promising for 1972, five were player models – Namath, Gabriel, Butkus, Lilly, and Plunkett. There was also a large and small NFLPA model and two small G-883 games. One was a tabletop game, while the other G-883L had legs. Putting legs on a G-883 certainly summed up Gotham's desperation, especially when compared to the sophisticated stand-alone rec room offerings from Coleco and Munro. But sticking legs on an old game was a lot cheaper and easier than designing an entirely new model. It was shaping up as another grim year for Gotham.

Over in the NFL things were far from grim. In addition to record television ratings, stadium attendance had topped the 10 million mark for

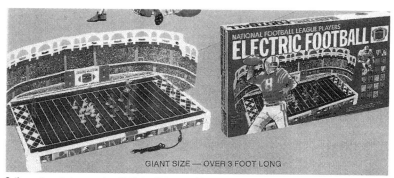

GIANT SIZE — OVER 3 FOOT LONG

Gotham attempts to compete with Tudor, Coleco, and Munro with the 38" x 21" National Football League Players Association model. 1972 Gotham sales catalog. (Collection of Roddy Garcia.)

the first time ever. But as the owners gathered in the paradise-on-earth backdrop of Hawaii for their annual meeting in March, Rozelle laid out a warning with his opening remarks. First, the commissioner said, there was an "unhealthy" and growing perception that the NFL was a business more than a sport. Helping foster this notion was the mounting number of lawsuits against the NFL that often cast the league in a negative light. When the fans perceived money as the overriding factor in professional football, according to Rozelle, they would turn away from the sport. The owners needed to be vigilant to not let this happen.

And second, Rozelle had Sunday afternoon concerns that needed immediate attention. The balance of the game had shifted to the defense – over 100 fewer touchdowns and 600 less points were scored in 1971 than in 1969. Rozelle feared that fans sitting through too many games with 7-0 and 6-3 scores would get bored and lose their interest in the NFL. He encouraged the owners and the competition committee to be proactive on the scoring decline. In other words, Rozelle expected action by the time the meeting adjourned.

Before addressing the scoring issue, the owners awarded the upcoming Super Bowl to Los Angeles, and the 1974 Super Bowl to Houston. The city of Miami had submitted bids and was still a favorite among both owners and fans. Unfortunately, the recent success of the Dolphins removed the city from serious consideration. No owner wanted to give a team home-field advantage in the biggest game of the year. Finally, before the meeting ended the owners voted to move the hash marks in 3 ½ yards to be in line with the goal posts. The idea behind the change was to open the field up for both the running and passing game. Kickers would also have less of an angle to contend with during field goals.

Another organization making football changes was Munro Games. In the April issue of *Playthings* the company paid for a prominent page 3 ad that announced a new, or one might say borrowed, electric football concept.

In April Munro promoted its new Individual Player Programming bases while also quietly renaming their new game "day/Nite Football." Courtesy of The Strong®, Rochester, New York.

It was called IPP, which was short for Individual Player Programming. It didn't take long, but Munro had taken Tudor's Total Team Control player base idea and given it a spin of its own. Actually it was more of a twist as the IPP bases came with a small dial that was adjusted to control the direction of the men. Turn it to the left, and the players went left; to the right, and they went right – theoretically at least. But the adjustments were easier to make on Munro's bases than on Tudor's.

Yet there was something else a little less obvious that Munro needed to do in its ad. That was to announce a change in the name of its flagship football game. It was no longer called Monday Nite Football; it was now called "day/Nite" Football. The "Monday" on the game frame had been covered up, while the "Mon" had been erased from the text in the ad. If the changes appeared hastily done, it's because they were done in great haste. Munro had kept its Monday Nite game a secret and so had the Aurora Plastics Corporation of Hempstead, New Jersey. (Aurora had created the 1960's HO slot car boom with its Thunderjet 500 cars and Model Motoring race sets and was now riding the success of Skittle Bowl.)

The difference was Aurora came to the Fair with an officially endorsed Monday Night Football game. They had approached ABC and made a deal to buy the rights to the name. Munro had decided the word Monday was in the public domain, and that by spelling night "N-I-T-E," they could get around any copyright and trademark issues. Unfortunately, Aurora's lawyers didn't see it that way, even though its Monday Night game was a "computerized" battery-operated game, not a vibrating football game. Munro didn't have much of a case and quickly agreed to change the name

Nick Trbovich and Bobby Hull examine a new hockey game. Trbovich liked being in the company of stars. In June of 1972 he bought Gotham...and Joe Namath. *Toy & Hobby World*, page 12, December 1971.

of its game. For the second straight year Munro's electric football line was off to a rocky start. Gone was the NFL connection that the Monday Nite name bestowed upon Munro.

A minor shock wave rippled through the toy world in June when Munro Games bought the financially endangered Gotham Pressed Steel Corporation. Under the terms of the deal, Gotham became a Munro subsidy that would operate out of Buffalo. Eddie Gluck, who was struggling with his health, retained the title of Gotham president even though he would not be moving with his company. The takeover made sense from the standpoint that, without any league licensing, both companies were going for player endorsements.

"We needed all the names we could get," said Don Munro, and Gotham had one name in particular that Trbovich wanted to add to his superstar endorser locker room – Joe Namath. Munro would continue to sell Joe Namath games under the Gotham name for the duration of 1972, but come 1973, Namath would officially be part of the Munro line.

Within weeks of the sale, it became apparent that the Namath name was going to be the most useful Gotham "part." The company wasn't just struggling from the outside; things inside the Gotham plant were in disarray as well. "Not one piece of official paper came with the Gotham purchase – nothing," said Don Munro. There was no history, no financial records, no designer blueprints or drawings. All that made it to Buffalo was the Gotham name, some machinery, and 20 boxes of sales catalogs. "The machinery was in terrible shape, and the tooling was junk," said Munro. "What we got was absolute junk." In what must have been a bittersweet journey, former Gotham factory manager Hal Lindberg traveled to Buffalo for a few weeks to set up Gotham's creaky machinery. Other than payroll checks mailed to Eddie Gluck, that was the end of Gotham's nearly fifty-year history in New York City.

NFL training camps were in full swing by the time the champion Cowboys defeated the College All-Stars 20-7 on July 29. And by the start of August, Nick Trbovich had found something else in the sporting world for Servotronics to buy – a World Hockey Association franchise in Ottawa. This new league was going into direct competition with the NHL in the fall and had already stolen a number of NHL stars with the promise of outrageous salaries. In many ways the Servotronics chairman and the WHA seemed like a perfect fit.

Munro's Day/Nite game in "night" mode. (Photo by Earl Shores.)

# 27 A SHOPPER'S DILEMMA: SUPER BOWL, DAY/NITE OR COMMAND CONTROL?

After six weeks of exhibition games, the NFL was finally ready to start the regular season on Sunday, September 17. Among the favored teams for the NFC title were the Redskins, Vikings, and Rams, while over in the AFC things were less clear-cut. Surprisingly, the Jets were being mentioned as a team with a chance to do great things, provided Namath stayed healthy. The Vikings were once again starting their season on *ABC Monday Night Football* and had five additional games scheduled for national telecast in 1972. Tudor was also off to a running start, having unveiled its *PRO!* electric football advertising campaign in the preseason. The company was going all out to promote NFL Strategy, NFL Game Plan, and Total Team Control NFL electric football with a full-color page in every NFL program. All three games were pictured with a sharp looking TTC No. 640 AFC model taking up the bottom left corner of the page. Absent from *PRO!* in 1972 were any ads from Coleco.

While things looked positive for Tudor from afar, both Norman and Lee had concerns with the new TTC bases. Despite repeated injection runs in Brooklyn, the quality was not up to Tudor's usual standards. The main problem was in the molding of moveable front legs, which came on a separate sprue of red polyethylene. A number of the sprues were not completely molded, leaving less than 22 useable sets of front legs. If these sprues were put into games, a boy would have to play with less than 11 players per team. This wasn't the type of problem a new electric football feature needed, especially in light of the intensifying competition between Tudor, Coleco, and Munro. Missteps weren't going to be as well tolerated by retailers as they were back in the days when Tudor's gorilla players were plodding around the miniature vibrating gridiron.

Beyond attendance figures and television ratings, perhaps nothing demonstrated the popularity of the NFL better in 1972 than the Sears

**Now you control the play by programming each individual player to go forward, left or right!**

NEW! TOTAL TEAM CONTROL

Steerable "legs" in the base of each player let you call the plays... secretly program your men "in the huddle"... then watch them slant, or sweep right, left, or go straight up the middle!

Your quarterback's dropping back to pass

but it's a fake! The halfback's coming around the end

The defensive line is fooled... can they react quickly enough?

Defensive backs charge in to stop the ball carrier

**SUPERBOWL**

**Electric Football®** $15⁹⁹

SOLD ONLY AT SEARS

- Dolphins and Cowboys clash on 37x20-inch field
- Giant 1½x2-foot high Superbowl VI poster

This year Sears brings a whole new dimension to electric football! Now you can actually "tell" each player what pattern to run, what defender to block, how fast he should move... to make the play go "all the way." You call each play by setting the adjustable "legs" on the players' bases for speed and direction. Then switch on the game and watch the vibrating metal field come alive. Includes 11 plastic players from each team molded in 5 realistic poses, 2 special quarterbacks that "run," "pass" or "kick," 3-tiered grandstand backdrop, goal posts, automatic timer, first-down marker with movable chain, 6 felt footballs, 4 goal-line flags. UL listed for 110-120-v., 60-c. AC.
79 N 65614L—Shipping weight 11 pounds .................................. $15.99

Both sets include 2 "triple threat" Quarterbacks

Sears' 1972 Super Bowl game. The Cowboys and Dolphins came with Tudor's new TTC bases. Sears 1972 *Christmas Book*, page 520. ©Sears, Roebuck and Co. 1972.

*Christmas Book.* Any shopper who followed a Winnie-the-Pooh guided tour of the featured items in the front of the catalog found a dramatic NFL presentation on pages 10 and 11. It was a full-color spread headed by the caption, "Look what Sears has done with the NFL Idea...it's one of the highlights of the 1972 Wish Book." With items for boys, dad, and the entire family, Sears claimed to have brought together its "largest ever collection of National Football League merchandise." Page 10 included a photo index of NFL items and the promise of eleven more pages of team blankets, sheets, towels, pajamas, jackets, and sweatshirts throughout the catalog. In just three short years, NFL Properties had gone from a single page of items, Larry Kent's original goal, to thirteen pages of items. It was the kind of success an organization might dream about, but never truly expect. Not even the NFL.

Overall, the massive NFL spread in Sears was good for Tudor. But at the same time, it was possible that among the growing number of NFL-licensed items was something that could pose a threat to Tudor's top spot at NFL Properties. It was going to be hard to compete against an NFL $3 t-shirt or a $4 sweatshirt. (There was also the increasing competition from Coleco and Munro.)

DAY-NITE
ELECTRIC FOOTBALL $24⁹⁹ without batteries

You control direction of 22 men on floodlighted, 40x25-inch metal field

Use dial on the base of every player to "program" them to move *individually* left, right or forward . . through any offensive or defensive pattern. Then watch as blocking forms and the "hole" opens . . pick out safest route and run your halfback through with Play Action Control rod as defensive opponent moves linebacker up for the tackle. Each team has eleven 3-D players plus quarterback for passing and kicking. With sprint track, timer. 32 in. high. legs fold. UL listed. 110-120-v., 60-c. AC. Uses 2 "D" batteries—order pkg. below.
79 N 65702L—Shipping weight 13 pounds . . . . . . . . . . .$24.99
49 N 8412—"D" Batteries. Pkg. of 4. Wt. 1 lb. . . .Pkg.   3.29

Individual Player Programming dial the direction you want each individual player to go

Play Action Control . . you move any one player on each team

498 [Sears] PSCO MKGAE

Munro's Day/Nite Electric Football game makes its debut on page 498 of the 1972 Sears *Christmas Book*. ©Sears, Roebuck and Co. 1972.

As in previous years, Sears gave Tudor a dynamic layout on page 500, including a Cowboys vs. Dolphins "demonstration" of how the new Total Team Control bases worked. In a close-up photo of a TTC base, Sears claimed that "Steerable 'legs' in the base of each player let you call the plays." It sounded amazing. Several generations of boys had dreamed about the day when electric football players would be "coach-able."

Tudor's Super Bowl again came with generic AFC and NFC markings, but Lee did put a large NFL shield at mid-field. This reflected a change the NFL had made to the real Super Bowl field in New Orleans. The Dolphins and Cowboys were replaying their game before a record crowd, as Lee had created a larger grandstand for this year's model. And included as a special item was a two-foot high Super Bowl VI poster. Even with the new bases and the larger grandstand, the Super Bowl price remained $15.99 for the third consecutive year.

Filling out the page was a TTC No. 635 game with the Lions and Rams and a small No. 515 NFL game with Jet and Raiders (none of Tudor's small games came with TTC bases in 1972). The final Tudor item on the page was NFL Strategy, which at $15.35, cost almost as much as the grander Super Bowl. One of the non-Tudor games on the page had direct links to the

**Electric Table Football Game**

Executive Command Control® rods let you direct player movement magnetically while plays are in progress. Control players of your choice . . vibrating playing field puts players in motion then you make them run, reverse, block and tackle by operating two control rods. Attractive wood-grain finished metal . . 38x21x32 in. 24 players (including passer and kicker). Pro-style goal posts, yardage markers, end zone flags, realistic scoreboard. UL listed: 110-120-volt, 60 cycle AC. Panel style legs. Partially assembled.
6 N 12591L—Shipping weight 31 pounds . . . . . . . . $22.44

376 Sears [logo]

Coleco's 1972 Executive Command Control game got squeezed into the bottom corner of page 376. Sears 1972 *Christmas Book.* ©Sears, Roebuck and Co. 1972.

NFL even though it was paying no licensing fees to NFL Properties. That was Aurora's Monday Night Football game.

On the opposite page, Tudor's electric baseball game found itself surrounded by five Munro games. Consisting of four hockey games and a floor model basketball game, all in full color, it was the largest display Sears had ever given Munro Games. Trbovich and Don Munro were justly proud of page 501, but they were even more excited about page 498, the first ever all-Munro Sears page. Taking up most of the top half of the page was Munro's Family Cup Hockey game, which at 48" x 30", was the largest table hockey game ever made. The Sears description highlighted the super large rink and "doll-like 3-D players" and went on to say, "You've never seen such realism in Game-room Hockey before." Family Cup was a stand-alone rec-room type game, complete with a wood-grain finish and wood legs that were "as solidly built and as beautifully finished as a piece of fine furniture." And at $49.99, it cost as much as a piece of actual furniture.

Next on the page was a Munro foosball soccer game, available with or without legs. And finally, there was the largest electric football game ever made, Day/Nite Electric Football. This was Munro's top-of-the-line model, complete with legs and a $24.99 price tag. The game was pictured in "Nite" mode with floodlights fully ablaze – electric football had never looked so realistic and inviting. Singled out as selling points were the Play Action Control rods, the Individual Player Program bases, and the floodlit 40" x 25" metal field. While it was true that Munro's Toy prototype games had metal fields, the games the company shipped in the fall had fiberboard fields. It was the design Munro knew best (all its hockey games were fiberboard), and fiberboard gave the Play Action rods the best chance of working. This page was much more impressive than Munro's hockey page, and for Trbovich it represented the future of Munro: large dramatic games that made dad and son stop and say, "I want that!!!"

But Munro and Tudor weren't the only companies selling electric football to Sears. Much earlier in the toy section, Coleco had a page of its own rec-room games, including another Executive Command Control

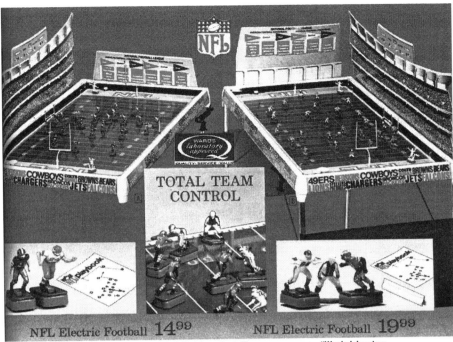

Tudor's offerings in the 1972 Montgomery Ward *Christmas Book.* The games were now "Wards laboratory approved" – whatever that meant. Page 281. ©Montgomery Ward, Inc. 1972.

electric football game, as well as a monster 50" x 25" stand-alone hockey game. This year's Executive football game came with a grandstand instead of the fancy timer of the previous year. Otherwise, it was identical to the 1971 model, right down to the wood-grain design on the frame. Leaving off the timer made the game a more affordable $22.44 – it was no longer the most expensive electric football game in the catalog. Coleco's new NHL Trophy Cup Hockey game would have been more impressive had the page been in color instead of black and white. The appeal of Coleco's new 3-D NHL players and oversized ice surface was swallowed by dim shades of gray. On the plus side, the game was almost $20 cheaper than Munro's Family Cup model.

Unfortunately, Coleco's football game, besides being presented in black and white, was stuffed into the bottom corner of the page with the description covering nearly the entire game. It was very easy to flip the page without even noticing the game was there. It may have been a fantastic product, but the presentation paled in comparison to Tudor's Super Bowl and Munro's Day/Nite game. Overall though, it was a landmark year for the NFL and electric football. Never had Sears devoted so much space to the league – or to a vibrating game.

Coleco had three electric football games on display in the J.C. Penney Christmas Catalog. J.C. Penney *Christmas 1972.* ©J.C. Penney, Inc. 1972.

The NFL didn't receive the same kind of coverage in the Ward Christmas catalog, yet Tudor did pretty well. There were two exclusive Ward NFL No. 627 games on page 281, including one with a feature that had never been seen before on a Tudor electric football game – legs. With the competition from Coleco and Munro mounting, Tudor had joined the battle for space in the rec room. Both Ward games included TTC bases and interconference team matchups. The tabletop No. 627 featured the Dolphins and Chiefs, while the No. 627L had the Dolphins and 49ers, along with four hand-painted referee figures and a plastic "scrimmage line separator." Wards' basic Tudor game was priced at $14.99. Adding legs cost another $5. Although Norman was getting close, he still hadn't crossed the $20 mark with an electric football game.

Tudor was the only brand of electric football game carried by Ward. Coleco was once again limited to supplying table hockey and basketball games in 1972. One of Coleco's hockey games had legs, furthering the trend of family room models. But by leaving off the wood-grain finish and the extravagant timer, Ward had managed to price the game at $19.88. Again, the $20 mark seemed to serve as the dividing line for affordability.

# Sears again pays honor to Tudor Metal

Tudor wins its 3rd consecutive Sears Excellence Award. From left to right: Sears' national merchandising manager John Waddle, Tudor's Norman Sas, Sears' toy buyer Clyde Peterson, and *Playthings'* publisher Harry Gluckert. Courtesy of The Strong®, Rochester, New York.

This line was evident in the J.C. Penney Christmas catalog as well. A large Coleco Command Control model with legs was priced at $19.99 (without legs it was still a somewhat pricey $16.44). Other options from the J.C. Penney catalog included the small entry-level Coleco Pro-Stars game ($6.44), a Tudor NFL TTC No. 635 game ($9.99), and a Gotham G-883L – yes, a small Gotham game with legs – for $9.99. A color page displayed the Coleco and Tudor games, while Gotham was relegated to the black-and-white side of Penney's two-page "Sports Center" football game layout. J.C. Penney was also selling the Aurora Monday Night football game and two other computer football games.

By late September all the catalogs were out, toy departments were opening up, and the selling season was working its way to a slow simmer. The NFL season was heating up too. On September 24, Joe Namath emphatically proved he was over his injury woes by throwing for six touchdowns and 490 yards (a new Jets passing record) during a 44-34 win over the Colts. For Munro Games this was great news. One of their superstars was making headlines.

As the fall moved on, Tudor got some prominent and welcome toy industry exposure thanks to the October issue of *Playthings*. A number of different types of sports games were pictured throughout "The Big Season For Games" article, but only Tudor was chosen to represent the electric football category. And it wasn't just the box of an electric football game (a Coleco Stanley Cup box was the face of table hockey in the article), it was a No. 640 AFC game fully set up and displayed in all its 3-D glory.

"One of the major attractions of game [toy store] counters during the Christmas season is high ticket, sports oriented items," declared the article, which quoted a Coleco spokesman giving credit to television sports coverage for the growth of sports game sales. This spokesman further added that electric football games and table hockey games were the best-selling games in the whole sports game category. Coleco may have gotten the quotes, but Tudor got the picture.

Two retailers who were favoring Coleco in early October were Kmart and J.C. Penney. Both began running print advertisements featuring Coleco electric football games with Kmart unloading the small Pro Stars game for less than $6. J.C. Penney was showing off the redesigned Command Control game for $10.88. (This game was not displayed in the Christmas catalog.) But it wasn't long before Sears and Ward put Tudor front and center in the electric football battle. By mid-October Sears had made the Super Bowl a prominent part of its toy ads, while Ward began steady promotion of the NFL No. 627 game. Both Tudor games were being advertised for $14.88. Munro was still fighting for visibility in retailer ads. The Day/Nite electric football game was only seen sporadically in W.T. Grant ads.

For some time now, Congress had been pressuring the NFL to reexamine its stance on blacking out home games, even going so far as to propose that NFL lift the local blackout when a game was sold out 48 hours before kickoff time. Finally in October, Rozelle responded by offering the coming Super Bowl as a "test case." If the 93,000-seat Coliseum in Los Angeles was sold out 10 days before the game, he would let the Super Bowl be televised within the usual 75-mile radius blackout area. Rozelle seemed to be stacking the deck, knowing full well that there were 16,000 unsold seats at the first Los Angeles Super Bowl in 1967. Obviously, those distant Coliseum seats hadn't moved any closer to the field in the interceding years. The commissioner was betting they would still be empty in 1973.

Rozelle, unfortunately, was not in attendance when Tudor won its third consecutive Sears Award of Excellence in early November. This year's luncheon took place at the New York Athletic Club, with Sears' John Waddle and Clyde Peterson again making the presentation to Norman. *Playthings* publisher Harry Gluckert was also

Thanks to Tudor being the NFL's top licensee, Norman Sas was part of an official NFL Properties visit to Hong Kong in the early 70's. Albert Sung hosted the visit, and also took this photo. Posed on the pavilion of the Hong Kong Lions club are L-R: the tour guide, NFLP President Bob Carey, NFLP attorney John Reiner, NFLP Vice President Peter French, NFLP Art Director Mike Gaines, and Norman Sas.

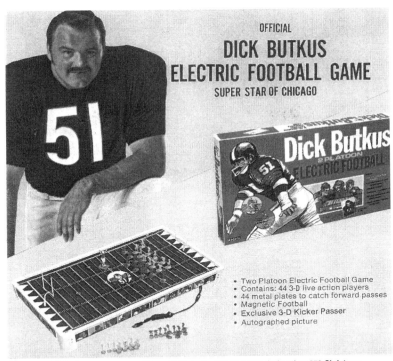

OFFICIAL
# DICK BUTKUS
# ELECTRIC FOOTBALL GAME
### SUPER STAR OF CHICAGO

- Two Platoon Electric Football Game
- Contains: 44 3-D live action players
- 44 metal plates to catch forward passes
- Magnetic Football
- Exclusive 3-D Kicker Passer
- Autographed picture

Gotham's Dick Butkus game was readily available in the Chicago area during the 1972 Christmas shopping season. From the 1972 Gotham sales catalog. (Collection of Roddy Garcia.)

on hand to acknowledge the significance of Tudor's achievement. The afternoon of celebration gave Norman a brief chance to remove himself from the intense electric football battle going on this fall out on the toy store shelves.

1972 was turning into the most remarkable year ever seen in electric football. Tudor still held the upper hand, with Sears and Ward both making electric football a regular feature of their November toy advertising. But Kmart was just as persistent, with a seemingly unlimited supply of inexpensive Coleco models. A retailer who seemed to enjoy the competition was Toys R Us who, like Sears, was carrying Tudor, Coleco, and Munro electric football games, and more than one model from each company. The most expensive game was Munro's Day/Nite, which Toys R Us was selling for $14.97. Next came Tudor's NFL No. 640 and Coleco's large Command Control game, both of which sold for $11.97. Lucky Toys R Us shoppers had some tough decisions to make. Were lights worth an extra $3? And if you only had $12 to spend did you want the NFL or the extravagance of Command Control? Electric football shopping was getting complicated.

On the Sunday before Thanksgiving, the Dolphins beat the Jets to clinch the AFC East. While it was unusual for a team to clinch a title before Thanksgiving, it was even more unusual for a team to head into the holiday without a loss. The Dolphins had achieved much of their perfect 10-0 record thanks to the play of 38-year-old backup quarterback Earl Morrall – the same Earl Morrall who led the Colts to Super Bowl III. Back in 1968 he'd filled in for the injured Johnny Unitas. This season it was for the injured Bob Griese.

Thanksgiving Day newspapers were weighty items, bulging with ads from retailers both large and small. Sears was doing heavy lifting for the Super Bowl game, using it prominently in its toy ads. And Ward was continuing to show off the NFL No. 627 game as a featured item. Tudor was also getting help from the Gibson Discount Center chain and the iconic Piggly Wiggly supermarket chain; both had ads for the No. 500 running throughout the South. Thanks to J.C. Penney and Kmart, Tudor's main competition over the holiday came from Coleco. Kmart was particularly aggressive, putting the Coleco Pro Stars model in a full-color insert that appeared in hundreds of Sunday newspapers throughout the country. The biggest surprise of the period came from Toys R Us, who didn't use electric football in any of its holiday weekend advertising.

Munro players with the new Individual Player Programming bases. (Photo by Earl Shores.)

Electric football continued to carry a very high profile as December opened. Tudor's NFL models were mentioned in a nationwide Associated Press article about NFL Properties on Sunday, December 3, a day that also happened to be a significant one for toy advertising. Both Gibson and Toys R Us ran full-color newspaper flyers that included electric football with Gibson promoting the Gotham G-883 for $4.97, while Toys R Us chose a Tudor NFL No. 620 with an "Everyday Low Price" of $11.97. (Pictured in close proximity to the No. 620 were a Coleco hockey game and a Munro basketball game.) In the background this day was Sears, who in many regions of the country quietly promoted its Super Bowl game in a "Pre-Holiday Sale" campaign.

Not only were a record number of retailers selling electric football, more retailers than ever were carrying multiple brands of games. Like Sears, J.C. Penney, and Toys R Us, the Woolco chain was selling games from three different manufacturers (Coleco, Tudor, and Gotham). For the bargain hunter, it was hard to beat Gotham's $3.99 G-883 game at Woolco. It was

$2 cheaper than a Tudor No. 500 and almost $12 less than a large Coleco Command Control game. Yet among all the wondrous options available to shoppers in electric football, Munro games were still hard to find. Outside of Sears and Toys R Us, only the W.T. Grant chain seemed to be making any effort in selling Munro models. In an ironic twist that must have driven Nick Trbovich crazy, Gotham electric football games were easier to find than Munro games – even with Munro deliberately ignoring its recently acquired subsidiary. Gotham's Bob Lilly game made it onto Gibson store shelves in Texas, Louisiana, Arkansas, and Oklahoma; several West Coast chains were still selling the Gabriel game, and the Dick Butkus game was available in the Chicago area.

Sears, Ward and Kmart all continued to feature electric football prominently in their December print ads, with the popularity of the game illustrated by the fact that prices were essentially unchanged since early October. Reinforcing electric football's popularity was a nationally published United Press International story which quoted a toy buyer from a prominent Ohio department store chain as saying that the game was a top seller this Christmas. In volume of sales it trailed only Monopoly and the Aurora Skittle line (Bowl, Pool, and Poker). The unfortunate exception in the category of price came from Munro. As the NFL season headed into the final weekend, Grant's had marked Munro's flagship Day/Nite game all the way down to the $10 mark.

Only the NFC West was undecided at this point, but there was still one monstrous question mark hanging over the season – could the 13-0 Miami Dolphins finish the regular season undefeated? The answer came on Saturday the 16th, when the Dolphins beat the Colts to finish with a perfect 14-0 record. Just a few hours, later the NFC West was decided when the 49ers pulled out a last-second 20-17 win over the Vikings.

After starting the season as a Super Bowl contender, the Vikings turned into one of the NFL's biggest disappointments, finishing out of playoff contention with a mediocre 7-7 record. Joining the Vikings as major disappointments were the Jets, who lost three of their last four games to also finish at 7-7. Namath, however, did earn first team All-Conference quarterback honors. The Rams also had a disappointing season, ending up with a sub-.500 record for the first time since 1965. Roman Gabriel struggled right along with his team, throwing more interceptions than touchdowns (15 versus 12 respectively). It wasn't a particularly good year to be a retailer with a large stock of Gotham Roman Gabriel electric football games.

One item that toy retailers were glad to have on their shelves was Aurora's Monday Night Football game. Wherever real electric football games were found, you could be sure that Aurora's game was nearby.

Tudor's 1972 "red leg" TTC bases. Tudor had molding issues, as can be seen by the uneven legs throughout the sprue. (Photo by Earl Shores.)

In fact, the games were side by side in many retailers. Interest was high in this new type of electric football, and sales were strong. Besides being more advanced than the vibrating models of Tudor, Coleco, Gotham, and Munro, the Aurora game was smaller, and often cheaper.

With just seven shopping days left until Christmas, retailers began hustling to clear out their toy inventory. During the final week, Sears Super Bowl models – where they could be found – were priced as low as $10.88. Ward joined in, dropping its large Tudor NFL games to $11, and large Coleco Command Control models could be bought at many different retailers for the same price. On the entry level, Woolco continued to unload its small Gotham games for $3.88. The Kiddie City chain was also handing out bargains in the entry level, pricing Tudor No. 500's at $3.99. Aurora's Monday Night game was on sale during this period too with W.T. Grant offering up the computerized competitor for just $5.88.

Electric football prices had gone about low as they could go when the NFL playoffs got under way on Saturday, December 23. For those who had their Christmas shopping out of the way, or just chose football over shopping, it was a memorable afternoon. In fact, it turned out to be a day that will forever be a part of pro football lore.

That's because on an icy, gray Pittsburgh afternoon, Steelers running back Franco Harris made his "immaculate reception" of a deflected last-second pass, running 42 yards for a touchdown. It gave the Steelers a 13-7 victory over the

While it was easy enough to slide a player onto Tudor's new TTC bases, it required patience and a gentle touch to get the player off the base without any damage. (Photo by Earl Shores.)

stunned Raiders, who to this day, still claim the catch was illegal because the ball bounced off a Steelers player. (In 1972 two offensive players could not make consecutive touches on a forward pass.) In the second game of the day, which was almost as thrilling but now mostly forgotten, the Cowboys began the fourth quarter trailing the 49ers 28-13. With the offense going nowhere and the game slipping away, Cowboys' coach Tom Landry summoned Roger Staubach from the bench to go in and play quarterback. Staubach rallied the team to a field goal and then a touchdown pass with 1:30 left in the game. Still trailing 28-23, the Cowboys tried an onside kick – which they recovered. Staubach quickly threw another touchdown, and the Cowboys defense intercepted a 49ers pass to preserve the 30-28 win. It was one of the most exciting days of football in NFL history.

It was unfair to expect the Sunday games to generate the same level of excitement that the Steelers and Cowboys produced, but there still was the matter of the Dolphins' perfect season, and the fact that it was December 24, Christmas Eve. The Washington defense proved to be in a very Scrooge-like mood, so the Redskins' 16-3 victory over the Packers did little to rouse the spirits. Fortunately, the Browns were ready to give rather than receive when they visited Miami, even edging out to a 14-13 lead early in the fourth quarter. The Dolphins countered with a touchdown and were assured a 20-14 win after intercepting a Browns pass with just seconds left in the game. For the Dolphins it was now 15 down and 2 to go.

Thanks to its size and features the Munro Day/Nite model was guaranteed to generate excitement on Christmas morning. (Photo by Earl Shores.)

This allowed Christmas to arrive in the afterglow of one of the most dramatic weekends in NFL history. It might not have been the best Christmas to receive an electric football game, but it certainly was one of the most exciting. Almost 40 different games available in 1972, including ones with lights, legs, referees, the most enormous fields ever created, and updated directional controls for each player. Tudor had marketed 14 different NFL models and that didn't even include the regionalized games that local retailers could request. With such an overwhelming number of games available it was getting harder to tell what made a game truly special. Obviously the Super Bowl was still unique, as was Munro's Day Nite model, but beyond these two models the marketplace was becoming a jumble. Just four years earlier in 1969, a total of 11 electric football games were available – and only 6 were professional models (five NFL and the AFL game). While the NFL's popularity rose steadily during this period, was there truly enough demand for a nearly 400% increase in the number of electric football games available? Could a boy even figure out which game he absolutely had to have?

The parade of televised holiday football continued on Christmas night, with the North-South Shrine All-Star game from Miami. (The Fiesta Bowl had kicked things off on Saturday.) Keeping things rolling on Wednesday night was the Blue-Gray All-Star, while the Peach Bowl finished out the weeknight prime time telecasts on Friday. But it was the weekend television schedule that would bring any dormant electric football games back to life. On Saturday, the Sun Bowl in El Paso would kickoff at just after 1:00 p.m. Eastern Time – and the final football whistle wouldn't blow until around 11:00 p.m. that evening when the Astro-Bluebonnet Bowl finished in Houston. In between would be the Gator Bowl and the East-West Shrine All-Star game. It all added up to over nine consecutive hours of televised football on a day that wasn't even New Year's.

This left football fans thoroughly warmed up for the NFC and AFC Championship games on Sunday. (In fact, their favorite television chairs might still be warm because they never bothered to get out of it.) Morning newspapers were filled with the usual pregame analysis and predictions, but there was another piece of significant NFL news to consider – and rejoice about if you lived in Los Angeles. According to commissioner Rozelle, the Los Angeles Coliseum would be officially sold out by Friday. As a result, for the first time ever, there would be no local television blackout of a Super Bowl game.

While the NFL finally got the blackout dilemma "right," the league still had issues in determining home-field advantage for the playoffs. As a result, the 15-0 Dolphins had to play a conference championship game in Pittsburgh to get to the Super Bowl. With Earl Morall directing the Dolphins in the first half and Bob Griese taking over in the second half, the team earned its 16th win and another trip to the Super Bowl with a 21-17 triumph over the Steelers. The Redskins made good use of their home-field advantage in routing the Cowboys 26-3. New Year's Eve celebrations in both Washington and Miami were going to be particularly lively this year.

There was one more game left to watch before the year ended, and that was the Sugar Bowl game between Penn State and Oklahoma. The game was on ABC, which found itself on the outside looking in during the afternoon's pro football proceedings. Kickoff would come just after 9:00 p.m., putting the end of the game near midnight. After eight hours of televised football, the year finally came to an end.

# Football

"Joe, I hate to talk behind your back but this game looks easy."

**ADVERTISED ON TV**

**MODEL 4203 — JOE NAMATH DAY/NITE FOOTBALL** One of the most popular of all electric vibra-action football games. Officially endorsed by Super Star JOE NAMATH, this large 25"x 40" game features real lights that illuminate the field for "Nite Time" action; 3 Dimensional hand painted "Dial-A-Play" players; Twin action quarterbacks that pass and kick; Play action controls; Windsprint track. GAME SIZE: W25"x L40"x H4" — Shpg. Wt. 10 lbs. - 2.7 cu. ft.

**MODEL 4301 — JOE NAMATH FLOOR FOOTBALL** (Not Shown) Fold away tubular steel legs with end panels are supplied. GAME SIZE: W25"x L40"x H32" — Shpg. Wt. 15 lbs. - 3.5 cu. ft.

**MODEL 4320 — JOE NAMATH PRO FOOTBALL** (Not Shown) GAME SIZE: W19"x L33"x H3" — Shpg. Wt. 6 lbs. - 1.5 cu. ft.

**MODEL 5302 — JOE NAMATH QUICK PLAY FOOTBALL** MUNRO is proud to present one of the most exciting, easy to play football board games to come along in years. Officially endorsed by Super Star JOE NAMATH and played on real Astro-Turf® by Monsanto, this distinctively packaged game is sure to be a "best seller".

Munro was betting heavily on Joe Namath in 1973. From the Munro sales catalog. (Collection of Earl Shores.)

# 28 MUNRO GOES DEEP AS THE ECONOMY CRUMBLES

**T**he final weekend of 1972 set a new record for televised football – 18 hours in 2 days. For those football fans who considered this total just an appetizer, there were another 8 consecutive hours scheduled for New Year's Day. Although the Cotton Bowl was first on the schedule, most eyes were on the Rose Bowl where 11-0 and top-ranked USC had a date with Ohio State. The Trojans didn't disappoint, trouncing the Ohio visitors 42–17. With the drama now drained from the day, only the true die-hard football fan would sit through the evening telecast of the Orange Bowl, especially after Nebraska ran out to a 20-0 halftime lead over Notre Dame. Nebraska didn't let up, leaving Notre Dame on the humiliating end of the 40-6 final score. When the Orange Bowl signed off, another record had been set – 10 football games had been televised nationally over the last 3 days. Or taking a more quantitative measurement, someone could have watched football on television during 26 of the previous 58 hours.

On the following Sunday, the Buffalo Chamber of Commerce ran a full-page ad in the *New York Times*. One of the companies featured in the ad was Servotronics, Inc., who proclaimed in bold typeface "We're Buffalo's Biggest Fan." The accompanying description introduced Servotronics as a Buffalo-born company that had grown and prospered by selling aerospace control components, fine cutlery, sporting goods, puzzles, and sports action games. In addition, Servotronics claimed that "the finest collection of professional athletes and organizations have endorsed our products." This was no exaggeration. The next sentence proudly ticked off those names – Joe Namath, Johnny Bench, Bobby Hull, the NBA, *ABC's Wide World of Sports*, and the *American Sportsman*. It was an impressive list. A signature finished the ad. Of course it was that of Nick Trbovich.

The *New York Times* went on to connect more dots in the growing sports and business relationship on Super Bowl Sunday, January 14, by reporting that the NFL had allotted 10,000 corporate tickets for this year's game in Los Angeles. Many businesses with NFL advertising connections – including Ford, Chrysler, and General Foods – were using Super Bowl trips as a reward for top performing employees, not to mention as a boys' club weekend for those with the keys to the executive washroom. Reported as one of the NFL's most important current clients was Sears, whose NFL shirts, jackets, sweatshirts, and "Youth Room" products were spreading the NFL brand, as well as bringing millions of dollars of revenue to NFL Properties. A company who played a significant role in making Sears an

## 515 NFL ELECTRIC FOOTBALL. NOW WITH TOTAL TEAM CONTROL™ NEW FOR '73

No. 515
Box Size: 16½"x27"x2⅛"
½ Doz. Ctn. Wt. 27 Lbs.
U.L. Listed 110 Volts, A.C. only.

Dolphins versus the Packers in their official pre-painted uniforms.

Full size gamefield.

- Individually controlled movement of every offensive and defensive player.
- New stronger Total Team Control™ bases. Side control for quicker and more accurate adjustment.
- 22 pre-painted NFL players in 5 realistic poses. Run real traps, end arounds, sweeps, slants, swing patterns and other NFL plays.
- Plus 2 triple threat quarterbacks that kick, pass and run.
- Colorful grandstand with adjustable scoreboard shows all 26 NFL teams.
- Steel gameboard for better play.
- Patented automatic timer that starts and stops with each play.
- Magnetic first down marker with movable 10 yard chain.
- Magnetic ball and down marker.
- Special control with printed dial and plastic knob.
- 4 goal line flags.
- Authentic NFL goalposts.
- Easy to apply player identification numbers.
- All 26 NFL teams available to consumer in official home and away uniforms directly through Tudor.
- U.L. listed safety plug and exclusive heavy duty switch.
- Officially endorsed by the NFL.
- All new full color package.

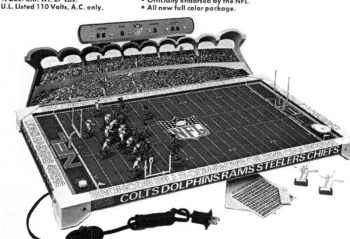

Lee Payne had redesigned Tudor's TTC bases for 1973. He had also redesigned Tudor's packaging. 1973 Tudor sales catalog. (Collection of Norman Sas.)

important NFL client was also receiving Super Bowl tickets. That company was run by Norman Sas.

Thanks to the lifting of the local television blackout, residents of a Super Bowl community got to watch a live telecast of the game for the first time ever. For more than three quarters, it was far from the most thrilling Super Bowl. The undefeated and underdog Dolphins (no, that is not a misprint) cruised to a 14-0 lead thanks to an unstoppable ground game. On nearly three out of every four offensive plays, the Dolphins handed the ball to a running back. The lead looked safe until Dolphins' kicker Garo Yepremian etched himself into football infamy by picking up his own blocked field goal and pathetically heaving it into the hands of Redskins' safety Mike Bass. Grateful for the gift from the football gods, Bass ran 49 yards for a touchdown. That made the score 14-7 with just 2:07 left in the game. After the kickoff the Dolphins were unable to sustain a drive and punted the ball back to the Redskins with just over a minute left on the clock. But the Redskins still couldn't handle the Dolphins' defense. Fittingly, the game ended with Washington quarterback Billy Kilmer being sacked for a 9-yard loss. It was the first time in NFL history that a team made it through a season unbeaten and untied.

On Thursday, February 1, just two days after the NFL held its draft, Eddie Gluck passed away at Columbia Presbyterian Medical Center in New York City. He was 70 years old. An obituary in the *New York Times* commemorated his passing, as did a *Toy & Hobby World* article that attributed his death to a "long illness." The unspecified illness was the likely reason Gluck sold his company to Servotronics, and it may also explain why Don Munro discovered Gotham's machinery and paperwork in such disarray once the sale was completed. *Toy & Hobby World* reported that Gluck was still president of Gotham at the time of his death, even though the company was now headquartered in Buffalo. Munro and Trbovich had allowed Gluck to keep his title as Gotham president despite the fact that he lived on Long Island and had little to do with the day-to-day operations of the company.

Word of Gluck's death would pass quickly through the showrooms at 200 Fifth Avenue when the Toy Fair got under way just a few weeks later. But just as quickly, thoughts would turn back to the business of selling toys. Tudor was responding to Coleco and Munro by coming to the Fair with a revamped line of electric football games, a new Tudor logo, and new packaging designs for the entire Tudor line. There was even a new name. From now on the company would be known as Tudor Games, not Tudor Metal Products. Lee Payne played a large part in all of these changes. He was also the designer of the full-page *Playthings* ad that introduced the "most spectacular Tudor ever" to the 1973 Toy Fair. This upbeat tone was a far cry from the dour "Warning to the Trade" Tudor issued 1971.

Lee Payne (seated) and his partner Vince Gambello working on Tudor's new packaging during the fall of 1972. (Collection of Roddy Garcia.)

One of the things upgraded this year were the Total Team Control bases. Redesigned TTC bases were heralded throughout the Tudor sales catalog as stronger, with "a quicker and more accurate method for adjustment." And just exactly how did Tudor achieve this better adjustment method? By doing some borrowing from Munro. The new bases still had the same Tudor shape, but now there was a dial mechanism with legs. Turning the dial adjusted the direction of the player. It was a much simpler task than turning the player upside down and pushing the front "legs" into position with a special tool. It was also the same design that Munro had on its IPP bases.

Tudor gave up two trademark features in moving to this dial-a-base design. The first lost feature was the tooth in the center of the base for mounting players. It was replaced by brackets on each end of the new base, which allowed the player to slide – sideways – into position for play. The center-mounting hole on each player was now obsolete, unless you had old bases (and Tudor did plan to keep making and selling the center-mount bases). The other lost feature was Tudor's unique paired-leg system

Tudor's new NFL Championship Electric Football game featuring the Dolphins, Steelers, Cowboys, and Redskins. Tudor sales catalog. (Collection of Norman Sas.)

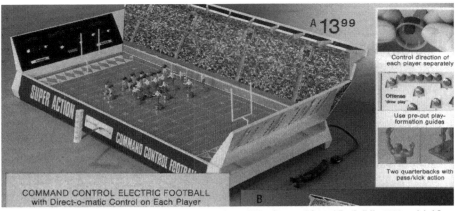

Coleco came to the Toy Fair with the new Super Action Command Control Football No. 5780 model. J.C. Penney *Christmas 1973*, page 8. ©J.C. Penney, Inc. 1973.

on the bottom of the base. Since 1967 there had been eight running legs on the bottom of each deluxe Tudor base – now there would be only four. It wasn't practical or economical to put eight legs on each dial. Any loss of speed would be made up for by increased directional control.

Besides redesigning the 1973 electric football line, Tudor did some consolidating as well. Norman eliminated the conference games, and also the College game, which hadn't sold particularly well. A single NFL model, the Dolphins-Packers No. 515, replaced both the AFC No. 510 and NFC No. 520 games. In the No. 600 level the colorful NFL No. 645, which came with a new Lee Payne-designed field and frame, replaced the old AFC No. 610 and NFC No. 620 models. Although it had a different color scheme, the No. 645 was patterned after the Ward NFL models of previous years. All 26 NFL team names were printed on the frame, and the field borrowed from Tudor's Super Bowl model by having a large NFL shield at midfield. The yard line numbers were now contained within bold circles, borrowing from real NFL teams of the era who often had elaborate markings on their fields (the Chiefs and Raiders for example). The major piece leftover from the old conference game was the grandstand, but with all the other changes the No. 645 looked like a totally new game.

Albert Sung had gotten word in late December to increase his production of Dolphins, Steelers, Redskins, and Cowboys. The reason why, now sat at the top of Tudor's revamped 1973 electric football line, and was called the No. 655 NFL Championship game. While the game had a newly designed Tudor frame and field design, its most distinctive feature was that it included all the teams from the recent NFC and AFC Championship games. With four championship teams, a lucky boy could now replay the three most important games from the 1972 NFL season – the NFC title game, the AFC title game, and the Super Bowl. Adding the championship atmosphere was another new

Lee Payne-designed field that was more colorful and creative than the previous Sears' Super Bowl model. Taking up most of midfield was a white circle, 20 yards in diameter, containing a large NFL shield. Framing this large circle were two smaller 10-yard diameter circles; the one on the left contained a red AFC logo, while the circle on the right contained a blue NFC logo.

This circle theme continued with the yard line numbers, where the odd numbers sat in red circles and the even numbers in blue circles. And there were even more circles on the orange-colored frame – twenty-six to be exact, each one containing the helmet of an NFL team. The final piece of the new game was a triple-decked grandstand, which had been borrowed from the Ward NFL models. Overall, the No. 655 was probably the best-looking game Tudor had made since the 1970 Chiefs-Vikings Super Bowl.

A final piece of realism on all of the new NFL games was having the hash marks line up with the goal posts. When the NFL made this rule change in March of 1972, Tudor was too far along in the production process to alter its game markings. The company had to wait until 1973 to finally bring the fields back into compliance with NFL rules.

Tudor's final new game came at the bottom of the electric football line. In fact the new Tudor No. 400 model

Munro's Nick Trbovich and the New York Jets' John Elliot at Munro's All-Star Hockey Night. Courtesy of The Strong®, Rochester, New York.

Toy buyers on the ice and dressed head to toe in Munro hockey gear at the All-Star Hockey Night. *Toy & Hobby World,* page 5, March 19, 1973.

might have been called the sub-economy model. Basically, it was a No. 500 game without a grandstand. It was also the only game in the 1973 line that didn't come with the new TTC bases as standard equipment. With the wholesale price of the No. 400 at $4.21, a savvy retailer could have an electric football game on the shelf that didn't break the $5 mark (the wholesale price of a No. 500 in 1973 was an even $5). Neither Coleco nor Munro could match such a price.

"Joe, I hate to talk behind your back but this game looks easy."

**MODEL 4203 – JOE NAMATH DAY/NITE FOOTBALL.** One of the most popular of all electric vibra-action football games. Officially endorsed by Super Star JOE NAMATH, this large 25″ x 40″ game features real lights that illuminate the field for "Nite Time" action; 3 Dimensional hand painted "Dial-A-Play" players; Twin action quarterbacks that pass and kick; Play action controls; Windsprint track. GAME SIZE: W25″ x L40″ x H4″ –

Munro had put Joe Namath's endorsement on the Day/Nite model. 1973 Munro sales catalog. (Collection of Earl Shores.)

Coleco rode into the Fair on a wave of record sales. The company was reporting $65 million in sales for 1972, a $17 million increase from 1971. Some of this money was used for a complete redesign of the Coleco showroom, including an expansion that added a second floor for the 1973 Fair. Displayed on the first floor – the sports floor – was *the* Stanley Cup Trophy. No toy buyer could walk through the showroom doors without understanding that there was a significant relationship between Coleco and the NHL. With approval from the Greenberg brothers, marketing vice president Brian Clarke had made a conscious decision to emphasize Coleco's NHL hockey games in 1973. And Coleco planned to get off to an early start by heavily promoting its Stanley Cup games during the NHL playoffs in April and May.

Part of Coleco's record proceeds had gone into signing NBA star Wilt Chamberlain to a personal endorsement deal. A tabletop basketball game and a backyard hoop set were going to receive Chamberlain's seal of approval – and national television support in the fall. Also scheduled to get a push from television was a new Coleco tabletop game called Bowl-A-Matic 300. (Professional Bowlers Association telecasts were an ABC network staple on winter Saturday afternoons.)

Practically overlooked this year was Coleco's shrinking electric football line. Football had not contributed significantly to Coleco's record sales figures, and some of the larger models were not selling well at all. In fact, there was going be inventory to carry over into 1973. So Coleco cut electric football down to just three games for the U.S. market. Gone entirely was the large 38" x 21" model that Coleco first introduced in 1970. Also gone were all the models with legs. Faring especially poorly in 1972 was Sears' "executive" Command Control game. Taking the place of the 38" x 21" game was Coleco's new Super Action Command Control 5780 model. It came with a relatively compact 36" x 18" field – and lots of plastic parts. Like Coleco's small 1972 models, both ends of the frame were now constructed entirely of plastic instead of metal. The plastic theme continued to a new end zone scoreboard, and an end zone standings board (Coleco used NFL city names instead of team names). Coleco's distinctive roof-covered 3-D grandstand was another victim of electric football budget cuts, having been replaced by a flat one-piece grandstand. This grandstand, when attached to the scoreboard and standings board, surrounded the field with a three-sided stadium. Coleco may have felt they had a winning and economical new design. But in relying so much on plastic, the new game seemed...less substantial. There was something to be said for the presence of metal in a toy.

Retained from the previous year was the end zone deficient 32" x 18" Command Control Touchdown game, as well as the 26" x 16" Pro Stars economy model without Command Control. Surprisingly, Coleco did offer

**MODEL 4316 – NATIONAL/AMERICAN** Officially endorsed by the National Football League Players Association. This extra large and exciting game features Dial-A-Play; 3 Dimensional hand painted players; Tiered grandstand and scoreboard; Twin-action quarterbacks that pass and kick. GAME SIZE: W25"xL40" xH40" – Shpg. Wt.- 10 lbs.-2.3 cu. ft.
**MODEL 4315 – NATIONAL/AMERICAN FLOOR MODEL** – Identical features to MODEL 4316 (above), plus fold away tubular steel legs with end panels permitting play anywhere and the convenience of easy storage. GAME SIZE: W25"xL40"x32" – Shpg. Wt. 18 lbs.-3.5 cu. ft.

The NFL Players Association endorsement was also now part of the Munro line. This NFLPA National/American electric football game came with faux floodlights. 1973 Munro sales catalog. (Collection of Earl Shores.)

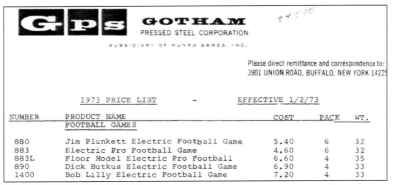

| NUMBER | PRODUCT NAME | COST | PACK | WT. |
|--------|--------------|------|------|-----|
| | FOOTBALL GAMES | | | |
| 880 | Jim Plunkett Electric Football Game | 5.40 | 6 | 32 |
| 883 | Electric Pro Football Game | 4.60 | 6 | 32 |
| 883L | Floor Model Electric Pro Football | 6.60 | 4 | 35 |
| 890 | Dick Butkus Electric Football Game | 6.90 | 4 | 33 |
| 1400 | Bob Lilly Electric Football Game | 7.20 | 4 | 33 |

**Gotham was now functioning as a subsidiary of Munro, with the Gotham electric football line down to five models. (Collection of Earl Shores.)**

up an electric football innovation despite reining in the rest of the line. Pressure from Tudor's and Munro's "programmable" bases led Coleco to come up with its own version of directional bases. And in doing so, the company created the first round player bases in electric football history. Instead of putting a directional dial in the player base, Coleco made the dial the base, adding a metal collar/ring for support. After three decades of rectangular and oval shaped electric football bases, Coleco's effort at going round was noble…but the players looked odd. There was something very unsettling about a scrimmage line of 22 round-based players. It looked like a chess game had broken out on an electric football field.

In previous years this player change might have gotten mention in one of Coleco's elaborate *Playthings* advertising spreads. But this year, the company had no ads at all in the toy industry's most important publication. And they didn't even hold a World of Sports Dinner. These things were all skipped despite a record sales year. Did success make these things no longer important, or was Coleco sensing a change in the sports game landscape?

Perhaps it was the heat they were feeling from Munro Games, who came to the Fair in a mood to spend money on promotion. First there was a two-page spread in *Playthings* titled "Munro Announces its 1973 Game Plan." Besides introducing a new line of Munro sports equipment, the company was introducing Joe Namath as an official company endorser. The Day/Nite Football game, which Munro claimed sold out completely in 1972, was now the Joe Namath Day/Nite game. And Joe wasn't confined to just football. He was also endorsing a new line of Munro pool tables. In the fall, both the pool tables and the Day/Nite games were going to be supported by television commercials featuring Namath.

But the *Playthings* ad was minor league compared with the audacious event Trbovich had planned for Toy Fair week. In attempting to upstage Coleco's World of Sports dinner, Trbovich had rented out the New York Rangers' practice rink on Long Island and invited toy buyers to ride Munro-chartered buses from downtown Manhattan to New Hyde Park. Once the

Coleco's new Direct-O-Matic bases. (Photo by Earl Shores.)

buyers arrived at the rink, there would be a hockey game – which the buyers would actually play in. Trbovich called the event the First Annual Munro All-Star Hockey Night.

It was an ingenious concept and a distinctive way to launch Munro's new line of hockey gear. The buyer-players were divided into "East" and "West" teams, and then completely outfitted with Munro hockey equipment; jerseys, pads, helmets, and hockey sticks. Coaching both teams was Rangers' captain Vic Hadfield. Actually suiting up to play with the buyers were two NFL players: John Elliot of the Jets and Bill Curry of the Oilers. No major injuries occurred during the event, which got glowing coverage from *Playthings* and *Toy & Hobby World*. Trbovich said he wanted to give buyers a "fun evening and a respite" from the hustle of the Toy Fair, and based on the ecstatic reactions from the lucky invitees who skated in Long Island, he'd done just that. Munro Games sent a message that it was a serious player in toys and sporting goods. As the happy but tired buyers boarded their buses for the return trip to Manhattan, a buoyant Trbovich promised that All-Star Hockey Night would be an annual Toy Fair happening. And with Coleco abandoning its Sports World dinner, Trbovich now owned one of the toy industry's "must attend" events.

Back in the Munro Games showroom the new and expanded electric football line was on display. Ten games were set up in the showroom, with the focus on Munro's three new Joe Namath models. Two of the Namath games were Day/Nite models: one was a floor model with legs, the other was a tabletop game. And for the faint of wallet (the wholesale price of the Namath Day/Nite was $13.50!), there was a Namath game without lights. These games came with painted players. Of course, one team was painted green and white and had a green and white no. 12 quarterback figure.

Something else Munro had acquired from Gotham was licensing for the NFL Players Association. As a result, there were four new Munro NFLPA games at the Fair. None of these games had lights, but two used the same oversized 40" x 25" frame as the Namath Day/Night models. Frames on these games featured a colorful red and white design, while the fields had a large red, white, and blue NFLPA logo at midfield, a red "National" end zone, and a blue "American" end zone. Painted Munro players were also a standard feature on these two large games. Finishing out the NFLPA line was a midsize game (33" x 19") and a small (28" x 19") game.

The Sears version of Day/Nite Football. Sears 1973 *Christmas Book*, page 519. ©Sears, Roebuck and Co. 1973.

In keeping an eye on the future, Munro had signed an endorsement deal with an NFL player whose star was on the rise – the Miami Dolphins' Super Bowl winning quarterback Bob Griese. In his first year as a Munro endorser, Griese was given an unlighted 38" x 21" game with painted players and a no. 12 quarterback figure (conveniently Namath and Griese wore the same number). Perhaps another Super Bowl victory would propel Griese to a larger Day/Nite model in 1974. Munro's entry-level game this year was the new 28" x 19" Super Pro model. What really added the "budget" designation to this game was the fact that it came with leftover Gotham players.

Not displayed in the showroom was the exclusive Day/Nite model Munro had created for Sears. This gave Munro a total of 11 electric football games for 1973 – four more games than Tudor planned to sell. But this total paled in comparison to the number of table hockey games Munro was offering. Buyers could choose from 24 different hockey games,

**You control the movement of every player on every play with improved TOTAL TEAM CONTROL**

A wheel in the base on each man turns his steerable "legs". . you secretly program your men "in the huddle". . then watch your team sweep left or slant right or go straight up the middle.

It looks like an end sweep. . no, it's a fake. The triple-threat QB still has the ball. He lobs a screen pass over the defensive line. . can the secondary recover in time?

**SUPERBOWL Electric Football** $15⁹⁹

Dolphins and Redskins clash on a 37½x20½-in. playing field . . each team in its official NFL uniforms

Now you can replay Superbowl VII—the game heard around the world (If you're a Redskin fan, you can even change the final score.)
Total Team Control lets you "tell" each player what pattern to run, what defender to block and where he should move . . to make the play "go all the way". You call each play by setting the wheel and adjusting the "legs" in the base of each player for speed and direction. Switch on the game and watch the vibrating metal field start the action.
Includes Superbowl field, 3-tier grandstand and scoreboard. Each team includes 11 plastic players molded in five 3-D positions plus a triple-threat quarterback that can "run", "pass" or "kick". Automatic timer starts and stops with each play. Also, magnetic 10-yard marker with ball and down indicator and goal-line flags. 6-ft. cord.
79 C 65736L—UL listed. 110–120-v., 60-Hz. AC. Shpg. wt. 11 lbs. . . . $15⁹⁹

**NFL Electric Football** $11⁹⁹

Lions battle Rams on a 31½x17½-inch playing field

Features the same improved Total Team Control as Superbowl game above. Vibrating metal field includes 2-tier grandstand and scoreboard. All 22 players molded in five 3-D positions and painted in the official colors of the Detroit Lions and the Los Angeles Rams. Each team has a triple-threat quarterback. Includes automatic timer, magnetic 10-yard marker with ball and down indicator and goal-line flags. 6-ft. cord.
79 C 65695C—UL listed. 110–120-v., 60-Hz. AC. Shpg. wt. 9 lbs. . . . $11⁹⁹

**NFL Electric Football** $8⁹⁹

Steelers and Cowboys meet on a 26½x15½-inch playing field

"Tell" each player where to move with Total Team Control as in Super bowl game above. Vibrating metal field has 2-tier grandstand and scoreboard. Each team has 11 players molded in five 3-D positions plus triple-threat quarterback. Includes automatic timer, magnetic 10-yard marker with ball and down indicator and goal-line flags. 6-ft. cord.
79 C 65707C—UL listed. 110–120-v., 60-Hz. AC. Shpg. wt. 5 lbs. . . . $8⁹⁹

Sears' Super Bowl game, along with an NFL No. 635, and an NFL No. 515 model. Sears 1973 *Christmas Book*, page 520. ©Sears, Roebuck and Co. 1973.

including a line of official World Hockey Association games. With Trbovich owning the WHA Ottawa Nationals, and long-time Munro endorser Bobby Hull now playing for the WHA Winnipeg Jets, this was a natural expansion for the company. And this 24-game total didn't even include the exclusive hockey games Sears had ordered! It was an ambitious lineup of games, even for the ever-ambitious Trbovich.

But this ambition had saddled Munro Games with the thoroughly obsolete line of Gotham games. Given Don Munro's stark assessment of what was inherited in the takeover, it was a wonder Munro Games even bothered to sell any game under the Gotham name in 1973. Munro had picked Gotham clean of its highest profile endorsers, leaving the electric football line to survive on the Jim Plunkett, Dick Butkus, and Bob Lilly models, as well as the ever-present entry-level G-883 game. Terminated in the takeover was the contract with Roman Gabriel, who suffered through a subpar season with the Rams in 1972. And by the time the season started, the quarterback would no longer be part of one of the NFL's most glamorous franchises. He would be throwing passes for one of the league's grittiest and most dreadful teams – the Philadelphia Eagles. Both Munro and the Rams threw Gabriel on the scrapheap.

These Gotham endorsers paled in comparison to the heavyweight names Aurora brought to the Fair to promote its Monday Night Football Game. At a series of Toy Fair luncheons, Cowboys quarterback Roger Staubach, retired Bears star Gale Sayers, and Monday Night Football commentator Howard Cosell all extolled the virtues of a game that turned out to be one of the top selling toys of 1972. And thanks to the game's success, more computer sports games were being unveiled at the Fair in 1973.

In fact, the most groundbreaking computer game ever invented made its Toy Fair debut in 1973. It was the Magnavox Odyssey. The Odyssey, in simple terms, was the first home electronic computer video game…in history. Magnavox had actually introduced the Odyssey during the fall of 1972, allowing the game to be sold only at authorized Magnavox television dealers. (The Odyssey creators' main objective was to help Magnavox sell more televisions.) A number of sports games were wired into the console, including video hockey, tennis, and football. But the game that really helped the Odyssey gain a retail foothold was video table tennis. Magnavox didn't know it at the time, but a company named Atari was about to unleash "Pong" (Atari's "borrowed" version of Odyssey's table tennis) on bars and arcades throughout the U.S. The resulting Pong-craze during the summer of 1973 would help both companies, in terms of profits and profiles. And Magnavox would eventually win some extra compensation from Atari in court. You might call it "interest" on a loaned idea. By the time the Fair ended, it was clear that the landscape of sports games was changing.

Another group evaluating a landscape change was the NFL owners. When they met in Phoenix in early April, they received news that the previous year's rule change – moving in the hash marks on the playing field – had the desired effect. More points were scored than in the 1971 season, and both the total number of touchdowns and field goals had increased. Yet an unintended side effect of the new rule was making the NFL more like electric football. Teams were running the ball more often. Increasing during the 1972 season were both the number of running plays and the total amount of rushing yardage. The Dolphins' pass/run ratio in the Super Bowl was no fluke, and the owners' concern was legitimate – did people want to watch NFL games if the ball was handed off on 70% of the plays?

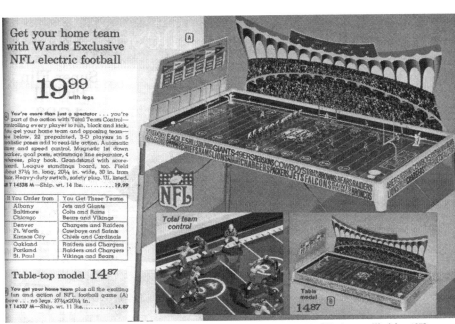

**Get your home team with Wards Exclusive NFL electric football**

# 19⁹⁹ with legs

You're more than just a spectator . . . you're part of the action with Total Team Control—controlling every player to run, block and kick. You get your home team and opposing team below. 22 prepainted, 3-D players in 5 realistic poses add to real-life action. Automatic timer and speed control. Magnetic 1st down marker, goal posts, scrimmage line separator, 4 referees, play book. Grandstand with scoreboard. League standings board, too. Field about 37¼ in. long, 20¼ in. wide, 30 in. from floor. Heavy-duty switch, safety plug. U.L. listed.
T 14538 M—Ship. wt. 14 lbs. . . . . . . . . . 19.99

| If You Order from | You Get These Teams |
|---|---|
| Albany | Jets and Giants |
| Baltimore | Colts and Rams |
| Chicago | Bears and Vikings |
| Denver | Chargers and Raiders |
| Ft. Worth | Cowboys and Saints |
| Kansas City | Chiefs and Cardinals |
| Oakland | Raiders and Chargers |
| Portland | Raiders and Chargers |
| St. Paul | Vikings and Bears |

**Table-top model 14⁸⁷**

You get your home team plus all the exciting fun and action of NFL football game (A) above . . . no legs. 37¾x20¼ in.
T 14537 M—Ship. wt. 11 lbs. . . . . . . . . . 14.87

**Total team control**

Table model 14⁸⁷

The electric football page from the 1973 Montgomery Ward *Christmas Catalog*, page 327. ©Montgomery Ward, Inc. 1973.

Before the meeting adjourned on April 5, the owners awarded New Orleans the 1975 Super Bowl and Miami got the game in 1976. Helping New Orleans land the game was the promise that construction on the city's new Superdome stadium would be completed by January 1975. It would be the first-ever indoor Super Bowl, but not the first-ever indoor NFL Championship game. That had taken place in the dirt and dung of Chicago Stadium back in 1933.

As May began, one of Nick Trbovich's ventures reached the end of the line. His WHA Ottawa Nationals had averaged less than 4,000 fans per game during the regular season. In fact, attendance was so bad that the team played two "home" playoff games in Toronto. The team was hemorrhaging money, and as the person with controlling interest in the team, Trbovich was the one with the most to lose. And these losses would end up on the books of Servotronics. So Trbovich sold his share of the team to a group of Toronto businessmen for $1.8 million. A 6% stake in the new ownership group was part of Servotronics' compensation.

The summer saw the NFL issue its first study on artificial turf injuries, and to the players' dismay, the league claimed there was no difference in the rate of major injuries between turf and grass. The study did show that turf had a higher rate of minor injuries (abrasions and contusions) but it wasn't a significant enough problem to put a moratorium on the installation of turf fields, as the players had requested. This was little consolation to the players who carried scarring from these "minor" abrasions well into the off-season.

Before the NFL preseason started in July, the league and the networks agreed to a new television contract. It was a four-year deal that would start in 1974, with CBS, NBC, and ABC paying a record $200 million for the television rights to the NFL. Under the new agreement, the league would receive an extra $10 million a year. It wasn't so long ago that this $10 million figure alone would have comprised a fat television deal.

The preseason opened on July 27 with the Dolphins defeating the College All-Stars in Chicago by a 14-3 score. By the time the second weekend of preseason games got underway, Coleco had announced record sales and earnings for the first half of 1973 ($41.8 and $3.2 million respectively).

Electric football was only a small part of this figure, but the company was clearly making the right decisions about what consumers wanted. With these types of sales figures, Coleco's clout with retailers – the shelf-space issue – would continue to grow.

On September 13, just three days before the regular season was set to open, Pete Rozelle announced that the NFL was lifting the television blackout for home games – at least for home games sold out 72 hours in advance. It was hardly a coincidence that just hours earlier, the House of Representatives passed a bill prohibiting the blackout of sold-out home games by a 336-37 margin. With the Senate's approval already on the legislation and President Nixon's signature guaranteed, the bill would soon be law. So in heading off the bill's official passage, Rozelle was engaging in damage control. But the decision would have immediate payoff for NFL fans. Eight of the twelve games played on opening day would be broadcast to the home fans.

The biggest surprise on opening day was the Bears' victory over the Cowboys, who were picked to battle the Redskins for the NFC East title. Nick Trbovich had to be smiling when the Jets took the field against the Packers in the first Monday night game of the season. What a fortuitous pairing for Munro Games – Namath and Monday night. Unfortunately, both the quarterback and team performed poorly in a 23-7 loss. Namath and Trbovich's luck would not get any better in week two. Although the Jets thrashed the Colts 34-10, Namath separated the shoulder of his throwing arm. Munro's star endorser was expected to be out of action for six to eight weeks. (In another significant event that day, the Raiders beat the Dolphins, ending the Miami winning streak at a record 18 games.)

In following the trend for "Game Room" models, JC Penney had asked Coleco for an electric football game with legs. J.C. Penney *Christmas 1973*, page 8. ©J.C. Penney, Inc. 1973.

The injury to Namath left Munro Games limping into the fall with its most prominent endorser on the sidelines and out of the headlines. Yet all the sports game makers got an industry boost from the September issue of *Playthings*. A six-page article titled "Games '73: Getting the Family Together" claimed that retailers were expecting a new category of games to do well this Christmas. "Family playroom games," as the article called them, "are designed to unite people in a sophisticated play situation and to provide extended fun." Examples of these games were Ideal's Toss Across, Aurora's Skittle line, and Coleco's sports games. Another example was Tudor's No. 655 NFL Championship game, which was prominently displayed in a photo of sports games on page 52. Both toy retailers and manufacturers were expecting the new category to become a "staple of the future." And in a dash of hubris, both retailers and manufacturers reported there was no ceiling on what a customer would pay for a family game. This kind of mindset went a long way to explaining $25 electric football games and $50 hockey games.

And games with those prices were again on view in the just published 1973 Sears *Christmas Book*. Taking up almost all of page 519 was Munro's $49.99 Family Cup Hockey game and a $24.99 NFLPA Day/Nite floor model electric football game with legs. It was a full-color page that gave both games vivid presentations – clearly they fit into the "family playroom game" category. Family Cup Hockey still had its supersize 48" x 30" rink and hand-painted 3-D players. The official NFLPA designation gave more color to the Day/Nite field with one end zone being blue and the other red. The wind-sprint track did not appear on this football game, but it was essentially the same Munro game that Sears had sold in 1972. Even the price was the same – which still didn't make the game a bargain.

A flip of the page gave the Christmas shopper a good look at Sears' 1973 Tudor line, with the Super Bowl again the top model. The game was the same as the year before, other than the new TTC bases and the Dolphins and Redskins. Sears held the line on the price of the game – for the fourth consecutive year a Super Bowl cost $15.99. Since it really hadn't gotten cheaper to manufacture this game, the profit margin was shrinking for both Tudor and Sears. It was a great item, and a popular one, but both the retailer and the maker were getting less out of the game than ever before.

Besides the Super Bowl, the other two Tudor electric football games filling out the page were the same as 1971 and 1972. The Lions-Rams No. 635 model was exactly the same as the previous two years (an advantage of this strategy was that Sears could sell any leftover stock the following year). And its price had dropped by $0.60 to $11.99. The only change on the $8.99 Sears No. 515 was an updated set of teams. In place of the Raiders and the Jets – who hadn't reached the playoffs since their victory in Super

Bowl III – were the Steelers and the Cowboys. With the Steelers on the rise in the NFL, and the Cowboys being perennial playoff participants, it was a smart pairing on Tudor's part. It would also prove to be a brilliant bit of Super Bowl foreshadowing.

Munro got its usual hockey game page opposite Tudor, with three hockey models (including a WHA game and a $24.89 floor model with legs) and a basketball game. But unlike 1971 and 1972, these three pages contained all the sports games being offered in the catalog. Coleco found its football and hockey games shut out of Sears because of meager sales in 1972. In fact, Sears was left with back stock of both the stand-alone Executive Command Control football game and the jumbo-sized NHL Trophy Cup Hockey game. The only Coleco sports game in the 1973 *Christmas Book* was the Bowl-A-Matic 300 game. Contrary to the recent *Playthings* article, it seemed that selling a family playroom game involved a bit more work than a manufacturer just naming a price.

NFL Properties, like the year before, was featured in the very front of the Sears catalog, although this year they weren't getting a personal endorsement from Winnie the Pooh. Perma-press NFL sheets took up most of page 12, while the bottom left-hand corner of the page provided an index of all the other NFL items in the catalog. A total of 24 Sears pages had NFL items, with 19 of those pages filled entirely with official NFL paraphernalia. From the "Quarterback Corner," a collection of NFL Home Fashions aimed at boys, to the 8 consecutive pages of jackets, sweatshirts, and sweaters, to the 9-page spread of bath towels, bedding, and curtains, it was another impressive year for NFL Properties.

Montgomery Ward gave Tudor a boost in 1973 by adding an NFL No. 515 to its electric football line. This meant Ward was now selling three Tudor models, with the new "budget" game pairing the Super Bowl champion Dolphins against the Packers. The $8.99 No. 515 joined two Ward No. 645 models, one with legs ($19.99) and one without ($14.87). Like the previous year, Ward had regionalized games, so there were a variety of team matchups available. Tudor was again including a scrimmage-line separator and four referee figures in its large Ward NFL games.

Just opposite Tudor on page 326 was Coleco. Shown off in full color were two new "Wards Exclusive" Coleco NHL Pro-Stars Hockey games – one was a $12.99 tabletop model, while the $15.88 version came with legs. A large headline over both games announced "Our lowest price in 10 years." Part of the reason for the cheaper price was a manufacturing change made by both Munro and Coleco. Instead of lithographed metal table hockey players, both companies switched over to plastic players. The players now came as blank, unprinted, ghostly white plastic shapes. Only after a player decal sheet was applied did the plastic slab turn into a recognizable hockey player.

One quarterback with kicking/passing action

Penney's was also selling the Gotham G-883L ("L" for legs). The G-883L was definitely the entry level of the "Game Room" category. J.C. Penney *Christmas 1973*, page 9. ©J.C. Penney, Inc. 1973.

Missing from Ward's catalog in 1973 was any type of Coleco basketball game. This was a bit of a surprise, considering that Coleco basketball had been a Ward anchor since 1970 and that the company was spending a tidy sum this year promoting its new Wilt Chamberlain model. In place of the basketball game were three soccer games. Apparently the fledgling North American Soccer League was making its mark.

The 1973 J.C. Penney Christmas catalog fielded four electric football games spread across two color pages. What was significant about these pages were their numbers, page 8 and page 9. J.C. Penney had put electric football up in the very front of its catalog. On page 8 there was a Coleco Super Action Command Control game for $13.99 and also a Super Action version with legs for $17.99. The Penney's catalog then mixed things up on page 9 with a Chiefs-Cowboys Tudor No. 635 model ($10.99) and a Gotham G-883 game with legs ($9.99). The reason for Coleco again being the featured electric football brand could be seen on page 7 where the retailer had three Coleco NHL hockey games, including a stand-alone Stanley Cup model. But this year Coleco had competition in hockey. Headlining the page was an oversized family room game from Munro called Tournament Hockey. Basically, it was the J. C. Penney version of Family Cup hockey with fewer features and "only" a $44.95 price tag. Perhaps Penney's toy buyers were among those chosen to take the ice during Munro's Hockey Night at Toy Fair.

Along with Sears and J.C. Penney, Toys R Us was fostering a healthy competition among the electric football manufacturers in 1973. With 48

Tudor wins its 4th consecutive Sears' Excellence Award. From left to right: Clyde Peterson (Sears), Norman Sas, Pete Rozelle, and Truman Coble (Sears). Courtesy of The Strong®, Rochester, New York.

stores nationwide and $130 million in annual sales, the retailer was now the biggest toy chain in the country. For toy makers, it was "a must" to have items on Toys R Us shelves. This allowed the chain to carry a wide range of electric football games from Tudor, Coleco, and Munro, including the largest and most expensive models from each company. Toys R Us was even selling the Munro Namath Day/Nite game for a heavily discounted $16.97. This price was just $3.47 above the quoted wholesale price – and $8 less than Sears was asking for a nearly identical Day/Nite game.

Other major toy retailers weren't as ambitious as Toys R Us and were content to stock less than a full range of electric football games. Kmart was selling both the Super Action and Touchdown Coleco Command Control models, as well as the Namath Day/Nite game for $19. Going exclusively with the Coleco line was Korvettes, while the Western Auto chain continued its loyalty to Tudor by carrying the No. 500 and the NFL No. 645. In the South and West the Gibson Discount Center chain was helping Munro clear out the last of the Gotham stock, including the Bob Lilly model, the G-883, and even the occasional Super Dome model. The entry-level G-883 was being sold for less than five dollars – the profit on this game was reduced to pennies.

In light of *Playthings'* cheerleading it was a bit surprising that Sears was not using the Super Bowl game to announce the openings of its ubiquitous

Toy Town departments. The retail giant waited until late October before it began promoting electric football in print, giving other toy sellers an unexpected and welcomed head start. Ward had already made Tudor's NFL No. 645 a steady part of its Christmas advertising, while J.C. Penney used Coleco's Touchdown Command Control game to promote its Toyland departments. Also leaning Coleco's way in the early going was Toys R Us, which started its fall electric football advertising with Coleco's Super Action game.

When Sears finally started advertising electric football, it was with full force. Throughout early November, Sears made the Super Bowl a featured toy in newspaper ads, selling the game for $12.99. So it was fitting for Tudor to win its fourth consecutive Sears Excellence Award during this same period. Rozelle was in attendance at this year's luncheon, which was held at the 21 Club in New York City. (A photo of Rozelle and a smiling Norman Sas would make it into the December issue of *Playthings*.) Ward was also making the early weeks of November a positive time for Tudor, as the retailer continued to use the NFL No. 645 in nearly all of its toy advertising.

But November was the month during which Munro would launch its most ambitious and expensive advertising campaign ever. Announced on page 65 in the November issue of *Playthings* was the "Watch Munro on the *Tonight Show*" promotion. It's not known how many hundreds of thousands of dollars Trbovich was spending to have "Johnny, Doc, and Ed telling millions of their fans about our (Munro's) big lineup of great games," but all through the Christmas shopping season the *Tonight Show* gang was going to promote Bobby Hull Hockey, Joe Namath Day/Nite Football, and Joe Namath pool tables. And besides the NBC Network package, Munro was once again promising "spot" saturation during local television shows. It was clear that Trbovich was determined to be one of the main players in the sports game market in 1973.

Between Munro Hockey Night at the Toy Fair and the *Tonight Show* ads, a lot of money was being thrown at promotion. The *Tonight Show* campaign even had some fortuitous timing as Namath returned to action for the Jets on November 18. Unfortunately, Broadway Joe's comeback wasn't going to be enough to rescue the Jets, who had already stumbled to a 3-7 record. This put them light years behind the 9-1 Dolphins (the Vikings had also sprinted to a 9-1 record in the NFC). But there was a much larger issue for Munro… and for Tudor, Coleco, and all other toy makers.

The U.S. economy was in a freefall.

# WATCH MUNRO ON "THE TONIGHT SHOW."

## It's part of a great big pre-Christmas TV package that will turn on millions of your best customers.

### We're on TV with Exclusive Bobby Hull Hockey.

Here's a game that's got everything. Safe plastic players in full color. Delayed Action Puck Dropper. Automatic Goal Indicator. Overhead Arena Scoreboard. And the biggest name in hockey behind it. With a combination like that you just can't miss your sales goal.

### We're on TV with Exclusive Joe Namath Day/Night Football.

Here's a game that will really brighten your Christmas season. It's got real lights. Variable speed vibrator. 3-dimensional "Dial-A-Play" players. Triple threat quarterbacks that run, pass, punt. Play action controls. A windsprint track. And the brightest star in football leading the way.

### We're on TV with Exclusive Joe Namath Pool Tables.

Here's a line of pool tables that will put something in *your* pocket. They've got handsome furniture styling. Live action cushions. Automatic ball returns. Smooth playing surface. Models to fit key price points. And Joe Namath's official endorsement.

### NBC Network! Spot Saturation!

This season Munro will be joining Johnny and his Gang on the top-rated "Tonight Show." Johnny, Doc and Ed will be telling millions of their fans about our big line-up of great games. And when Johnny and his Gang tell it, they sell it!

And we not only have a big network TV package, we have a big local TV package, too. Lots of local spots from now right up until Christmas.

We've got the games. We've got the personalities. We're on network TV. We're on local TV. We're off to the biggest year in our history. Join Johnny and Munro in '73. And join in on the fun, games and profits!

Munro Games, Inc.
A Subsidiary of Servotronics, Inc.
3901 Union Road, Buffalo, N.Y. 14225.
(716) 633-5990

Despite the struggling economy Munro had bought ads during The Tonight Show to promote its line of games. Courtesy of The Strong®, Rochester, New York.

**EARL SHORES | RODDY GARCIA**

# 29 THE 1973 ENERGY CRISIS

I n mid-October, the Organization of Arab Petroleum Exporting Countries (OAPEC) placed an embargo on oil shipments to the United States. The reason for the embargo was pretty straightforward – it was to punish the United States for giving military support to Israel after Israel was attacked by Egypt and Syria on Yom Kippur (the Yom Kippur War). There was no immediate effect on the U.S. economy and, in fact, the Dow Jones Industrial Average hit a nine-month high on October 26. But over the next six weeks, the Dow declined 198 points (20% of its value) with the dollar losses at the New York Stock Exchange totaling $97 billion. Gasoline and home fuel prices also rose dramatically during this period. Gas station lines often stretched for blocks, and gasoline shortages were as common as turkeys as Thanksgiving approached.

Throughout the Thanksgiving Day weekend things appeared pretty normal – that is, if you confined yourself to perusing newspaper toy advertisements. Sears, Ward, and Toys R Us all ran national ads featuring electric football, with Sears promoting the Tudor Super Bowl game in numerous newspapers from coast to coast for $12.99. Ward finished a strong second in the ad numbers game, having its NFL No. 645 model priced at a very competitive $12.77. The most intriguing ads came from Toy R Us, which ably covered the cities where its stores were located. It was no coincidence that the retailer chose to feature the Day/Nite game for $16.97 just as Munro's *Tonight Show* television promotion was getting into full swing.

The only hint that something might be amiss in electric football and the whole family-room-sports-game phenomenon described by *Playthings* came from the Sears Catalog Surplus Store in suburban Chicago on Black Friday. There you could find last year's Coleco Executive Command Control football game for $9.99, which was a far cry from the 1972 Sears *Christmas Book* price of $22.44. Also available at the Surplus Store was

Munro and Tudor were competing on the shelves of Toys R Us in 1973. *Oakland Tribune*, page 34, November 27, 1973.

last year's Coleco NHL Trophy Hockey game. Its $16.99 price was a 50% savings over what the game cost in 1972.

Bringing the holiday weekend to a sober conclusion was President Nixon, who went on television Sunday evening to outline the energy conservation measures the country would have to undertake in the coming weeks. Among the energy actions the President called for were lowered highway speeds, a Sunday ban on gasoline sales, and a very Scrooge-like ban on residential outdoor Christmas lights. Then on Tuesday, President Nixon signed the Emergency Petroleum Allocation Act, which gave the federal government control of oil distribution, as well as pricing and marketing controls for petroleum. If an oil shortage wasn't enough to push the national psyche into a fragile state, the leader making these pronouncements had the raven of Watergate perched over the White House door. Bills to impeach the president had been introduced into Congress, there was very public talk of resignation, and a November Gallup Poll had Nixon's approval rating at 27%. Compounding the president's woes was something else that happened on Tuesday – the public finally got to "hear" the infamous 18-minute gap in Nixon's Oval Office Watergate tapes.

So as the Christmas season approached, the usual jolly holiday spirit was much harder to come by. It was no different in the world of toys, where toy makers had been receiving limited allocations of plastic. These allocations delayed the delivery of popular Christmas items, and sent the cost of plastic soaring. Production costs became so overwhelming that Fisher Price and Marx actually dropped items from their holiday lines. In a newspaper interview, Toy Manufacturers of America president Henry Coords called it the greatest shortage of raw material since World War II.

Surprisingly, the struggling economy did not produce an automatic decline in toy sales. Retailers around the country were reporting generally strong sales figures, as well as sold out items. The one difference retailers were noticing from previous years was that parents were not waiting until the last minute to stroll the toy store aisles. Fearing a shortage, shoppers had been out early in December to make sure Santa would leave more than disappointment on Christmas morning. Popular items like Baby Alive and the Evel Knievel stunt cycle had already disappeared from toy shelves. And thanks to the oil crisis, there was little hope of restocking these hot items.

For the moment, the oil allocation issue was having only a limited impact on the supply of electric football games. All of the players and almost all of the games had already been produced. Games were either in stores or on warehouse shelves – the only vulnerable part of the supply chain was the cost of fuel to move the games from the factory to the retailer. Although shipping was getting more expensive, shoppers were unlikely to see any price increase this year. A number of retailers were already having problems moving the games they had.

Sears continued promoting its Super Bowl in December, with the game holding a steady $13.99 price. Also seeing electric football as an important item was Toys R Us, which ran ads and a color newspaper flyer featuring both the Munro Namath Day/Nite game ($16.97) and the Tudor NFL No. 515 model ($8.96). Toys R Us distributed a second color flyer in December, this one advertising Coleco's Super Action Command Control ($13.97) and Tudor's NFL No. 635 ($11.97).

Munro knew it had a serious problem when the flagship Day/Nite electric football game turned up in the Sears Surplus Store at the height of the Christmas shopping season. *The Herald*, Section 2, page 4, December 10, 1973.

# Get more teams and have more fun!

Your favorite NFL Teams now available in Home and Away uniforms… player numbers available too (order form in rule book).

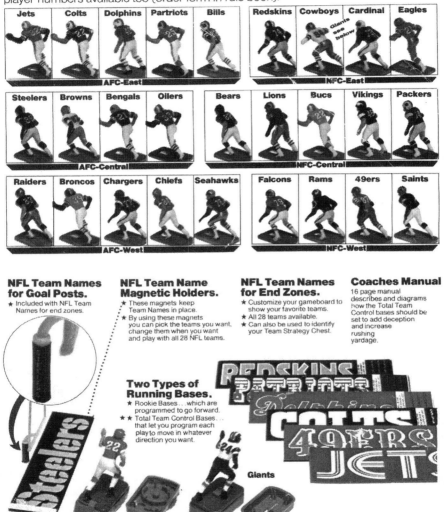

## NFL Team Names for Goal Posts.
★ Included with NFL Team Names for end zones.

## NFL Team Name Magnetic Holders.
★ These magnets keep Team Names in place.
★ By using these magnets you can pick the teams you want, change them when you want and play with all 28 NFL teams.

## NFL Team Names for End Zones.
★ Customize your gameboard to show your favorite teams.
★ All 28 teams available.
★ Can also be used to identify your Team Strategy Chest.

## Coaches Manual
16 page manual describes and diagrams how the Total Team Control should be set to add deception and increase rushing yardage.

## Two Types of Running Bases.
★ Rookie Bases…which are programmed to go forward.
★★ Total Team Control Bases… that let you program each play to move in whatever direction you want.

A late 70's Tudor team page insert. This was found in a 1978 Super Bowl game. These are Haiti players with white shoes (except for Chiefs and Giants players at the bottom of the page).

# Haiti Picks Up Hong Kong's Fumble

A Haiti-painted black shoe Oakland Raider circa 1974-77: Fred Biletnikoff.

A Haiti-painted black shoe Tampa Bay Buccaneer, circa 1976.

**D**espite the best efforts of the authors, there is still much mystery surrounding the Tudor NFL teams that were made in Haiti during the mid-1970's. Norman Sas, Lee Payne, and Albert Sung were all asked on numerous occasions about the timing of the Haiti switchover, but none of them had a recollection that was definitive enough to put into the timeline of the book. (There are photos placing Norman Sas and a contingent from NFL Properties in Hong Kong for a factory inspection in 1973.) The Haiti players were distinctive for the bright bone-white coloring of their plastic and also the details present in their molding. Finishing off these figures, at least the earliest versions with black shoes, was some of the best painting ever seen in commercially produced electric football players.

Haiti black shoe Steelers and white shoe Rams. (Photo by Earl Shores.)

A Haiti-painted black shoe Minnesota Viking, circa 1974-77.

A Haiti-painted black shoe Atlanta Falcon, circa 1974-77.

Tudor's sales catalogs from the period offer few clues. Most of the player photos were still from the early 1970's, and the player images in the game photos were too small to reveal any details. Christmas catalogs from the period were also of little help. Again the player images were too small to draw any definite conclusions.

Another complicating factor is that teams arriving from Haiti would have been mixed in with Tudor's standing inventory of Hong Kong teams. That meant it would have been possible to send an order to Brooklyn for four teams and end up receiving three Hong Kong teams and a Haiti team – and a year later, the order could be reversed. So the year a Haiti team was produced, and the year they actually arrived at your door, could be two different things.

What is definitive about Tudor's Haiti players is this:

Norman had become increasingly unhappy with the players coming from Hong Kong. Much of his dissatisfaction came from Tudor's lack of control over the molding process, which led to subtle and not so subtle variations in the players through the years. Adding to the molding issue was the fact that player painting had also gotten sloppier over time. The 1967-68 period was already being viewed as the golden age of player painting when the Packers and Browns still carried their intricate and distinctive triple-stripe sleeve patterns. In fairness, Albert Sung's painters had to paint a lot more teams than in 1967, but Rams' horns and Eagles' wings had started engulfing entire helmets; jersey colors consistently dripped into the flesh colors, and more and more players were wearing green shoes. After Norman pleaded for improvement and saw very little, he knew it was time to come up with a different way of making the players.

Tudor's solution was to make its own set of molds directly from Lee's brass master players and then mold the players in the U.S. A plastics manufacturer in New Jersey had been chosen to mold the players, and all of these New Jersey players were then shipped to Haiti for painting and packaging. (Unfortunately, neither Norman nor Lee could remember the name of the molder.) Norman was pleased with the batches of NFL teams that arrived in Brooklyn. From the molding to the painting, he felt the Haiti players were a superior product to the Hong Kong players. And the Haiti players became Norman's favorites.

As the 1980's began, player production and painting was shifted back to Hong Kong (and eventually into China). Costs were the overriding factor for returning to Asia. Norman Sas again turned to Albert Sung, who supervised the team painting for Tudor throughout the company's final years in Brooklyn.

A bag from a black shoe Haiti Raiders team. Note that the bags says "Painted and Packaged in Haiti." The players were actually molded in New Jersey.

A photo of a company outing for Hong Kong team painters and their families during the early 1980's. It was taken at the Hong Kong Life Guard Club at Repulse Bay. The tallest man in the back row (6th from the left) is Albert Sung. Standing to his immediate right are his daughter and his wife. (Courtesy of Albert Sung.)

Tudor's NFL No. 645 would have been a nice Christmas morning "find." This is a Lee Payne photo that was used in the 1973 Tudor sales catalog. (Collection of Roddy Garcia.)

But there were signs that the gasping economy was taking a toll on electric football. On the second Monday of the month, the Sears Catalog Surplus Store was advertising that it had another electric football game for sale – Munro's Day/Nite game. It was now priced at $16.99, or $8 less than the catalog price. But the sale price only told part of the story. The real story was that Sears already considered the Day/Nite game a bust, even though the Christmas shopping season still had two weeks remaining. Sears knew that a $25 electric football was going to be a tough sell in the best of times (see the Coleco Executive model). And once gasoline and heating oil prices started taking a giant bite out of American households, a game that expensive just wasn't viable. Dismal catalog orders and frustrated toy department managers convinced Sears to do all that it could to unload the game before Christmas was over. Matching the Toys R Us Day/Nite game price was good place to start.

By the following weekend, some Sears and Ward stores had their top electric football games selling at the $10 mark. Kmart joined in dropping the Super Action Coleco game to the same price. But there was a difference in these price drops. For Kmart, these discounts covered all the stores in the chain. The discounts for Sears and Ward were regional. A lot of Super Bowl games were still $11.88, and some Ward No. 645's were being sold for as much as $14.88.

The real tumble in electric football prices took place as the shopping season entered its final week. Around the country Ward began pricing the No. 645 near $10; Kmart took the Super Action Coleco down to $8. For the final weekend of shopping J.C. Penney dropped the Touchdown Coleco model all the way down to $6.88, a price that represented a 40% discount. Holding pretty steady at this point was Sears' Super Bowl, which still commanded an $11.88 price even at this late date. And it turned out that Sears wasn't the only retailer having problems moving the Munro Day/Nite game. Kmart, W.T. Grant, and the California-based White Front chain had all dropped the game to the $13 mark.

As retailers tried hard to empty out their electric football inventory, the NFL playoffs began on Saturday, December 22. In typically blustery Minnesota winter weather, the favored Vikings beat the wild card Redskins 27-20. Later in the day, Oakland healed a bit of the scar left from the "Immaculate Reception" by blowing out the Steelers 33-14. On Sunday, the Dolphins made it to the AFC championship game for the third straight year by dominating the Bengals 34-16 on a balmy Miami afternoon. And in the final game of the weekend, the 12-2 Rams were forced to travel to Dallas to play the 10-4 Cowboys. The Cowboys used their undeserved home-field advantage fully in a 27-17 victory.

When Christmas arrived on Tuesday, there was little question that consumer belt tightening had occurred in electric football. There were surely disappointed boys on Christmas morning, who woke up to find a Tudor No. 500 or a smaller entry-level Coleco game under the tree instead of the more expensive model that had been asked for. But some boys woke up to pleasant surprises. Those with procrastinating parents may have ended up with a top-of-the-line Tudor or Munro game, which their parents picked up for just a few dollars more than a No. 500. Regardless of the costs, a Tudor Super Bowl or NFL No. 645 model with a local team would have been a great find on Christmas morning. But perhaps the "best" Tudor game in 1973 was the beautiful four-team NFL Championship No. 655, which allowed an ambitious boy to replay the final three games of the 1972 NFL season. Besides the extra teams, the game had an exciting field and frame design that was better looking than Sears' Super Bowl.

The hardest hit and most discounted games where those made by Coleco and Munro. Munro Games had bet its season on Joe Namath – and lost. The Namath Day/Nite model was still a beautiful game, but it's hard to imagine that an endorser who appeared in only six games for a mediocre NFL team could have done much to boost sales. Especially with the game being one of the most expensive electric football models ever sold – in an economy that was skidding toward recession. These were not outcomes Munro Games had considered back in the heady days of the Toy Fair

Another Christmas morning surprise – Tudor's new TTC bases. (Photo by Earl Shores.)

and All-Star Hockey Night. It's possible the *Tonight Show* ad campaign salvaged a situation that could have been much worse, but the company had fallen into such disarray that nobody knew how many Munro electric football games had been actually shipped. And if Munro Games couldn't figure out what was going on with its own line, they surely cared little about their burdensome Gotham subsidiary. Christmas of 1973 represented the true end of Gotham Pressed Steel. Games with the Gotham name were still out there on toy store shelves, but no more would ever be made. Only the retailers stuck with Gotham stock cared about what happened to these games. It was a sad end for one of the NFL's original licensees. But it was, unfortunately, a very typical toy company demise.

While it may have been a good Christmas to receive an electric football game (a big game that is, and not a Gotham model) it was not a good Christmas to be a toy retailer selling the games. It was clear that even though there were only 25 different electric football models available this year (compared with 38 in 1972), there were too many games for the oil-distressed economy of 1973. Yet despite the growing problems of electric football, toy retailers were reporting that one of the top-selling Christmas items was, in fact, a football game. That game was Aurora's battery-powered Monday Night Football. Perhaps its $8 price, compact size, and computerized play was just right for the struggling economy.

The year limped into its final weekend with televised football offering a massive dose of reality dodging diversion. Coming first on Friday night was the Peach Bowl, followed on Saturday by the Sun Bowl, the Astro-Bluebonnet Bowl, the East-West Shrine All-Star game, and finally the Gator Bowl. With the kickoff times strung out from 1:00 to 8:30 p.m., over 10 consecutive hours of football was available to anyone who could sit still that long. Sunday, December 30 served up the NFL championship doubleheader, where both the AFC and NFC games ended in identical 27-10 scores. The winners were the Dolphins and Vikings. It seemed a fitting Super Bowl matchup. Including playoff victories, both teams had identical 14-2 records.

New Year's Eve of 1973 had more than just Guy Lombardo and Dick Clark to make it special. The Sugar Bowl in New Orleans had No. 1 Alabama playing No. 3 Notre Dame. Both teams were undefeated – an Alabama win would clinch a national title. It turned out to be a tense and exciting game, with Notre Dame edging Alabama 24-23. The Fighting Irish left the field claiming that they were number one. But it was a claim that would have to wait until the final whistle on New Year's Day.

The entrance to the Tudor Toy Fair showroom in 1974. This photo was taken by Lee Payne. (Collection of Roddy Garcia.)

# 30 A RECESSION SCRAMBLES THE ECONOMY AND THE TOY WORLD

hio State and Penn State both started New Year's Day feeling that the No. 1 ranking was within their grasp. Ohio State had been the top-ranked team for a large chunk of the season but tumbled down the rankings after an unfortunate tie with Michigan. Penn State was 11-0 and carrying a large chip on its shoulder from insulting poll results of previous seasons. An impressive bowl victory by either team could give them a legitimate claim to the top spot. The Buckeyes must have thought they had a chance after thumping USC in the Rose Bowl 42-21. Penn State, on the other hand, knew its 16-9 victory over LSU in the Orange Bowl wasn't going to be enough to sway the sportswriters who voted in the Associated Press poll. But it's likely that no team playing on New Year's Day had a chance, as Notre Dame was anointed the nation's top team thanks to its upset of Alabama.

Throughout the country, people were eagerly awaiting the wave of optimism that comes with a brand new year. Unfortunately, it didn't take long before this wave spent itself on the shores of reality. In football there was speculation on Joe Namath's future and whether he could withstand the pounding of another season for the now mediocre Jets. Would he retire or would he try out a new option – the newly formed World Football League. The NFL's newest competitor was promising an elevated pay scale and a twenty-game schedule starting in July. There was speculation that the former University of Alabama star would be a perfect marquee signing for the WFL's Birmingham franchise.

And just days into 1974 the president stoked the oil-inspired uncertainty descending upon the U.S. by signing into law a 55 mph national speed limit. It would be the second major national oil-conservation measure enacted during the first week of January. The country would soon be on year-round Daylight Savings Time.

The tough issues facing the country seemed a world away as NFL fans, owners, and executives gathered in Houston for a week of Super Bowl festivities. It was a game that promised to be an exciting one as the Vikings and Dolphins were clearly the two best teams in the league (many knowledgeable fans disregarded the Dolphins' status as 6-point favorites). And in the hotels throughout Houston – like the Shamrock Hotel where National Football League Properties and its clients occupied 450 of the 650 rooms – deep-pocketed guest wined and dined with a blind eye to the economy. At least they did for a couple of days. On Wednesday, January 9, the stock market lost more than 3% of its value. With the New Year just weeks old, stock values for Eastman Kodak, Johnson & Johnson, and Xerox were already down 10%. Suddenly, many executives attending the Super Bowl found themselves having something less than a grand time.

Unfortunately, the Super Bowl game itself did little to distract those watching from the worries of the outside world...unless you were a Dolphins fan. The 24-7 score didn't do justice to the Dolphins' domination of the Vikings. Miami quarterback Bob Griese threw only 7 passes all day, completing 6, as the Dolphins ran the ball 55 times against the hapless and helpless Vikings' defense. Carrying the ball on 33 of those attempts was running back Larry Csonka, who picked up 145 yards and the Super Bowl MVP trophy. It was not a very exciting game to watch, even if you had seats on the 50-yard line. As a result, Nielsen ratings dropped a full point from the previous year making it the second straight year that Super Bowl television ratings had declined. And this result was no fluke. Aside from Monday Night Football, Nielsen ratings for the NFL on both CBS and NBC were declining. In fact since 1971, CBS had lost an average of 2.2 million viewers per game. Media "experts" chalked up this decline to an over-saturation of sports on television – 11% of all television programming was now dedicated to sports.

January finished with the NFL draft on the 29th. This happened to be a week later than the inaugural WFL draft. For the first time since 1966, the NFL would compete with another league for college players. The new league also planned to hold a second draft in March...for out-of-contract NFL players. Most NFL owners were not overly concerned by the prospect of a new league. They would believe it when they saw it.

Year round daylight savings time did little to brighten January, as the economy continued to perform dismally. Toy companies suffered too, with the industry's biggest worry being about shortages of oil-based plastics. By the end of the month one-time toy heavyweight Remco (who had once made large plastic toys like the Mighty Matilda Aircraft Carrier and Mr. Kelley's Car Wash) had closed its doors and filed for bankruptcy. Topper, of Johnny Lightning fame, was still in deep financial trouble, and toy

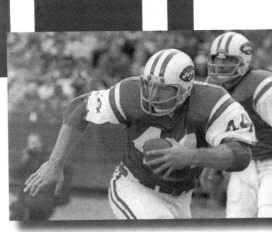

Tudor's new logo with a peak into the waiting area of the Toy Fair showroom. Photo by Lee Payne. (Collection of Roddy Garcia.) Jets' running back John Riggins (right) was used as the model for Tudor's player image.

stock prices had continued to slide. Coleco's stock had lost over $20 and was down to $7 a share. Just a year earlier, when Nick Trbovich proclaimed in the *New York Times* that Servotronics was "Buffalo's biggest fan," the company's stock was selling for $14 a share. Servotronics stock in January of 1974 was now worth only $5. During the same period Mattel's stock dropped from $12.50 to $4 a share, and Hasbro also suffered a steep decline, going from $11.75 to $4.

But without question the strongest indicator of how poorly toys were doing came in the form of a hypothetical stock portfolio created by *Playthings* in August of 1969. Consisting of an imaginary $1,000 invested in each of twelve different major toy makers (Coleco, Hasbro, Mattel, and Remco were included), this portfolio started with a value of $12,000. By January of 1974, over 70% of the portfolio's value had evaporated. This $12,000 figure was down to a meager $3,463.88.

So the Toy Fair opened on February 11 with an uncertain atmosphere in most showrooms. There had been an increase in wholesale toy volume and also an overall increase in toy profits for 1973, but the outlook for the coming year was going to be quite different. Many companies were carrying large inventories of unsold items from the previous year. This happened after a number of major retailers refused to reorder toys as the Christmas season wound down. When these retailers opted for empty

Lee Payne and Mike Ledyard of Payne Associates at work in the wee hours of the morning setting up the 1974 Tudor Toy Fair showroom. (Photo by Vince Gambello. Collection of Roddy Garcia.)

shelves over unsold inventory of their own, many toy manufacturers, even with a plastic shortage, ended up making too many items. Trimming this old inventory, profitably, was going to be a challenge in 1974.

One way to deal with excess inventory was to scale back a toy line. Mattel, who suffered through an excess of Hot Wheels after the die-cast car market cooled off, was coming to the 1974 Fair with 250 items. This was exactly half the number of items the company had in its 1972 showroom.

A category that was reported to have done well in 1973 was sports games, both the tabletop and stand-alone models. In fact, some toy "visionaries" were predicting even greater success for the coming year. Yet this success story seemed to come from the burgeoning air hockey segment of sports games more than electric football or traditional table hockey games. With three companies splitting the market, thousands of electric football games were being sold, yet nobody was getting rich. In fact the market was oversaturated with games before the economy went in the tank. So *Playthings* proclamations to the contrary, there truly was a "limit" to what shoppers would pay for a "family game." Norman Sas himself had witnessed firsthand the outcome of so many different sports games being on store shelves.

While visiting an Abraham & Strauss store in New York City during the Christmas season, Norman came across a mother and a son studying a large display of Coleco sports games. (Abraham & Strauss sold Coleco games exclusively). "It was impressive, they had every Coleco model on a big display," said Sas. When the little boy passed by Norman, the mother asked the child whether he saw anything he liked. The boy's reply – "Nah,

## 600
## ELECTRIC FOOTBALL

Box Size: 18" x 32¼" x 3"
½ Doz. Ctn. Wt. 33 lbs.
U.L. Listed 110 Volts A.C. only

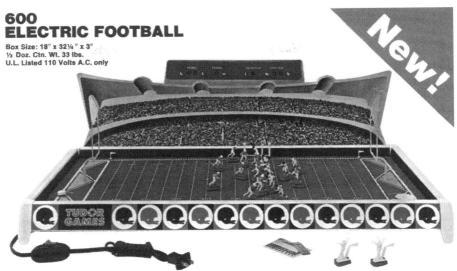

Tudor was looking to make more affordable games in 1974. The result was a generic non-NFL No. 600 model. 1974 Tudor sales catalog. (Collection of Norman Sas.)

I got most of them already" – stayed with Sas for many years. "It was clear that there were just too many games," said Sas. "All the sports game makers were starting to have unsold games."

A diluted market and a struggling economy did not make it a good time to be in electric football. This was illustrated dramatically by the lack of advertising in *Playthings* from Tudor, Coleco, or Munro. In past years, both Coleco and Munro had multipage Toy Fair layouts promoting their games. This year they had nothing – not a single word of paid advertising. Tudor's usual full-page Toy Fair ad was also missing, as was the company's smaller ad in the manufacturers' index. Considering this manufacturer's ad had run in every *Playthings* issue for the last 30 years, its absence was a momentous event. If ever there was a sign of belt tightening in the toy industry, this was it.

And Tudor made another momentous change in 1974 – they downsized the Sears' Super Bowl for 1974. With the oil embargo still in effect, every part of toy making had become more expensive. So Tudor had to figure out a way to balance profitability and affordability for its most recognizable model. The easiest way to accomplish this was to make the game smaller. Instead of being a large 37" x 20" game, the new Super Bowl would be a midsize model based on Tudor's No. 635 frame. It would also turn out to be the most inexpensive Super Bowl ever sold.

In light of the shrinking Super Bowl, it was a little surprising that Tudor would come to the Fair with two additional electric football games. But these items had been planned well before the oil crisis, and Norman elected to go ahead and let the production process continue as planned for 1974. This meant Tudor had eight electric football games on display in its showroom,

16⁹⁹

**Bowl-A-Matic 300**
- A 3¾-ft. long bowling alley right in your own home!

ITS FUN FOR BEGINNERS AND VETERANS ALIKE. You can share in the fun with a bowling alley in your own home. Remote-control Bowl-A-Matic 300 has all the features of the real thing. Automatic pin setter sets up the pins, and the automatic ball return lets you play for hours. If you miss a strike, try for a spare! Durable molded plastic and wood alley with pin set and ball return is 13 in. wide, 45 in. long. Colorful, tough molded plastic pins are individually activated by the ball. Alley is easy to assemble—instructions and hardware included. Any number can play. Ages 7 to adult. *Mailability restricted—read about shipping, page 298.*
X 924-3718 A—Mailing weight 15 lbs.................................. 16.99

Coleco was looking in directions other than electric football in 1974. One of its most successful 1973 items was the Bowl-A-Matic 300. J.C. Penney *Christmas 1973*, page 11. ©J.C. Penney, Inc. 1973.

including the new No. 600 and No. 640 model. Both were generic games without NFL endorsement – the No. 600 being a 31" x 17" midsize model, while the No. 640 was a large model. Each cost $1.50 less than its NFL brethren on the wholesale level, giving Tudor more affordable generic options throughout its electric football line. Affordability was certainly a concern in 1974 given that the wholesale prices of the company's electric football games had gone up an average of 14% per game. Also rising in 1974 was the cost of Tudor's individual NFL teams. It was the first price increase ever, as the teams had remained $1.50 since they were introduced in 1967. Now a team would cost $2 – a 33% increase.

The rest of the electric football lineup consisted of the same models from the previous year. In the entry-level category, there were the generic No. 400 and No. 500 models, while the NFL was represented with four games: the small Dolphins-Packers No. 515; the midsize custom team combination No. 635; the large custom team combination No. 645; and the NFL Championship No. 655 with the Dolphins, Raiders, Cowboys, and Vikings. It was still a formidable collection, even in a sagging economy.

Another sign of changing times in the Tudor showroom was the display of three foosball soccer games carrying the endorsement of the North American Soccer League. The newest "major" league to be added to the American sports scene was starting to be noticed by a previously indifferent American public.

For Coleco, electric football sales had diminished significantly due to the economy and increased competition. (Table hockey sales had declined also.) The meager profit almost wasn't worth the effort of marketing the games – at least in the U.S. But Coleco wasn't ready to scrap electric football. The game could still coast to shelf space and sales on the back of Coleco's newer "must have" items. So once again there was no World of Sports dinner. Instead, there was a reception featuring famed puppeteer Shari Lewis who, along with her sidekick Lamb Chop, would demonstrate Coleco's new line of Junior Chef food toys. Lewis was the spokesperson for this new line, and she and her puppets were going to be featured in a Junior Chef television ad campaign. Pictures of Lewis and Lamb Chop were also on every Junior Chef box.

Another Coleco television ad campaign was being cranked up in the sports line, but it wasn't electric football or table hockey that was going to benefit from the promotion. It was the company's Bowl-A-Matic 300 game that was going to get the push from the tube. Also prominently featured in the showroom was a new line of air hockey games. These Power-Jet Hockey games were all set to compete with one of the hit items of the previous Christmas – Aurora's Brunswick Air Hockey Game.

All that was left in the American Coleco electric football line were two models. There would be no pro football players in the showroom, no television campaign, and no stadium program ads to promote the line. It was almost as if electric football had become an afterthought. In 1971 Coleco claimed Command Control would make other electric football games obsolete. Just three short years later, the company was acting as if its own electric football games were obsolete.

At least Coleco recognized changes in the marketplace and adjusted its electric football presence with a purpose. Munro, on the other hand, had no plan for electric football – or seemingly for any other part of its business. Don Munro had resigned his presidency of both Munro Games and Munro Limited, opting to limit his involvement with the company to that of a consultant. The company staggered into the Fair like a football player who had played a full season without his helmet.

"I could see it coming, we had too much growth too fast," said Munro. Besides Munro Games in Canada and the U.S., Servotronics now owned two knife companies, a tool-and-die company, a jigsaw puzzle company, and a Chicago sporting goods company. "The products, like the Day/Nite game, were great, but there weren't enough people in Servotronics to keep up with the expansion." A prime example of a thoughtless acquisition was the purchase of Gotham Pressed Steel. Whether it was done to eliminate a competitor or to help out the ailing Eddie Gluck, Munro Games got next to nothing it could use from the deal. The equipment was basically useless, and the paperwork was nonexistent. And as of 1974, Gotham officially ceased to exist. Five decades of toy history vanished off the face of the earth.

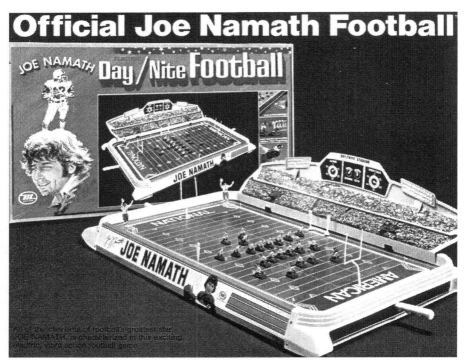

# Official Joe Namath Football

### Joe NAMATH Day/Nite Football

All of the charisma of football's greatest star, JOE NAMATH, is characterized in this exciting electric, vibra action football game.

**Exhibit A for Munro's financial struggles. A 1974 Joe Namath Day/Nite model that didn't have lights. 1974 Munro sales catalog. (Collection of Earl Shores.)**

Overexpansion had occurred within the company too. The City Star Hockey line that Munro Games offered in 1972 and 1973 – which allowed retailers to personalize table hockey games with the name of a local NHL or WHA star – created a giant logistical nightmare for the company. And Munro piled on itself in 1973 by marketing regionalized hockey games, which let the retailer pick the team combinations.

"We were offering the customer 10 different types of hockey games with 10 different labeling possibilities," said Don Munro. Creating color lithograph labels for 100 different game models was a very expensive undertaking. If a retailer wanted only 100 games with its city's star, the wholesale price per game had Munro Games barely breaking even. "We had to hope somebody else would buy another 1000 games [with that particular star] so we could make a profit."

Combine this faulty production plan with Servotronics' careless collection of companies, and it was no surprise that Munro Games was having problems. Sprinkle in the nose-diving economy, and the result was devastating. Nick Trbovich's grand ambitions were scattered like peanut shells under a stadium seat. Just a year earlier the company was at Toy Fair basking in the triumph of Munro Hockey Night. But like the gladiator

# Now! Munro brings you Hover-Glide Hockey ...the Air-Action game

Available at better Toy and Department stores everywhere

A new dimension in hockey games... The puck actually floats on a cushion of air at speeds faster than real hockey. You defend and attack the goals with hand-held shooters. Believe us, Hover-Glide Hockey is great family fun. Or Gordie Howe and family wouldn't have endorsed it!

**Munro... America's 1st name in family room action games**

With its electric football line in decline, Murno was putting most of its resources into air-powered hockey games. (Collection of Earl Shores.)

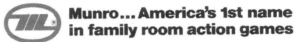

battles of the Roman Coliseum, this event now seemed to be part of a very distant and once glorious past.

Munro Games brought to the Fair a drastically paired down electric football line. It was down to just four games – a large (40" x 25") Namath model, a small (33" x 19") Namath model, an NFL Players Association game, and a small non-electric mechanically vibrating Bob Griese game. Munro's cost-cutting hit the large Namath model hard. The game was now without its trademark battery-operated floodlights, and also missing was the distinctive double-decked grandstand. Neither Namath model had the same visual flair as the earlier Day/Nite games.

Spared from the budget ax were Munro's hand-painted players and "Dial A Play" bases. Both were featured on the large and small Namath games. But even with only four games to produce and sell, Munro still had major problems in electric football. Despite the pre-Christmas *Tonight Show* ads, many retailers were saddled with unsold inventories of electric football games. Setting an example of how to deal with the problem of excess inventory was the Wisconsin-based Prange-Way Discount chain. In a post-Christmas clearance sale they were liquidating top-of-the-line Munro models for as little as $4. Munro's football games were creating a lot of red ink for retailers around the country. And these retailers would certainly not make shelf space for any new Munro football games in 1974.

Football wasn't the only place where Munro cut back, as there were ten fewer table hockey models for 1974. Some of the resources that would have gone to football and hockey in previous years had been diverted to the only real hopeful spot in the Munro showroom – air hockey. Munro Games was unveiling a brand new line of Gordie Howe Hover Glide Hockey games. The biggest of the three models was a 5-foot long 175-pound arcade-style monster.

The company was betting its future on air hockey. Brunswick introduced the concept in 1972, and whacking a plastic puck across a 6-foot cushion of air quickly became a popular pastime in arcades, bars, and bowling alleys throughout North America. (Brunswick also copyrighted the term "air hockey," forcing competitors to come up with "equivalent" names.) For 1973 Brunswick was able to scale down air hockey for home use, and the game became a surprisingly hot Christmas item. This success didn't go unnoticed, and, as always happened in toys, there were going to be imitators for 1974. Munro, Coleco, and Ideal were now all aiming for a piece of the air hockey market. But no one had as much riding on air hockey as Munro Games. Coleco and Ideal were much bigger companies with a broader range of items.

In 1973 Munro had a "Game Plan" for retailers, including a schedule of print and television advertising. Surely with the bulk of its efforts turned over to air hockey there was a similar plan for the coming year? There was not. With the company descending into disarray and debt, no one had bothered to come up with an advertising plan for 1974. There were no ads forthcoming in *Playthings*, and no elaborate *Tonight Show* television campaigns featuring Gordie Howe or Joe Namath. The games would simply be shipped to the retailers who wanted them, and it was hoped eager consumers would do the rest.

This level of product support didn't seem adequate, even in the heady February optimism that pervades Toy Fair. Brunswick was already in its showroom with a tabletop air hockey game that was slated to sell for less

A prototype Lee Payne-designed Tudor box that was never put into production. Photo by Lee Payne. (Collection of Roddy Garcia.)

than $30. Since Munro, Coleco, and Ideal were conceptually a year behind Brunswick, this would be the only tabletop air hockey game on the market in 1974. As it did with electric football in 1971, Munro seemed to be arriving at the air hockey party very much on the late side.

Finally in mid-March, the oil embargo on the U.S. was lifted. But oil supplies were still going to remain tight and prices high for months to come. The damage of the embargo was cascading throughout the world economy, leaving inflation in U.S. running at almost 15% for the first two months of 1974. Most economists felt a recession was inevitable. And it could be years before the country recovered from the shock of this oil shortage.

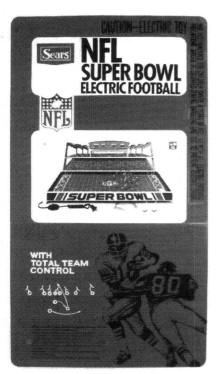

The prototype box for the new Sears Super Bowl. Designed by Lee Payne, this is what the actual boxes looked like in 1974. Photo by Lee Payne. (Collection of Roddy Garcia.)

Feeling a different kind of shock in March were the NFL owners. The Players Association presented them with a list of 57 demands for the new players' contract. Included in the demands were an increase in pension payments, an increase in the minimum NFL salary, and the elimination of the Rozelle rule, which the players said limited their ability to move to another team (Rozelle currently had the power to order "compensation" – either in money or in flesh – when a player signed with a new team). Negotiations on the contract were set to start in a couple of weeks.

But before these talks got underway, the NFL owners suffered another shock – something they hoped was an outrageous April Fool's Day joke. Newspaper headlines around the country on April 1 announced that three offensive stars from the Super Bowl champion Miami Dolphins – Paul Warfield, Jim Kiick, and Super Bowl MVP Larry Csonka – had signed with the Toronto franchise of the WFL. It was a package deal, with the three players signing for three years for a total sum of $3 million. With each player earning approximately $333,000 a year, they were now the highest paid players in pro football history (eclipsing Namath's current $250K figure). This figure was well beyond the NFL average player salary of $28,000. All three players were in their option year with Miami for 1974, so they couldn't play for Toronto until 1975. That made them the first "lame duck" players in NFL history. The very next day, Oakland's starting quarterback Ken Stabler signed with the WFL's Birmingham franchise. Since his option year didn't come until 1975, he would spend two years in lame duck player limbo.

Earlier in the year Commissioner Rozelle had vowed that the NFL would maintain a low profile with regard to the WFL. But the new league now had the commissioner's and the owners' undivided attention. In fact the fallout from the signing was so massive that Csonka was given the opportunity to explain his decision in the *New York Times* Sunday "Opinion" section. So by the time the NFL owners gathered on April 26 to select expansion cities, they had hustled to sign 25 of the 26 number-one picks from the January draft. They also offered raises to a number of veteran players and secured them to long-term contracts. Just as the AFL had done, the WFL was escalating NFL payrolls.

By the meeting's end, Tampa had a new NFL franchise, and the league had nine new rules to liven up play. Among the major changes were moving the goal post back to the end line, moving kickoffs back to the 35-yard line, and instituting a fifteen-minute overtime period to decide a tie game. Overtime would be of the sudden death variety – the first team to score wins. The owners' position on the Players Association's demands remained unchanged. They saw no reason to bother talking with the players about their outrageous demands.

| PARTS | Replacement Cost |
|---|---|
| Bag of 11 NFL uniformed figures (BASES NOT INCLUDED) | $ 2.00 |
| Bag of 11 "red" or "blue" prepainted figures (MODEL #500) (BASES NOT INCLUDED) | 1.50 |
| Bag of 11 white or yellow unpainted figures (BASES NOT INCLUDED) (If you want to paint your favorite college or high school teams) | 1.25 |
| Bag of 22 Standard player bases | 1.75 |
| Complete set of 24 Total Team Control™ player bases | 3.00 |
| Please Note: Total Team Control™ player bases are not sold singly | |

A sign of the economic times – Tudor's teams now cost $2.00. 1974 Tudor Rule Book.

A few years earlier it would've been easy to imagine Coleco and Munro in a bidding war for the WFL's licensing rights, with the winning company marketing official WFL electric football games. But even beyond the troubles caused by the oil embargo, the electric football market had changed. Coleco's ambitions with the game were now much diminished. The company seemed content to pick off entry-level sales through select discount chains and let its deluxe Command Control games fill the pricing space between Tudor's small and large NFL models. The way things were going at Munro, someone might buy the WFL rights and then misplace them in a file cabinet drawer. Norman could care less about the WFL. His main concern was that the NFL players and owners start talking again.

Progress was made in the labor situation when federal mediators stepped in and got the players and owners to sit down together in late May. As a good will gesture, the owners offered to cover the players' health

In addition to Munro's struggles, Bob Griese would be handing off to a lame duck Miami backfield in 1974. (Photo by Roddy Garcia.)

insurance payments until July. All the mediators could wring out of this session was an agreement by both sides to meet three times a week starting on June 9. Before these new talks started, the owners gave Seattle an expansion team. Memphis had been an expansion frontrunner until the WFL moved its Toronto franchise to the city. The owners also took a stand in the public relations battle surrounding the labor talks by publishing a report from the NFL Management Council, which claimed that the NFL teams did not experience a windfall of money in 1973. In fact, two teams lost money during the previous year, with the average per team profit figure being $472,000. The report also claimed the average player salary was just over $36,000, about a third higher than a previously reported figure. It's unclear whether this report got the public behind the owners, but the players saw the report as a very deliberate attempt to undermine their position. Labor talks broke off again on June 26 after resuming for just two weeks. A strike seemed imminent.

What was no longer imminent, but an accepted fact, was that the U.S. was in a recession. Inflation was running at 10% for the year – layoffs and unemployment were widespread throughout the country. Toy stocks continued to drop with Coleco and Servotronics losing more than half of their value since January. Coleco was now down to 3 ¼, Servotronics was trading at 2, and the *Playthings* portfolio had fallen further to $2,519.13. Not helping the confidence of the country was a distracted president who was fighting off a subpoena to release his Oval Office tapes to the Watergate special prosecutor. Finally on July 1, the NFL players' strike became a reality.

Picket lines were set up at team training camps – the striking players carried signs saying "No Freedom-No Football." Immediately, the owners vowed to open the camps and play the exhibition season with rookie and free agent players. This really wasn't the best time for an NFL strike. With so many people out of work and struggling to make ends meet, it was going to be hard for the players to earn much sympathy. Let's face it; they were getting paid to play a kid's game…who could walk away from that? Of course the players' plight was far from that simple, but emotions have a way of making important details disintegrate. Out-of-work season ticket holders weren't going to be very understanding of players who walked away from an available job. (Not to mention screwing up one of life's bright spots, the professional football season.)

Another reason why this wasn't such a great time to go on strike was the WFL. The new league was set to start its season on July 10; perhaps football fans would flock to watch the new league while the NFL players and owners' squabbled over their riches. But the WFL wasn't going to be able to flood television screens with games. All the major networks had NFL contracts, and strike or no strike, they weren't going to jeopardize that relationship. So the WFL ended up signing with the independent TVS Network for a series of Thursday night games. Although technically a national network, there were no dedicated TVS stations anywhere in the country. TVS depended on local independent television stations, most of which had call numbers on the UHF dial, to take its programming feed. So the number of markets carrying the TVS game would vary from week to week. This made it harder to sell advertising for the league, and also made the contract not especially lucrative. WFL teams were expecting $100K each from TVS; each NFL team now received over $2 million in television revenue.

Attendance was strong for the first week of WFL games, making the cancellation of the annual College All-Star game all the more painful for the NFL. It was the first time in 41 years that the game would not be played. Since the proceeds from the game went to Chicago-area charities, it was another black eye for the league, especially the players (the NFLPA was offering a donation of $10,000 in lieu of the cancellation). The players and owners met for seven hours on July 12, but when no progress was made the owners announced that no more games would be cancelled. Rookies, free agents, and players not supporting the strike would comprise NFL team rosters for the duration of the strike.

In the days leading up to the NFL Hall of Fame game between the Bills and Cardinals, the WFL had 64,000 fans turn out in Philadelphia, another 61,000 in Birmingham, and 46,000 in Jacksonville. Meanwhile the first weekend of NFL exhibition games saw total attendance down by over 250,000 people from the same weekend in 1973. It was estimated that the owners lost $1.8 million from gate receipts alone – there would also be losses from concession and parking. And television ratings were down more than 50%. Sponsors were not happy. Clearly the fans weren't

Sears' electric football page with the new and smaller Super Bowl model. Sears 1974 *Christmas Book*, page 531.
©Sears, Roebuck and Co. 1974.

in the mood to "buy" the replacement NFL. In acknowledgement of the substandard quality of their product, the NFL owners offered refunds to season ticket holders who did not want to pay for exhibition games.

Anyone tied to the NFL's fortunes had to be concerned. Norman had experienced NFL labor disputes before, but this one had a much more bitter edge to it. The players and owners seemed so far apart it was hard to envision how they would reconcile. With proof of fan anger in the meager attendance figures and television ratings, the NFL was far from the marketing juggernaut it had been in previous years. Throw in the recession and 1974 had the potential to be a disastrous year for Tudor. The way the economy was going, the increased mail-order price ($2) for NFL teams wouldn't even be at a break-even point by Christmas. And who could measure the fan backlash at the NFL if the regular season started with replacement players? By Christmas, Norman might be wishing he had WFL teams to sell. At least the new league would have finished its season.

Despite professional football's ascending role in American culture, and the soap-opera quality engulfing the 1974 season, a much more important

## TABLE MODEL ELECTRIC FOOTBALL ...3 CHOICES!

**NFL Electric Football Games (A)-(C) have these features:**

- 22 pre-painted players in 5 authentic positions, that run reel traps, end arounds, sweeps, slants and swing patterns
- Two triple-threat quarterbacks that kick, pass and run
- Automatic timer that starts and stops with each play
- Magnetic first down marker with movable 10-yd. chain
- 4 colorful goal line flags • Authentic NFL goal posts
- UL Listed safety plug and exclusive heavy-duty switch
- Easy to apply identification numbers for each player
- Rugged steel gameboard • Magnetic ball and down marker
- Colorful grandstand with adjustable scoreboard

### Deluxe Electric Football

**17⁹⁹**

**A** Wards Exclusive NFL Electric Football Game, with your choice of teams. YOU be the coach! Total team control lets you mastermind every run, kick, and block! Wheel in the base of each player lets you pre-program speed and direction of his legs, to obey your commands! You get your home team and opposing team; see below. Jumbo size playing field about 37¾x20¾x3 in. Includes NFL Playbook written by NFL staff, deluxe grandstand, and league standings board. For ages 8 yrs. and up.
48 G 14564 M—Ship. wt. 11 lbs. ................... 17.99

**B** Wards Exclusive! Our most popular NFL electric football game. Slightly smaller field than (A); about 31½x17¼x3 in. Just the right size for a card table. Includes standings board, scoreboard, Play book and choice of teams (below). For ages 8 yrs. and up.
48 G 14565 M—Ship. wt. 8 lbs. 4 oz. ................ 14.94

**When you order (A) or (B) you get these teams:**

| If you order from | You get these teams |
|---|---|
| Albany | Jets/Giants |
| Baltimore | Redskins/Cowboys |
| Chicago | Bears/Lions |
| Denver | Rams/49'ers |
| Ft. Worth | Redskins/Cowboys |
| Kansas City | Chiefs/Cards |
| Oakland | Raiders/Chargers |
| Portland | Rams/49'ers |
| St. Paul | Vikings/Packers |

**C** Budget NFL electric football game. Playing field about 27x16 in. Teams: Bears and Lions. Does not include Play book, standings board or choice of teams. For ages 8 yrs. and up.
48 G 14539 M—Ship. wt. 4 lbs. 8 oz. ................ 9.96

**14⁹⁴** ⓑ

**9⁹⁶** ⓒ

The electric football page (379) from the 1974 Montgomery Ward *Christmas Catalog.* ©Montgomery Ward, Inc. 1974.

matter quickly rose to make the NFL's problems seem trivial. President Nixon resigned on August 9 after newly released Oval Office tapes showed that the he'd played an active role in covering up the Watergate break-in. Impeachment proceedings were already speeding through Congress, so Nixon sought to avoid the inevitable by stepping down. It was the first time in United States' history that a sitting president resigned, and it shook the country. And this came on top of Nixon's vice president, Spiro Agnew, resigning in October of 1973 after pleading no contest to tax evasion and money laundering charges. People were deeply cynical of their leaders and resentful of the betrayal of trust by Nixon. There was also Cold War-inspired fear. With the country in disarray, the Russians might see us as vulnerable. Newly sworn-in President Gerald Ford inherited a situation that no other American president had ever faced.

In the wake of Nixon's resignation, the NFL players decided to have a fourteen-day cooling off period. All the players would report to camp, while the union continued to negotiate with the owners. The NFLPA had been struggling to maintain unity. It was estimated that 25% of established NFL players were already in camp, including star quarterbacks Roger

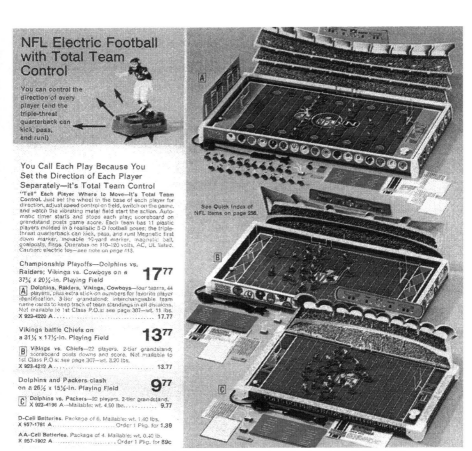

## NFL Electric Football with Total Team Control

You can control the direction of every player (and the triple-threat quarterback can kick, pass, and run!)

**You Call Each Play Because You Set the Direction of Each Player Separately—it's Total Team Control**

"Tell" Each Player Where to Move—It's Total Team Control. Just set the wheel in the base of each player for direction, adjust speed control on field, switch on the game, and watch the vibrating metal field start the action. Automatic timer starts and stops each play; scoreboard on grandstand posts game score. Each team has 11 plastic players molded in 5 realistic 3-D football poses; the triple-threat quarterback can kick, pass, and run! Magnetic first down marker, movable 10-yard marker, magnetic ball, goalposts, flags. Operates on 110-120 volts, AC, UL listed. Caution: electric toy—see note on page 413.

Championship Playoffs—Dolphins vs. Raiders; Vikings vs. Cowboys on a 37¼ x 20½-in. Playing Field **17⁷⁷**

[A] Dolphins, Raiders, Vikings, Cowboys—four teams, 44 players, plus extra stick-on numbers for favorite player identification. 3-tier grandstand; interchangeable team name cards to keep track of team standings in all divisions. Not mailable to 1st Class P.O.s; see page 307—wt. 11 lbs.
X 923-4220 A . . . . . . . . . . . . . . . . . . . . . . . . . . . . . . . . 17.77

Vikings battle Chiefs on a 31¼ x 17½-in. Playing Field **13⁷⁷**

[B] Vikings vs. Chiefs—22 players. 2-tier grandstand; scoreboard posts downs and score. Not mailable to 1st Class P.O.s; see page 307—wt. 3.20 lbs.
X 923-4212 A . . . . . . . . . . . . . . . . . . . . . . . . . . . . 13.77

Dolphins and Packers clash on a 26½ x 15½-in. Playing Field **9⁷⁷**

[C] Dolphins vs. Packers—20 players. 2-tier grandstand.
X 923-4196 A—Mailable: wt. 4.50 lbs. . . . . . . . . . . 9.77

D-Cell Batteries. Package of 6. Mailable: wt. 1.40 lbs.
X 957-1761 A . . . . . . . . . . . . . . . . . . . . Order 1 Pkg. for 1.39
AA-Cell Batteries. Package of 4. Mailable: wt. 0.40 lb.
X 957-1902 A . . . . . . . . . . . . . . . . . . . . Order 1 Pkg. for 89c

See Quick Index of NFL items on page 256.

Including J.C. Penney, Tudor had a sweep of the major mail-order catalogs in 1974. J.C. Penney *Christmas 1974*, page 415. ©J.C. Penney, Inc. 1974.

Staubach, Bob Griese, Terry Bradshaw, and John Hadl. After the cooling off period expired on August 28 with no agreement, the players chose to remain in camp and play the season rather than go back on strike.

The owners were happy the players were in camp and also happy about some news coming out of the WFL. Of the 64,000 fans that attended the Philadelphia Bell game on July 25, only 6,000 paid for their tickets. Over 58,000 seats had been given away. It turned out that similar sleight-of-hand calculations had been happening throughout the league, so attendance figures were basically lies. There were also rumors that a number of teams were paying their players erratically, if at all. And things were not going to get any better for the WFL as the "real" league finally geared up for play.

When the NFL season finally got underway on September 15, there were many unanswered questions. Could the Dolphins win a third consecutive

Super Bowl...with a lame duck backfield and wide receiver? Were the players in shape after the abbreviated time spent in training camps? And what unforeseen outcomes would the new rule changes bring? Another worry for the owners was the impact of the strike on game-day attendance and television ratings. They were also concerned about the blackout policy (lifting the television blackout when home games sold out 72 hours in advance) on season ticket sales. Last year's anti-blackout legislation went into effect just as the season started – and well after season ticket holders had made their final payments.

There were also a lot questions in the toy world as the main shopping season slipped into low gear. The obvious question was how much money would people be willing to spend on toys during the Christmas shopping season. *Playthings* gazed into the consumer crystal ball in its September issue and predicted that games over $10 would be a "tough" sell unless it was an air hockey game. This was a far cry from the 1973 prediction of there being "no limit" on what consumers would shell out for family games. Reflecting the changes in the toy landscape was the new Sears catalog where a $300 Munro air hockey game took up most of page 6 as a "featured item." Further in the catalog there was a full-color page of air hockey games, including a stand-alone $100 Munro game, and the $29.49 tabletop Brunswick game. Beyond the emergence of air hockey, another milestone item was on page 409 – a Magnavox Odyssey electronic game system. This was the first time Magnavox had made the Odyssey available beyond authorized Magnavox television dealers. Page 409 marked the introduction of home video games to the toy buying masses.

Although a handful of foosball soccer games were sprinkled throughout the toy section, football games were still holding a prominent spot. Seven football games occupied page 531, with Tudor having four of those games. But the space dedicated to the company's three electric football games had shrunk from the previous year. A smaller Tudor Super Bowl game was an obvious reason for diminished space, but larger forces were at work here. Electric football sales were just not what they once were. Still, the Super Bowl was the main item on the page (accompanied by an NFL No. 515 and NFL No. 635). In contrast to the Super Bowl, which was cheaper than the previous year's, the other two Tudor electric football games had increased in price by almost a dollar. This left the cost differential between two equal size games – the NFL No. 635 and the new Super Bowl – at just two dollars. Shoppers had to decide if having a "Super Bowl" on the side of the game was worth this extra amount. Considering that consumer spending was down and the Consumer Confidence Index was at a record low, $2 loomed as a significant sum of money.

One thing Tudor didn't have to compete with in Sears this year was electric football games from any other company. Sears' toy buyers didn't take on any Munro football games because they still had leftover stock from 1973. So anybody shopping the famous *Christmas Book* for ele ctric football would end up with a Tudor game. It was the first time ever that Tudor had complete electric football domination of Sears.

Yet Munro Games was still very prominent in Sears, and with more than just air hockey games. On the page just opposite from Tudor sat four Munro table hockey games, including an official World Hockey Association game. Munro was still skating ahead in the family room category – the oversized $49.99 Family Cup hockey game filled nearly a third of the page. It was hard to imagine shoppers in the current economy spending that much on a table hockey game, especially when a number of air hockey models were less expensive. But clearly Munro's dreams of challenging Tudor for electric football prominence were over.

NFL Properties once again was a dominant force in Sears with over 20 pages of NFL merchandise. This year the scope of items expanded to include children's furniture and NFL wood-burning craft sets; it's safe to say that market over-saturation wasn't just limited to electric football. Some unfortunate manufacturers were going to find out in 1974 that an NFL logo didn't guarantee success.

Montgomery Ward countered Sears with six football games, all featured in color on page 379. The three electric football games on the page belonged to Tudor. After two years of sporadic sales, Ward decided to eliminate the floor model with legs from its electric football line. But they did keep the NFL No. 645, Tudor's largest model. The teams would again be "regionalized" according to a shopper's particular area of the country, although a boy in Baltimore would not be thrilled to find out that the Redskins were his "home" team. In keeping the No. 645, Ward had increased the price to $17.99 – a 20% markup from 1973. Ward also brought in a smaller NFL No. 635 model this year, describing it as "our most popular NFL game," even though it never appeared in the 1973 catalog. At $14.94 it was the same price as Sears' Super Bowl game. Rounding out electric football in Ward was the NFL No. 515, which at $9.96 just scraped the magic $10 mark. Tudor had one more game on the page, that being NFL Strategy. Two other strategy games – Aurora's Monday Night Football, and Mattel's Talking Football – finished out the Ward football page.

An interesting development at Ward was its abandonment of Coleco. On the color page next to electric football was just a single table hockey game… made by Munro. The rest of the page followed the family game room theme, even down to the "no limit" pricing. Ideal's air hockey entry, the stand-alone Hurricane Hockey, crossed the $50 mark. But it was topped by a monstrous "Ward's Exclusive" game – the wood-grain finished, six-foot long Bowl-A-Matic 600. Unlike the foosball game bordering Munro's single hockey offering, this was not a game you could fold up when you were finished. It was a 110-pound monster that required a serious space commitment from the shopper. And that was on top of the $97 monetary commitment. The market for such a game was limited, even before the recession. The final game on the page seemed the most realistic offering, both in price and playability. That was the tabletop Brunswick Air Hockey game, a nice deal at $27.88.

Another major Christmas catalog where Tudor had almost total domination in 1974 was J.C. Penney. The four-team NFL Championship No. 655 was Penney's featured game, accompanied by an NFL No. 635, an NFL No. 515, and both NFL Strategy models (standard and junior editions). A new card-based game called Pro Draft was the only non-Tudor item on the football page. Tudor now had total electric football supremacy in all the major U.S. Christmas catalogs. It was a fantastic position to have for the Christmas shopping season. Considering the swooning economy, the only thing that seemed certain in 1974 was uncertainty.

That theme carried over to the NFL as well. Attendance for the first three weeks of the season was down 8% from 1973, and only 3 of 13 games sold out during the first weekend of October. It was hard to pinpoint what was keeping fans away – the economy, the strike, or the blackout rule.

Sears had leftover Munro Day/Nite games from 1973 and was determined to get rid of them – even at a loss. The Sears Catalog Surplus Store, October 1974. *The Economist*, page CSR 5, October 20, 1974.

NFL owners and execs were very concerned. But luckily the NFL powers-that-be had one less thing to be worried about. That would be the WFL.

WFL teams were hemorrhaging money at this point with the Detroit and Jacksonville franchises already defunct. Two other teams, including the major market New York Stars, had relocated to new cities. And of the ten teams left, most were not meeting their payroll obligations. In fact, the NFL's Kenny Stabler was in the process of suing his future WFL team for "breach of contract" after his bonus payments stopped being delivered. The league's misery mounted in mid-October, when the Philadelphia Bell reported a paid crowd of 750 for a game with Shreveport (the relocated Houston franchise). It was not a pretty sight to see a crowd this sparse in a stadium that annually held over 100,000 fans for the Army-Navy game. By month's end, the commissioner and founder of the league, Gary Davis, would be forced out by the WFL owners.

Another organization in serious trouble was Munro Games. Sears had yet to use electric football in any kind of print advertising, but when they finally did on October 20, it was devastating for Munro. The Sears Catalog Surplus store in Chicago was unloading leftover Day/Nite games for $9.99, or $7 less than last year's Surplus store price (and $15 less than the original asking price). This $9.99 figure was less than what new Munro electric football games were selling for, and the new games didn't even have real floodlights. Not that it was easy to find any Munro football games.

"Games were made, but who knows what happened to them," said Don Munro, "It was such a confusing period." For a number of reasons, distribution of Munro's stock was erratic. As fuel prices drove the cost of shipping ever higher, the company fell behind on its bills. Shipping companies started to refuse making deliveries for Munro Games. Sometimes games, especially electric football games, never made it out of the warehouse. Air hockey was the future, and table hockey was the game the company had been founded on. Major retailers like Sears, Toys R Us, and the True Value Hardware chain had significant orders in for both types of games, with Sears featuring Munro's Pro Hockey game prominently in its fall toy advertising. If Munro wanted to stay in business it could not let these retailers down. When the delivery budget got thin, air hockey and table hockey took priority. Those games would get on the truck. Electric football was left on the loading dock.

**NEW YORK EXCHANGE**

| | Closing 10/9/74 | Closing 9/9/74 | Closing 9/10/73 |
|---|---|---|---|
| Bradley* | 6¾ | 6¼ | 56⅛ |
| Coleco** | 1⅞ | 2½ | 10⅝ |
| Consolidated Foods (Tyco) | 11½ | 12⅞ | 31 |
| Damon | 7½ | 8¼ | 40⅞ |
| General Mills | 29½ | 36⅝ | 58½ |
| Ideal | 3⅛ | 3¼ | 5⅛ |
| Masco | 20⅝ | 29½ | 54 |
| Mattel | 2 | 2 | 4¼ |
| Murray Ohio | 18¾ | 18½ | 27¼ |
| Nabisco | 24½ | 24⅜ | 43 |
| National Ind. | 3½ | 3⅝ | 2½ |
| Owens-Illinois | 30½ | 32¼ | 34⅞ |
| Quaker Oats | 15¼ | 13¼ | 36⅜ |
| Tonka | 8⅛ | 9⅝ | 19⅝ |

**Illustrating the toll the economy had taken on the toy world was a stock table published in the November issue of *Playthings*. Page 14, November 1974. Courtesy of The Strong®, Rochester, New York**

Perhaps the major reason that Munro electric football games never made it out of the warehouse in 1974 was simply because nobody wanted them. Retailers still had thousands of unsold Munro electric football games from the previous Christmas and simply didn't want any more items from the company. It didn't help that Munro's stripped-down games were much less appealing than models from previous years. (Many games were now stocked with old Gotham players.) It also didn't help that Joe Namath and the Jets were off to a 1-7 start. There was just little demand for the Munro electric football line.

The company was very fortunate to have Toys R Us still selling its games. But like Sears, the chain was not selling Munro's electric football line. This left Tudor as the main electric football game supplier for Toys R Us. Coleco electric football games were being sold by the toy superstore, but they weren't featured in any Toys R Us advertising. The only game getting space in the chain's newspaper ads was Tudor's NFL No. 515, whose price fell just under the $10 mark. In promoting only a single model, and a small one at that, Toys R Us plainly had less enthusiasm for electric football than in the golden years of the 1971-73 period. Larger Tudor NFL games were still available at the retailer, but the bulk of the account seemed focused at the $10 price point.

What Toys R Us was selling from Munro Games was Bobby Hull table hockey and the new line of Hover Glide air hockey games. But in both areas, Munro was in major battles with other companies. On the table hockey front, Munro was still head-to-head with long time rival Coleco. Neither company had gained any advantage from the "family room" competition. And this category ultimately turned out to be a red-ink generator for both Coleco and Munro. Air hockey, on the other hand, was clearly THE hot category in 1974 – it was very reminiscent of electric football in 1972. Four different companies were in on the fun including Munro, Coleco, Ideal, and the originator, Brunswick. It didn't take a marketing genius to see that the air hockey pie was probably not going to be big enough for all of them. But all the companies were willing to roll the dice on the concept. Munro, at this point, was betting the house.

Aside from Toys R Us' measured promotion of electric football, another indicator of the category's troubles came in early November. Actually, it was an event that didn't happen that told the tale. For the first time in four years Tudor did not win an Excellence Award from Sears. It wasn't that Tudor didn't still make a quality game or couldn't supply Sears' stores with all the games they needed. The Super Bowl simply hadn't sold as well in previous years. And Tudor wasn't the only Sears toy supplier who had disappointing sales the previous Christmas. Some companies didn't even exist anymore. While Tudor was far from that predicament, it was a disappointment not to receive an award from Sears.

An additional concern for Norman was that both Sears and Ward waited until early November to promote electric football. Tudor's new Super Bowl game appeared more often in Sears' ads as the month went on, but this did little to assuage Norman's mounting frustration. That's because the image of the game being used by the retailer was usually small and dark and totally inaccurate. Although it was hard for most shoppers to figure out what they were looking at (other than something that cost $13.99), anyone with a little electric football savvy could see that this game was actually last year's model. The game Sears was selling was significantly different from the game it was advertising.

Thanksgiving came late in 1974, arriving on November 28. This meant it would be December by the time people returned to work after the traditional four-day break, and also that a full week had been cut from the Christmas shopping season. It was a given that shoppers were going to spend less this year, and the lost shopping days were going to have a major impact on retailers. Electric football games were scarce in holiday advertising this year, and when the games did appear, they followed the trend of the fall. Most of the electric football games being advertised were Tudor No. 500's and No. 400's, ranging in price from $4.99 to $7. On the rare occasions that larger NFL games did make it into print they were highly discounted. Sears had the Super Bowl as low as $9.99 while Ward dropped the NFL No. 645 all the way down to $8.88. Games from Coleco and Munro were almost invisible during the weekend. Toys R Us, in what seemed to be an ominous statement about electric football's current status, didn't even bother to advertise the game during the holiday period.

A few days later the WFL limped into its World Bowl championship game with only nine teams left in the league and an estimated $20 million in losses. The game was played on Thursday night, December 5, in order to avoid getting overrun in the television ratings by college football or the NFL. Earning the WFL title was the Birmingham Americans, who defeated the Florida Blazers 22-21. Unfortunately, being WFL champs wasn't enough to stop the local sheriff's deputies from confiscating Birmingham's team uniforms on Friday morning. The company who created and supplied the uniforms was still owed $30,000.

This particular Friday didn't turn out to be a very good one for the economy either. After losing 41 points during the week, the Dow Jones Industrial average closed at 577.60. It was a twelve-year low, and a stunning figure – the Dow had lost 42% of its value over the last fourteen months. Investors were scared as there seemed to be an unrelenting stream of bad economic news. Inflation was running at 11%, and new government figures put the jobless rate at 6.5%, the highest level since 1961. In just the last three weeks, the auto industry alone had laid off almost 190,000 workers. Even Sears was resorting to layoffs thanks to slow sales and increased inventories.

But even in a recession, there was still Christmas shopping to be done. Toys R Us had just put out a color newspaper flyer with the lone electric football game being the No. 515 for $9.86. (Accompanying the game was a cartoon drawing of Toy R Us mascot Geoffrey the Giraffe playing electric football.) And a number of Ward stores were running a three-day half-price toy sale. Included were Tudor's NFL No. 645 for $8.49 and the NFL No. 515 model for an unbelievable $4.48. The No. 515 was a true steal. With NFL teams from Tudor now costing $2 apiece, the Ward price meant that a shopper got the game board, the grandstand, and all the accessories for just $0.48! With the wholesale price on this game being $7.25 (and the No. 645 costing $11.90 wholesale), Ward was taking a financial hit to move these games.

Any football fan who chose a checkout line over the NFL on Sunday may have regretted the decision. By late Monday night, all eight playoff teams were in place. This rendered the final weekend of the season meaningless. But there still was plenty of drama in the Christmas shopping season. Stores were reporting fewer shoppers in their aisles, and as expected, these shoppers were spending less than in previous years. One exception was the Gibson Discount Chain. As people found less and less green in their wallets, the super discount merchants became more attractive. For much of the fall, Gibson's stores had been offering Coleco's Touchdown Command Control game for as little as $5 while blowing out Gotham's Jim Plunkett game for $3.97.

To keep shoppers coming through their doors, major retailers continued offering deep discounts on toys. During the second weekend of the month, Sears' Super Bowl and Ward's No. 645 games could both be found for less than $10. But it was over the next week that the bottom began to fall out of sports game pricing. On Monday, December 16, Munro saw its brand new WHA All-Star Hockey game go on half-price clearance for $6.49 at the Chicago area Sears Surplus Store – another failed item from a struggling company. This was also a day when Tudor's NFL No. 635 could be found for $6.96 in the Kresge store chain. J.C. Penney put electric football at 50% off on Tuesday, with special

Most of the electric football games being advertised in 1974 were priced around the $10 mark. *Oakland Tribune*, page 51, November 21, 1974.

Wednesday discounts seeing the No. 500 being sold for as low as $2.99. Yet it was another Wednesday sale that summed the state of electric football in 1974.

At a Sears Surplus Store in Grand Prairie, Texas, the Super Bowl was on sale for $6.50. It was only for one day, in one area of the country, and only from 6:00–9:00 p.m., but it was an unheard of event. Sears' Super Bowl games never ended up in the surplus stores, and never ended up selling for $8 less than the catalog price. At least the Super Bowl was in good company. This same surplus store was selling Aurora's Monday Night Football game for half-price ($4.50) during the same three-hour sale period. While it's possible to view the Texas sale as an outlier, it broke new and unwanted ground for Tudor.

By contrast, Illinois store managers were breathlessly recounting to a local newspaper reporter how impossible it was to keep Brunswick's Air Hockey game in stock. The local Sears was completely out of stock, while

Another sign of the economic times – the Super Bowl is offered for ½ price in Sears Catalog Surplus Store. *Grand Prairie Daily News*, page 3, December 18, 1974.

Toys R Us had sold an entire 50 game shipment during a single Saturday afternoon. A $30 price tag for the games was no obstacle.

With just five shopping days left until Christmas, J.C. Penney stores were in permanent toy clearance mode, pricing all their No. 500's below the $5 mark. Ward began discounting all its toys by 25% on the 19th and quickly extended the discounts to the 50% range. Local toy stores and chains then jumped on the discounting bandwagon, making the final shopping days of 1974 unlike any seen before in electric football. Tudor NFL No. 515 games were going for $5, while Tudor's flagship NFL Championship model could be bought for as little as $9. These same retailers were selling the NFL No. 635 for $7.99, and some even dropped the No. 500 model below the $3 mark. Coleco games suffered the same discounted fate, getting slashed to at least half-price and sometimes even more.

Some surprising exceptions to the avalanche of electric football clearance sales came from Toys R Us and retailers with Munro Joe Namath models. Electric football never appeared in Toys R Us advertising after the first week of December. The retailer seemed comfortable enough with the overall level of sales that it didn't feel the need to push the game. And for whatever reason, Munro sellers were reluctant to drop the Namath model much below $10, even late in the month when it was obvious the game wasn't moving.

For shoppers who procrastinated, there were extraordinary toy bargains to be had beyond electric football. Also going for half-price in the final shopping days were GI Joe's, Aurora HO racecar sets, Tyco train sets, Monopoly, Battleship, and even Lincoln Logs. So Tudor was in good company, even if it was a bad situation. Never in modern toy-industry history had there been such a mass Christmas season liquidation. Yes, there had always been last-minute discounting in previous years, but the array of items had never been as broad or the discounts as deep as they were in 1974.

The half-price toy frenzy was in high gear when the NFL playoffs opened on Saturday, December 21. Viking weather – snow flurries and 21-degree temperatures – greeted the St. Louis Cardinals in Minnesota, who after taking a 7-0 lead, let the host Vikings run off thirty unanswered points. The score at the final gun was 30-14. Later in the day at Oakland the Raiders ended the Dolphins' two-year reign as NFL champions. After trailing for most of the game, the Raiders completed a touchdown pass with 26 seconds left in the game for a 28-26 victory. The WFL-bound trio of Larry Csonka, Jim Kiick, and Paul Warfield, all played their final game in a Dolphins uniform. On Sunday the Steelers rumbled out to a 29-7 halftime lead before finishing off the Bills by a 32-14 score. Finally, under sunny southern California skies, the Rams defeated the Redskins 19-10 thanks to a 59-yard touchdown return of an intercepted pass.

Determined toy shoppers still had two more days of half-price madness to complete their Christmas lists. Bargains were plentiful and available at even the largest retailers. Electric football games were there for the taking at prices that would have been bargains back when Gotham's first NFL game appeared in 1961. But when Christmas finally came on Wednesday, would electric football still be a welcomed item? Yes, but it was no longer the gift against which all other Christmas gifts would be measured. The football-game landscape had changed significantly since Tudor introduced the miniature NFL.

Things were much simpler on Christmas morning of 1967. Tudor had five electric football models, while Gotham had three. The big "life-changing" electric football games of the day were the Gotham Big Bowl or the Tudor Browns-Giants No. 620. Next in line were the Sears NFL No. 618 and the Colts-Packers No. 510. If you found one of these games under your tree, it had been a great Christmas. There were no doubts or questions. But after Coleco's entry into electric football in 1970, the choices seemed to escalate exponentially. And by 1972, Munro had helped push the number of different electric football models to almost forty. This glut of games during the 1971-73 period meant kids had pretty much seen it all in electric football, and there really wasn't much new going on within the 15 games available in 1974 to grab their attention. Command Control, floodlights, and "family room games" had all failed to alter the course of electric football. Despite all the innovation of the period, electric football was still a game decided by the mostly random movement of vibrating figures. The TTC concept provided better directional control, yet it was far from the X and O precision drawn up on a football coach's blackboard.

Those nine-year-olds who had been blown away by the Tudor No. 620 in 1967 were now teenagers. Their interest had moved beyond vibrating games. As a result, newer football strategy games offering a

The No. 655 model still held onto the early promise of Tudor's 1967 NFL line. Photo by Lee Payne. (Collection of Roddy Garcia.)

more sophisticated challenge had come into the marketplace. Aurora's Monday Night Football game fit this bill, as did Mattel's Talking Football and Tudor's own NFL Strategy line. The apex of these strategy games took advantage of an emerging technology – computer circuitry. Bringing computers into the home were electronic calculators, the Magnavox Odyssey, and Computamatic Football games. Kids were being exposed to sophisticated games at an earlier age. The nine-year-old boy of 1974 was simply harder to impress than his 1967 counterpart.

And what would impress him was nowhere to be found during the liquidation days leading into Christmas. The hot item was Brunswick's tabletop air hockey game. The combination of play and price proved a perfect combination for the 1974 recession, and the games were sold out long before Santa loaded his sleigh. Some disappointed shoppers bit the monetary bullet and shelled out an extra $10 to purchase Munro's least expensive Hover Glide Hockey game or an extra $20 for Ideal's Hurricane Hockey game. Coleco's line of Power-Jet Hockey games also benefited from the overwhelming demand for Brunswick's game. But all of these other games had the disadvantage of being freestanding models with legs.

A large part of Brunswick's appeal was its ability to be stored under a bed or in a closet.

So this year as the NFL championship weekend approached there was more "thwacking" than "buzzing" going on in living rooms across the country. But any kid flicking the switch of an electric football game this year was most likely to be flicking on a game made by Tudor. The company's total control of the Sears, Ward, and J.C. Penney catalogs, along with a push from Toys R Us,

The "must-have" sports action game of 1974: Brunswick Air-Hockey. Montgomery Ward 1974 *Christmas Catalog*, page 378. ©Montgomery Ward, Inc. 1974.

meant that Tudor dominated Christmas in a way that it hadn't since the late 1960's. With Coleco moving away from electric football and Munro focusing its scattered resources on air hockey, Tudor had its biggest share of electric football sales in years. That some of those sales came at half price really didn't matter at this point.

Surprisingly, there was no televised football on Christmas Day to reignite any sagging electric football sentiments. It would be a two-day wait until Saturday before football again became an overwhelming presence with the Peach Bowl, Sun Bowl, East-West Shrine game, and the Fiesta Bowl all scheduled to be played over an eight-hour stretch starting at noontime. Then it was on to NFL Championship day on Sunday. Few were surprised when the home Vikings outlasted the Rams 14-10 for their second straight NFC championship. Out in Oakland, the Raiders hosted the Steelers and carried a 10-3 lead into the fourth quarter. Then the Steelers erupted for 21 points and a 24-13 victory. The history of the two conference champions couldn't have been more different. After just 14 seasons in the NFL, the Vikings were heading to the Super Bowl for the third time. For the Steelers, who joined the NFL in 1933, this was their first appearance in any type of NFL title game. Awaiting both teams in New Orleans was an aging and obsolete Tulane Stadium. The city's much-hyped and larger-than-life Superdome was over budget and well past its construction deadline.

Two more collegiate games would be televised before the year's end, the Gator Bowl on Monday night and the Sugar Bowl on New Year's Eve. Unfortunately, this year's Sugar Bowl would have no impact on the college rankings, and little of the "must-watch" quality of last year's contest. Both Nebraska and Florida had 8-3 records.

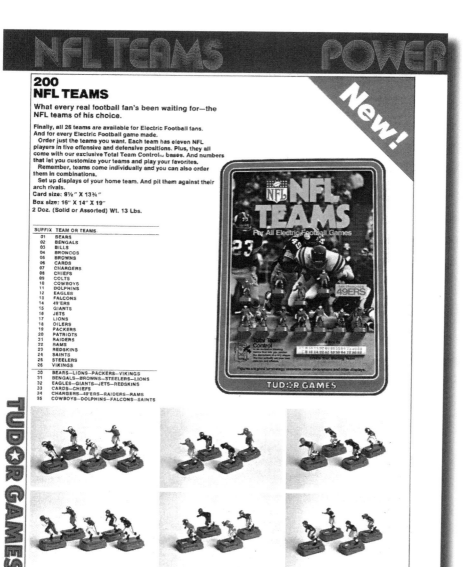

## 200
## NFL TEAMS

What every real football fan's been waiting for—the NFL teams of his choice.

Finally, all 26 teams are available for Electric Football fans. And for every Electric Football game made.

Order just the teams you want. Each team has eleven NFL players in five offensive and defensive positions. Plus, they all come with our exclusive Total Team Control™ bases. And numbers that let you customize your teams and play your favorites.

Remember, teams come individually and you can also order them in combinations.

Set up displays of your home team. And pit them against their arch rivals.

Card size: 9½" X 13¾"
Box size: 16" X 14" X 19"
2 Doz. (Solid or Assorted) Wt. 13 Lbs.

| SUFFIX | TEAM OR TEAMS |
|--------|---------------|
| 01 | BEARS |
| 02 | BENGALS |
| 03 | BILLS |
| 04 | BRONCOS |
| 05 | BROWNS |
| 06 | CARDS |
| 07 | CHARGERS |
| 08 | CHIEFS |
| 09 | COLTS |
| 10 | COWBOYS |
| 11 | DOLPHINS |
| 12 | EAGLES |
| 13 | FALCONS |
| 14 | 49'ERS |
| 15 | GIANTS |
| 16 | JETS |
| 17 | LIONS |
| 18 | OILERS |
| 19 | PACKERS |
| 20 | PATRIOTS |
| 21 | RAIDERS |
| 22 | RAMS |
| 23 | REDSKINS |
| 24 | SAINTS |
| 25 | STEELERS |
| 26 | VIKINGS |
| 30 | BEARS—LIONS—PACKERS—VIKINGS |
| 31 | BENGALS—BROWNS—STEELERS—LIONS |
| 32 | EAGLES—GIANTS—JETS—REDSKINS |
| 33 | CARDS—CHIEFS |
| 34 | CHARGERS—49'ERS—RAIDERS—RAMS |
| 35 | COWBOYS—DOLPHINS—FALCONS—SAINTS |

The Company that Turns a Game into a Sporting Event.

In 1975 Tudor began selling NFL teams "over-the-counter." 1975 Tudor sales catalog. (Collection of Norman Sas.)

# 31 A NEW TYPE OF GAME CHALLENGES ELECTRIC FOOTBALL

**N**ew Year's Day had a very intriguing lineup of games, thanks in large part to Oklahoma whose season was already over. The Sooners finished undefeated – and on NCAA probation – leaving them ineligible for any type of bowl game. A major question throughout the entire 1974 college season was whether Oklahoma should be eligible to be ranked in the polls. The Associated Press poll, which used the votes of sports writers, didn't have an issue with Oklahoma's probation and ranked the team No. 1. But the United Press International poll – a poll where college football coaches did the voting – had banned Oklahoma from its rankings. Coming into the final bowl day, UPI had Alabama first, Ohio State second, and USC third. All of these teams were playing on January 1, with Ohio State and USC facing off in the Rose Bowl. Only Alabama was undefeated. Ohio State already had a loss, while USC had a tie and a loss marring its score sheet.

The day started with the Cotton Bowl at 2 p.m., followed by the Rose Bowl and the Orange Bowl. USC edged out Ohio State 18-17, leaving a simple task for Alabama. If Alabama beat Notre Dame in the Orange Bowl, they would be No. 1 – the legitimate top-ranked team. Alabama certainly owed one to Notre Dame. No one on the team had forgotten how the Irish took the national title last year by beating Alabama in last year's Sugar Bowl. But Alabama couldn't avenge last season's humiliation, losing again to Notre Dame, this time by the score of 13-11. That left the UPI poll wide open, and, in a bit of a surprise, it was USC who was given the top spot. Their 55-24 thrashing of Notre Dame at the end of November was a major influence on the coaches who voted.

Over in the NFL, the Steelers had been installed as four-point favorites by the time the fans and league executives started assembling in New Orleans. As part of official NFL Super Bowl week business, the league named an MVP – Oakland quarterback Ken Stabler. This announcement came just days after a judge released Stabler from his WFL contract. Even with the season long over, there was no respite for the WFL from its seemingly endless string of troubles. Three teams were now facing property liens, and the IRS was set to auction the assets of the Portland franchise. And what could highlight the differing status of the two leagues more than a Super Bowl in the Big Easy? Advertisers were paying NBC $107,000 per 30-second spot, while the city was expecting an extra $15 million in revenue from the event (part of this coming from 1,500 private jets that were scheduled to arrive during the weekend).

Unfortunately, New Orleans again experienced unseasonably cold weather on game day. The thermometer didn't hover near freezing as it had in 1972, but between the 40-degree air temperature and the damp overcast skies it was an unpleasant day to be outside (and this was supposed to have been the first indoor Super Bowl). Conditions were so bad that over 1,000 people with tickets decided to stay in their hotel rooms or private jets to watch the game on television. It was a Super Bowl record for no-shows.

And no matter where you watched the game from, the first half was one thing – ugly. With the field wet and heavy from flooding rain in the preceding days, players from both teams looked like they needed skates to negotiate the conditions. After taking a 2-0 halftime lead, the Steelers cruised to a 16-6 win. Eight turnovers made the game a sloppy one, which didn't feel as close as the score suggested. That was due to the Steelers' dominating defense. The Vikings' offense gained only 119 yards (17 on the ground and 102 through the air), and didn't score a single point. Minnesota's lone touchdown came from the recovery of a blocked punt. It was the first title for the Steelers in the 42-year history of the franchise. The Vikings became the first team to suffer three Super Bowl losses.

Monday-morning quarterbacks usually thrive in the workplace the day after a Super Bowl, but silence would reign at auto plants throughout the U.S. Thanks to acres of unsold and unwanted cars, Ford had laid off 85,000 workers for the week of January 13. General Motors and American Motors were dealing with their own inventory issues, so industry-wide a total of 274,000 autoworkers were temporarily or indefinitely out of work. When these unemployment numbers were combined with the most recent inflation rate (13.7% for the final quarter of 1974), the depth of the recession truly came into focus. In fact the very next day, President Ford gave a national address asking for a $16 billion tax cut to stimulate the economy. Within his proposal was an individual tax rebate as well as tax increases on oil and natural gas. President Ford also asked for "personal sacrifices" in energy conservation.

While Congress worked on measures to keep the economy afloat, bad news continued to mount in February. A record 5.7 million people were

Tudor's new team packs, which included TTC bases and player numbers. 1975 Tudor sales catalog. (Collection of Norman Sas.)

collecting unemployment, and a menacing moniker was now being used to describe this period of high inflation, high unemployment, and flat economic growth. The term economists were using was "stagflation."

Over at the Toy Fair, stagflation had a simple translation – a very difficult time to be in toys. Issues of *Playthings* were down to 80 pages, and the *Playthings* portfolio was now down to $1,767.33, having loss 85% of its value since 1969. (Yes, this value was imaginary, but it was a dramatic fall from the $12,000 starting point.) *Playthings'* editor and publisher Harry Gluckert usually chose his words carefully, but the editorial titled "The Toy Industry Is Running Scared" eviscerated toy retailers, going so far as to accuse them of having "given up on the idea of making profit." Parker Brothers' president Randolph Barton offered a succinct summation of toy industry fears, saying that 1975 would be "the toughest profit year we ever looked at."

The cover of the 1975 Coleco sales catalog. There was no sign of electric football.

A large part of what made it tough was again dealing with excess inventories. Many toy retailers, as in 1973, did not place reorders during the latter part of the year. But some retailers went even further in 1974, *refusing* to accept previously arranged deliveries. It was a desperate way to assure empty store shelves for the New Year, and it hurt toy makers badly. The decline in sales during the final and critical fiscal quarter had pushed many toy companies into the red for the entire year. And inventories aside, overall expectations for 1975 were tempered by rising production costs – from the plastic the toys were made of to the energy needed to run a factory to the fuel needed to transport a toy – all of these things were going to rise in 1975.

The state of the toy industry was accurately reflected in electric football, as Tudor, Coleco, and Munro all decided not to place ads in *Playthings*. Tudor was at the Fair showing the same eight-game electric football lineup as 1974, but they did have one new electric football item – NFL teams for store display. It would be the first time that Tudor allowed its NFL teams to be available at the retail level. Now a boy could walk into a local store and check out a hanging rack of NFL teams. Instead of waiting weeks for his favorite team to come in the mail, he could have them in a just few minutes. (If the stock was good, that is.) Each package contained a single NFL team complete with TTC bases and number sheet. Retailers could set their own price – the wholesale per-team price was $1.95. Large yellow print on

Munro's 1975 Bob Griese model. 1975 Munro sales catalog. (Collection of Earl Shores.)

the packaging made it clear that the teams were "for all electric football games." To make this concept even more enticing to retailers, Tudor had put together prepackaged geographical assortments of teams. For example, a San Francisco toy store could order the West Coast assortment of the 49ers, Raiders, Rams, and Chargers. A Midwest assortment included the Browns, Bengals, Steelers, and Lions.

In the showroom, there were no obvious signs of the toll the recession was having on Tudor. In fact, the number of soccer games the company was offering increased. Yet backstage at Toy Fair, Norman already knew that electric football sales were going to take another hit. Sears had asked for only two electric football games from Tudor. After five consecutive years of offering three Tudor models for Christmas, the country's largest toy seller decided it wanted fewer electric football games cluttering its warehouses. But without question the biggest sales blow came from Ward. For 1975, Ward told Norman "no thanks" – they didn't want any games from Tudor. No electric football, no NFL Strategy...nothing. After having nearly an entire Ward page in 1973 and three electric football games in 1974, Tudor found itself completely shut out of one of its most reliable outlets. The last time Ward published a Christmas catalog without a Tudor electric football game had been 1961.

Filling in for Tudor at Ward would be Coleco. Coleco wasn't doing anything special with electric football. The company was given the electric football slot thanks to the success of its Bowl-A-Matic, pinball, and air hockey offerings. By all outward appearances it seemed that Coleco was ignoring electric football in the U.S., as the game wasn't even pictured in the current sales catalog. The company was selling three different games in 1975 – a 32" x 18" Super Action Command Control model and two 26"-long economy Pro-Stars models (with and without Command Control). Thanks to declining sales numbers, as well as nonexistent profits when electric football games needed to be liquidated each December, Coleco and

**The ad says it all. Brunswick had the most wanted game for Christmas of 1974. *Playthings*, page 22, March 1975. Courtesy of The Strong®, Rochester, New York.**

Ward had become kindred spirits. Neither wanted to be heavily vested in the game anymore.

Coleco's focus had turned elsewhere by this point. The company now had three distinct components, with the toy division overseeing air hockey, table hockey, electric football, and the expanding line of Shari Lewis' Junior Chef items. Still the backbone of the company was the pool division, but a new Coleco division was getting lots of money for research and development. This was the electronics division. They had helped create the Bowl-A-Matic game, several Coleco pinball games, and they had been watching the success of the Magnavox Odyssey closely. There was a feeling within Coleco that electronic toys were the future. Still, Coleco executives weren't tipping their hand about the direction of the company. No Coleco items were being promoted in *Playthings*, not even the half dozen Power-Jet Hockey games that would populate Sears, Ward, and Toys R Us during 1975.

Brave faces in the Munro Games showroom tried to send a signal that all was well, but it was already common knowledge at Toy Fair that Servotronics had lost almost $3 million in 1974. And the Munro subsidiary was being blamed for most of this loss. So in 1975 there were no Munro toy-buyer hockey scrimmages or promises of *Tonight Show* television advertising. There weren't even any ads in *Playthings*. There was just an ever-shrinking line of sports games. The electric football line held steady at four models with Munro keeping the large and small Joe Namath games, as well as the Vibra Action Bob Griese model. But the NFL Players Association game was gone. In its place was something described as "newly designed for the volume market." But upon closer inspection, there was clearly nothing "new" about Super Pro Football. It was simply a Bob Griese game with an electric motor, a grandstand...and old Gotham players.

While rumors had Joe Namath going to the reorganized World Football League, Munro had no choice but to remain vested in his Jets' persona. 1975 Munro sales catalog. (Collection of Earl Shores.)

# TUDOR GAMES

TUDOR GAMES,INC. 176 JOHNSON STREET BROOKLYN, N.Y. 11201 (212) 624-0910
SHOWROOM: 200 FIFTH AVENUE NEW YORK, N.Y. 10010 ROOM 526 (212) 675-8280

## ORDER FORM

BILL TO        SHIP TO

| DATE. | ORDER NO. | DEPT. NO. | WHEN SHIP | SHIP VIA | SALESMEN |
|-------|-----------|-----------|-----------|----------|----------|
|       |           |           |           |          |          |

## No. 200 N.F.L. TEAMS INDIVIDUAL ORDERING SHEET

MINIMUM PACKING: 24 PCS.      MINIMUM PACK WEIGHT: 13 LBS.

| QUANTITY | SUFFIX | TEAM | | QUANTITY | SUFFIX | TEAM |
|----------|--------|------|---|----------|--------|------|
|  | 01 | BEARS |  |  | 15 | GIANTS |
|  | 02 | BENGALS |  |  | 16 | JETS |
|  | 03 | BILLS |  |  | 17 | LIONS |
|  | 04 | BRONCOS |  |  | 18 | OILERS |
|  | 05 | BROWNS |  |  | 19 | PACKERS |
|  | 06 | CARDS |  |  | 20 | PATRIOTS |
|  | 07 | CHARGERS |  |  | 21 | RAIDERS |
|  | 08 | CHIEFS |  |  | 22 | RAMS |
|  | 09 | COLTS |  |  | 23 | REDSKINS |
|  | 10 | COWBOYS |  |  | 24 | SAINTS |
|  | 11 | DOLPHINS |  |  | 25 | STEELERS |
|  | 12 | EAGLES |  |  | 26 | VIKINGS |
|  | 13 | FALCONS |  |  | 27 |  |
|  | 14 | 49 'ERS |  |  | 28 |  |

## SPECIAL PREPACKED ASSORTMENTS

MINIMUM PACKING: 24 PC. CARTON      MINIMUM PACK WEIGHT: 13 LBS.

| QUANTITY | SUFFIX | NOTE: TEAMS ONLY PACKED EVENLY |
|----------|--------|--------------------------------|
|  | 30 | BEARS - LIONS - PACKERS - VIKINGS |
|  | 31 | BENGALS - BROWNS - LIONS - STEELERS |
|  | 32 | EAGLES - GIANTS - JETS - REDSKINS |
|  | 33 | CARDS - CHIEFS |
|  | 34 | CHARGERS - 49 'ERS - RAIDERS - RAMS |
|  | 35 | COWBOYS - DOLPHINS - FALCONS - SAINTS |

All prices FOB factory, Brooklyn, N. Y.

The wholesale/retailer order form for Tudor's new team packs. (Collection of Earl Shores.)

Most toy buyers and retailers had a simple question for Munro Games at this point – why even bother with electric football? There were so many leftover games from 1974. Most had ended up in clearance sales and they still didn't sell. Things had gotten so bad at the Buffalo plant that thousands of games had been shipped without artwork. Essentially these games were naked; a kid didn't even know what model he had. To make things worse, Gotham players were being substituted freely, even in games that were supposed to come with painted players. Electric football was a charade at this point – why would Munro continue?

The answer was hope...and air hockey. Sears had a significant order in for Munro's largest air hockey models and several table hockey games. By

```
30   BEARS—LIONS—PACKERS—VIKINGS
31   BENGALS—BROWNS—STEELERS—LIONS
32   EAGLES—GIANTS—JETS—REDSKINS
33   CARDS—CHIEFS
34   CHARGERS—49'ERS—RAIDERS—RAMS
35   COWBOYS—DOLPHINS—FALCONS—SAINTS
```

TUD◊R GAMES

**Tudor's geographical team groups. 1975 Tudor sales catalog. (Collection of Norman Sas.)**

maintaining the "breadth" of its sports game line through this rough period, air hockey could be the company's lifeline. And once the economy picked up, Munro would be better positioned to sell electric football again. But this was hope of the most desperate kind. All someone had to do was walk through the corridors of Toy Fair to see where the game world was heading.

One of the "must see" showrooms this year was Aurora's. Toy buyers flooded through the doors to secure orders for Aurora's tabletop Brunswick Air Hockey game. Giant black letters on a shiny gold card-stock page in *Playthings* explained why: "Aurora Turns Air Into Gold." On the flip side, the page returned to a traditional white hue and ran the headline: "Retailers who stocked up [in 1974] had a golden year." Aurora had completely sold out of the game during Christmas – it was THE item for 1974. Retailers didn't have a hope of reordering the game once it disappeared from their shelves. Compare this to the glut and slashed-to-the-bone prices of electric football games. And Aurora was promising a million dollars for Air Hockey television advertising in 1975, claiming it was "the largest budget ever set aside for a single game in toy business history." The company was promising a "gold rush" for the coming year, and you needed to get on board early to cash in. No smart retailer would miss such an opportunity.

Aurora also had another game that held its own nicely in 1974 – Monday Night Football. It was a little lost in the air hockey hype, but it was a game retailers welcomed to their aisles. The game was priced right, just under $10, and didn't take up a lot of shelf space. Munro's fortunes would have been radically different with such a game.

Perhaps the showroom leaving the biggest footprint at the Fair was Magnavox. They were introducing two new improved Odyssey models

## $15⁹⁷

### Super Bowl Electric Football Game

NFL's Steelers and Vikings clash on
31½x17½-inch playing gridiron

**Sold only at Sears.** Total Team Control lets you "tell" each player what pattern to run, what defender to block, to make the play "go all the way". Switch on the game and watch the vibrating metal field start the action.

Exclusive Super Bowl field, 2-tier grandstand and scoreboard. Each team includes 11 plastic players with official uniforms and steerable "legs", molded in five 3-D positions plus a triple-threat quarterback. Automatic timer starts and stops. Magnetic 10-yard marker with ball and down indicator and goal line flags. UL listed; 110–120-volt, 60 Hz. AC. 6 watts. 6-foot cord. Ages 8 and up.

79 C 65538C—Shipping weight 8 pounds .............................. $15.97

## $8⁸⁷

### Electric Football Game

Two teams clash on a 26½x15½-inch playing field. "Tell" each player where to move with Total Team Control. Vibrating metal field has grandstand and scoreboard. Each team has 11 plastic players molded in five 3-D positions plus a triple-threat quarterback. Automatic timer, 10-yard marker, down indicator, flags. UL listed; 110–120-v., 60-Hz. AC. 6 watts. 6-foot cord. Ages 8 years and up.

79 C 65536C—Shipping weight 4 pounds .................................. $8.87

Sears decided to carry only two electric football games in 1975, the Super Bowl and the No. 500. The 1975 Sears *Christmas Book*, page 542. ©Sears, Roebuck and Co. 1975.

and were also going to allow the game console to be sold through a variety of retailers. No longer did a consumer have to find an authorized Magnavox dealer or a Sears catalog to buy an Odyssey. An electronic game had finally broken out into the shopping mainstream, and the toy world would never be the same.

Shortly before the NFL owners met in mid-March, the WFL declared that it was alive and well and planning a season for 1975, even though nobody was sure how many teams the league would have. (The WFL hadn't even been organized enough to have a draft yet.) This must have been less than reassuring to NFL refugees Csonka, Kiick, and Warfield. Their contracts were guaranteed even if the league folded. But for their teammates, only deep pay cuts would allow the WFL to move forward.

Rozelle opened the NFL meeting bluntly, saying "1974 brought problems of a greater magnitude than at any time in league history." Hanging over the NFL was the unfinished labor agreement, and a court case that pitted the players against the owners over the legality of the "Rozelle rule." Adding to the league's labor and legal woes were declining attendance figures (down 4.6% for the season). Just as worrisome were the 1.1 million stadium no-shows. This figure was a record and represented 11% of 1974's total paid attendance. League officials felt the no-show problem could be blamed on the demise of the home-game blackout rule, but their concern over the rest of the NFL's mounting problems was real. If the fans thought that too much of the "real world" was creeping into football – that is, the rich greedy owners and the spoiled selfish players were no longer motivated by the love of the game – the NFL's popularity would decline. Obviously the purity of professional football was an illusion. But it was an illusion that both the owners and players needed to maintain for the sake of their own bottom lines.

By meeting's end, the owners had not come up with any labor solutions. An easier problem to solve was the site of the 1977 Super Bowl, which was awarded to Pasadena, California, home of the 100,000-seat Rose Bowl stadium. It would be the first time that a city without an NFL team was allowed to host the game.

On March 29 President Ford signed into law the largest tax cut in U.S. history ($22.8 billion). The new law also extended unemployment benefits by 13 additional weeks. Right on the heels of this economic good news, the WFL held a press conference presenting the "NEW World Football League." Eleven teams – including one with the trio of Dolphin defectors – would play a 20-game season. The league also promised to pay back all its debts. This was going to be a difficult task because the "new" WFL didn't have a television contract. Adding to the intrigue was a $4 million WFL offer to Joe Namath from a revived Chicago franchise.

The WFL's shaky status had to be a disappointment to the 68 NFL players who became free agents on May 1. This number was a record – there had only been 115 free agents in the entire history of the league (with the free agency concept dating back to 1959). Unfortunately the players' prospects, in terms of pay and choices, were much diminished thanks to the WFL's near implosion in 1974.

One player who did stand to profit from being a free agent was Namath, as included in his offer from the WFL was a certified check for $500,000. After spending several weeks considering the prospect of a half million dollars in cash, Namath turned the fledgling league down. There were executives in the NFL (anonymous ones) who thought that the Jets might have been better off if Namath had signed with the new league. At the moment, as the highest paid player in the NFL, Joe posed a unique problem. No other team would be eager to sign him because his salary meant the Jets would be asking for momentous compensation in terms of players and draft picks. Any team signing Namath would, thanks to the Rozelle rule, probably end up in the uninviting position of playing compensation roulette with the commissioner. Yet shelling out another record salary for an aging and oft-injured player – even if he was the 1974 NFL Comeback Player of the Year and named Joe Namath – was an enormous gamble for the Jets.

In other years Munro Games would have kept an anxious eye on Namath's status, but this year it really didn't matter what happened to the quarterback. He wasn't going to be able to single-handedly rescue Munro from its mostly self-inflicted problems. And Munro's use of its star was questionable from the outset. Was the endorsement of an NFL quarterback really going to make people run out and drop a couple hundred dollars on a pool table? The obvious answer was "no." Namath could not rescue the sinking Munro sports line. He was probably wondering if Munro would ever pay him for the Namath games they sold in 1974.

Despite a small rise during the spring in the Consumer Confidence Index, the economy was still struggling mightily with recession. Industrial layoffs were hurting the middle class, and inflation was running at over 10% for the year. Food prices, in particular, rose sharply in May, adding to inflation worries. Major retailers like Sears, Ward, J.C. Penney, and Woolworth's, all had declining profits, with Sears reporting a 61% decline for the first quarter of 1975. The NFL was also lamenting the effects of the economy, claiming that eight teams lost money in 1974. With the league experiencing an overall increase in revenue and each team earning $2.28 million from television and radio rights, the Players Association loudly disputed the notion that any NFL team could have losses.

In July, the NFL players reported to their training camps (without a contract), and before the month ended, the Jets made Joe Namath the highest paid player in football history. His two-year contract, at $450,000 per year, eclipsed even the extravagant money that lured away Kiick, Csonka, and Warfield to the WFL. And speaking of the WFL newcomers, a healthy crowd of more than 25,000 saw Jim Kiick score a last-minute touchdown for the victorious Memphis "Dolphins" on August 2. But without a national television contract, it was questionable as to how many people beyond those in the stands even knew the three former NFL stars made their WFL debut. More ominous signs came from Philadelphia, where only 3,300 people showed up that very same night to watch a Bell victory over the visiting Hawaiians. At least the sight of an empty WFL stadium wasn't televised nationally. But it didn't take long for the new WFL to start crumbling. On September 2, the Chicago Wind – the team that offered $4 million to Namath – was shut down by the WFL.

Montgomery Ward went to a single electric football game in 1975...and that game was from Coleco. Montgomery Ward 1975 *Christmas Book of Values*, page 373. ©Montgomery Ward, Inc. 1975.

Yet unrest wasn't limited to the new league. After two weeks of federally mediated negotiations between the NFL owners and players, the players voted on September 10 to reject the latest contract offer. Within days, the Patriots went on strike, refusing to play their final exhibition game against the Jets. And by September 17, just four days before the start of the regular season, the Jets, Redskins, Giants, and Lions joined the strike. Three additional teams considered striking, while three others, the Oilers, Dolphins, and Vikings, voted not to. Thanks to the endless contract negotiations, a number of players currently viewed the Players Association as the problem. This led to deep divisions within many teams. Highlighting the divide was a walkout by Minnesota's defensive stars Alan Page and Jim Marshall after the Vikings voted 21-19 not to strike.

Fortunately, there were cooler heads on both sides. A temporary agreement between the players and owners came the next day when the owners promised to make a serious contract offer by the following Monday. Not all the players were happy with this truce. A federal mediator had to spend five hours convincing the Patriots to go along with the agreement. But finally the season was ready to start, divided locker rooms and all. After playing just a single regular season game, the players voted overwhelmingly to reject the owners' new proposal, but they did not go out on strike. The season would continue.

September seemed to be the month for sober reflection. The current *Playthings* carried an article lamenting the failure of family action games – the same games that were once hailed "as the messiah for the game industry."

Belonging to this category were the stand-alone electric football and table hockey games that Munro Games and Coleco enthusiastically pushed forward during the sports game boom of the early 70's. Unfortunately, Munro's oversized Family Cup games and Coleco's Trophy line turned out to be red-ink generators. (Family Cup would soon be available in the Sears Surplus Store for $19.99, which was $30 less than the 1974 Sears catalog price.) *Playthings* neatly summed up the problems of the games in the family action game category: "These highly technical, involved mechanisms proved disappointing...the category was not well thought out enough."

In other words, Command Control wasn't very realistic, and neither the IPP nor TTC bases made electric football players run with chalkboard precision. Just because a game was bigger and more elaborate, it didn't improve the overall concept. Electric football was still just electric football, and table hockey was still just table hockey. Big beautiful action games were wonderful on Christmas morning, but after a few weeks of taking up a large chunk of the living room, a family was stuck with a monstrous item that nobody wanted to play with anymore. It was too big to fit under the bed, and the legs had to come off no matter where it was stored. Ultimately, there was a large disassembled item in the attic or the basement. And over the coming months no amount of longing glances could resurrect the game – or the long lost euphoria of Christmas morning.

*Playthings* didn't mention the economy, but it certainly didn't help that some of largest and most expensive sports action games ever made were introduced at the beginning of a recession. The one exception in the family action category was air-powered hockey games. They turned into a "must have" item, so much so that major retailers like Sears, Ward, and Penney were making air hockey the focal point of their toy departments in 1975. This enthusiasm was apparent in the current Sears *Christmas Book*, where two full-color pages were devoted to air hockey. From 7-foot long 175-pound stand-alone behemoths to tabletop models, Sears was covering the entire range of air hockey offerings. The retailer even turned over half of a page to foosball, thanks to Pelé – "the world's greatest soccer player" – who was now playing for the New York franchise of the North American Soccer League.

But beyond air hockey and foosball, the Sears toy section reflected the failure of the family action game category. For 1975, both electric football and table hockey were confined to page 542; it was the first time since 1961 that there wasn't an individual page dedicated to each type of game. Tudor had two electric football games, the scaled-down Super Bowl, which had the prime spot at the top of the page and a No. 500 model. In addition, Tudor's NFL Strategy and Electric Baseball claimed space on the page. Pictured just to the right of Tudor's electric football models were a large

Penney's still held with a three game electric football lineup – all Tudor models. J.C. Penney *Christmas 1975.* ©J.C. Penney, Inc. 1975.

and a small Munro hockey game. It was a demotion for both companies.

A surprising change in a different part of the catalog was that Sears had jettisoned the Odyssey. In its place was a new Sears' exclusive – Atari Pong for $98.95. Sears had gotten rid of Magnavox's version of electronic table tennis and replaced it with the game and name that everybody knew. There wasn't a whole lot of difference between the Magnavox and the Atari in terms of play, but it was an astute move on Sears' part. It was also a more profitable arrangement. What was not a surprise in 1975 was having the economy shake out some of the NFL's numerous licensees from the *Christmas Book*. This year there were only sixteen pages of NFL items – five less than in 1974.

Over in Ward, the slowing sales of electric football and table hockey games prompted a dramatic change. While air-powered hockey games got a full-color page, there was only a single electric football game for sale in the 1975

Christmas catalog – and no table hockey games whatsoever. And oddly, that electric football game was a large Coleco Command Control 5799 game, complete with legs and the original 1970 Coleco frame and grandstand design. (Ward obviously hadn't consulted *Playthings* about the downward trend in family action games.) This Coleco configuration hadn't been seen in the American market since the 1973 J.C. Penney Christmas catalog. Ward's decision to sell this particular model was puzzling, for long past were the days when boys lingered over a catalog page dreaming of Command Control glory. The only "new" feature on the game was the Direct-O-Matic players, and as directional bases went, they weren't very good.

But upon looking closely at the two preceding Ward pages, it was easy to see that they were packed with Coleco items. Three Coleco Power-Jet Hockey games dominated page 371, and Coleco made a clean sweep of page 372 with four pool tables and an arcade-sized Coleco Bowl-A-Matic 600 game. So the reason for Ward selling a large and elderly Command Control electric football game was simple – Coleco was supplying the game on the cheap. It's likely that Coleco approached Ward offering to throw electric football in with all the other Coleco items for next to nothing. The $14.88 price for the game supplied evidence of such a deal and made Coleco's top-of-the-line model cheaper than two of the three Tudor games Ward sold in 1974. And if Ward ended up having a half-price electric football clearance sale this Christmas, they would still come out with a little profit. It was clear from the layout that electric football was a second-string player in 1975. Ward had positioned the game on an orange background next to an orange Coleco pinball machine. It was very easy to turn the page and not even notice the game was there. The last time Ward had offered only a single electric football game in its Christmas catalog was 1961 (a single Gotham model). And you had to go all the way back to 1955 to find a Ward Christmas catalog without a table hockey game. But Coleco was hardly suffering by the omission of its trademark item. The Power-Jet Hockey line was making table hockey seem quite old-fashioned.

Another new item for Ward this year was the Magnavox Odyssey ($99.99). The game had been a nice seller for Sears during the previous Christmas, and Ward was eager for the chance to cash in on the home video game trend. Profits would be tougher this year because it was the first time Magnavox unleashed the game to more than just selected retailers. But there was surely plenty of money still to be made with the Odyssey.

Only in the J.C. Penney Christmas catalog did electric football get the traditional pre-recession treatment in 1975. Just like in the old days, Tudor had three games with the four-team No. 655 NFL Championship game as the top model. It was priced just a shade under $20, while the NFL No. 635 carried a $15.88 tag. Tudor's entry-level NFL model, the Packers-Dolphins No. 515, was

$11.88. From outward appearances, only J.C. Penney still had faith in electric football as an anchor toy item.

Unfortunately, the football players who put their faith in the WFL found themselves unemployed on October 22. After 11 games and another $10 million in losses, the league could go on no more. Obviously the NFL was ecstatic to see the new league finally implode. But the WFL had already done its damage by increasing NFL payrolls. Rozelle immediately issued a season-long ban on signing WFL players, but by early November a federal judge overturned this NFL policy. Rozelle finally agreed that WFL players could be signed after getting clearance from his office. NFL teams were given until midnight November 26, the day before Thanksgiving, to sign orphaned WFL players. But a still active NFL policy was going to discourage most teams from dipping heavily into the WFL pool – the Rozelle rule. It wasn't clear whether a player's old NFL team could make a free agent compensation claim. Any team signing Csonka, Kiick, or Warfield might be asked to give the Dolphins draft picks and players.

The Magnavox Odyssey became one of the hot Christmas items in 1975. Even the $100 price tag didn't scare buyers away. Montgomery Ward 1975 *Christmas Book of Values*, page 297. ©Montgomery Ward, Inc. 1975.

As the Christmas shopping season loomed on the horizon, retailers were anxious not only about the state of mind of shoppers, but also about another condensed shopping season. Thanksgiving was falling on November 27, which, like 1974, meant that it would be December by the time consumers returned to work after the holiday. A shortened shopping season was a challenge in the best of economic times. But there was the possibility of a positive Christmas season. Inflation was starting to fall, the Dow was up 35% from the start of the year, and the Consumer Confidence Index had been on a slow rise throughout the year. There were still some negative indicators hanging around, like the 8.6% unemployment rate and the declining savings rate (from 10.6% to 7.8% of after tax income). Retailers had little idea what the next four weeks would hold. All were hopeful, yet justifiably nervous.

Regardless of how the selling season went, electric football was going to have its lowest Christmas season profile in many years. For the second year in a row there was no Sears Award of Excellence for Tudor, and the retailer wasn't featuring the Super Bowl very prominently in its newspaper ads. Most of the time there was only a description of the game and price ($12.99), without a photo. And given the limited space Ward devoted to electric football in its catalog, it was no surprise that Ward's toy ads using the game were sparse. When the Coleco game did appear, it was for the highly discounted price of $9.99.

As in 1974, Toys R Us was focusing its marketing on the Tudor NFL No. 515, whose price remained under $10. But like Sears and Ward, electric football was overshadowed at Toys R Us by air hockey. In an advertising booklet published over the Thanksgiving weekend, Toys R Us promoted four air-powered hockey games – two from Munro, one from Coleco, and one from Brunswick – versus a single NFL No. 515. It wasn't so long ago that Toys R Us was using multiple electric football games in every single print ad. Toys R Us also ran single page ads over the holiday weekend, ads which included a $9.86 NFL No. 515 model. Joining Toys R Us as the only other major retailer to advertise electric football over Thanksgiving of 1975 was Ward.

Despite the economy, the snub from Ward, and the lack of advertising support from Sears, J.C. Penney, or any number of other formerly supportive retailers, Tudor was still in the most favorable position among electric football makers. From the local auto part store to the Gibson Discount Center chain, to the Sears catalog, Tudor electric football games were still easily found. And not surprisingly, the most frequently promoted Tudor games were the No. 400, the No. 500, and the NFL No. 515. Very few of Tudor's large NFL games made it into toy ads, thanks to their nearly $20 price tag. Especially rare was a print sighting of the NFL Championship No. 655 game. In the retail climate of Christmas 1975, the $10 NFL No. 515 seemed to be priced just right.

Coleco electric football models had sporadic availability outside the Ward catalog. Some Command Control games were being sold at nearly clearance prices before Thanksgiving while the economy model held its price line at $6. And it was the small Pro Stars game without Command Control that was advertised most often – with "often" being a relative term. There really wasn't much Coleco football to see this year. But Coleco wasn't overly concerned about electric football these days. The Power-Jet Hockey line was clearly the item of profit for Coleco.

Munro was delivering on most of its Hover Glide hockey orders and table hockey games, but they had stopped manufacturing electric football games months ago. Most of what was out in retail circulation now was leftover stock from 1974. As a result, Munro electric football games were not easy to find. Many chains had tried to liquidate their Munro electric football stock well before the Christmas season started (the Philadelphia-based John Wanamaker's chain was unloading large Munro games in October for $8). Many of the retailers that still carried Namath electric football

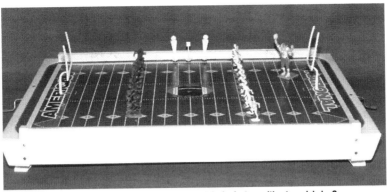

At Munro things had gotten so out of hand that games left the factory without any labels. Can you imagine waking up to a "naked" Bob Griese model on Christmas morning...especially when you wanted Air-Hockey?

games had titles like "Bargain Basket," and "Bargain Center." It was a sad convergence that Namath games had sunk to such an ignominious point while Namath himself suffered through the most disappointing season of his career. After starting the season at 2-1, the Jets lost nine of the next ten games. For the season, Namath would complete only 48% of his passes and throw almost twice as many interceptions as touchdown passes.

As December moved forward, retailers gleefully reported double-digit sales increases over 1974. Sears, Ward, Woolworth's, and Macy's were all reporting strong overall sales, and toys were no exception. Air hockey games led the way, but this year they had competition from an unexpected item, and one that had a much larger profit margin – electronic games. The Magnavox Odyssey, whose basic version was priced at $99, was already sold out at many retailers, including Macy's, Ward, and Wanamaker's. Sales managers at these stores were astounded that games costing nearly triple digits were in such heavy demand, but they were grateful. And for more than just the profit. Big-ticket electronic sales seem to be a sure sign the recession was waning.

With Odyssey turning into a hot item, was Sears regretting its decision to stop selling the game? Not at all. The Atari Pong home electronic game had proven every bit as attractive and lucrative as the Odyssey. Most Sears' stores were completely sold out by early December, with Sears running apology ads in local newspapers due to Pong shortages.

By mid-December the Super Bowl game was still holding at $12.97 despite its sporadic appearance in Sears toy ads. And overall it seemed that Tudor electric football games were holding their value well this year with most discounts being limited to a dollar or two. The surge in consumer spending was a big part of the increased demand for Tudor's games, but Munro and Coleco were not experiencing the same kind of sales increases. Both companies were again seeing their electric football games being offered for clearance prices. On December 21, the final day of the NFL season, Munro's Joe Namath games and Coleco's Super Action Command Control games could be found for less than $9. And it wasn't uncommon to find them going for as little as $7. The economy might have been recovering, but electric football sales were not, at least for Coleco and Munro.

Air hockey games were going strong up to the final week of shopping, and then they seemed to reenact the electric football market of 1974. With so many different models available, not all of them sold equally well. Like the previous year, it was the tabletop-sized games that had the most appeal. So as Christmas closed in, retailers found themselves with a glut of large stand-alone hockey games – particularly Munro models. Discounts came fast and furious with $20-$40 being slashed off already competitive prices. Savvy last-minute shoppers were treated to some of the best air hockey bargains ever seen.

President Ford did his part to further the economic recovery on Tuesday, December 23, by signing an extension of the recently enacted tax cuts. This would carry the new cuts into 1976, giving the average family more money to spend in the New Year. It was most likely just a coincidence, but Macy's flagship store on Fifth Avenue reported this day as the most profitable one in the company's history.

Christmas landed on Thursday, just two days before the start of the NFL playoffs. So it would seem to be another ideal year for an electric football game, considering they were still prominently mentioned in the Dear Santa letters printed by local newspapers. But times were continuing to change – it was quite possible that electric football wasn't the biggest item on a Christmas list anymore. If a Magnavox Odyssey or air hockey game were your top choices, but Santa left "only" electric football, then Christmas was a disappointment. There was no way around the fact that electric football just was not as exotic and exciting as it once was, especially when pitted against the Odyssey and Pong. Further proof of this came from the Christmas catalogs, which were giving electric football treatment to other items while clearly pulling back on the game itself.

No football games were televised on Christmas Day, but both the Sun Bowl and Fiesta Bowl were televised on Friday afternoon. So it is likely that many electric football games were still buzzing by the time the NFL playoffs got under way on Saturday, although any boy with an NFL No. 515 might have been disappointed because the Dolphins on his game missed the playoffs for the first time in five years. Edging out the Dolphins were the surprising Colts who, after winning only two games in 1974, managed ten wins in the current season. But the Colts playoff run only lasted until Saturday afternoon. After leading the home Steelers 10-7 in the third quarter, the Colts gave up three unanswered touchdowns in a 28-10 defeat. In the day's late game, the 12-2 Rams took a 28-9 halftime lead over the visiting Cardinals and never looked back. Finally the Rams would play an NFC championship game on their home field.

So if the Vikings beat the wild card Cowboys on Sunday – and the 12-2 Vikes were heavily favored – they had to travel to balmy Los Angeles for the title game. The advantage provided by the Artic-like Minnesota weather would be missing this year. Unfortunately, the weather didn't freeze the Cowboys who won the game on a controversial touchdown with 24 seconds left. During the 50-yard "Hail Mary" pass – and this pass is acknowledged as the "original" Hail Mary – the Cowboys' Drew Pearson appeared to get open by pushing the Vikings' Nate Wright to the ground. The Vikings faithful in Metropolitan Stadium were incensed and littered the field with debris as the 17-14 loss sunk in.

Almost as exciting, yet fortunately not as controversial, was the late game in Oakland. The Raiders led 31-14 early in the fourth quarter, then held off a furious Bengal rally for a 31-28 win – and a trip to Pittsburgh the following Sunday. It's possible that one of the biggest events of the year in professional football happened on Tuesday, December 30, in a Minneapolis courtroom. On that day a Federal judge ruled that the Rozelle rule violated federal antitrust laws by limiting the players' ability to seek better employment opportunities. And the judge went further to say that the rule had damaged the careers of the 15 NFL players who filed the suit. Rozelle's prophetic 1972 warning of pro football being perceived as more of a business than a sport never seemed more true.

The year would end with a nationally televised doubleheader of the Peach Bowl, and the first Sugar Bowl ever played in the Superdome. Earning a very happy New Year's in New Orleans was Alabama, who defeated Penn State 13-6. The victory gave the Crimson Tide an 11-1 record...and also a chance of ending up as the nation's top team.

Lynn Swann soars over Mark Washington to make an acrobatic catch in Super Bowl X on January 18, 1976. The Steelers defeated the Cowboys 21-17 and Swann was the game's MVP. (AP Photo/NFL Photos)

# 32 CHANGES CONTINUE IN THE TOY WORLD

**O**hio State had a simple task on New Year's Day – win the Rose Bowl and become the undefeated and undisputed national champions of college football. UCLA, however, had other ideas and gave the Buckeyes a thorough 23-10 beating. This left the door open for the Oklahoma Sooners, who gladly stepped through it with a 14-6 win over Michigan in the Orange Bowl. Despite both teams having identical 11-1 records, Oklahoma was voted the nation's top team by both the AP and UPI polls. Ohio State dropped to the fourth spot. A 12-0 Arizona State team finished second.

New Year's Day offered up the usual eight-plus hours of televised football, and the day ended up being a rewarding one to spend sedentary on the couch. But the NFL wouldn't play for three more days, and there were no other televised college football games to bridge the gap this year. It was easy to imagine electric football games being packed away rather than played with during this lull in the action.

The Rozelle rule outcome made it a less than happy start to the New Year for the NFL hierarchy. In not having the ruling go into effect immediately, the judge offered the league a chance to appeal the decision and, more importantly, a chance to "reconsider" its stance on compensation. From any viewpoint, it was a major victory for the players in their quest for something most working Americans took for granted – the freedom to find a better job. Encouraged by the ruling, the players were determined to push the owners even harder for labor concessions.

But the main focus for NFL fans right now was championship Sunday. In Pittsburgh the wind chill dipped to minus 14, serving up a frozen field, frostbitten fingers…and thirteen turnovers. Somehow the Steelers survived eight of those turnovers to beat the Raiders 16 -10. It was the sixth time in nine years that a Raiders season ended one heartbreaking game shy of the Super Bowl. Over in the NFC and out in the comfortable sunshine of Los Angeles, the Rams started the championship game as 7-point favorites. Unfortunately, "7" turned out to be the total number of points the Rams would score – the Cowboys scored 37. In victory the Cowboys became the first wild card team to reach a Super Bowl.

The NFL's 10th Super Bowl was scheduled for Sunday, January 18, in Miami. As usual, it was a case of things getting bigger each year, with record ticket costs (face value of $20), a record number of media personnel (1,735), and a record number of private jets (50) flying into Miami on game day. Chrysler, Ford, Nestlé, American Express, and Coca Cola were all entertaining important clients during Super Bowl week, but outdoing them all was Lincoln-Mercury. The luxury carmaker was not only brining its top 600 salespeople and families to the game, they were renting a cruise ship and taking everybody to the Bahamas. It was an extravagant new standard for Super Bowl week corporate entertainment.

Munro had put a lot of money and hope into its air-powered hockey line, only to see the games put on sale at the end of 1975. *The Morning Herald*, page 25, December 18, 1975.

On the Orange Bowl field – its disintegrating Poly Turf surface had been patched and glued in the days leading up to the game – the Steelers were slight favorites. Luckily the game did not mirror the desperate state of the playing surface. Instead, it turned out to be the most entertaining and well-played Super Bowl game to date, with the Steelers holding off the Cowboys for a 21-17 victory. Pittsburgh wide receiver Lynn Swann was the game MVP. Three of his catches, including a fourth-quarter touchdown, were so acrobatic that they are forever a part of Super Bowl lore. But even with Swann's heroics the game went down to the final play, which ended with the Steelers intercepting a potential Cowboys' touchdown pass. One of the game's little known legacies is that it would be the last outdoor Super Bowl ever played on artificial turf.

By now the sales figures were coming in from the Christmas period, and it wasn't just the retailers' imaginations that shoppers were spending more freely. The Commerce Department announced that retail sales for December increased 15.5% compared with the same period in 1974. And for the four-week period ending on December 27, Sears was reporting $1.77

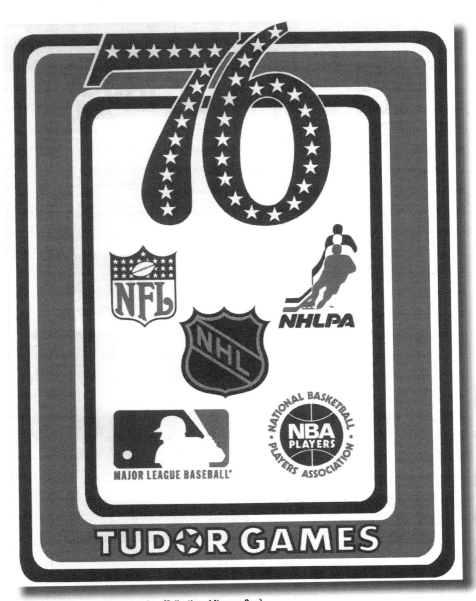

The cover of Tudor's 1976 sales catalog. (Collection of Norman Sas.)

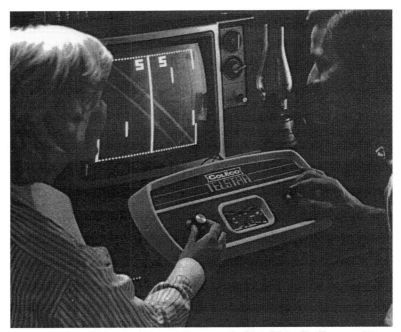

Coleco came to the 1976 Toy Fair with its own video game – the Coleco Telstar. *Playthings*, page 331, February 1977. Courtesy of The Strong®, Rochester, New York.

billion in gross sales – this was an 11.5% increase over 1974 and the highest four-week figure in company history. For the same period, J.C. Penney reported an 18.1% increase in sales from 1974, while Ward had to "settle" for a 10.4% increase. (The most impressive sales increase was reported by the S.S. Kresge chain – 28.8%.) These increases left retailers and toy makers feeling pretty good about the coming year, especially when January sales figures continued showing double-digit increases. Adding to the optimism was the Dow Jones average, which climbed 50 points through the opening weeks of January to hit the 900 mark for the first time in two years.

As the Toy Fair geared up for its annual two-week run, there was an almost buoyant atmosphere in the hallways. It had been a great year for toys, the sales figures from Sears, J.C. Penney, and Ward made that very clear. And this year most toy makers were carrying very little inventory over into 1976. But the key word here is "most." There were exceptions of course, and one company that still had inventory both on retailers' shelves and in its warehouse was Munro Games. Rumors put Servotronics' 1975 losses in the $5 million range, with most of this amount coming from the Munro subsidiary. Sales of the air-powered Hover Glide hockey line had been so poor that retailers had no choice but to put the games on clearance in the weeks leading up to Christmas.

Munro's most glaring mistake in air hockey was not creating a tabletop model. Brunswick, Ideal, and Coleco all were marketing a model that fit neatly on a dining room table. Munro's best effort in this category was Glide Hockey (notice the word "hover" is missing from the title), which was actually a game without any air power. Needless to say, this game required a lot of muscle and still didn't play very well – even with a rolling ball-bearing puck and an extra-slick playing surface. And surprisingly it wasn't priced that much cheaper than games that actually had air blowing up through their "ice." So Munro really couldn't compete in the most competitive category of air hockey. That left the company in the same position it had defaulted to in electric football – the maker of large and expensive games. Unfortunately the "large game" segment of both markets was the least profitable place to be. Munro should have already learned that lesson through the failure of the Day/Nite electric football line. Something else Munro should have learned from electric football was to not dive impulsively into a market as the tide of interest was going out. But the allure of air hockey proved too tempting. As a result, the company's financial health was on life support.

With money a major problem, there were no Munro ads in *Playthings*. The company was contracted to supply a table hockey game to Sears and was also still attempting to continue marketing Hover Glide games, but electric football had vanished. Besides the games not selling, the star of Joe Namath was fading from the sporting universe. His presence on Munro's flagship electric football game only seemed to emphasize the desperate shape the company was in. Namath's picture was still on the games because Munro had no ideas and no money. It's even questionable as to whether Namath knew he was still endorsing an electric football game. Already resigned from his consulting duties was Don Munro. Not only was he disgusted with the dysfunctional organization Munro Games had become, he knew at this point there was little chance of the company surviving 1976.

A company whose fortunes were headed in the opposite direction was Coleco. This year Coleco showed off its diversification by arriving at the Fair with a home video game system – the Coleco Telstar. It would come wired with three different games (tennis, handball, and hockey) and be available at many different retailers. Montgomery Ward, Toys R Us, and even the Western Auto chain had already agreed to carry the Telstar. And thanks to the wide distribution of so many other Coleco items, the new video game system was assured space almost anywhere Coleco wanted it. A suggested retail price of $60 made it one of the most affordable home video games ever offered. Telstar was priced to sell. Retailers were going to be happy to have the game. A whole new stream of revenue was opening up for Coleco.

Coleco's Power-Jet Hockey line was not doing badly, either, finishing second in sales only to Brunswick Air Hockey. What made Power-Jet

**A page from the 1976 Tudor sales catalog (Collection of Norman Sas.)**

Hockey games so formidable was that they were widely available through major toy retailers like Sears, Ward, J.C. Penney, and Toys R Us. This was as close to "everywhere" as you could get (like Tudor with electric football). Table hockey, once one of Coleco's prime items, now found itself overshadowed by air hockey. It would still be available; shoppers would just have to look a little harder to find it. Table hockey wasn't pulling in the profit of air hockey, but Coleco had no thoughts of giving up on its once signature game.

Electric football was a different story. Long gone were the days when Coleco expected significant revenue from the game, and it was clear that electric football was now just riding on the back bumper of Coleco's more glamorous and profitable products. All you had to do was look at the

**EARL SHORES | RODDY GARCIA**

models Coleco brought to the Fair – the 5780 Command Control game and the nearly miniature 5755 Pro Stars game – to see that the company's heart was no longer in electric football. It was hard to believe that these two withered games descended from the same grandiose sports action aspirations that created the "Coleco World of Sports" back in 1970. Summing up the uninspired state of Coleco electric football was the game Ward was planning to sell in the fall – the same 5799 Command Control model it sold in 1975. In sports action terms the game was a dinosaur. The design hadn't changed in five years. Coleco could argue that games like Mouse Trap and Monopoly hadn't changed in decades, but these were classic toys. The same could hardly be said about any Coleco electric football game. The only reason for Coleco continuing to dabble in electric football at this point was to simply take shelf space away from Tudor. Otherwise the company was doing little to show that it cared about the game. Coleco wasn't even bothering to promote the game in its 1976 sales catalog.

Despite Coleco's unwillingness to give up its meager market share, the company's plunge into home video games was, unofficially at least, ceding the sports action game category back to Tudor. The days of running multipage *Playthings* spreads promoting sports games were long gone. Also gone for Coleco's sports games were the days of expensive television ads. Adding Coleco's apathy to Munro's debt and disorganization meant one thing for electric football: Tudor was the last one standing.

It might seem that Norman was especially clairvoyant in deciding to scale down the Tudor electric football line for 1976, but the decision to discard the generic No. 640 and No. 600 models was simply a bottom-line decision. Neither game had been very popular during the two years each had been offered. Also not finding a solid niche were the hanging NFL Team retailer packages. Stores just weren't willing to find the space for the players. The team packs were a high-maintenance item, and it was difficult to put together a team display in the same aisle where the games were sold. These aisles were usually full of sports games, which came in large boxes. So the retailer team packs were retired after just a single year.

Tudor had six games on display in its showroom, including four NFL games (No. 515, No. 635, No. 645, and NFL Championship No. 655), as well as the generic No. 400 and No. 500 models. Except for the Championship game, all the other NFL models would come with regional team combinations. None of these models were exactly new, and this was reflected in Tudor's sales catalog. Game photos dated back to 1973, while the player photos came from a layout Lee did back in 1971. There weren't even any announcements about the two new NFL expansion teams that would be added to the Tudor team line this year. In the past, not refreshing the catalog could be viewed as a way to keep costs down. The same could be said for 1976, but Tudor had another reason not to bother to update the catalog – there wasn't anyone left to compete with. If retailers wanted electric football and wanted electric football games that would actually sell, they would contact Tudor.

One of the showrooms receiving plenty of traffic this year was Magnavox. The company had run a full-page ad in the February issue of *Playthings* aimed directly at any toy buyer who was considering stocking up on Atari's Pong or the new Coleco Telstar system. "Selling the number one home video game is as easy as playing it" read the headline, and the ad further emphasized the Odyssey's top-dog status by adding the line: "First in sales because it's first in features." The Odyssey was expanding beyond the basic 100 and 200 models to include a 300, 400, and a 500 system. There was even going to be a Magnavox television with a built-in Odyssey game. Heavy ad support was promised for all retailers, but at this point, video games were practically selling themselves. And thanks to the increased competition from multiple game makers, video games were going to be more affordable than ever.

In 1976 Lee Payne became the Director of Industrial Design at Georgia Tech. This marked the end of his 16-year run with Tudor. (Collection of Roddy Garcia.)

During a Super Bowl week press conference, Commissioner Rozelle referred to this time in professional football as "a very negative period," citing the labor conflict and court battles facing the NFL. Legal costs for 1975 were estimated at $3.5 million, and the litigation and labor issues were being blamed for the 10% drop in attendance. So it was a less than ebullient group of owners who gathered in California for their annual mid-March meeting. Newly elected NFLPA president Dick Anderson was scheduled to address the owners about the players' concerns, but before he even spoke a word, the players filed a lawsuit for back damages caused by the Rozelle rule. Needless to say Anderson got a chilly reception. Also receiving a cold shoulder were the owners of the Birmingham and Memphis WFL franchises who came to the meeting hoping to get their teams admitted to the NFL. Not surprisingly, both applications were turned down. Now that Memphis had no league to play in, it was speculated that Csonka, Kiick, and Warfield would finally become NFL free agents. (The "personal services" clause in their contracts had obligated them to the Memphis owner despite the WFL folding.) Before the meeting ended, the owners awarded the 1978 Super Bowl to New Orleans and scheduled an expansion draft for Seattle and Tampa Bay teams on March 30. The regular college draft would take place a week a later.

In the days leading up to the college draft, the Browns signed Paul Warfield, and the Giants signed Larry Csonka. So all eyes now turned to the Dolphins –

In four years Munro went from electric football trendsetter to bankruptcy. The elaborate Day/Nite game never brought Nick Trbovich and Don Munro the success they had hoped for. (Collection of Earl Shores.)

would the team demand compensation for either player? When the draft ended, neither the Dolphins nor the league had taken any action against the Browns and Giants. The message being sent was clear – the Rozelle rule was no longer being enforced. There was no league announcement, no clarification, and no legalese statement reserving judgment or action. There was just…nothing. All the NFL players who were set to become free agents on May 1 were now free beyond their wildest dreams.

Besides Warfield and Csonka, another prominent football groundbreaker was on the move in the spring of 1976. That person's name was Lee Payne. Since his redesign of Tudor's showroom and packaging in 1973 – for which he won a "Package of the Year" award from *Packaging Design* magazine – Lee's contributions to the Tudor line had been shrinking. Clearly the status of electric football in the toy world was not what it once was, and innovation throughout the mechanical sports action game genre had come to a standstill. But Lee's decision to move on had less to do with electric football than it did with the fact that he was always looking for a new challenge. The one he was taking on this time was the biggest of his life. He had agreed to become the Director of Industrial Design at Georgia Tech. This meant that both his family and Lee Payne Associates would be uprooted to Atlanta. There, Lee would attempt to revive a struggling academic program and also run a business. His long-standing relationship with Tudor would finally come to a close.

By the time the first NFL training camp got underway – credit new Eagles coach Dick Vermeil for getting into the Bicentennial spirit by breaking out the pads on July 4 – it was clear that free agency wasn't destroying the NFL.

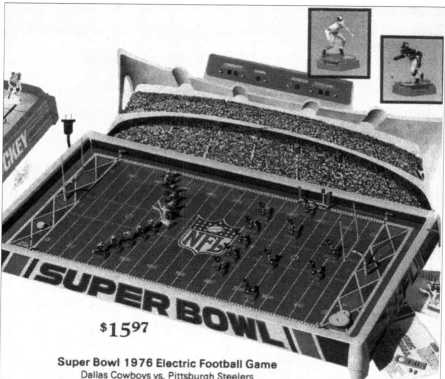

# $15⁹⁷

### Super Bowl 1976 Electric Football Game
#### Dallas Cowboys vs. Pittsburgh Steelers

Two NFL Teams in official Super Bowl uniforms run plays using your strategies.

HOW TO PLAY: Total Team Control dials in each platform base let you set direction for each player. Tackles, ends, guards, backs, in five poses, move left, right or straight, make sharp turns, wide arcs or end sweeps. Switch on game and field vibrates sending players off in your patterns. You set the pace for each play with speed-control dial. Automatic timer starts and stops with each play. Players may be removed from bases for strategy sessions or display.

WHAT YOU GET: Metal gridiron playing field 31⅝x17⅜x3 in. high. Grandstand 12 in. high with adjustable scoreboard. 24 plastic figures with 2 triple-threat quarterbacks, magnetic 10-yd. marker with movable chain marker, magnetic ball, down marker, 4 goal line flags.

ELECTRICAL INFORMATION: UL listed: 110–120-volt, 60-Hz. AC. 6 watts. 6-foot cord. Not recommended for ages under 8.

FOR AGES: 8 years and up.

ORDERING INFORMATION:
79 N 65538C—Shpg. wt. 8 lbs.........$15.97

### Electric Football Game

HOW TO PLAY: Total Team Control bases determine movement in each figure. Players move left, right, straight, making sharp turns, wide arcs or sweeps. 2 quarterbacks carry ball, pass and kick by hand lever. Switch on and metal field vibrates sending players off. You control speed with dial, automatic timer starts, stops with each play.

WHAT YOU GET: Metal field, 26⁷⁄₁₆x15⅜ in. wide, stand with scoreboard, 24 plastic players, 10-yd. marker, down indicator.

ELECTRICAL INFO: UL listed; 110–120-v., 60-Hz. AC. 6 w. 6-ft. cord. Not for ages under 8.

FOR AGES: 8 years and up.

ORDERING INFORMATION:
79 N 65536C—Shpg. wt. 4 lbs. .......$9.97

### $9⁹⁷

The 1976 Sears *Christmas Book* with the Tudor Super Bowl and No. 500 model. Sears 1976 *Christmas Book*, page 483. ©Sears, Roebuck and Co. 1976.

Unfounded were fears that major market teams (the Giants, Jets, and Rams) and warm weather teams (Dolphins, Chargers, and Rams) would sign all the top free-agent players. In fact John Riggins, who was considered the top free-agent running back, moved from the Jets to the Redskins. Still, there were plenty of other issues for the owners to worry about. The NLRB had found the NFL guilty of illegal and unfair labor practices during the 1974 players strike. A 69-page report by Judge Charles Schneider did not paint a flattering portrait of the league hierarchy, concluding that the NFL had unlawfully denied the NFLPA access to information about player injuries, player contracts, stadium leases, and the league's contract with commissioner Rozelle. Schneider further ruled that three union officials, including former union president Bill Curry, were jettisoned from their teams because of union activity. These players were to be reinstated with back pay.

On Thursday, July 15, some remarkable news came out of Buffalo. But it wasn't the anticipated story of O.J. Simpson being traded to the Los Angeles Rams. This story came from the business world, and to many in toys it wasn't a surprise. Servotronics announced that it would consolidate most of Munro's production to the Munro Games plant in Burlington, Ontario. Only the Tucco Puzzle division would continue operating in Arcade, New York. Most of the inventory and the equipment at the Arcade plant would be liquidated. The vast and mostly unoccupied facility would then serve as "a warehouse and distribution center for servicing United States customers." Obviously a large number of Munro workers would soon be joining the ranks of the unemployed, although the company wouldn't reveal exactly how many jobs would be lost. For those working on the Munro shop floor, this turn of events was hardly a surprise. Everybody on the inside knew the company was in deep, deep trouble.

The reason for this drastic action was simple – Servotronics needed cash. It turned out that over $12 million worth of loans to Munro Games had been called after the company stopped making payments on its debt. Besides the American Stock Exchange suspending all trading of Servotronics stock, the lack of payments had prompted two major U.S. banks – Citibank and Manufacturer's Traders Trust Co. – to sue Servotronics for payment of the loans. Under pressure from the Securities & Exchange Commission, Servotronics filed a new financial statement on Wednesday, July 21. This time the company's losses for 1975 totaled not $5 million, but $9.5 million, with Munro Games being blamed for $8.9 million of that figure. It was a massive financial hole that had been papered over by creative accounting. And the losses were continuing to mount through the first half of 1976, conservatively adding $3 million more of debt. The liquidation of the Arcade plant would hopefully allow Munro to work out a debt agreement with the banks.

While these decisions gave Servotronics a chance to save its skin, the U.S. version of Munro Games, the one that traced its lineage back to Don Munro Sr. and the birth of table hockey, now ceased to exist. Under the new plan the Canadian plant would continue making air hockey and table hockey games, shipping them to Arcade for distribution in the states. But electric football was finished. The Burlington plant had no electric football production scheduled for 1976. The leftover inventory was all there would ever be of Munro electric football. It was the most spectacular flameout ever seen in sports games: from Day/Nite electric football – one of the landmarks of electric football innovation – to the collection agency in just four short years.

A lone Coleco electric football in the 1976 Montgomery Ward *Christmas Catalog*, page 359. ©Montgomery Ward, Inc. 1976.

Servotronics' restated earnings were published in the *Wall Street Journal* on Thursday, July 22, and the very next evening the Steelers defeated the College All-Stars in Chicago 24-0. Actually the game was stopped in the third quarter when monsoon rains flooded the field. Soon thousands of fans flooded the field, using the waterlogged artificial turf as a giant Slip'n Slide. When several groups of fans tore the goal posts down, the game was called. It was a sad ending to what turned out to be the final NFL-College All-Star game ever played.

The rest of the NFL exhibition season got under way on July 31, and proved uneventful until the end of August when there was an official vote on a player contract. The players rejected the new proposal, citing the similarity of the proposed compensation rules to the old Rozelle rule. Since the Rozelle rule had been declared illegal, the players weren't about to sign a contract that would essentially legalize it. While the vote made it appear that the players were united, there was a lingering and growing distrust of the NFLPA. Membership had declined to the point where less than 60% of eligible NFL players now belonged to the union. Feeding the antiunion feeling was a rift between players who wanted a hardline stance against any kind of limitations on player movement (the position of NFLPA executive director Ed Garvey), and those players who felt it was reasonable for teams to expect compensation. But despite these misgivings, there was no talk of a strike. The season would again move forward without a new player contract.

Thirteen NFL games were played on opening day, Sunday, September 12, including an AFC championship game rematch between the Steelers and the Raiders. The Raiders got a bit of revenge by scoring 24 fourth-quarter points

J.C. Penney continued to sell three electric football games. And this year they were selling Division sets of NFL teams. J.C. Penney *Christmas 1976*, page 393. ©J.C. Penney, Inc. 1976.

and stunning the Steelers 31-28. Monday night's game featured the promising matchup of the Bills and Dolphins. Ratings for *Monday Night Football* had risen 6% in 1975 – over 40 million people were now tuning in to see the NFL on a weeknight – and this game was certain to draw similar numbers. But neither O.J. Simpson's return to the Buffalo lineup or a home crowd of 77,000 could prevent the Bills from losing to the Dolphins for the 13th straight time.

Christmas catalogs from Sears, Ward, and J.C. Penney had just begun their journeys to households across the country, and by the following week Sears celebrated its 90th anniversary by opening the "Big Toy Box" section of its retail stores. In the Sears catalog, Tudor's Super Bowl was the focus of page 483. It was the same No. 635-based game of the previous two years, and the retailer even kept the price the same as 1975 ($15.97). Positioned on the page just below the Super Bowl was the No. 500 model, whose price had increased by more than a dollar this year to $9.97. Tudor landed two more items on the page, including NFL Strategy and electric baseball. All these Tudor offerings competed with a very lonely Munro hockey game. Sears' toy buyers probably wished they'd picked another supplier for table hockey. There were serious questions about how many games Munro would be able to deliver during the Christmas season.

The J.C. Penney Divisional team sets. J.C. Penney *Christmas 1976*, page 393. ©J.C. Penney, Inc. 1976.

This was the second straight year that Sears stuffed all the sports games onto a single page. And for the second straight year, electronic games and air hockey games got the kind of backing electric football and table hockey used to receive. Four different Pong games were laid out across a color two-page spread, with prices ranging from $65-$99. Air-powered hockey games were also positioned across multiple pages, and there were even two different Pelé soccer games, including an air-powered Coleco version that was a hybrid of table and air hockey. But while the economy continued to improve and the demand for electronic games continued to grow, shakeout from the recession was still ever present. Consumers had become much pickier, and this was reflected in Sears only having twelve pages devoted to NFL-licensed items. It was the lowest NFL page count since 1972.

The direction of the toy world was easy to see in the 1976 Ward Christmas catalog. Featured in full color on page 6 was the brand new Ward Video World of Sports. This exclusive cost $57.88 and could play three different games – tennis, hockey, and handball. (What the ad didn't reveal was that the new console was actually a Coleco Telstar system with a Ward label.) Elsewhere there was a two-page video game spread including the Magnavox 400 model and two other Pong clones. Comparing Ward's treatment of electronic games versus the sports action category in 1976 – a single Coleco electric football model and no table hockey – and the retailer's view was clear. Other than air hockey, traditional sports action games were hardly worth bothering with. In fact there were more soccer games (3) in the Ward catalog than electric football.

The only retailer still keeping the faith in electric football was J.C. Penney. In what might be viewed as a last stand, Penney devoted an entire color page to football, mixing in Tudor's NFL Strategy and Cadaco's classic Foto-Electric Football with three Tudor NFL electric football models. Tudor's offerings were almost the same as the previous year – the NFL No. 655, the NFL No. 635 (Dolphins and Jets this year), and a No. 515 with the Redskins and Chiefs. But the No. 655 had been scaled back to include just two teams, the Rams and Cowboys. The reason J.C. Penney eliminated the two AFC teams from the game was simple – to keep it under $20. Although the retailer had given up on selling regionalized games this year, there was still a way to get your favorite teams. Sears and Ward may have been scaling back electric football, but Penney had come up with a new Tudor item to sell – divisional sets of teams. All 28 NFL teams were available, organized by each of the six divisions in the league. Numbers and bases were included with each set. It was a beautiful page that stayed true to the colorful sports action advertising tradition started by Sears back in its 1962 catalog.

In mid-October, a verdict was rendered on the NFL's final appeal of the Rozelle rule. Agreeing that the rule was restrictive and illegal was a federal appeals court judge in St. Louis, who went on to say that the issue should be resolved by collective bargaining between the players and owners. Both sides welcomed the ruling – it seemed to bring genuine hope to finally resolving the player contract. Thankfully, the action out on the field at this point in the season was much more interesting than courtroom proceedings. On the top of the standings three teams – the Colts, Cowboys, and Raiders – were all 8-1. Just as fascinating was the bottom of the standings where both the Giants and the expansion Tampa Bay Buccaneers were 0-9. The Giants finally got a win on November 14 over the Redskins. Tampa, unfortunately, didn't have the same luck, and by the time Thanksgiving arrived on November 25 the Buccaneers were 0-11.

Coming into the holiday weekend almost equally winless was electric football. The game was nearly invisible in toy ads this year, being totally shut out by Sears, Ward, and J.C. Penney. Of the major toy retailers, only Toys R Us was bothering at all, advertising the Tudor No. 400 for the inflation-driven price of $9.58. Western Auto was still a Tudor stalwart, using both the NFL No. 635 and No. 400 in a number of its fall ads. Again, the inflationary prices were a bit shocking – the No. 635 was $19.99, while the No. 400 was $9.99. And the invisibility trend continued in full over Thanksgiving break. On a weekend that had once been the high-water mark of electric football advertising, the game now could hardly be found. Only Toys R Us maintained this decades-old tradition, running a color toy flyer on Sunday that included Tudor's NFL No. 515 for $11.87.

Coleco electric football games may have been on the shelves competing with Tudor, but the Coleco item getting the biggest push from Toys R Us was the Telstar video system. Toys R Us had given the Telstar a price a tag of less than $50. This was one of the lowest Telstar prices in the entire country – and one that was going to elicit silent curses from Atari and Magnavox. Coleco was determined to have Telstar make a big splash in video games. Still prominent at Toys R Us was Coleco's Power-Jet Hockey line, although this was another market segment where competition had withered profits. What Coleco had to compete with was the Brunswick tabletop game and Ideal's stand-alone Hurricane Hockey – both were going for under $20. So Coleco, of course, had to sell its tabletop Power-Jet Hockey game for under $20. This put air hockey at the same price point as Tudor's large football games. Also under $20 in 1976 was Coleco's Bowl-A-Matic 300.

What couldn't be found at Toys R Us this Christmas season was anything carrying a Munro Games logo. Few retailers wanted anything to do with Munro – even before the factory closed in July. Now the leftover stock of football and hockey games was almost entirely in the hands of toy liquidators. If a Munro item was found in 1976, it was likely on clearance. Personifying the fate of Munro was its lead endorser Joe Namath, whose diminishing skills and injuries had relegated him to the Jets' bench. All he could do was watch as an agile rookie from Alabama named Richard Todd became the Jets "quarterback of the future." Namath would finish the season with 4 touchdown passes...and 16 interceptions. On top of that, he probably didn't get a dime from Munro.

The December issue of *Playthings* had toy insiders predicting that the industry was on the cusp of an electronics boom that would last for years. All someone had to do to come up with such a forecast was scan the December newspaper ads. None of the big three – Sears, Ward, or J.C. Penney – was using electric football in its Christmas advertising. Instead, the featured item for most toy retailers was a video game. Whether a Coleco Telstar, a Magnavox Odyssey, Atari Pong, or some lesser-known clone, video games were as common as long-time classics like Life or Sorry.

From drug stores, to hardware stores, to auto part stores, even to farm supply stores, you could find a video game on the shelves of nearly every category of retailer. As for the big chains, Sears, Kmart, and Target were heavily invested in Atari Pong, while Telstar was the main system for Ward and Toys R Us. The Odyssey could be found at J.C. Penney, Ward, and a number of major upscale department store chains. But the top-selling video game of 1975 was in for a stiff challenge thanks to the aggressive pricing and distribution savvy of Atari and Coleco. Why make a special trip to the department store when you could pick up a video game with your aspirin at the drugstore? People's, PayLess, Skaggs, Osco, or Eckerd, it didn't matter where you were in the country. Pick a chain, and Coleco or Atari had it covered.

All of these stores were places where, not so long ago, electric football had been a premium

The Montgomery Ward Video World Of Sports game. This was actually a Coleco Telstar system that Ward licensed as an exclusive item. The Telstar was a best seller during the Christmas season. ©Montgomery Ward, Inc. 1976.

Christmas item. In most cases electric football was still on the nearby shelves, but the game was easily overlooked, especially in the video game mania that had prices dropping into the $50-$70 range. Compared with the $100 prices of the previous year, video games were a bargain in 1976.

As Christmas Day closed in, toy retailers of all shapes and sizes were hoping for another good Christmas season. And one lucky toy maker already had an inkling of how profitable this year would be. Reporting a record $36 million in sales and earnings for the third quarter of 1976 was Coleco. This figure was an 80% increase from third quarter sales of 1975, and the company now predicted a record $100 million in sales for the year. Only a tiny percentage of this total came from electric football. A full-page ad in the December issue of *Playthings* told the whole story: "Telstar by Coleco No.1 in video games."

When the NFL season came to a close on December 12, the AFC West was the division of opposites. Finishing at the top, one win short of

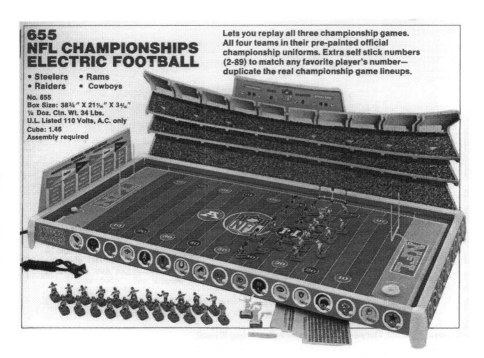

**655**
**NFL CHAMPIONSHIPS**
**ELECTRIC FOOTBALL**

Lets you replay all three championship games. All four teams in their pre-painted official championship uniforms. Extra self stick numbers (2-89) to match any favorite player's number— duplicate the real championship game lineups.

• Steelers  • Rams
• Raiders   • Cowboys

No. 655
Box Size: 38¾" X 21⅞" X 3¼"
¼ Doz. Ctn. Wt. 34 Lbs.
U.L. Listed 110 Volts, A.C. only
Cube: 1.46
Assembly required

Even in 1976 the NFL No. 655 still carried the aura of a "grand" game. But 1976 would be its last year of existence. It would not be part of the Tudor line in 1977. 1976 Tudor sales catalog. (Collection of Norman Sas.)

perfection, were the 13-1 Raiders. Sitting at the bottom, at 0-14, were the expansion Tampa Buccaneers, who became the first NFL team to have a winless season. The Raiders were favorites to wrest the AFC crown from the Steelers, by virtue of their league-best record. But first the Raiders would have to face the upstart Patriots, while the Steelers wrestled with the potent offense of the Baltimore Colts. Playing for the NFC title were the usual suspects – the Cowboys, Redskins, Vikings, and Rams. Minnesota again had the best record, making it likely that the NFC title would be decided in the icebox known as Metropolitan Stadium.

The playoffs started at noon on Saturday the 18th in Bloomington, Minnesota. Although the weather was unseasonably mild – 40 degrees – the Redskins were never in the game. After taking a 35-6 lead into the fourth quarter, the Vikings cruised to a 35-20 victory. Out in Oakland, the Raiders' season was rescued by Ken Stabler, who threw a touchdown pass with 10 seconds left to lift the team to a 24-21 win. On Sunday afternoon, the Steelers set a team playoff scoring record in a 40-14 dismantling of the Colts. But it was a costly win as both starting running backs, Franco Harris and Rocky Bleier, were lost to injury. The final game of the weekend saw the Rams' defense keep the Cowboys out of the end zone during the final two minutes for a tense 14-12 triumph. Once again the Rams would have to travel to Minnesota for an NFL championship game.

As Monday morning quarterbacks around the country discussed the weekend's results, the Christmas shopping season rounded into the home stretch. Electric football was still mentioned in Santa letters, but the game was trying hard to stay afloat in the froth of home video systems (also scarce in toys ads this season was Aurora's Monday Night game). Despite Coleco's gaudy quarterly sales figures, large Command Control games had been on clearance prices for most of the shopping season. Discounters with names like Railroad Salvage, Toy Outlet, and Nichols Discount Center were unloading Command Control models for as little as $6.50. This price undercut Ward's Coleco football game by almost $10 and was also less than what small Coleco electric football models usually cost.

Munro existed in name only at this point. The few games that made it onto retailers' shelves would have no bearing on the company's bottom line. These games were either leftover stock from long ago or part of July's grand clearance (incredibly, three-year-old Day/Nite games could still be found for sale). Their existence had long been written off as a loss. And it seemed that only a few unfortunate retailers were stuck with small Munro Namath games. For some reason the price hovered around the $10 level despite the game's small size and the quarterback's fading star.

Tudor electric football games seemed to be holding their value in 1976, although ad appearances were too scarce to commit this statement to fact. What is fact is this: Tudor electric football games weren't being offered relentlessly in toy sales. This put Tudor's games in much better shape than many air hockey games, which were heavily discounted in the final week of shopping. Sears dropped the tabletop Brunswick model to the same price as Tudor's Super Bowl and even slashed $20 off a $60 Coleco stand-alone game. Finally, on December 23rd, Ward went into its half-price toy clearance mode, while J.C. Penney advertised a 20%-30% sale on all remaining toys. Both chains were including air hockey in their discounts, which left the price of some of the deluxe models slashed by almost $100. But it did seem that Ward finally got the right price on their Command Control football game – $8. And certainly they had plenty of these games still in stock. The last-minute discounts at J.C. Penney would make any leftover Tudor games very attractive. An NFC Championship game would cost less than Sears' Super Bowl.

Surprisingly, prices on video games also dropped during this time. With so many video makers sharing the market, there were more than enough games to meet demand. So as the days wound toward Christmas, the clone Tele-Match systems and Telstar were being sold for less than $50. Most of these bargains came from drugstore chains that didn't want to carry the

1976 Sears' Super Bowl Game with Haiti Steelers and Cowboys. (Photo by Earl Shores.)

games into 1977. Their limited shelf space was valuable, and they couldn't afford to have items – even home video games – lingering around. These chains wanted the games out the door by the time the whistle blew on that final New Year's Day bowl game.

Christmas came on Saturday morning in 1976, and the "bleep-blip" of home video games echoed in more living rooms than ever before. Six Million Dollar man action figures were keeping the world safe from evildoers, while rubberized recoiling Stretch Armstrong limbs were whacking the heads of little brothers in every state. But was electric football still a welcome delivery from the jolly man dressed in red? As in previous years, it would depend on your expectations. A Tudor NFL game easily substituted for that Munro table hockey game that Sears couldn't deliver, but probably not for an air hockey game. (Although with the economy improving and the price of hockey dropping, it wasn't out of the question for Santa to bring both football and hockey this year.) Unfortunately, even Tudor's four-team NFL championship No. 655 model was not going to be a good swap for a video game.

And it finally reached the point where a Coleco or a Munro electric football game wasn't a good substitute for anything. Both companies' games were so outdated and unattractive that they were guaranteed to be abandoned long before the kids went back to school. It was hard to ignore the unfulfilled promise that lingered over these games. One company didn't care about electric football, and the other was out of business. It could be argued that Munro cared little about electric football before their demise. Even kids could figure this out.

Keeping games buzzing was the Fiesta Bowl at 4 p.m. on Christmas Day. And the NFL Conference Championship games would be played the very next day, an occasion that might have even saved Coleco and Munro models from the final "clean up." Any boy fortunate enough to have received a four-team NFL No. 655 game found himself owning three of the four teams playing on Sunday (Steelers, Raiders, and Rams). A Sears' Super Bowl would leave you with one team (Steelers), as would a J.C. Penney NFC Championship game (Rams). But as realistic as they were, none of Tudor's games came with the 12-degree air and frozen field that the Rams faced in Minnesota. Again, the conditions seemed to affect the California team more than the home team, who blocked a field goal and a punt for a 24-13 victory. Out in the more reasonable weather of Oakland, the Steelers didn't put up much of a fight without Harris and Bleier. The 24-7 score summed up just how dominant the Raiders were in defeating the champions of the previous two Super Bowl games. For the Raiders, it would be a second trip to the Super Bowl while the Vikings were heading to appearance number four. Both teams had something in common in their Super Bowl history – neither had a victory. One team was going to overcome that stigma in two weeks. Thanks to their 15-1 record, the Raiders were favored to earn their first Super Bowl title.

Despite there being almost a week left in 1976, the televised bowl game schedule was light. Only the Gator Bowl on Monday, and Friday's Peach and Astro-Bluebonnet Bowl remained. The Sugar Bowl, which this year featured top-ranked Pitt, had given up on New Year's Eve and moved back to its traditional New Year's Day slot. That left Saturday with a full slate of four bowl games. Scheduled to kickoff at noon was the Sugar Bowl. Ending somewhere around midnight would be the Orange Bowl.

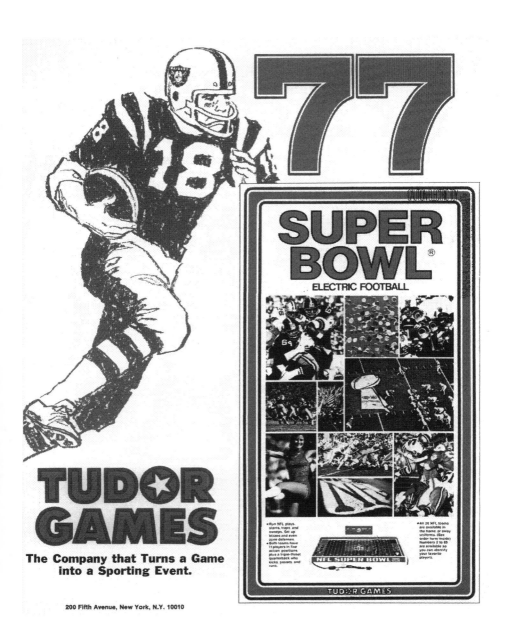

Cover of the 1977 Tudor sales catalog. (Collection of Norman Sas.)

# 33 TUDOR MAKES A COMEBACK

**P**itt settled any national title debates by midafternoon on New Year's Day, dismantling Georgia 27-3. Maryland entered the day undefeated and ranked fourth, but then lost to Houston in the Cotton Bowl. Heavyweights USC and Michigan were going at it in the Rose Bowl, but both teams already had a loss. And by early evening Michigan had two, losing to the Trojans by a 14-7 score. The final game of the day, the Orange Bowl, featured two teams that weren't even ranked in the top ten. Compared to recent New Year's Day football offerings, January 1, 1977, came up a little short. But at least there were 12 hours of televised football.

Next came a full week of football hype that culminated with the Super Bowl on the following Sunday. For Vikings' fans (including both authors, who adopted the team in the late 60's so as to not be permanently scarred by their wretched hometown NFL teams) January 9 served as proof that God was not a football fan. That was probably the easiest way to swallow the Raiders' 32-14 demolition of the horned men from the north, who now owned a humiliating 0-4 Super Bowl record. It still hurts to admit a simple fact – the Raiders were the better team. And that's all that will be said about Super Bowl XI.

Christmas of 1976 turned out to be a great one for retailers. December sales were up from the previous year by double digits at Sears, Ward, and J.C. Penney (12.4%, 10.7%, and 12.5% respectively). Consumers clearly were feeling more optimistic about the economy, and toys had more than done their part to lift retail sales. In fact, when the Toy Fair opened in February, the Toy Manufacturers Association reported that $3.1 billion of toys had been sold on the wholesale level in 1976 – a 14% increase from 1975. Profits were up as well, and most toy makers were feeling very good about 1977.

Highlighting the toy industry's exhilaration was a significant increase in trade publication advertising pages. *Playthings*, *Toys*, and *Toy & Hobby*

# 660
# SUPER BOWL

### With Total Team Control™

No. 660
Box Size: 38¾" X 21⅞₆" X 3⁵₁₆"
¼ Doz. Ctn. Wt. 32 Lbs.
U.L. Listed 110 Volts, A.C. only
Cube: 1.46
Assembly required

Both teams in their fully painted official
Super Bowl uniforms. Extra self stick numbers
(2-89) to match any favorite player's number—
duplicate the real Super Bowl game lineups.

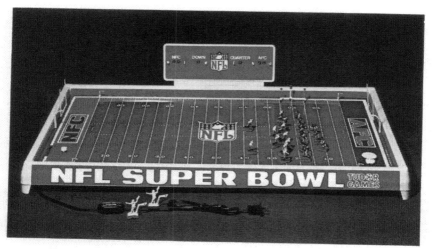

The new Tudor Super Bowl game. It had a new model number (No. 660), and was no longer a Sears'
exclusive item. From the 1977 Tudor sales catalog. (Collection of Norman Sas.)

*World* all swelled to page counts not seen since the pre-recession days.
And some toy makers were taking their recent success to new heights –
both Fisher Price and Mattel were increasing their television budgets by
30% for 1977 (Mattel's television budget now stood at $20 million.)
More electronic games were going to be offered in the coming year, yet the
big item, at least according to the TMA prognosticators, would be home
pinball machines. From tabletop models to full-size arcade versions, there
would be a pinball game for every budget and taste.

One company who had no intention of competing in the electronic or
pinball segment of the toy marketplace was Tudor. With Munro out of
business and Coleco focusing its energies elsewhere, 1976 had turned out
to be a nice year for the company. And this lack of competition made it
clear to Norman that there was no longer a need for an extensive line of
football games. So Tudor came to the Fair with just three electric football
models in 1977. The most interesting of the three was Tudor's new flagship
electric football game – the No. 660 Super Bowl. Sears had finally lost its
exclusive on the Super Bowl. Tudor was still giving the retailer an exclusive
Super Bowl model (the same No. 635-sized game from previous years), but
this year a Super Bowl could be found anywhere Tudor electric football

# 500
# ELECTRIC FOOTBALL
## with Total Team Control™

The best selling Electric Football game.
Individually controlled movement of every offensive
and defensive player. Total Team Control bases.
Side controls for quicker and more accurate adjustment.

Box Size: 27" x 16½" x 2"
½ Doz. Ctn. Wt. 27 Lbs.
U.L. Listed 110 Volts, A.C. only.

Cube: .50
Assembly required

Tudor's redesigned No. 500. The 1977 Tudor sales catalog. (Collection of Norman Sas.)

games were sold. And that even meant in other Christmas catalogs – J.C. Penney was already on board to sell the new Tudor game.

The new Super Bowl was different from the Sears' Super Bowl in a number of ways. Based on the 38" x 21" No. 620 frame, it was larger. There were also some differences in frame and field design, as the end zones would spell out AFC and NFC instead of having the standard No. 635 red, white, and blue diamond pattern. And the new game would cost more than the Sears' model. But there was a change on both Super Bowls that was made possible only through the demise of Munro and the disinterest of Coleco. Neither game would have a grandstand. Only a scoreboard would be included, and it would read NFC and AFC – gone were the interchangeable NFL team names.

Omitting a grandstand hadn't been a consideration since Gotham introduced its Yankee Stadium inspired G-1500 in 1961. From that point on, Tudor had to compete with Gotham's Big Bowl, Gotham's Super Dome, Coleco's terraced 3-D grandstand, and ultimately the double-decked floodlit architecture of Munro. For boys who grew up in the 60's studying the Sears and Ward catalogs like sacred texts, this return to simplicity was stunning. It wasn't the logical place to which electric football was supposed to evolve. But the logic of a 10-year-old doesn't go far in the ultracompetitive toy world. Tudor's decision not to include a grandstand on either of its Super Bowl models was a smart cost-cutting move, even if it kicked mud in the face of nostalgia.

As for Tudor's other two electric football models, the NFL No. 515 kept its grandstand and remained unchanged for 1977, while the No. 500 received a complete makeover. Tudor was attempting to modernize the No.

Coleco sales had set a record in 1976 thanks to the Telstar system. Courtesy of The Strong® Rochester, New York

500 using brighter field accents, as well as end zones garishly emblazoned in a white-on-red "HOME" and "GUEST" design. Furthering the update was a red and white bull's-eye design at midfield, and, like the Super Bowl, the No. 500 would now only include a scoreboard (the last time Tudor designed a No. 500 without a grandstand was 1963). New players were the final updated feature of the No. 500, with one team molded in yellow plastic and the other molded in red. It certainly was a different look for Tudor. In fact, it was so different that it almost didn't look like a Tudor electric football game.

The company was offering up a curious explanation for the overhaul of the No. 500. In both the sales catalog and a blurb in *Playthings* the company was proclaiming 1977 the 30th anniversary of electric football. That seemed to be a case of "marketing math" more than real math, since Norman Sas was still studying at MIT in 1947. Another curious aspect of Tudor's marketing plan in 1977 was to focus more on the NFL and the drawing power of pro football than on the actual electric football games in the company line. In the Tudor sales catalog, NFL football was touted as "the best known, best advertised product in the history of sports." A further juxtaposition of television facts – "93% of all boys and 91% of all girls between the ages of 8 and 13 have seen NFL games on television or in person" – gave the catalog a peculiar tone. Tudor was clearly taking a conservative approach to the Toy Fair and 1977. That was evident in the shrinking line and the lack of toy trade advertising. Considering the flux of the electric football market over the last three years, this caution was well founded.

Coleco, on the other hand, was ready to flaunt its success in electronics. The company sold over a million Telstar units in 1976 and increased its overall sales by 60% (sales totaled a record $116 million for the year). So a full-page *Playthings* ad proclaimed "Coleco Telstar – No. 1 in video games." Coleco was introducing six new Telstar games in 1977, and pinball was on its agenda too, as a licensing deal had been signed to make a *Happy Days* "The Fonz" pinball machine. Both The Fonz and Telstar were going to get heavy support from television advertising, and there was even going to be a television campaign for Power-Jet Hockey, despite the fact that air hockey was a fading market. Pretty much ignored at this point was long-time Coleco staple table hockey. But that was "star" status compared to electric football. Coleco had again agreed to supply Ward with the outdated 5799 Command Control game, only because Ward was taking on over a dozen Coleco items, including the full Telstar line and an exclusive *Welcome Back, Kotter* pinball game. Beyond the Ward model, it seemed unlikely that Coleco was manufacturing any more electric football games. Overstock could meet the meager demand of 1977.

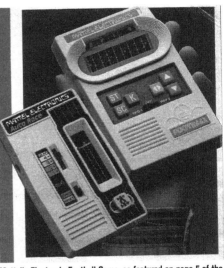

Mattel's Electronic Football Game, as featured on page 5 of the 1977 J.C. Penney Christmas catalog. ©1977 J.C. Penney, Inc.

With Munro's New York factory completely liquidated, the 1977 Toy Fair marked the official point where Tudor took back the electric football market. Coleco might argue that they ceded electric football to Tudor without putting up a serious fight, but they would be viewing the last seven years through rose-colored binoculars. During the course of 1976, Coleco overwhelmed the Magnavox Odyssey with the same "World of Sports" tactics they'd unveiled on electric football back in 1970. Through product saturation, distribution muscle, and television advertising, the Telstar had pushed the Odyssey – the original home video game – into nearly second-class status. (It was telling that banks around the country were using the Odyssey as an enticement for new accounts.)

But Tudor had weathered the Coleco charge, including multipage trade ads, NFL program ads, television commercials, and even gimmicks like Command Control. Ultimately, Coleco never seemed to sweat electric football details in the same way that Tudor always did. Instead of chasing down the impossible – fully controllable players – Coleco could have stuck to the basics and made a thoroughly finished product. More realistic players, more realistic goal posts, and more colorful fields might have gained them more sales than a faulty magnetic magic wand. As a result, Tudor never relinquished the top spot in electric football. That Tudor was able to fend off a powerhouse toy maker like Coleco for half a dozen years was an authoritative testament to the marketing muscle of the NFL, Norman's toy savvy, and Lee Payne's creative flair.

Even though the direct competition between Tudor and Coleco was greatly diminished, an item on display at the 1977 Toy Fair would prove to be a major challenge to both companies. And if the breadth of the threat wasn't readily apparent to Norman Sas or Brian Clarke, there was a reasonable explanation. The company making the item – Mattel – had little idea of what the impact of its new game would be.

The public notice for Munro's summer liquidation. *The Toronto Star*, page C10, July 18, 1977.

In Mattel's first foray into electronic games they had teamed up with Rockwell International to create two hand-held calculator sized games – Electronic Auto Race and Electronic Football. Both games were LED based, allowing a player to maneuver his or her race car or running back (both represented by a red blip) through packs of oncoming automobiles or tacklers (more red blips). For Toy Fair, Mattel was running a full-page *Playthings* ad which finished by saying, "If you want to be #1, make it with Mattel in '77." The company had no idea just how much Electronic Football would validate this pronouncement.

Just as the Fair wrapped up in late February, the NFL was finally able to wrap up the biggest crisis the league had ever faced – the labor contract. On the 25th both the players and owners ratified a new labor contract. Included in the deal were at least $15 million in payments to former players and the elimination of the long-despised option clause. The Rozelle rule was also eliminated. Under the new rules, a player was free to move to another team when his contract was up, but the original team could keep the player by matching the highest salary offer. And in lieu of the Rozelle rule there was now a compensation formula based on the player's salary. Another part of the contract was that all NFL players had to pay dues to the NFLPA even if they didn't become a member. This was aimed at

The electric football page in the 1977 Sears *Christmas Book* (page 538). ©Sears, Roebuck and Co. 1977.

strengthening the union, whose membership had declined to just 300 players during the labor impasse. The settlement also meant that when the owners met in March, they had – to everyone's relief – nothing major on their agenda. Among the easily approved issues was the sale of the 49ers to the Ohio-based DeBartolo family. Another formality for the owners was awarding the 1979 Super Bowl to Miami.

Few in the NFL were surprised when the Jets put Joe Namath on waivers at the beginning of April. The Jets really didn't want to pay his $495,000 salary anymore, and neither did any other teams around the league (a trade with the Rams had just fallen through). Waivers meant that anyone could claim Joe, but as a veteran player he could reject the teams he didn't like. Once claimed, the Jets would get nothing in return; yet by putting Namath on waivers the Jets owed him nothing. It was a given that any team who signed Namath would pay him a lot less than his current salary.

The timing was coincidental, but a company who once sold Namath-endorsed products was in trouble again, this time north of the border. On April 4 Servotronics reported $9.5 million worth of losses for 1976. It was also no secret that losses were mounting for the first quarter of 1977. So two days later, a Canadian bank called in a Munro Games Ltd. loan. Servotronics didn't have the cash to cover the loan, so the final piece of Munro Games was forced into receivership. The Clarkson Company of Toronto, the "receiver," would liquidate all the Munro assets. Through the bankruptcy and liquidation of Munro, Servotronics and Nick Trbovich could stay in business.

Joe Namath's fortunes turned out better than that of his former business partner. The Rams eventually signed him to a contract on May 12 for $150,000. Namath's only guarantee for signing the contract was a chance to compete for the starting quarterback job. It was more than a little ironic to have Broadway Joe hoping for a Hollywood ending to his football career. Back when Namath signed with the Jets in 1964, he had shifted the pro football landscape. By comparison, his Los Angeles signing was almost anonymous.

A four-page color spread in the July issue of *Playthings* reported that the electronic toy and game category brought in sales of over $315 million during the previous year. Estimates from the television game category (Odyssey, Telstar, and clones) had 4 million units being sold in 1976, with expectations of 8-10 million units moving off the shelves by the end of this year. Featured in the article were the new Odyssey 5000, the new Telstar Arcade model, and Mattel Electronic Football.

Coleco's strangely sideways positioned electric football game in the 1977 Montgomery Ward Christmas catalog (page 429). ©Montgomery Ward, Inc. 1977.

Before July finished, the contents of Munro's Ontario factory were put up for auction. It was a sad final chapter for the 42-year-old company. From Sears Award of Excellence winner in 1970 to bankruptcy in 1977 – the once proud creator of table hockey was no more. And with the loss of the company came a loss for two different communities. In Ontario, that count was 12 full-time workers and nearly 100 seasonal workers. A few days after the auction, workers from the Danbury Auctioneers began emptying unwanted Munro file boxes onto the floor of the vacant factory. As they carried out their tedious assignment, a man walked up and asked them to please stop. That man was Don Munro – the files they were dumping had been his personal archive. Munro quickly gathered up the papers and loaded as many boxes as he could into his car. His home in Burlington became the final resting place of Munro Games.

The NFL preseason moved on without any drama this year, but not without change. There would be no College All-Star game in 1977. Thanks to declining attendance, resistance from coaches (for having their top draft picks subject to injury and not in team camp), and the slip-and-slide fiasco of the previous year, *Chicago Tribune* Charities decided not to sponsor the game anymore. Another sporting institution had come to an end after 43 years.

NFL Electric Football with Total Team Control You can control the direction of every play and player!

B Superbowl Football

18⁸⁸

C NFL Football

13⁸⁸

J.C. Penney now had the largest Super Bowl game, and the only one being made with a grandstand. J.C. Penney Christmas catalog, page 417. ©1977 J.C. Penney, Inc.

When the regular NFL season got underway on September 18, the Raiders were favored to repeat as AFC champions. Over in the NFC, the Vikings were seen as too old to be a serious contender, leaving the conference open to the Rams, Redskins, or Cowboys. The Raiders cruised to a 24-0 victory over the Chargers in week one, but of the NFC favorites, only the Cowboys got off to a winning start. With Joe Namath at quarterback, the Rams' offense managed only a single touchdown during a 17-6 loss to the Falcons.

The start of the NFL season meant that the delivery of Christmas catalogs was already under way. Like the previous year, the Sears *Christmas Book* contained only two Tudor electric football games – the No. 635-sized Super Bowl game and the redesigned No. 500 game. Both games became part of Sears' catalog history thanks to a missing feature. Sears had never sold an electric football game without a grandstand. Never. When Sears began selling electric football back in 1955 its first model was the Gotham G-940 – which came with two metal end zone grandstands. Any boy who just ten years earlier ogled a Big Bowl or a Browns-Giants No. 620 would have been shocked by the plainness of the games in 1977. But times had changed, as had the toy landscape.

The Super Bowl was priced at $18.49, while the No. 500 just crossed over the $10 barrier. Both games were stuffed up against the top edge of page 538, taking up less catalog space than previous years. Yet 1977 was still shaping up as a promising year for Tudor. Of the eight items shown on the page, Tudor manufactured six. In addition to electric football there was electric baseball, Tudor bowling, Tudor table hockey, and a new NFL magnetic dart game. Table hockey was not part of the Tudor line in 1977 – Sears had to put in a special order with Norman to have a game manufactured. Sears' toy buyers were smart enough to have written off Munro Games long before the company fell into receivership.

Sears made the Tudor Super Bowl a regular item in its newspaper ads in 1977. The Super Bowl and the Batmobile. *Chronicle-Telegram*, page B-2, November 20, 1977.

Elsewhere in the catalog, electronic games continued to take up the kind of space once reserved for electric football and air hockey. Sears' newest electronic console game for 1977 was the color graphic and cartridge-based Tele-games System (actually an Atari 2600). The realism of this new game was touted as turning your television into a video arcade. With the price at $179.99, and additional game cartridges costing $19.95, the Tele-games System needed to live up to this promise to have any chance of success. Sears was still carrying the Pong line, at what now seemed like bargain prices – all it took now was $20 to enter the world of electronic games. Not receiving the same support as the Tele-games system were Mattel's handheld Electronic Football and Auto Race games. Both of Mattel's offerings provided a portable electronic game for about the cost of a Tele-games cartridge.

Ward also followed the electronic game trend. Page three of its catalog featured a Bally Arcade cartridge video game console…for $269! (Cartridges sold for $20-$25.) A $27 Pong-clone video game took up the entire back cover of the catalog, and on the spread of pages preceding the back cover Coleco had four new Telstar models on display. The most expensive Coleco game was the cartridge-based color-graphic Telstar Arcade, which came with a built-in pistol and steering wheel. It was listed at just a few cents under $100. Next in line was the Telstar Galaxy, a color game with six built-in sports games. The four battle games of the $70 Telstar Combat were not in color, but the Telstar Colormatic brought the most basic of

Pong games into color (for $44.44). In all, Ward had devoted four full pages to television computer games – not counting the space devoted to the new Mattel hand-held games. This was a far cry from the tiny area Ward used for electric football. Buried in the bottom corner of page 429 was a Coleco electric football game – the same 5799 Command Control model from the previous two years. Only this year the game was turned up at nearly a ninety-degree angle and photographed from directly overhead. This view made it hard to tell you were looking at an electric football game – which may have been the way Ward wanted it. Coleco and Ward were much more interested in selling Telstar systems than electric football games. Table hockey was once again completely missing from Ward.

Over in the J.C. Penney catalog, however, electric football was still holding a prominent place. For sale on page 417 was a large Super Bowl game – with grandstand – and a grandstand-equipped NFL No. 515 model. Penney's larger and better-appointed Super Bowl cost only $0.39 more than its Sears' cousin, while the No. 515 hovered around the $14 mark. Also available on the page were all 28 NFL teams (again in conference sets), Tudor's NFL Strategy and Tudor's NFL magnetic dart game. This gave the company five of the six items on the page. The final item was a football tossing "Mr. Quarterback," giving Penney the only "all football" page in the major Christmas catalogs. Both Sears and J.C. Penney were giving Tudor a running start to the 1977 Christmas season.

But J.C. Penney was not overlooking the electronic game category. The catalog's back cover was devoted to the Telstar Arcade game and on page 4 there was a cartridge-based RCA video game. (Unfortunately the $140 RCA Studio II Home TV Programmer was programmed in old-fashioned black and white.) Not far from electric football, a two-page spread of home video games featured two Telstar models and a $150 television video game from a company called APF. Yet it was on page 5 of the catalog where J.C. Penney did something really different from Sears and Ward. Shown in almost life-size color photos were both of Mattel's new electronic games – Auto Race and Electronic Football. The size of the display let shoppers really get a good look at the games and also signaled that these items were special. Auto Race, at $19.95, was the cheaper of the two games, but Football ($29.95) had a scoreboard that not only kept the score, it kept the time, the downs, the yard line, yards to go, and even played the sporting-event "charge" theme. An extra $10 seemed like a bargain for such exotic features.

It was clear that all three major retailers saw electronics as the future. Air hockey games were given less space in each catalog; the desperation of the genre was summed up neatly in Brunswick's newest game – Glow-in-the-Dark Air Hockey. (When there's nowhere else to go, you make the

New video game console with programmed microprocessor cartridges

Console comes with cartridge No. 1: Road Race, Quick Draw and Tennis

Cartridge No. 2: 8 combinations based on 5 games. Comes with 2 remote controls that attach to console. Tennis, Hockey, Handball, 2 Target Games (1 to 4 players).

Cartridge No. 3 has 6 new and different games. 4 Pinball games (for 1 or 2) with flipper action 2 moving Target Games—Shoot the Bear and Shooting Gallery

99⁸⁸

Coleco had created the Telstar Arcade for 1977, which featured a pistol and a steering wheel. Montgomery Ward *Christmas 1977*, page 429. ©Montgomery Ward, Inc. 1977.

game glow.) But these games weren't yet as deep in the dustbin as table hockey. Its journey over the last five years from action game staple to action game afterthought was astonishing. Sears and Penney were each carrying only a single model (Tudor and Coleco respectively). And Ward had abandoned the game completely even though it was carrying over a dozen Coleco items.

In mid-October the Denver Broncos intercepted seven Ken Stabler passes in hanging a 30-7 defeat on the Raiders. The loss ended the Raiders' 17-game winning streak and put the Broncos on top of the AFC West division with a 5-0 record. Just down the coast in Los Angeles the Rams climbed above the .500 mark for the first time with a 14-7 win over the Saints. Joe Namath witnessed the game from the bench, replaced by the younger and more mobile Pat Haden. Halloween night marked the midpoint of the NFL season, and after the Cardinals humiliated the Giants 28-0 on *Monday Night Football*, 15 of the league's 26 teams were still in the running for the playoffs. Included were the Raiders, who over the weekend took revenge on the Broncos (both teams were now 6-1).

With the calendar turning to November, the Christmas selling season was just starting to shift into high gear. And a surprising item was getting featured in toy world advertising – electric football. Toys R Us was using the game in its ads (the $10 No. 500 model), as was Woolco (big Super Bowl), and Sears. In fact, Sears would feature Tudor's Super Bowl in almost every toy newspaper ad run in November. Sometimes the game got a large photo, sometimes it was a small one, and sometimes Tudor was competing with a Tele-games system or a Mattel Electronic Football game. But amazingly the one constant toy for Sears through its November and early December advertising was electric football. Norman hadn't gotten this kind of support from the retailer since the early 1970's. Super Bowl games of all kinds were selling well this Christmas season, even in a world that was obviously going electronic.

It was no surprise that Coleco had a strong footprint in Toys R Us with the chain selling all of the Telstar systems, as well as table hockey, Power-Jet Hockey, pool tables, and The Fonz pinball machines. Coleco, as usual, had again muscled its leftover electric football games into Toys R Us, but the heavily discounted Pro-Stars games had little to offer. And Ward surely didn't appreciate seeing large Command Control games pop up on toy liquidator shelves for less than $10. But electric football's declining sales hardly worried Coleco.

Thanksgiving came early in 1977, making the Christmas shopping season a long and potentially lucrative one for retailers. Yet as the days of December moved forward, something unexpected happened in the world of home video games. Because so many different games were available, sales started to slump. Overwhelmed by Telstar and Pong clones was the Magnavox Odyssey – as a result some Odyssey's were being sold for less than $25. And after Atari released its 2600 to the general public in late fall, a large number of major retailers found themselves all selling the identical video game system. (This included Sears, whose Tele-games console was an Atari 2600.) It was not an enviable position to be in. Even with the strong economy, toy retailers were not seeing their shelves empty as quickly as they had hoped. So they did what they had to do – they held huge clearance sales.

Sears, Ward, and J.C. Penney all had toy sales, with Ward being the most aggressive in clearing its inventory. (Sears was discounting only "selected toys.") Upper-end Telstar systems were cut by a minimum of $20, with some Ward locations chopping the price of the $100 Telstar Arcade in half as Christmas neared. This pricing did not help the more expensive cartridge game systems, prompting Sears to lower its Tele-games system by $20. But at $159, the game was still more expensive than an Atari 2600 at Target ($139.97), or even at a Walgreen's pharmacy ($145). There was still profit to be made from electronic games, but things had become very competitive in 1977. Video games were being sold by almost every kind of retailer – toy stores, department stores, drug stores, auto part stores, and hardware stores. It was hard to find a retailer that wasn't selling a video game.

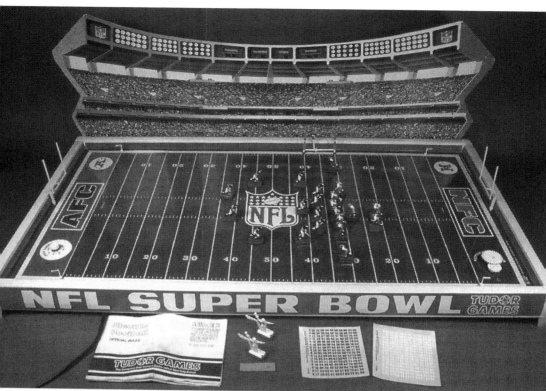

The J.C Penney 1977 Super Bowl game, as it might have looked on Christmas morning. The Vikings and Raiders were black shoe Haiti teams. It would be the last electric football game that Tudor made with a grandstand. (Photo by Earl Shores.)

Among the games that did not have trouble making the cash register ring were Mattel's Electronic Football and Tudor's Super Bowl. With the push from Sears and its marketing plan focused on a single game, Tudor had nearly sold through its entire Super Bowl inventory by Christmas. It was a pleasant and unexpected development for electric football to make a comeback when other mechanical sports action games, like table hockey and air hockey, were in decline. But Tudor electric football, after nearly thirty years on toy shelves, was again a solid selling item.

While Tudor served as a link to football games of the past, Mattel's new football game clearly represented the future. No marketing campaign was needed for Electronic Football, as hand-held computer games became the hot toys of 1977 (Mattel's Auto Race and Blip by Tomy were among the top-selling Christmas items). Mattel's timing for a hand-held computer football game was perfect. At the moment, they were the only company making such a game – no one else had "borrowed" the concept yet. So Mattel's electronic games rarely even made it to the shelf because people were waiting in lines for toy stores to open. The number of games Mattel could sell depended solely on how many computer chips the company had.

At least Mattel could get its games to the stores, even if they disappeared quickly. Long predicted for success this Christmas was anything related to the Star Wars movie, which had broken all Hollywood box office and earnings records since being released in July. Unfortunately, the extended licensing negotiations between 20th Century-Fox and Kenner left Kenner without enough time to get its Star Wars line into production. So at Christmas, Kenner was forced into the unusual and somewhat unfortunate arrangement of selling Star Wars gift certificates instead of merchandise. (Everyone in the toy industry knows that a company needs to capitalize when a market is hot…maybe this Star Wars thing would be all played out by the following Christmas.) Luckily for Kenner, people really did want the merchandise the company promised to deliver in 1978. A company with a different kind of Christmas problem was Ideal. After four years of having the toys of daredevil Evel Knievel lead its sales – his line earned about $25 million in 1976 – Ideal now couldn't give these toys away. The reason? Knievel was serving a six-month jail term for assaulting his former press agent with a baseball bat. He was no longer the type of hero parents wanted as a role model for their children.

Much more acceptable heroes took the field on Saturday, December 24, when the AFC playoffs started. With Christmas falling on a Sunday, the NFL had decided to play games on Saturday and Monday. Although one of the most memorable games in NFL history had been played on Christmas Day (the Dolphins' sudden-death win over the Chiefs in 1971) Rozelle and the league decided not to risk any controversy by playing on the holiday in 1977. (Perhaps Rozelle worried that the NFL couldn't compete with all the video games that would be occupying television screens on Christmas Day.) In Baltimore, the Colts and Raiders exchanged leads eight times before the Raiders put the game away in the second period of overtime. The final score was 37-31. Out in the mile-high city of Denver, the surprising 12-2 Broncos defeated the Steelers 34-21.

Finally it was time for Santa – who was now running a help wanted ad for an elf with an electrical engineering degree – to make his rounds. It's hard to imagine a Star Wars gift certificate being a big hit on Christmas morning. Maybe it would be great in a couple of months for breaking the midwinter doldrums, but in the instant gratification glory of Christmas morning, any kind of gift certificate would probably end up in the corner with the underwear and socks. Electronic games were what most kids wanted. Television video games or a hand-held game would do fine, although even the basic Pong tennis game was starting to look a bit dated.

The spike in electric football sales in 1977 is still puzzling. Throughout the shopping season Sears had offered its Super Bowl game at sale prices, sometimes for as low as $14.88. So maybe it was familiarity and

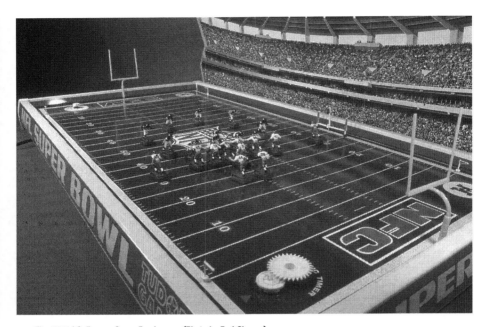

The 1977 J.C. Penney Super Bowl game. (Photo by Earl Shores.)

affordability that allowed electric football to compete against the more exotic electronic offerings of the season. It may have also been helpful that the Mattel Electronic Football was in high demand, leaving electric football as the default football item. Rather than have no football game at all under the tree, electric football would do. By far, the best-looking Tudor game for 1977 was the J.C. Penney Super Bowl. With its large field and large grandstand, it was a worthy successor to Tudor's early Super Bowl models. It captured the grandeur and glory that was always at the heart of electric football, continuing to supply the innocence and inspiration offered by Gotham's Yankee Stadium and Gotham's Big Bowl, as well as the original NFL No. 620, NFL No. 510, and Jets-Colts Super Bowl models. All of Tudor's new games without grandstands – the No. 500, Super Bowl, and Sears' Super Bowl – looked naked, in large part because kids were used to seeing electric football games with grandstands. And just a few years earlier, they had indeed been very grand.

While a Super Bowl or NFL No. 515 model may still have been viewed as an exciting gift, the No. 500, despite its update, was less inspiring. With bright red and white graphics, red and yellow players, and no grandstand, it seemed to have less realism than its predecessors. In fact, its design scheme seemed to carry a comic-book element, as if to be noticed in a world going video, electric football needed more flash than realism.

Any boy receiving a Coleco electric football game would know that little thought had gone into the gift. It wasn't even a good backup football game. The amount of playing time a Coleco electric football game would get, especially if there were, say, a Coleco Telstar system in the same house, could be measured with an egg timer.

It was another Christmas where beeps and blips would surpass the buzz, although having the holiday sandwiched by the NFL playoffs surely extended the buzzing into Monday afternoon. In the early game the Cowboys trounced the Bears 37-7. After waiting almost a decade to get a home playoff game with the Vikings, the Rams couldn't get revenge for the three NFL seasons that ended in the Artic-like air of Minnesota. Instead, their season ended in the mud of the Los Angeles Coliseum, where tropical rains turned the field into a bog. The Rams never led during the 14-7 loss. Even though the Vikings intercepted three Pat Haden passes, the Rams' quarterback was never in danger of being replaced by his backup, Joe Namath. On New Year's Day the Broncos would host the Raiders, and the Cowboys would host the Vikings. Those matchups were for certain. Less certain was whether the bleeps, blips, and buzzes would continue for another week.

# Our Super Bowl was Sold Out!!

**For 1977 we produced more Super Bowls than ever before and we sold them all. With this as a background we expect our 50th Anniversary year to be a big winner. Please plan to see us at Toy Fair and get your orders in early.**

**The Company that turns a game into a sporting event!**   Room 520

Tudor's ad in the February 1978 issue of *Playthings* (page 389). 1977 was good year for Tudor. Courtesy of The Strong®, Rochester, New York. (Collection of Earl Shores.)

**EARL SHORES | RDDDY GARCIA**

# 34 HAND-HELD ELECTRONIC GAMES OVERTAKE ALL

On the first day of 1978 the traditional college bowl games stepped aside to allow the NFL to crown its conference champions. In the early game, the Cowboys exposed the Vikings defense for what it was – a once-great unit, now past its prime. The outcome of the game was never in question with the 23-6 score actually flattering the Vikings. In the AFC game, the Broncos surprised the Raiders 20-17 with the help of a questionable fumble ruling. This left Denver quarterback Craig Morton set to face his former team in the Super Bowl on January 15.

Several firsts were accomplished in Super Bowl XII. It was the first Super Bowl ever played indoors. And because the weather in the Superdome was under human control, the kickoff was pushed back to 6:00 p.m. Eastern Time. This made the game the first ever prime time Super Bowl. Like the previous three New Orleans' Super Bowl games, this one also fell into the category of lackluster. The Broncos had as many turnovers as completions (8) in a 27-10 loss to the plainly superior Cowboys. But with the Super Bowl now established as a major event on the U.S. calendar, television viewers did not tune out as "America's Team" went for a romp on the Superdome's artificial grass. According to Nielsen 86 million people viewed the game, making it the second most-watched television program ever.

By the time the Super Bowl was played, Sears, J.C. Penney, and Kmart had posted record sales gains for December. All three had registered over 20% increases against the previous December, with Ward not far behind at 18.3%. Ward was also reporting a sharp increase in toy sales for the month, which was no surprise considering that they had offered the deepest discounts as the Christmas shopping season entered its final days. A number of other retail chains, including the May department store chain and Woolworth were reporting double-figure sales increases. It had been a good Christmas for retailers.

# NFL Super Bowl
## Electric Football with Total Team Control™

Both teams in their fully painted official Super Bowl uniforms. Extra self stick numbers (2-89) to match any favorite player's number— duplicate the real Super Bowl game lineups.

No. 660
Box Size: 35¹³/₁₆"x19⁵/₁₆"x3³/₈"
¹/₂ Doz. Ctn. Wt. 36 Lbs.
U.L. Listed 110 Volts, A.C. only
Cube: 1.40
Assembly required

Tudor's newly re-sized No. 660 Super Bowl game. It was 3" shorter than the 1977 model. From the 1978 Tudor sales catalog. (Collection of Norman Sas.)

1977 had also been a great year for Tudor. The Super Bowl line, including the Sears' models, sold out completely. It was the first time since the early 1970's that Tudor sold through its inventory, leading to a confident feeling as the company headed into its 50th year of existence. *Playthings* had already interviewed Norman for a 50th anniversary article (to run in the February Toy Fair issue), and Tudor was set to run a full-page *Playthings* ad announcing the Super Bowl sell-out. A large piece of optimism came from elsewhere in the toy world – Coleco had officially given up on electric football. Unlike Joe Namath's retirement announcement on January 25, there was no media event marking Coleco's exit from the gridiron. Tudor appeared to have clear sailing into 1978.

But just a few days after Namath's goodbye, Tudor, and Norman in particular, were hit with some very sad news. Elmer Sas passed away on January 29, just two days after his 90th birthday. So the Toy Fair opened for Norman with the optimism of the previous year being tempered by the death of his father, the company's founder.

Even though the Super Bowl line had sold out, Tudor had planned to scale back again in 1978. The Super Bowl game the company was showing at the Fair was slightly smaller than the 1977 model. This size reduction was accomplished by simply eliminating the surrounding sideline border from the No. 620-size field. Cleverly, the playing field remained the same size while the frame of the game shrunk by several inches to 35" x 19" dimensions. Tudor also redesigned the NFL No. 515 model. Part of the changes included removing the grandstand and renaming the game the NFL No. 520. But the primary component of the redesign was brighter and louder graphics on the field and frame.

Another new element for Tudor was packaging all their games with new "team boxes" where players could be safely stored. At least now there would be less dog-chewing casualties in the miniature NFL. Norman told *Playthings* that football was the main thrust of 1978 – this included electric football, NFL Strategy, and a new NFL Quarterback game, which was essentially NFL Strategy "lite." For the moment, Norman added, electronic games were not for Tudor. But he was keeping his eye on them.

And they weren't hard to find at the 1978 Toy Fair. Coleco, who claimed to be "No. 1 in electronic fun," was expanding the Telstar line and also jumping into the hand-held market with an electronic football game. Thanks to Telstar's success, Coleco had expanded into a larger showroom at 200 Fifth Avenue. Also finding electronics profitable was Mattel, which set a sales record in 1977. Electronic Auto Race and Football played a big part in that record, and this year Mattel was planning to have a total of seven hand-held electronic games on toy store shelves by the fall.

Retailers were delighted with the hand-held electronic category. The games were an easy sale. Often the demand was so great that they barely sat on the shelf. And the profit margin was high. But there were several other reasons for ordinary toy retailers to be very, very excited. Mattel Electronic Football sold well in June and December – the same could not be said for electric football or any other kinds of football games. And many of the people buying the games were adults who didn't have kids. They were purchasing the game for themselves! So a whole new demographic was

Tudor's new NFL No. 520 model. From the 1978 Tudor sales catalog. (Collection of Norman Sas.)

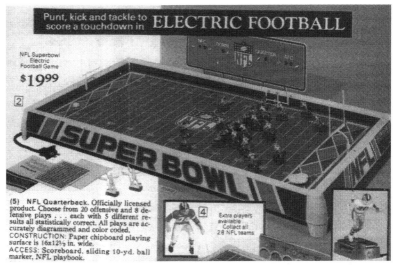

Punt, kick and tackle to score a touchdown in ELECTRIC FOOTBALL

NFL Superbowl Electric Football Game

$19.99

(5) NFL Quarterback. Officially licensed product. Choose from 20 offensive and 8 defensive plays . . . each with 5 different results all statistically correct. All plays are accurately diagrammed and color coded. CONSTRUCTION: Paper chipboard playing surface is 16x12½ in. wide. ACCESS: Scoreboard, sliding 10-yd. ball marker, NFL playbook.

Extra players available. Collect all 28 NFL teams

The electric football page in the 1978 Sears Christmas Book (page 599). The Super Bowl is now at the $20 mark. The Cowboys' player is the first white shoe player to appear with in a Tudor photo. ©Sears, Roebuck and Co. 1978.

prowling the toy store aisles. These "big kids" not only had the money for a $30 game, they didn't have to deal with a parent who could say no. This new electronic game customer was a retailer's dream.

For Tudor, there was reason for optimism in 1978. The company had gotten a good push from Sears and J.C. Penney during the previous year, and now they were the only electric football maker left. And it was still good to be part of the NFL Properties. The league's profile had never been higher – a prime time, Nielsen record-setting Super Bowl proved that unequivocally. As a result of being the last electric football maker standing, Norman had been approached by Montgomery Ward. A Tudor Super Bowl game would appear in the 1978 Ward Christmas catalog. The last time Tudor had appeared in Ward was 1974.

After so many years spent worrying about what electric football competitors were doing, the summer of 1978 was a pleasant change. Electric football was Tudor. The situation was almost the same as it had been 30 years earlier when Norman first invented the game. But as Norman had perceptively mentioned to *Playthings*, he had a watchful eye on all those hand-held electronic games being made by Mattel and Coleco, especially now that Coleco had a football game of its own. Was it possible that Coleco could pose a bigger threat to Tudor now that the company was out of electric football?

When the Sears *Christmas Book* came out in September, Norman was quite pleased. Of the eight sports games displayed on page 599, Tudor manufactured seven. The main item was the Sears' Tudor Super Bowl, which now carried a $19.99 price tag. A No. 500 model with an $11.47 list price sat right below the Super Bowl, and this year Sears had also decided to compete with J.C. Penney by selling sets of extra NFL teams. The second most expensive Tudor item on the page was a game that wasn't even listed in the sales catalog. With Munro out of business and Coleco focused on electronics, Sears had asked Tudor to again make a table hockey game. It was the large 37" x 21" model – bigger than any football game Tudor was making in 1978 – and cost $18.97. With the page in full color, it was a very nice layout for Tudor. The Super Bowl and hockey games looked sharp, as did all the other Tudor games that filled out the page: NFL Strategy, NFL Quarterback, Electric Baseball, and Tudor Bowl. It gave Norman hopeful thoughts for the coming Christmas season. And Sears wasn't finished with Tudor. After being shut out since 1974, Tudor had won another Sears Excellence Award, thanks in large part to the sold out 1977 Super Bowl.

Tudor was also getting a push from Ward this year. They, too, were selling the Tudor Super Bowl, with the game pictured on page 451 being Tudor's standard Super Bowl model. (The Sears' model had special artwork on the frame and in the end zones.) At $18.44, the Ward model was $1.55 less than the Sears' Super Bowl. But the pricing didn't matter at all to Norman. He was the sole supplier of electric football games for two of the largest retailers in country. Actually, it was more than that in 1978. Tudor was the sole supplier of electric football. Period. Any retailer in the country who wanted to carry electric football would be selling a Tudor Super Bowl No. 660, a Tudor NFL No. 520, or a Tudor No. 500.

Montgomery Ward goes back to Tudor in 1978, selling the No. 660 Super Bowl game. Montgomery Ward 1978 Christmas catalog (page 451). ©Montgomery Ward, Inc. 1978.

As the fall went on, Sears did not give Tudor's Super Bowl game nearly the same type of ad support as the year before. In 1977 it was hard to find a Sears' toy ad page that didn't have electric football; this year the situation was reversed. But in fairness, at least Sears did offer some ad support. The same could not be said of Ward, Toys R Us, J.C. Penney, and other long-time electric football strongholds. Retailers both large and small had simply abandoned electric football. Other than Sears, it was almost impossible to find an electric football game in any retailer's toy advertising. And just what types of items were pushing Tudor's games aside? Electronic games – both the console and hand-held models.

Electric football didn't even get a reprieve over the Thanksgiving Day holiday. As an ad item in 1978, it was missing in action. Slipping ad support would lead to a sales decline for Tudor in the best of years, but unfortunately this was not just any Christmas. It was the Christmas when hand-held electronic game sales exploded. In fact, Mattel had sold more electronic games in the first nine months of the year than all of 1977.

As Christmas neared there were massive shortages of all the popular hand-held electronic games. Retailers were in a frenzy begging toy makers for any scraps they could spare. But toy makers, incredibly, had underestimated the demand for hand-held games. In a case of simple math, there just weren't enough computer chips to make any more games. Texas Instruments, the country's top chipmaker, was now in overdrive trying to supply extra chips to desperate toy companies.

Coleco's popular 1978 Electronic Quarterback game. (Collection of Earl Shores.)

Perhaps the most desperate group of all were Christmas shoppers, who now bounced from store to store in an aggravated funk, pursuing the Holy Grail items of the 1978 toy world. Mattel's Electronic Football, Basketball, and Auto Race games had all long disappeared from the toy store shelves. Other hot sellers like Milton Bradley's Simon, Hasbro's Merlin, Coleco's Electronic Quarterback, and Coleco's Quiz Wiz games were impossible finds by early December. The more expensive television console game systems were also having a good year. Their costs had dropped significantly with some Coleco Telstar and clone systems being sold at the $20 mark. But that market wasn't in full frenzy mode like hand-held games. A lot of consoles were purchased in the waning days of the shopping season to make up for the inevitable disappointment there was going to be when a child discovered that his or her "must have" item was not under the Christmas tree.

An item that was in good supply during the Christmas season was electric football. That's because even though Tudor had the electric football market all to itself, and even had Sears and Ward, it was a difficult Christmas to be selling the game. And in taking stock of the situation, Norman realized that Tudor's competition with Gotham, Munro, and Coleco back in the early 70's was starting to look like the good old days.

A unanimous conclusion from retailers around the country declared Mattel's Electronic Football as the most popular game for Christmas 1978. Not only was it the top-selling game, it was the top-selling toy. Mattel would later report that Electronic Football grossed $25 million at the wholesale level for 1978. This figure made it the biggest selling item in *toy history*. As if this wasn't enough football competition for Tudor, one of the other top-selling games for Christmas was Coleco's Electronic Quarterback. Coleco had obviously "borrowed" from Mattel to create the game, but something Coleco had done differently was to price its game aggressively and undercut Mattel at the cash register.

When Mattel's Football game was available, it was priced in the $20-$25 range (the Ward Christmas catalog had it listed for $19.99). Coleco's Quarterback game, which also sold out in 1978, was often under $18. This pricing was nothing but a headache for Tudor, as it put the electronic games at the same price point as Tudor's Super Bowl. And Coleco's Quarterback was usually selling for less than the Super Bowl. It's impossible to measure how many Mattel and Coleco sales would have been Tudor sales just a couple years earlier, but it's clear that the number was significant. Plus these computer games were brand new. The technology was modern and intoxicating. Electric football, other than appearances, hadn't changed much in 30 years. And the vibrating concept of the game was based on 40-year-old technology.

After all his years at Tudor, Norman knew well the fickle nature of the toy business. To sell out your line one year and then get blitzed by a competitor the next – this was all part of the game. And it really hadn't been a disastrous year for Tudor. Electric football was still selling. But the electronics genre offered up a different type of competition. It wasn't like Eddie Gluck getting the NFL, or Coleco starting its "World of Sports," or Munro putting floodlights on a game and running Joe Namath commercials during the *Tonight Show*. Something from outside of electric football was stealing the market, and it was also something from technology's cutting edge. And this technology was raising consumers' sports game expectations to a level that electric football could never match. It made electric football seem old-fashioned – which, truth be told, it was. Norman could feel a real change taking place. The hand-held electronic game bubble would likely pop sometime in time future, but Norman couldn't see boys reverting back to electric football after having held a Mattel or a Coleco electronic football game in their hands. For this new generation, electric football would always be a game whose time was past.

The cover of Tudor's 1979 sales catalog. (Collection of Norman Sas.)

EARL SHORES | RODDY GARCIA

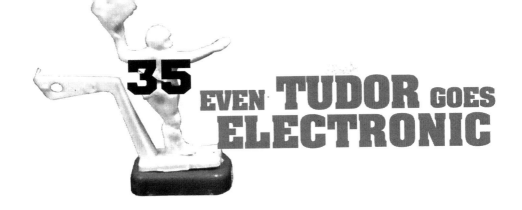

# 35 EVEN TUDOR GOES ELECTRONIC

lectric football's slide into the Christmas-present category of "ordinary" was under way. Tudor's longtime ties with the NFL were offering little in the way of a Hail Mary, even with the league's profile locked into what seemed to be a permanent state of ascendancy. The NFL's new 16-game schedule and riveting Super Bowl in Miami between the Cowboys and Steelers couldn't change the "electronics generation" perception that electric football was a game from the past. (The Steelers prevailed 35-31, as the Cowboys became the first team to score more than 30 points and lose a Super Bowl.)

With the company's main product overwhelmed by uncertainty, Tudor approached the coming Toy Fair with the exact same lineup as 1978. That meant only three electric football games were on display – the No. 500, the NFL No. 520, and the Super Bowl. Norman hadn't bothered with any *Playthings'* ads this year. He knew they would get lost in the electronics deluge that was overtaking the toy industry. Everyone wanted a piece of the electronics market. If you were in, it was almost like having a license for printing money.

Mattel had done so well over the last two years that it was bringing 247 new items to the 1979 Toy Fair. One of those toys was Mattel Electronic Football II, a more complex version of the original game. Coleco had a number of new items for the Fair, including a series of "Head-to-Head" hand-held electronic sports games. These games would allow two human players to play against each other instead of just against the computer. Coleco was also set to rake in additional profits after Sears decided it wanted its own piece of the hand-held game market. The company had agreed to let Sears re-brand and sell Coleco's Electronic Quarterback as the Sears Electronic Touchdown game.

But as always happens with popular toy items, there were imitators. Lots of them. By *Playthings'* own count, 120 new electronic games were set to debut at the 1979 Fair. And most of these games had nothing new to

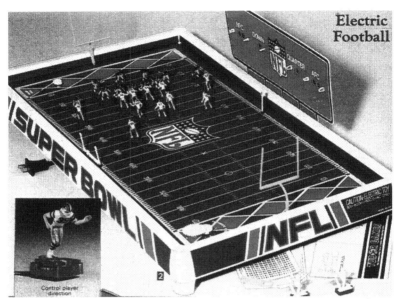

Electric Football

Sears' 1979 Super Bowl game. Sears was also selling the No. 500 and Tudor Divisional team sets. Sears 1979 *Wish Book,* page 634. ©Sears, Roebuck and Co. 1979.

offer. They were just another football or baseball clone to add to the ever-expanding electronic game pile.

The year unfolded with electronic games dominating the toy world. *Playthings'* March issue devoted four full pages to covering electronics at the Toy Fair, while the April issue gave electronic games the cover and an eight-page feature article. In an interesting development, one of the toy manufacturers quoted in this article was Norman. He offered a keen assessment of the future of electronic games: "As technology increases, the products will get more sophisticated and the chips will have more capacity," said Norman, adding something that no electronics manufacturer wanted to hear. "Prices will also have to come down eventually."

By the fall of 1979 Norman's prediction was holding up as the first generation of electronic sports games all carried cheaper price tags than the previous year. But it was the new games that carried the premium – Mattel Football II and Coleco's Head-to-Head games. They were the exciting "new and improved" games, overshadowing their older siblings. Yet things were going to get interesting as Christmas got closer. A lot more electronic football games were on the shelves this year, and many of these were made by companies whose names were not Mattel or Coleco.

Tudor still had the Sears *Christmas Book*, which was running almost a full page of Tudor games. The Super Bowl game was the headliner with the

No. 500, NFL Strategy, and Tudor electric baseball filling out the rest of the page (a Coleco hockey game was the final item). But unfortunately, electric football was nearly invisible in Christmas advertising. Sears no longer actively promoted the game, and for the first time in nearly a decade Toys R Us left electric football completely out of its ads. Electronic games took electric football's place, with knock-off sports games selling for as little as $15. That was now about what a Tudor NFL No. 520 cost. The only major retailer giving electric football a push was Woolco, which seemed not to be as heavily involved with electronics as other retailers.

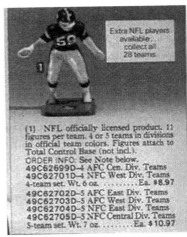

Sears' NFL Divisional team sets in 1979. Sears 1979 *Wish Book*, page 634. ⁰Sears, Roebuck and Co. 1979

Beyond the dated vibrating game concept, there was also the size issue. An electronic football game was much easier to store than an electric football game. With the price point the same, Tudor was in an uphill battle with the practical parent. Just three years ago an electric football game was at least 27" long. Now, a kid could hold an amazing action football game in the palm of his hand.

During the Christmas shopping season retailers reported that electronic games accounted for over 25% of all toys sales. The big three of electronic games – Mattel, Coleco, and Milton Bradley – were dominating the market, although this year Coleco's Head-to-Head Football was giving Mattel Football II a serious challenge. But a funny thing happened to electronic game makers just as their profits were overflowing – Texas instruments again ran out of the computer chips that powered the games. So instead of a glut of games, there was a shortage. Mattel, Coleco, and Milton Bradley began allocating their hot games based on how much of the total company line a retailer was carrying. Retailers who did not get what they wanted from the big three began to fill in the gaps in their electronic inventory with cheaper and less sophisticated knock-off games that used older (and readily-available) computer chips.

One of the companies stepping into electronic games at this point was a bit of surprise – Tudor. In the fall of 1979 Tudor managed to get its new NFL Electronic Football Game out on the market. The game was a first – it was the first game officially licensed by a professional sports league. Unfortunately an NFL endorsement just didn't seem to mean a whole lot for an electronic game. The players were just blips. It wasn't as if Tudor had painted NFL blips while Mattel or Coleco had unpainted ones. Having

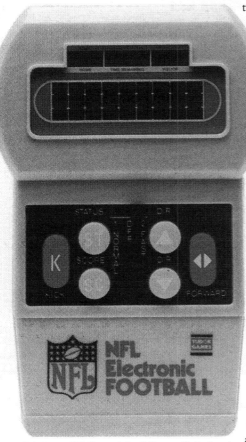

Tudor's 1979 NFL Electronic Football game. (Collection of Norman Sas.)

the NFL logo on the case didn't make the game any more exciting. And the game Tudor was selling wasn't particularly special. It was simply the equivalent of a 1978 Mattel or Coleco game.

Another unfortunate fact for Tudor was that it didn't have the distribution "weight" to get its new electronic games placed next to its electric football games. Those larger retailers who were still carrying Tudor electric football games were also carrying extensive lineups of Mattel or Coleco items. If Mattel or Coleco Electronic Football games were on the shelves, there was little room for Tudor's new offering. So Tudor's NFL Electronic Football games were relegated to the aisles of discounters like Murphy's Mart.

Obviously, Norman's decision to go into electronics was a concession to the times and the snowballing direction of sports games. It was an easy decision on the one hand, as there seemed to be no ceiling to the demand for electronic games – at least in 1979. Profits were there to be made. But for the inventor and perpetual guardian of electric football to start selling electronic football and knowingly undercut the already sagging sales of the item Tudor was most identified with...well, it wasn't an easy decision. In the past when challenges from Coleco and Munro seemed to be on the verge of shifting the sports game market, Norman kept to his belief that electric football would carry Tudor through any difficult times. It had done so for three decades, and there was no reason to doubt the appeal of the game. But with electronics, things were different. The game market was changing in ways never seen before. Some industry analysts were saying it was the biggest change in toys since the advent of plastics. Putting a Tudor Electronic Football game on the market showed that Norman had doubts about his game. When and if electronic games cooled down, electric football would not return to the prominence it had in 1977. Expectations had changed. Electronic games were all about having control. Sitting idly over a game watching 22 vibrating figures – that was pretty old fashioned.

For Christmas 1979, it was again a story of shortages. The best-selling item this year was Milton Bradley's electronic Simon game. In some areas of the country it was sold out by November, never to be restocked. In football, retailers were giving the sales edge to Coleco's Head-to-Head Football over Mattel's Football II. And in more bad news for Tudor, retailers were unanimous in proclaiming electronic football games as the leading sellers in the entire sports game genre. It turned out that

The box from Tudor's 1979 NFL Electronic Football game. (Collection of Earl Shores.)

electric football wasn't the only sports game being squeezed by electronics this year. One of the hot items from just a few years earlier was nearly invisible in 1979. Air powered hockey had also been swept aside by the tidal wave of electronic games.

Electronic games were dominating toy store shelves, but Tudor still had its Super Bowl. One of teams included in the Super Bowl – the white shoe Haiti Rams. (Photo by Earl Shores.)

The brass master that was used to make Tudor's "Quarterbacks of the NFL" line. This includes the figures sized for electric football, and Tudor's line of 3"-tall collectible figures. Norman Sas displayed the figure on his desk during Tudor's final years. (Collection of Roddy Garcia.)

# 36

# THE 1980's AND TUDOR'S FINAL DAYS

O ver 300 electronic games were on the market in 1980, including two NFL hand-held models from Tudor. The No. 800 was the company's entry level game, while the more sophisticated No. 850 was the "Deluxe" model. Both games appeared in the Tudor sales catalog on page two – electric football wasn't seen until page three. This placement was no accident. Tudor was still making three electric football games (the No. 500, the NFL No. 520, and the Super Bowl) but the number of retailers who wanted electric football was declining. Many were eagerly awaiting the next big thing. It was again coming from Mattel, as the toy giant took its massive profits and leaped into the television console video game market. Mattel's new game system – called Intellivision, as in "intelligent television" – was designed to take down the popular Atari 2600. Intellivision would have better graphics and smoother on-screen action. It would also have an official NFL football game...and a $300 list price.

Tudor and electric football still got a substantial presentation from Sears in 1980 with a page that was almost identical to the previous year's *Christmas Book*. But the final 15 pages of the catalog were taken up entirely by electronic games. Twelve of those pages consisted solely of hand-held models. The NFL and NFL Properties were also doing fine in 1980. NFL-licensed items took up the first 33 pages of the Sears catalog (including girls' flannel nightgowns). Somewhere off in his retirement, Larry Kent was smiling from ear-to-ear.

Finally late in the year, oversaturation became a problem in the hand-held game market. Mattel's once soaring earnings were dropping, thanks to sales and rebates that priced its electronic football games under $10. Milton Bradley's Simon game was also struggling, thanks to Simon clones and Milton Bradley's own Super Simon and Pocket Simon models. Consumers were getting picky with electronic games – the exception was Coleco's still

# 850 New for 1980!
# NFL Deluxe Electronic Football

The ultimate hand held Electronic Football Game. Precision designed to provide NFL Realism, challenge and fun.

No other Electronic Football Game has more features compare them:

- Like in the Pros teams change field direction at end of each quarter.
- Individual four way direction control of both quarterback and receiver.
- Two minute warning sounds before end of half and game.
- Continuous information display—down, yards to go, time, field position.
- Instant automatic set up after each play.
- Quarter display—shows 1st, 2nd, 3rd and 4th quarters.
- Constant ball position field marker—shows which side of 50 yd. line ball is on.
- Four speed or skill levels to choose from.
- Running back moves forward, reverse and laterally left and right.
- Safety
- Kickoff/Punts/Field Goals
- Runback/Rushing
- Passes/Intercepts
- 15 minute quarters
- Adaptor Jack for 110V AC—6V DC plug in adaptor

One or two can play and it's exciting to be in control, deciding when to run, pass or kick. The computerized defense is good and you've got to be better than your opponent to win.

Ages 8 to Adult

No 850
Box Size: 7½"x5½"x2"
8 Doz. Ctn. Wt. 51 lbs.
Cube: 9.042
4 penlite batteries required

**The new 850 NFL Deluxe Electronic Football Game from Tudor. The electronics market was booming. Tudor couldn't afford to not be part of it. 1980 Tudor sales catalog. (Collection of Norman Sas.)**

popular Head-to-Head line – the clone games were being marked down to bargain basement prices. In the end, it was a tough year to be heavily vested in hand-held electronic games.

On the flip side, 1980 was the year of the Atari 2600. The Atari was still priced between $130-150, but with the help of the home version of the arcade-hit Space Invaders, the 2600 became a hot item for Christmas, leaving the pricier Intellivision game decidedly earthbound in terms of sales. (There was also a football game for the Atari…where the men looked like invaders from space.) Electric football once again received very little ad support at Christmas, especially with major retailers trying to unload the mountains of unwanted hand-held electronic games. But even with the issue of oversupply, electronic games accounted for 10% of all the toys sold in 1980. In monetary terms this worked out to an astounding $375 million in total sales.

Tudor's concession to the hand-held electronic concept illustrated the uphill battle the company faced against the computer game onslaught. Even with support from Sears and a shakeout in the oversaturated hand-held market in 1981, electric football sales continued to fade. In 1982 Tudor abandoned its electronic games while giving the Super Bowl a complete redesign. Tudor also started selling "Quarterbacks of the NFL," which were a line of pre-painted electric football quarterback figures. The new players would be sold in complete sets – bags of 14 NFC quarterbacks or 14 AFC quarterbacks would be available from both Tudor and Sears. Thanks to a sharp and detailed paint job the quarterbacks added the first new piece of realism to electric football in some time.

But Tudor also brought out five new soccer games in 1982. This left the company that invented vibrating football with nearly twice as many soccer

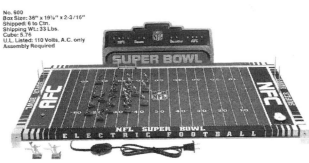

# 600 New!
# NFL Super Bowl
## with Total Team Control

No. 600
Box Size: 36" x 19⅛" x 2-3/16"
Shipped: 6 to Ctn.
Shipping Wt.: 33 Lbs.
Cube: 5.76
U.L. Listed: 110 Volts, A.C. only
Assembly Required

- Total Team Control—adjustable bases allow game players to secretly set the offensive and defensive football figures to run in any direction desired
- 22 players in 5 action poses plus 2 triple threat quarterbacks that kick, pass and run
- Both teams in their fully painted Super Bowl uniforms
- Self sticking identification numbers 2 to 89 allow for duplication of actual Super Bowl lineups
- Adjustable scoreboard
- Automatic timer—starts and stops with each play
- Magnetic first down marker with movable 10 yard chain
- Speed control
- Safety plug and heavy duty switch
- Recommended for ages 8½ to adult
- Steel gameboard
- All 28 NFL teams in official home and away uniforms are available to consumer by ordering directly from Tudor

Tudor's 1982 Super Bowl game. It was the final configuration of this model. 1982 Tudor sales catalog. (Collection of Norman Sas.)

games as football games. The Super Bowl revamp, unfortunately, failed to stimulate sales, in part because Tudor's top-of-the-line game now cost $28. For parents who could remember a $5 No. 500 model, electric football hardly seemed like a bargain anymore.

Norman knew that he had to look beyond electric football to keep Tudor viable, so in 1983 the company came out with two new product lines. The first new item actually made the cover of the 1983 Tudor sales catalog. These were Tudor's NFL Team Mascots. They were totally different from anything the company had ever done before – Tudor had never sold an item that wasn't supposed to be played with. These miniature versions of NFL team mascots were being marketed as collectibles. Three different sizes would be offered for this first year of production – a small plastic figure, a 7"-tall stuffed figure, and an 11" stuffed figure. Designing the Mascots line was Mike Gaines from NFL Properties. He had worked closely with Norman since the earliest days the NFL-Tudor partnership. (And once again overseeing Tudor's player production as well as the production of the NFL Mascots was Albert Sung.)

Next, Tudor had created an oversized set of the Quarterbacks of the NFL. The new figures were 3" tall – more than twice the height of a standard electric football player – and would be sold individually instead of in a set. There were 28 different quarterbacks in all, with one for each team in the NFL. The players were meticulously painted and numbered just like actual NFL quarterbacks. For example, the 49ers figure was no. 16, or Joe Montana; the Steelers figure was no. 12, or Terry Bradshaw. While there was little mystery about the quarterback's identities, there were

Tudor's 1982 "Quarterbacks of the NFL" electric football figures. From L-R: the Vikings, Falcons, and Giants. (Photo by Earl Shores)

no player names on the new figures. (Tudor would have to pay the NFL extra to license individual player images.) Each quarterback was blister-packaged on a 4" x 7" card that retailers would display on hanging racks in their stores. And like the NFL Mascots, they weren't to be played with. They, too, were being sold as collectibles.

Electric football's decline continued in 1984, with games and both types of Tudor NFL quarterbacks recording disappointing sales figures.

The cover of the 1983 Tudor sales catalog introducing the NFL Team Mascot line of figures. (Collection of Norman Sas.)

By contrast, sales of Tudor's NFL Mascots, now called "Huddles," were taking off. Sears and Montgomery Ward both gave the Huddles a full page in their respective Christmas catalogs, and the Huddles ended up occupying seven of the twelve pages in the 1985 Tudor sales catalog. Thanks to the Huddles' success, Tudor's three remaining electric football games were all jumbled together on page two of the sales catalog.

It was a state of affairs that would have been unfathomable just a decade earlier. Electric football's long and storied legacy was now down to a single page. But electric football wasn't the only toy struggling in 1985. During this same period of time the video game market collapsed from overproduction and lousy decision making. Intellivision and Atari consoles and games were being unloaded for next to nothing. Coleco had suffered its own video game disaster with Colecovision, whose debut came just as the console video game market was crashing. But even the smoldering clearance sale wreckage left by the implosion of the video game market wasn't going to revive electric football. Red LED blips and crudely animated television screen "players" had completely changed the sports action game paradigm.

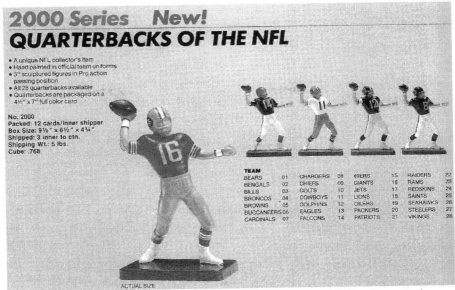

## 2000 Series   New!
# QUARTERBACKS OF THE NFL

- A unique NFL collector's item
- Hand painted in official team uniforms
- 3" sculptured figures in Pro action passing position
- All 28 quarterbacks available
- Quarterbacks are packaged on a 4½" x 7" full color card

No. 2000
Packed: 12 cards/inner shipper
Box Size: 9½" x 8½" x 4¾"
Shipped: 3 inner to ctn.
Shipping Wt.: 5 lbs.
Cube: .768

**TEAM**

| BEARS | 01 | CHARGERS | 08 | 49ERS | 15 | RAIDERS | 22 |
| BENGALS | 02 | CHIEFS | 09 | GIANTS | 16 | RAMS | 23 |
| BILLS | 03 | COLTS | 10 | JETS | 17 | REDSKINS | 24 |
| BRONCOS | 04 | COWBOYS | 11 | LIONS | 18 | SAINTS | 25 |
| BROWNS | 05 | DOLPHINS | 12 | OILERS | 19 | SEAHAWKS | 26 |
| BUCCANEERS | 06 | EAGLES | 13 | PACKERS | 20 | STEELERS | 27 |
| CARDINALS | 07 | FALCONS | 14 | PATRIOTS | 21 | VIKINGS | 28 |

ACTUAL SIZE

Tudor's 3"-tall collectible NFL quarterback figures. From the 1983 Tudor sales catalog. (Collection of Norman Sas.)

Fortunately for Tudor, Huddles sales were benefiting from a recent craze that had swept the U.S. Now helping to counterbalance Coleco's disastrous forays into video games and home computers (the infamous "Adam") were the astounding sales figures from the company's Cabbage Patch dolls. As a result, Tudor's Huddles became one of NFL Properties' top selling items in 1985.

Tudor expanded in 1986, adding a line of college football Huddles. That meant the company had a sales catalog with four vibrating games – the Super Bowl, the No. 500, Electric Baseball, and Electric Horse Racing – going up against eight pages of Huddles. And electric football sales weren't going to be helped by the Super Bowl game crossing the $30 mark for the first time ever. The Huddles line kept Tudor going in 1987, a year where the "discounted" Toys R Us price for a Super Bowl game was $35.99. This was an outlay that proved too steep for what electric football had become in the eyes of many toy shoppers – a piece of nostalgia. The final straw for Norman was Black Monday, October 19, 1987, when the U.S. stock market declined more than 22%. It was the largest one-day percentage loss in history, and markets around the globe also

A winning game plan...

The 1985 Sears catalog with Tudor's Super Bowl and painted quarterback figures. Sears *Wish Book '85*, page 585. ©Sears, Roebuck & Co. 1985.

suffered major losses. One of the biggest losers that day and in the coming weeks was the Hong Kong stock market. With so much of the Tudor line now originating in the Far East – the Huddles came exclusively from this region – Norman knew that the challenges of 1988 would be brutal.

During the late 70's and early 80's, the NFL had truly become "America's Game," yet the company who helped jump-start NFL Properties two decades earlier had been left behind. Tudor was now like many aging NFL stars whose moments of greatness were a thing of the past. As a true toy veteran, Norman could have squeezed one more year out of Tudor on guile

The Tudor factory today. It's now a building of luxury condominiums called "The Toy Factory." (Photo by Robin Shores.)

alone. But something that contributed to Tudor's long-time success was Norman's ability to be a hard-eyed realist. And in 1988 he had no illusions about the future. There were still profits to be culled from the Huddles line, but Tudor, at least since Norman took over in 1948, had always been about sports action games. A real market for the type of game Tudor was famous for hadn't existed since the late 1970's. So in 1988, the 60th year of Tudor's existence, the 63-year-old Sas decided to sell the company. Forty-three years at 176 Johnson Street in Brooklyn and almost 40 years in electric football would all come to an end. The new owner, the Superior Toy & Manufacturing Co., would move everything – "lock, stock, and barrel" – to Chicago.

"It was time to go," said Sas. "Nothing lasts forever."

It might be argued that 40 years in the toy business comes pretty close.

Miggle's innovative helmet stamp process produced detailed reproductions of NFL team logos. (Photo by Earl Shores.)

# 37 BEYOND BROOKLYN

**B**uying Tudor was just one of several ambitious moves made by Superior Toy in 1988. The company was expanding, with a five-year plan and significant financing from Continental Bank in Chicago. In addition to Tudor, Superior purchased New Jersey-based HG Toys, and also a new $1.2 million warehouse in Rockford, Illinois. By early 1989 Tudor and HG Toys were together under one roof at Superior's new 2020 Harrison Avenue address. (The company also had plants operating in Chicago and Peoria.)

After cataloging tractor trailers full of Tudor equipment, Superior warehouse production manager Kathy Holford assembled an archive room of Tudor's entire line, including electric football games dating back to 1949. Superior's President Mike Landsman then made the trip from Chicago to inspect the display and decide what parts of the Tudor line would be put into production. For 1989 Landsman decided to produce the iconic and now forty year-old No. 500 model, as well as the current version of the Super Bowl. Superior's Peoria division would produce the NFL Huddles line.

Superior was leaning heavily on Kmart and Toys R Us to reestablish electric football in the toy world, but the retailers were having trouble making a dent in their Tudor inventory. The 1989 Christmas shopping season was barely underway when Continental Bank unexpectedly called Superior's $23 million loan.

"For no reason and out of the blue they called the loan," said Landsman. "We had a plan and an agreement...to this day I still don't know why the loan was called." Landsman was pushed out of the company and the bank brought in its own people. "It wasn't fair what they did to Mike," said Holford. "He had put his heart and soul into that company for decades."

Many of the people brought in to run Superior were coming from a recently bankrupt and now defunct toy company – Coleco. In the atmosphere of uncertainty triggered by Landsman's ouster, the Coleco castoffs did little to win the trust of Superior's employees. "I didn't care for them, and didn't associate with them," said Holford.

Production of electric football came to a halt under the new management. The only games available were the ones left on store shelves. In February of 1990 Continental Bank brought in former Coleco chief financial officer Paul Meyer to rescue Superior and appease clamoring creditors. Meyer had left Coleco just weeks after the company filed for bankruptcy and reorganization in June of 1988. (His resignation also came just weeks after Coleco appointed a new chief executive officer. The new CEO's name was Brian Clarke.)

Miggle Toys warehouse manager Kathy Holford, January 1996. (Photo by Roddy Garcia.)

Meyer's tenure at Superior got off to a rocky start. On March 9th three Superior creditors filed a court petition forcing the company into a Chapter 7 bankruptcy (the ultimate outcome of Chapter 7 is liquidation). The largest creditor in the filing was Leaf, Inc., which supplied gumballs for Superior's extremely profitable line of gumball machines. In the petition Leaf claimed it was owed $1.25 million.

With Continental Bank intimately involved in Superior's day-to-day operations, financing was quickly arranged to convert the bankruptcy from a Chapter 7 to a Chapter 11. (Under Chapter 11 the company could remain operational while restructuring its debt.) During the Chapter 11 filing, which took place on March 27, it was revealed that Superior Toy was more than $20 million in debt.

Continental Bank was already infamous for having received a $4.5 billion bailout from the Federal Deposit Insurance Corporation in 1984, thanks to its dealings with a notorious and unscrupulous energy loan specialist in Oklahoma called Penn National Bank. Despite government oversight and 'the largest ever "too big to fail" bank bailout, Continental Bank's current condition was far from sound. And now it was coming under federal scrutiny for again being involved in risky loan deals. Almost 10% of Continental Bank's assets – or $3 billion – were in highly leveraged transactions (known in financial world shorthand as "HLT's"). These HLT's were used for mergers and corporate buyouts, an example being Superior buying Tudor and HG Toys. A bank with a 10% HLT load in

In the early 1990's when Superior Toy was in bankruptcy and not making electric football, this mysterious and unauthorized Monday Night Football game appeared on the shelves of discount retailers in the U.S. ABC was not amused and the game was quickly removed from the market.

1990 was very unusual. By contrast, the highly respected J.P Morgan & Co. had a 1990 HLT load of just 1.8%.

During extended legal wrangling in the summer of 1990, Leaf claimed that Continental Bank had siphoned off more than $1 million from Superior, paying itself instead of creditors. Leaf also discovered that their own law firm, Sidley & Austin, had been advising Continental Bank on how to recover debt from Superior. As a result, Leaf was suing Sidley & Austin for conflict of interest.

This all made 1990 a very tangled time in the courtroom and at Superior. Among the creditors whose payments had stopped was Norman Sas. Tudor had been bought on "paper" – that is, Norman had received very little cash up front for his company. Payments were to come out of Superior's future earnings, but at this point, the company wasn't even acknowledging its largest creditors.

# ELECTRIC FOOTBALL NEWS

$1.00          (The Official Newsletter of Tudor NFL Super Bowl Electric Football)          Spring 1994
★★★★★★★★★★★★★★★★★★★★★★★★★★★★★★★★★★★★★★★★★★★★★★★★★★★★★★★★★★★★★

### FROM THE COMMISSIONER'S DESK . . .
*by Commissioner Michael Landsman*

Greetings to all Tudor NFL Super Bowl Electric Football players across the country. My name is Michael Landsman and I am the president of Miggle Toys, Inc. For those of you who are not familiar with me or my company, Miggle Toys, Inc. is a toy manufacturer based out of Illinois, and most importantly to you, we are the ones responsible for last year's resurrection of Tudor NFL Super Bowl Electric Football.

The Miggle Newsletter announcing the return of electric football. (Collection of Earl Shores.)

# First and goal

The 1960s phenomenon of electric football games,
where you *always* ran and *never* passed

BY EARL SHORES
PHOTOS BY THE AUTHOR

In 1968, Santa brought the NFL into my living room. I remember my trembling fingers lining up the Cleveland Browns and New York Giants for a Christmas morning kickoff—a harsh intrusion of reality for my parents, since kickoff came at 6 a.m. The game's electric *bzzz* must have seemed like the alarm clock from hell, but it was a sound they were used to hearing by the end of January.

Santa had left electric football games before, but none was like Tudor's NFL Football Model no. 620. Its enormous green field, modern single-post goals, end zone N-F-L lettering, clip-on grandstand with detailed crowd scene, and scoreboard that could display any NFL team—hey, I could almost smell the grass.

By the late 1960s, electric football games were everywhere; it seemed like every kid had one. Tudor Metal Products Company, of Brooklyn, New York, was the giant in the field, having built games since the mid-1950s. Their tin-lithographed players of earlier days evolved into paint-'em-yourself plastic figures in the 1960s, but the electric *bzzz* remained a constant.

However, when Tudor obtained a late-1960s license from the National Football League, an electric football landmark was marked. Electric football games had developed true-to-life identities, making them even more appealing to young kids who idolized Unitas, Namath, and Jurgenson.

As a collector of electric football games, I've discovered many interesting elements about this unsung collectible. Not only do many games feature early NFL licensing, they're also great fun to play with, and they make wonderful conversation pieces. It's amazing how many people have fond (or frustrated) memories concerning their own electric football games. Read on and remember yours.

### SIMPLICITY AND ACTION

By today's video game standards, electric football games are primitive, but their simple technology thrilled generations of kids. Most included only the absolute basics: an electric relay mounted under the game vibrates the field, and players move when vibrations reach their bases. You can regulate vibration intensity by turning the "speed control knob."

Wound too tight, the game is quiet and players hardly move. Too loose, and it's cacophony. The optimal noise-to-speed ratio was a matter of personal preference—and often depended on mom and dad's tolerance.

Kids with a desire to win learned the "secrets" behind electric football. The main one involved "tapping." Taught to me by my next-door neighbor, this technique involved tapping lightly on the field to make the players move. It slowed things down a bit, but a shrewd tapper could alter his rhythm to modify the course of players.

Electric football. Any kid who had one during the late 1960s remembers 'em. They were loud, obnoxious toys that rarely worked as advertised—but were incredible fun nonetheless!

**Electric football's profile was also rising in the world of toy collecting.**
*Collecting Toys,* pages 52-55, October 1994 (Vol. 2 No. 5).

So by summer's end Leaf and a committee of creditors were suing Continental Bank for $50 million. Charges in the suit included fraud, racketeering, breach of fiduciary responsibility, and unfair competition.

As staffing got thinner and thinner at Superior, Kathy Holford found herself overseeing the Rockford warehouse. Then finally on December 7, 1990, her decades of experience and institutional memory were deemed unnecessary. She was relieved of her responsibilities, with "relief" being a large part of the emotions she felt. After Kathy's departure Superior stumbled into 1991 still in Chapter 11 and still in corporate limbo. In April a broker for the bank began taking sealed bids for the entire company, or at least whatever was left. It was no secret that things were disappearing from the warehouse. "A lot of the company went out the backdoor," said Landsman with a sigh.

This attempt to sell the company failed, and Superior lasted, in name at least, until December 26, 1991. On the day after Christmas, Superior Toy filed for Chapter 7 bankruptcy. The assets of the company would be sold off in a bankruptcy court, and the creditors would then get in line to try recoup whatever they could. One creditor who didn't bother to get in line despite being owed millions of dollars was Norman Sas.

It was in federal bankruptcy court that Mike Landsman purchased the Superior Toy assets designated as Tudor Games. He purchased it "as is," meaning there was no guarantee as to what or even how much of the old Tudor Mike now owned. Kathy Holford had already agreed to be part of the new company, now called Miggle Toys, and Mike and Kathy returned to the Rockford warehouse to see what they could salvage. Mike knew that when he left Superior, Tudor was intact. And when Kathy left the warehouse on her last day, Tudor was mostly intact. Some of the Tudor

The authors' display of games at the 1996 Miggle Convention in Chicago. (Photo by Ernesto Verdeja.)

inventory had been sold off in lots during Chapter 11, but the archive room and Tudor's paperwork still remained in place when Kathy left her 2020 Harrison Avenue office for a final time.

Mike and Kathy were not ready for what they found. Much of what Mike thought he bought was missing, and a number of areas in the building were totally closed off...they weren't even allowed to go see if some of the Tudor stock was simply in a different location. Kathy was shocked, as her carefully constructed archive room was mostly cleaned out, and Tudor's paperwork had been ransacked and scattered about like confetti from a ticker-tape parade. It was a devastating moment, and it took some very deliberate effort for Mike and Kathy to gather themselves, and decide what exactly they should focus on. Quickly it was decided. They would focus on teams, parts, and tooling...and how to move forward.

"We weren't worried about where we'd been," said Kathy. "We were worried about where we were going."

And they needed to sort out the Tudor remnants quickly, as the plant had been sold and new owners were chomping at the bit to take over. Anything not removed from the building would end up auctioned off or in a dumpster. During a second solo trip to the plant, Kathy developed a composite plan of all the tooling and inventory Mike would need to get Miggle Toys and electric football going again. It was going to be a very big job, and require more work and capital than Mike had anticipated.

The Miggle Super Bowl game and Monday Night Football stadium in the 1998 J.C Penney *Christmas Catalog.* Page 557. ©J.C. Penney, Inc. 1998.

It took until 1993 for Miggle Toys to get electric football back on the market, and even this roll out was low key as Mike and Kathy got production and inventories up to full speed. One of the most important things Mike accomplished was getting the NFL back on board. As a result Miggle was able to have a highly visible start to 1994.

Miggle was given permission to set up their NFL Super Bowl game in the pressroom at the 1994 Super Bowl in Atlanta, an event that was reported in the first ever Miggle newsletter, the *Electric Football News.* In the newsletter, which Mike included in every Miggle game and team order, he introduced himself to the electric football community, titling himself as the "commissioner." And in a bold and very forward thinking move Mike encouraged people to contact Miggle. Not only could Mike get content for future newsletters, he could also find out exactly who was still interested in electric football.

Miggle Toys President Mike Landsman addressing those gathered at the 1996 Miggle Convention. (Photo by Earl Shores.)

What Mike discovered was, not only were there people still playing electric football, the game had been around long enough to now be considered a "collectible." In fact, Mike's resurrection of electric football coincided with a toy-collecting boom, evidenced by the existence of three different publications covering the hobby (*Toy Shop*, *Toy Trader*, and the glossy full-color *Collecting Toys*). Electric football collector Mark Newell had even been interviewed in the Miggle newsletter.

When *Collecting Toys* published "First and goal" in its October 1994 issue – including a two-page spread of a 1968 NFL No. 620 – the response was overwhelming. Letters flooded into the magazine and connections were made all across the now expanding world of electric football. NFL teams were available from Miggle, and Mike got the Super Bowl game into the J.C. Penney Christmas catalog, as well as Back to Basics, a toy catalog that specialized in selling classic American toys. Miggle's successful comeback year with Tudor finished in Chicago in January 1995, with the first-ever electric football "Super

**Break through the endzone or ozone!**

**J. Monday Night Football Lighted Stadium.** Get ready for great night games with this Electric Football stadium. It really lights up the action. Realistic crowds, markings and a working score board add to the excitement. Requires 8 "AA" batteries, not included. Ages 8 years and up.
19337 ..............................$79.99

Miggle's Deluxe NFL Electric Football Game in the 2000 Sears Wish Book. Page 141. ©Sears, Roebuck and Co. 2000.

Dedicated electric football fans gather at 2000 Miggle Convention in Washington, D.C.

Bowl." Four "teams" were picked from videos submitted to Miggle. Winning that first championship were Mark and Bill Klingbeil, who would become pillars of the contemporary electric football community.

Mike was able to get electric football into more retailers in 1995, including Toys R Us, and he planned a more ambitious electric football gathering that he hoped would draw attention to his next Super Bowl. At the prestigious Hyatt Regency Hotel in downtown Chicago, Miggle held the first ever Electric Football National Convention in January of 1996 (reports at the time titled it as the "first"). The Chicago press had full coverage, with the *Sun-Times* featuring Mike on its cover just days before the event opened. It was the first true gathering of the electric football nation. From league and solitaire players, to figure and stadium makers, to painters and collectors, the entire spectrum of electric football turned out for what many viewed as an once-in-a-lifetime event. Attendees read like a who's who in electric football's past and future: Myron Evans, Chuck Jones, Lavell Shelton, Byron Jackson, David Nickles, Mark Newell, Reginald Rutledge, and Larry Walker. Mark and Bill Klingbeil were also there, successfully defending their Super Bowl title.

Tudor Games logo in 2012. (Courtesy of Doug Strohm and Tudor Games.)

Mike turned his convention into an annual event, which became a high point for electric football each year. In the meantime, Miggle continued to sell its games in J.C. Penney, Sears, Back to Basics, and Toys R Us. In 1997 Miggle introduced an ABC Monday Night Electric Football Game, complete with a giant wraparound stadium, and floodlights. (Unlike Munro 25 years earlier, Miggle had gotten an official deal with MNF.) The stadium and games were sold separately, which was a good thing because the combined cost of the two items was almost $150. An electronic scoreboard became part of the Miggle line in the late 90's, as did stamped helmets. Instead of painting the team logo on the helmets, Miggle now had a process where a very detailed replica of the NFL team logos could be "stamped" on the helmet. Mike and Miggle received well-deserved plaudits from all corners of the electric football community for this innovation.

Miggle tried to make its mark in 2000 by producing a giant stand alone "Deluxe NFL Electric Football Game." It was the largest electric football game ever made, measuring in at 48" by 24." With an all-wood cabinet, it outclassed Coleco's faux wood grain models of the early 1970's, and certainly would have been a great fit back in the long-forgotten "Game Room" era of electric football. Sears was selling the game, as was Back to Basics. It was truly a beautiful item with a Super Bowl-sized $379 price tag.

One of Miggle's major triumphs of the period was its website, which included an online chat board where electric football fans and coaches could make contact with each other. A challenge for hobbyists who played the game seriously was developing a set of universally accepted rules, as well as standards for players and bases. Leagues and playing styles had evolved regionally over time. Despite the sophistication of play, there were rule and equipment variations that made inter-regional play a challenge. To keep the playing field even, Mike had turned to handing out stock Miggle equipment to his Super Bowl participants. The coaches had to make the best of what they got – the results were amazing.

Tudor Games President Doug Strohm and author Earl Shores at the 2013 International Toy Fair in New York City. (Photo by Denise Strohm Chrystowski.)

That Mike was able to keep Miggle and electric football going for more than a decade into the new millennium years of Xbox 360, Playstation 3, and Wii, is quite a testament to his devotion to the game. He attempted to keep up with the hobbyists who were looking for "more" from electric football by making special bases, paints, and player poses. And he also took "requests," eventually making a line of 1967 "Big" players, as well as recreating the hallowed Tudor No 620 model. Even after losing the NFL license in 2007 Mike kept moving forward, quickly lining up licensing agreements with the Rose Bowl and prominent college teams.

But by 2011, after spending almost twenty years as the face of electric football and fifty years in the toy business, Mike was ready to move on. In February of 2012 he sold Miggle Toys and the Tudor line to Ballpark

Classics, Inc., a Seattle-based maker of Major League Baseball-licensed tabletop baseball games. Ballpark president Doug Strohm officially made Tudor Games the name of his company, astutely using the six-decade union between "Tudor" and "electric football" to provide immediate brand recognition in the toy world. Thanks to the vision of Doug Strohm electric football is still available, and seems to be in very good hands for the future. (www.TudorGames.com)

For those enthusiastic and exuberant electric football devotees who first gathered in Chicago in 1996, the Miniature Football Coaches Association is what many envisioned. (In fact, the MFCA was founded in 2007 by some of those early convention attendees.) Guided by Lynn Schmidt in 2013, the MFCA provides not only organization, but also a unique mixture of professionalism and welcome to anyone interested in electric football. Whether you're a "pro" looking for serious competition, or haven't touched an electric football game since the 1970's, the MFCA will welcome you aboard and help get you started. Like Doug Strohm they are keeping electric football alive and moving forward. (www.miniaturefootball.org)

As of the spring of 2013, electric football's status is this: Sixty-four years after the first Tudor electric football game rolled off the production line, the game is still available. That's longer than Mouse Trap®, longer than Barbie®, longer than Hot Wheels®, longer than Etch-A-Sketch®, longer than Play-Doh®, longer than GI Joe®, longer than the Hula Hoop®, and Mr. Potato Head®.

It's a toy legacy worth remembering – and one worth celebrating.

# ACKNOWLEDGEMENTS

**T**his book was started decades ago, in that innocent time when hours were spent studying the Sears Christmas *Wish Book*. To think that our younger selves would eventually wind up talking to and getting to know many of the men who were responsible for some of the best and warmest memories of childhood...is totally astounding. Sometimes dreams do come true.

But while electric football was often about dreaming, the toy business was and still is a real life endeavor that often, like life, involves harsh and unpleasant outcomes. One of the unpleasant life outcomes we experienced while putting this book together was having most of its key contributors pass away before a truly worthy version was finalized. The sadness of these losses will always be part of this project. It is our hope that we can repay the generosity of everyone who contributed by making sure their stories are told.

This book would not have been possible without Norman Sas, who spoke with us on so many occasions and put up with us asking the same questions over and over and over. Not only did he provide us with a treasure trove of Tudor materials, he offered us perspective, guidance, and encouragement at every step. We were grateful for his patience too, as the end point of this project was always seemingly just beyond our grasp. He was a true gentleman, and we will always treasure the warmth and kindness he offered through the years. It was our privilege to work with him and tell his story. We feel incredibly fortunate that he and his family were able to see an advance copy of the book before his passing in June 2012.

We are also grateful for all of Lee Payne's contributions. It was exciting to learn about the physical process involved in bringing 3-D players to electric football, and to also get a feel for how much of an artist Mr. Payne truly was. (He was a very keen businessman as well.) His talents were not lost on several generations of sports-minded boys. (Mr. Payne passed away in 2003.)

Also providing invaluable information about the nuts and bolts of manufacturing and painting Lee's players was Albert Sung. He oversaw the entire Tudor NFL team operation in Hong Kong for many years, and shared with

The authors setting up a photo shoot for the book. (Photo by Terri Garcia.)

us a number of electric football photos and stories that can best be described as one-of-a-kind. (Mr. Sung passed away in 2006.)

Many thanks to Roger Atkin, the former NFL Properties executive who provided critical puzzle pieces about the formation of NFL Enterprises, as well as the relationship between the NFL and Tudor. As someone who worked closely with Larry Kent and John Carney, Mr. Atkin was able to help us understand the roles those two played in building NFL Properties into a licensing powerhouse.

Earl and Roddy working together in the early days of the project. (Photo by Terri Garcia.)

And on to the competitors. It was a pleasure to have had a number of conversations with Don Munro Jr., who not only provided the wonderful story about his electric football conversation with Norman, but also detailed information about the workings of the toy business. Of course he was able to provide an insider view on the troubles of the Servotronics-Munro partnership, and its subsequent demise. His story of gathering up personal files from the post-auction debris of Munro's liquidated factory is hard to forget. He was very generous in sharing the paperwork he salvaged that day. Our conversations with Mr. Munro (who passed away in 1999), would have never taken place without the help of table hockey historian Rob Raven. We are grateful to Rob for sharing his friendship with Don Munro.

From the Coleco side, Brian Clarke, who went on to become CEO of Coleco in 1988, was incredibly open and magnanimous about the good old days of electric football. (Mr. Clarke is actually pictured in a 1972 Coleco *Playthings* ad.) In a single yet vibrant and wide-ranging conversation, Mr. Clarke was able to fill in many gaps in our story. (Mr. Clarke succumbed to cancer in 2006.)

Both Mr. Munro and Mr. Clarke were gentlemen – it seems to go with the era – offering nothing but praise for Tudor and Norman Sas. And they told their own stories in a very "just-the-facts" manner; at no time did it feel like they were trying to exaggerate the achievements of their respective companies. This strain of gentlemanly humility ran deep in Norman Sas too, and it's an endearing quality that made us determined to tell the story of all the great Toy Men – Eddie Gluck included – who were part of electric football.

Another gentleman and accomplished toy man who contributed not only to the book, but also to the "present" of electric football, is Mike Landsman. We are grateful for Mike's honesty in recounting his trials at Superior Toy and the subsequent difficulties of getting electric football back into the public eye. And we are grateful to Mike for connecting us with Kathy Holford, who ran the warehouses for both Superior and Miggle Toys. Kathy's detailed recollection and ground floor viewpoint are a treasured part of our story. Kathy, tragically, lost her life in a car accident.

Much of the toy history in this book was reconstructed in the Lower Level of the Science, Industry, and Business Library at 34th & Madison Avenue in New York City. It houses the largest collection of toy industry journals in the country, and is truly the Olduvai Gorge of American toy history. The library's *Playthings* holdings stretch from 1912 to 2006. Many long and fruitful days were spent thumbing through the pages of *Playthings*.

Gail Sniegowski's editorial input was vital in assembling our text. She polished our words and also sharpened our focus on the true story of electric football. We are grateful for all of her contributions and her encouragement.

Finally, we have Michael Kronenberg to thank for making this book look *amazing*. He's an incredible artist, and a fellow electric football enthusiast who "sees" the game as we see it. It's hard to imagine this book without Michael's contributions. We are thankful that our original cover shouted "amateur" so loud that when Michael saw it, he had just a single thought: "These guys need help!!"

To a time when the greatest football games were played on your living room floor...

# ABOUT THE AUTHORS

Earl Shores, Norman Sas, Roddy Garcia. Florida, February 2010.

Earl Shores and Roddy Garcia have been chasing the story of electric football for almost two decades. They have authored numerous articles about the game for publications ranging from the *Beckett Football Monthly* to *Toy Shop*, and have been interviewed by print and video media on both the national and local level. (The *Chicago Sun-Times* called them the "country's foremost collectors of electric football games.") During Mr. Shores' long and accomplished writing career he has covered the International Toy Fair in New York City, and written about sports and toys for *Sports Illustrated*, *Highlights for Children*, the *Washington Post*, the *Philadelphia Inquirer*, the *Chicago Tribune*, *Toy Shop*, and *Sports Collector's Digest*. He also spent time as a Contributing Writer for *Eastern Surf Magazine*.

After meeting in 1994, Shores and Garcia developed a remarkable friendship based on their love of toys, the Bud Grant-era Vikings, and the Beatles. (Both wives claim that the pair are actually long-lost brothers.) They have been lucky enough to share many special experiences together, including the one above, finally meeting the creator of electric football – Norman Sas.

# NOTES

Events in this book have been reconstructed from a number of sources, including newspaper and magazine reporting of the time, as well as personal recollections by the participants involved. All efforts have been made by the authors and publisher to give an accurate portrayal of the historical events described. However, personal memories often fade over time, and unfortunately many of people within the pages of this book have long since passed away. Some of their views and "voices" had to be reconstructed or inferred from the sources that were available. All dialogue comes from direct quotes - there are no "made up" conversations in this book.

Every effort was made to make sure the information used was confirmed and correct at press time. But do to the inherent difficulties involved when writing about historical events, the authors and publisher do not assume and hereby disclaim any liability to any party for any loss, damage, or disruption caused by errors or omissions, whether such errors or omissions resulted from negligence, accident, or any other cause.

---

Citations from the *New York Times*, *Washington Post*, *Los Angeles Times*, and *Chicago Tribune* were acquired from the ProQuest Historical Newspapers online research database, while other newspapers citations were acquired from NewspaperArchive.com. The numbering of pages through these databases does not always align with page numbering in the actual newspapers. For example, an article that appears on page 1 in a newspaper may be numbered page 5 in a historical newspapers database – being that it was the fifth article entered into the database for this particular newspaper issue.

## Abbreviations

| | |
|---|---|
| CT | *Chicago Tribune* |
| CCB | *Crain's Chicago Business* |
| LAT | *Los Angeles Times* |
| NYT | *New York Times* |
| MW | *Montgomery Ward* |
| PT | *Playthings* |
| SI | *Sports Illustrated* |
| THW | *Toy & Hobby World* |
| WP | *Washington Post* |
| WSJ | *Wall Street Journal* |

## Chapter 2

*Tudor had invented and manufactured a cardboard toy:* Tudor Walkie-Talkie Toy Fair ad, *Playthings*, February 1945.

*Tudor was carrying the expense of a new Brooklyn factory:* "Tudor Metal Products Corp. Buys New Factory," page 212, *PT*, November 1945.

*The changes were announced:* "Tudor Metal Products Announces New Officers," page 114, *Playthings*, July 1948.

*Throughout the pages:* Norman A. Sas, *Characteristics and Problems of the Toy Manufacturer*, Thesis (B.S.), Department of Business and Engineering Administration, Massachusetts Institute of Technology, May 1947.

*The ultimate aim:* ibid.

## Chapter 3

*The first Toy Fair was held in 1902:* "American Toy Fair – 75th year and going strong," page 62-63, *PT*, February 1978.

*New York City's Toy District:* "Toy Center on Fifth Ave. Is Quiet, but Not for Long," page C8, *NYT*, June 11, 2003.

## Chapter 4

*Tudor's 1937 Electric Auto Race*: Photo of Eugene Levay and game: page 42, *PT*, May 1937. "Electric Auto Race Offers Fun And Thrills": page 204, *PT*, April 1939.

*The electric horse race had the unfortunate luck*: "New Tudor Number Ready For Fair," page 264, *PT*, March 1941. Tudor ad: page 251, ibid.

*On Sunday, college football coverage expanded*: "Sports Section 5," pages 1-5, *NYT*, Sunday, October 12, 1947.

*The crowds major college football powers were drawing*: "New Record For Crowds": page 50, *NYT*, November 25, 1946.

*Attracting 70,060 spectators*: "Yankees and Browns Play Thrilling Draw Before Record Crowd of 70,060," page 33, *NYT*, November 24, 1947.

*Television manufacturer DuMont was enticing buyer*: DuMont advertisement: page A-9, *The Bridgeport Sunday Post*, November 2, 1947.

*During the fall of 1947, television programing*: "Television," page X10, *NYT*, November 9, 1947; "Television": page X10, *NYT*, November 16, 1947; "Television": page X10, *NYT*, November 23, 1947.

*Norman's gut must have felt pretty good as 1948 wound down*: "Programs On The Air": page 62, *NYT*, November 25, 1948; "Football Crowds Bigger This Year": page 38, *NYT*, December 10, 1948

*NFL title was decided in a snowstorm so intense*: "Eagles Win National Football League Title in Driving Snowstorm": page 33, *NYT*, December 20, 1948.

*The Browns had no trouble winning*: "Browns Rout Buffalo, Annex All-America Honors 3d Year in Row," page 34, *NYT*, December 20, 1948.

*Tudor's full-page ad in the Toy Fair issue*: "Tudor! A Name for Quality and Service," page 146, *PT*, March 1949.

*Tonole was essential*: "Joe Tonole New Sales Manager For Tudor Metal Products," *PT*, August 1945.

*Exposure in the Toy Fair issue*: "New Tudor Electric Football Game," *PT*, March 1949.

*Norman had already registered the name Electric Football*: Reg. No. 2,244,533, United States Patent and Trademark Office.

*To promote the new game*: Norman Sas, personal interview.

*Tonole went back to Playthings for promotion*: "Tudor's Electric Football Game," *PT*, September 1949.

*One of those early retailers*: "Men Actually Move in New Electric Football Game!," page 34, *NYT*, September 11, 1949.

*DuMont network planned to televise five Notre Dame football games*: "The Field of Television: News and Notes: Football," page X9, *NYT*, June 5, 1949.

*NBC was also jumping on the college football bandwagon*: "In The Field of Television: News and Notes — Football": page X9, *NYT*, September 11, 1949.

*Fifteen NFL games would be televised*: "Radio-Video 15 Professional Football Games Scheduled for Television by ABC": page 42, *NYT*, August 30, 1949.

*College football's popularity*: "Notre Dame Routs No. Carolina, 42-6": page S1, *NYT*, November 13, 1949.

*The NFL Bulldogs and AAFC Yankees*: "Yankees Turn Back Hornets," page 22, *NYT*, November 14, 1949; "Cardinals Roll Up Record Score Defeating Bulldog Eleven": page 22, *NYT*, November 14, 1949.

*Only though radio*: "Facts, Figures on Today's Game," page A11, *LAT*, December 18. 1949.

## Chapter 5

*He was there as a courtesy*: Norman Sas, personal interview.

*Another part of the agreement*: Levay, Eugene. "Vibrating Propelling Device." U. S. Patent 2,167,985. Issued August 1, 1939.

*And what Norman was able to achieve*: Cahalane, M.A. "Toy Foot Ball Game Board." U. S. Patent 593,512. Issued November 9, 1897.

*A finger snap propulsion*: Pell, J. L. E., "Game Apparatus." U. S. Patent 808.111.

*Rubino even proposed*: Rubino, Robert. " Football Game." U. S. Patent 1,603,717. Issued October 19, 1926.

*In a 1933 patent*: Sargent, E. H. "Football Game." U. S. Patent 1,929,757. Issued October 10, 1933.

*And by 1937 player locomotion had evolved*: Swart, H.A. "Game." U. S. Patent 2,101,764. Issued December 7, 1937.

*Electrical vibrations were considered*: Hackman, J. R. "Vibration Device." U. S. Patent 2,152,689. Issued April 4, 1939.

*Stores around the country*: Haak Brothers advertisement, page 6, *Lebanon Daily News* (PA), January 26, 1950; West Side News toy ad: page 4, *The Daily Courier*, February 2, 1950.

*Tonole again sought the influence of Playthings*: "Tudor's Electric Football Game": page 289, *PT*, February 1950.

*A full-page Tudor ad*: "Tudor Tru-Action Electric Games," page 323, *PT*, March 1950.

*Tudor had the game on store shelves*: Abraham & Straus Tudor Electric Baseball ad, page 66, *NYT*, April 23, 1950.

*DuMont was broadcasting six Notre Dame contests*: "Arries Lands Notre Dame Contract," page B3, *WP*, April 14, 1950.

*The NFL wasn't as prolific*: "Fifteen Pro Grid Games Slated for Television Network This Fall," page C1, *LAT*, June 14, 1950.

*Browns fans in Ohio*: "Tune In WXEL Channel 9, The Game of a Lifetime on Television!" page 6, *The Sandusky Register-Star News*, September 16, 1950.

*It had taken eleven week*s: "Football Takes Over On Air Next Weekend," page L4, *WP*, September 24, 1950.

*The price of a game*: Tudor No. 500 priced at $5.95, W. H. Hardware ad, page 22, *Dixon Evening Telegraph* (Dixon, IL), November 23, 1950.

*Other items electric football was competing against*: "The Lionel Joe Dimaggio Television Show," page 125, *PT*, September 1950.

*In an unusual but astute move*: Tudor ad, page 63, *PT*, December 1950.

*Television maker Admiral sponsored the game*: "Admiral Buys Pro Title Game," page B9, *WP*, December 14, 1950.

## Chapter 6

*Norman's mother Martha*: "Obituary 7," page 22, *NYT*, January 19, 1951.

*The full-page ad*: "It's no too late YET," *PT*, March 1951.

*DuMont bought the television rights*: "Pro Football and DuMont Sign a $475,000 TV Pact," page 54, *NYT*, May 22, 1951; "DuMont Due To Handle Pro Football": page B11, *NYT*, August 30, 1951.

*By early September*: "TV Set Sales Boom On Pacific Coast," page 28, *NYT*, September 29, 1951.

*Fearing declining attendance*: "TV Football Plan Being Worked Out," page 38, *NYT*, July 26, 1951.

*But neither team did*: "Penn Not On NCAA Schedule," page 17, *WP*, September 6, 1951.

*"The only non-women's garment"*; Strouss-Hirshberg's ad: page11, *New Castle News* (PA), September 21, 1951.

*By mid-October*: "Sears Toy Town," page 12, *San Mateo Times*, October 17, 1951.

*Not that the world of football*: "Pro Football Sued By U. S. On TV Curb," page 1, *NYT*, October 10, 1951.

*But after the Rams attendance declined*: "Pro Football Dip Noted," page 33, *NYT*, November 3, 1950.

*New York City fans got to see*: "Attention New York: Pro Football On Television," page 36, *The Troy Record* (Troy, NY), November 8, 1951.

*First ever coast-to-coast*: "Lions-Packers Televised Today," page 24, *WP*, November 22, 1951.

*The Justice Department had issued*: "Government Says TV Restrictions Are Illegal," page 10, *WP*, November 24, 1951.

*Football fans got an eyeful*: "On Television," page 7, *NYT*, December 1, 1951.

*In 1951 electric football was more than holding its own*: Sears Toy Town ad, page 13, *The Morning Herald* (Uniontown, PA), December 12, 1951; Korbacker's toy ad: page 7, *Mansfield News-Journal* (OH), December 14, 1951; Montgomery Ward ad: page 8, *The Winona Republican-Herald*, December 19, 1951.

*Fewer and fewer No 500's*: "Browns Are Favored Over Rams," page S1, *NYT*, December 23, 1951.

*Tudor's No. 500 prove to be so popular*: Hill's Toys ad, page 2, *Evening Times* (Cumberland, MD), January 29, 1952; Downstairs Store Toy ad: page 20, *Charleston Daily Mail*, February 12, 1952.

*At the Toy Fair in March*: "Toy Fair Here Sets Attendance Mark," page 35, *NYT*, March 11, 1952.

*The financially struggling New York Yanks*: "News Of TV and Radio," page X11, *NYT*, January 27, 1952.

*And these games*: "TV Fans Here Get to See Grid Giants Contests," page 9, *The Oneonta Star*, May 24, 1952.

*Viewers of the 53 DuMont stations*: "Ram Eleven Choice In All-Stars Game," page 21, *NYT*, August 14, 1952

*The NCAA had paid $50,000*: "Football Hurt By Television," page B3, *NYT*, May 9, 1952.

*And as a result of the study*: "College Football Limiting TV Again," page 40, *NYT*, June 3, 1952.

*"Is no longer a sport, it's big business"*; "Pro Football Crowds Increasing But Few Clubs Profit, Bell Says," page 42, *NYT*, October 10, 1952.

*On Thanksgiving Day*: "Bears, Dallas Also Meet; Both Are On TV Here," page 21, *WP*, November 27, 1952.

*Found on page seven*: "Giants Favorites Against Steelers," page S7, *NYT*, November 30, 1952.

*Toys were getting bigger and more expensive*: Sears Toy ad, page 14, *The Frederick Post (MD)*, December 4, 1952.

*The cattle's method of movement*: Bonanno, J. L. (Et Al). "Toy Railroad Trackside Accessories." U. S. Patent 2,882,644. Issued April 21, 1959.

*The arrival of Tudor shipments*: Skinner Chamberlain ad: page 16, *The Evening Tribune* (Albert Lea, MN), December 3, 1952.

*1953 opened with*: "On Television," page 30, *NYT*, January 1, 1953.

*Toy Fair continued to reflect the growing postwar*: "6,000 Buyers Visit American Toy Fair," page 37, *NYT*, March 10, 1953.

*Lionel was reporting that*: "Experience Of '52 Spurs Toy Buying," page 50, *NYT*, March 11, 1953.

*Sweating through the early months*: "Bell Hedges on TV Destroying N.F.L.," page 29, *NYT*, February 27, 1953.

*With the help of DuMont*: "Saturday Games Will Show Here," page 21, *WP*, May 14, 1953.

*Under the terms of the deal*: " More TV Football Seen This Season": page 43, *NYT*, May 14, 1953; "Westinghouse Announces NFL Television," page 15, Reno Evening Gazette, July 17, 1953.

*An extra $40,000 payment*: "A Risky Business," page 33, *NYT*, January 30, 1964.

*In college football*: "N.B.C. To Televise 11 Gridiron Games," page 13, *NYT*, June 20, 1953.

*Tudor's game was again a featured lay-away item*: "Korbacker's Lay-Away Now Toys": page 8, *Mansfield News-Journal* (OH), November 6, 1953.

*Roy's merchandise had become a staple of Sears*: "Santa Comes to Sears": page 7, *El Paso Herald Post*, November 11, 1953.

*Under the direction of marketing manager Larry Kent*: "News of the Advertising and Marketing Fields": page F16, *NYT*, October 5, 1952.

*Joe Tonole passed away*: "Obituaries 2," page 27, *NYT*, November 6, 1953; "Trade Mourns Passing of Joseph J. Tonole": page 93, *PT*, December 1953.

*Judge Grimm handed down a verdict*: "Home TV Ban Upheld," page 33, *WP*, November 13, 1953.

*A record 130 station*: "Brown-Detroit Game on Video": page 36, *Oakland Tribune*, December 25, 1953.

*The following weekend*: "Line-Up of Bowl Football Games," page S8, *NYT*, December 27, 1953.

## Chapter 7

*Television money had allowed*: "1953 Pro Football Best Financially," page 29, *NYT*, December 23, 1953.

*College football had done well too*: "Bowl Games Awaited by TV Millions," page 1, *WP*, January 1, 1954.

*Incorporated in 1930*: "New Incorporations," page 40, *NYT*, January 31, 1930.

*In the mid-1930's Gotham created*: Gotham Toy Ice Hockey ad, *PT*, March 1937.

*By 1940 Gotham's toy line*: Gotham Toy Fair Showroom photo, page 22, *PT*, May 1940.

*In Playthings' advertisements*: Gotham ad, page 49, *PT*, February, 1941.

*Yes, it was the same Eddie Gluck*: "Eddie Gluck In The Army," page 35, *PT*, December 1942.

*And it was the same Eddie Gluck*: "Eddie Gluck Vice President Of Gotham Pressed Steel," page 176, *PT*, December 1945.

*By 1928 he had moved on*: "Brooklyn Is A Real Menace To Hansonites," page 22, *Syracuse Herald*, December 14, 1928.

*Gluck to finish his career*: "Kinston, Albany Tied for State League Lead," page 13, *Middletown Times Herald* (NY), November 15, 1934.

*There were no special announcements*: Gotham ad, page 234, *PT*, March 1954.

*Another thing about to change*: "National Football League Amends Rule on Control for Games," page 34, *NYT*, January 28, 1954.

*DuMont eagerly renewed its NFL television contract*: "National Football Loop To Telecast Many Games," page 17, *Syracuse Post Standard*, April 29, 1954.

*ABC took college football away from NBC*: "Football Pact Signed by NCAA," page 24, *NYT*, April 24, 1954.

*It was May when Gluck finally*: Gotham ad, *PT*, May 1954.

*And the following month*: "Gotham Making 6 New Items," page 161, *PT*, June 1954.

*So in an innovative move*: "Big Four Football Starts Saturday," page S8, *NYT*, August 22, 1954.

*D.C. football fans got their first taste*: "TV Fans Have Pick of Series, U.S. and Canadian Football," page 17, *WP*, October 2, 1954.

*Eddie Gluck had gotten his Gotham electric football*: "Sale-Buy on Wards Lay-Away Plan," page 23, *Charleston Daily Mail* (W. VA), October 10, 1954.

*Tudor's No. 500 was the dominant model*: "Educator Approved Prestige Toys – Ed Guth

Hobbies," *Syracuse Herald-Journal*, November 25, 1954.

*In fact, it usually wasn't even pictured*: "Wards 1954 Christmas Book," page 5, *Miami Daily News-Record* (OK), November 29, 1954.

*Almost seven million sets were sold*: "Sales Of TV Sets Hit New Highs," page F1, *NYT*, December 26, 1954.

*And five televised bowl games the following Saturday*: "Five Bowl Games On TV Here Today," page 10, *WP*, January 1, 1955.

## Chapter 8

*DuMont cancelled its telecast*: "Pro Bowl TV Dropped," page 31, *WP*, January 14, 1955.

*DuMont's on-air presence*: Charles H. Grant, "The DuMont Television Network," The Radio History Society, Inc., Monograph Number 1, February 2000.

*In covering the Toy Fair*: "Santa Claus Here For 1955 Preview," page F1, *NYT*, March 6, 1955.

*Tudor's new high impact Styrene figures*: Modica Jr, J., "Playing Piece For Game," U.S. Patent 2,772,512. Issued December 4, 1956.

*Norman announced the new upgrades*: "What will Tudor be showing at the Fair? Plenty!" *PT*, March 1955.

*The updated No. 500 was displayed at a New York City TGC*: "Toys Are 'Real McCoy," page 28, *WP*, August 9, 1955.

*The Pro Bowl debacle*: "DuMont To Drop Two TV Programs," page 35, *NYT*, August 15, 1955.

*Both CBS and NBC*: "Top Teams Will Be on Football TV," page C6, *WP*, August 21, 1955.

*Commissioner Bell admitted that*: "NFL To Curb Saturday TV Programs," page 12, *The Titusville Herald* (PA), September 23, 1955.

*There on page 202*: "Exciting Electric Football Game," page 202, *Sears 1955 Christmas Book*.

*Ward was still involved*: "Electric Football," page 234, *MW Christmas Book, 1955*.

*Toy shoppers across the country*: "Montgomery Ward 'Buy Now On Lay-Away Plan,'" page 25, *The Times Record* (Troy, NY), November 3, 1955.

*And Ward had upgraded and modernized*: "New Fixtures Help Boost Ward's Toy Sales," page 558, *PT*, March 1956.

*There was an electric football game*: "Sears Happi-Time Toy Town," page 17, *Ironwood Daily Globe* (MI), November 24, 1955.

*Roy Rogers Sports Kit*: ibid.

*But on the plus side*: "Big Rise Forecast For Electronics," page 41, *NYT*, December 19, 1955.

*Arthur Daley of NYT*: "The Pros and Cons of Pro Football," SM 17, *NYT*, November 20, 1955.

## Chapter 9

*Norman, who had recently won*: "Toy Mfrs. Ass'n Officers and Directors," page 124, *PT*, January 1956.

*A record 1,655 manufacturers*: "Toy Show Sets Record," page 32, *NYT*, March 16, 1956.

*Another change in the industry*: "The Growing Menace of the Discount House," page 69, *PT*, May 1954.

*Things were looking up for the NFL*: "CBS Plans Pro Football Regional TV," page 13, *WP*, February 27, 1956.

*It didn't hurt that the Parents' Magazine seal*: "TGC Selects 104 'Prestige Toys,'" page 89, *PT*, May 1956.

*Sears opened many of its Toy Town departments*: "Sears Happi-Time Toy Town Lay-Away," page 11, *The Salina Journal* (KS), October 3, 1956.

*Ward continued to feature electric football*: "Montgomery Ward Buy Now on Lay-Away Plan," page C-6, *The Hammond Times* (IN), November 9, 1956.

*Sears had the G-940*: "Sears Santa's Here," page 24, *Hamilton Daily News Journal* (OH), November 22, 1956.

*Ward did its share*: "Christmas Toy Sale," page 9, *Globe-Gazette* (Mason City, IA), December 5, 1956.

*Over 39 million sets*: "The Growth of Television Is the Great Spectacular," page A11, *WP*, December 29, 1956.

*So many unsold sets*: "Glut Of TV Sets Widens Lay-Offs," page 25, *NYT*, December 29, 1956.

*One of the unique boy's items being sold*: "L.A. Rams Authentic Football Kit," page K9, *LAT*, November 25, 1956.

*In the days leading up to Christmas*: "On Television," page 35, *NYT*, December 22, 1956. "Redskins, Colts Vie On TV Today," page B5, *LAT*, December 23, 1956.

*In spite of the number of bowl games*: "Schedule of Bowl Games," page 32, *NYT*, January 1, 1957.

*For the first time in ten years*: "Tickets Go Begging In Miami," page C4, *WP*, December 30, 1956.

*NFL Pro Bowl got caught up*: "Pro Bowl Not on TV As Promised," page A9, *WP*, January 12, 1957.

*CBS decided to continue*: "N.Y. Giants, Bear's Title Favorites," page C7, *WP*, September 29, 1957.

*It was another season where pro games*: "TV College Football Opener Pits Maryland, Texas A & M," page 32, *Lima News* (OH), September 1, 1957.

*Sears christened the opening of Toy Town*: "Sears Happi-Time Toy Town," page 6, *Reno Evening Gazette*, October 9, 1957.

*Ward made Gotham*: "Ward Wonderland of Toys," page 8, *The Ada Evening News* (OK), November 3, 1957.

*Payless Drug Store chain*: Payless ad, page 13, *Oakland Tribune*, November 20, 1957.

*Ward caught on to this trend*: "Ward Wonderland of Toys," page 11, *Evening Times* (MD), November 29, 1957.

*Ward broke the $5*: "Wards Christmas Gift Sale," page 3, *Big Spring (Texas) Herald*, December 5, 1957.

*Christmas sales were struggling*: "Many Cities Show Lag In Yule Sales," page 175, *NYT*, December 22, 1957.

*Even hitting $4.28*: Stotter's ad, page 14, *Chester Times* (PA), December 19, 1957.

*New York Times' television critic*: "TV: Assignment Southeast Asia," page 29, *NYT*, December 23, 1957.

## Chapter 10

*Sales figures made it clear*: "1957 Chain Sales Topped '56 By 5.1%," page 42, *NYT*, January 16, 1958.

*Toy volume*: "Discounts Reduce Profit From Toys," page 79, *NYT*, January 6, 1958.

*There was optimism as toy makers*: "Toy Makers Here for 2 Show Expect 10% Rise in Sales in '58," *NYT*, March 9, 1958.

*Tudor brought to the Fair*: "The Big 3," page 95, *PT*, March 1958.

*Gotham, without a hint of irony*: "Rules and Instructions for Gotham All-Star Vibrating Electric Football G-880," 1958.

*The new contract*: "CBS Airs NFL Tiffs," page C-5, *Independent Star-News* (CA), September 14, 1958.

*The NFL gave both networks*: "Time-Out for Commercial," page S3, NYT, September 14, 1958.

*Sears had the deluxe G-940*: "Electric Football Game," page 346, *Sears 1958 Christmas Book*.

*Ward was showing off*: page 415, *MW Christmas Book 1958*.

*As low as $3.99*: "Bargain City U.S.A.," page 31, *Chester Times* (PA), December 4, 1958.

*But in areas with less electric football*: Firestone Store ad, page 48, *Tucson Daily Citizen*, December 22, 1958.

*More than 84% of the U.S. population owned a television*: "U.S. Television Sets Outnumber Bathtubs," page A23, WP, September 16, 1958.

*When Colts fullback Alan Ameche*: Michael MacCambridge, "Legacy of the Greatest Game Can Be Found in What Followed," NFL.Com, December 25, 2008.

*Early in the New Year*: "December Sales Set Records for Sears, Montgomery Ward; Spiegel Also Gained," page 48, NYT, January 8, 1959.

*Also adding to the good news*: "Yule Surge Sets Retail Sales Record," page C12, WP, January 11, 1959.

*Summing up the NFL's stature*: Arthur Daley, "Sport of *The Times*: The Foot in Football," page 36, NYT, January 6, 1959.

*In March of 1959*: Letter from Roger Atkin, NFL Properties vice president of Retail Sales, nominating Pete Rozelle to the Licensing Industry Hall of Fame, December 1996.

*George Halas Co. store*: Display ad 68, page C3, CT, November 10, 1949.

*Rozelle had been*: "Rozelle New Ram Manager," page C1, LAT, April 9, 1957.

*Sold out of the Rams' store*: Michael MacCambridge, America's Game, page 145, Anchor Books 2005.

Rams uniform kit: Display 191, page K9, LAT, November 25, 1956

*$30 million in sales in 1958*: "Larry Kent and Lou Banks Promoted By Roy Rogers Firm," page 100, PT, July 1959.

*The connection between the two men*: Roger Atkin, former NFL Properties vice president of Retail Sales, personal interview.

*Kent's letter*: Larry Kent of Roy Rogers Enterprises to Rams general manager Pete Rozelle, letter dated March 13, 1959, Roger Atkin, personal interview.

*Eight of Nielsen's top ten television shows*: Tim Brook and Earle Marsh, page 1458, *The Complete Directory to Prime Time and Cable TV Shows 1946-Present*, Ballantine Books 2003.

*The Toy Fair had come and gone*: "Business Brisk As Toy Fair Opens," page 48, NYT, March 10, 1959.

*Successful negotiations were carried out*: "5 Pro Football Exhibitions Will Be Televised," page A15, WP, July 11, 1959; "Pro Grid League Again to Televise," page 12, Coshocton Tribune (OH), July 29, 1959.

*Another event taking place*: "Larry Kent and Lou Banks Promoted By Roy Rogers Firm," page 100, PT, July 1959.

*A few weeks later*: "Roy Rogers Licensees Meet To Hear of Promotion Plans," page 136, *PT*, August 1959.

*Sears had the G-940 for 789*: page 405, Sears *Christmas Book*, 1959.

*The mainstay item of all Sears' ads*: "Sears Happi-Time Toy Town," page 5, *Reno Evening Gazette*, November 5, 1959.

*Ward didn't use electric football*: "Toy Wonderland Now Open," page 13, *The Sun-Standard* (IL), October 29, 1959.

*The company had bought airtime*: "Marx Saturation TV Campaign Opens in Oct.," *PT*, April, 1959.

*Also heavily into television this year*: "A Powerful Lionel Promotion To Help You Sell," page 56, *PT*, September 1959.

*But by early fall*: "Makers of Toys Work Overtime," page F1, *NYT*, September 13, 1959.

*League gave verbal approval on October* 1: Roger Atkin, personal interview.

*The contract created NFL Enterprises*: Pete Rozelle to acting NFL Commissioner Austin Gunsell, letter and NFL Enterprises proposal agreement, dated October 26, 1959.

*Hosting ABC's telecast*: "Television Preview," page D23, *WP*, November 26, 1959.

*As December began*: "Toy Shipments Rise 10%," page C10, *WP*, December 1, 1959.

*No. 500 under the $5 mark*: Arthurs Toy Shops ad, page 11B, *The Fresno Bee* (CA), December 8, 1959.

*Austin Gunsell received a letter*: NFL Enterprises vice president and general manager Larry Kent to Austin Gunsell, letter dated December 21, 1959.

*Wards shifted to 50%*: "Clearance Our Entire Stock Of Toys," page 14, *The Lima News* (OH), December 22, 1959.

## Chapter 11

*Page 137*: "Eugene Levay," page 137, *PT*, January 1960.

*History was being made*: "NFL Must Grow, page 34, *Tuscon Daily Citizen*, January 14, 1960; "Giants Ask A.F.L. Head for Help," page 41, *NYT*, ibid.

*The NFL's new commissioner was*: "Ram Official Heads Pro Football," page 1, *NYT*, January 27, 1960.

*Receiving a call from Kent*: Norman Sas, personal interview.

*Gotham was dealing with a recent move*: New York City Department of Finance, Office of the City Register, Document 102/1911, Deed, Bronx Block 2574, Lot 82, February 25, 1969.

*Buying pucks, players and gears from Munro*: Don Munro Jr., personal interview.

*Tudor was going all out*: Tudor ad, pages 10-11, *PT*, March 1960.

*Toy Fair ran for ten days*: "Toy Fairs Shape New World for Children," page F1, *NYT*, March 6, 1960.

*In early April*: "Charles Anderson, Steel Executive, 74," page 33, *NYT*, April 12, 1960.

*The AFL boldly moved forward*: "$10,625,000 TV Deal For New Football League," *WP*, June 10, 1960.

*Rozelle expressed his desire*: "Rozelle Decries Lack Of Harmony," page 27, *NYT*, July 16, 1960.

*The AFL got the jump on the NFL*: "American Football League Kicks Off Season," page C4, *WP*, September 4, 1960.

*The retailer had even opened up*: "Happi-Time Toy Town Is Now Open," page 22, *Reno Evening Gazette*, September 20, 1960.

*An ordinary G-940*: 'Thrill-A-Minute Electric Football Game," page 451, Sears *Christmas Book*, 1960.

*The first officially NFL licensed item*: "Approved by the National Football League Complete Outfit $10.47," page 394, Sears *Christmas Book*, 1960.

*NFL Enterprises getting a big push*: There's gold in the sidelines," pages 16-17, *Parade*, November 13, 1960.

*Sears even dropping the G-940 to $5.66*: "Sears Gifts for Everyone," page 6C, *High Point Enterprise* (NC), November 24, 1960.

*The New York Titans and Dallas Texans*: "Television Highlights," page D23, *WP*, November 24, 1960.

*Only 14,000 New Yorkers showed up*: "Titans Triumph as Texan Rally Falls Short," page 36, *NYT*, November 25, 1960.

*Electric football sales were "terrific"*: "Race Cars Hot Items in Young Fry Gifts," page 2, *Albuquerque Tribune*, December 22, 1960.

## Chapter 12

*After considering Minnesota's dismal*: "Mississippi Is Chosen," page 31, *NYT*, January 6, 1961.

*With the weekend finally over*: "20 Week-end Hours of Running and Tackling Leave a Critic Kicking," page 59, *NYT*, January 3, 1961.

*Rozelle declined*: "NFL Won't Consider Game With Suing Rivals From AFL," page A16, *WP, Times Herald*, January 16, 1961.

*However, the league was being warned*: "Rozelle Says TV Plan Must Benefit Public," page C2, *WP, Times Herald*, February 19, 1961.

*Most of the 1,500 manufacturers*: "Attendance and Selling Heavy As Toy Makers Show '61 Lines," page 45, *NYT*, March 14, 1961.

*A price war had broken out*: "Toy Trade Finds No Fun Or Profit," page F1, *NYT*, December 18, 1960.

*So despite record toy sales for 1960*: "Toy Sales Boom But Profits Fall," page 47, *NYT*, January 9, 1961.

*There was genuine concern*: "Jobbers, Retailers Review 1960's Sales, Profits and Problems," page 446-448, *PT*, March 1961.

*Was being announced*: "Go Gotham," *Toys & Novelties*, March 1961.

*A dramatic two-page spread*: "Nationally Advertised," *PT*, March 1961.

*NBC agreed to pay the league $615,000*: "Pro Football's Covered A Lot of Ground on TV," *WP, Times Herald*, April 8, 1961.

*Appearing in the April issue of Playthings*: "Your Ticket To 'Big Ticket' Sales," *PT*, April 1961.

*This same issue*: "Tudor Schedules Nat'l Magazine Ads," page 103, *PT*, April 1961.

*Not only was he the Titans quarterback*: "Dorow Gets New Post," page 47, *NYT*, December 20, 1960.

*Rozelle had already announced*: "Vikings Get Player Lists From NFL Clubs," page 16, *San Mateo Times (CA)*, January 25, 1961.

*At the spring owners' meeting*: "C.B.S. Gets Rights To Pro Football," page 43, *NYT*, April 27, 1961.

*Gotham ran a bold full-color*: "What's New? Everything!" *PT*, June 1961.

*On page 88*: "Official Nat'l League Football Game Introduced by Gotham," page 88, *PT*, June 1961.

*Federal Judge Allan K. Grim*: "TV Pact Voided By Court," page 1, *NYT*, July 21, 1961.

*Within days of the ruling*: "AFL Claims Deal on TV Different," page D3, *WP*, July 22, 1961.

*During an appeal*: "NFL Plea To Save Package TV Denied," page A16, *WP*, July 29, 1961.

*Gotham continued to ramp up*: "SIZZLING!" *PT*, August 1961.

*Gluck had landed the NFL G-1500*: "Instant Cold Is In the Bag," page D12, *WP*, August 26, 1961.

*Tudor focused on hockey*: "Your Ticket To 'Big Ticket' Sales," *PT*, September 1961.

*Gotham again went full-color*: "Pro-Action," *PT*, September 1961.

*A special pullout section from Ideal Toys*: "Ideal Toys," page 114-115, *PT*, September 1961.

*Sears, on the other hand*: page 371, *Sears 1961 Christmas Book*.

*A Gotham Professional Football G-880*: page 388, *MW Christmas Catalog 1961*.

*President Kennedy signed into law*: "President Signs Bill For Pros to Pool TV," page C2, *WP*, October 1, 1961.

*Sears began running newspaper ads*: "Sears Days Sale," page 13, *The Press-Courier* (CA), October 18, 1961.

*The AFL would get on the air first*: "Sports Today On TV, Radio," *WP*, November 23, 1961.

*By mid-afternoon*: "Titans Rally to Defeat Bills Here, 21-14; Packers Turn Back Lions 17-9," page 42, *NYT*, November 24, 1961.

*Some ads even featured a second image*: page 6, *Oneonta Star* (NY), November 24, 1961.

*It was advertising Gotham didn't have to pay for*: "Indoor Sports Games Booming On Yule Market," page 17, *The Daily Courier* (PA), November 24, 1961.

*The ad ran on page 86*: "Family Fun with Tudor," page 86, *SI*, November 27, 1961.

*Just days earlier*: "Dorow Stars As Titans Whip Bills," *WP*, November 24, 1961.

*Sales were strong*: "Tudor Broaden Sales and Service By Appointing Reps for 6 Areas," page 69, *PT*, December 1961.

*But Gotham would not go away*: "Gotham Using TV Spots Prior To Pro Telecasts," page 79, *PT*, December 1961.

*Gotham got a strong endorsement*: "Imaginative Sporting Games That The Whole Family Can Enjoy..." page E1, *SI*, December 11, 1961.

*Gotham had Sears using the G-1500*: "Exciting NFL's Electric Football Games $14.95," page 18, *The New Mexican*, December 14, 1961.

*It was so cold*: "Fans Battle Cold But Fail To Win," page 16, *NYT*, January 1, 1962.

## Chapter 13

*Lee Payne was hired*: Lee Payne, personal interview.

*Actually, Payne was more than dangerous*: Lee Payne, personal interview; "North Augusta Team Received Letters," page 5, *Aiken Standard And Review*, December 17, 1951.

## Chapter 14

*The NFL finally signed*: "NFL Signs $9.3 Million TV Pact: All 14 Clubs Will Share Equally," page A20, *WP*, January 11, 1962.

*But the Colts and Steelers*: "Pro Teams Take Full Advantage of Television," page C3, *WP*, December 31, 1961.

*Besides appearing in Sears*: "G-1500 Official National Football League Electric Football Game," page 23, *NFL Enterprises Catalog 1962*.

*A full-page Tudor ad*: "there's a new dimension in electric sport games!" *PT*, February 1962.

*Payne attended a Princeton-Yale football game*: Lee Payne, personal interview.

*The new games*: "there's a new dimension in electric sport games and tudor's got it!" *PT*, March 1962.

*A full-page color ad*: "Only as Gotham," *PT*, February 1962.

*In a clever layout*: "Look sharp and see...what's been going on at Gotham?" *PT*, March 1962.

*Gotham also landed*: "New Styling Gives New Look To Gotham Pressed Steel's Racing and Bowling Numbers," page 488, *PT*, March 1962.

*Also doing some hard thinking by the end of the Fair*: "Strong '61 Sales Picture Clouded By Reports of Declining Profits," pages 368-373, *PT*, March 1962; "Toy-Price Battle Hurts Retailers," page 95, *NYT*, January 8, 1962.

*It was on March 31*: NFL Enterprises vice president and general manager Larry Kent to Austin

Gunsell, letter and contracts dated December 21, 1959.

*He had resigned from Roy Rogers*: "Kent Marketing Director For Scientific Industries," page 69, *PT*, December 1961.

*In the April issue*: "Only at Gotham," *PT*, April 1962.

*Photo of the Gotham Toy Fair Showroom*: "Here and the Toy Fair," page 97, *PT*, April 1962.

*Tudor had purchased*: "Tudor Scores Again," *PT*, April 1962.

*Proceeded to run another color two-page ad*: "hit from Gotham," *PT*, June 1962.

*But more significant was the headline*: "Gotham's Pro Action Sports Game Line Scheduled for Network TV," page 136, *PT*, June 1962.

*A new electric Tank Battle game*: "Just Out From Gotham," *PT*, July 1962.

*Promoting the new G-980*: "Gotham crashes through with something new," *PT*, August 1962.

*Even bigger news was printed page 179*: "TV Star Art Linkletter to Present Commercials on Gotham's Hockey," page 179, *PT*, August 1962.

*Mattel was spending a toy-industry record*: "$5 Million Plus Biggest Broadcast Buy In Toy History," *PT*, September 1962.

*Sears had the Gotham G-1500*: "National League Electric Football," page 344, *Sears 1962 Christmas Book*.

*There was good news for Tudor*: "All American Football," page 366, *MW Christmas Catalog 1962*.

*The Playthings advertising battle continued*: "Gotham Pro-Action Sports Games," *PT*, September 1962.

*Tudor kept things simple*: "New games, styling, realism, packaging," *PT*, September 1962.

*Sears finally started promoting the G-1500*: "Sears Toy Town," page 13, *The Daily Mail* (MD), November 8, 1962.

*Got a promotional push from J.C. Penney*: "Toyland," page 14, *Anderson Daily Bulletin* (IN), November 22, 1962,

*Sears set the benchmark price*: "Sears Toy Town," page A-10, *El Paso Herald-Post*, November 22, 1962.

*Retailers seemed unsure how to handle the No. 600*: "The Best to You From Buffums'," page L-3, *Long Beach Independent*, November 22, 1962.

*SI felt the need to enter the fray*: ""Beneath The Christmas Tree," page E1, *SI*, December 10, 1962.

*Examples of price cutting*: "Thrifty Acres Toytown," page 18, *The Holland Sentinel* (MI), December 13, 1962.

*The G-1500 then appeared*: "Sears Last Minute Life Savers," page 2, *Logansport Pharos-Tribune* (IN), December 20, 1962.

*He upheld the league's legal right*: "Judge Upholds TV Blackout," page C7, *WP*, December 29, 1962.

*By early October*: "Bills Place Dorow on Waivers," page 52, *NYT*, October 3, 1962.

## Chapter 15

*Sears reported record sales*: "Sidelights: December Sales Set Sears Peak," page 10, *NYT*, January 8, 1963.

*But the Sears retail paradigm*: "Sears Earnings Record For Year," page 10, *NYT*, March 28, 1963.

*That was the formation of a new NFL-owned*: personal interview, Roger Atkin.

*During the 1959-60 television season*: Tim Brook and Earle Marsh, pages 1366-69, *The*

*Complete Directory to Prime Time and Cable TV Shows 1946-Present*, Ballantine Books 2003.

*Kent envisioned a bright future*: page A21, "Sideline Big Business For Pro Clubs," *WP*, March 18, 1963.

*In Rogers' eyes*: "He Could Always Move Merchandise," *SI*, July 27, 1998.

*Tudor started its advertising*: "So what's new?" page 44, *PT*, February 1963.

*A color four-page layout*: "Sales Excitement Tudor," *PT*, March 1963.

*A small article*: "Tudor Now Offering 2 New Electric Games," page 443, *PT*, March 1963.

*Look at the 1963 Tudor catalog*: *Tudor Sales Catalog No. 63, 1963*.

*NBC paid $926,000*: "N.B.C. Purchases Football Rights," page 71, *NYT*, April 26, 1963.

*Playthings' coverage of the Toy Fair*: "At the Toy Shows," *PT*, April 1963.

*A small photo feature*: "Changeable 'Tote Board' in Tudor's New Electric Horse Racing Game," page 119, *PT*, April 1963.

*Gotham finally had its 1963*: "High Styling, Slide Action Features Of Gotham's New Hockey Game," page 136, *PT*, April 1963.

*Lee had kicked the quest*: Lee Payne, personal interview.

*Gotham finally fired up*: "Are we insisting on customer dissatisfaction," *PT*, June 1963.

*Norman answered back*: "How Big Should A Football Player Be?" *PT*, September 1963.

*Kicking off earlier than ever*: "Television Football Schedule in Area," page L2, *WP*, September 8, 1963.

*Ward had Tudor's No. 600 model*: "Deluxe Electric Football Game," page 318, *MW Christmas Catalog 1963*.

*Sears had made the NFL G-1500*: "National League Electric Football," page 100, *Sears 1963 Christmas Book*.

*Most prominent of the NFL Properties' sellers*: "Exclusive: S.F.A.'S official Pro Jackets for boys – endorsed by the National Football League," page 5, *NYT*, November 19, 1963.

*Schlafer's in suburban Green Bay*: "Packer Backers!" page B13, *Appleton Post-Crescent* (WI), September 12, 1963.

*Most Sears Toy Town and Ward Toyland departments*: "Sears Happi-Time Toy Town," page 20, *The Panama City Herald*, October 2, 1963; "Montgomery Ward Early Santa Sale," page 10, *Clovis News-Journal* (NM), October 13, 1963.

*Life for most Americans*: "Back To Normal For Radio And TV," page 75, *NYT*, November 26, 1963.

*There was loud and immediate criticism*: "Vocal Critics Upset That N.F.L. Will Play a Full Slate," page 97, *NYT*, November 24, 1963.

*Most stadiums had normal attendance*: "Pro Football Attendance Unaffected," page 35, *NYT*, November 25, 1963.

*Sears finally started promoting electric football*: "Visit Sears Toytown," page 73, *Pasadena Star-News* (CA), November 28, 1963.

*Sears continued*: "Sears Toytown," page 50, *Lebanon Daily News* (PA), December 11, 1963.

*Toy clearance sales appeared*: "Montgomery Ward Toys Reduced!" page 2, *The Ada Evening News* (OK), December 19, 1963.

*It was estimated the $80 million worth of slot cars*: "Makers of Toys Voice Optimism," page 147, *NYT*, December 15, 1963.

*Most electric football games were still in use*: "Bowl Lineup," page B9, *WP*, December 25, 1963.

*SI named Pete Rozelle*: "Pete Rozelle Named Year's Top Sportsman," page A13, *WP*, December 31, 1963.

## Chapter 16

*Although the exact earnings for toys*: "Sales Mark Set By Chain Stores," page 39, *NYT*, January 17, 1964.

*Rozelle waved his magic marketing wand*: "C.B.S.-TV to Pay $28.2 Million For 2-Year Pro Football Rights," page 1, *NYT*, January 25, 1964.

*The NFL double-header was born*: "Network to Televise Two N.F.L. Games on Some Sundays," page 37, *NYT*, January 28, 1964.

*NBC, who was still smarting*: "Football Rights Bought By N.B.C.," page 59, *NYT*, January 30, 1964.

*In a just a single week*: "The Great TV Bonanza," page S12, *NYT*, February 2, 1964.

*ABC and the Ford Motor Company*: "A.B.C. To Televise 5 N.F.L. Games in '64," page 79, *NYT*, February 11, 1964.

*Major League Baseball attempted to get in*: "Baseball Clubs Propose TV Deal," page 67, *NYT*, February 12, 1964.

*By early March*: "National Football League Say It Won't Show Friday Games," page 40, *NYT*, March 3, 1964.

*Loss leader pricing*: "Where Do We Go from Here?" page 50, *PT*, January 1964.

*Picket lines protesting the increasing production*: "Visions of Christmas Sales Captivate Toy Buyers," page 51, *NYT*, March 10, 1964.

*Painting the usual rosy picture*: "Toy Industry Sees Sales Surge in '64," page 53, *NYT*, March 10, 1964.

*"MattelZapoppin"*: "MattelZapoppin in '64," page 218-26, *PT*, March 1964.

*Marx had a large spread*: "A Simple Statement about Marx TV in 1964," *PT*, March 1964.

*Topper Toys*: "Johnny Seven O.M.A.," *PT*, March 1964.

*Another company with a multipage*: "The Best Selling Football Games For The Last 15 Years..." *PT*, March 1964.

*For the first time ever*: Tudor Catalog 64, Tudor Sales Catalog 1964.

*Gluck had only a short*: "Gotham Pressed Steel Sees Big Year For Pool Table Line," page 452, *PT*, March 1964.

*The NFL television bandwagon*: "$1.8 Million Bid by C.B.S. Wins Rights to N.F.L. Championship," page 59, *NYT*, April 18, 1964.

*Gotham finally got around to*: "Gotham Pressed Steel," *PT*, June 1964.

*It also didn't get a mention*: "Gotham's Floor Model Pool Table," page 97, *PT*, June 1964.

*By early summer*: "Hanging Windows Used For Pavilion," page R1, *NYT*, June 21, 1964.

*In July of 1964*: Lee Payne, personal interview and resume.

*A relative newcomer to the Christmas catalog fray*: "J.C. Penney Distributing A Promotional Catalogue," page 31, *NYT*, January 1, 1964.

*Sears devoted the most space*: page 124, *Sears 1964 Christmas Book*.

*Since Ward*: page 276, *MW Christmas Catalog 1965*.

*Ward had new NFL boys' pajamas*: page 128, ibid.

*Lined up Saks Fifth Avenue*: "Display Ad 3," page 4, *NYT*, September 25, 1964.

*One unique item Kent had licensed*: "Aladdin School Lunch Kits," page 96, *Pasadena Independent Star-News*, August 30, 1964.

*How much a lunchbox would add*: "Larry Kent, 86, Marketer of the NFL Merchandise," page A17, *NYT*, July 27, 1999.

*Many Sears retail stores*: "Toytown Lay-Away Sale," page 69, *San Antonio Express*, October 1, 1964.

*Ward joined the sale-pricing bandwagon*: "Montgomery Ward Money Save Specials," page 6, *Winona Daily News* (MN), October 22, 1964.

*Game day attendance*: "New York Is a Football Festival And for 124,960 Good Reasons," page 60, *NYT*, November 10, 1964.

*Sears had the NFL G-1400*: "Sears Toytown Table Top Fun," page 17, *The Sheboygan Press*, November 11, 1964.

*Ward was more sporadic*: "Ward Money Saver Specials," page 13, *Leader-Times* (PA), November 11, 1964.

*Gluck was relying on a brief press release*: "Sports Games Sure-To-Score," page 7, *The Gettysburg Times*, November 25, 1964.

*Sears continued to push*: "Say Merry Christmas With Gifts from Sears, page 9, *The Charleston Gazette* (WV), December 11, 1964.

*Tudor's No. 500 model*: "Ward Giant Toyland Sale," page T-3, *Manitowoc Herald-Times* (WI), December 14, 1964.

*As Sears ad in Washington state*: "Say Merry Christmas With Gifts from Sears, page 11, *The Daily Chronicle* (WA), December 21, 1964.

*Three consecutive days of televised football*: "Post Season Games Bowl Picture," page D2, *WP*, December 25, 1964.

## Chapter 17

*The Orange Bowl would be played at night*: "30 Color Cameras Turn To Football," page 26, *NYT*, December 31, 1964.

*The very next day*: "Namath Accepts A $400,000 Pact To Play For Jets," page S1, *NYT*, January 3, 1965.

*A league owned film company*: "This Is NFL Films," pages 44-50, *Forbes Small Business*, January 25, 2004.

*Sears and Ward again set sales records*: "Sears and Ward's Set Sales Marks," page 40, *NYT*, January 7, 1965.

*Profits made by several 1964 toys*: "Toy Buyers Crowd Showrooms Here," page 56, *NYT*, March 9, 1965.

*Tudor was giving the Magnetic Quarterback*: "Tudor magnetic quarterback," page 24, *PT*, March 1965.

*What was modestly described*: "Gotham Has the Big Play," page 19, *NFL Properties Catalog 1965*.

*Gluck did finally present the NFL Big Play*: "Gotham's Game Will Tie In with NFL TV Program," page 102, *PT*, April 1965.

*Recently completed Atlanta structure*: "Atlanta Stadium Opened," page 57, *NYT*, March 30, 1965.

*Atlanta's vision*: "Pro Football Expansion," page S6, *NYT*, June 6, 1965.

*The AFL announced*: "Atlanta: Its Pro Football Prospects," page 25, *NYT*, June 10, 1965. "Marching to Georgia," page 25, ibid.

*At a special meeting*: "N.F.L. Owners Agree to Put a Team in Atlanta for 1966 Football Season," *NYT*, June 22, 1965.

*They called an audible and looked further south*: "Miami Gets A.F.L. Franchise for '66," page 25, *NYT*, August 17, 1965.

*A United Press International article*: "Pro Football War Going On Other Places Besides Field," page 15, *The Sheboygan Press*, August 24, 1965.

*MCA acted as the league's agent*: "A.B.C.-TV May Sign Football League," page 47, *NYT*, April 23, 1960.

*MCA, whose client list*: "Hollywood Colossus; MCA Future is Big Riddle to Industry," page 29, *NYT*, December 17, 1961.

*MCA got out from under*: "M.C.A. Will Drop Its Talent Office," page 34, *NYT*, July 9, 1962.

*Mincolla had spent ten years*: "Frank Mincolla Leaves MCA; Opens Own Office In New York," page 81, *PT*, December 1962.

*Namath performed like a typical raw rookie*: "Joe Namath Disappointed in His Play," page B2, *WP*, September 20, 1965.

*On page 442*: "Crowd fills 3 sides of double-deck stands," page 442, *Sears 1965 Christmas Book*.

*He discovered something startling*: John Carney, personal interview, May 1999.

*And the ever-growing Gibson Discount Center chain*: "$8.7 Million in Toys Bought at Gibson Show," page 46, *PT*, November 1964.

*Norman's pitch to Carney was pretty simple*: Norman Sas, personal interview.

*Lee told Norman he could refine the players*: Lee Payne, personal interview.

*By the name of Johnny Hero*: "The All-American Athlete Johnny Hero," page 520, *Sears 1965 Christmas Book*.

*Thanks to Larry Kent*: "Famous NFL Players Will Promote Gotham's Electric Football Game," page 58, *PT*, November 1965.

*The Wooward & Lothrop department store*: "Hey Fellows, Beat Redskins Star Dick Shiner At His Own Game With The New Gotham Big Play Football Game," page D5, *WP*, October 29, 1965.

*Instead, the NFL G-1500*: "Sear Lay-Away For Christmas," page 4, *Corpus Christi Times*, October 27, 1965.

*The G-1500 and a Gotham pool table*: "Sears Toytown," page 13, *The Evening Capital* (MD), November 16, 1965.

*Eddie Gluck had sent out press release packages*: "Pro Sports Techniques Move into Family Fun Home Leagues," page 9E, *Racine Journal Times* (WI), November 24, 1965.

*Sears continued to do its part*: "Sears Holiday Sale," pages 14-15, *Salina Journal* (KS), November 25, 1965.

*Ward had a much smaller*: "Ward 3 Day Toyland Specials," page 22, *The Lima News* (OH), November 18, 1965.

*Gibson Discount Center chain*: "Exciting Electric Football," page 22, *Brownwood Bulletin* (TX), November 25, 1965.

*Both leagues were holding their college player drafts*: "Pro Football Set For Draft Today," page 36, *NYT*, November 27, 1965.

*Giant Tiger Discounters*: "Tudor Electric Football Game," page 21, *Chronicle-Telegram* (OH), December 2, 1965.

*Sears was still giving the G-1500*: "3-Dimensional Electric Football Sets," page B-12, *The Modesto Bee*, December 15, 1965.

*Ward had the large Tudor No. 600*: "Montgomery Ward Christmas Sale," page 7, *Oakland Tribune*, December 15, 1965.

*Namath even got a nod of approval*: "Namath Has Proved That Price Was Right," page 67, *NYT*, November 25, 1965.

*The game was part of clearance sales*: "Sears Last Minute Gifts," page 2-B, *The Register* (VA), December 22, 1965.

*Retailers had now reduced the price*: "Newberry's Gift Sale," page 2, *Union-Bulletin* (WA), December 15, 1965.

*New York City area Arbitron*: "Good Day for Football," page 55, *NYT*, December 28, 1965.

*A new two-year television contract*: "C.B.S. Will Pay $18.8 Million A Year to Extend Football Deal," page 49, *NYT*, December 30, 1965.

*A glorious three-day football weekend*: "TV Football Fans Plan This Weekend With Care," page 41, *NYT*, December 31, 1965.

## Chapter 18

*Of the 111 players drafted by both leagues*: "Pro Football Goes Into Orbit: Pays $7-Million for 20 Stars," *NYT*, January 9, 1966.

*Less than happy group of AFL owners*: "Football League Will Meet Today," page S2, *NYT*, January 16, 1966.

*The city of New Orleans*: "New Orleans Plans All-Purpose Superdome," page C3, ibid.

*Norman was given the electric football contract*: Norman Sas, personal interview.

*The television gravy train continued*: "C.B.S. Pays $4-Million for 2 N.F.L. Title Games," *NYT*, February 15, 1966.

*Over 4.6 million people paid to see an NFL game*: "N.F.L. Won't Pick 16th City Till June," *NYT*, February 18, 1966.

*A presentation by Harris Poll head*: "To Poll or Not to Poll," page 38, *NYT*, February 22, 1966.

*Toy sales had set another record*: "007 Infiltrating Toy Industry as Sales Rise; Further Gains Seen," page F1, *NYT*, March 6, 1966.

*Sears, Ward and Woolworth also set sales records*: "Chain Stores Raise Sales to New High," page 59, *NYT*, January 21, 1966.

*Mattel showed up with 25 new toys*: "Over 25 New Spring Numbers Added to the Mattel Line," page 157, *PT*, February 1966.

*Eldon had a complete new line*: "New! Champion Games," *PT*, March 1966.

*Only a small photo*: "Sealright Publicizing Gotham's NFL Electric Football Game," page 431, *PT*, March 1966.

*A new manufacturing arrangement with Canadian table hockey giant Munro*: Don Munro Jr., personal interview.

*To promote these new games*: "So What's New? Tudor '66" *PT*, March 1966.

*A man walked into the Tudor suite*: Albert Sung, letter, June 14, 2004.

*In early April*: Raiders' Director Gets Foss's Post," *NYT*, April 9, 1966.

*The NFL owners attended to*: "N.F.L. To Raise Posts To 20 Feet Above Bar," page 82, *NYT*, May 18, 1966.

*Giants made a significant change*: "Football Giants Sign Pete Gogolak of the Bills for $32,000," ibid.

*Yes*: "Thurlow Asserts He'll Stay Here: page 54, *NYT*, May 20, 1966.

*He was going back to a two-piece design*: Lee Payne, personal interview.

*His solution was to take a $300,000 second mortgage*: New York City Department of Finance, Office of the City Register, Document 73/212, Mortgage, Bronx Block 2574, Lot 82, June 1, 1966.

*Then on June 6, word leaked out*: "National and American Football League Officials Are Holding Peace Talks," page 60, *NYT*, June 7, 1966.

*On June 8*: "National and American Leagues Will Merge Into 26-Team Circuit," page 78, *NYT*, June 9, 1966.

*Norman held onto the rights*: Norman Sas, personal interview.

*Sears had a new toy buyer*: ibid.

*Al Davis resigned as AFL commissioner*: "New Pact To Last At Least 3 Years," page 30, *NYT*,

July 26, 1966.

*One complete set was going to Hong Kong*: Albert Sung, e-mail, April 29, 2004.

*The final three went to*: Lee Payne, John Carney, personal interview.

*Combining the NFL and AFL television schedules*: "N.F.L. And A.F.L. Will Flood TV Screens With 159 Games," page 191, NYT, August 28, 1966.

*In early September*: "Millions Invested To Promote NFL Products," page 14, *The Lowell Sun* (MA), September 2, 1966.

*Just few days later*: "Advertising: Keeping in Step With Football," page 70, NYT, September 12, 1966.

*NFL Properties' biggest ever promotion*: The National Football League Teams announce their Selections of Official 1966 Training Table Foods," *Life*, September 16, 1966.

*The Training Table Food program*: "New! Official Training Table Bread!" page 7-A Kingsport Times-News (TN), September 23, 1962; "Viking's Training Table Bread," page 7, *Brainerd Daily Dispatch* (MN), October 12, 1962.

*Equal to the beating the NFL took in the Nielsen ratings*: "Sullivan Signals Mason To Return; Packers and Colts Lose," page S8, NYT, September 12, 1966.

*Gotham's NFL Big Bowl was still*: "NFL Big Bowl Electric Football, page 562, *Sears 1966 Christmas Book*.

*Taking up the top third*: "Over 3 Ft. Long! Action-packed Electric Football," page 317, *Wards 1966 Christmas Catalog*.

*One of NFL Films' earliest ventures*: "Triple-Action 8mm Projector," page 330, ibid.

*The Higbee's Team Shop*: "Lorain boy mascot of Browns," page 37, *Chronicle-Telegram* (OH), October 7, 1966.

*Final piece of the NFL-AFL merger*: "Congressional Approval of Pro Football Merger Hastens Expansion Plans," page 34, NYT, October 22, 1966.

*Before a national television audience*: "3 Interceptions By Wilson Vital," page 66, NYT, November 1, 1966.

*Who met in early November*: "Merged League to Meet Today To Chart Super Bowl and Draft," page 69, NYT, November 9, 1966.

*Ward had started in October*: "Ward Toyland Specials," page 9, *Anderson Daily Bulletin* (IN), October 14, 1966.

*Sears waited until almost November*: "Sears Toytown is Open," page 13, *Austin Daily Herald* (MN), October 27, 1966.

*Gluck sent out another deluge*: "New Games Cater to Knowledgeable Fans," page B 10, *The Post-Crescent* (WI), November 24, 1966.

*Luckily for Gluck, Sears made the G-1500*: "Sears Electric Football," page A-7, *The Modesto Bee* (CA), November 24, 1966.

*Television was confirming its ever-growing popularity*: "TV Viewers Still Not Wearied Of Heavy Diet of Pro Football," page 60, NYT, November 30, 1966.

*It would be unheard of today*: "2 Networks Get First Super Bowl," page 1, NYT, December 14, 1966.

*The game had been on the network's television schedule*: "Schedule of Area Television Games," page M2, WP, September 11, 1966.

*Also discounted during the final shopping week*: "Sears Gifts for Him," page 5, *The Press-Courier* (CA), December 18, 1966.

*The Tudor accordion No. 600*: "Montgomery Ward Christmas Sale," page C-6, *Albuquerque Journal*, December 14, 1966.

# Chapter 19

*Critically acclaimed television documentary*: "Sonny, Money, and Merger," page 54, *NYT*, January 6, 1967.

*Newest franchise would be named the Saints*: "New Orleans Eleven To 'March In' as Saints," *NYT*, January 10, 1967.

*Commissioner Rozelle admitted*: "Rozelle Says the Price Is Wrong as Sale of Tickets Lags," *NYT*, January 15, 1967.

*Both CBS and NBC*: "The Million-Dollar Game," page 52, *NYT*, December 23, 1966.

*Officially adopting the new single-standard*: "Fair-Catch Rule Changed By N.F.L.," page 33, *NYT*, February 23, 1967.

*When Toy Fair opened*: "Toy Prices Will Rise as Fads Decline," page 145, *NYT*, March 5, 1967.

*Tudor's official kickoff*: "NFL Joins TUDOR's Champions – Watch'em go!" page 109, *PT*, March 1967.

*Four-paragraph feature*: "Tudor Set for 1967 Kickoff With Electric Football Games," page 324, *PT*, March 1967.

*It was his decision to produce African-American players*: Norman Sas, personal interview.

*During the month's final days*: "Football Teams Get Product Ties," page 126, *NYT*, March 26, 1967.

*Pro football owners*: "Cincinnati Receives Pro Football Franchise," page 60, *NYT*, May 25, 1967; "3 Other Cities Bid For Title Affair," page 57, *NYT*, May 26, 1967.

*The pro football preseason once again*: "Elevens To Test Foes of Future," page 51, *NYT*, June 23, 1967.

*Larry Kent and NFLP*: "A Family Guide to Football," *Life*, September 8, 1967.

*Sports games in Sears received a beautiful full-color*: pages 460-61, *Sears 1967 Christmas Book*.

*Had again used the Gotham factory as collateral*: New York City Department of Finance, Office of the City Register, Document 221/104, Mortgage, Bronx Block 2574, Lot 82, June 13, 1967.

*Tudor's NFL got a more impressive presentation*: "Wards NFL electric football with 3-Ft. Grandstand...Scoreboard," page 275, *Wards 1967 Christmas Catalog*.

*Another Larry Kent Life magazine promotion*: "This Is Football," *Life*, September 29, 1967.

*Some of the biggest companies in the U.S.*: "Advertising: Merchandising Kickoff Nears," page 61, *NYT*, July 13, 1967.

*Sears was already using Tudor's NFL No. 613*: "Sears Bike Sale," page 18, *Corpus Christi Times*, October 24, 1967.

*A new set of production-size masters*: Albert Sung, letter June 20, 2004. Don Munro Jr., personal interview.

*In the early weeks of November*: "Sears Toy Town is open," page 20, *The Anderson Herald* (IN), November 8, 1967.

*Ward was running the No. 500*: "Montgomery Ward Christmas Bargain Days," page 9, *The Portsmouth Herald* (NH), November 15, 1967.

*Sears continued having the No. 613*: "Sears Greatest Road Race Sale," page 46, *Wisconsin State Journal*, November 23, 1967.

*Norman was pleased with the visibility*: "Outstanding Toy Buys at Sears Low Prices," page 48, *Tucson Daily Citizen*, December 12, 1967; "Montgomery Ward Gift Sale," page 20, *Union-Bulletin* (WA), December 13, 1967

*On December 23*: "Saturday TV Programs," page D4, *WP*, December 23, 1967.

*This was the league's "prime" television game*: "Cleveland, Dallas Game on Television," page C1, *WP*, December 24, 1967.

*Namath was spectacular*: "Namath Throws 4 Scoring Passes," page 40, *NYT*, December 25, 1967.

*The early game on December 31*: "NFL, AFL Games On TV," page E1, *WP*, December 31, 1967.

## Chapter 20

*Dedicated football fans*: "4 Games Launch Flood of Footballs," page B1, *WP*, December 30, 1967.

*Taking place amid the other hoopla*: "Pro Football Association Assumes Status of Independent Union," page 45, *NYT*, January 11, 1968.

*Demand number one*: "N.F.L. Players Union Outlines Six-Point Plan for Immediate Negotiations," page S2, *NYT*, January 14, 1968.

*Any coach with consecutive Super Bowl victories*: "Lombardi Quits as Packers' Coach, but Stays With Club," page 41, *NYT*, February 2, 1968.

*During the meeting*: "Hirsch, Motley and Trippi Among Seven Named to Pro Football Hall of Fame," page 58, *NYT*, February 20, 1968.

*A 1967 Harris Poll*: "The Winds of Change," page 142, *NYT*, July 23, 1967.

*The newly opened New York City office of NFLPA*: "Players Open Office," page 34, *NYT*, February 24, 1968.

*Toy Fair opened on March 11*: "Toy Industry Talking of Profit and Sociology," page F1, *NYT*, March 10, 1968.

*Their advertising budget was going to be $15 million*: "Advertising: Talking Big on Toys," page 62, *NYT*, March 5, 1968.

*Tudor ran a color two-page spread*: "New AFL Electric Football, Plus..." *PT*, March 1968.

*Did anyone really care that the Houston Oilers*: "Oilers Put Feet First, Test New Shoes," page S2, *NYT*, April 14, 1968.

*Rozelle had extracted a second Monday night game*: "N.F.L. Doubles Its Monday Night TV," page S7, *NYT*, April 21, 1968.

*A frustrated Players Association*: "Positions Harden in Contract Talks," page S6, *NYT*, April 28, 1968.

*A voice vote by the NFL and AFL owners*: "Pro Football's Super Bowl Game Awarded to Miami Again," page 55, *NYT*, May 15, 1968.

*On May 23*: "Negotiations Between NFL Players and Owners Halted," page 56, *NYT*, May 24, 1968.

*NFL owners and players decided to resume their negotiations*: "Football Talks To Resume Today," page 51, *NYT*, June 28, 1968.

*Talks continued through July 2*: "N.F.L. Players Reject Owners' Offer," page 44, *NYT*, July 3, 1968.

*In the Packers camp*: "N.F.L. Players Try to Report to Camps but Are Barred," page 47, *NYT*, July 11, 1968.

*This "Ice Bowl" prototype*: Lee Payne, personal interview and photograph.

*Finally, a settlement was reached*: "N.F.L. Club Owners and Players Group Reach Agreement," page 38, *NYT*, July 11, 1968.

*On the third night*: "TV Covering the Chaos in Chicago," page 47, *NYT*, August 31, 1968.

*Most cities would see over 50 pro football games on television*: "Schedule of Area Television Games," page G2, *WP*, September 15, 1968.

*This did not sit well with Johnny Carson*: page F17, *LAT*, September 10, 1968.

*Best example of the antiwar influence*: "From The Ocean's Depths To The Stratosphere...GI

Joe," page 505, *Sears 1968 Christmas Book*.

*If Joe wanted some ammo*: "Talking GI Joe," page 269, *MW Christmas Catalog 1968*.

*It was the same generic Big Bowl*: "Big Bowl Electric Football," page 468, *Sears 1968 Christmas Book*.

*Over in the Ward Catalog*: "Wards NFL Electric Football," page 311, *MW Christmas Catalog 1968*.

*Having success with the Team Shop*: "Prange's Teams Up With NFL and Opens a Packer Shop," page B3, *Sunday Post-Crescent* (WI), September 3, 1967.

*A record 90 NFL licensees*: "New N.F.L. Franchise A Blanket, Not a Team," page F9, *NYT*, November 10, 1968.

*Sears, Ward, and J.C. Penney were already featuring electric football*: "Sears Toy Town is Open," page 50, *Tucson Daily Citizen*, October 1, 1968. "Montgomery Ward Toyland Is Open," page D-2, *Albuquerque Journal*, October 2, 1968; "Penney's Toyland," page 7-A, *The Times Recorder* (OH), October 6, 1968.

*Pete Rozelle and the NFL*: "Football Loop Promoting Monday TV," page 59, *NYT*, October 25, 1968.

*From the depths of the Cowboys' sorrows*: "Sunday and Monday," page 51, *NYT*, November 6, 1968.

*So many calls came into the NBC switchboard*: "Jets Cut for 'Heidi'; TV Fans Complain," page 1, *NYT*, November 18, 1968.

*Retailers who regretted passing on Tudor's miniature NFL*: "Save At Gibson's," page 4-A, *The San Antonio Light* (TX), November 7, 1968.

*Boys had begun walking right into the factory office*: Norman Sas, personal interview.

*Using newspaper ads to announce when new shipments arrived*: "Another Shipment N.F.L. Electric Football Game by Tudor," Tri-State Discount Center, page 11-D, *Kingsport Times-News* (TN), December 1, 1968.

*Sears continued*: "Sears Toy Town," page 4 A, *The Times* (IL), December 12, 1968.

*An article about the toy industry*: "Toy Sales Propelled By Science," page F1, *NYT*, December 15, 1968.

*Toy clearance sales at Sears and Ward*: "Sears Saturday Savers," page 12, *The Daily Plainsman* (SD), December 20, 1968; "Montgomery Ward Toy Clearance Save 30% To 50%," page D-5, *The Arizona Republic*, December 22, 1968.

*By the time Commander Frank Borman signed off*: "3 MEN FLY AROUND THE MOON ONLY 70 MILES FROM SURFACE," headline page 1, *NYT*, December 25, 1968.

*Time magazine named the Apollo 8 astronauts*: "Men Of The Year," *Time*, January 3, 1969.

*But the last days before the holiday*: "Late Shopping Spree," page 62, *NYT*, December 26, 1968.

*And Sears, Ward, and J.C. Penney would all report*: "Store Chains Life December Sales," page 35, *NYT*, January 3, 1969.

*The Tangerine Bowl launched a six-day period*: "The Bowl Picture," page D1, *WP*, December 28, 1968.

*Las Vegas sports analyst*: "Colts listed as 17-point Favorite of 7-1 Choice Over Jets in Super Bowl," page 35, *NYT*, December 31, 1968.

## Chapter 21

*A frustrated Namath*: "Namath's Super Confidence Shakes Crowd," page E5, *LAT*, January 11, 1969.

*It's usually not a good idea*: "Does Pete Rozelle Run Pro Football? Ask Joe Namath," page SM 30, *NYT*, August 17, 1969.

*Over 50 million viewers*: "It was a Super Day For Television," page 50, *NYT*, January 13, 1969.

*One person who viewed the upset from a very good seat*: Norman Sas, personal interview.

*In both Playthings and Toy & Hobby World*: "Gotham brings Santa back with the hottest action Sport Game for Spring and Summer Sales!" page 33, *PT*, January 1969. Page 55, *THW*, January 6, 1969.

*A once retired coach*: "Lombardi's Aim: Instant Winner," page 41, *NYT*, February 7, 1969.

*He was now the head of his own*: Lee Payne, personal interview.

*Gotham was still having financial issues*: New York City Department of Finance, Office of the City Register, Document 102/1911, Mortgage, Bronx Block 2574, Lot 82, February 25, 1969.

*Ideal, Remco, Kenner, and Hasbro*: "Advertising: Toy Makers Are Taking to the Networks," page F16, *NYT*, March 16, 1969.

*It was no accident that space-themed toys*: " Toy Ideas Come From Outer Space," page F15, *NYT*, March 2, 1969.

*Apollo 9 was scheduled to lift off*: "Apollo Joined To Moon Module In Space First," page A1, *WP*, March 4, 1969.

*Tudor was playing up its link*: "Go To The pro," *PT*, March 1969.

*There was only one electric football change in 1969*: *Tudor 1969 Sales Catalog*.

*A full-page Gotham ad challenged the toy world*: "If these 3 Action Games don't make money for you then the other 9 will," page 87, *PT*, April 1969.

*Gotham's new game was*: "Has Joe Namath Sold Out?" Gotham Pressed Steel 1969 Catalog.

*A joint NFL-AFL meeting*: "Super Bowl Game Is Shifted," page 64, *NYT*, March 20, 1969.

*During meeting that began on April 30*: "Pro Football Owners Agree to New Playoff System Involving Eight Teams," page 58, *NYT*, May 1, 1969.

*A week later*: "New Face of Pro Football," page 63, *NYT*, May 12, 1969.

*Another one of Pete Rozelle's visions was fulfilled*: "It's a Seller's Market in Football TV," page 60, *NYT*, May 28, 1969.

*The owners met again*: "Pro Alignment Still Unsettled," page 50, *NYT*, June 4, 1969.

*Joe Namath retired from football*: "Namath, Told to Sell Bar, Quits Football," page 1, *NYT*, June 7, 1969; "Courage of Convictions Could Throw Namath for $5-Million Loss," page 40, ibid.

*On July 18*: "Namath Agrees to Sell His Bar; Will Return to Jets Tomorrow," page 1, *NYT*, July 19, 1969.

*American astronaut Neil Armstrong*: "Astronauts Land On Plain; Collect Rocks, Plant Flag," page 1, *NYT*, July 21, 1969.

*Over 70,000 fans filled the Yale Bowl*: "Jets Beat Giants, 37-14; Namath Completes 14 of 16 Passes, 3 for Scores," page 40, *NYT*, August 18, 1969.

*Gluck claimed the demand*: "Big Demand For Namath Game," page 29, *THW*, September 1, 1969.

*For both leagues*: "Pros Entering Last Season Before Merger Ends Old Order of Two Leagues," page S1, *NYT*, August 24, 1969.

*Hovering majestically about the Super Dome*: "Super Bowl Electric Football," page 472, *Sears 1969 Christmas Book*.

*Over in Ward*: "Wards NFL electric football," page 361, *MW Christmas Catalog 1969*.

*Larry Kent had finally gotten his wish*: "Pick your favorite football team...and get an official NFL or AFL Sweatshirt plus an action Poster!" page 213, *Sears 1969 Christmas Book*.

*Many Sears stores*: "Grand Opening of Sears Toy Department," page A-10, *El Paso Herald-Post*, September 24, 1969.

*Ward also featured Tudor's NFL models*: "Ward 'Circus Of Toys' Now Open," page 3, *Walla Walla Union-Bulletin*, October 7, 1969.

*Sears' toy ads focused solely on the NFL No. 618*: "The Big Toy Box at Sears," page 7, *The Sun* (AZ), October 10, 1969.

*Retailers like the Gibson Discount Chain*: "AFL and NFL Electric Football Game also NHL Hockey Game," page 9B, *Ogden Standard-Examiner* (UT), November 5, 1969.

*Gluck caught a break*: "Gimbels toy world is the place to watch children glow," page 56, *NYT*, November 9, 1969.

*Placed it right between two other electric football games*: Santa Is Here, He's Waiting to greet all children at Gimbels this Saturday," page 20, *NYT*, November 21, 1969.

*Featuring NFL games in their holiday advertising*: "Wolf Kubly Hirsig Special Christmas Magic!" page 117, *Capital Times* (WI), November 27, 1969; "Montgomery Ward Big Sale," page 31, *Morgantown Dominion News* (WV), ibid; "Kmart Merry Christmas Discount Buys," page 7, *Syracuse Herald-Journal*, ibid.

*The No. 618 was often the feature item*: "Sears Action Games," page C-4, *Alton Evening Telegraph* (IL), December 8, 1969.

*Also, the long intradivision rivalry between the Browns and the Giants*: "Giants, Browns Player Here Today," page S7, *NYT*, December 21, 1969.

*On Monday morning*: "Montgomery Ward Toy Clearance All Toys 1/2 Price While They Last!" page 32, *Abilene Reporter News*; "Sears Final Toy Clearance," page 3A, *The Victoria Advocate* (TX), December 22, 1969.

## Chapter 22

*Jimmy the Greek made the Vikings 13-point favorites*: "Viking Are Made 13-Point Favorites," page 45, *NYT*, January 6, 1970.

*According to Nielsen ratings*: "More Eyes On Football" page 171, *NYT*, February 15, 1970.

*One of NFL Properties special guests*: Norman Sas, personal interview.

*NFL Films' Steve Sabol has described*: NFL Films, *Full Color Football No. 5*, January 28, 2010.

*Rozelle took it upon himself*: "Pro Elevens Realigned as Giants Stay in Group With Redskins and Eagles," page 37, *NYT*, January 17, 1970.

*On January 26 Rozelle announced*: "Pro Football Gets Four-Year TV Pact," page 50, *NYT*, January 27, 1970.

*The very next morning*: "Steelers Select Bradshaw, Passes, as First Choice in Pro Football Draft," page 73, *NYT*, January 28, 1970.

*Parts of the NFL and AFL had already combined*: "New Players Group Formed," page 187, *NYT*, January 11, 1970.

*The new 84,000-seat domed stadium*: "Pangs of Prosperity," page 177, *NYT*, February 8, 1970.

*In 1969, toy manufacturers spent*: "Advertising: Toy Buyers View Commercials," page 76, *NYT*, February 26, 1970.

*An interest by toy makers in the occult*: "Witches, Zodiac, Occult Newest Trend for Toys," page F1, *NYT*, March 8, 1970.

*The brothers felt the company could be more profitable*: Brian Clarke, personal interview.

*Coleco bought Playtime Products*: "Coleco Industries Buys Playtime Products for Cash," page 118, *PT*, January 1966.

*And Klauber Games*: "Coleco Plans to Buy Klauber," page 98, *PT*, September 1968.

*Coleco purchased Eagle Toys*: "Coleco to Buy Eagle Toy," page 10, *PT*, November 1968.

*In 1968, Eagle did a quarter of its total business*: Brian Clarke, personal interview.

*That vision was "The Coleco World of Sports"*: "New. A Coleco World Of Sports In Official

Team Action Games," *PT*, February, 1970.

*Greenberg had Eagle Toys purchase*: "Coleco Canadian Subsidiary Buys Injection Mold Firm," page 186, *THW*, March 3, 1969.

*In this Pro Stars line*: Coleco 1970 World of Sports Catalog.

*In preparing to meet the anticipated nationwide demand*: "Coleco Opens Huge Shipping Center," page 14, *PT*, February 1968.

*A West Coast production and distribution facility*: "Coleco Expands In The West," page 8, *THW*, November 3, 1969.

*A four-page full-color Playthings layout*: "New. A Coleco World Of Sports In Official Team Action Games," *PT*, February 1970.

*$6 million of electric football and $300,000 of licensing fees*: Norman Sas, personal interview.

*The redesigned No. 500*: Tudor Sales Catalog 1970.

*Gluck had an ad*: "Score with Gotham's Family of Sports Stars," page 265, *PT*, March 1970.

*This family stars had expanded*: "Gotham's 'Family Of Stars' Games," *Gotham Catalog 1970*.

*NFL Properties took out a half page ad*: "NFL," page 154, *PT*, March 1970.

## Chapter 23

*By the end of the gathering*: "Halas, Hunt Head N.F.L. Conferences," page 61, *NYT*, March 20, 1970.

*Player Association President John Mackey*: "Football Players to Seek New Contract," page 52, *NYT*, March 28, 1970.

*When the NFL owners broke off contract talks*: "Negotiating Snag Charged To N.F.L.," page 62, *NYT*, June 19, 1970.

*The Players Association instructed veteran NFL players*: "N.F.L. Players Told: Skip Camp Awhile," page 44, *NYT*, July 10, 1970.

*Players and owners aired their grievances in the media*: "It's Fourth Down and 100 Yards to Go as Pro Football Pension Dispute Hardens," page 138, *NYT*, July 19, 1970.

*Both sides agreed to federal mediation*: "All-Star Football Game to Be Played, Players Disclose," page 26, *NYT*, July 25, 1970.

*But just two days before the game*: "N.F.L. Labor Negotiations Are Recessed Indefinitely at Request of Owners," page 66, *NYT*, July 29, 1970.

*Rozelle "summoned" the owners*: "Rozelle Assumes Role Of Mediator," page 24, *NYT*, August 4, 1970.

*Vince Lombardi died of stomach cancer*: "Vince Lombardi, Dead at 57," page 1, *WP*, September 4, 1970.

*Howard Cosell narrated*: "Special on Vince Lombardi Scheduled by ABC Tonight," page 33, *NYT*, September 4, 1970.

*The first regular season game of the merged NFL*: "4-Day Weekend, Starting Friday, Gets 182-Game NFL Season Under Way," page S4, *NYT*, September 13, 1970.

*Nielsen ratings had the game*: "Monday Football A Success On TV," page 63, *NYT*, September 23, 1970.

*Page 488 in Sears*: "Super Bowl Electric Football," page 488, *Sears 1970 Christmas Book*.

*It was the Ward NFL No. 627*: "Wards NFL electric football," page 423, *MW Christmas Catalog 1970*.

*Ward's reason for taking on the Coleco game*: "NHL NEW! Table Hockey: Ward Exclusive," page 422, ibid.

*Within issues of PRO!*: "Time Out!" page 43, *PRO!*, October 4, 1970.

*Carefully placed within the zany world of Team Shop*: "From Our House To Yours," page 84, ibid.

*Taking his place*: "NFL Merchandising Chief," page 43, *NYT*, July 17, 1970.

*By late September*: "Sears Big Toy Box Opening," page 8A, *The Anniston Star* (AL), September 24, 1970.

*Ward wasn't far behind*: "Montgomery Ward 'Circus of Toys' Now Open!" page 8, *The Lawton Constitution* (OK), October 7, 1970.

*For Sears it was the Super Bowl and NFL No. 619*: "Big Toy Box Sale," page 37, *The Gastonia Gazette* (NC), October 21, 1970.

*Kmart was selling Gotham's Joe Namath*: "Kmart Midnight Magic Sale," *Charleston Daily Mail* (WV), September 30, 1970.

*It moved through the fall*: "Monday Night Football Hits Paydirt," page S7, *NYT*, October 25, 1970.

*Tudor received Sears' prestigious*: Tudor Wins Sears 'Excellence' Award," page 6, *THW*, December 7, 1970.

*The Super Bowl being the lead item*: "Big Toy Box Sale," page 16, *The Hutchinson News* (KS), November 13, 1970.

*Tudor was getting just as much support from Ward*: "Montgomery Ward 'Circus of Toys' Now Open!" page 11, *Raleigh Register* (WV), November 18, 1970.

*Coleco's models were finally*: "Kmart," page 6B, *The Cedar Rapids Gazette*, November 11, 1970.

*Toys R Us was aggressively expanding*: "Toys R Us the Children's discount Supermarts," page A-6, *The Daily Report* (CA), November 12, 1970.

*An ad campaign in National Hockey League Programs*: "Play the game the pro-stars play!" page 41, *National Hockey League Official Magazine* (Philadelphia Flyers Version), November 15, 1970.

*Sears and Ward did their share*: "Big Toy Box Sale," page 68, *The News-Palladium* (MI), November 25, 1970; "Montgomery Ward Giant Toy Sale" page A-8, *The New Mexican* (NM), November 27, 1970.

*Coleco got a strong push*: "Kmart Bombshells," page 39, *Oshkosh Daily Northwestern* (WI), November 28, 1970.

*The Namath game*: "Korvettes Veteran's Day Values," page E-7, *The Economist* (IL), November 8, 1970.

*Both J.C. Penney and the Gibson Discount Center chain*: "Action Toys," page 12, *Appleton Post Crescent*, November 29, 1970; "Gotham NFLPA Superdome Electric Football," page 38, *Colorado Springs Gazette*, November 29, 1970.

*Gluck had sent out a press release*: "Toyland will delight kids of any age," page C-5, *Alton Evening Telegraph* (IL), November 25, 1970.

*A full-color J.C. Penney insert*: "Action Toys," page 26, *Jefferson City Post Tribune*, December 1, 1970.

*More electric football requests in Dear Santa letters*: "Expensive Gifts Replace Kids' Visions of Sugarplums," page 1, *Tucson Daily Citizen*, December 19, 1970.

*And Toys R Us with the Roman Gabriel game*: "Table Top Sports, Too!" page 175, *The Oakland Tribune*, November 22, 1970.

*Coleco's muscle couldn't stop these same retailers*: "Kmart Discount Toys," page 28, *Bakersfield Californian*, December 9, 1970.

*A nationally televised game between the 49ers and the Raiders*: "NFL Season to End With 182 Game," page 152, *NYT*, December 20, 1970.

*Over the weekend J.C. Penney had offered*: "Christmas Toy Clearance!" page 2-E, *Kingsport Times-News* (TN), December 20, 1970.

*The Gibson Discount Center*: "Suggestions For Late Shoppers," page 28, *Grand Prairie Daily News* (TX), December 20, 1970.

*Tudor's NFL models were also in great demand*: "Sears Last Minute Gifts," page 8, *Sheboygan Press*, December 22, 1970.

*Just two days before Christmas*: "Ward Toy Sale," page A11, *The New Mexican*, December 22, 1970.

## Chapter 24

*The Cornhuskers*: "Writers Pick Nebraska," page D3, *WP*, January 4, 1971.

*All the way down to the Poly Turf*: "...But Artificial Turf Could Be Real Consideration," page S1, *NYT*, January 17, 1971.

*Jimmy The Greek*: "Unitas, Poly Turf, Keys in Bowl Odds," page 44, *NYT*, January 4, 1971.

*Nielsen ratings making Super Bowl V*: "Advertising: Bowl Is Super on TV, Too," page 47, *NYT*, January 27, 1971.

*Munro Games president Don Munro Jr. called Norman*: Don Munro Jr., personal interview.

*Trbovich initiated the construction of a new*: "Munro Games Expands Plants, Adds Two Key Personnel," page 14, *THW*, September 15, 1969.

*Munro Games enlarged its reputation*: "Presentation of the coveted Sears Roebuck's Symbol of Excellence," page 2, *Munro 1971 Sales Catalog*.

*Don Munro still had memories*: Don Munro Jr., personal interview.

*A very stark ad*: "Notice To The Trade," page 151, *PT*, March 1971.

*Hosting a "World Of Sports" dinner*: "Coleco World of Sports," page 38, *PT*, April 1971.

*Besides television commercials*: "Coleco's TV and Print Campaign for 1971," *Coleco Sales Catalog 1971*.

*In the new sales catalog*: page 2, *Munro 1971 Sales Catalog*.

*A schedule of commercials for the fall*: "Munro Games East Coast TV Advertising For 1971," Munro Sales Catalog Insert.

*Tudor had two new games for 1971*: page 4, *Tudor 1971 Sales Catalog*.

*A full-page ad for NFL Strategy*: page 199, *PT*, March 1971.

*Gluck continued to expand*: "Family of Sports Super Stars," page 25, *PT*, March 1971.

*He had already been to Tokyo*: Don Munro Jr., personal interview.

## Chapter 25

*The NFL owners served up a surprise*: "New Orleans Selected As '72 Super Bowl Site," page 29, *NYT*, March 24, 1971.

*When the NFL owners met again*: "NFL Owners Agree to Three Changes in Rules," page 48, *NYT*, May 27, 1971.

*There were many unique features*: "Rozelle Feels Labor Discord Will Not Block Season's Start," page 28, *NYT*, May 28, 1971.

*Players and owners finally signed*: "NFL Players Agree On Bargaining Contract," page 48, *NYT*, June 18, 1971.

*This generic Super Bowl design*: Norman Sas, personal interview.

*Anyone skimming a PRO! program*: "Coleco keeps your kids at home," page 76, *PRO!* , Volume 2, Number 1, 1971.

*Another first time PRO! advertiser was Tudor*: "NFL Strategy," page 1D, ibid.

*Joe Namath threw an interception*: "Namath Hurts Knee, Lost At Least Till November," page S1, *NYT*, August 8, 1971.

*A sign of how much American culture was changing*: "CBS Line-UP for Fall Omits Once-Prized Country Comedies," page 91, *NYT*, March 17, 1971.

*The network decided to move its hour-long biweekly news show*: "CBS Is Shifting Its Weekly News Hour in Fall," page 75, *NYT*, March 12, 1971.

*Montgomery Ward opened some of its Toyland*: "Toyland Is Open," page 4, *Tucson Daily Citizen*, September 8, 1971.

*Sears was not far behind*: "Sears Big Toy Box Opening," page 2-A, *Gazette Telegraph* (CO), September 15, 1971.

*The day the 1971 NFL season opened*: "NFL Season Gets Under Way Today," page S1, *NYT*, September 15, 1971.

*Tudor's redesigned Super Bowl*: "Super Bowl Electric Football," page 102, *Sears 1971 Christmas Catalog*.

*On the opposing page*: "Professional Hockey with all these features:" page 103, ibid.

*A mere 96 pages later*: "Sports Table games with legs…set up almost anywhere," page 198, ibid.

*NFL Properties now had over four pages*: pages 102, 285, 425, 491-493, ibid.

*Tudor supplemented its Sears success*: "NFL Electric Football Wards exclusive…" page 431, *MW Christmas Catalog 1971*.

*Even though Coleco didn't get a game*: "New! NHL Stanley Cup Hockey," page 430, ibid.

*Throughout the fall Sears and Ward*: "The Big Toy Box Action game Sale," page 15, *The Altoona Mirror*, October 21, 1971. "Montgomery Ward Unbeatable Toy Buys," page 8, *WP*, November 4, 1971.

*J.C. Penney, Toys R Us, and the Gibson Discount Centers*: "Toyland is Open," page 2A, *The Victoria Advocate* (TX), October 22, 1971; "Toys R Us Is Your Shop: Fun And Games For Every Kid!" page L34, *WP*, November 21, 1971; "Where You Always Buy The Best For Less," page 24, *The Billings Gazette*, October 24, 1971.

*For 1971 Kmart had cozied up with Coleco*: "Kmart Storewide Discount Days," page 24, *Waterloo Daily Courier* (IA), November 3, 1971.

*There was little surprise*: "Monday Night Passes the Screen Test," page S2, *NYT*, November 14, 1971.

*Tudor won its second consecutive*: "Tudor Wins 2nd Sears Symbol of Excellence," page 11, *THW*, December 1971.

*This time giving Munro Games*: "Aggressive Expansion Plans Announced by Munro Games," page 12, *THW*, December 1971.

*A good thing that few retailers*: "Grants Known For Values," page 6, *Newport Daily News* (RI), November 8, 1971.

*Hundreds of press releases*: page 9, *Daily Messenger* (NY), November 22, 1971; "A Look At Toyland 1971 Reveals That Even Children Can't Escape Adult World," page 6, Section Three, *The Gettysburg Times*, November 24, 1971.

*Gluck caught a break*: "Toys R Us Is Your Shop: Fun And Games For Every Kid!" page L34, *WP*, November 21, 1971.

*Sears and Ward continued to make electric football*: "Big Toy Box Sale," page 125, *Ogden Standard Examiner* (UT); "Ward Christmas Value Days," page 3-E, *Iowa City Press-Citizen*, November 25, 1971.

*Toys R Us favored the No. 500*: "Toys R Us," page 35, *WP*, November 25, 1971.

*Kmart gave Coleco serious visibility*: "Kmart Big Toy Sale," page 50, *Florence Morning News*;

page 5, *Ogden Standard Examiner* (UT); page 18, *Des Moines Register*; page 59, *El Paso Herald*, November 25, 1971.

*SI published and article*: "Shopwalk: NFL Properties can help you with an autograph but not a new toupee," page E2, *SI*, December 20, 1971.

*At Sears, the Super Bowl*: "Sears Christmas Gifts," page A-7, *Chronicle-Telegram* (OH), December 19, 1971.

*And by Wednesday*: "Riding Toys from the Big Toy Box at Sears," page 2-A, *Gazette Telegraph*, December 22, 1971.

*Over in Ward*: "Ward Last Minute Gift Sale," page 3, *The Daily Inter Lake* (MT), December 19, 1971.

*Discounts on Coleco models*: "Kmart Last Minute Gift Discounts," page 7-B, *The Danville Bee* (VA), December 22, 1971.

*Deep discounts on its larger NFLPA game*: "Lazarus Lima Mall," page 14, *The Lima News* (OH), December 22, 1971.

*Some Joe Namath games*: "American Toy Savings!," page 25, *Newport Daily News* (RI), December 12, 1971.

## Chapter 26

*By the time Orange Bowl signed off*: "Television," page 37, *NYT*, January 1, 1972.

*New kinds of turf were producing an alarming number of injuries*: page D1, *LAT*, September 30, 1971.

*Concerns about artificial turf*: "Makers Dispute Astroturf Study," page 56, *NYT*, November 3, 1971.

*Dolphins coach Don Shula*: "Shula Wants to Pull the Rug Out," page 14, *NYT*, January 1, 1972.

*Nielsen ratings were up*: "65 Million Saw Super Bowl," page 21, *NYT*, January 26, 1972.

*A Gallup poll*: "The No. 1 Sport? It's Now Football," page S1, *NYT*, January 16, 1972.

*Similar results came from an NFL-funded*: "Kuhn Tackles Rozelle on No. 1 Sport Claim," page 46, *NYT*, February 1, 1972.

*Coleco held its World of Sports Dinner*: "Coleco's World of Sports dinner set," page 13, *PT*, February 1972.

*Some major companies were shaking off*: "Profits On Toys Seesaw," page F5, *NYT*, March 5, 1972.

*It was unveiled in a four-page color spread*: "The Coleco Way..." *PT*, April 1972.

*A national ad campaign*: Coleco Toys/Games/Sporting Goods 1972.

*Trbovich was determined to announce the game*: "Announcing Munro Monday Nite Football," pages 206-207, *PT*, March 1972.

*High speed assembly lines*: Don Munro Jr., personal interview.

*Munro's wholesale prices*: Munro Games 1972 Price List, from Don Munro Jr.

*Only three Tudor games were going to have*: Tudor 1972 Sales Catalog.

*Instead on page 217*: "New for '72 NHLPA Players Hockey," page 217, *PT*, March 1972.

*Two new endorsers were added*: Gotham Sales Catalog 1972.

*Rozelle laid out a warning*: "Problems Facing NFL Analyzed," page 51, *NYT*, March 21, 1972.

*The owners awarded the upcoming Super Bowl*: "Los Angeles Gets 1973 Super Bowl," page 37, *NYT*, March 22, 1972.

*Voted to move the hash marks*: "Owners In NFL, Adopt New Rule," page 48, *NYT*, March 24, 1972.

*In the April issue of Playthings*: "New direction in Football I.P.P.," *PT*, April 1972.

*Munro Games bought the financially endangered*: "Eddie Gluck Dies After Long Illness," page 2, *THW*, March 19, 1973.

Nick Trbovich had found something else: "Servotronics Announces Purchase," page 2, The Titusville Herald (PA), August 9, 1972.

## Chapter 27

*The NFL was finally ready to start*: "Rerun of NFL's Longest Day," page S1, *NYT*, September 17, 1972.

*Tudor was also off to a running start*: "Do you have enough brains to play NFL football," page 2B, *PRO!*, Volume 3 No. 4, September 24, 1972.

*Found a dramatic NFL presentation on pages 10 and 11*: "Look What Sears has done with the NFL Idea...it's one of the highlights of the 1972 Wish Book," pages 10-11, *Sears 1972 Christmas Catalog*.

*Sears gave Tudor a dynamic layout*: "Superbowl Electric Football," page 500, ibid.

*It was the largest display Sears had ever given Munro games*: "Sears Professional Hockey," page 501, ibid.

*They were even more excited about page 498*: "You've never seen such realism in Game-room Hockey before," page 498, ibid.

*Coleco had a page of its own*: "NHL Trophy Cup Hockey," page 376, ibid.

*Two exclusive Ward NFL No. 627 games*: "NFL Total Team Control," page 281, *MW Christmas Catalog 1972*.

*Coleco was once again limited*: "NHL Stanley Cup Hockey," page 280, ibid.

*This line was evident the J.C. Penney Christmas catalog*: "Electric Football," pages 430-431, *J.C. Penney Christmas 1972*.

*Joe Namath emphatically proved he was over his injury*: "Namath Throws for Six Touchdowns as Jets Top Colts, 44-33, page 51, *NYT*, September 25, 1972.

*A number of different sports games*: "The Big Season for Games," pages 72-77, *PT*, October 1972.

*Two retailers who were favoring Coleco*: "Kmart October Discount Days," page 41, *The Capitol Times* (WI), October 4, 1972; "It's all fun and games in Penneys Toyland, opening October 6th," page 26, *Tucson Daily Citizen*, October 5, 1972.

*By mid-October*: "Sears Lay-Away Toy Sale," page 14, *The Baytown Sun* (TX), October 25, 1972; "Only At Wards!" page 11, *Salina Journal* (KS), October 19, 1972.

*The Day/Nite electric football game*: "Grants Fights Inflation," page 38, *The Cumberland Times* (MD), October 22, 1972.

*Rozelle responded by offering*: "Blackout Policy Is Eased by NFL," page 47, *NYT*, October 13, 1972.

*Tudor won its third consecutive Sears Award*: "Sears again pays honor to Tudor Metal," page 34, *PT*, December 1972.

*A retailer who seemed to enjoy the competition was Toys R Us*: "Toys R Us!," page 18-K, *Oakland Tribune*, November 2, 1972; "Toys R Us!," page B16, *WP*, November 16, 1972.

*The Dolphins beat the Jets*: "Unbeaten Team Clinches Title With Rally," page 51, *NYT*, November 20, 1972.

*Sears was doing heavy lifting for the Super Bowl game*: "Sears Annual After Thanksgiving Sale," page 16-C, *Florence Morning News* (SC), November 23, 1972.

*Ward was continuing*: "Montgomery Ward We Fill Santa's Orders," page 10, *Las Cruces Sun-News* (NM), November 23, 1972.

*Tudor was also getting help from Gibson*: "Gibson's Toyland is now Open!," page C-9, *El Paso Herald*, November 23, 1972.

*Kmart was particularly aggressive*: "Kmart 7 days of Christmas Discounts," page 75, *Pasadena Star News*; page 89, *Charleston Gazette Mail* (WV); page 73, *Abilene Reporter News* (TX); page 115, *Cedar Rapids Gazette*, November 26, 1972.

*Tudor's models were mentioned*: "Want A Miami Lamp?" page 11D, *High Point Enterprise* (NC), December 3, 1972.

*Gibson promoting the G-883*: "Gibson's Christmas Gift Hints," page 111, *Abilene Reporter News*; page 55, *Grand Prairie Daily News* (TX), December 3, 1972.

*Toys R Us Chose the NFL No. 620*: "Toy R Us," page X10, *CT*; Page Q10, *LAT*; page 222, *The Oakland Tribune*, December 3, 1972.

*For the bargain hunter*: "Woolco Gift Center," page 15, *Greeley Tribune* (CO), December 19, 1972.

*Only the W.T. Grant chain*: "Grants Toy Sale," pages 6A, *News-Herald* (FL), December 2, 1972.

*Gotham's Bob Lilly game*: "Say Merry Christmas With Gifts From Gibson's," page 8-9, *Northwest Arkansas Times*, December 13, 1972.

*West Coast chains still selling the Gabriel game*: "White Front Discount Sale," page A27, *The Fresno Bee*, December 10, 1972.

*The Dick Butkus game*: "Goldblatt's Toys," page 22, *The Chicago Defender*, November 4, 1972.

*A nationally published*: "Astute Shoppers Fair Best For Christmas," page 9, *Zanesville Times Recorder*, December 14, 1972.

*As the NFL season head into the final weekend*: Grants Christmas Gift Specials," pages 8-9, *Delta Democrat-Times* (MS), December 7, 1972.

*Sears Super Bowl models*: "Super Bowl Electric Football," page B-3, *Chronicle Telegram* (OH), December 20, 1972.

*Ward joined in*: "Last Minute Toy Bargains," page 2-A, *The Abilene Reporter-News*, December 23, 1972.

*Coleco Command Control models*: "Kmart," page 73, *The Billings Gazette*, December 17, 1972.

*Woolco continued to unload its small Gotham games*: "Woolco Big Toy Sale," page 19-A, *Greeley Tribune* (CO), December 22, 1972.

*The Kiddie City chain*: "Toy-A-Gram," page 1-C, *San Antonio Express*, December 20, 1972.

*Aurora's Monday night game was on sale*: "Grants Christmas Sale," page 23, *Tucson Daily Citizen* (AZ), December 20, 1972.

*No local television blackout of a Super Bowl game*: "Rozelle Seen Lifting Super Bowl Blackout," page S1, *NYT*, December 31, 1972.

## Chapter 28

*The Buffalo Chamber of Commerce*: "There's still room at the top...New York State," page 184, *NYT*, January 7, 1973.

*The NFL had allotted 10,000 corporate tickets*: "Business in a Front Seat For Today's Super Bowl," page 1, *NYT*, January 7, 1973.

*Eddie Gluck passed away*: "Sonny Gluck, Who Played On Original Celtics, Dead," page 32, *NYT*, February 3, 1973; "Eddie Gluck Dies After Long Illness," page 2, *THW*, March 19, 1973.

*From now on the company would known as Tudor Games*: "Introducing For The First Time The Newest Stupendous Most Exciting Spectacular Tudor Ever," page 48, *PT*, March 1973.

*Redesigned TTC bases*: Tudor Games '73 Catalog.

*The No. 655 NFL Championship game*: ibid.

*Coleco rode into the Fair on a wave of record sales*: "Coleco 1972 sales record $65 million," page 16, *PT*, March 1973.

*A complete redesign of the Coleco showroom*: "Coleco redesigns showroom," page 66, *PT*, May 4, 1973.

*Displayed on the first floor*: "Coleco exhibits Stanley Cup," page 15, *PT*, March 1973.

*Signing NBA star Wilt Chamberlain*: "Coleco creates adult look," page 240-241, *PT*, March 1973.

*First there was a two-page spread*: "Munro Announces Its 1973 Game Plan," pages 212-213, *PT*, March 1973.

*Glowing coverage from Playthings and Toy & Hobby World*: "Munro puts their buyers on ice (literally)," page 38, *PT*, April 1973; "Spirits High, Action Lively At 1st Annual Munro Hockey Night," page 2, *THW*, March 19, 1973.

*This gave Munro a total of 11 electric football games*: Munro 1973 Sales Catalog and Price List.

*At a series of Toy Fair luncheons*: "1973 Toy Fair struck by star fever; attendance was up," page 35, *PT*, April 1973.

*Magnavox had actually introduced the Odyssey*: "Magnavox Dealers Introduced To Product Innovations," page 6, *The Daily Herald* (IL), July 27, 1972; "Odyssey The Electronic Game Of The Future," page B-8, *The Sun* (AZ), November 18, 1972

*More points were scored*: "NFL to Weigh Sudden-Death Tiebreaker," page 222, *NYT*, March 11, 1973.

*Before the meeting adjourned*: "NFL Sites are Picked For '75, '76 Super Bowl," page 49, *NYT*, April 4, 1973.

*Trbovich sold his share of the team*: "Ottawa Gets New Owners," page 6, *Daily Messenger* (NY), May 3, 1973.

*The NFL issued its first study on artificial turf injuries*: "Artificial Turf Gets Tie In Study," page 64, *NYT*, June 28, 1973.

*The league and the networks agreed*: "TV Pact Is Put At $200-Million," page 20, *NYT*, July 20, 1973.

*Coleco had announced record sales*: "Leonard Greenberg named to Coleco chairmanship," page 21, *PT*, August 1973.

*The NFL was lifting the television blackout for home games*: "Congress Votes To Limit TV Ban On Football Games," page 1, *NYT*, September 14, 1973.

*Namath separated his shoulder*: "Joe Suffers A Shoulder Separation," page 43, *NYT*, September 24, 1973.

*A six-page article*: "Games, '73: Getting The Family Together," pages 48-53, *PT*, September 1973.

*Taking up almost all of page 519*: "Day-Nite Electric Football," page 519, *Sears 1973 Christmas Book*.

*A flip of the page*: "You control the movement of every player on every play with improved Total Team Control," page 520, ibid.

*Munro got its usual hockey game page*: "You control all the action from ice level with Sears Professional Hockey Game," page 521, ibid.

*NFL Properties*: "Handy Index To Other NFL Items In This Book," page 12, ibid.

*Ward was now selling three Tudor models*: "Get you home team with Wards Exclusive NFL electric football," page 327, *MW Christmas Catalog 1973*.

*Just opposite Tudor on page 326*: "Our lowest price in 10 years," page 326, ibid.

*J.C. Penney had put electric football up in the very front*: "Football Family Fun, it's not like being up in the stands...it's like being on the field!" pages 8-9, *J.C. Penney Christmas 1973*.

*Toys R US was a fostering a healthy competition*: "Toy R Us," page 8, *The Sun-Standard* (IL), October 11, 1973.

*With 48 stores nationwide*: "Supermarket For Toys Get a Big Play," page 221, *NYT*, December 9, 1973.

*Toys U Us was even selling the Munro Namath Day/Nite*: "Toy R Us," page C5, *WP*, November 23, 1973.

*Kmart was selling*: "Kmart's Christmas Toyland Now Open," page 76, *North Adams Transcript*, October 24, 1973.

*The Western Auto chain continued its loyalty to Tudor*: "These Are the Games People Play," page 8, *Western Auto Christmas Catalog 1973*.

*In the South and West the Gibson Discount Center*: "Gibson's Fall Festival," page 2, *The Ada Evening News* (OK), October 11, 1973; "Gibson's Toyland," page 6B, *Corsicana Daily Sun* (TX), November 23, 1973; "Christmas Savings," *Abilene Reporter*, November 28, 1973.

*Ward had already made Tudor's*: "Montgomery Ward Toyland Is Open," page 11, *The Lima News* (OH), October 18, 1973.

*J.C. Penney used Coleco*: "The fun starts October 19 at Penney's Toyland," page 20, *The Montana Standard*, October 19, 1973.

*When Sears finally started advertising*: "Great Toys At Sears Low Prices," page A-2, *The Sandusky Register* (OH), November 1, 1973.

*So it was fitting*: "Number Four," page 30, *PT*, December 1973.

*Announced on page 65*: "Watch Munro on 'The Tonight Show'" page 65, *PT*, November 1973.

*Namath returned to action*: "Namath Back but Jets lose by Foot," page 73, *NYT*, November 19, 1973.

## Chapter 29

*Over the next six weeks*: "Dow Hits 2-Year Low In Broad Stock Retreat," page B9, *LAT*, December 4, 1973.

*Sears promoting the Tudor Super Bowl*: "Games At Sears Low Prices," page 4C, *Fort Pierce News Tribune*, November 22, 1973.

*Ward finished a strong second*: "Open Every Night Till 10:00 p.m.," page 58, *Kingsport Times* (TN), November 22, 1973.

*The most intriguing ads*: "Toy R Us," page C5, *WP*, November 23, 1973.

*There you could find*: "Sears Catalog Surplus Store," page B-12, *The Herald* (IL), November 23, 1973.

*President Nixon, who went on television Sunday*: "Sunday Sales and Holiday Lights to Be Forbidden," page 65, *NYT*, November 26, 1973.

*President Nixon signed*: "Oil Allocation Act Signed As Nixon Ends Opposition," page 93, *NYT*, November 28, 1973.

*Compounding the president's woes*: "Tape Played in Court: Noise, Chatter – and Big Gap," page A1, *NYT*, November 28, 1973.

*Toy makers had been receiving allocations of plastic*: "Oil Pinch Hits Toy Industry," page 3, *Evening Capital* (MD), December 8, 1973.

*In a newspaper interview*: "Never before were toys so scarce..." page 24, *The Lowell Sun* (MA), November 29, 1973.

*The struggling economy did not produce*: "Fear And Fantasy: Material Shortages, Christmas Gift Buying Boost Toy Sales," page B1, *The Fresno Bee*, December 13, 1973; "Merchants report Christmas sales up after a slow start," *The Lowell Sun* (MA), December 12, 1973.

*Sears continued promoting its Super Bowl*: "Great Toys At Sears Low Prices," page 16, *The*

*Daily Times* (PA), December 12, 1973.

*Also seeing electric football as an important item*: "Toys R Us," pages 67-69, *Daily Review* (CA), November 29, 1973.

*Toys R Us even distributed a second color flyer*: Toys R Us, pages O12-13, *LAT*, December 2, 1973.

*On the second Monday of the month*: "Sears Catalog Surplus Store," page 4 Section 2, *The Herald* (IL), December 10, 1973.

*Kmart joined in*: "Kmart Happy Holidays Gift Guide," page 10-A, *Florence Morning News* (SC), December 14, 1973.

*A lot of Super Bowl games were still $11.88*: "Great Games At Sears Low Prices," page 12, *The Newark Advocate* (OH), December 18, 1973.

*Ward began pricing the No. 645*: "Wards Exclusive 38x20" Table Top Electric Football Game," page 21, *Union-Bulletin* (WA), December 20, 1973.

*Kmart took the Super Action Coleco down to $8*: "Kmart Doorbusters," page 37, Burlington *Daily Times-News* (NC), December 20, 1973.

*For the final weekend of shopping*: "We're lowering our already low prices on big name toys," page 10A, *The High Point Enterprise* (NC), December 20, 1973.

*Holding pretty steady at this point*: "Sears Last Minute Gift Suggestions," page 3A, *Playground Daily News* (FL), December 23, 1973.

*Sears wasn't the only retailer*: "Kmart Last Minute Gift Sale," page 10-A, *The Galveston Daily News*, December 23, 1973; "White Front Christmas Sale," page 22, *Press-Telegram* (CA), December 21, 1973.

*Toy retailers were reporting*: "Fear And Fantasy: Material Shortages, Christmas Gift Buying Boost Toy Sales," page B1, *The Fresno Bee*, December 13, 1973.

*Over 19 consecutive hours of football*: "Sports Today," page 21, *NYT*, December 29, 1973.

## Chapter 30

*Notre Dame was anointed the nation's top team*: " Irish Rated No. 1, But Falter on TV," page 35, *NYT*, January 4, 1974.

*Speculation on Joe Namath's future*: "What Play Will Namath Call: Retire, Sign Again, or Jump," page 59, *NYT*, December 11, 1973.

*The newly formed World Football League*: "New Pro Football League Plans to Start in 1974 With 12 Teams," page 61, *NYT*, October 4, 1973.

*Signing into law a 55 mph national speed limit*: "Nixon Approves Limit of 55 M.PH.," page 1, *NYT*, January 3, 1974.

*And in hotels throughout Houston*: "Houston Unruffled By Striking It Rich," page 206, *NYT*, January 13, 1974.

*The stock market lost more than 3%*: "Prices of Stocks Plunge 26.99 In 3d Largest Drop Since '62," page 53, *NYT*, January 10, 1974.

*The 24-7 score*: "Dolphins Rout Vikings, 24-7, to Win 2d Super Bowl in Row," page 33, *NYT*, January 14, 1974.

*Nielsen ratings dropped a full point*: "David Walther Enters California 500 Race," page C2, *CT*, January 4, 1974.

*Nielsen ratings for the NFL*: "Changing Face of U.S. Sports: TV Saturation and Its Effects," page 45, *NYT*, July 23, 1974.

*A week later than the inaugural WFL draft*: "WFL Mobilized for Contract War With College Draft Tuesday," page 199, *NYT*, January 20, 1974.

*One-time toy heavyweight Remco*: "Remco closes doors once and for all," page 47, *PT*, January 1974.

*Coleco's stock had lost over $20*: "Stock Market Prices for 47 Leading Toy Companies," page 22, *PT*, January 1974.

*Servotronics stock in January*: ibid.

*A hypothetical stock portfolio created by Playthings*: "The Playthings Portfolio," page 12, *PT*, August 1969.

*By January of 1974*: "The Playthings Portfolio," page 22, *PT*, January 1974.

*There had been an increase in wholesale toy volume*: "Industry reports banner year in '73 despite problems," page 146. *PT*, February 1974.

*A category that was reported to have done well in 1973*: "750 Companies Show Wares at 71st Fair," page 39, *NYT*, February 18, 1974.

*Tudor would come to the Fair*: Tudor Games '74 Catalog.

*A reception featuring famed puppeteer Shari Lewis*: "Coleco to host reception for Shari Lewis and puppets," page 86, *PT*, February 1974.

*Munro Games brought to the Fair*: Munro Games Limited 1974 Game Price List, Effective Date: May 24, 1974.

*In a post-Christmas clearance*: "Prange's East Towne January Clearance," page 10, *The Capital Times* (WI), January 2, 1974.

*Brunswick was able to scale down air hockey*: "Brunswick brings ice hockey into family playrooms," page 87, *PT*, October 1973.

*The oil embargo was finally lifted*: "Nixon To Allow Stations To Sell Gas On Sundays," page 1, *NYT*, March 20, 1974.

*Feeling a different kind of shock in March*: "NFL Players Open Negotiations With 57 Demands on League," page D7, *WP*, March 17, 1974.

*Newspaper headlines around the country*: "Csonka, Warfield and Kiick to Go to WFL," page 43, *NYT*, April 1, 1974.

*Ken Stabler signed with the WFL's Birmingham franchise*: "Stabler of Raiders Joins WFL for '76," page 51, *NYT*, April 3, 1974.

*Csonka was given the opportunity*: "Opinion: Why Csonka Jumped to the New League," page 220, *NYT*, April 7, 1974.

*By the time the NFL owners gathered*: "NFL Owners Meet Tuesday to Decide on Expansion," page 235, *NYT*, April 21, 1974.

*Tampa had a new NFL franchise*: "NFL Accepts Tampa," page 51, *NYT*, April 25, 1974.

*The owners offered to cover*: "Owners Break Ice In NFL," page 13, *NYT*, May 31, 1974.

*The owners gave Seattle an expansion team*: "Seattle New Club In NFL," page 35, *NYT*, June 5, 1974.

*Publishing a report from the NFL Management Council*: "NFL Clubs Dispel 'Myths' of Big Profits," page 29, *NYT*, June 7, 1974.

*Labor talks broke off again*: "NFL Players' Strike Looms as Talks Break Off," page 59, *NYT*, June 27, 1974.

*U.S. was in a recession*: "Living Costs Increase Highest in 27 Years" page A1, *LAT*, June 22, 1974.

*Coleco and Servotronics losing more than half of their value*: "Stock Market Prices for 43 Leading Toy Companies," page 16, *PT*, August 1974.

*The Playthings portfolio*: "The Playthings Portfolio," ibid.

*Picket lines were set up*: "NFL Players Strike," page 37, *NYT*, July 1, 1974.

*The WFL ended up signing with the independent TVS Network*: "WFL Needs Television Contract to Survive; Does Television Need the WFL?" page 221, *NYT*, April 7, 1974.

*Attendance was strong for the first week of WFL games*: "WFL Openers Create Set of Paradoxes," page 25, *NYT*, July 12, 1974.

*It was the first time in 41 years*: "All-Star Game Off; Strike Is Blamed," page 21, *NYT*, July 11, 1974.

*First weekend of NFL exhibition games*: "NFL's Preseason Crowds Are Off By 256,748; Gate Down $1.8-Million," page 17, *NYT*, August 5, 1974; "Significant Decline Noted for Giants and Jet Games," page 21, *NYT*, August 6, 1974.

*NFL players decided to have a fourteen-day cooling off period*: "Players Halt Strike 14 Days; Report to Camps Wednesday," page 31, *NYT*, August 12, 1974.

*Also happy about some news coming out of the WFL*: "6,000 Not 64,000 Paid To See Bell-Stars Game," page 16, *NYT*, August 5, 1974.

*Similar sleight-of-hand calculations had been happening*: "WFL Sharks Reveal 44,000 Free Tickets," page 24, *NYT*, August 6, 1974.

*When the NFL season finally got underway*: "Lame-Duck Players Among Questions NFL Openers Will Try to Answer," page 221, *NYT*, September 15, 1974.

*Playthings gazed into the consumer crystal ball*: "Games can really be your pie in the sky," page 60-65, *PT*, September 1974.

*Reflecting the changes in the toy landscape*: "Pro-style Hockey Game," page 6, *Sears 1974 Christmas Book*.

*Seven football games*: "You're the head coach with these Electric Football Game," page 531, ibid.

*On the page just opposite from Tudor*: "Sports Action Games lead the league in family fun," page 530, ibid.

*Children's furniture and NFL wood-burning craft sets*: "NFL Team Furniture for all you football fans," page 504; "NFL Woodburning Set," page 506, ibid.

*All featured on page 379*: "Table Model Electric Football...3 Choices!" page 379, *MW Christmas Catalog 1974*.

*On the color page next to electric football*: "New Games For The Family Room and Den," page 378, ibid.

*Tudor had almost total domination*: "NFL Electric Football with Total Team Control," page 117, *J.C. Penney Christmas 1974*.

*Attendance for the first three weeks*: "Crowds Drop as New Leaders Arise in Early NFL Action," page 50, *NYT*, October 8, 1974.

*WFL teams were hemorrhaging money*: "Two Teams Are Dropped By WFL," page 33, *NYT*, October 11, 1974.

*Including the major market New York Stars*: "Stars Receive WFL Approval To Move Franchise to Charlotte," page 31, *NYT*, September 25, 1974.

*Philadelphia Bell reported a paid crowd of 750*: "750 See Bell Lose," page 53, *NYT*, October 17, 1974.

*By month's end*: "Davidson Out as WFL Commissioner," page 53, *NYT*, October 30, 1974.

*The Sears Catalog Surplus Store*: "Sears Catalog Surplus Store," page 5, *Suburban Economists*, October 20, 1974.

*This left Tudor as the main electric football game*: "Toys R Us," page 51, *Oakland Tribune*, November 21, 1974.

*What Toys R Us was selling from Munro Games*: "Toys R Us," page SG3, *LAT*, November 24, 1974; "Toys R Us," page A24, *WP*, November 14, 1974.

*Sears and Ward waited until early November*: "Sears," page 47, *Ogden Standard Examiner*, November 5, 1974; "When Wards Cuts Prices You Save A Bundle," pages 10-11, *The Lawton Constitution*, November 1, 1974.

*Most of the electric football games being advertised*: "Western Auto Christmas Gifts," page 16, *The Yuma Daily Sun* (AZ); "Grand Auto Toy Sale," page 23, *The Argus* (CA), November 28, 1974; "J.C. Penney 20% off these selected toy," page 21, *Altoona Mirror*, November 29, 1974.

*Sears had the Super Bowl down to*: "Sears Toy Box," page D-3, *Herald Times-Reporter* (WI), November 28, 1974.

*Ward had dropped the No. 645*: "Values From Our Toy Department," page 9, *Big Spring Herald* (TX), November 29, 1974.

*Toy R Us, in what seemed to be an ominous statement*: "Toys R Us," page SG3, *LAT*, November 24, 1974; "Toys R Us," page 70, *Van Nuys Valley News*, November 28, 1974.

*That wasn't enough to stop the local sheriff's department*: "WFL Champions' Uniforms Seized," page C3, *WP*, December 7, 1974.

*The Dow Jones*: "Dow Stock Average Drops 9.46 Points To 12-year Low as Volume Increases," page 39, *NYT*, December 7, 1974.

*The auto industry alone*: "Auto Makers Set Widened Layoffs," page 41, *NYT*, November 23, 1974.

*Even Sears was resorting to layoffs*: "Sears to Idle Up to 2% Or 8,000 in Field Staff Due to Dim Outlook," page 8, *WSJ*, November 27, 1974.

*Toys R Us had just put out*: "Toys R Us," page 216, *The Oakland Tribune*, December 1, 1974.

*A number of Ward stores*: "Toys 1/2 Price," page 9, *Herald Times-Reporter* (WI), December 6, 1974.

*Gibson's had been offering*: "Gibson's Toy Sale," page 9, *Ogden Standard Examiner*, October 13, 1974; Gibson' Red Tag Sale," page 3, *Clovis News-Journal*, December 11, 1974.

*During the second weekend of the month*: "Sears Toy Sale," page 15, *The Billings Gazette*, December 15, 1974; "Prices Slashed Save 10% to 50% Off," page 7A, *The Lawton Constitution*," December 14, 1974.

*Munro saw its brand new WHA*: "Sears Catalog Surplus Store," page 8, *The Herald* (IL), December 16, 1974.

*Tudor's NFL No. 635*: "Kresge's Santa's Bombshells," page 14, *The Daily Mail* (MD), ibid.

*J.C. Penney put electric football*: "Our Year-End Sales galore," page 14, *News-Journal* (OH), December 17, 1974.

*At a Sears Surplus Store*: "Sears Catalog Surplus Store," page 3, *Grand Prairie Daily News* (TX), December 18, 1974.

*By contrast, Illinois store managers*: "Santa please bring me air hockey," page 1, *The Herald* (IL), December 18, 1974.

*J.C. Penney stores were in permanent toy clearance*: "JC Penney The Christmas Place," page 13, *Lebanon Daily News* (PA), December 18, 1974.

*Ward began discounting all its toys*: "Stumped for ideas? Try these," page 6, *News-Journal* (OH), December 19, 1974; "Lucky you, It's as Sell-out Sale," page 16, *News Tribune* (MO), December 22, 1974.

*Tudor NFL No. 515*: "Town & Country Midnight Sale," page 2, *The Morning Herald* (PA), December 20, 1974.

*Tudor's flagship NFL Championship model*: "Wal-Mart Discount City Toys up to 50% Off!" page 9, *The Ruston Daily Leader* (LA), December 19, 1974; "Kids Town This Is It!!" page 8, *Syracuse Herald Journal*, December 21, 1974.

*Coleco games suffered the same fate*: "Grant City 50% Off Sale," page 14, *The Daily News* (PA), December 21, 1974.

*Munro sellers were reluctant to drop the Namath model*: "King's Self-Service Dept Stores," page 23, *The Cumberland News* (MD), December 19, 1974.

## Chapter 31

*The Associated Press poll*: "AP Votes Oklahoma Top Team," page C1, *WP*, January 4, 1975.

*It was USC who was given the top spot*: "Bryant Joins Trojan Parade," page D1, *WP*, January 3, 1975.

*The league named an MVP*: "Stabler Named Most Valuable," page 31, *NYT*, January 10, 1975.

*Just days after a judge released Stabler*: "Ken Stabler Freed From WFL Pact," page 38, *NYT*, January 7, 1975.

*No respite for the WFL*: " Unhappy 'Super Sunday' for the WFL," page 193, *NYT*, January 12, 1975.

*Advertisers were paying NBC*: "Minute TV Commercial to Cost Super Bowl Sponsor $214,000," page 194, *NYT*, January 12, 1975.

*The city was expecting an extra $15 million*: ibid.

*Ford had laid off 85,000 workers*: "22 Of Ford Plants To Shut For Week," page L1, *NYT*, January 11, 1975.

*The most recent inflation rate*: "Inflation Worse, A Revision Shows," page 39, *NYT*, February 21, 1975.

*Depth of the recession*: "Consumer Prices Rose 12.2% in '74, Worst Since '46," page 81, *NYT*, January 22, 1975.

*President Ford gave a national address*: "Drastic Reversal: President Calls For 'Sacrifice' to Help 'Nation In Trouble,'" page 69, *NYT*, January 14, 1975.

*The term economists were using was "stagflation"*: "New Stagflation Era?" page 184, *NYT*, January 19, 1975.

*Playthings portfolio was now down to*: "The Playthings Portfolio," page 14, *PT*, January 1975.

*Playthings' editor and publisher Harry Gluckert*: "The Toy Industry is Running Scared!!!" page 4, *PT*, January 1975.

*Parker Brothers' president Randolph Barton*: "A Tough Year In Toy Making," page F2, *NYT*, February 16, 1975.

*NFL teams for store display*: Tudor Games '75.

*Servotronics had lost almost $3 million in 1974*: "Servotronics Loss For Year Put at $9.5 Million, *Buffalo Evening News*, July 22, 1976.

*Giant black letters on shiny gold card-stock page*: Aurora Turns Air Into Gold," *PT*, February 1975.

*The WFL declared it was alive and well*: "WFL Head: League Will Play," page 55, *NYT*, March 13, 1975.

*Rozelle opened the NFL meeting bluntly*: "'74 Problems Reviewed by NFL Clubs," page 45, *NYT*, March 18, 1975.

*On March 29 President Ford signed into law*: "Ford Approves Tax Cuts, Saying He Has No Choice; Bars A New Spending Rise," page 1, *NYT*, March 30, 1975.

*WFL held a press conference*: "WFL Is Replaced by 'NEW' WFL," page 64, *NYT*, April 17, 1975.

*The WFL's shaky status had to be a disappointment*: "Record Player Reshuffling: 68 Set to Be Free Agents," *NYT*, April 27, 1975.

*One player who did stand to profit*: "An Overture Of $500,000 To Namath," page 64, *NYT*, May 1, 1975.

*A small rise during the spring*: "Consumer Confidence Is Found Rising," page 52, *NYT*, May 22, 1975.

*Major retailers like Sears*: "Retailers Face Frugal Shopper," page 43, *NYT*, June 30, 1975.

*The NFL was also lamenting the effects*: "NFL Says 8 Clubs Lost Money in '74," page 23, *NYT*, July 1, 1975.

*The Jets made Joe Namath*: "All Smiles in Jet Camp As Namath Signs, Drills," page 21, *NYT*, July 31, 1975.

*A healthy crowd of 25,000*: "Southmen Win, 27-26 on Kiick's Tally," page 164, *NYT*, August 3, 1975.

*Didn't take long for the new* WFL: "WFL Drops Chicago Club," page 30, *NYT*, September 3, 1975.

*After two weeks of federally mediated negotiations*: "Players' Group Reject Offer Of Contract," page 51, *NYT*, September 11, 1975.

*Four days before the start of the regular season*: "Jets and Redskins Join Patriots' Strike," page 31, *NYT*, September 17, 1975.

*A temporary agreement*: "Football Teams End Their Strike," page 77, *NYT*, September 19, 1975.

*The players voted overwhelmingly to reject*: "New Pact In NFL Is Failing," page 43, *NYT*, September 26, 1975.

*The current Playthings carried an article*: "Board Games out in front for '75 race," pages 36-41, *PT*, September 1975.

*This enthusiasm was apparent in the current Sears Christmas Book*: pages 441, 541, *Sears 1975 Christmas Book*.

*Both electric football and table hockey*: "Super Bowl Electric Football Game," page 542, ibid.

*A new Sears' exclusive*: "Sears Tele-Games Electronic Games," page 410, ibid.

*Air-powered hockey games got a full-color page*: "Only At Wards Deluxe Jet Hockey," page 371, *MW Christmas Book Of Values 1975*.

*Only a single electric football game*: "Command Control Electric Football," page 373, ibid.

*Another new item for Ward this year*: "Odyssey Electronic Game," page 297, ibid.

*Only in the J.C. Penney Christmas catalog*: page 444, *J.C. Penney Christmas 1975*.

*Football players who put their faith in the* WFL: "Money Ills Force WFL to Disband," page 51, *NYT*, October 23, 1975.

*Rozelle immediately issued a season-long ban*: "Rozelle Orders a Season Ban On Signing of WFL Players," page 19, *NYT*, October 25, 1975.

*Rozelle finally agreed to that WFL players could be signed*: "NFL Set To Process WFL Pool," page 45, *NYT*, November 7, 1975.

*There was the possibility of a positive Christmas season*: "The Spending Riddle," page 59, *NYT*, November 28, 1975.

*The retailer wasn't featuring the Super Bowl*: "Sale from the Big Toy Box," page 2, *Sheboygan Press*, November 21, 1975.

*Ward's toy ads using the game were sparse*: "Toys, Toys, Toys," page E3, *The New Mexican*, November 9, 1975.

*In an advertising booklet*: "Toys R Us," pages T10-T11, *CT*, November 30, 1975.

*Joining Toys R Us as the only other major retailer*: "Montgomery Ward Saturday Specials," page 32, *Kingsport Times News* (TN), November 29, 1975.

*To the Gibson Discount Center chain*: "Toys," page 45, *Emporia Gazette* (KS), November 29, 1975.

*It was the small Pro Stars game*: "Toyland Santa Special," page 79, *Florence Morning News* (SC), December 4, 1975.

*Philadelphia-based John Wanamaker*: "Electric Football Games By Monrow, Yours at less than our wholesale cost," page A13, *Courier Times* (PA), October 20, 1975.

*Many of the retailers that still carried Namath*: "Walls Bargain Center," page 8B, *The Lawton Constitution*(OK), December 10, 1975.

*Retailers gleefully reported double-digit*: "Christmas Spending Is Up But Not On Credit," F1, *NYT*, December 14, 1975.

*Sales managers at these stores*: "Electronic Games Bringing a Different Way to Relax," page 33, *NYT*, December 25, 1975; "Christmas craze is TV ping pong," page D7, *Courier Times* (PA), December 21, 1975; "Merchants report good Christmas sales," page 1, *Greeley Tribune* (CO), December 23, 1975; "Stockings were filled with gifts from local stores," page 14, *The Times-Standard* (CA), December 28, 1975.

*Sears running apology ads*: "Sears Notice," page 6, *Kokomo Tribune* (IN), December 17, 1975.

*The Super Bowl game was still holding*: "Toys Kids Want at Sears Everyday Low Prices," page 12, *The Sunday Freeman* (NY), December 21, 1975.

*Munro's Joe Namath games*: "S. Klein Price Reduced! Christmas Toys," page 32, *Courier Times* (PA), December 20, 1975; "Play Town Last Call," page A18, *Courier Times* (PA), December 21, 1975.

*Coleco's Super Action Command Control*: "Railroad Salvage," page 6, *The Transcript* (MA), December 20, 1975.

*Retailers found themselves with a glut of large stand-alone hockey games*: "Town & Country Great Savings on Air Hockey Games," page 25, *The Morning Herald* (PA), December 18, 1975; "Kiddie City Late Shoppers Sale!" page A11, *Courier Times* (PA), December 21, 1975; "Big Town Super Mart," page 33, *Chronicle Telegram* (OH), December 21, 1975.

*President Ford did his part to further the economic recovery*: "Ford Signs Tax Cut Bill; Starts Colorado Vacation," page 1, *NYT*, December 24, 1975.

*Macy's flagship store on Fifth Avenue*: "Holiday Sales Up Throughout The U.S.," page 1, *NYT*, December 24, 1975.

*On that day a Federal judge ruled*: "Rozelle Rule Found In Antitrust Violation," page 27, *NYT*, December 31, 1975.

## Chapter 32

*It was a case of things getting bigger*: "Steelers Favored Over Cowboys Today in Super Bowl at Miami," page 161, *NYT*, January 18, 1976.

*On the Orange Bowl field*: "Super Bowl Grows Into Oversized Revel," page S3, *NYT*, January 11, 1976.

*Retail sales for December*: "Retail Sales in the Nation Soared 3.4% in December," page 43, *NYT*, January 10, 1976.

*Sears was reporting*: "Sears Roebuck Sets Mark for Four Weeks," page 50, *NYT*, January 6, 1976.

*Adding to the optimism*: "Wall Street rally best since 1938, analysts report," page H7, *CT*, January 10, 1976.

*Tudor's solution*: Norman Sas, personal interview.

*Rumors put Servotronics losses in the $5 million range*: "Amex Halts Trading In Servotronics Stock, Awaits Certain Data, page 22, *WSJ*, April 26, 1976; Servotronics to Defer Payment, page 17, *WSJ*, February 13, 1976.

*Already resigned from his consulting duties*: Don Munro Jr., personal interview.

*Tudor had six games on display*: Tudor Games 76.

*The company had run a full-page ad*: "Selling The Number One Home Video Game Is As Easy As Playing It," page 190, *PT*, February 1976.

*During a Super Bowl press conference*: "Can't Find Czars Like Pete," page 163, *NYT*, January 18, 1976.

*Newly elected NFLPA president Dick Anderson*: "Football Union Clears Air, Prods Owners to Negotiate," page 56, NYT, March 19, 1976.

*The message being sent was clear*: "The Rozelle Rule Is Dead: Long Live the Free Agents," page 169, NYT, April 11, 1976.

*For which he won a "Package of the Year," award*: "Top Packages of the Year: 1974 Edition," *Packaging Design*, January 1974.

*He agreed to become Director of Industrial Design*: Lee Payne, personal interview.

*By the time the first training camps go underway*: "Several Pro Football Camps to Open Tomorrow With No Heavy Clouds Hanging Over ''76 Season," page S3, NYT, July 4, 1976.

*Free agency wasn't destroying the NFL*: "Free-Agent Rule Fails to Hurt NFL," page 50, NYT, August 4, 1976.

*Other issues for the owners to worry about*: "NFL Held In Labor Code Violation," page 38, NYT, July 2, 1976.

*Servotronics announced that it would consolidate*: "Munro Games To Consolidate Canadian Plant," *Buffalo Evening News*, July 16, 1976.

*Servotronics needed cash*: "Servotronics and Unit May File for Chapter 11 If Required to Pay Debt," page 6, WSJ, July 6, 1976.

*Under pressure*: "Ailing Servotronics Firm Notes $9,501,702 Loss," *Buffalo Courier-Express*, July 22, 1976.

*Servotronics restated earnings*: "Digest of Corporate Earnings," page 19, WSJ, July 22, 1976.

*Actually the game was stopped in the third quarter*: "Game Halted by a Rainstorm Is the First in NFL History," page 135, NYT, July 25, 1976.

*The players rejected the new proposal*: "NFL Players Reject New Pact Offer," page 56, NYT, September 1, 1976.

*Ratings for Monday Night Football*: "Pro Football: A Full Slate For Openers," page 179, NYT, September 12, 1976.

*In the Sears catalog*: "Super Bowl 1976 Electric Football Game," page 483, *Sears 1976 Christmas Book*.

*Four different pong games*: "TELE-GAMES...challenging games you play on your own TV," pages 390-391, ibid.

*Air-powered hockey games were positioned*: "Great additions to any GAME ROOM," pages 486-489, ibid.

*This exclusive*: "Exclusive Wards Own Video World of Sports," page 6, *MW Christmas 1976*.

*A two-page video game spread*: "Imagine! Odyssey 4000 by Magnavox," pages 272-273, ibid.

*Comparing Ward's treatment of electronic games*: "Electric Football," page 359, ibid.

*Penney devoted an entire color page to football*: "NFL Electric Football with Total Team Control," page 393, *J.C. Penney Christmas 1976*.

*A verdict was rendered on the NFL's final appeal*: "Rozelle Rule Again Is Held To Be Invalid," page 62, NYT, October 19, 1976.

*Only Toys R Us*: "Toys R Us," page 18, WP, November 21, 1976.

*Western Auto was still a Tudor stalwart*: "Christmas Gifts Western Auto," page 27, *Las Cruces Sun-News* (NM), November 16, 1976.

*Running a color toy flyer on Sunday*: "NFL Electric Football," page O10, CT, November 28, 1976.

*The Coleco item getting the biggest push*: "Toys R Us," page 18, WP, November 21, 1976.

*The December issue of Playthings*: "Electronics starring on the game and toy circuit," cover, pages 30-31, PT, December 1976.

*Sears:* "Tele-Games," page 63, *Hagerstown Daily Mail*, December 15, 1976.

*Kmart:* "Holiday Values," page 95, *Pasadena Star News*, December 15, 1976.

*Target:* "Play 4 exciting games on your TV screen with Super Pong," page 14, *The Cedar Rapids Gazette*, December 16, 1976.

Toys R Us: "Toys R Us," page 32, *Oakland Tribune*, December 19, 1976.

*Odyssey could be found at J.C. Penney:* "Odyssey 300 by Magnavox," page 19, *Tri-City Herald* (WA), December 16, 1976.

*People's:* "Thousands of Gifts for Late Santas," page 24, *The Cumberland News*, December 23, 1976.

*Skaggs:* "Old Fashioned Christmas Toy, Game and Doll Sale," page C-12, *The Post-Register* (ID), December 5, 1976.

*Osco:* "Toys To Please Every Girl and Boy!" page 20, *Daily Journal* (WI), December 3, 1976.

*Were hoping for another good Christmas season:* "Retail Sales Gains Lower In November Big Chains Report," page 79, *NYT*, December 3, 1976.

*Reporting a record $36 million:* "Coleco reports sales & earnings," page 16, *PT*, December 1976.

*A full-page ad:* "Telstar by Coleco no. 1 in video games," page 54," *PT*, December 1976.

*Railroad Salvage:* "Railroad Salvage," page 9, *The Berkshire Eagle* (MA), December 11, 1976.

*Toy Outlet:* "Toy Outlet The Ugly Store with the Beautiful Prices" page B-4, *The Post-Crescent* (WI), December 7, 1976.

*Three-year-old Day/Nite games:* "Walls Bargain Center," page 3A, *The Ada Evening News* (OK), December 22, 1976.

*The price hovered around $10:* "Play Town Great Toys Great Hours," page 14, *The Times Record*, December 9, 1976.

*Sears dropped the tabletop Brunswick:* "Sears Toy Gifts of Value," page 36, *The Times Herald Record* (NY), December 22, 1976.

*Ward went into its half-price toy clearance:* "1/2" Price Toy Sale," page 6, *Portsmouth Herald* (NH), page 6, December 23, 1976.

*J.C. Penney advertised:* "JC Penney The Christmas Place," page 7, *Muscatine Journal* (IA), December 22, 1976.

*Most of these bargains came from drug stores:* "The Akron," page A-7, *Pasadena Star News*; "Fay's Drugs for the Last Minute Shopper," page 22, *Syracuse Post Standard*," December 23, 1976.

*Thanks to their 15-1 record:* "Raiders Are Favorites by 5 1/2 Points In Super Bowl Struggle With Vikings," page 34, *NYT*, December 28, 1976.

## Chapter 33

*Christmas of 1976:* "Big Store Chains Report Strong Sales In December," page 60, *NYT*, January 7, 1977.

*When Toy Fair opened:* "'76 Toy Sales hit record high," page 40, *Tri-City Herald* (WA), February 16, 1977.

*Highlighting the toy industry's exhilaration:* " Advertising: It's Television Time for Tinkertoy," page 50, *NYT*, February 8, 1977.

*Fisher Price and Mattel were increasing their television budgets:* "Advertising: Some Toy Makers Budgets Going Up," page 79, *NYT*, February 23, 1977.

*The big item, according to TMA prognosticators:* "Another Toy Fair, another year," page 111, *PT*, February 1977.

*Tudor came to the Fair with just three electric football games: Tudor Games 77* (sales catalog).

A blurb in *Playthings*: "Tudor's introductions mark 30th year of electric football," page 152, *PT*, March 1977.

*The company sold over a million Telstar units*: "Coleco reports great success with Telstar; plans to beef up promotional spending," page 34, *PT*, October 1977.

*Sales totaled a record $116 million*: "Coleco reports profitable year," page 23, *PT*, March 1977.

*A full-page Playthings ad*: "Coleco Telstar No. 1 In Video Games," page 331, *PT*, February 1977.

*Coleco was introducing six new Telstar games*: "Coleco introduces Telstar items among others at New York fair," page 39, *PT*, April 1977.

*A television campaign for Power-Jet Hockey*: "Coleco scores with new TNT Power Jet Hockey Game," page 90, *PT*, March 1977.

*In Mattel's first foray into electronic games*: "Preview 1977: Barbie continues SuperStar role at Mattel," page 152, *PT*, February 1977.

*Mattel was running a full-page ad*: "Mattel is #1," *PT*, February 1977.

*The NFL was finally able to wrap up*: "Players Unit And Owners Ratify Pact, page 36, *NYT*, February 26, 1977.

*Few in the NFL were surprised*: "Jets Put Namath on Waivers," page C1, *WP*, April 2, 1977.

*On April 4 Servotronics reported*: "Companies List Earning Reports," page 53, *NYT*, April, 1977.

*The final piece of Munro Games*: "Hockey-game firm is in receivership," page C 11, *The Toronto Star*, May 24, 1977.

*Joe Namath's fortunes turned out better*: "Namath Reaches Agreement With Rams," page 42, *NYT*, May 13, 1977.

*A four-page color spread in the July issue*: "Electronics: toy circuit's flashing future," pages 34-37, *PT*, July 1977.

*The contents of Munro's Ontario factory*: "Munro Games LTD. Auction," page C 10, *The Toronto Star*, July 15, 1977.

*Munro quickly gathered up the papers*: Don Munro Jr., personal interview.

*Only two Tudor electric football games*: "Action Games," page 538, *Sears 1977 Christmas Book*.

*Page three of its catalog*: "Bally Arcade," page 3, *MW Christmas 1977*.

*A Pong-clone video game*: "APF Electronic TV Fun Game," back cover, ibid.

*Coleco had four new Telstar models*: pages 434-435, ibid.

*Coleco electric football game*: "Electronic football," page 429, ibid.

*For sale on page 417*: "Football Fun For the Whole Family," page 417, *J.C. Penney Christmas 1977*.

*On page J.C. Penney did something really different*: "Mini Computer Games from Mattel Electronics," page 5, ibid.

*Glow-in-the Dark Air Hockey*: page 420, ibid.

*Toys R Us was using the game*: "Toys R Us," page I25, *LAT*, November 6, 1977.

*Sears*: "Sears Toys," page 3-A, *Gazette-Telegraph* (CO), November 5, 1977.

*Some Odyssey's were being sold for less than $25*: "Radio Hospital Magnavox," page 19, *The Lima News* (OH), December 3, 1977.

*Sears*: "Sears Holiday Sale," page 27, *The Orange County Register* (CA), December 11, 1977.

*Ward*: "Toy Clearance! 33% to 50% off!" page 3, *Charleston Daily Mail* (WV), December 9, 1977.

*J.C. Penney*: "Toy Sale. And we've got all the best names," page 19, *Alton Telegraph* (IL), December 16, 1977.

*Some Ward locations chopping the price*: "Toy Clearance," page 4, *The Courier News* (AR), December 19, 1977.

*Sears to lower its Tele-Games*: "Sears Holiday Gifts," page 60, *Pasadena Star News*, December 20, 1977.

*More expensive than an Atari 2600 at Target*: "Save $35 on Atari's programmable video game," page 18, *The Cedar Rapids Gazette*, December 15, 1977.

*Or even at a Walgreen's pharmacy*: "The Christmas Shopper's Center," page 11, *The Daily Review* (CA), December 20, 1977.

*Left Kenner without enough time to get its Star Wars line*: "Toying With Christmas Bills," page 35, *WP*, December 9, 1977; "Kenner begins plans for 'Star Wars' line," page 91, *PT*, September 1977.

*Ideal now couldn't give these toys away*: "Assault by Knieval Halts Boom In Ideal's Daredevil Toy Sales," page D1, *NYT*, December 9, 1977.

*Even though the Vikings intercepted three Pat Haden passes*: "Rams' Haden Sways Doubters," page 49, *NYT*, December 21, 1977.

## Chapter 34

*The first ever prime time Super Bowl*: "Super Bowl a Cultural Phenomenon in Prime Time," page C12, *NYT*, January 9, 1978.

*According to Nielsen*: "86 Million Saw Super Bowl, Most Ever for Sports Event," page C20, *NYT*, January 18, 1978.

*Sears, J.C. Penney, and Kmart had posted record sales*: "Retailers Report Surprise at High Figures," page C6, *WP*, January 6, 1978.

*Tudor was set to run a full-page Playthings ad*: "Our Super Bowl was Sold Out," page 389, *PT*, February 1978.

*Unlike Joe Namath's retirement*: "Namath Is Retiring From Pro Football," page A1, *NYT*, January 25, 1978.

*Elmer Sas passed away*: "Deaths," page 30, *NYT*, January 31, 1978.

*Norman told Playthings*: "Tudor Games hitting 50 and looking ahead," page 87, *PT*, February 1978.

*Coleco, who claimed to be #1 in electronic fun*: "See Why Coleco Is #1 In Electronic Fun!," page 329, ibid.

*Retailers were delighted with the hand-held category*: "Electronic Games Get Retail Play," page F1, *NYT*, December 24, 1978.

*Of the eight sports games displayed*: "Punt, kick, and tackle to score a touchdown in Electric Football," page 599, *Sears 1978 Christmas Book*.

*Tudor had won another Sears Excellence Award*: "Sears awards Tudor for supplier excellence," page 38, *PT*, November 1978.

*Tudor was also getting a push from Ward*: "What's Your Game," page 451, *MW Christmas 1978*.

*Other than Sears*: "Values from the Big Toy Box Family Game bonanza," page 118, *Frederick News Post*, November 27, 1978.

*Mattel had sold more electronic games*: "Electronic Games Get Retail Play," page F1, *NYT*, December 24, 1978.

*There were massive shortages*: "Toy Shortage Bigger Than Usual," page 10, *The Pharos-Tribune* (IN), December 3, 1978.

*A unanimous conclusion*: "Best selling toys in 1978," pages 100-101, *PT*, January 1979.

*Mattel would later report*: "Zip! Zap! Zounds!," page B1, *WP*, February 27, 1979.

*The Ward Christmas catalog had it listed for $19.99*: "Challenge the Champs," page 459, *MW Christmas 1978*.

*Was often under $18*: "Coleco Electronic Quarterback," page 28, *Titusville Herald* (PA), November 11, 1978.

## Chapter 35

*Tudor approached the coming Toy Fair*: *Tudor Games '79*.

*Mattel had done so well*: "Mattel entering '79 with 247 new items; electronics and softuf highlighted," page 147, *PT*, February 1979.

*By Playthings' own count*: "Electronics: big entry into market by outside firms," pages 26-32, *PT*, April 1979.

*Devoted four full pages to covering electronics*: "Electronics set pace at '79 Toy Fair," pages 52-55, *PT*, March 1979.

*The April issue gave electronics the cover*: "Electronics: big entry into market by outside firms," pages 26-32, *PT*, April 1979.

*Tudor still had the Sears Christmas Book*: "Electric Football," page 634, *Sears 1979 Christmas Book*.

*Giving electric football a push was Woolco*: "Woolco Grand Opening," page 10-A, Galveston Daily News, November 2, 1979.

*Retailers reported that electronic games*: "Electronic Games A Big Winner For the Holiday," page D1, *NYT*, November 15, 1979.

*Texas Instruments again ran out of chips*: "Companies Placing Chips On Electronic Game Boom," page F1, *WP*, December 9, 1979.

*Relegated to the aisles of discounters*: "Murphy's Mart Christmas Grand Opening," page 13, *The Daily News* (PA), November 21, 1979.

*The best-selling item this year*: "The 10 Best Sellers," page B6, *NYT*, December 7, 1979.

*Retailers were unanimous in proclaiming electronic football*: "Companies Placing Chips On Electronic Game Boom," page F1, *WP*, December 9, 1979; "Electronic Games A Big Winner For the Holiday," page D1, *NYT*, November 15, 1979.

## Chapter 36

*Over 300 electronic games were on the market*: "Electronic-Games Race," page SM45, *NYT*, December 14, 1980.

*Two NFL hand-held models from Tudor*: *Tudor Games 1980*

*Mattel's new game system*: "Test Play Mattel Electronics Intellivision Master Component," page 55, *NYT*, October 26, 1980.

*With a page that was almost identical*: "Action Games for the sports-minded family," page 647, *Sears 1980 Christmas Book*.

*Oversaturation became a problem*: "A Troubled Season in Toyland," page D1, *NYT*, December 23, 1980.

*Electronic games accounted for*: "Electronic-Games Race," page SM45, *NYT*, December 14, 1980.

*In 1982 Tudor finally abandoned its electronic games*: *Tudor Games 1982*.

*Tudor's top-of-the-line game cost*: "Table top Sports Games," page 628, *Sears 1982 Christmas Book*.

*The first new line actually made the cover*: "Tudor Games...And Collectibles. Great Fun For 1983," *Tudor Games 1983*.

*Tudor had created a line of figures*: "Quarterbacks Of The NFL," page 2, *Tudor Games 1983*.

*Complete sets of NFC and AFC quarterbacks*: "Quarterbacks Of The NFL," page 585, *Sears 1984 Christmas Book*.

*Seven of the twelve pages in the 1985 Tudor sales catalog*: "Makers of Sports Events," *Tudor Games 1985*.

*The video game market collapsed*: "Mattel Agrees To Restructure Its Bank Debt," page 4, *WSJ*, March 15, 1984; "Warner Sells Atari To Tramiel," page D1, *NYT*, July 3, 1984.

*Helping to counterbalance*: "Coleco Discontinues Its Adam Computer Line," page F1, *LAT*, January 3, 1985.

*Astounding sales figures*: "Cabbage Patch Still No. 1," page 11, *CT*, December 24, 1984.

*Huddles became one of NFL Properties'*: "The NFL Means Business," page 15, *Del Rio News Herald*, October 19, 1985.

*Tudor expanded in 1986*: *Tudor Games 1986*.

*Toys R Us price for a Super Bowl*: "We've Still Got Hot Toys," page 91, *Capital Times* (WI), December 2, 1987.

*It was the largest one-day*: "Bedlam On Wall St.," page 1, *LAT*, October 19, 1987.

## Chapter 37

*The company was expanding*: personal interview, Mike Landsman.

*Superior purchased New Jersey-base HG Toys*: "Toy firm playing acquisition game," page A6, *CT*, January 6, 1989.

*Continental unexpectedly called Superior's $23 million loan*: "Financial stress puts screws to Cont'l strategy," page 3, *CCB*, April 9, 1990.

*Superior warehouse production manager*: personal interview, Kathy Holford.

*Now defunct toy company*: "Coleco Agrees to Sell Hasbro Most Assets For $85 Million in Cash Plus Warrants," page A3B, *WSJ*, June 16, 1989.

*In the atmosphere of uncertainty*: ibid.

*In February of 1990*: "Superior Toy caught in push for liquidation," page 40, *CCB*, March 26, 1990.

*Meyer had left Coleco*: "Coleco's Financial Chief, Paul Meyer, Will Resign," page 47, *WSJ*, September 8, 1998.

*Coleco's appointment of a new*: "Coleco Fails To Fend Off Chapter 11," page D1, *NYT*, July 13, 1988.

*Three Superior creditors had filed a court petition*: "Local toy company forced into bankruptcy," page 70, *CCB*, March 19, 1990.

*The bank quickly arranged for financing*: "Superior Toy files for Chapter 11," page 4, *CT*, March 28, 1990.

*Continental Bank was already infamous*: "Continental Illinois National Bank and Trust Company," pages 545-565, *Managing the Crisis: The FDIC and RTC Experience, Volume One, Part II*, U.S. Government publication, December 1997.

*Almost 10% of Continental Bank's assets*: "Financial stress puts screws to Cont'l strategy," page 3, *CCB*, April 9, 1990.

*During extended legal wrangling*: "Leaf suit 1st volley in Gumball Case," Page B4, *CT*, July 13, 1990.

*By summer's end Leaf and a committee of creditors*: "Toy company creditors sue Continental for $50 million,"" page B5, *CT*, August 28, 1990.

*Then finally on December 7, 1990*: personal interview, Kathy Holford.

*In April a broker for the bank*: "Local toymaker is going on block," page B3, *CT*, April 12, 1991.

*On the day after Christmas*: Steege (trustee for estate of Superior Toy) vs. Accountant Professional Staff, Inc., Playtex Family Services, Corp.; Chapter 7, No. 90 B 04481, Adv. No. 93 A 01350, United States Bankruptcy Court For The Northern District of Illinois, Eastern Division, April 16, 1994 Decided.

*One creditor who didn't bother to get in line*: personal interview, Norman Sas.

*It was in federal bankruptcy court*: personal interview, Mike Landsman.

*The archive room and Tudor's paperwork*: personal interview, Kathy Holford.

*Mike and Kathy were not ready for what they found*: personal interview, Mike Landsman; personal interview, Kathy Holford.

*The plant had been sold and new owners were*: personal interview, Kathy Holford.

*During a second solo trip*: personal interview, Kathy Holford.

*Miggle newsletter*: *Electric Football News*, Miggle Toys, Inc., Spring 1994.

*When Collecting Toys published*: "First and Goal," pages, 52-55, *Collecting Toys*, October 1994.

*With the Sun-Times featuring Mike*: "Charged Up: Football Game Makes Return," *Chicago Sun-Times*, January 17, 1996.

*In 1997 Miggle introduced*: "New Fun Products Displayed," page A-5, *The Telegraph*, July 13, 1997.

*Miggle tried to make its mark*: "Deluxe NFL Electric Football Game," page 141, *Sears Wish Book* 2000.

*In February of 2012*: "Gaming World Vibrates With News Of Electric Football Acquisition," www.tudorgames.com, February 9, 2012.

Photos from Super Bowl V by Lee Payne.